EVERY VOTE EQUAL:
A State-Based Plan for Electing the President by National Popular Vote

John R. Koza
Barry Fadem
Mark Grueskin
Michael S. Mandell
Robert Richie
Joseph F. Zimmerman

FOREWORDS BY

John B. Anderson	Birch Bayh	John Buchanan
Tom Campbell	Gregory G. Aghazarian	Saul Anuzis
Laura Brod	James L. Brulte	B. Thomas Golisano
Joseph Griffo	Ray Haynes	Robert A. "Bob" Holmes
Dean Murray	Thomas L. Pearce	Christopher Pearson

NATIONAL POPULAR VOTE PRESS
www.NationalPopularVote.com
Third Edition — First Printing

Yale University Press is gratefully acknowledged for permission to use figure 2.13 from *The People's President: The Electoral College in American History and Direct-Vote Alternative* by Neal R. Peirce and as the copyright owner of that figure.

First edition — First Printing (February 6, 2006)
First edition — Second Printing (February 17, 2006)
First edition — Third Printing (March 6, 2006)
First edition — Fourth Printing (March 13, 2006)
First edition — Fifth Printing (April 5, 2006)
First edition — Sixth Printing (May 8, 2006)
First edition — Seventh Printing (July 6, 2006)
First edition — Eighth Printing (December 20, 2006)
Second edition — First Printing (December 20, 2008)
Third edition — First Printing (January 5, 2011)

ISBN-13 978-0-9790107-2-9

National Popular Vote Press
Post Office Box 1441
Los Altos, California 94023
www.every-vote-equal.com
www.NationalPopularVote.com
Phone: 650-472-1587
Email: info@NationalPopularVote.com

CHAPTER-LEVEL TABLE OF CONTENTS

DETAILED TABLE OF CONTENTS

BIOGRAPHIES

GREGORY G. AGHAZARIAN served in the California State Assembly from 2002 to 2008. He was named Assembly Republican Caucus Chairman in 2006.

JOHN B. ANDERSON served in Congress as a Republican Representative from Illinois from 1961 to 1981. He was Chairman of the House Republican Conference for 10 years. In 1980, he ran for President as an Independent and won 6.6% of the national vote. He is a professor of law at Nova Southeastern University and is the President of the Board of Directors of The Center for Voting and Democracy (Fair Vote) in Washington, D.C.

SAUL ANUZIS is former chairman of the Michigan Republican Party and currently a member of the Republican National Committee.

BIRCH BAYH was a member of the Indiana House of Representatives from 1955 to 1963, its Speaker from 1961 to 1962, and a United States Senator from Indiana from 1963 to 1980. He is currently partner in the law firm of Venable LLP in Washington, D.C. Senator Bayh authored two amendments to the U.S. Constitution—the 25th Amendment on presidential and vice-presidential succession, and the 26th Amendment lowering the voting age to 18.

He also sponsored and led the efforts to adopt a federal constitutional amendment on direct nationwide election of the President in the 1960s and 1970s.

LAURA BROD served in the Minnesota House of Representatives from 2003 to 2010 and was the Ranking Republican member of Minnesota's House Tax Committee. She is the Minnesota Public Sector Chair for ALEC (American Legislative Exchange Council), Governing Board member of the Council of State Governments, Executive Committee Member of the Midwest Legislative Conference, and an Aspen-Rodel Fellow.

JAMES L. BRULTE represented California's 31st senate district, from 1996 to 2004 and served as the Senate Republican leader from 2000 to 2004. He was previously the Republican Leader of the California State Assembly from 1992 to 1996.

JOHN BUCHANAN is an ordained Baptist minister who has served churches in Virginia, Tennessee, Alabama, and Washington, D.C. A life-long Republican, he was Alabama Republican State Finance Director and Jefferson County Chairman prior to his service for sixteen years as the first Republican to represent Birmingham in the Congress in the city's history. A legislative consultant and public interest advocate, he has served as Chairman of the Council for the Advancement of Citizenship and as National Vice-Chairman of the Republican Mainstream Committee. Presently, he is Chairman of the Board of Managers of the Nexus Group.

TOM CAMPBELL earned his bachelor's and master's degrees in economics simultaneously at the University of Chicago, a law degree from Harvard University, and a Ph.D. in economics from the University of Chicago. He served as law clerk to U.S. Supreme Court Justice Byron White, a White House Fellow in the Office of the Chief of Staff, and Executive Assistant to the U.S. Deputy Attorney General. He was a law professor at Stanford University Law School for 19 years, beginning in 1983. He was elected as a California state senator once and elected five times to represent the Silicon Valley area of California in the United States House of Representatives. Campbell served as Director of the California Department of Finance under Governor Arnold Schwarzenegger. He is currently the Bank of America Dean and Professor at the Haas School of Business at the University of California Berkeley. His book, *Separation of Powers in Practice,* published by Stanford University Press in 2004, examines the constitutionally defined roles and powers of the judicial, legislative, and executive branches of government, in the context of some of America's most contentious policy issues.

BARRY F. FADEM is a partner in the law firm of Fadem & Associates in Lafayette, California. He specializes in all aspects of campaign and election law, and provides expert consultation in the area of initiatives and referendums. He is President of National Popular Vote.

B. THOMAS GOLISANO is an American businessman and philanthropist. He is the founder and Chairman of Paychex, the second-largest payroll processor in the United States. He is also the founder of the B. Thomas Golisano Foundation, an organization dedicated to serving those with developmental disabilities.

JOSEPH GRIFFO is New York State Senator (Republican) representing parts of Lewis, Oneida and St. Lawrence counties since 2007. He was Oneida County Executive from 2003 through 2006 and Mayor of Rome, New York, from 1992 through 2003.

MARK GRUESKIN is a shareholder at Isaacson Rosenbaum P.C. in Denver and chairs the firm's Public Law and Policy practice.

RAY HAYNES was first elected to the California State Assembly in 1992. He served in the California State Senate from 1994 to 2002, including as Senate Republican Whip. In 2000 he served as National Chairman of the American Legislative Exchange Council (ALEC). Haynes was again elected to the Assembly in 2002. He is a graduate of the University of Southern California Law School.

ROBERT A. "BOB" HOLMES, PH.D. (Columbia University) is Emeritus Distinguished Professor of Political Science (Atlanta University), former Director of the Southern Center for Studies in Public Policy, and a retired Democratic State Representative (after 34 years of service) in the Georgia General Assembly. He has served as Co-Chair of the Georgia Commission to Revise the State Election Code, an expert witness on voting rights and reapportionment and redistricting cases in several southern region federal district court cases for the ACLU Voting Rights Project and the Southern Poverty Law Center, and an international election observer on election teams in Africa. Dr. Holmes is the author or editor of more than 25 books and more than 60 book chapters and journal articles. His most recent publication is *Maynard Jackson: A Biography.*

JOHN R. KOZA, originator of the plan described in this book, received his Ph.D. in computer science from the University of Michigan in 1972. He published a board game involving Electoral College strategy in 1966. From 1973 through 1987, he was co-founder, chairman, and CEO of Scientific Games Inc., where he co-invented the rub-off instant lottery ticket used by state lotteries. In the 1980s, he and attorney Barry Fadem (see above) were active in promoting adoption of lotteries by various states through the citizen-initiative process and legislative action. He taught a course on genetic algorithms and genetic programming between 1988 and 2003 at Stanford University, where he has been consulting professor in the Department of Computer Science, Department of Electrical Engineering, and Department of Medicine. He is Chair of National Popular Vote.

MICHAEL S. MANDELL has been an associate with the law firm of Perkins Coie Brown & Bain in Phoenix and is currently the general counsel to the Arizona State Senate. He received his J.D. with honors from Arizona State University, where he was an editor of the *Arizona State Law Journal.*

DEAN MURRAY (Republican, Conservative Party) is a member of the New York State Assembly for the third district. He was a Tea Party organizer before being elected to the Assembly in February 2010. He was described by FOX News as the first Tea Party candidate elected to office in the United States.

THOMAS L. PEARCE served as a Republican Michigan state representative from 2005–2010. During his time in the Michigan House, he was appointed Dean of the Republican Caucus, having led several faith-based initiatives in Lansing. Prior to serving in the House, he was the executive director of the North Kent Service Center and served as director of development at Mel Trotter Ministries.

CHRISTOPHER PEARSON is in his third term as a state representative from Burlington, Vermont. He has served on the House Government Operations committee, which has jurisdiction over the state's election laws. Prior to serving in the statehouse, he was the director of the Presidential Election Reform program at FairVote. He began working in politics as a campaign and Congressional aide for then-Congressman Bernard Sanders (I-VT).

ROBERT RICHIE has been the executive director of FairVote—The Center for Voting and Democracy (www.fairvote.org), a non-profit organization dedicated to advancing fair elections, since its founding in 1992. His political writings have appeared in many newspapers and in eight books, including the feature essay in Whose Votes Count. He has been a guest on C-SPAN, NBC News, National Public Radio, CNN, FOX, and MSNBC.

Richie has addressed numerous events, including the annual conventions of the National Association of Counties, and National Conference of State Legislatures and has drafted several pieces of federal and state legislation.

JOSEPH F. ZIMMERMAN is Professor of Political Science at the State University of New York at Albany. He has authored *Interstate Cooperation: Compacts and Administrative Agreements (2002), Interstate Relations: The Neglected Dimension of Federalism (1996), Contemporary American Federalism: The Growth of National Power (1992), The Initiative: Citizen Law-Making (1997), The Referendum: The People Decide Public Policy (1997),* and *The Recall: Tribunal of the People (1997).*

ACKNOWLEDGMENTS

The authors are especially grateful to Paul F. Eckstein of Perkins Coie Brown & Bain in Phoenix for his invaluable advice in the early stages of formulation of their proposal.

Chris Pearson of the Center for Voting and Democracy (Fair Vote) in Washington, DC, made numerous valuable contributions to this book including researching items for this book.

The authors appreciate legal comments from

- Catherine Carroll,
- Edward DuMont,
- Kevin O. Faley,
- Tom Goldstein,
- Martin S. Lederman,
- Spencer Overton,
- Jamin Raskin,
- Leonard Shambon,
- Sonja Starr,
- Laurence H. Tribe, and
- Eugene Volokh.

In addition, the authors gratefully acknowledge the following people who were helpful in preparation of this book:

- David Andre,
- Christie Carter at the Vermont State Archives,
- Susan Cumberpatch,
- Neil Erikson at the Nebraska Secretary of State's office,
- Deb Fadem,
- Kate Gottfredson,
- Terri Hudoba,
- Adam Johnson,
- David Johnstone,
- Lee W. Jones,

- Natalie Marie Koss,
- Alex Michael,
- Bob Michaud, *Reference Librarian, Maine State Law and Legislative Reference Library,*
- John Mountjoy, *Director, National Center for Interstate Compacts, The Council of State Governments,*
- William Mydlowec,
- Elisabeth Higgins Null,
- Timothy Sahd of the Cook Political Report in Washington, DC,
- Ernie Sowada and Amy Bunk of the Office of the Federal Register at the National Archives and Records Administration,
- Matthew J. Streeter,
- Barbara Wardenburg of the League of Women Voters of Mountain View, California, and
- Natalie Young-Lee.

Danielle Terrazas of Color Story Studio in Mountain View, California, did the typesetting and preparation of this book.

FOREWORD
By John B. Anderson

I believe the occupant of the nation's highest office should be determined by a nationwide popular vote by legally registered voters.

The current system of allocating electoral votes on a statewide winner-take-all basis divides us on regional lines, undercuts accountability, dampens voter participation, and can trump the national popular vote. The system is not based on majority rule, and it fails to provide political equality.

The anti-democratic nature of the Electoral College is deeply grounded in our history. The Framers distrusted democracy and saw the Electoral College as a deliberative body that would pick the best candidate. However, the lofty view of the Founding Fathers was based on a wildly mistaken understanding of the way our political system would evolve.

Many believe that the Electoral College was included in the Constitution to satisfy the last-ditch efforts of the "states' righters" of 1787 to preserve as much of the Articles of Confederation as possible. This group was intent on denying direct popular election of the President and preserving the power of the states. Just as they had succeeded in establishing a provision allowing state legislatures to elect the members of the U.S. Senate, they wanted the primary power to elect a President to be lodged in the states—not in a mass electorate of individual voters.

The initial impact was to give slave states additional weight. The infamous constitutional provision counting slaves as three-fifths of a person for the purpose of apportioning Representatives in Congress (and apportioning electoral votes) was designed to favor Southern states. Slaves could not vote, but they could give their owners extra power in both congressional and presidential elections. It is no accident that slave-owning Virginians served as President for thirty-two of the nation's first thirty-six years.

The rule for apportioning electoral votes according to the number of each state's members of Congress is anti-democratic because it makes electoral power in the presidential race dependent on the population of a state, rather than on its number of voters. For this reason, there is no national incentive to spur turnout in a state and expand the franchise. Majority rule and political equality are fundamental tenets of democracy. The power of one's vote should be equal, no matter where one lives. Candidates for our most important national office should have incentives to speak to everyone. In the past century, we have amended the Constitution to elect Senators directly, to guarantee women's right to vote, and to lower the voting age to 18. We have passed the Voting Rights Act to provide access to the ballot regardless of race or ethnicity. The Electoral College has escaped the move to greater democracy only because of institutional inertia and misguided, parochial considerations.

A large majority of Americans have consistently supported direct election of the President for many years, and it is time to listen to them. This book describes the "Agreement Among the States to Elect the President by National Popular Vote," an innovative approach that is a politically practical way to achieve the goal of nationwide popular election of the President. It has my enthusiastic support.

FOREWORD
By Birch Bayh

On January 10, 1977, I introduced S.J. Res.1, a proposed Amendment to the Constitution to abolish the Electoral College and provide for direct election of the President and Vice President of the United States. As Chairman of the Senate Subcommittee on Constitutional Amendments, I held five days of hearings on this and related proposals that year, receiving testimony from 38 witnesses and hundreds of pages of additional statements and academic studies. This series of hearings was not the first time the Subcommittee on Constitutional Amendments undertook a review of the workings and implications of the Electoral College. In fact, my Subcommittee held its first hearing on the process of electing the President on February 28, 1966, and had amassed a record on the need for electoral reform of nearly 2,600 pages prior to the 1977 hearings.

At the end of this process, I was even more firmly convinced that the Electoral College had outlived whatever positive role it once played as a choice of convenience and compromise. Long overdue, the President and Vice President should be chosen by the same method every other elective office in this country is filled—by citizen voters of the United States in a system which counts each vote equally. In 1979 we came close to getting S.J.Res.1 through the Senate but in the end we could not get enough votes to end the filibuster blocking the Resolution. Our effort, like many before it, was relegated to the Congressional history books.

Unfortunately, Congress has continued to block this basic reform that has long-standing, overwhelming public support. Gallup polls have shown strong public support for nationwide popular election of the President for over five decades.[1] Numerous other polls have confirmed a high level of public support for this reform. Polls consistently show 60–80% of Americans believe they should be able to cast votes in the direct election of the President. That is why I unequivocally support this

---

[1] Gallup News Service. 2000. Americans have historically favored changing the way presidents are elected: Historical polling data show majority favored abolishing electoral college system more than 50 years ago. November 10, 2000.

new strategy to provide for the direct election of the President and Vice President. This new approach is consistent with the Constitution but does not rely on the arduous process of a Constitutional Amendment.

Today more than ever, the Electoral College system is a disservice to the voters. With the number of battleground states steadily shrinking, we see candidates and their campaigns focused on fewer and fewer states. While running for the nation's highest office, candidates in 2004 completely ignored three-quarters of the states, including California, Texas, and New York, our three most populous states. Why should our national leaders be elected by only reaching out to 1/4 of our states? It seems inherently illogical, and it is.

Opponents of the direct election often point to the wisdom of the Founding Fathers in drafting the Constitution. No question, the Founders had incredible wisdom and foresight, but they were dealing with a much different society and the Electoral College was designed for the realities of the 18th century. The landmass of the country was huge; travel and communication were arduous and primitive; and education was limited at best. Lack of information about possible Presidential candidates among the general public was a very real consideration. Also, there were issues involving slavery. At the time, 90% of the slave population lived in the South. Since the slaves could not vote, without the weighted vote of the Electoral College, the South faced electoral domination from Northern states. While not the first choice of any Founder, the Electoral College system solved these tricky considerations with a compromise which allowed them to complete the monumental task of creating our country's Constitution.

However, it soon became apparent that the Electoral College process devised by the Founders was flawed. In 1804, the initial Electoral College system was changed through the adoption of the 12th Amendment. Additional weaknesses became apparent. In the 1800s, there were three instances when the popular vote winner lost the Presidency. In 1824, John Quincy Adams was a minority vote winner over Andrew Jackson, as were Rutherford B. Hayes over Samuel J. Tilden (1876), and Benjamin Harrison over Grover Cleveland (1888). This anomaly is not that rare in the Electoral College system. In fact, a small shift of votes in one or two states would have thrown the election to the second-place vote winner five additional times in the last 60 years.

For example, in 1976, Jimmy Carter won a nationwide popular vote victory of 1.7 million votes. However, a change of only 25,579 votes in the states of Ohio and Mississippi would have reelected President Gerald Ford in the Electoral College. With a switch of 18,488 votes in the states of Ohio and Hawaii, the Electoral College normally would have produced a Ford victory. However, because a renegade elector from Washington state cast his vote for non-candidate Ronald Reagan, the final electoral vote count would have been Carter – 268, Ford – 269, and Reagan – 1. Under this scenario, with no candidate receiving the necessary 270 electoral votes, the President would have been chosen by the House of Representatives.

In recent history, we all remember the 2000 election, which awarded the Presidency to the candidate who came in second in the popular vote. In 2004, President Bush defeated Senator Kerry by more than 3 million votes nationwide. However, it is easy to overlook that a change of less than 60,000 votes would have put Ohio in the Kerry column under the Electoral College system and would have elected him President.

In the final analysis, the most compelling reason for directly electing our president and vice president is one of principle. In the United States every vote must count equally. One person, one vote is more than a clever phrase, it's the cornerstone of justice and equality. We can and must see that our electoral system awards victory to the candidates chosen by the most voters. In this day and age of computers, television, rapidly available news, and a nationwide public school system, we don't need nameless electors to cast our votes for president. The voters should cast them directly, themselves. Direct election is the only system that counts every vote equally and where the voters cast their ballots directly for the candidates of their choice. It has the additional virtue of operating in the way most Americans think the electoral process operates—and is expected to operate.

It is heartening to see the Every Vote Equal strategy described in this book which will correct the flawed system we maintain for electing our top two leaders. Our federation of states must band together to solve this long-standing, vexatious problem. Since Congress has repeatedly refused to act, it's refreshing to know states have the ability under the Constitution to step up and create the sensible solution Americans have long been supporting. I hope you will join me in supporting this important effort.

The election of President of the United States should not be a contest between red states and blue states. The President should be chosen by a majority of our citizens, wherever they may live. Direct popular election would substitute clarity for confusion, decisiveness for danger, and popular choice for political chance.

FOREWORD
By Gregory G. Aghazarian

Every four years a presidential election takes place. Our votes are cast. Our votes are counted. But, do they count?

The truth of the matter is that we, the people, do not directly elect the President. The Electoral College elects the President. Every four years, each state appoints electors who in turn elect a president. Under the U.S. Constitution, each state legislature has the complete and total power as to how it appoints its electors (Article II, section 1, clause 2). The current practice in 48 states is to appoint electors, winner-take-all, based on the outcome of each state's popular vote. This sounds simple enough, but the problem is that the current practice ensures that a large majority of Americans have no say in choosing their chief executive.

Most states are solidly "red" or "blue." This means that no matter how much money or time a presidential candidate spends in states like Texas and Wyoming or New York and Vermont, the result is a foregone conclusion. Consequently, no money or time is spent in these states. Instead, virtually everything goes into a small group of "battleground" states. In 2008, two-thirds of the collective presidential campaigns' time and money was dedicated to just 6 states, with 98% going to only fifteen states. Over two-thirds of us just had to sit back and watch.

The real problem with the current winner-take-all practice is that it encourages the wholesale dismissal of the hopes, dreams and aspirations of over 200,000,000 Americans. Issues which are vital to states like Montana and California are routinely disregarded. Under the current system, they do not matter. Issues which are vital to states like Ohio and Pennsylvania are overemphasized. Under the current system, they do matter. It is difficult to imagine that the Founding Fathers intended the disenfranchisement of so many states and the empowerment of so few in their quest to form a more perfect union.

There is a better way. *Every Vote Equal* eloquently lays out the blueprint for a truly democratic and efficient way to elect the President of the United States. Through detailed historic, legal and statistical analysis, this book sets forth a comprehensive and compelling case for each state, pursuant to its constitutional powers, to appoint its electors based on the outcome of the national popular vote. The winner of the election would be the candidate who gets the most popular votes in each of the 50 states plus the District of Columbia. Every state would matter, because every vote would matter. No longer would the issues of a small handful of states dominate presidential elections. Candidates for President would need to be in tune and in touch with all Americans regardless of their address.

The time has come for a national popular vote system.

FOREWORD
By Saul Anuzis

As former chairman of the Michigan Republican Party, I am asking you to consider a bipartisan, truly representative and a more fair process to elect the president of the United States. Our president.

It is the National Popular Vote bill, which would guarantee the presidency to the candidate who receives the most popular votes in all 50 states, and I support it.

This bill has passed multiple chambers around the country in a bipartisan manner. As someone who has run twice for Chairman of the Republican National Committee and is an active "movement conservative," I'm often times challenged about the fact that I'm supporting something that's not blatantly partisan.

Good public policy is good politics, and sometimes good public policy can be bipartisan.

The National Popular Vote plan does not abolish the Electoral College. Instead, it uses the state's existing authority to change how the Electoral College is chosen. The change would be from the current state-by-state approach to a national popular vote approach that would guarantee the presidency to the candidate who receives the most popular votes in all 50 states and the District of Columbia.

The shortcomings of the current system stem from the winner-take-all rule (that is, awarding all of a state's electoral votes to the candidate who receives the most popular votes in each state).

Because of the winner-take-all rule, a candidate can win the presidency without winning the most popular votes nationwide. This has occurred in four of the nation's 56 presidential elections. As an example, a shift of fewer than 60,000 votes in Ohio in 2004 would have defeated President Bush despite his nationwide lead of over three million votes.

This is a state rights issue and we, the people, have the right to decide how and who is elected president.

The U.S. Constitution gives the states exclusive and plenary control over the manner of awarding their electoral votes. The winner-take-all rule is not in the Constitution. It was not the Founders' choice and was used by only three states in the nation's first presidential election in 1789. Maine and Nebraska award electoral votes by congressional district—

a reminder that an amendment to the Constitution is not required to change the way the president is elected.

Under the National Popular Vote, all the electoral votes from the enacting states would be awarded to the presidential candidate who receives the most popular votes in all 50 states. The bill would take effect only when enacted by states possessing a majority of the electoral votes—that is, enough electoral votes to elect a president (270 of 538). As of the end of 2010, the National Popular Vote Bill has been passed by 30 legislative chambers in 20 states. The most recent poll of Michigan voters found that 73 percent or our citizens support this concept. A 2007 national poll showed 72 percent supported it.

The National Popular Vote bill has passed in states having almost a quarter of the electoral votes necessary to bring this into effect. This proposal would guarantee that every vote matters, that every state is relevant. Every community would have the same value to every candidate for president in every election.

This is a serious proposal that deserves serious consideration and debate. The "knee-jerk" reaction against this bill and the ease in which some can "demonize" this issue without serious study or consideration is frustrating. I encourage everyone who cares about our country to read about the "myths," study and understand the intent of our Founding Fathers, and then make a decision as to whether or not this proposal deserves your support.

FOREWORD
By Laura Brod

Like many conservatives, I view most "election reforms" through a skeptical eye. I share a reverence for the Constitution and our founding documents. I believe that the Founders not only got it right, but that they were visionary and creative in their approach.

In all truthfulness, when I first saw the National Popular Vote Plan, I defaulted to a "No" position on the concept. But, I was curious enough to read the legislation, re-read the Constitution, and re-read some relevant Federalist Papers. After evaluating the pros and cons of the current winner-take-all approach and coming to a better understanding of the states' exclusive right to award electors, I moved toward a position of support of both the concept and the legislation.

The concept has too often been referred to by opponents as a "partisan" or even "liberal" effort to eliminate the Electoral College in an attempt to tarnish the issue and scare away those of us on the right side of the political spectrum. But, this description could not be further from the truth.

The National Popular Vote Bill is not a Democratic bill or Republican bill. It is not even a liberal or conservative bill. The National Popular Vote Bill is a bill for Americans interested in both preserving our Electoral College and reforming the shortcomings of our current state-by-state "winner-take-all" system that awards all the electors of one state to the candidate who wins in that particular state. In particular, the "winner-take-all" system has led to a concentration of campaign efforts and policy attention in a few states at the expense of many states. The idea that Presidential candidates and campaigns should seek votes from a broad swath of our country—rather than only focusing on what might move a few voters in the few battleground states—is actually quite non-partisan and has appeal across the political spectrum.

The National Popular Vote plan rightfully utilizes the states' rights, as explicitly spelled out in Section 1, Article II of the United States Constitution in which the Founders specifically gave authority to the states to award their electoral votes as they see fit and to achieve the best influence of the citizens of their state. This is an important states' right designed by the Founders as one of the checks and balances within our republican form of government. It is a state's right that the National Popular Vote Plan recognizes and a right that I support.

The National Popular Vote legislation is not the legislation of the past that many remember. This proposal does not abolish the Electoral College that is crucial to the stability of our republic. It preserves the Electoral College while at the same time utilizing each state's right to award their electors.

The National Popular Vote is an agreement among states that simply changes how they award their own electoral votes.

I am one of a growing number of conservatives who support the National Popular Vote legislation because, contrary to what some folks suggest in rhetorical opposition; the many conservative supporters of the idea know that the National Popular Vote plan is not in conflict with the Constitution and certainly not an end run around the Constitution. In actuality, the legislation is an exercise of power by the states that is explicitly granted by the Constitution.

Legislators across this great country—in red states and blue states, large states and small states—are supporting the National Popular Vote Plan because they are bound by one thing: the fact that their states are "fly-over" states. The great majority of states are effectively ignored in presidential elections. Legislators know this is not good for their state, their citizens, or their entire slate of candidates down the ballot. In fact, that is not good for our country generally. Policies important to the citizens of "flyover" states are not as highly prioritized as policies important to "battleground" states when it comes to governing.

Right now, battleground states enjoy political influence which is less related to the number of their electoral votes and more related to the closeness of the elections. In order to win electoral votes, candidates care what voters in the few battleground states think and want far more than they do voters in the many fly-over states. The hunt for electoral votes leads to an elevation of the importance and perceived immediacy of political and policy issues connected to battleground states. Meanwhile, policy issues more broadly appealing to citizens throughout the country get set aside. Why should the status of the economy or a volatile local issue in a battleground state have the potential to determine the Presidency for the entire country? Why should issues important to the few battleground states get addressed, while other issues important to the many fly-over states are ignored?

Reforming our state-based system of elections through an agreement of the states for a National Popular Vote keeps the stability of our republican form of government by preserving our Electoral College, keeps the checks and balances in place to ensure the protection against so-called mob rule, ensures that voters in every state matter in every election, and keeps the states' rights intended by the Founders securely intact.

The National Popular vote plan being discussed by legislatures across the country does exactly that.

FOREWORD
By James L. Brulte

California voters recently joined other states in stripping the state legislature of its power to draw legislative and congressional districts and allowing a citizen's commission to redraw these lines. Voters did this in part because they knew that with politicians creating safe legislative seats, competition would be diminished, and as a result, politicians of both major parties could ignore their communities with impunity. Unfortunately, our nation's Electoral College provides on the national level what many citizens are trying to eliminate on our state level.

Most states in the union are not in play in Presidential Elections. California, for example, has not voted for a Republican nominee for President since George H. W. Bush carried the state in 1988. Texas has been reliably Republican since 1980. In fact only 16 states have been considered swing states in recent presidential elections, while the remainder are relegated to spectator status.

While this might be fine for the partisans who actually run presidential elections (shrinking the number of states in which their candidates need to compete), it is not good for the citizens of most of the states in the nation.

For example, in 2008 after both parties chose their presidential candidates, all 300 of the campaign events with major-party nominees took place in just 19 states. And from September 24th, two days before the first general election debate until election day, 99.74% of all advertising took place in just 18 states.

While this might be great for the states involved, the rest of the nation suffers as candidates of both major political parties ignore them during the general election. Why is this a problem? Because during the course of campaigns, political candidates are educated about local, regional, and state issues and they take this knowledge with them once they are elected. And with a nation as large and diverse as ours, it is critical that presidential candidates be educated about all our states, not just the lucky 16 swing states.

Fortunately, our founding fathers anticipated the dynamic nature of our country and provided for each state to choose how its presidential electors are chosen. The National Popular Vote provides the necessary incentives to encourage presidential candidates of both major parties to campaign in every state in the union. This is better than the current approach for electing the President. It is better for the candidates, it is better for the citizens of the individual states, and it is better for the nation as a whole.

FOREWORD
By John B. Buchanan

The founder of my party, Abraham Lincoln, described the American political system as "Government of the people, by the people, for the people." Yet in the first presidential election of the twenty-first century, once again the presidential candidate who won the popular vote lost the election, and the will of the people who cared enough to be present and voting was frustrated rather than fulfilled. In the next election the then incumbent President won the popular vote, but a change in the electoral vote of a single state could have cost him the election.

Denying the American people the right to determine by their votes who the President and Vice-President shall be is a flaw in our system, and one that needs fixing. It is time for "the world's greatest democracy" to in fact become one at the highest level of elective office as is already the case at all other levels.

As a member of Congress I voted in support of the direct election of the president and nearly saw the system change during my tenure. At the time it was a controversial idea, but not overburdened by the partisan bickering so much as regional concerns. Many of my colleagues in Southern states, for example, believed the Electoral College system, as it stood, benefited their state.

Today, any discussions, although there have been too few, seem to give rise to partisan concerns. Yet this is not, nor should it be, either a regional or a partisan matter. We should rather be guided by patriotism and principle to do what is right for our country and for the American people as a whole. When we look at the method by which we elect the president, we should have a system that is fair, guarantees votes are counted equally, puts residents of each state on equal footing, and promotes vote-seeking across the nation.

Today, the Electoral College system means that campaigns are focused on dangerously few states. In 2004, over two-thirds of the country was completely neglected during the one nationwide political contest. Candidates spend more and more money to reach fewer and fewer voters. In the close states, which do get attention, under the winner take all system of allotting electoral votes practiced by most states, all who end up on the losing end of even a 50.1% to 49.9% statewide vote are denied the right for their votes to count toward the election of the candidate of their choice at the national level in a national election. Hence, too many people in too many places have no meaningful role in the election process.

In 1969, I was one of 337 members of the U.S. House of Representatives who passed an amendment for direct election of the president. We had overwhelming support and outside help from the US Chamber of Commerce, the American Bar Association, and others who agreed this was a needed change to our system. Unfortunately the effort went down in the Senate. Yet from that time to the present, a large majority of the American people has continued to support the direct election of the president.

Since 1969, Congress has not taken meaningful action to address this issue. While doing away with the Electoral College would be my preference, that requires a Constitutional amendment. Yet the states themselves have the power to achieve the result of the popular election of the President and Vice-President without such an amendment. The time has come for them to act.

The strength of our country and its democracy lies in the public. The people have supported the direct election of the president for over fifty years. In this book, Dr. Koza suggests a way for states to come together and make it happen. If every vote counts equally, if every voter has an equal say in the election of the president and can cast a meaningful vote, then we can better address issues of confidence in our political system, and in fact and fully become a true democracy.

I strongly support and applaud any good-faith effort to make the direct election of the president a reality and commend to you the intriguing approach offered in the "Agreement Among the States to Elect the President by National Popular Vote" described in this book.

I want your vote and my vote to count in the most important elections of all. It can happen. It should happen. If enough of us care enough, it will be done.

FOREWORD
By Tom Campbell

California has 35,893,799 residents. Wyoming has 506,520 residents. California casts 55 electoral votes for President. Wyoming casts 3. The result: A Wyoming voter is worth 4 times a California voter in selecting America's President. If a Third World country, coming into democratic principles out of tyranny, announced a scheme with some citizens worth 4 times as much as others in their governance, it would be told to try again. Indeed, America would tell it to try again!

No Californian should accept the present way we elect Presidents. No American should accept it.

The ingenious approach put forward in this book provides, for the first time, a solution that is achievable. It does not rely on unrealistic assumptions. It can be implemented, if the very people who are relatively disenfranchised in our country will only be awakened to how to do it.

FOREWORD
By B. Thomas Golisano

Seventy-five percent of voters polled in the United States think the way we elect our President should be changed.

Under our current system, a candidate can win the White House without receiving the most votes nationwide. This has actually happened a number of times in our history, and it is likely to happen again.

The current system awards all the state's electoral votes to the candidate who gets the most votes in that particular state. This is called the "winner-take-all" rule. By the way, this method of awarding electoral votes is not a part of the U.S. Constitution. It is strictly a matter of state laws that were adopted on a piecemeal, state-by-state basis.

Unfortunately the winner-take-all rule creates a problem where the candidate with the most votes can actually lose the election. Would you call that democratic?

We can easily change to a system where the candidate with the most votes always wins.

In fact, the process is already underway. Once states representing a majority of electoral votes approve, the process will change, and the President will be elected by the national popular vote.

In fact seven states have already approved this legislation, called the National Popular Vote bill. We are already at a quarter of the votes needed to approve the bill. In 2010, the New York State Senate voted 52 to 7 to go to the National Popular Vote. Republicans supported the change 22 to 5, Democrats 30 to 2. Talk about non-partisanship.

There are some other very important reasons for this bill to be passed.

Have you noticed how the media categorizes our states into two groups: Battleground and fly-over states? A battleground state is a state where the vote for candidates is undecided. The state could go either way. A fly-over state is a state where the outcome is a foregone conclusion for one candidate or the other.

Unless you live in one of the few battleground states, your particular vote doesn't matter. The presidential candidates don't need to consider your issues as they "fly over" your state on the way to the few states that swing presidential elections.

In 2008, candidates concentrated 98% of their ad money and visits in just 15 states.

In summary, we have the option to guarantee that the choice of the American people wins the election. Every American's vote should count. Candidates will pay attention to the needs and concerns of all 50 states not just a few battleground states. And we can do this while preserving the states' power over how we pick our President.

The President we choose represents this entire nation. We should all count when making that choice. This is the world's greatest democracy. Our presidential election should truly be democratic. Please join me and 75% of Americans in supporting the National Popular Vote bill because it's the right thing to do.

FOREWORD
By Joseph Griffo

Presidential elections should be a time when the entire nation is galvanized into action through a vibrant democracy because every citizen has a voice in setting the nation's direction for the next four years.

Sadly, that is not the reality. By October, 12 to 15 swing states are all that matters in presidential campaigns. Much of the nation is shunted into red or blue piles. We in New York know how it feels to be treated as if we were politically irrelevant: my entire state and its voters are ignored by one party and taken for granted by the other. That's not the democracy I want to leave as my legacy to the future. I want to help create a vibrant new democracy that sparks activism instead of abetting apathy.

The National Popular Vote Bill detailed in *Every Vote Equal* will ensure that the voice of the people is heard at every level of government. Isn't that what common sense tells us should happen in the first place?

The current system does not serve the people. According to research by National Popular Vote, presidential candidates concentrate over two-thirds of their advertising money and campaign visits in just six very close states, and over 98 percent of their advertising money in just 15 battleground states. Something is wrong with this picture.

Elections are the cornerstone of our democracy. There is nothing more important in the American system of government than elections that attract voters to examine the challenges of our time. And elections must deal with all the people and all the issues, not just those important to a small handful of states.

The current system of electing a president effectively disenfranchises millions of Americans because they live in states where one candidate or the other has a safe majority. At a time when America needs its citizens to be involved in government, we need to ensure that every vote counts and that the popular vote is the true measure of victory.

For these reasons and more I am proud to be the lead sponsor of the National Popular Vote bill in the New York Senate. We passed the bill in 2010 by a vote of 52-7, but the Assembly didn't get the bill through in 2010. I will continue to push this legislation until New York is on board with the effort. The American people support the principle of a popular vote for President, and I believe New York and the country will be well served once we make this reform a reality.

FOREWORD
By Ray Haynes

Elected officials know how to get elected to office. They know how to raise the necessary resources to get their message out to the voters. They know where to find the people who will work on their campaigns. They know what messages to communicate to voters, and how to communicate those messages. They know the rules that determine what they must do to get elected. The "science" of getting elected requires those who pursue public office to know the rules of elections, discover how voters vote, where their likely voters are located, what messages will persuade these voters to vote, and how best to communicate those messages to voters. It requires them to know where to find the money to communicate those messages, where to find the people who will help communicate those messages, and where those messages can be most effectively communicated to maximize the chances of getting elected.

The art of politics is marshaling the resources available, and using the knowledge obtained, and the rules of the election, to maximize the opportunity for getting elected. Elected officials, and those who help them get elected, spend a lot of time and effort attempting to get elected. They have limited resources (reports to the contrary notwithstanding). Therefore, no one can expect them to spend time or money in places where the expenditure of financial, public relations, or operational resources will not affect the outcome of an election. They work within the rules provided to communicate with the voters whose votes will make a difference in the election in the most effective way.

In most elections, a candidate runs in one district, or state, and if he or she gets the most votes in that district or state, he or she wins. People understand that process. Since the United States Constitution awards presidential electors on the basis of the congressional representation in each state, and since most states award their electors to the winner of the popular vote in that state, Presidential candidates end up running 50 separate elections in the 50 different states. The goal? Win enough states to get 270 electoral votes for president. In my opinion, our Founding Fathers could have set up any number of ways to choose the president.

They chose this one, and I see no reason to change it. The Electoral College, and its allocation of presidential electors to the states based on the number of congressional representatives, has worked quite well for over 200 years.

These rules, however, have led to elections that a lot of people don't understand. Why do candidates spend a lot of time in Ohio, Florida, New Mexico, Wisconsin, Missouri, Pennsylvania, or a few other states, and virtually no time in most of the other states? Why are the citizens of some states virtually pummeled with political advertisements, while others are literally ignored? The reason is, of course, the rules of the game. A candidate can spend millions in California and New York, and not change the electoral outcome, and thousands in New Mexico and become president. We cannot expect our presidential candidates to do things that will not change the outcome of an election, and quite frankly, spending money in some states will not change a single electoral vote.

The good news is our Constitution grants the states the right to award those electors on any basis the state chooses. While the rules each state has adopted up to this point have skewed the allocation of political resources up to this time, there is no reason that the states cannot change those rules, without changing the Constitution, in order to encourage presidential candidates to run a more national campaign. I believe we should be circumspect in changing the Constitution. Elected officials, and voters, in the various states should not, however, be afraid of changing the rules of elections in ways the Constitution allows, in order to correct perceived problems in the electoral process.

The National Popular Vote proposal does just that. The proposal does not change the Constitution, or the method of awarding electors to the various states. If it did, I personally would have found it problematic. It respects the Electoral-College system as established in the Constitution, and the role of the various states in the awarding of their presidential electors. It preserves the fundamental framework provided by the United States Constitution in the election of the President.

It also changes the rules by which the states award their electors, by going to each of those states, and convincing the elected officials and the voters in those states, to award their electors to the candidate that wins the popular vote in all 50 states. It changes the rules by which the electors are awarded to the candidates, and therefore, it will change the decisions a candidate makes when trying to allocate resources in that candidate's campaign.

How will the National Popular Vote proposal affect a candidate's decisions?

First, it will require the candidate to campaign in more places, and in more states. No longer will 10, 12, or 15 states determine the outcome of a presidential campaign. Candidates will allocate their resources to change the minds of voters in more places, because now the votes of each voter in each state could change the outcome in the national election. Today, presidential candidates spend millions to pick up a thousand votes in Florida, Pennsylvania, or Ohio. Under National Popular Vote, that money may get spent to change the minds of voters in Washington State, or Georgia, or Texas, or New York, because those votes will now affect the awarding of electoral votes. Since the states will now agree to award their electors to the candidate that receives the most votes in all 50 states, candidates will devote their resources to receiving the most votes nationwide, and not just the most votes in Missouri or Wisconsin.

Second, it will add more legitimacy to the outcome of the presidential election. People still don't really understand how someone can win an election without winning the most votes. No other election in the country works that way. Governors, Senators, and State Legislators throughout the country win office by winning the most votes. People understand that, and do not question that outcome. The National Popular Vote proposal coincides with the beliefs of most voters on how elections should be decided.

Finally, it preserves the Electoral-College system, and the flexibility that comes with a true federalist proposal. Our federal system has set up a workable framework for elections and governance, granting the states a substantial amount of power to organize their elections and their internal rules in the ways that make sense to the various states. The National Popular Vote proposal respects that process. It sets up a system that makes sense, but allows for changes from the states if the states find that the changes the proposal has implemented are not working. It avoids the inflexibility that a constitutional amendment would impose, and protects the rights and powers of the individual states. It is the blending of common sense and constitutional flexibility that I believe our Founding Fathers contemplated when they drafted the Electoral-College framework.

I support this concept because it will change the rules, and therefore the behavior of the candidates, in ways that will add legitimacy to the election of our President. It preserves the rights of states, and the integrity of the framework established by our Founding Fathers. Finally, it maintains a level of flexibility that allows the states to rethink the process should the individual states discover that the process is not working as they thought it would. The National Popular Vote proposal is in keeping with the best political traditions of our country, innovation in elections and governance with a strong respect for the constitutional framework which established this country. I believe it is a proposal we all can, and should, support, and I intend to do what I can to persuade elected officials and voters of the wisdom of this approach.

FOREWORD
By Dr. Robert A. "Bob" Holmes

The struggle to achieve voting fairness and political equality has continued since the founding of the United States in 1789. Many voting rights issues were first discussed and resolved in the states many years before they were finally applied nationwide, such as granting former slaves and women the right to vote. The states are continuing to serve as "laboratories" for developing new and creative solutions to make this nation a more democratic system of government. The National Popular Vote legislation is another opportunity for states to take a leadership role in changing the current archaic and undemocratic method used to elect the President of the United States.

Perhaps the most important issue of voting inequality in the nation today is the method used to choose the President, particularly the awarding of states' Electoral-College votes using the winner-take-all method. Article I, Section 2 of the U.S. Constitution gives the 50 states the exclusive authority to decide how to allocate their electoral votes in presidential elections. Originally, the Electoral College was created to allow a group of "chosen wise men" whose numbers were determined by the size of the congressional delegation from the various states to meet after the general election at their state capitols to vote for the candidate whom they believed should be President. While competing political parties have come and gone, and there have been changes in the methods for choosing members of the Electoral College, the allocation of these electoral college votes among the candidates has remained a plenary power of the 50 individual state legislatures. Forty-eight states and the District of Columbia use the winner-take-all method while two states, Maine and Nebraska, assign their votes based on congressional districts. Under the current system, four of the 56 presidential elections (1 of each 14) have been "won" by the candidate who finished second in terms of the total national popular vote of the electorate. Further, a change of less than 1 percent in one or two states would have led to the same results in five of the last 12 presidential elections.

In fact, two of the first three elections in the 21st century provide good examples of a major flaw in the current system. In the 2000 contest, Democratic presidential candidate Al Gore won 537,000 more votes than his Republican opponent George Bush, but the latter became President. Then in the 2004 election, President Bush won more than 3 million more popular votes than Democrat John Kerry, but Kerry would have won the Presidency if he had received only 60,000 more votes in Ohio.

The winner-take-all rule (used in 48 states and Washington, D.C.) awards all of the Electoral-College votes to the candidate who receives the most popular votes in the state (or the District of Columbia). This method of awarding electoral votes is the primary culprit of undemocratic outcomes in presidential elections.

A second major problem of the current system is that both major party candidates regularly ignore about 35 of the 50 states in their campaigns because the polls show they are either far ahead in some states or way behind their opponent. Thus, neither candidate has any incentive to campaign in states that are reliably Republican (red) or Democrat (blue) in voting for presidential candidates. Therefore, candidates spend 98% of their financial resources and campaign activities in only 15 states that are considered competitive battlegrounds (which, in practice, means less than a 5% difference in the polls between candidates). And even worse, persons who vote for the losing candidate in their state have their votes awarded to the winning candidate who receives all of the Electoral-College votes in the state!

The current system of electing the President is similar to the method used to elect the Governor of Georgia until 1962. Georgia used the county "unit system" and allocated units (similar to electoral votes) to each county based on their population. The largest counties (including Fulton with 300,000) had a maximum of six units to vote for Governor, while the smallest counties (some having only 2,000 residents) were guaranteed a minimum of one unit. Thus, six of the smallest counties (with a combined total of less than 20,000 people) had more voting power than one county with more than 300,000 people.

Fortunately, the U.S. Supreme Court declared the county unit system used to elect the Governor of Georgia unconstitutional because it violated the political equality doctrine of "one person, one vote." Yet in the 21st century, the President of the United States is still elected by an inequitable Electoral-College vote system that is clearly inequitable. It is important to know that none of the more than 200 nations in the world uses such an anti-democratic method to elect their head of state.

The national popular vote method of electing the President provides a new innovative and creative method that will produce much-needed reform that will guarantee that all future Presidents will be chosen based on the candidate receiving the most national popular votes cast in the 50 states and the District of Columbia.

Recent polls taken between 2008 and 2010 in 32 states show that the American electorate overwhelmingly supports the idea of the direct election of the President by a national electorate, not 51 separate political jurisdictions. In every one of the 32 states where polls were conducted, there was a minimum of 67% who favored the new system over the current method. Also, the actions of many state legislators have already resulted in six states and the District of Columbia enacting the National Popular Vote bill (over a quarter of the electoral votes required). The bill has been approved by 30 legislative bodies in 20 states.

Under the national popular vote method, all of the Electoral-College votes of states that enact legislation to join the interstate compact would agree to cast their electoral college votes for the candidate who receives the most national popular votes. The compact would be activated when the number of states that adopt the legislation constitute a majority (270) of the electoral-college votes (538) required to elect the President.

The public and their elected state legislators understand that the new method would make every vote equal in each state and would likely achieve two other democratic outcomes: (1) cause all Presidential candidates to campaign in all of the states just as they do to win their party's nomination, and (2) generate greater voter interest and turnout in presidential elections because election data show that fewer people turn out in solid red and blue states compared to competitive states. For example, when North Carolina and Virginia (which had been red states for 50 years) became competitive in the 2008 election, voter turnout increased by 8% and 10%, respectively.

Under a national popular vote, candidates would have to pay attention and respond to the policy priorities and concerns of voters in the 50 states, not just 15 states.

Many organizations that have for decades been at the forefront of electoral reform in this nation have recently endorsed the national popular vote legislation because they recognize that the current system of electing the President is the antithesis of the fundamental democratic principles of "one person, one vote" and "every vote equal." Among these organizations are: the American Civil Liberties Union, Common Cause, Fair Vote, The League of Women Voters, the National Association for the Advancement of Colored People, the National Black Caucus of State Legislators, the National Coalition on Black Civic Participation, and many others. Their support resolutions passed at their national conventions included phrases stating the justification for their support, such as: "It would effectively ensure that no future President would be elected without having received the most popular votes" and "It would guarantee that each American vote in this process would count equally."

The National Popular Vote legislation is the most significant proposed election reform in this nation since the Voting Rights Act of 1965 because it will ensure that the principle that every vote should be equal will apply in the election of the President of the United States. This excellent treatise provides a detailed historical, legal, and political analysis of attempts at presidential election reform and also effectively answers the questions and criticisms (myths) made by opponents. More importantly, it provides the best solution to democratize the process of electing the President. In sum, it is an idea whose time has come, and I urge the reader to contact their state legislators and get involved in their state to ensure that this great idea reaches fruition.

FOREWORD
By Dean Murray

Playwright Tom Stoppard once said, "It's not the voting that's democracy, it's the counting." That's the case when it comes to electing a President in our country—thanks to the Electoral College.

In school, we were all taught about the democratic principal of "one man, one vote." That's the case in every election we have here in New York—for school boards, state legislators, and even our governor and U.S. Senators. The only exception to this, however, is for our President.

When it comes to presidential elections, New York is usually completely ignored by candidates from both parties—except for fundraising stops in New York City and the Hamptons. Why? For the simple reason that rarely, if ever, is the Empire State considered a "battleground" or "swing" state.

The Tea Party is the most powerful movement to hit this country in years. We have successfully transformed politics as usual and given voice to the concerns and issues of ordinary taxpayers and working people.

However, the long-term impact of the Tea Party is threatened by a presidential election process that systematically silences voters throughout the country.

The 2012 presidential election will leave fully two-thirds of the voters in the country wondering what is happening. When the general election campaign rolls around in the summer and fall of 2012, the presidential candidates, whoever they are, will ignore voters as they focus their campaigns exclusively on the swing states. Whether you align yourself with the Tea Party, Republicans, Democrats, Libertarians, or Greens, whether you are conservative, liberal, or moderate, the candidates and the campaign will pass you by unless you live in one of a handful of states.

In both 2004 and 2008, candidates spent 98% of their resources in just 15 closely divided battleground states. They concentrated over two-thirds of their resources in just six states. Simply put, the millions and millions of dollars spent advertising and polling and visiting and organizing in this small group of states means that their votes are more important than those of us who live in fly-over country.

This marginalization of the majority of our country is why I support and have sponsored the national popular vote legislation in New York. This proposal, once enacted, will guarantee the Presidency to the candidate receiving the most popular votes in all 50 states.

A vote should be a vote regardless of where it was cast. A voter in Ohio shouldn't be more important than a voter in Kansas. Miami shouldn't trump Main Street. Every voter should be heard, and every vote should count equally.

America can make this happen.

The National Popular Vote bill preserves the Electoral College and the intent of the Constitution. It recognizes that it is the exclusive right of the states, not Congress, the President, or anyone else, to decide how to award their electoral votes. The Constitution makes this perfectly clear under Article II, Section 1.

The current system that allows vast areas of the country to be completely disregarded during the general election was not one that was envisioned by the Founding Fathers. Forty-eight of the 50 states use the winner-take-all rule for allocating their electoral votes (as opposed to just three states in the first election). Under this rule, the candidate who wins the most popular votes in a given state receives all the electoral votes. As a result, the overwhelming majority of Americans are rendered irrelevant when electing their President because they live in a "safe state" where the Republican or Democrat candidate for President is comfortably ahead or hopelessly behind.

The National Popular Vote bill would take effect only when enacted by states possessing a majority of the electoral votes—that is, enough electoral votes to elect a President. When the bill is in effect, all the electoral votes from the states that enacted the bill would be awarded, as a bloc, to the presidential candidate who receives the most popular votes in all 50 states.

A national popular vote based on the candidate receiving the most votes in the country would encourage candidates to court voters of every party, in every state, and to reach out across our great nation. Candidates would be forced to listen to the concerns of Americans everywhere, not just where it counts politically under today's system.

The Tea Party movement is about many things. Perhaps the most important is that our voices and our values be heard by our government.

President Dwight D. Eisenhower said "The future of this republic is in the hands of the American voter." The best way to make that happen in the long term is to make every vote count. A national popular vote for President, where every vote counts and every vote counts equally, ensures that no-one will be marginalized or overlooked in the future.

FOREWORD
By Tom Pearce

In 2008, the state of Michigan had 17 electoral votes. As a state with nearly twice the population of the average state, not to mention twice the problems, Michigan should have had a strong voice in the presidential election. You would have expected both candidates to fight long and hard for our vote.

Not so. In fact, John McCain pulled out of Michigan four weeks before the election, ceding Michigan's electoral votes to Barack Obama. As a Republican I was disappointed, of course. But as a citizen of this great state, I was outraged.

Of course, Michigan was the victim of a policy that actually rewards presidential candidates for ignoring the majority of states. The winner-take-all system of awarding electoral votes treats election results in more than thirty states as a foregone conclusion.

The result? No campaign stops, no campaign dollars, and no incentive to represent the needs of Michigan voters at a national level.

If every single voter in Michigan had cast his or her vote for Barack Obama, the outcome would have been exactly the same. The winner-take-all system of awarding electoral votes effectively disenfranchises every voter beyond those needed to establish a plurality. In 2008, the people of Michigan spoke, and nobody listened.

When I think of blue states or red states, Michigan doesn't exactly come to mind. Our presidential vote totals are typically close. We recently flipped the state House, and the Governor's office. Michigan isn't a one-party state like Utah or Massachusetts. Even moderate states like Michigan are being cast aside as the list of battleground states continues to shorten.

This is a high-school civics lesson gone wrong.

We see the impact of this political calculus at a national level. Compare the response to hurricane Katrina (in Louisiana, a "safe" state) to the federal response to hurricanes in Florida (a "swing" state) under Presidents of both parties. President Obama only became angry about the BP oil spill once it reached Florida's shores.

Thankfully, hurricanes and oil spills aren't a problem here in Michigan. We have an equally urgent disaster, however, in the form of unemployment. Our people need jobs, and deserve respect from the executive branch in accordance with our population. This is no time to be taken for granted.

Fortunately, the U.S. Constitution gives the states the means to remedy the shortcomings of the present system, and restore a voice to voters in states like Michigan. The winner-take-all rule, which may have once made sense, can be continued or discontinued at our, or any state's discretion. It is not mentioned anywhere in the Constitution, much less mandated.

The National Popular Vote compact leverages the power accorded to the states by the Constitution to ensure that every vote counts equally. Under this system, states agree to award their electoral votes to the candidate who wins the most votes in all fifty states. This would give Michigan a voice commensurate with its population.

When states like Michigan are getting lost in our electoral system, it's time for a change. The National Popular Vote initiative is long overdue, and it has my full support.

FOREWORD
By Christopher Pearson

By the time I became familiar with the National Popular Vote bill I already liked the idea of a popular vote for president. There is something so basic about one person, one vote. I didn't need much convincing.

As I learned more about this proposal for state action I began to appreciate how far-reaching the impacts of this bill would be. Living in Vermont, we are all familiar with the organized treks of campaign volunteers to the swing state of New Hampshire. This occurs at the time of the New Hampshire primary and then, because New Hampshire has been a battleground state for several cycles; the trek occurs again in the fall campaign. As somebody who has worked on Vermont campaigns, it is frustrating to lose good volunteers to our neighbor to the East.

There is nothing special about New Hampshire's voters. They just happen to be evenly divided. They aren't solid blue or solid red. The end result in New Hampshire is up for grabs, and so the candidates and their teams do everything they can to get the four electoral votes New Hampshire offers. Candidates do next to nothing to earn the three votes we hold here in Vermont.

Our three electoral votes get completely taken for granted because we are a reliably blue state. Thirty-four other states are similarly reliable for one party or the other. Examining election results makes it obvious that more and more Americans are effectively left out of our process. This isn't some fluke of the last few cycles—it's a trend that's been continuing for 50 years. It's obvious to most Americans that our electoral system is broken.

Vermont isn't ignored because we're a small state. And we don't get any meaningful bonus because we're little, despite what we learned in high-school civics. The bottom line is candidates either care about earning your votes or they don't. Because we're a safe "blue" state, Democrats running for the White House know they have us, and the Republicans know they couldn't possibly win us. Therefore, nobody polls us, nobody visits us, and campaigns are organized to get our people on the phone to Ohio or knock on the doors in New Hampshire.

But the impact of National Popular Vote goes way beyond the basic fairness of every vote counting equally; that only scratches the surface.

Does anybody really believe a sitting president doesn't consider his re-election when his administration hands out stimulus money? Or makes trade policy? Or energy policy? Is it a coincidence that President Bush, a free trader, put a tariff on steel—an industry that just happens to be important in Pennsylvania? I doubt it.

A close examination of everything from policy decisions to travel schedules of a president reveals a strong bias to the states that happen to be up for grabs in the Electoral College. While most states wrestle with budget deficits and soaring costs I hope you might take a bit of time and right a fundamental flaw in American politics. The impact will be far-reaching and positive for generations to come.

WHAT PEOPLE ARE SAYING ABOUT NATIONAL POPULAR VOTE

"Innovative new proposal ... Legislatures across the country should get behind it."
— New York Times Editorial — March 14, 2006

"The Sun-Times News Group backs the concept and applauds the National Popular Vote group for thinking outside the box."
— Chicago Sun Times Editorial — March 1, 2006

"The Legislature [should] do the right thing and endorse the new compact."
— Minneapolis Star Tribune Editorial — March 27, 2006

"This book describes the 'Agreement Among the States to Elect the President by National Popular Vote'—an innovative approach that is a politically practical way to achieve the goal of nationwide popular election of the President. It has my enthusiastic support."
— John B. Anderson (R–Illinois and Independent presidential candidate)

"The President and Vice President should be chosen by the same method every other elective office in this country is filled—by citizen voters of the United States in a system which counts each vote equally.... I unequivocally support this new strategy to provide for the direct election of the President and Vice President. This new approach is consistent with the Constitution.... It's refreshing to know states have the ability under the Constitution to step up and create the sensible solution Americans have long been supporting."
— Birch Bayh (D–Indiana)

"The people have supported the direct election of the President for over fifty years. In this book, Dr. Koza suggests a way for states to come together and make it happen.... I strongly support and applaud any good-faith effort to make the direct election of the President a reality and commend to you the intriguing approach offered in the 'Agreement Among the States to Elect the President by National Popular Vote' described in this book."
— John Buchanan (R–Alabama)

"The ingenious approach put forward in this book provides, for the first time, a solution that is achievable. It does not rely on unrealistic assumptions. It can be implemented, if the very people who are relatively disenfranchised in our country will only be awakened to how to do it."

–Tom Campbell (R–California)

"What makes the National Popular Vote plan particularly promising is how neatly it fits in with American traditions. A century ago it was states that first established women's suffrage and direct election of U.S. Senators. Under the U.S. Constitution it is states that have the power to fix our broken presidential election system. This book provides the roadmap."

–Chellie Pingree (Former President of Common Cause, U.S. Representative)

"This isn't a Democratic or Republican issue to me. It's important that people have faith that in the election of the most important office in the world that their vote will count. I'm proud to sponsor legislation that will hopefully result in presidential candidates showing up and working to meet voters in my state."

– Kirk W. Dillard (Illinois State Senator and former Chairman of DuPage County Republican Party)

1 | Introduction

In elections for President and Vice President of the United States, every vote should be equal. Every person's vote should be equally important, regardless of the state in which the vote is cast. The presidential and vice-presidential candidate who receive the most popular votes throughout the United States should win those offices. The current system for electing the President and Vice President does not satisfy these principles. This book presents a politically practical way by which action at the state level can bring presidential elections into conformity with these principles.

This chapter

- describes what the U.S. Constitution says—and does not say—about presidential elections (section 1.1),
- highlights three significant shortcomings of the current system for electing the President and Vice President of the United States and identifies the common cause of all three problems (section 1.2),
- identifies nationwide popular election as a remedy for the shortcomings of the current system (section 1.3),
- notes the fortuitous convergence of factors favoring reform at the present time (section 1.4),
- provides a roadmap to the remainder of this book (section 1.5), and
- identifies additional sources of information (section 1.6).

1.1 WHAT THE U.S. CONSTITUTION SAYS—AND DOES NOT SAY—ABOUT PRESIDENTIAL ELECTIONS

The method of selecting the President and Vice President of the United States is not set forth in detail in the U.S. Constitution. In fact, the Founding Fathers never reached agreement on a complete system for selecting the President. Aside from scheduling and administrative provi-

1

sions,[1] the U.S. Constitution specifies only four aspects of presidential elections:

- **Indirect Election:** The Constitution specifies that the President and Vice President are to be chosen every four years by a small group of people who are individually referred to as presidential "electors." The electors are often collectively referred to as the "Electoral College," although this term does not appear in the Constitution.

- **Allocation of Electoral Votes to the States:** The Constitution specifies that each state is entitled to one presidential elector for each of its U.S. Representatives and Senators. Today, there are a total of 538 electoral votes.[2]

- **Majority of Electoral College Required for Election:** The Constitution specifies that a presidential or vice-presidential candidate must win a majority of the electoral votes in order to be elected to office (that is, 270 of the 538 electoral votes). In the absence of such a majority, the U.S. House of Representatives chooses the President, and the U.S. Senate chooses the Vice President.[3]

---

[1] The Constitution contains provisions concerning setting the date for appointing presidential electors, setting the date for the meeting of presidential electors, recording the electoral votes, and counting the electoral votes by Congress. For the reader's convenience, appendix A contains the provisions of the U.S. Constitution relating to presidential elections.

[2] The total of 538 electoral votes corresponds to the 435 U.S. Representatives from the 50 states *plus* the 100 U.S. Senators from the 50 states *plus* the three electoral votes that the District of Columbia received under the 23rd Amendment to the Constitution (ratified in 1961). Every 10 years, the 435 U.S. Representatives are reapportioned among the states in accordance with the latest federal census, thereby automatically reapportioning the electoral votes among the states. The number of U.S. Representatives is set by federal statute.

[3] More precisely, a majority of the presidential electors "appointed" are required for election. There have been several occasions when a state has failed to appoint its presidential electors. For example, New York failed to appoint its electors for the nation's first presidential election in 1789, and 11 southern states failed to appoint their electors for the 1864 election during the Civil War. In the event that no candidate receives an absolute majority of the number of presidential electors who are "appointed" for a particular presidential election, the Constitution provides that the House of Representatives chooses the President (with each state casting one vote regardless of the size of its congressional delegation) and that the Senate chooses the Vice President (with each Senator casting one vote).

- **The Way That the Presidential Electors Cast Their Votes:** Under the original Constitution, each presidential elector cast two votes. The leading candidate became President, and the second-place candidate became Vice President. Under the 12th Amendment to the Constitution (ratified in 1804), each presidential elector casts a separate vote for President and Vice President.

As can be seen from the above, the U.S. Constitution is silent about many of the most politically important features of presidential elections, most notably including:

(1) **Who Votes for the Presidential Electors?** Do the nation's voters, for example, have any direct voice in choosing the presidential electors?

(2) **How Are Votes Counted for Presidential Electors?** Regardless of who may be entitled to vote for the presidential electors, are the votes to be counted on a statewide basis? By congressional district? In regional multi-member districts? In specially created presidential elector districts? In a proportional way? In some other way?

The Constitution does not answer these (and other politically important) questions about the conduct of presidential elections. Instead, the Founding Fathers created a system with considerable built-in flexibility. The Constitution leaves these questions to be decided by the individual states. It provides:

> "Each State shall **appoint,** in such **Manner as the Legislature thereof may direct,** a Number of Electors, equal to the whole Number of Senators and Representatives to which the State may be entitled in the Congress...."[4]
> [Emphasis added]

The above delegation of power to the states concerning presidential elections is unusually unconstrained. It contrasts significantly with the limitations contained in the Constitution on state power over congressional elections.

---

[4] U.S. Constitution. Article II, section 1, clause 2.

"The Times, Places and Manner of holding Elections for Senators and Representatives, shall be prescribed in each State by the Legislature thereof; **but the Congress may at any time by Law make or alter such Regulations**...."[5] [Emphasis added]

Accordingly, the U.S. Supreme Court has characterized state power concerning the manner of appointing presidential electors as "supreme," "plenary,"[6,7] and exclusive. As the Court wrote in 1892:

"In short, the appointment and mode of appointment of electors belong **exclusively** to the states under the constitution of the United States."[8]

In a 1919 case involving a state statute entitled "An act granting to women the right to vote for presidential electors," the Maine Supreme Judicial Court wrote:

"[E]ach state is thereby clothed with the **absolute power to appoint electors in such manner as it may see fit, without any interference or control on the part of the federal government,** except, of course, in case of attempted discrimination as to race, color, or previous condition of servitude...."[9] [Emphasis added]

Over the years, the states have used the Constitution's built-in flexibility concerning presidential elections in a remarkable variety of ways. Many of the most familiar features of present-day presidential elections

---

[5] U.S. Constitution. Article II, section 4, clause 1.

[6] In the 1892 case of *McPherson v. Blacker*, the U.S. Supreme Court wrote, "[F]rom the formation of the government until now the practical construction of the clause has conceded **plenary** power to the state legislatures in the matter of the appointment of electors" (146 U.S. 1 at 36) [Emphasis added].

[7] In the 2000 case of *Bush v. Gore*, the U.S. Supreme Court wrote, "The individual citizen has no federal constitutional right to vote for electors for the President of the United States unless and until the state legislature chooses a statewide election as the means to implement its power to appoint members of the Electoral College. U.S. Const., Art. II, §1. This is the source for the statement in *McPherson v. Blacker*, 146 U.S. 1, 35 (1892), that the State legislature's power to select the manner for appointing electors is **plenary;** it may, if it so chooses, select the electors itself, which indeed was the manner used by State legislatures in several States for many years after the Framing of our Constitution. *Id.*, at 28–33." (531 U.S. 98. 2000) [Emphasis added].

[8] *McPherson v. Blacker.* 146 U.S. 1 at 29. 1892.

[9] *In re Opinion of the Justices.* 107 A. 705. 1919.

were not in widespread use immediately after ratification of the Constitution.

   (1) **Who Votes for the Presidential Electors?** In the nation's first presidential election in 1789, only four states gave the voters a direct voice in electing the presidential electors. In most states, there was no election at all, and the legislature simply "appointed" the presidential electors. By 1836, the voters elected the presidential electors in all states except South Carolina. No state legislature has appointed presidential electors since Colorado did so in 1876.[10]

   (2) **How Are Votes Counted for Presidential Electors?** In 1789, only three states awarded their electoral votes using the system that is now in almost universal use throughout the United States—that is, the statewide "winner-take-all" rule. Under this rule, a majority (or, nowadays, a plurality) of each state's voters controls the election of 100% of the state's presidential electors. In 1789, Virginia permitted the voters to elect presidential electors in specially created presidential elector districts, thereby creating the possibility that minority sentiment within the state would control some of the state's electoral votes. At various times in other states, voters elected presidential electors from congressional districts or from multi-member regional districts. Various indirect methods have been used occasionally, including a miniature state-level electoral college in Tennessee to choose the state's members of the national Electoral College.[11] Today, the voters in Maine and Nebraska elect presidential electors by congressional district.

    In short, there was no consensus among the Founding Fathers in favor of two of the most politically salient features of present-day

---

[10] Section 2.2 covers the history of methods of selecting presidential electors.

[11] As detailed in section 2.2.2, in 1796, in Tennessee, specific citizens from various groups of counties were named in the state law establishing this system. The specifically named individuals then chose the presidential electors for their part of the state. In 1828, the New York legislature created an indirect system in which the presidential electors who were elected by the voters from each of the state's congressional districts selected the state's two senatorial presidential electors (section 2.2.4).

presidential elections—namely voting by the people and the statewide winner-take-all rule. These features are not mandated by the U.S. Constitution. These features were not implemented by amending the U.S. Constitution. Instead, these now-familiar features came into existence because the states used the flexibility that the Founders built into the Constitution to make these features part of our political landscape. These features are strictly a matter of state law.

The piecemeal adoption by the states of the winner-take-all rule is particularly instructive. As the U.S. Supreme Court noted in 1892, many of the Founding Fathers considered the district system (such as that used by Virginia in the nation's first presidential election) to be "the most equitable."[12] However, as early as the nation's first competitive presidential election (1796), it had become clear to political observers that the district system diminished a state's political influence because it fragmented the state's electoral votes. As historian Noble Cunningham wrote:

> "The presidential election of 1796 had been extremely close, and in examining the results of that contest Republican Party managers had been struck by the fact that **Adams' 3-vote margin of victory in the electoral college could be attributed to 1 vote from Pennsylvania, 1 from Virginia, and 1 from North Carolina.** In each of these states, the Republicans had won an impressive victory, amassing in the three states a total of 45 electoral votes. The loss of 3 votes in these strongly Jeffersonian states was due to the district method of electing presidential electors. **In looking for ways to improve their chances for victory in the next presidential election, Republican managers thus turned their attention to state election laws.**"[13] [Emphasis added]

On January 12, 1800, Thomas Jefferson (the losing Republican[14] candidate from the 1796 election) wrote James Monroe (then a member of the legislature in Jefferson's home state of Virginia):

---

[12] *McPherson v. Blacker:* 146 U.S. 1 at 29. 1892.

[13] Cunningham, Noble E., Jr. In Schlesinger, Arthur M., Jr. and Israel, Fred L. (editors). 2002. *History of American Presidential Elections 1878–2001.* Philadelphia, PA: Chelsea House Publishers. Pages 104–105. See section 2.2.3 for additional details on the 1796 election.

[14] Jeffersonians were originally called Anti-Federalists, later Republicans or Democratic-Republicans, and eventually Democrats.

"On the subject of an election by a general ticket [the statewide winner-take-all rule], or by districts, most persons here seem to have made up their minds. All agree that an **election by districts would be best, if it could be general; but while 10 states chuse either by their legislatures or by a general ticket, it is folly & worse than folly** for the other 6. not to do it."[15] [Emphasis added; spelling and punctuation as per original]

Thus, although the statewide winner-take-all system may not have been "best," Virginia changed from its original district system to the winner-take-all system, thereby ensuring Jefferson 100% of his home state's electoral votes in the 1800 elections.

Over a period of years, more and more states gravitated to the statewide winner-take-all rule to avoid the "folly" of fragmenting their electoral votes. By 1836, all but one state had adopted the statewide winner-take-all rule.[16] Except for Florida in 1868, Colorado in 1876, and Michigan in 1892, all states used the statewide winner-take-all rule between 1860 and 1972.

More recently, Maine (since 1972) and Nebraska (since 1992) have awarded one electoral vote to the candidate who carries each congressional district in the state and two electoral votes to the presidential candidate carrying the state.[17] The present-day state laws in Maine and Nebraska are reminders of the flexibility that the Founders built into the U.S. Constitution. They are reminders that the manner of conducting presidential elections is strictly a matter of state law. Most importantly,

---

[15] The January 12, 1800 letter is discussed in greater detail and quoted in its entirety in section 2.2.3. Ford, Paul Leicester. 1905. *The Works of Thomas Jefferson.* New York: G. P. Putnam's Sons. 9:90.

[16] The South Carolina legislature elected the state's presidential electors until 1860, so South Carolina's electoral votes were also cast as a solid bloc. See chapter 2 for a detailed history of the proliferation of the statewide winner-take-all rule.

[17] In all 13 presidential elections in which the district system has been used by Maine and Nebraska, the presidential candidate carrying the state has carried all of the state's congressional districts. The reason why the congressional district system has not produced a division of the electoral votes in Maine and Nebraska is that Maine has only two congressional districts and Nebraska has only three. The presidential candidate carrying a state with only a few districts is apt to carry each of the state's individual districts. Thus, in terms of the practical political outcome, the statewide "winner take all" rule is universal throughout the United States despite the Maine and Nebraska laws.

they are reminders that the now-prevailing statewide winner-take-all rule may be changed, at any time, by the states—merely by passage of a state law.

1.2 SHORTCOMINGS OF THE CURRENT SYSTEM

The current system for electing the President and Vice President of the United States has three major shortcomings:

- **Voters Are Effectively Disenfranchised in Two Thirds of the States in Presidential Elections.** Under the now-prevailing statewide winner-take-all rule, presidential candidates do not campaign in states in which they are far ahead because they do not receive any additional electoral votes by winning such states by a larger margin. Similarly, candidates ignore states where they are far behind because they have nothing to gain by losing those states by a smaller margin. Instead, presidential candidates concentrate their public appearances, organizational efforts, advertising, polling, and policy attention on states where the outcome of the popular vote is not a foregone conclusion. In practical political terms, a vote matters in presidential politics only if it is cast in a closely divided battleground state. To put it another way, the question of whether a voter matters in presidential politics depends on whether *other* voters in the voter's own state happen to be closely divided. In the five most recent presidential elections (1988–2004), about two thirds of the states have been non-competitive, including six of the nation's 10 most populous states (California, Texas, New York, Illinois, New Jersey, and North Carolina), 12 of the 13 least populous states,[18] and the vast majority of medium-sized states.
- **The Current System Does Not Reliably Reflect the Nationwide Popular Vote.** The statewide winner-take-all

---

[18] There are 13 states with just one or two U.S. House members (and hence three or four electoral votes). Of the 13 smallest states, only New Hampshire has been competitive in recent presidential elections (having gone Republican in 1988, 1992, and 2000 and having gone Democratic in 1996 and 2004). The small states tend to be non-competitive in presidential elections because they are apt to be one-party states.

rule makes it possible for a candidate to win the Presidency without winning the most popular votes nationwide. This has occurred in one of every 14 presidential elections (as detailed in section 1.2.2). In the past six decades, there have been six presidential elections in which a shift of a relatively small number of votes in one or two states would have elected (and, of course, in 2000, did elect) a presidential candidate who lost the popular vote nationwide.

*   **Not Every Vote Is Equal.** The statewide winner-take-all rule creates variations of 1000-to-1 and more in the weight of a vote (as illustrated in section 1.2.3).

1.2.1 Voters in Two Thirds of the States Are Effectively Disenfranchised

Most people who follow political news are aware of the fact that presidential campaigns are concentrated on a tiny handful of battle-ground states; however, few are aware of the extreme degree of this concentration.

Although there is no single definition of a "battleground" state, these states can be readily identified by examining where presidential campaigns pay close attention to public opinion, where they spend their advertising money, and where they campaign.

In terms of polling, presidential candidates pay hardly any attention to the concerns of voters in states that are not closely divided in presidential elections. As Charlie Cook reported in 2004:

> "Senior Bush campaign strategist Matthew Dowd pointed out yesterday that the Bush campaign hadn't taken a national poll in almost two years; instead, it has been polling 18 battle-ground states."[19]

Kerry similarly pursued an 18-state strategy in 2004.

Battleground states can be readily identified by "following the money." Fully 99% of the $237,423,744 reported advertising expenditures in the last month of the 2004 presidential campaign was spent in only 17

---

[19] Cook, Charlie. 2004. Convention dispatches—As the nation goes, so do swing states. Charlie Cook's Political Report. August 31, 2004.

Table 1.1 THE 17 STATES RECEIVING 99% OF THE ADVERTISING MONEY

PER CAPITA AD SPENDING	STATE	AD SPENDING
$4.45	New Mexico	$8,096,270
$4.30	Nevada	$8,596,795
$4.16	Ohio	$47,258,386
$4.02	Florida	$64,280,557
$3.73	New Hampshire	$4,608,200
$3.22	Iowa	$9,412,462
$3.00	Pennsylvania	$36,813,492
$2.70	Wisconsin	$14,468,062
$2.18	Minnesota	$10,734,683
$1.70	Maine	$2,171,101
$1.63	Colorado	$7,015,486
$1.36	Michigan	$13,518,566
$1.22	West Virginia	$2,213,110
$0.67	Oregon	$2,280,367
$0.42	Missouri	$2,361,944
$0.32	Hawaii	$388,095
$0.20	Washington	$1,198,882
	Total	**$235,416,458**

states. Table 1.1 lists the 17 states in order of per capita spending.[20] The nine states where per capita spending exceeded $2.00 correspond to the top-tier battleground states and account for seven eighths (87%) of the $237,423,744. Five states (Florida, Iowa, Ohio, Pennsylvania, and Wisconsin) account for three quarters (72%) of the money.

A mere 1% of the money was spent in the remaining 34 of the 51 jurisdictions entitled to vote in presidential elections. The 1% was split among 11 jurisdictions, while nothing at all was spent in 23 states.

Advertising expenditures were similarly concentrated during the earlier part of the presidential campaign period.[21]

Candidate travel is another way to identify battleground states. The major-party presidential or vice-presidential candidates appeared at 307

---

[20] The period covered was October 2 to November 4, 2004. See FairVote. 2005. *Who Picks the President?* Takoma Park, MD: The Center for Voting and Democracy. www.fairvote.org/whopicks. See also http://www.cnn.com/ELECTION/2004/special/president/campaign.ads/.

[21] An article by Chuck Todd in the *New York Times* (November 3, 2004) reported that five states accounted for 66% of the TV ad spending over the entire campaign period ($380 million of the $575 million spent).

Table 1.2 THE 16 STATES RECEIVING 92% OF THE VISITS BY THE PRESIDENTIAL AND VICE-PRESIDENTIAL CANDIDATES

STATE	CAMPAIGN EVENTS
Florida	61
Ohio	48
Iowa	37
Wisconsin	31
Pennsylvania	23
Michigan	19
Minnesota	14
Colorado	10
Nevada	7
New Hampshire	6
New Mexico	6
Oregon	5
Missouri	5
Arizona	4
New Jersey	4
California	2
Total	**282**

campaign events in the last month of the 2004 campaign. These 307 events were concentrated in 27 states.[22] If one excludes from consideration the six states receiving only one visit,[23] the home states of the four candidates,[24] and the District of Columbia (where all four candidates had day jobs),[25] 92% of the 307 campaign events were concentrated in just 16 states (as shown in table 1.2). Two thirds (200 of the 307) of the events were concentrated in Florida, Ohio, Iowa, Wisconsin, and Pennsylvania (the same five states that accounted for three quarters of the money).

As can be seen from table 1.2, 35 (over two thirds) of the 51 jurisdictions entitled to vote in presidential elections cumulatively received

---

[22] For simplicity, we often refer to the District of Columbia as a "state" in this book. The 23rd Amendment provides that the District of Columbia's three electoral votes "shall be considered, for the purposes of the election of President and Vice President, to be electors appointed by a state."

[23] Hawaii, Kansas, Maine, Maryland, West Virginia, and New York.

[24] There were four events in Texas (Bush's home state) and Massachusetts (Kerry), three in Wyoming (Cheney), and two in North Carolina (Edwards).

[25] There were six events in the District of Columbia.

Table 1.3 NINETEEN CLOSE STATES IN THE 2000 PRESIDENTIAL ELECTION

STATE	ELECTORAL VOTES	DEMOCRATIC PERCENTAGE
Louisiana	9	46.06%
Arizona	8	46.72%
West Virginia	5	46.76%
Arkansas	6	47.20%
Tennessee	11	48.04%
Nevada	4	48.14%
Ohio	21	48.18%
Missouri	11	48.29%
New Hampshire	4	49.33%
Florida	25	50.00%
New Mexico	5	50.03%
Wisconsin	11	50.12%
Iowa	7	50.16%
Oregon	7	50.24%
Minnesota	10	51.29%
Pennsylvania	23	52.15%
Michigan	18	52.63%
Maine	4	52.75%
Washington	11	52.94%
Total	**200**	

only 8% of the campaign visits. Almost half of the states received no visits at all.

In short, polling, advertising, and campaigning are not merely skewed toward about a dozen and a half states in presidential campaigns, but the remaining two thirds of the states are, for all practical purposes, *excluded* from the campaign. They are mere spectators in the election process.

Not surprisingly, this concentration of polling, advertising, and travel corresponds closely to the states where the presidential election was close. Table 1.3 shows the 19 states in which the two-party vote for President was between 46% and 54% in the 2000 presidential election, starting with the least Democratic state.[26]

---

[26] Not all of the states in the tables are full-fledged battleground states. The 2004 Kerry campaign made efforts to pick up three states that Bush had carried in 2000 (Missouri, Colorado, and Nevada), and the 2004 Bush campaign made similar efforts to reverse the 2000 results in Delaware, Washington, New Jersey, and Oregon. Nonetheless, as the 2004 campaign progressed, it became apparent that none of these states would actually change hands. By the end of the campaign, there were few actual battleground states.

Table 1.4 SIXTEEN CLOSE STATES IN THE 2004 PRESIDENTIAL ELECTION

STATE	ELECTORAL VOTES[27]	DEMOCRATIC PERCENTAGE
Missouri	11	46.33%
Colorado	9	47.35%
Florida	27	47.47%
Nevada	5	48.67%
Ohio	20	48.75%
New Mexico	5	49.42%
Iowa	7	49.54%
Wisconsin	10	50.20%
New Hampshire	4	50.68%
Pennsylvania	21	51.13%
Michigan	17	51.73%
Minnesota	10	51.76%
Oregon	7	51.97%
New Jersey	15	53.13%
Washington	11	53.60%
Delaware	3	53.82%
Total	**182**	

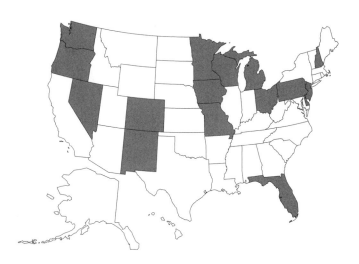

Figure 1.1 Sixteen close states in the 2004 presidential election

---

[27] Some states in tables 1.3 and 1.4 have a different number of electoral votes because of the reallocation of electoral votes resulting from the 2000 federal census.

Table 1.4 and figure 1.1 show the 16 states in which the two-party vote for President was between 46% and 54% in the 2004 presidential election, starting with the least Democratic state.

The 16 states in table 1.4 and figure 1.1 together represent 182 electoral votes—34% of the total (538).

Because each state receives one electoral vote for each of its U.S. Representatives, the Founding Fathers expected that the Constitution's formula for allocating electoral votes would give the most populous states the greatest amount of influence in presidential elections. Glances at tables 1.1 through 1.4 and figure 1.1 show that the Founders did not achieve this objective. Large states are not necessarily important in presidential elections. Six of the nation's 10 most populous states (California, Texas, New York, Illinois, New Jersey, and North Carolina) are non-competitive in presidential elections. Non-competitive states—regardless of their size or number of electoral votes—simply do not matter in presidential elections.

The Founders' intended allocation of political influence in favor of the most populous states was not achieved because of the cumulative effect of the nearly universal adoption by the states of the winner-take-all rule. Political power resides in the scattered collection of states of various sizes where the popular vote happens to be closely divided—that is, the battleground states. In short, the Founders' attempt to allocate political influence was trumped by the decisions—taken separately by the individual states—to adopt the winner-take-all rule.

The less populous states are similarly affected by the statewide winner-take-all rule. As part of the political compromise that led to the Constitution, the Founding Fathers intended to confer a certain amount of extra influence on the less populous states by giving every state a bonus of two electoral votes corresponding to its two U.S. Senators.[28] Again, tables 1.1 through 1.4 and figure 1.1 show that the Founding Fathers did not achieve their objective. Because small states are apt to be one-party states, 12 of the 13 (92%) least populous states are non-competitive in presidential elections. Non-competitive states—with or without a bonus of two extra electoral votes—simply do not matter in

---

[28] In present-day terms, about 81% of the current pool of 538 electoral votes are allocated according to population. The 13 smallest states collectively possess about 4% of the nation's population and have 8% of the electoral votes (44 of 538).

presidential politics. The Founders' intended allocation of political influence was not achieved because the political effect of the mathematical bonus provided by the Constitution was trumped by the nearly universal adoption by the states of the winner-take-all rule.

The effective disenfranchisement of voters in two thirds of the states has additional negative effects.

First, the absence of a meaningful presidential campaign in two thirds of the states diminishes voter turnout in those states. A 2005 Brookings Institution report entitled *Thinking About Political Polarization* pointed out:

> "The electoral college can depress voter participation in much of the nation. Overall, the percentage of voters who participated in last fall's election was almost 5 percent higher than the turnout in 2000. Yet, most of the increase was limited to the battleground states. Because the electoral college has effectively narrowed elections like the last one to a quadrennial contest for the votes of a relatively small number of states, people elsewhere are likely to feel that their votes don't matter."[29,30]

Second, diminished voter turnout in presidential races in non-competitive states weakens the candidates of the state's minority party for state and local offices, thereby making the state even less competitive in the future. In turn, political divisiveness may be increased because a lack of competition may increase the influence of each party's fringe elements.

The number of battleground states has been declining for many decades, and this decline appears to be continuing, as detailed in *The Shrinking Battleground* by the Center for Voting and Democracy.[31]

---

[29] Nivola, Pietro S. 2005. *Thinking About Political Polarization.* Washington, DC: The Brookings Institution. Policy Brief 139. January 2005.

[30] Voter turnout is adversely affected in non-competitive states because voters of both parties in non-competitive states realize that their votes do not matter in presidential elections. As reported by the Committee for the Study of the American Electorate, "Turnout in battleground states increased by 6.3 percentage points, while turnout in the other states (and the District of Columbia) increased by only 3.8 percentage points." Committee for the Study of the American Electorate (2004). "President Bush, Mobilization Drives Propel Turnout to Post-1968 High." November 4, 2004.

[31] FairVote. 2005. *The Shrinking Battleground: The 2008 Presidential Election and Beyond.* Takoma Park, MD: The Center for Voting and Democracy. www.fairvote.org/shrinking.

Table 1.5 PRESIDENTIAL ELECTIONS IN WHICH THE CANDIDATE WITH MOST POPULAR VOTES DID NOT WIN THE PRESIDENCY

YEAR	CANDIDATE WITH THE MOST POPULAR VOTES NATIONWIDE	CANDIDATE WITH THE MOST ELECTORAL VOTES	POPULAR VOTES FOR THE CANDIDATE WITH THE MOST POPULAR VOTES	POPULAR VOTES FOR THE CANDIDATE WHO PLACED SECOND IN THE POPULAR VOTE	POPULAR VOTE DIFFERENCE
1824	Andrew Jackson	John Q. Adams	151,271	113,122	38,149
1876	Samuel J. Tilden	Rutherford B. Hayes	4,288,191	4,033,497	254,694
1888	Grover Cleveland	Benjamin Harrison	5,539,118	5,449,825	89,293
2000	Al Gore	George W. Bush	50,992,335	50,455,156	537,179

1.2.2 The Current System Does Not Accurately Reflect the Nationwide Popular Vote

Of the 55 presidential elections between 1789 and 2004, there have been four elections—approximately once every five decades—in which the candidate with the most popular votes nationwide did not win the Presidency (table 1.5).[32]

In the past six decades, there have been six presidential elections in which a shift of a relatively small number of votes in one or two states would have elected a presidential candidate who lost the popular vote nationwide. In 1976, for example, Jimmy Carter led Gerald Ford by 1,682,970 votes nationwide; however, a shift of 3,687 votes in Hawaii and 5,559 votes in Ohio would have elected Ford. As shown in table 1.6, there has been an average of one problematic election each decade.[33]

In 2004, President George W. Bush was ahead by about 3,500,000 popular votes nationwide on election night; however, the outcome of the election remained in doubt until Wednesday morning because it was not clear which candidate was going to win Ohio's 20 electoral votes. In the end, Bush received 118,785 more popular votes than Kerry in Ohio,[34] thus winning all of the state's 20 electoral votes and ensuring his reelection.

[32] Congressional Quarterly. 2002. *Presidential Elections 1789–2002*. Washington, DC: CQ Press.
[33] Congressional Quarterly. 2002. *Presidential Elections 1789–2002*. Washington, DC: CQ Press.
[34] Ohio Certificate of Ascertainment, December 6, 2004.

Table 1.6 SIX PROBLEMATIC PRESIDENTIAL ELECTIONS IN THE PAST SIX DECADES

YEAR	POPULAR VOTE WINNER	ELECTORAL VOTE WINNER	NATIONWIDE POPULAR VOTE LEAD	ELECTORAL VOTES RECEIVED BY NATIONWIDE POPULAR VOTE WINNER	ELECTORAL VOTES RECEIVED BY ELECTORAL VOTE WINNER	POPULAR VOTE SWITCH THAT WOULD HAVE CHANGED THE OUTCOME
2004	Bush	Bush	3,319,608	286	286	59,393 in Ohio
2000	Gore	Bush	537,179	267	271	269 in Florida
1976	Carter	Carter	1,682,970	297	297	5,559 in Ohio and 3,687 in Hawaii
1968	Nixon	Nixon	510,645	301	301	10,245 in Missouri and 67,481 in Illinois
1960	Kennedy	Kennedy	114,673	303	303	4,430 in Illinois and 4,782 in South Carolina
1948	Truman	Truman	2,135,570	303	303	3,554 in Ohio and 42,835 in New Jersey

However, if 59,393 Bush voters in Ohio had switched in 2004, Kerry would have ended up with 272 electoral votes (two more than the 270 required to be elected to the Presidency). The 59,393 Bush voters in Ohio were decisive, whereas Bush's 3,500,000-vote nationwide lead was irrelevant.[35] The illusion of closeness in 2004 resulted from the statewide winner-take-all system used in Ohio—not because the election was genuinely close on the basis of the nationwide popular vote.

Given the relative closeness of the five most recent presidential elections and the current closely divided political environment, additional problems with the electoral system should be considered probable.

---

[35] Ohio was not the only key state in the Electoral College in 2004. A switch of 6,743 votes in Iowa (with 7 electoral votes), 4,295 in New Mexico (with 5 electoral votes), and 10,784 in Nevada (with 5 electoral votes) would have given George W. Bush and John Kerry each 269 electoral votes. If this switch of 21,822 popular votes had occurred, the presidential election would have been thrown into the House of Representatives (with each state casting one vote and states with an equal division casting no vote), and the vice-presidential election would have thrown into the Senate (with each Senator having one vote).

Interestingly, the 1991 book *Wrong Winner: The Coming Debacle in the Electoral College* by David Abbott and James P. Levine[36] predicted that emerging political and demographic trends would lead to an increasing number of elections in which the candidate with the most popular votes nationwide would not win a majority in the Electoral College.

1.2.3 Not Every Vote Is Equal

There are numerous examples of large disparities in the value of votes under the statewide winner-take-all system. For example, Gore won five electoral votes by carrying New Mexico by 365 popular votes in the 2000 presidential election, whereas Bush won five electoral votes by carrying Utah by 312,043 popular votes—an 855-to-1 disparity in the importance of a vote.

In 2000, George W. Bush received 2,912,790 popular votes in Florida, whereas Al Gore received 2,912,353—a difference of 537 popular votes. Meanwhile, Gore had a nationwide lead of 537,179 popular votes. Gore's shortfall of 537 votes in Florida was less than 1/1000th of Gore's nationwide lead of 537,179 votes. However, under the winner-take-all rule in effect in Florida, Bush's 537-vote lead in Florida entitled him to all of Florida's 25 electoral votes, thereby giving him the Presidency.[37]

The large differences in the value of a vote in various states in presidential elections has the additional negative side effect of increasing the likelihood of contested presidential elections and recounts. Because the statewide winner-take-all system divides the nation's 122,000,000 popular votes into 51 separate pools, it regularly manufactures artificial crises even when the nationwide popular vote is not particularly close. There are fewer opportunities for razor-thin outcomes when there is one single large pool of votes than when there are 51 separate smaller pools.

The 2000 presidential election is remembered as having been close because George W. Bush's popular vote in Florida was a mere 537 more than Gore's statewide total. There was, however, nothing particularly close about the 2000 election on the basis of the nationwide popular vote. Al Gore's nationwide lead of 537,179 popular votes was larger than, for

---

[36] Abbott, David W. and Levine, James P. 1991. *Wrong Winner: The Coming Debacle in the Electoral College.* Westport, CT: Praeger.

[37] George W. Bush received 271 electoral votes when the Electoral College met in December 2000—one more than the minimum required for election.

example, Nixon's lead of 510,314 in 1968 and Kennedy's lead of 118,574 in 1960.[38] The closeness of the 2000 presidential election was an artificial crisis manufactured by Florida's use of the statewide winner-take-all system. In the controversial 1876 presidential election, Democrat Samuel J. Tilden received 4,288,191 popular votes—254,694 more than the 4,033,497 popular votes received by Rutherford B. Hayes. Tilden's lead of 3.05% was substantial. It was, for example, greater than George W. Bush's popular vote lead of 2.8% in 2004. The 1876 election is remembered as having been close because Hayes's one-vote lead in the Electoral College resulted from his winning several states by extremely narrow margins:

- 889 votes in South Carolina,
- 922 votes in Florida,
- 1,050 votes in Oregon,
- 1,075 votes in Nevada, and
- 2,798 votes in California.[39]

The closeness of the 1876 election was an artificial crisis created by the statewide winner-take-all system—it was not due to anything particularly close about the nationwide popular vote for President.

The six problematic presidential elections in the past six decades (table 1.6) are reminders that the operation of the winner-take-all system in 51 separate jurisdictions makes razor-thin margins more likely and electoral fraud more rewarding. As Senator Birch Bayh said in a Senate speech in 1979:

"[O]ne of the things we can do to limit fraud is to limit the benefits to be gained by fraud.

"Under a direct popular vote system, one fraudulent vote wins one vote in the return. In the electoral college system, one fraudulent vote could mean 45 electoral votes, 28 electoral votes."[40]

---

[38] Congressional Quarterly. 2002. *Presidential Elections 1789–2002*. Washington, DC: CQ Press. Pages 146 and 148.

[39] Congressional Quarterly. 2002. *Presidential Elections 1789–2002*. Washington, DC: CQ Press. Page 125.

[40] *Congressional Record*. March 14, 1979. Page 5000.

1.3 NATIONWIDE POPULAR ELECTION AS A REMEDY FOR THE SHORTCOMINGS OF THE CURRENT SYSTEM

Nationwide popular election of the President is the only system that

- makes all states competitive,
- guarantees that the candidate with the most popular votes nationwide wins the Presidency, and
- makes every vote equal.

The authors of this book believe that George W. Bush's lead of 3.5 million popular votes in 2004 should alone have guaranteed him the Presidency in 2004—regardless of who ended up carrying Ohio. Similarly, Al Gore's lead of 537,179 alone should have been sufficient to elect him as President in 2000—regardless of whether one candidate or the other carried Florida by 537 votes.

1.4 FORTUITOUS CONVERGENCE OF FACTORS FAVORING REFORM AT THE PRESENT TIME

There is, at the present time, a fortuitous convergence of factors favoring reform of the current system.

First, the public has come to realize that voters are effectively disenfranchised in presidential elections in about two thirds of the states. Because of the closeness of the last five presidential elections, the media has spotlighted the operation of the winner-take-all rule and the notion of reliably "red" states, reliably "blue" states, and battleground states. In addition, the six problematic presidential elections in the past six decades (table 1.6) have further focused public attention on the mechanics of the Electoral College.

Second, neither major political party gains a partisan advantage from the small states. The small states have been equally divided between the major political parties in the five most recent presidential elections (1988 through 2004).

- Six of the 13 smallest states (Alaska, Idaho, Montana, North Dakota, South Dakota, and Wyoming) have almost always given their combined 19 electoral votes to the Republican presidential candidate.[41]

---

[41] Among the six Republican-leaning small states, the one exception was that Clinton carried Montana in 1992.

- Six other small jurisdictions (Delaware, the District of Columbia, Hawaii, Maine, Rhode Island, and Vermont) have almost always given their combined 21 electoral votes to the Democratic presidential candidate.[42]
- One small state (New Hampshire) is a battleground state that has gone Republican three times and Democratic twice.

As it happens, the small states are disadvantaged by the statewide winner-take-all rule to a considerably greater degree than the larger ones. Overall, two thirds of the states have been politically non-competitive in the last five presidential elections, whereas 92% (12 of the 13) of the smallest states have been non-competitive.

The 13 smallest states have a combined population of 11,448,957.[43] Coincidentally, Ohio has almost the same population (11,353,140) as the 13 smallest states combined. Excluding the one competitive small state (New Hampshire) from consideration, the Constitution gives 40 electoral votes to the 12 non-competitive small states (16 electoral votes warranted by population and 24 bonus electoral votes). The Constitution gives Ohio only 20 electoral votes—half as many as the 12 non-competitive small states. If it were true that the two-vote bonus enhanced the influence of small states, the 12 small states should exert considerably more influence than Ohio in presidential elections. This is not, of course, the case. The battleground state of Ohio (with its "mere" 20 electoral votes) is very important in presidential elections, whereas the 12 non-competitive small states (with their seemingly hefty cache of 40 electoral votes) are irrelevant.[44] Table 1.2 (on 2004 campaign events) dramatically shows the irrelevance of the 12 non-competitive small states in presidential elections—there was not one visit by any major-party presidential or vice-presidential candidate to those states. Almost none of the $237,423,744 in table 1.1 was spent in the 12 non-competitive small states.

---

[42] Among the six Democratic-leaning small states, the three exceptions were that, in 1988, George H. W. Bush carried Delaware, Maine, and Vermont.

[43] Unless otherwise stated, population figures in this book refer to the 2000 federal census.

[44] The 12 non-competitive small states have 16 electoral votes warranted by population plus 24 bonus electoral votes, for a total of 40.

The nearly universal use by *other* states of the winner-take-all rule has trumped the voices of the 11 million people in the 12 non-competitive small states and has also trumped the potential benefit of the two-vote bonus that each state receives in the Electoral College.

In short, the two-vote bonus established by the Constitution to enhance the influence of the small states exists today in *form;* however, the nearly unanimous use by the states of the winner-take-all rule robs these bonus electoral votes of any political *substance.* If, hypothetically, the Constitution had given each state a bonus of *four* electoral votes (instead of just two), the 12 non-competitive small states would then collectively have 64 electoral votes (16 warranted by population plus 48 bonus electoral votes). Even then, these states still would not have any meaningful influence in presidential elections. A competitive state, such as Ohio with only 20 electoral votes, would remain far more important in terms of practical politics than the 12 non-competitive small states. Political power in a system based on the statewide winner-take-all rule comes from being a closely divided battleground state—not from mathematical bonuses.

The argument that the Electoral College confers an enormous amount of influence on the most populous states is another superficially plausible and arithmetically correct argument that simply does not reflect political reality. A large state (such as California, Texas, or New York) receives electoral votes approximately in direct proportion to its population. The Constitution allocates 81% of the electoral votes according to population.[45] If size mattered, the nation's three most populous states (California, Texas, and New York) would be at center stage in presidential elections. But this is not the case. The political reality is that these three largest states suffer from the same spectator status as the 12 non-competitive small states—none has mattered in presidential elections for decades. If, hypothetically, California, Texas, and New York were to suddenly each acquire 10 extra electoral votes, they still would not matter in presidential elections. Presidential candidates would continue to take the

---

[45] Out of the 538 electoral votes, the 435 corresponding to the 435 U.S. Representatives are allocated according to population.

non-competitive states for granted and to concentrate on the closely divided battleground states.

Civics books often recite the argument that a vote in a small state is worth more than a vote in a large state because of the bonus of two electoral votes that each state receives in the Electoral College. The argument is that a Wyoming vote is worth 3.74 times that of a California vote because one electoral vote corresponds to 164,594 people in Wyoming, compared to 615,848 people in California.[46] This argument is arithmetically and legally correct, but it does not reflect political reality. A vote in a small state such as Wyoming and a vote in a large state such as California simply do not matter because everyone knows, well in advance of the voting in November, which candidate will win the electoral votes from those states. From the perspective of presidential candidates operating under the winner-take-all system, a vote in Wyoming is equal to a vote in California in presidential elections—*both are equally worthless.*

Third, there has been long-standing support for nationwide popular election among the public and from members of Congress in both political parties from small, medium, and large states in all parts of the country. As shown in appendix S of this book, there has been at least one Senator or Representative in each of the 50 states who has either sponsored a bill for nationwide popular election or voted for nationwide popular election of the President in a roll call vote in Congress.

1.5 ROADMAP OF THIS BOOK

Chapter 2 of this book describes the current system of electing the President, including the federal constitutional and statutory provisions that govern presidential elections (section 2.1). Section 2.2 reviews the history of the various methods that the states have used over the years to elect their presidential electors, and section 2.3 discusses present-day methods.

---

[46] Wyoming has a population of 493,782 (according to the 2000 federal census) and has three electoral votes (one warranted by population plus its two-vote bonus). California (with a population of 33,871,648) has 55 electoral votes (53 warranted by population plus its two-vote bonus). Thus, one electoral vote corresponds to 164,594 people in Wyoming, compared to 615,848 people in California.

The chapter also discusses the certification of the popular vote for President by the states (section 2.4), the meeting of the Electoral College in mid-December (section 2.5), the certification of the votes cast by the presidential electors (section 2.6), and the counting of the electoral votes in Congress (section 2.7). The chapter also covers write-in voting for President (section 2.8), voting for individual presidential electors (section 2.9), fusion voting in presidential races (section 2.10), unpledged presidential electors (section 2.11), and faithless presidential electors (section 2.12).

Chapter 2 identifies five salient features of present-day presidential elections that did not exist or that were not prominent at the time of ratification of the U.S. Constitution, namely

- popular voting for presidential electors,
- the non-deliberative nature of the Electoral College,
- the statewide winner-take-all rule,
- nomination of presidential candidates by political parties, and
- the short presidential ballot.

As chapter 2 demonstrates, these present-day features of the system evolved over a period of many decades as a result of the piecemeal passage of laws by individual states and the emergence of political parties. As summarized in section 2.13, none of these features is contained in the U.S. Constitution or any federal law. None reflects a consensus of the Founding Fathers. None came into being because of the adoption of any federal constitutional amendment. Instead, these features came into existence because the states used the built-in flexibility of the Constitution to make them part of our present-day political landscape.

Chapter 3 examines the three most prominent approaches to presidential election reform that have been proposed in the form of a federal constitutional amendment, including

- fractional proportional allocation of electoral votes (section 3.1),
- district allocation of electoral votes (section 3.2), and
- nationwide popular election (section 3.3).

Each of these three proposed approaches is examined in light of three criteria:

- whether the proposed approach accurately reflects the nationwide popular vote;
- whether the proposed approach makes every state competitive; and
- whether every vote is equal.

Chapter 4 examines the two most prominent approaches to presidential election reform that can be enacted at the state level (i.e., without a federal constitutional amendment and without action by Congress), namely

- the whole-number proportional approach (section 4.1), and
- the congressional-district approach (section 4.2).

Again, each proposed approach is examined in light of the above three criteria.

Chapter 5 provides background on interstate compacts—the contractual arrangement authorized in the Constitution by which states can act in concert to address an issue that cannot be readily solved by unilateral action. The chapter begins with the constitutional basis for interstate compacts starting with the Articles of Confederation (section 5.1), the legal standing of compacts (section 5.2), and the history of compacts (section 5.3). The chapter then covers the wide variety of subjects addressed by compacts (section 5.4), the variety of parties that may participate in compacts (section 5.5), the procedures for drafting, negotiating, and formulating compacts (section 5.6), the methods by which a state may adopt an interstate compact (section 5.7), and the contingent nature of compacts (section 5.8). Section 5.9 discusses congressional involvement in interstate compacts and the process of congressional consent; section 5.10 discusses the effect of congressional consent; section 5.11 gives examples of compacts that are contingent on the enactment of federal legislation; and section 5.12 gives examples of compacts that do not require congressional consent. Section 5.13 discusses enforcement of compacts; section 5.14 discusses amendments to compacts; section 5.15 discusses the duration of compacts and the process of terminating and withdrawing from compacts; section 5.16 discusses administration of compacts; and section 5.17 discusses the style of drafting compacts. Section 5.18 compares treaties and compacts; section 5.19 compares uniform state laws and compacts; and section 5.20 compares federal multi-state commissions and compacts. The future of interstate compacts is discussed in section 5.21.

Chapter 6 presents the authors' proposal to reform the presidential election process—an interstate compact entitled the "Agreement Among the States to Elect the President by National Popular Vote." The compact is a proposed state law. The compact would not become immediately effective when any one or two states enact it. Instead, the compact would come into effect only after it is enacted by states collectively possessing a majority of the electoral votes (i.e., 270 of the 538 electoral votes).

The proposed compact would not change any state's internal procedures for conducting or counting its presidential vote. After the people cast their ballots in early November of presidential election years, the popular vote counts from all 50 states and the District of Columbia would be added together to obtain a national grand total for each presidential slate. At the present time, the Electoral College reflects the voters' state-by-state choices for President or, in the cases of Maine and Nebraska, the voters' district-wide choices. The compact would change the Electoral College from an institution that reflects the voters' state-by-state choices or district-wide choices into a body that reflects the voters' nationwide choice. Specifically, the proposed compact specifies that each member state will award all of its electoral votes to the presidential candidate who received the largest total number of popular votes in all 50 states and the District of Columbia. Because the compact would become effective only when it encompasses states collectively possessing a majority of the electoral votes, the presidential candidate receiving the most popular votes in all 50 states and the District of Columbia would be guaranteed enough electoral votes in the Electoral College to be elected.

Note that membership in the proposed compact is not required for the popular votes of a state to count. Every state's popular vote is included on an equal footing in the nationwide total regardless of whether the state is a member of the compact. Note also that the political complexion of the states belonging to the compact does not affect the outcome produced by the compact. The presidential candidate receiving the most popular votes in all 50 states and the District of Columbia is ensured enough electoral votes (that is, at least 270 of the 538) to be elected to the Presidency regardless of what states happen to belong to the compact.

Chapter 7 outlines a possible timeline for securing adoption of the proposed interstate compact.

Chapter 8 addresses several legal questions concerning the proposed interstate compact, namely

- Is the subject matter of the proposed compact appropriate for an interstate compact (section 8.1)?
- May the citizen-initiative process be used to enact interstate compacts in general (section 8.2)?
- May the citizen-initiative process be used to enact a state law concerning the manner of choosing presidential electors (section 8.3)?
- Does the proposed compact encroach on the power of non-member states (section 8.4)?
- Does the proposed compact impermissibly delegate a state's sovereign power (section 8.5)?
- Is the six-month blackout period for withdrawals from the proposed compact enforceable (section 8.6)?

Chapter 9 addresses various administrative aspects of the proposed interstate compact.

- Does the proposed compact impose any significant additional financial cost or administrative burdens on a state's election officials (section 9.1)?
- How would recounts be handled (section 9.2)?

Chapter 10 is the epilogue.

1.6 SOURCES OF ADDITIONAL INFORMATION

There is a large literature analyzing the arguments for and against the current electoral system and possible alternatives. This book limits its discussion of the various possible approaches to three criteria that seem particularly pertinent to the electoral system at the present time—namely whether a particular approach makes every state competitive in presidential elections; whether the approach accurately reflects the nationwide popular vote; and whether the approach makes every vote equal.

Additional information is available from a variety of sources. The congressional hearings held in 1967,[47] 1969,[48,49,50] 1975,[51] 1977,[52] 1979,[53] 1993,[54] and 1999[55] contain numerous detailed discussions of the current system and its alternatives from various experts, members of the public, organizations, and members of Congress. Books on these same subjects include:

[47] U.S. Senate Committee on the Judiciary. 1967. *Election of the President: Hearings on S.J. Res. 4, 7, 11, 12, 28, 58, 62, 138 and 139, 89th Congress; and S.J. Res. 2, 3, 6, 7, 12, 15, 21, 25, 55, 84, and 86.* 89th Congress, 2nd Session and 90th Congress, 1st Session. February 28–August 23, 1967. Washington, DC: U.S. Government Printing Office.

[48] U.S. House of Representatives Committee on the Judiciary. 1969. *Electoral College Reform: Hearings on H.J. Res. 179, H.J. Res. 181, and Similar Proposals to Amend the Constitution Relating to Electoral College Reform.* 91st Congress, 1st Session. February 5, 6, 19, 20, 26, and 27; March 5, 6, 12, and 13, 1969. Washington, DC: U.S. Government Printing Office.

[49] U.S. Senate Committee on the Judiciary. 1969. *Electing the President: Hearings on S.J. Res. 1, S.J. Res. 2, S.J. Res. 4, S.J. Res. 12, S.J. Res. 18, S.J. Res. 20, S.J. Res 25, S.J. Res. 30, S.J. Res 31, S.J. Res 33, S.J. Res 71, and S.J. Res 72 to Amend the Constitution Relating to Electoral College Reform.* 91st Congress, 1st Session. January 23–24, March 10, 11, 12, 13, 20, 21, April 30, May 1–2, 1969. Washington, DC: U.S. Government Printing Office.

[50] U.S. Senate Committee on the Judiciary. 1969. *Direct Popular Election of the President: Report, with Additional Minority, Individual, and Separate Views on H.J. Res. 681, Proposing an Amendment to the Constitution of the United States Relating to the Election of the President and Vice President.* 91st Congress, 1st Session. Washington, DC: U.S. Government Printing Office.

[51] U.S. Senate Committee on the Judiciary. 1975. *Direct Popular Election of the President: Report (to Accompany S.J. Res. 1).* 94th Congress, 1st Session. Washington, DC: U.S. Government Printing Office.

[52] U.S. Senate Committee on the Judiciary. 1977. *The Electoral College and Direct Election: Hearings on the Electoral College and Direct Election of the President and Vice President (S.J. Res. 1, 8, and 18): Supplement.* 95th Congress, 1st Session. July 20, 22, and 28, and August 2, 1977. Washington, DC: U.S. Government Printing Office.

[53] U.S. Senate Committee on the Judiciary. 1979. *Direct Popular Election of the President and Vice President of the United States: Hearings on S.J. Res. 28, Joint Resolution Proposing an Amendment to the Constitution to Provide for the Direct Popular Election of the President and Vice President of the United States.* 96th Congress, 1st Session. March 27 and 30, April 3 and 9, 1979. Washington, DC: U.S. Government Printing Office.

[54] U.S. Senate Committee on the Judiciary. 1993. *The Electoral College and Direct Election of the President: Hearing on S.J. Res. 297, S.J. Res. 302, and S.J. Res 312, Measures Proposing Amendments to the Constitution Relating to the Direct Election of the President and Vice President of the United States.* 102nd Congress, 2nd Session. July 22, 1992. Washington, DC: U.S. Government Printing Office.

[55] U.S. House Committee on the Judiciary. 1999. *Proposals for Electoral College Reform: Hearing on H.J. Res. 28 and H.J. Res. 43.* 105th Congress, 1st Session. September 4, 1997. Washington, DC: U.S. Government Printing Office.

- *Wrong Winner: The Coming Debacle in the Electoral College* by David Abbott and James P. Levine (1991),[56]
- *Choice of the People? Debating the Electoral College* by Judith A. Best (1996),[57]
- *The Case Against Direct Election of the President: A Defense of the Electoral College* by Judith Vairo Best (1975),[58]
- *Why the Electoral College Is Bad for America* by George C. Edwards III (2004),[59]
- *The Importance of the Electoral College* by George Grant (2004),[60]
- *Securing Democracy: Why We Have an Electoral College*, a collection of articles edited by Gary L. Gregg II (2001),[61]
- *The Electoral College* by Suzanne LeVert (2004),[62]
- *The Politics of Electoral College Reform* by Lawrence D. Longley and Alan G. Braun (1972),[63]
- *The People's President: The Electoral College in American History and Direct-Vote Alternative* by Neal R. Peirce (1968),[64]
- *Enlightened Democracy: The Case for the Electoral College* by Tara Ross (2004),[65]

---

[56] Abbott, David W. and Levine, James P. 1991. *Wrong Winner: The Coming Debacle in the Electoral College.* Westport, CT: Praeger.

[57] Best, Judith A. 1996. *Choice of the People? Debating the Electoral College.* Lanham, MD: Rowman & Littlefield.

[58] Best, Judith Vairo. 1975. *The Case Against Direct Election of the President: A Defense of the Electoral College.* Ithaca, NY: Cornell University Press.

[59] Edwards, George C. III. 2004. *Why the Electoral College Is Bad for America.* New Haven, CT: Yale University Press.

[60] Grant, George. 2004. *The Importance of the Electoral College.* San Antonio, TX: Vision Forum Ministries.

[61] Gregg, Gary L. II (editor). 2001. *Securing Democracy: Why We Have an Electoral College.* Wilmington, DE: ISI Books.

[62] LeVert, Suzanne. 2004. *The Electoral College.* New York, NY: Franklin Watts.

[63] Longley, Lawrence D. and Braun, Alan G. 1972. *The Politics of Electoral College Reform.* New Haven, CT: Yale University Press.

[64] Peirce, Neal R. 1968. *The People's President: The Electoral College in American History and Direct-Vote Alternative.* New York, NY: Simon and Schuster.

[65] Ross, Tara. 2004. *Enlightened Democracy: The Case for the Electoral College.* Los Angeles, CA: World Ahead Publishing Company.

- *Choosing a President,* a collection of articles edited by Paul D. Schumaker and Burdett A. Loomis (2002),[66]
- *History of American Presidential Elections 1878–2001* an 11-volume collection of articles edited by Arthur M. Schlesinger, Jr. and Fred L. Israel (2002),[67]
- *A History of the Presidency from 1788 to 1897*[68] and *A History of the Presidency from 1897 to 1916* by Edward Stanwood (1924),[69] and
- *The Electoral College* by Lucius Wilmerding (1958).[70]

Among books that have come out since the 2000 presidential election, the 2004 book *Enlightened Democracy: The Case for the Electoral College*[71] contains some of the clearest arguments supporting the existing system. On the other side of the argument, the 2004 book *Why the Electoral College Is Bad for America*[72] is noteworthy because it closely examines and analyzes many of the most commonly invoked arguments in favor of the existing system—such as protection of federalism and protection of state interests.

The Center for Voting and Democracy (FairVote) published two insightful reports on presidential elections in 2005:

- *The Shrinking Battleground: The 2008 Presidential Election and Beyond*[73] and
- *Who Picks the President?*[74]

---

[66] Schumaker, Paul D. and Loomis, Burdett A. (editors). 2002. *Choosing a President.* New York, NY: Chatham House Publishers.

[67] Schlesinger, Arthur M., Jr. and Israel, Fred L. (editors). 2002. *History of American Presidential Elections 1878–2001.* Philadelphia, PA: Chelsea House Publishers. 11 volumes.

[68] Stanwood, Edward. 1924. *A History of the Presidency from 1788 to 1897.* Boston, MA: Houghton Mifflin Company.

[69] Stanwood, Edward. 1916. *A History of the Presidency from 1897 to 1916.* Boston, MA: Houghton Mifflin Company.

[70] Wilmerding, Lucius, Jr. 1958. *The Electoral College.* Boston, MA: Beacon Press.

[71] Ross, Tara. 2004. *Enlightened Democracy: The Case for the Electoral College.* Los Angeles, CA: World Ahead Publishing Company.

[72] Edwards, George C. III. 2004. *Why the Electoral College Is Bad for America.* New Haven, CT: Yale University Press.

[73] FairVote. 2005. *The Shrinking Battleground: The 2008 Presidential Election and Beyond.* Takoma Park, MD: The Center for Voting and Democracy. www.fairvote.org/shrinking.

[74] FairVote. 2005. *Who Picks the President?* Takoma Park, MD: The Center for Voting and Democracy. www.fairvote.org/whopicks.

This book's bibliography contains numerous additional references to books about particular problematic elections (e.g., 1800, 1876, and 2000) as well as the history and operation of the present system over the years.

2 | How the Electoral College Works

The current system for electing the President and Vice President of the United States is governed by a combination of federal and state statutory and constitutional provisions. This chapter discusses the:
- federal constitutional and federal statutory provisions governing presidential elections (section 2.1),
- history of various methods for choosing presidential electors (section 2.2),
- current state laws governing the election of presidential electors (section 2.3),
- certification of the popular vote by the states (section 2.4),
- meeting of the Electoral College (section 2.5),
- certification of the votes cast by a state's presidential electors (section 2.6),
- counting of the electoral votes in Congress (section 2.7),
- write-in votes for president (section 2.8),
- state laws permitting a voter to cast separate votes for individual candidates for presidential elector (section 2.9),
- fusion voting (section 2.10),
- unpledged electors (section 2.11),
- faithless presidential electors (section 2.12), and
- five major changes that have been implemented without a federal constitutional amendment (section 2.13).

2.1 FEDERAL CONSTITUTIONAL AND STATUTORY PROVISIONS
The President and Vice President of the United States are not elected directly by the voters. Instead, the President and Vice President are elected by a group of 538 people who are known individually as "presidential electors" and collectively as the "Electoral College." Each political party nominates its own candidates (typically long-standing party activists) for the position of presidential elector.

Presidential electors are chosen separately by each state and the District of Columbia on the Tuesday after the first Monday in November in presidential election years. The 538 presidential electors cast their votes for President and Vice President in mid-December in separate meetings held in the 50 state capitals and the District of Columbia.

The U.S. Constitution provides:

> "The executive Power shall be vested in a President of the United States of America. He shall hold his Office during the Term of four Years, and, together with the Vice President, chosen for the same Term, be elected, as follows:

> "Each State shall appoint, in such Manner as the Legislature thereof may direct, a Number of Electors, equal to the whole Number of Senators and Representatives to which the State may be entitled in the Congress...."[1]

For the reader's convenience, appendix A contains the provisions of the U.S. Constitution relating to presidential elections, and appendix B contains the relevant provisions of federal law.

The number of seats in the House of Representatives is set by federal statute. There are currently 435 U.S. Representatives. There are, in addition, two Senators from each state. Consequently, the 50 states together have 535 electoral votes. The District of Columbia acquired three electoral votes as a result of the ratification of the 23rd Amendment to the U.S. Constitution in 1961. Thus, in total, there are currently 538 electoral votes. If all 538 electors are appointed, 270 electoral votes (i.e., a majority of 538) are required to elect the President and the Vice President.

After each decennial federal census, the 435 seats in the United States House of Representatives are reapportioned among the 50 states. The 2000 federal census determined the distribution of electoral votes among the states for the 2004 and 2008 presidential elections. The 2010 census will determine the distribution of electoral votes for the 2012, 2016, and 2020 presidential elections.

Table 2.1 shows the distribution of electoral votes among the 51 jurisdictions that appoint presidential electors. Because each state has two Senators and at least one Representative, no state has fewer than three

---

[1] U.S. Constitution. Article II, section 1, clauses 1 and 2.

electoral votes. The average number of electoral votes is about 11. The states with the most electoral votes are California (55), Texas (34), and New York (31). There are 13 states with three or four electoral votes.

Table 2.1 DISTRIBUTION OF ELECTORAL VOTES AMONG THE 50 STATES AND THE DISTRICT OF COLUMBIA

JURISDICTION	REPRESENTATIVES	SENATORS	ELECTORAL VOTES
Alabama	7	2	9
Alaska	1	2	3
Arizona	8	2	10
Arkansas	4	2	6
California	53	2	55
Colorado	7	2	9
Connecticut	5	2	7
Delaware	1	2	3
District of Columbia	0	0	3
Florida	25	2	27
Georgia	13	2	15
Hawaii	2	2	4
Idaho	2	2	4
Illinois	19	2	21
Indiana	9	2	11
Iowa	5	2	7
Kansas	4	2	6
Kentucky	6	2	8
Louisiana	7	2	9
Maine	2	2	4
Maryland	8	2	10
Massachusetts	10	2	12
Michigan	15	2	17
Minnesota	8	2	10
Mississippi	4	2	6
Missouri	9	2	11
Montana	1	2	3
Nebraska	3	2	5
Nevada	3	2	5
New Hampshire	2	2	4
New Jersey	13	2	15
New Mexico	3	2	5
New York	29	2	31
North Carolina	13	2	15
North Dakota	1	2	3
Ohio	18	2	20

Table 2.1 DISTRIBUTION OF ELECTORAL VOTES AMONG THE 50 STATES AND THE DISTRICT OF COLUMBIA (cont.)

JURISDICTION	REPRESENTATIVES	SENATORS	ELECTORAL VOTES
Oklahoma	5	2	7
Oregon	5	2	7
Pennsylvania	19	2	21
Rhode Island	2	2	4
South Carolina	6	2	8
South Dakota	1	2	3
Tennessee	9	2	11
Texas	32	2	34
Utah	3	2	5
Vermont	1	2	3
Virginia	11	2	13
Washington	9	2	11
West Virginia	3	2	5
Wisconsin	8	2	10
Wyoming	1	2	3
Total	**435**	**100**	**538**

The Electoral College meeting in mid-December is governed by the 12th Amendment to the U.S. Constitution:

"The Electors shall meet in their respective states, and vote by ballot for President and Vice-President, one of whom, at least, shall not be an inhabitant of the same state with themselves; they shall name in their ballots the person voted for as President, and in distinct ballots the person voted for as Vice-President, and they shall make distinct lists of all persons voted for as President, and of all persons voted for as Vice-President, and of the number of votes for each, which lists they shall sign and certify, and transmit sealed to the seat of the government of the United States, directed to the President of the Senate."

The Constitution further provides:

"The Congress may determine the Time of chusing the Electors, and the Day on which they shall give their Votes; which Day shall be the same throughout the United States."
[Spelling as per original]

Federal election law establishes the date for the choosing of presidential electors. In 2004, the date was Tuesday, November 2.

"The electors of President and Vice President shall be appointed, in each State, on the Tuesday next after the first Monday in November, in every fourth year succeeding every election of a President and Vice President."[2]

The date for the meeting of the Electoral College is established by federal election law. In 2004, the designated day for the meeting of the Electoral College was Monday, December 13.

"The electors of President and Vice President of each State shall meet and give their votes on the first Monday after the second Wednesday in December next following their appointment at such place in each State as the legislature of such State shall direct."[3]

This statute was enacted in 1934 after the 20th Amendment (ratified in 1933) changed the date for the presidential inauguration from March 4 to January 20.

The people have the right, under the Constitution, to vote for United States Representatives. The 17th Amendment (ratified in 1913) gave the people the right to vote for United States Senators (who were elected by state legislatures under the original Constitution). The people, however, have no federal constitutional right to vote for President or Vice President or for presidential electors. Instead, the Constitution provides:

"Each State shall appoint, in such Manner as the Legislature thereof may direct, a Number of Electors, equal to the whole Number of Senators and Representatives to which the State may be entitled in the Congress...."[4]

As the U.S. Supreme Court observed in the 1892 case of *McPherson v. Blacker:*

"The constitution does not provide that the appointment of electors shall be by popular vote, nor that the electors shall be voted for upon a general ticket, nor that the majority of those who exercise the elective franchise can alone choose the electors."[5]

---

[2] United States Code. Title 3, chapter 1, section 1.

[3] United States Code. Title 3, chapter 1, section 7.

[4] U.S. Constitution. Article II, section 1, clause 2.

[5] *McPherson v. Blacker.* 146 U.S. 1 at 27. 1892.

The full text of the Court's decision in *McPherson v. Blacker* can be found in appendix O.

In 2000, the U.S. Supreme Court in *Bush v. Gore* reiterated the principle that the people have no federal constitutional right to vote for President.

> "The individual citizen has no federal constitutional right to vote for electors for the President of the United States unless and until the state legislature chooses a statewide election as the means to implement its power to appoint members of the Electoral College."[6]

There is only one state where the right of the people to vote for presidential electors is guaranteed by a state constitution. The Colorado Constitution provides:

> "The general assembly shall provide that after the year eighteen hundred and seventy-six the electors of the electoral college shall be chosen by direct vote of the people."[7]

2.2 HISTORY OF METHODS OF SELECTING PRESIDENTIAL ELECTORS

In 1787, the Constitutional Convention considered a variety of methods for electing the President and Vice President, including election by

- state governors,
- Congress,
- state legislatures,
- nationwide popular vote, and
- electors.

The delegates debated the method of electing the President on 22 separate days and held 30 votes on the topic.[8,9] As described in George Edwards's recent book:

> "The delegates were obviously perplexed about how to select the president, and their confusion is reflected in their voting. On July 17, for example, the delegates voted for selection of

---

[6] *Bush v. Gore.* 531 U.S. 98. 2000.

[7] Section 20 of the article of the Colorado Constitution governing the transition from territorial status to statehood.

[8] Peirce, Neal R. 1968. *The People's President: The Electoral College in American History and Direct-Vote Alternative.* New York, NY: Simon and Schuster. Pages 28–57.

[9] Longley, Lawrence D. and Braun, Alan G. 1972. *The Politics of Electoral College Reform.* New Haven, CT: Yale University Press. Pages 22–41.

the president by the national legislature. Two days later they voted for selection by electors chosen by state legislatures. Five days after that, they again voted for selection by the nation legislative, a position they rejected the next day and then adopted again the day after that. Then, just when it appeared that the delegates had reached a consensus, they again turned the question over to a committee. This committee changed the convention's course once more and recommended selection of the president by electors...."[10]

The Constitutional Convention never agreed on a method for choosing the presidential electors. The matter was simply turned over to the states.

The U.S. Constitution gave the states considerably more discretion in choosing the manner of appointing their presidential electors than it did in choosing the manner of electing their U.S. Representatives and Senators. The states' power to chose the manner of conducting congressional elections is subject to congressional oversight. Article I, section 4, clause 1 of the U.S. Constitution provides:

> "The Times, Places and Manner of holding Elections for Senators and Representatives, shall be prescribed in each State by the Legislature thereof; **but the Congress may at any time by Law make or alter such Regulations,** except as to the Places of chusing Senators." [Emphasis added]

In contrast, article II, section 1, clause 2 of the U.S. Constitution gives Congress no comparable oversight power concerning a state's choice of the manner of appointing its presidential electors.

> "Each State shall appoint, in such Manner as the Legislature thereof may direct, a Number of Electors, equal to the whole Number of Senators and Representatives to which the State may be entitled in the Congress...."

As the U.S. Supreme Court wrote in *McPherson v. Blacker:*

> "In short, the appointment and mode of appointment of electors belong **exclusively** to the states under the constitution of the United States."[11] [Emphasis added]

---

[10] Edwards, George C., III. 2004. *Why the Electoral College Is Bad for America.* New Haven, CT: Yale University Press. Pages 79–80.

That is, the states have plenary power in choosing the manner of appointing their presidential electors. Of course, the state's power in this area is limited by various general constitutional limitations, such as the equal protection clause of the 14th Amendment, the 15th Amendment (outlawing the denial of vote based on race, color, or previous condition of servitude), the 20th Amendment (women's suffrage), the 24th Amendment (outlawing poll taxes), and the 26th Amendment (18-year-old vote).

2.2.1 THE FIRST AND SECOND PRESIDENTIAL ELECTIONS

The states employed three distinct methods for choosing presidential electors in the nation's first presidential election (1789), including

- appointment of all the state's presidential electors by the legislature,
- popular election by district, and
- statewide popular election.

In five of the 10 states that participated in the first presidential election, the legislatures simply designated themselves as the appointing authority for all of the state's electors. Thus, the voters had no direct involvement in choosing presidential electors in Connecticut, Delaware, Georgia, New Jersey, and South Carolina.

Massachusetts used a more complicated system; however, a majority of the legislature[12] effectively retained the power to choose all of the state's 10 presidential electors. In each of the state's eight congressional districts, the voters cast ballots in a popular election for their choice for the district's presidential elector. However, the actual selection of the presidential elector for each district was then made by the state legislature from among the two elector candidates receiving the most popular votes in each district. The state legislature also chose the state's two senatorial electors.

Appointment of presidential electors by a state legislature did not seem as odd in 1789 as it would today. In 1789, the states legislatures had the power to elect United States Senators[13] and, in most states, the state's Governor.

---

[11] *McPherson v. Blacker.* 146 U.S. 1 at 35. 1892.

[12] Sitting in a joint convention of both houses.

[13] Under the original constitution, United States Senators were elected by state legislatures. The ratification of the 17th Amendment in 1913 permitted the voters to elect Senators.

In four of the 10 states that participated in the first presidential election, the voters chose all of the presidential electors.

In Virginia (which, at the time, had 10 congressional districts and hence 12 electoral votes), the state was divided into 12 presidential elector districts. Each voter cast a vote for an elector in his district.

In New Hampshire, Maryland, and Pennsylvania, presidential electors were elected in a statewide popular vote. This method (sometimes called the "general ticket" system) resembled the modern-day system in that a majority of the state's voters controlled all of the state's electoral votes. It differed from the present-day system in that the names of the presidential and vice-presidential candidates did not appear on the ballot. Instead, each voter cast votes for individual candidates for presidential elector. For example, in a state with five electoral votes (such as New Hampshire), a voter could (and ordinarily would) cast a vote for five individual candidates for presidential elector. In Maryland, all the state's voters voted for three electors from the Eastern Shore and five from the Western Shore.

In summary, nine of the 10 states chose presidential electors in a way that permitted a majority to control all of the state's presidential electors. In six states, a legislative majority controlled all of the state's electors. In three states, a popular majority controlled all of the state's electors. Only Virginia used a system that, under normal circumstances, was likely to produce a division of the state's electoral votes.

The Supreme Court noted the "disadvantage" of such "division of their strength" in 1892 in *McPherson v. Blacker*:

> "The district system was largely considered the most equitable, and Madison wrote that it was that system which was contemplated by the framers of the constitution, although it was soon seen that its adoption by some states might place them at a disadvantage by a division of their strength, and that a uniform rule was preferable."[14]

Three of the original 13 states did not participate in the nation's first presidential election. Rhode Island and North Carolina did not ratify the Constitution in time to participate. In New York, the legislature could not agree on a method for choosing presidential electors, so New York

---

[14] *McPherson v. Blacker*. 146 U.S. 1 at 29. 1892.

did not cast any votes in the first presidential election. The missing votes mattered little because George Washington received a vote from all of the 69 presidential electors who voted in the Electoral College in 1789.[15]

In 1792, the Massachusetts legislature loosened its grip on the choice of presidential electors and permitted the voters to elect all of the state's presidential electors directly. The state was divided into four regional multi-member districts for the purpose of electing the state's 16 electors.[16] Under the 1792 plan in Massachusetts, the legislature would become involved in the choice of presidential electors only in the event that a presidential elector candidate failed to receive a majority of the popular votes cast in a district.

In 1792, George Washington again received a vote from all of the presidential electors who voted.

2.2.2 THE FIRST COMPETITIVE PRESIDENTIAL ELECTION

In the early years of the republic, Thomas Jefferson led the opposition to the policies of the ruling Federalist Party.

George Washington's decision not to run for a third term in 1796 opened the way for a contested presidential election between the country's two emerging political parties.

In the summer of 1796, the Federalist members of Congress caucused and nominated John Adams of Massachusetts as their candidate for President and nominated Thomas Pinckney for Vice President. Meanwhile, the opposition caucus in Congress (originally called the Anti-Federalists, later the Republicans or the Democratic-Republicans, and eventually the Democrats) voted to support the candidacies of Thomas Jefferson of Virginia for President and Aaron Burr for Vice President.[17,18,19]

In preparation for the 1796 presidential election, the legislature of the newly admitted state of Tennessee created a state-level electoral

---

[15] In addition, two presidential electors from Maryland and two from Virginia failed to vote in the Electoral College in 1789.

[16] As a consequence of the 1790 federal census, Massachusetts became entitled to choose 16 presidential electors in the 1792 presidential election (as compared to 10 in the 1789 election).

[17] Peirce, Neal R. 1968. *The People's President: The Electoral College in American History and Direct-Vote Alternative.* New York, NY: Simon and Schuster. Page 63.

[18] Grant, George. 2004. *The Importance of the Electoral College.* San Antonio, TX: Vision Forum Ministries. Pages 23–26.

[19] The congressional caucus was replaced by the national nominating convention during the 1820s.

college to choose the state's members of the national Electoral College. The legislative act asserted that its aim was that the presidential electors

"be elected with as little trouble to the citizens as possible."[20]

To this end, the legislature specifically named, in the statute, certain prominent local persons from Washington, Sullivan, Green, and Hawkins counties to select one presidential elector from their part of the state. Then, it named another group of individuals from Knox, Jefferson, Sevier, and Blount counties to select their area's presidential elector. Finally, it named yet another group from Davidson, Sumner, and Tennessee counties to select a presidential elector from their district.

For the 1796 election, Massachusetts switched from multi-member elector districts to a system in which the voters elected the presidential electors by congressional district (with the legislature being involved only in the event that a presidential elector candidate failed to receive a majority of the popular votes cast in his district). Under the 1796 plan, the state legislature appointed the state's two senatorial electors.

Maryland used a district system in 1796.

The Founding Fathers anticipated that the Electoral College would act as a deliberative body wherein the presidential electors would exercise independent and detached judgment as to the best persons to serve as President and Vice President. Hamilton wrote in *Federalist 64*:

"As the select assemblies for choosing the President … will in general be composed of the most enlightened and respectable citizens, there is reason to presume that their attention and their votes will be directed to those men only who have become the most distinguished by their abilities and virtues."

The Founding Fathers' lofty expectations that the Electoral College would be a deliberative body were dashed by the political realities of the nation's first competitive presidential election.[21] In 1796, both political parties nominated candidates for President and Vice President on a centralized basis (the party's caucus in Congress). Both parties campaigned throughout the country for their nominees. It was only logical that the presidential

---

[20] Laws Tenn. 1794, 1803, p. 209; Acts 2d Sess. 1st Gen. Assem. Tenn. c. 4.
[21] White, Theodore H. 1969. *The Making of the President 1968*. New York, NY: Atheneum Publishers. Page 471.

electors associated with each political party would be expected to cast their votes in the Electoral College for the party's nominees.

As the Supreme Court observed in *McPherson v. Blacker*:

> "Doubtless it was supposed that the electors would exercise a reasonable independence and fair judgment in the selection of the chief executive, but experience soon demonstrated that, **whether chosen by the legislatures or by popular suffrage on general ticket or in districts, they were so chosen simply to register the will of the appointing power** in respect of a particular candidate. In relation, then, to the independence of the electors, the original expectation may be said to have been frustrated."[22] [Emphasis added]

Table 2.2 shows the distribution, by state, of the 71 electoral votes received by John Adams and the 68 electoral votes received by Thomas Jefferson in the nation's first contested presidential election in 1796.[23,24]

In 1796, presidential electors were effectively chosen by state legislatures in nine of the 16 states.[25] Despite the distinguished qualifications of both Adams and Jefferson, there was no hint of independent judgment by any of the presidential electors chosen by the legislatures. As table 2.2 demonstrates, all 66 presidential electors from these nine states voted in unison for Jefferson or Adams in accordance with "the will of the appointing power"—that is, the will of the legislative majority.

In the one state (New Hampshire) in which the voters elected the state's presidential electors in a statewide popular election in 1796, all of the state's presidential electors voted for Adams. That is, the voters were "the appointing power," and they chose electors who faithfully did their bidding.

---

[22] *McPherson v. Blacker.* 146 U.S. 1 at 36. 1892.

[23] Congressional Quarterly. 2002. *Presidential Elections 1789-2002.* Washington, DC: CQ Press. Page 176.

[24] The table simplifies the results of the 1796 election by presenting only the number of electoral votes received by Adams and Jefferson. Thirteen different people received electoral votes in the 1796 election. Under the original Constitution, each presidential elector cast two votes. The candidate with the most electoral votes (provided that it was a majority of the electors appointed) became President. The second-ranking candidate (if he received a majority of the electors appointed) became Vice President.

[25] This count treats Tennessee as a state in which the legislature, in effect, chose the state's presidential electors. When Tennessee's three presidential electors cast their votes in the Electoral College in 1796, they unanimously supported Thomas Jefferson— the candidate who was popular with a majority of the Tennessee legislature.

All of the presidential electors in Massachusetts voted for their home state candidate, Adams. All four presidential electors in Kentucky voted for Jefferson.

In three of the 16 states (Virginia, North Carolina, and Maryland), the electoral votes were fragmented because the presidential electors were elected from districts. One elector from Virginia, one from North

Table 2.2 ELECTORAL VOTES FOR ADAMS AND JEFFERSON IN THE NATION'S FIRST CONTESTED PRESIDENTIAL ELECTION (1796)

STATE	ELECTORAL VOTES	ADAMS	JEFFERSON	METHOD OF ELECTING PRESIDENTIAL ELECTORS
Connecticut	9	9		Legislature
Delaware	3	3		Legislature
Georgia	4		4	Legislature
Kentucky	4		4	Popular voting in elector districts
Maryland	11	7	4	Popular voting in districts
Massachusetts	16	16		Popular voting in congressional districts (with the legislature choosing the two senatorial electors)
New Hampshire	6	6		Popular voting statewide
New Jersey	7	7		Legislature
New York	12	12		Legislature
North Carolina	12	1	11	Popular voting in elector districts
Pennsylvania	15	1	14	Popular voting statewide
Rhode Island	4	4		Legislature
South Carolina	8		8	Legislature
Tennessee	3		3	Presidential electors chosen by county electors chosen by the state legislature
Vermont	4	4		Legislature
Virginia	21	1	20	Popular voting in 21 elector districts
Total	**139**	**71**	**68**	

Carolina, and four electors from Maryland voted differently from the majority of their state's electors. These presidential electors were not demonstrating independence or detached judgment—they were merely voting in accordance with "the will of the appointing power" at the level of the district that elected them.

Although Pennsylvania employed the general ticket system in 1796, its electoral votes were divided because voters were required to cast separate votes for the 15 positions of presidential elector. As Stanwood reported in *A History of the Presidency from 1788 to 1897*:

> "In Pennsylvania, the vote was extremely close. There were ... two tickets, each bearing fifteen names. The highest number polled by any candidate for elector was 12,306; the lowest of the thirty had 12,071. Thus 235 votes only represented the greatest difference; and two of the Federalist electors were chosen."[26]

Fourteen of Pennsylvania's presidential electors (13 Anti-Federalists and one Federalist) duly voted for their party's designated nominee for President. One of the two Federalist electors from Pennsylvania in 1796 did not, however, vote as expected.

Samuel Miles cast his vote in the Electoral College for Thomas Jefferson—instead of John Adams.[27] A Federalist supporter complained in the December 15, 1796, issue of *United States Gazette*:

> "What, do I chufe Samuel Miles to determine for me whether John Adams or Thomas Jefferfon is the fittest man to be President of the United States? No, I chufe him to **act,** not to **think.**" [Emphasis as per original; spelling as per original].[28]

The expectation that presidential electors should "act" and not "think" has remained strong ever since political parties began nominating their presidential candidates on a centralized basis. Of the 21,915 electoral votes cast for President in the 55 presidential elections between 1789 and 2004, only 11 were cast in an unexpected way. Moreover, among

---

[26] Stanwood, Edward. 1924. *A History of the Presidency from 1788 to 1897*. Boston, MA: Houghton Mifflin Company. Page 48.

[27] Peirce, Neal R. 1968. *The People's President: The Electoral College in American History and Direct-Vote Alternative*. New York, NY: Simon and Schuster. Page 64.

[28] This piece was signed "CANDOUR."

these 11 cases in 217 years, the vote of Samuel Miles for Thomas Jefferson in 1796 remains the only instance when the elector might have thought, at the time he cast his unexpected vote, that his vote might affect the national outcome.[29]

In summary, the Electoral College never operated as the deliberative body envisioned by the nation's Founding Fathers. In the nation's first two presidential elections, the Electoral College was a rubberstamp of the national consensus in favor of George Washington. By the time of the nation's first contested presidential election (1796), the Electoral College had become a rubberstamp that simply affirmed "the will of the appointing power" of each separate jurisdiction. Thus, in practice, the Electoral College had the form, but never the substance, of a deliberative body.

2.2.3 THE SECOND COMPETITIVE PRESIDENTIAL ELECTION

Thomas Jefferson lost the Presidency in the nation's first competitive election (1796) by a mere three electoral votes (table 2.2). As Cunningham wrote in *History of American Presidential Elections 1878–2001*:

> "The presidential election of 1796 had been extremely close, and in examining the results of that contest Republican Party managers had been struck by the fact that Adams' 3-vote margin of victory in the electoral college could be attributed to 1 vote from Pennsylvania, 1 from Virginia, and 1 from North Carolina. In each of these states, the Republicans had won an impressive victory, amassing in the three states a total of 45 electoral votes. The loss of 3 votes in these strongly Jeffersonian states was due to the district method of electing presidential electors. **In looking for ways to improve their chances for victory in the next presidential election, Republican managers thus turned their attention to state election laws.** No uniform system of selection of presidential electors prevailed. In some states electors were chosen by the state legislature; in others they were elected on a general ticket throughout the state; in still others they were elected in districts. This meant that the party that controlled the state legislature was in a position to enact the system of

---

[29] As discussed in greater detail in section 2.12, all but one of the other instances of faithless electors are considered grand-standing votes. One electoral vote (in 2004) was cast by accident.

selection that promised the greatest partisan advantage. Thus, in January 1800 the Republican-controlled legislature of Virginia passed an act providing for the election of presidential electors on a general ticket instead of districts as in previous elections. By changing the election law, Republicans in Virginia, confident of carrying a majority of the popular vote throughout the state but fearful of losing one or two districts to the Federalists, ensured the entire electoral vote of the Union's largest state for the Republican candidate."[30] [Emphasis added]

Vice-President Thomas Jefferson (soon to be a candidate for President in the 1800 election) summed up the reasons for Virginia's switch from the district system to the statewide winner-take-all system in a January 12, 1800, letter to James Monroe:

"On the subject of an election by a general ticket, or by districts, most persons here seem to have made up their minds. All agree that an election by districts would be best, if it could be general; but while 10 states chuse either by their legislatures or by a general ticket, **it is folly & worse than folly** for the other 6. not to do it. In these 10. states the minority is entirely unrepresented; & their majorities not only have the weight of their whole state in their scale, but have the benefit of so much of our minorities as can succeed at a district election. This is, in fact, ensuring to our minorities the appointment of the government. To state it in another form; it is merely a question whether we will divide the U S into 16. or 137. districts. The latter being more chequered, & representing the people in smaller sections, would be more likely to be an exact representation of their diversified sentiments. But a representation of a part by great, & a part by small sections, would give a result very different from what would be the

[30] Cunningham, Noble E., Jr. In Schlesinger, Arthur M., Jr. and Israel, Fred L. (editors). 2002. *History of American Presidential Elections 1878-2001*. Philadelphia, PA: Chelsea House Publishers. Pages 104–105. The quotation from Cunningham contains a small error. Pennsylvania did not use a district system in 1796. The split vote in Pennsylvania resulted from the closeness of the statewide popular vote, as explained in section 2.2.2.

sentiment of the whole people of the U S, were they assembled together."[31] [Emphasis added; spelling and punctuation as per original]

Thus, in 1800, Virginia ended its "folly" and adopted the statewide winner-take-all system to replace the district system used in the state in the first three presidential elections. As a result of this change in Virginia's election law, Jefferson received all of Virginia's electoral votes in the 1800 election.[32]

Meanwhile, Virginia's "folly" of dividing its electoral votes did not go unnoticed by the Federalist Party in Massachusetts. In the 1796 election, Adams had succeeded in winning all his home state's electoral votes under the congressional-district approach. The Jeffersonians, however, were making such significant inroads into Massachusetts that the Federalist-controlled legislature feared that the Jeffersonians might win as many as two districts in Massachusetts in the upcoming 1800 election.[33]

---

[31] Ford, Paul Leicester. 1905. *The Works of Thomas Jefferson.* New York: G. P. Putnam's Sons. 9:90.

[32] The remainder of Thomas Jefferson's January 12, 1800, letter to James Monroe is interesting in that it discusses the political calculations in the decisions by the New York and New Jersey legislatures not to permit the voters to participate in choosing the state's president electors. The letter continues, "I have today had a conversation with 113 [Aaron Burr] who has taken a flying trip here from N Y. He says, they have really now a majority in the H of R, but for want of some skilful person to rally round, they are disjointed, & will lose every question. In the Senate there is a majority of 8. or 9. against us. But in the new election which is to come on in April, three or 4. in the Senate will be changed in our favor; & in the H of R the county elections will still be better than the last; but still all will depend on the city election, which is of 12. members. At present there would be no doubt of our carrying our ticket there; nor does there seem to be time for any events arising to change that disposition. There is therefore the best prospect possible of a great & decided majority on a joint vote of the two houses. They are so confident of this, that the republican party there will not consent to elect either by districts or a general ticket. They chuse to do it by their legislature. I am told the republicans of N J are equally confident, & equally anxious against an election either by districts or a general ticket. The contest in this State will end in a separation of the present legislature without passing any election law, (& their former one is expired), and in depending on the new one, which will be elected Oct 14. in which the republican majority will be more decided in the Representatives, & instead of a majority of 5. against us in the Senate, will be of 1. for us. They will, from the necessity of the case, chuse the electors themselves. Perhaps it will be thought I ought in delicacy to be silent on this subject. But you, who know me, know that my private gratifications would be most indulged by that issue, which should leave me most at home. If anything supersedes this propensity, it is merely the desire to see this government brought back to it's republican principles. Consider this as written to mr. Madison as much as yourself; & communicate it, if you think it will do any good, to those possessing our joint confidence, or any others where it may be useful & safe. Health & affectionate salutations."

Thus, the Massachusetts legislature eliminated the district system and, just to be safe, eliminated the voters and decided to choose all of the state's presidential electors themselves for the 1800 presidential election.[34] Similarly, the Federalist-controlled New Hampshire legislature feared losing the statewide vote to the Jeffersonians under the state's existing statewide winner-take-all popular election system and decided to choose all of the state's presidential electors themselves.

Cunningham describes election law politics in New York and Pennsylvania in 1800 as follows:

> "In New York, Republicans introduced a measure to move from legislative choice to election by districts, but the proposal was defeated by the Federalists, an outcome that ultimately worked to the advantage of the Republicans when they won control of the legislature in the state elections of 1800. In Pennsylvania, a Republican House of Representatives and a Federalist Senate produced a deadlock over the system to be used to select electors, and the vote of that state was eventually cast by the legislature in a compromise division of the 15 electoral votes, eight Republican and seven Federalist electors being named." [35,36]

2.2.4 THE EMERGENCE OF THE CURRENT SYSTEM

The method of choosing presidential electors varied from state to state and from election to election over the next several decades.

Chief Justice Melville Fuller of the U.S. Supreme Court recounted the history of methods used to appoint presidential electors between 1804 and 1828 in his opinion in *McPherson v. Blacker*:

---

[33] Cunningham, Noble E., Jr. In Schlesinger, Arthur M., Jr. and Israel, Fred L. (editors). 2002. *History of American Presidential Elections 1878–2001*. Philadelphia, PA: Chelsea House Publishers. Page 105.

[34] Congressional Quarterly. 2002. *Presidential Elections 1789–2002*. Washington, DC: CQ Press.

[35] Cunningham, Noble E., Jr. In Schlesinger, Arthur M., Jr. and Israel, Fred L. (editors). 2002. *History of American Presidential Elections 1878–2001*. Philadelphia, PA: Chelsea House Publishers. Page 105.

[36] It is interesting to note that, by the time of the nation's second competitive presidential election (1800), both of the states (Pennsylvania and New Hampshire) in which presidential electors were elected in a statewide popular vote in 1796 had switched to a system of legislative election of the state's presidential electors. That is, no state used a statewide popular vote system in the 1800 presidential election.

"[W]hile most of the states adopted the general ticket system, the district method obtained in Kentucky until 1824; in Tennessee and Maryland until 1832; in Indiana in 1824 and 1828; in Illinois in 1820 and 1824; and in Maine in 1820, 1824, and 1828. Massachusetts used the general ticket system in 1804, ... chose electors by joint ballot of the legislature in 1808 and in 1816, ... used the district system again in 1812 and 1820, ... and returned to the general ticket system in 1824 ... In New York, the electors were elected in 1828 by districts, the district electors choosing the electors at large.... The appointment of electors by the legislature, instead of by popular vote, was made use of by North Carolina, Vermont, and New Jersey in 1812."[37]

By 1824, presidential electors were chosen by popular vote (either by districts or statewide) in 18 of the 24 states. State legislatures chose presidential electors in Delaware, Georgia, Louisiana, New York, South Carolina, and Vermont.

By 1832, the people, rather than the state legislatures, chose presidential electors in 22 of the 23 states, with South Carolina being the only exception.[38]

By 1832, Maryland was the only state where presidential electors were elected by district. Maryland changed to a statewide system in 1836. In 1836, presidential electors were elected on a statewide basis in all of the states (that is, either by the people or, in the case of South Carolina, by the legislature).

As previously noted, the Founding Fathers did not advocate the use by the states of a statewide winner-take-all system to allocate their electoral votes. Nonetheless, once the states acquired the exclusive power to choose the manner of appointing their presidential electors, it was probably inevitable that they would realize the disadvantage of dividing their electoral votes and that they would consequently gravitate to the unit rule. Thus, the Constitution's grant of the power to the states to choose the manner of allocating their electoral votes resulted in the emergence throughout the country of a system that the Founding Fathers never envisioned. This fundamental change in the system for electing the President did not come about from a federal constitutional amendment but,

[37] *McPherson v. Blacker.* 146 U.S. 1 at 32. 1892.

instead, from the use by the states of a power that Article II of the U.S. Constitution specifically granted to them. As Stanwood noted in *A History of the Presidency from 1788 to 1897,*

> "the [statewide] method of choosing electors had now become uniform throughout the country, **without the interposition of an amendment to the Constitution.**"[38] [Emphasis added]

The South Carolina legislature last chose presidential electors in 1860. Since the Civil War, there have been only two instances when presidential electors have been chosen by a state legislature. In 1868, the Florida legislature did so because reconstruction was not complete in Florida in time for the presidential election. In 1876, Colorado did so because it was admitted as a new state in the midst of the presidential election.

By 1876, the principle that the people should elect presidential electors was so well established that the Colorado Constitution specifically addressed the exceptional nature of the appointment of the state's presidential electors by the legislature in 1876:

> "**Presidential electors, 1876.** The general assembly shall, at their first session, immediately after the organization of the two houses and after the canvass of the votes for officers of the executive department, and before proceeding to other business, provide by act or joint resolution for the appointment by said general assembly of electors in the electoral college, and such joint resolution or the bill for such enactment may be passed without being printed or referred to any committee, or read on more than one day in either house, and shall take effect immediately after the concurrence of the two houses therein, and the approval of the governor thereto shall not be necessary."[39]

---

[38] Stanwood, Edward. 1924. *A History of the Presidency from 1788 to 1897.* Boston, MA: Houghton Mifflin Company. Page 165. See also Busch, Andrew E. 2001. The development and democratization of the electoral college. In Gregg, Gary L. II (editor). 2001. *Securing Democracy: Why We Have an Electoral College.* Wilmington, DE: ISI Books. Pages 27–42.

[39] Section 19 of the article of the Colorado Constitution governing the transition from territorial status to statehood.

The next section of the Colorado Constitution then mandated a segue from legislative appointment to popular election of presidential electors by providing that after 1876:

"[T]he electors of the electoral college shall be chosen by direct vote of the people."[40]

The inclusion of the above section in the Colorado Constitution was a congressional condition for Colorado's admission to the Union.

2.2.5 DEVELOPMENTS SINCE 1876

Since 1876, the norm has been that a state's voters directly elect presidential electors in a statewide popular election under the winner-take-all system (with only the three exceptions described below).

The first exception arose as a consequence of the controversial 1888 presidential election. In that election, President Grover Cleveland received 5,539,118 popular votes in his re-election campaign, whereas Republican challenger Benjamin Harrison received only 5,449,825 popular votes.[41] Despite Cleveland's margin of 89,293 popular votes, Harrison won an overwhelming majority of the electoral votes (233 to Cleveland's 168) and was elected President. In the 1890 mid-term elections, the Democrats won political control of the then-usually-Republican state of Michigan. Under the Democrats, Michigan switched from the statewide winner-take-all system (then prevailing in all the states) to an arrangement in which one presidential elector was elected from each of Michigan's 12 congressional districts; one additional presidential elector was elected from a specially created eastern district (consisting of the 1st, 2nd, 6th, 7th, 8th, and 10th congressional districts); and the state's final presidential elector was elected from a western district (consisting of the state's other six congressional districts). The Republicans contested the constitutionality of the change to the district system before the U.S. Supreme Court in the 1892 case of *McPherson v. Blacker* mentioned earlier in this chapter. In that case, the Court upheld Michigan's right to choose the method of allocating its electoral votes. As a result, in the 1892 presidential election, Democrat Grover Cleveland received

---

[40] Section 20 of the article of the Colorado Constitution governing the transition from territorial status to statehood.

[41] Congressional Quarterly. 2002. *Presidential Elections 1789–2002.* Washington, DC: CQ Press. Page 128.

five electoral votes from Michigan, and Republican Benjamin Harrison received the other nine. When the Republicans regained political control in Michigan, they promptly restored the statewide winner-take-all system.

The second exception arose in 1969 when Maine adopted a system in which the state's two senatorial presidential electors are awarded to the presidential slate winning the statewide vote and one additional presidential elector is awarded to the presidential slate carrying each of the state's two congressional districts.

The third exception arose in 1992 when Nebraska adopted Maine's system of district and statewide electors. Nebraska law provides:

"Receipt by the presidential electors of a party or a group of petitioners of the highest number of votes statewide shall constitute election of the two at-large presidential electors of that party or group of petitioners. Receipt by the presidential electors of a party or a group of petitioners of the highest number of votes in a congressional district shall constitute election of the congressional district presidential elector of that party or group of petitioners."[42]

In practice, the approach currently used in Maine and Nebraska has never resulted in a political division of either state's presidential electors. The reason is that, in states with only a few congressional districts (two in Maine and three in Nebraska), the presidential candidate carrying the state is very likely to carry all of the state's congressional districts.

2.2.6 THE SHORT PRESIDENTIAL BALLOT

Until the middle of the 20th century, voters generally cast separate votes for individual candidates for presidential elector. In other words, in a state with 20 electoral votes, the voter was entitled to cast 20 separate votes. Inevitably, some voters would accidentally invalidate their ballot by voting for more than 20 candidates—something that was especially easy to do on the paper ballots that were in general use at the time. Other voters would accidentally vote for fewer than 20 electors (thereby diminishing the value of their franchise). Still other voters would mistakenly vote for just one presidential elector (thereby drastically diminishing

[42] Nebraska election law. Section 32-1038.

their franchise). A small number of voters intentionally split their ticket and voted for presidential electors from opposing parties (perhaps because they liked or disliked individual candidates for presidential elector). One result of these "bed sheet" ballots was that a state's electoral vote would occasionally become split between two political parties. For example, in 1916, Woodrow Wilson received one of West Virginia's electoral votes, with Charles Evans Hughes receiving seven. In 1912, Wilson received two of California's electoral votes, with Theodore Roosevelt receiving 11. The statewide winner came up short by one electoral vote in California in 1880, in Ohio and Oregon in 1892, in California and in Kentucky in 1896, and in Maryland in 1904.[43] The Federalists elected two presidential electors in Pennsylvania in 1796 (one of whom was the faithless elector Samuel Miles).

The *short ballot* was developed to simplify voting. It enables a voter to cast a single vote for a presidential slate composed of the name of a candidate for President and the name of a candidate for Vice President. By 1940, 15 states had adopted the short ballot. The number increased to 26 states by 1948 and to 36 by 1966.[44]

The presidential ballot in Ohio in 1948 was particularly confusing. Ohio employed the short ballot for established political parties. The newly formed Progressive Party (supporting Henry Wallace for President) failed to qualify as a regular party in Ohio in time for the 1948 presidential elections. Consequently, the individual names of its 25 candidates for presidential elector appeared on the ballot. In the confusion caused by this hybrid system, an estimated 100,000 ballots were invalidated because voters mistakenly voted for some individual presidential electors while also voting for either Democrat Harry Truman or Republican Thomas Dewey. Truman carried Ohio by 7,107 votes.

Vermont used a combination of the short presidential ballot and the traditional long ballot until 1980. Figure 2.1 shows a 1964 sample presidential ballot in Vermont. As can be seen, the voter had the option of casting a straight-party vote for all three of a party's presidential electors; voting for one, two, or three individual candidates for presidential elector on

---

[43] Congressional Quarterly. 2002. *Presidential Elections 1789–2002*. Washington, DC: CQ Press. Pages 158–159.

[44] Peirce, Neal R. 1968. *The People's President: The Electoral College in American History and Direct-Vote Alternative*. New York, NY: Simon and Schuster. Page 120.

Figure 2.1 1964 presidential ballot in Vermont

the ballot; or voting for one, two, or three write-in candidates for presidential electors.

Since 1980, all states have employed the short presidential ballot. Nonetheless, it is still possible today, in some states, to cast write-in votes for individual presidential electors (section 2.8), to cast votes for unpledged presidential electors (section 2.11), and, on an exceptional basis, to cast separate votes for individual candidates for presidential elector (section 2.9).

2.3 CURRENT METHODS OF ELECTING PRESIDENTIAL ELECTORS

As stated previously, the people have no federal constitutional right to vote for President or Vice President of the United States. In Colorado, the people have a state constitutional right to vote for presidential electors. In all the other states, the people have acquired the presidential vote by means of state law.

In this book, we will frequently refer to the laws of Minnesota to illustrate the way in which one state implements the process of electing the President and Vice President. As a convenience for the reader, appendix D contains the provisions of Minnesota election law that are relevant to presidential elections.

Section 208.02 of Minnesota election law gives the people of Minnesota the right to vote for presidential electors.

> "Presidential electors shall be chosen at the state general election held in the year preceding the expiration of the term of the president of the United States."

In Minnesota, the presidential ballot is prepared and printed by county auditors in accordance with state law. Accordingly, when a voter walked into a polling place in Hennepin County, Minnesota on November 2, 2004, he or she received a "short presidential ballot" resembling the sample ballot shown in figure 2.2 containing nine presidential slates, including the Republican slate consisting of George W. Bush for President and Dick Cheney for Vice President and the Democratic slate consisting of John F. Kerry and John Edwards.

As demonstrated by figure 2.2, Minnesota's presidential ballot is silent as to the existence of the Electoral College or the state's 10 electoral votes. The ballot simply reads,

> "U.S. President and Vice President—Vote for one team."

The linkage between a vote cast for a presidential slate on Minnesota's ballot and the state's 10 presidential electors is established by state law.

> "When Presidential electors are to be voted for, a vote cast for the party candidates for president and vice-president **shall**

Figure 2.2 2004 presidential ballot in Minnesota

be deemed a vote for that party's electors as filed with the secretary of state."[45] [Emphasis added]

Thus, a voter filling in the oval next to the names of George W. Bush and Dick Cheney on November 2, 2004, was not directly casting a vote for Bush and Cheney but, instead, for a slate of 10 Republican candidates for presidential elector who, if elected on November 2, 2004, were expected to vote for Bush and Cheney when the Electoral College met on December 13, 2004.

[45] Minnesota election law. Section 208.04, subdivision 1.

Minnesota law outlines the procedure by which the Minnesota Secretary of State becomes officially informed of the names of the persons running for President and Vice President and the names of the candidates for presidential elector:

> "Presidential electors for the major political parties of this state shall be nominated by delegate conventions called and held under the supervision of the respective state central committees of the parties of this state. On or before primary election day the chair of the major political party shall certify to the secretary of state the names of the persons nominated as Presidential electors and the names of the party candidates for president and vice-president."[46]

Thus, it is the state chair of each major political party in Minnesota who officially informs the Minnesota Secretary of State as to the name of the person nominated for President by the party's national convention, the name of the person nominated for Vice President by the party's national convention, and the names of the 10 persons nominated for the position of presidential elector by the party's state convention.

Twenty-nine states follow Minnesota's approach of nominating elector candidates at state party conventions. In six other states and the District of Columbia, the state party committee (or district committee) nominates the party's presidential electors. Many of the remaining states permit each party in the state to choose its method for itself. In Pennsylvania, each party's presidential nominee directly nominates the elector candidates who will run under his name in the state.[47]

Minnesota law also provides the procedure by which the county auditors become officially notified of the names of the persons running for President and Vice President:

> "The secretary of state shall certify the names of all duly nominated Presidential and Vice-Presidential candidates to the county auditors of the counties of the state."[48]

---

[46] Minnesota election law. Section 208.03.

[47] Berns, Walter (editor). *After the People Vote: A Guide to the Electoral College.* Washington, DC: The AEI Press. Page 11. See section 2.12 for Pennsylvania law.

[48] Minnesota election law. Section 208.04, subdivision 1.

Laws in the other states and the District of Columbia operate in a broadly similar way to accomplish the above objectives.

There are currently three major types of presidential ballots that a voter encounters in presidential elections:

- Presidential ballots in eight states (Arizona, Idaho, Kansas, North Dakota Oklahoma, South Dakota, Tennessee, and Virginia) explicitly mention the names of all of the candidates for presidential elector associated with each presidential slate. For example, the 2004 presidential ballot in North Dakota (figure 2.3) makes it clear that a vote for "Bush-Republican" is, in fact, a vote for the Republican Party's three candidates for presidential elector in 2004-namely Betsy Dalrymple, Evan Lips, and Ben Clayburgh. Curiously, in North Dakota, the name of the candidate for Vice President does not appear on the ballot even though the ballot is headed by the words "President & Vice President of the United States—Vote for no more than one team."
- Presidential ballots in most states mention that the voter is voting for presidential electors but do not explicitly identify the electors. Figure 2.4 shows the 2004 ballot for Michigan. It refers to "Presidential: Electors of President and Vice President of the United States—4 Year Term."
- Oregon's presidential ballot is unusually explicit and informs the voter: "Your vote for the candidates for United States President and Vice President shall be a vote for the electors supporting those candidates."
- Presidential ballots in many states[49] make no reference at all to the existence of the Electoral College or presidential electors.

2.4 CERTIFICATION OF THE PRESIDENTIAL VOTE BY THE STATES

After the popular voting for presidential electors takes place on the Tuesday after the first Monday in November, the votes cast by the people are counted at the precinct level. The vote counts are then aggregated at the local level (e.g., city, town, village, township, or county) and are finally aggregated at the statewide level.

---

[49] Including Minnesota, Alaska, Florida, Georgia, Illinois, Iowa, Maryland, North Carolina, Texas, Washington, and West Virginia.

SAMPLE BALLOT
GENERAL ELECTION BALLOT - NOVEMBER 2, 2004
COUNTY OF BURLEIGH   STATE OF NORTH DAKOTA

INSTRUCTIONS TO VOTER

To vote for the candidate of your choice, you must completely blacken the oval (⬛) opposite the name of the candidate.
To vote for a person whose name is not printed on the ballot, write or paste that person's name in the blank space provided for that purpose and completely blacken the oval opposite the space provided (⬛).

PARTY BALLOT

President & Vice President of the United States
Vote for no more than ONE team

- NADER — Independent { Mathew Reister, Patrick Jund, Mary Jund }
- BADNARIK — Libertarian { Roland Riemers, James Foster, Keith Hanson }
- PEROUTKA — Constitution { Charlene Nelson, Leland Wetzel, Herb Mittelstedt }
- KERRY — Democratic-NPL { Jocelyn Burdick, Heidi Heitkamp, Roland Redlin }
- BUSH — Republican { Betsy Dalrymple, Evan Lips, Ben Clayburgh }

Member of House of Representatives
8TH DISTRICT
Vote for no more than TWO names

- Dwight Wrangham — Republican
- Jeff Delzer — Republican
- Ken Baker — Democratic-NPL
- Muriel Kisse — Democratic-NPL

Governor and Lt. Governor
Vote for no more than ONE set of names

- Joseph A. Satrom & Deb Mathern — Democratic-NPL
- John Hoeven & Jack Dalrymple — Republican
- Roland Riemers & Mitchell S. Sanderson — independent nomination

Secretary of State
Vote for no more than ONE name

- Douglas Melby — Democratic-NPL

Attorney General
Vote for no more than ONE name

- Wayne Stenehjem — Republican
- Bruce Schoenwald — Democratic-NPL

Commissioner of Insurance
Vote for no more than ONE name

- Terry Barnes — Democratic-NPL
- Jim Poolman — Republican

Commissioner of Agriculture
Vote for no more than ONE name

- Roger Johnson — Democratic-NPL
- Doug Goehring — Republican

Public Service Commissioner
Vote for no more than ONE name

- Ron Gumeringer — Democratic-NPL
- Kevin Cramer — Republican

Figure 2.3 2004 presidential ballot in North Dakota

Minnesota law specifies that the state canvassing board shall ascertain the number of votes cast for each presidential slate in the state.

"The state canvassing board at its meeting on the second Tuesday after each state general election shall open and canvass the returns made to the secretary of state for Presidential electors, prepare a statement of the number of votes cast for the persons receiving votes for these offices, and **declare the person or persons receiving the highest number of votes for each office** duly elected. When it appears that more than the number of persons to be elected

Figure 2.4 2004 presidential ballot in Michigan

as Presidential electors have the highest and an equal number of votes, the secretary of state, in the presence of the board shall decide by lot which of the persons shall be declared elected. The governor shall transmit to each person declared elected a certificate of election, signed by the governor, sealed with the state seal, and countersigned by the secretary of state."[50] [Emphasis added]

---

[50] Minnesota election law. Section 208.05.

Thus, it is the above section of Minnesota election law that establishes the statewide winner-take-all system in Minnesota.

Minnesota law (in common with the laws of many states) calls for the use of a lottery in the event of a tie vote for presidential electors. In some states (including Maine and Michigan), the state legislature would break a tie among presidential electors. For example, Maine law provides:

"If there is a tie vote for presidential electors, the Governor shall convene the Legislature by proclamation. The Legislature by joint ballot of the members assembled in convention shall determine which are elected."[51]

Although elections are primarily controlled by state law, various federal laws also govern presidential elections. For example, federal law requires each state to create seven "Certificates of Ascertainment" certifying the number of votes cast for each presidential slate. One of these certificates is sent to the Archivist of the United States in Washington, D.C., and six are supplied to the presidential electors for their use during the meeting in mid-December. Title 3, chapter 1, section 6 of the United States Code specifies:

"It shall be the duty of the executive of each State, as soon as practicable after the conclusion of the appointment of the electors in such State by the final ascertainment, under and in pursuance of the laws of such State providing for such ascertainment, to communicate by registered mail under the seal of the State to the Archivist of the United States a certificate of such ascertainment of the electors appointed, setting forth the names of such electors and the canvass or other ascertainment under the laws of such State of the number of votes given or cast for each person for whose appointment any and all votes have been given or cast; and it shall also thereupon be the duty of the executive of each State to deliver to the electors of such State, on or before the day on which they are required by section 7 of this title to meet, six duplicate-originals of the same certificate under the seal of the State...."

---

[51] Maine 21-A M.R.S, section 732. The State of Maine claims a copyright in its codified statutes. All copyrights and other rights to statutory text are reserved by the State of Maine.

STATE of MINNESOTA

EXECUTIVE — DEPARTMENT

TIM PAWLENTY
GOVERNOR

CERTIFICATE OF ASCERTAINMENT
OF APPOINTMENT OF ELECTORS
FOR PRESIDENT AND VICE PRESIDENT
OF THE UNITED STATES
FOR THE STATE OF MINNESOTA

To: John W. Carlin
     Archivist of the United States
     National Archives and Records Administration
     c/o Office of the Federal Register (NF)
     8601 Adelphi Road
     College Park, MD 20740-6001

I, Tim Pawlenty, Governor of the State of Minnesota, do hereby certify the following:

In accordance with Article 2, Section 1 of the Constitution of the United States, the Legislature of the State of Minnesota directed that the electors for President and Vice President of the United States be elected at the General Election conducted on November 2, 2004.

At the General Election held in this State on November 2, 2004, the following persons received the greatest number of votes cast for the office of Electors for President and Vice President of the United States, and are duly elected to fill such office:

Figure 2.5 First page of Minnesota's 2004 Certificate of Ascertainment

Figures 2.5, 2.6, and 2.7 show the first three pages of Minnesota's 2004 Certificate of Ascertainment (with all eight pages being shown in appendix E). Minnesota's Certificate of Ascertainment is signed by the Governor and Secretary of State, bears the state seal, and was issued on November 30, 2004 (four weeks after the voting by the people on November 2).

The second page of Minnesota's Certificate of Ascertainment (figure 2.6) shows that 1,445,014 popular votes were cast for each of the 10 presidential electors associated with the presidential slate consisting of John Kerry for President and John Edwards for Vice President of the

State of Minnesota
Certificate of Ascertainment, 2004, Page 2 of 8

Minnesota Democratic-Farmer-Labor Party
Electors pledged to John F. Kerry for President of the United States
and John Edwards for Vice President of the United States.
These candidates for presidential elector each received 1,445,014
votes:

Sonja Berg, of St. Cloud
Vi Grooms-Alban, of Cohasset
Matthew Little, of Maplewood
Michael Meuers, of Bemidji
Tim O'Brien, of Edina
Lil Ortendahl, of Osakis
Everett Pettiford, of Minneapolis
Jean Schiebel, of Brooklyn Center
Frank Simon, of Chaska
Chandler Harrison Stevens, of Austin

I further certify that the returns of the votes cast for Presidential Electors at the General Election were canvassed and certified by the State Canvassing Board on the 16th day of November, 2004 in accordance with the laws of the State of Minnesota, and that the number of votes cast for each candidate for Presidential Elector at the General Election is as follows:

Green Party of Minnesota
Electors pledged to David Cobb for President of the United States
and Pat LaMarche for Vice President of the United States.
These candidates for presidential elector each received 4,408 votes:

Scott Bol
Kellie Burriss
Michael Cavlan
Amber Garlan
Jenny Heiser
Molly Nutting
Douglas Root
Mark Wahl
Annie Young
Dean Zimmermann

Figure 2.6 Second page of Minnesota's 2004 Certificate of Ascertainment showing that the Kerry-Edwards slate received 1,445,014 popular votes and carried the state

Minnesota Democratic-Farmer-Labor Party. All 10 elector candidates received the identical number of votes because Minnesota law specifies that a vote cast for the Kerry-Edwards presidential state "shall be deemed" to be a vote for each of the 10 presidential electors associated with that slate.[52]

---

[52] Minnesota election law. Section 208.04, subdivision 1.

State of Minnesota
Certificate of Ascertainment 2004, Page 3 of 8

Republican Party of Minnesota
Electors pledged to George W. Bush for President of the United States
and Dick Cheney for Vice President of the United States.
Each elector received 1,346,695 votes:

> George Cable
> Jeff Carnes
> Ronald Eibensteiner
> Angie Erhard
> Eileen Fiore
> Walter Klaus
> Michelle Rifenberg
> Julie Rosendahl
> Lyall Schwarzkopf
> Armin Tesch

Socialist Equality Party
Electors pledged to Bill Van Auken for President of the United States
and Jim Lawrence for Vice President of the United States.
These candidates for presidential elector each received 539 votes:

> Nathan Andrew
> Dan W. Blais
> William J. Campbell-Bezat
> Christopher M. Isett
> Cory R. Johnson
> Cynthia B. Moore
> Thomas G. Moore
> Stephen M. Paulson
> Emanuele Saccarelli
> James Strouf

Figure 2.7 Third page of Minnesota's 2004 Certificate of Ascertainment showing that the Bush-Cheney slate received 1,346,695 popular votes

Similarly, the third page of Minnesota's Certificate of Ascertainment (figure 2.6) shows that 1,346,695 popular votes were cast for presidential electors associated with the presidential slate consisting of George W. Bush and Dick Cheney of the Republican Party.[53]

---

[53] Minnesota's 2004 Certificate of Ascertainment goes on to report the votes cast for candidates of the Better Life Party, Libertarian Party, Green Party, Constitution Party, Christian Freedom Party, Socialist Equity Party, and Socialist Workers Party.

The Certificate of Ascertainment reflects Minnesota's use of the winner-take-all system of awarding electoral votes. In particular, the second page (figure 2.6) of the certificate states that the 10 presidential electors associated with the presidential slate consisting of John Kerry for President and John Edwards for Vice President of the Minnesota Democratic-Farmer-Labor Party

> "received the greatest number of votes for the office of Electors of President and Vice President of the United States and are duly elected to fill such office."

In the two states that use the district system (Maine and Nebraska), the Certificate of Ascertainment shows the statewide vote (which decides the state's two senatorial electors) as well as the district vote (which decides the presidential elector for each congressional district). Maine's 2004 Certificate of Ascertainment is shown in appendix F, and Nebraska's 2004 Certificate of Ascertainment is shown in appendix G.

Controversies about the voting for presidential electors generally focus on the issuance of the Certificate of Ascertainment in the contested state. Title 3, chapter 1, section 5 of the United States Code creates a "safe harbor" date six days before the scheduled meeting of the Electoral College for resolving disputes concerning the November voting for presidential electors. Title 3, chapter 1, section 5 of the United States Code states:

> "If any State shall have provided, by laws enacted prior to the day fixed for the appointment of the electors, for its final determination of any controversy or contest concerning the appointment of all or any of the electors of such State, by judicial or other methods or procedures, and such determination shall have been made at least six days before the time fixed for the meeting of the electors, such determination made pursuant to such law so existing on said day, and made at least six days prior to said time of meeting of the electors, shall be conclusive, and shall govern in the counting of the electoral votes as provided in the Constitution, and as hereinafter regulated, so far as the ascertainment of the electors appointed by such State is concerned."

This "safe harbor" date played a central role in the decision of the U.S. Supreme Court in *Bush v. Gore*[54] concerning the disputed counting of the popular votes in Florida in the 2000 presidential election. Many states finalize their Certificate of Ascertainment in late November. Maine's 2004 Certificate of Ascertainment (shown in appendix F) was issued on November 23, 2004. Almost all states have a law setting a specific deadline for finalizing the canvassing of their statewide elections (sometimes with an earlier deadline for presidential electors). Appendix T lists these deadlines.

Most states regard the federal "safe harbor" date established by Title 3, chapter 1, section 5 of the United States Code as a deadline for finalizing their Certificate of Ascertainment. For example, New York's 2004 Certificate of Ascertainment (shown in appendix H) was issued on December 6, 2004 (i.e., six days before the scheduled December 13 meeting of the Electoral College). States tend to regard the federal "safe harbor" date as a deadline if there is any controversy about the presidential vote count in the state. For example, various issues were raised about the presidential voting in Ohio in 2004, and Ohio finalized its Certificate of Ascertainment on December 6, 2004.

On the other hand, if there is no controversy involving a state's presidential vote, some states fail to finalize their Certificate of Ascertainment until the day that the Electoral College meets. For example, in 2004, 14 states finalized their Certificate of Ascertainment on December 13, 2004. Appendix J shows the date on which each state's Certificate of Ascertainment was finalized.

2.5 MEETING OF THE ELECTORAL COLLEGE

The U.S. Constitution[55] specifies that electors must meet on the same day throughout the United States.

Federal law specifies the particular day for the meeting of the Electoral College (December 13 for the 2004 presidential elections).

> "The electors of President and Vice President of each State shall meet and give their votes on the first Monday after the second Wednesday in December next following their

[54] *Bush v. Gore.* 531 U.S. 98. 2000.
[55] U.S. Constitution. Article II, section 1, clause 4.

appointment at such place in each State as the legislature of such State shall direct."[56]

State law, in turn, specifies the place and time of the meeting of the Electoral College. For example, Minnesota law provides:

"The Presidential electors, before 12:00 [P.]M. on the day before that fixed by congress for the electors to vote for president and vice-president of the United States, shall notify the governor that they are at the state capitol and ready at the proper time to fulfill their duties as electors. The governor shall deliver to the electors present a certificate of the names of all the electors. If any elector named therein fails to appear before 9:00 a.m. on the day, and at the place, fixed for voting for president and vice-president of the United States, the electors present shall, in the presence of the governor, immediately elect by ballot a person to fill the vacancy. If more than the number of persons required have the highest and an equal number of votes, the governor, in the presence of the electors attending, shall decide by lot which of those persons shall be elected."[57]

2.6 CERTIFICATION OF VOTES OF THE PRESIDENTIAL ELECTORS

Federal law requires that the presidential electors sign six separate Certificates of Vote reporting the outcome of their voting for President and Vice President. Of the seven Certificates of Ascertainment created by each state, one is sent to the National Archivist in Washington, D.C., and six are given to the presidential electors for use at their meeting. At the Electoral College meeting, the electors attach one Certificate of Ascertainment to each of the six required "Certificates of Vote."

"The electors shall make and sign six certificates of all the votes given by them, each of which certificates shall contain two distinct lists, one of the votes for President and the other of the votes for Vice President, and shall annex to each of the certificates one of the lists of the electors which shall have been furnished to them by direction of the executive of the State."[58]

---

[56] United States Code. Title 3, chapter 1, section 7.
[57] Minnesota election law. Section 208.06.
[58] United States Code. Title 3, chapter 1, section 9.

Figure 2.8 Minnesota 2004 Certificate of Vote

In addition, federal law[59] specifies that one of these sets of documents be sent to the President of the Senate in Washington, D.C.; two be sent to the Secretary of State of the United States; two be sent to the Archivist of the United States in Washington, D.C.; and one to the federal district court in the judicial district in which the electors assemble. In the event that no certificates are received from a particular state by the fourth

---

[59] United States Code. Title 3, chapter 1, section 11.

Wednesday in December, federal law[60] establishes procedures for sending a special messenger to the local federal district court in order to obtain the missing certificates.

In Minnesota in 2004, the Kerry-Edwards presidential slate received the most votes in the statewide popular election held on November 2, 2004. Thus, all 10 Democratic-Farmer-Labor Party presidential electors were elected. Figure 2.8 shows Minnesota's 2004 Certificate of Vote.

In Minnesota, the presidential electors vote by secret ballot. In accordance with the 12th Amendment to the Constitution, each presidential elector is to cast one vote for President and a separate vote for Vice President. As can be seen in figure 2.8, all 10 of Minnesota's presidential electors voted for John Edwards for Vice President. However, one of the 10 electors also voted for John Edwards for President. That vote was apparently accidental because, after the count was announced, all 10 electors said that they had intended to vote for John Kerry for President. The result of this error was that John Kerry officially received only 251 electoral votes for President in 2004 (with John Edwards receiving one electoral vote for President and George W. Bush receiving 286). The vote for Edwards for President in 2004 was, apparently, the only electoral vote ever cast by accident.[61]

2.7 COUNTING OF THE ELECTORAL VOTES IN CONGRESS

Federal law specifies that the electoral votes are to be counted on January 6th of the subsequent year.

> "Congress shall be in session on the sixth day of January succeeding every meeting of the electors. The Senate and House of Representatives shall meet in the Hall of the House of Representatives at the hour of 1 o'clock in the afternoon on that day, and the President of the Senate shall be their presiding officer. Two tellers shall be previously appointed on the part of the Senate and two on the part of the House of Representatives, to whom shall be handed, as they are opened by the President of the Senate, all the certificates and

---

[60] United States Code. Title 3, chapter 1, sections 13 and 14.

[61] See section 2.12 for a discussion of the related issue of faithless electors.

papers purporting to be certificates of the electoral votes, which certificates and papers shall be opened, presented, and acted upon in the alphabetical order of the States, beginning with the letter A; and said tellers, having then read the same in the presence and hearing of the two Houses, shall make a list of the votes as they shall appear from the said certificates; and the votes having been ascertained and counted according to the rules in this subchapter provided, the result of the same shall be delivered to the President of the Senate, who shall thereupon announce the state of the vote, which announcement shall be deemed a sufficient declaration of the persons, if any, elected President and Vice President of the United States, and, together with a list of the votes, be entered on the Journals of the two Houses."[62]

The 12th Amendment to the Constitution governs the counting of the electoral votes by Congress. In order to be elected president, a candidate must receive "a majority of the whole number of Electors appointed." Assuming that all 538 electors are appointed, 270 electoral votes are necessary for election. The 12th Amendment states in part:

"[T]he President of the Senate shall, in the presence of the Senate and House of Representatives, open all the certificates and the votes shall then be counted;—The person having the greatest number of votes for President, shall be the President, if such number be a majority of the whole number of Electors appointed...."

In the event that no candidate receives the required majority, the 12th Amendment provides a procedure (appendix A) for a "continent election" in which the House of Representatives chooses the President (with each state having one vote), and the Senate chooses the Vice President (with each Senator having one vote).

The President and Vice President are inaugurated on January 20th in accordance with the terms of the 20th Amendment (ratified in 1933).

---

[62] United States Code. Title 3, chapter 1, section 15.

2.8 WRITE-IN VOTES FOR PRESIDENT

Write-in votes for the offices of President and Vice President are inherently more complex than those for any other office because when the people go to the polls in November, they are voting for candidates to fill the office of presidential elector—not for candidates to fill the office of President and Vice President of the United States.

Minnesota law permits a voter to cast presidential write-in votes in two ways.

- **Advance Filing of Write-Ins:** Under this approach, supporters of a write-in presidential slate may file a slate of presidential electors prior to the election. Such advance filing makes write-in voting more convenient because it enables the voter to write in the name of a presidential slate, without having to write in the names of 10 (in the case of Minnesota) individual candidates for presidential elector.
- **Election-Day Write-Ins:** Under this approach, there is no advance filing, and the voter must write in the names of up to 10 individual presidential electors.

Minnesota law implements the method of advance filing of write-ins as follows:

"(a) A candidate for state or federal office who wants write-in votes for the candidate to be counted must file a written request with the filing office for the office sought no later than the fifth day before the general election. The filing officer shall provide copies of the form to make the request.

"(b) A candidate for president of the United States who files a request under this subdivision must include the name of a candidate for vice-president of the United States. The request must also include the name of at least one candidate for Presidential elector. The total number of names of candidates for Presidential elector on the request may not exceed the total number of electoral votes to be cast by Minnesota in the presidential election."[63]

---

[63] Minnesota election law. Section 204B.09, subdivision 3.

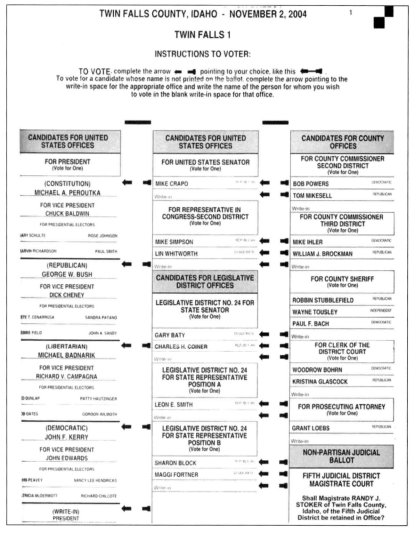

Figure 2.9 2004 presidential ballot in Idaho

Minnesota's 2004 Certificate of Ascertainment (appendix E) shows that 1, 1, 2, 2, and 4 votes were cast for the presidential electors associated with the five officially declared write-in slates in the presidential election in Minnesota in 2004.

Many other states permit advance filing of write-ins.

Election-day write-ins (without advance filing) are permitted in fewer states. This method is allowed in Minnesota as the consequence of a 1968

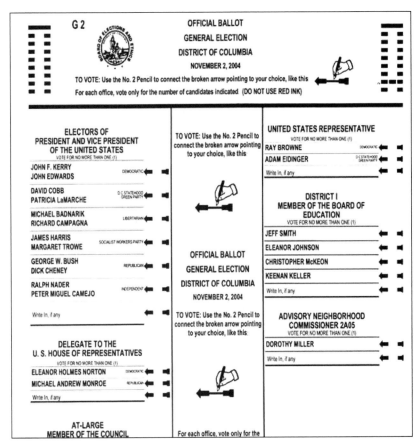

Figure 2.10 2004 presidential ballot in the District of Columbia

opinion of the Minnesota Attorney General.[64] That ruling declared that a presidential write-in vote may be cast in Minnesota by writing between one and 10 names of persons for the position of presidential elector. The Minnesota Attorney General also ruled that a pre-printed sticker containing the names of between 1 and 10 presidential electors may be employed in Minnesota. Given the small amount of space available for a write-in for president on Minnesota's ballot (figure 2.2), a pre-printed sticker is the most practical way to cast such a vote.

A similar small space (figure 2.9) is provided on the ballot for presidential write-ins in Idaho (which has four electoral votes) and the District of Columbia (figure 2.10).

---

[64] Op. Atty. Gen., 28c-5. October 5, 1968.

In Minnesota, it is possible for an individual candidate to receive votes for the office of presidential elector in Minnesota in three ways:

- by appearing as one of the electors nominated by a political party under section section 208.03;
- by appearing on a list of electors filed in advance under subdivision 3 of section 204B.09; and
- by receiving a write-in vote for the position of presidential elector (e.g., on a pre-printed sticker) as permitted by the 1968 Attorney General's opinion.

When the Minnesota State Canvassing Board meets, all votes cast for a particular individual for the office of presidential elector are added up. The 10 elector candidates receiving the most votes are elected to the office of presidential elector. In other words, there can be a fusion of votes from more than one source.

2.9 SEPARATE VOTING FOR INDIVIDUAL PRESIDENTIAL ELECTORS

Notwithstanding the now-universal use of the short presidential ballot, it is still possible for a voter to cast separate votes for individual candidates for the office of presidential elector in some states.

Section 23–15–431 of Mississippi election law entitled "Voting irregular ballot for person whose name does not appear on voting machine" provides:

"Ballots voted for any person whose name does not appear on the machine as a nominated candidate for office, are herein referred to as irregular ballots. In voting for presidential electors, a voter may vote an irregular ticket made up of the names of persons in nomination by different parties, or partially of names of persons so in nomination and partially of persons not in nomination, or wholly of persons not in nomination by any party. Such irregular ballots shall be deposited, written or affixed in or upon the receptacle or device provided on the machine for that purpose. With that exception, no irregular ballot shall be voted for any person for any office whose name appears on the machine as a nominated candidate for that office; any irregular ballot so voted shall not be counted. An irregular ballot must be cast in its appropriate place on the machine, or it shall be void and not counted."[65]

In addition, Mississippi election law concerning "Electronic Voting Systems" provides:

"No electronic voting system, consisting of a marking or voting device in combination with automatic tabulating equipment, shall be acquired or used in accordance with Sections 23-15-461 though 23-15-485 unless it shall ...

"(c) Permit each voter, at presidential elections, by one (1) mark or punch to vote for the candidates of that party for President, Vice-President, and their presidential electors, or to vote individually for the electors of his choice when permitted by law."[66]

Although Mississippi law permits such "irregular" voting, Mississippi's 2004 Certificate of Ascertainment (appendix I) and the state's 2000 Certificate indicate that no such votes were actually cast in the state in either the 2004 or 2000 presidential elections.

2.10 FUSION VOTING IN NEW YORK

Fusion voting is a major aspect of partisan politics in the state of New York. In New York, candidates for political office may appear on the ballot in the general election as nominees of more than one political party. For example, George Pataki has run for Governor as the candidate of both the Republican Party and the Conservative Party. That is, Pataki's name appeared more than once on the same ballot. Under New York election law, the votes that a candidate receives on each ballot line are added together in a process called *fusion*.

One of the political effects of fusion is that it enables a minor party to make a nominee of a major political party aware that he or she would not have won without the minor party's support. In the past, fusion voting played an important role in Minnesota politics prior to the merger that

---

[65] Mississippi election law. Section 23-15-431.

[66] Mississippi election law. Section 23-15-465. Similar statutory provisions are applicable to other voting systems that may be used in Mississippi (e.g., optical mark-reading equipment).

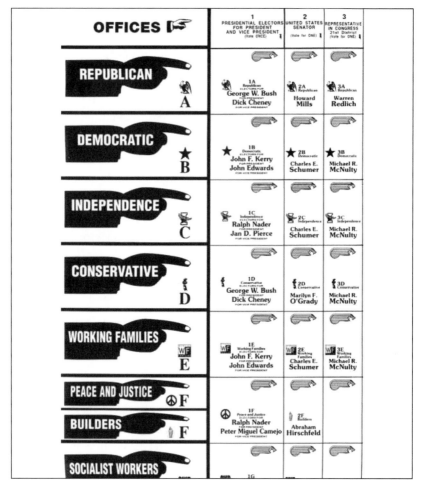

Figure 2.11 2004 New York presidential ballot

resulted in the formation of that state's present-day Democratic-Farmer-Labor Party.

New York is not the only state that currently allows fusion voting. For example, fusion voting is currently permitted under Vermont election law.

Figure 2.11 shows the 2004 New York presidential ballot. As can be seen, the Bush-Cheney presidential slate ran with the support of both the Republican Party and the Conservative Party, and the Kerry-Edwards slate ran with the support of the Democratic Party and Working Families Party.

STATE OF NEW YORK, ss:

Statement of the whole number of votes cast for all the candidates for the office of ELECTOR OF PRESIDENT and VICE-PRESIDENT at a General Election held in said State on the Second day of November, 2004.

The whole number of votes given for the office of ELECTOR OF PRESIDENT and VICE-PRESIDENT was **7,448,266** of which

		REPUBLICAN	CONSERVATIVE	TOTAL
George E. Pataki	received	2,806,993	155,574	2,962,567
Alexander F. Treadwell	received	2,806,993	155,574	2,962,567
Joseph Bruno	received	2,806,993	155,574	2,962,567
Charles Nesbitt	received	2,806,993	155,574	2,962,567
Mary Donohue	received	2,806,993	155,574	2,962,567
Rudolph Giuliani	received	2,806,993	155,574	2,962,567
Charles Gargano	received	2,806,993	155,574	2,962,567
Joseph Mondello	received	2,806,993	155,574	2,962,567
J. Patrick Barrett	received	2,806,993	155,574	2,962,567
John F. Nolan	received	2,806,993	155,574	2,962,567
Robert Davis	received	2,806,993	155,574	2,962,567
Peter J. Savago	received	2,806,993	155,574	2,962,567
Maggie Brooks	received	2,806,993	155,574	2,962,567
Catherine Blaney	received	2,806,993	155,574	2,962,567
Howard Mills	received	2,806,993	155,574	2,962,567
John Cahill	received	2,806,993	155,574	2,962,567
Rita DiMartino	received	2,806,993	155,574	2,962,567
Libby Pataki	received	2,806,993	155,574	2,962,567
Stephen Minarik	received	2,806,993	155,574	2,962,567
Raymond Meier	received	2,806,993	155,574	2,962,567
Thomas M. Reynolds	received	2,806,993	155,574	2,962,567
Adam Stoll	received	2,806,993	155,574	2,962,567
Herman Badillo	received	2,806,993	155,574	2,962,567
Jane Forbes Clark	received	2,806,993	155,574	2,962,567
James Garner	received	2,806,993	155,574	2,962,567
Shawn Marie Levine	received	2,806,993	155,574	2,962,567
Viola J. Hunter	received	2,806,993	155,574	2,962,567
Laura Schreiner	received	2,806,993	155,574	2,962,567
Carmen Gomez Goldberg	received	2,806,993	155,574	2,962,567
Bernadette Castro	received	2,806,993	155,574	2,962,567
Cathy Jimino	received	2,806,993	155,574	2,962,567

Figure 2.12 Third page of New York's 2004 Certificate of Ascertainment

When fusion voting is applied to presidential races, the question arises as to how to handle the presidential electors associated with the candidate. New York law permits two parties to nominate a common slate of presidential electors. For example, the Republican and Conservative parties nominated the same slate of presidential electors for the 2004 presidential election. Similarly, the Democratic and Working Families parties nominated the same slate of presidential electors.

Figure 2.12 shows the third page of New York's 2004 Certificate of Ascertainment indicating that the Bush-Cheney presidential slate received

2,806,993 votes on the Republican Party line and an additional 155,574 votes on the Conservative Party line, for a grand total of 2,962,567 votes. Similarly, the fourth page of New York's 2004 Certificate of Ascertainment (appendix H) shows that the Kerry-Edwards presidential slate received 4,180,755 votes on the Democratic Party line and an additional 133,525 votes on the Working Families Party line, for a grand total of 4,313,280 votes.

The second page of New York's 2004 Certificate of Ascertainment states that the 31 presidential electors shared by the Democratic Party and the Working Families Party (i.e., the Kerry-Edwards electors)

"were, by the greatest number of votes given at said election, duly elected elector of President and Vice-President of the United States."

The presidential ballot in New York in 2004 (figure 2.11) shows that the presidential election in New York is indeed conducted on the basis of distinct presidential slates. Ralph Nader appeared on the ballot in New York as the presidential nominee of both the Independence Party and the Peace and Justice Party. Nader, however, ran with Jan D. Pierce for Vice President on the Independence Party line but with Peter Miguel Camejo for Vice President on the Peace and Justice Party line. Thus, there were two different "Nader" presidential slates in New York in 2004, each with a different slate of presidential electors. The Nader-Pierce presidential slate received 84,247 votes on the Independence Party line (shown on the fifth page of the Certificate of Ascertainment in appendix H). The Nader-Camejo presidential slate received 15,626 votes on the Peace and Justice Party line (shown on the sixth page of the Certificate of Ascertainment in appendix H). Because there were two distinct presidential slates and two distinct slates of presidential electors, there was no fusion of votes between the Independence Party and the Peace and Justice Party.

2.11 UNPLEDGED PRESIDENTIAL ELECTORS

Unpledged electors were a prominent feature of presidential voting in many southern states immediately before and after passage of the civil rights legislation of the mid-1960s.

In 1960 (figure 2.13), for example, Alabama's presidential ballot contained 11 separate lines, each with the name of one candidate for the office of presidential elector and a separate lever that the voter could pull.[67] The 11 electors of the Alabama Democratic Party appeared under the party's rooster logo and the slogan "White Supremacy-For the Right." Similarly, there were lists of 11 elector candidates for the Alabama Republican Party and 11 elector candidates for each of several other political parties in Alabama that year. The name of no presidential or vice-presidential candidate appeared anywhere on the 1960 Alabama presidential ballot.

Current Mississippi law provides for unpledged presidential electors:

"(1) When presidential electors are to be chosen, the Secretary of State of Mississippi shall certify to the circuit clerks of the several counties the names of all candidates for President and Vice-President who are nominated by any national convention or other like assembly of any political party or by written petition signed by at least one thousand (1,000) qualified voters of this state.

"(2) The certificate of nomination by a political party convention must be signed by the presiding officer and secretary of the convention and by the chairman of the state executive committee of the political party making the nomination. Any nominating petition, to be valid, must contain the signatures as well as the addresses of the petitioners. Such certificates and petitions must be filed with the State Board of Election Commissioners by filing the same in the office of the Secretary of State not less than sixty (60) days previous to the day of the election.

"(3) Each certificate of nomination and nominating petition must be accompanied by a list of the names and addresses of persons, who shall be qualified voters of this state, equal in number to the number of presidential electors to be chosen. Each person so listed shall execute the following statement which shall be attached to the certificate or petition when the same is filed with the State Board of Election Commissioners:

---

[67] The 1960 Alabama presidential ballot is shown in appendix K of Peirce, Neal R. 1968. *The People's President: The Electoral College in American History and Direct-Vote Alternative.* New York, NY: Simon and Schuster. The 1960 Alabama presidential ballot is reprinted as figure 2.13 in this book with the permission of Yale University Press.

Figure 2.13 1960 Alabama presidential ballot

GENERAL ELECTION JEFFERSON COUNTY	GENERAL ELECTION JEFFERSON COUNTY	GENERAL ELECTION JEFFERSON COUNTY
NATIONAL STATES RIGHTS PARTY — Column 3	PROHIBITION PARTY — Column 4	REPUBLICAN PARTY — Column 5
GEORGE E. ALLEN ☐	L. E. BARTON ☐	ROBERT S. CARTLEDGE ☐
ANNETTE M. BARTEE ☐	WILLIAM E. BROWN ☐	CHARLES H., JR. CHAPMAN ☐
LODWICK H. BARTEE ☐	L. J. CHAMBLISS ☐	J. N. DENNIS ☐
LEE J. CROWDER ☐	LEONA B. FRAME ☐	CECIL DURHAM ☐
THERMAN De LEE ☐	JOE FROST ☐	W. H. GILLESPIE ☐
MRS. LILA EVANS ☐	KATHRYNE E. GARDNER ☐	PERRY O. HOOPER ☐
WILLIE BAZZELL GARRETT ☐	O. A. GARDNER ☐	W. J. KENNAMER ☐
JOHN DOUGLAS KNOWLES ☐	A. D. PECK ☐	TOM McNARON ☐
SANFORD D. RUDD ☐	PHOEBE SHOEMAKER ☐	MRS. JOHN SIMPSON ☐
JACK ANDREW TOMLINSON ☐	C. B. STEWART ☐	T. B. THOMPSON ☐
ERNEST WILSON ☐	R. DREW WOLCOTT ☐	GEORGE WITCHER ☐

Figure 2.13 1960 Alabama presidential ballot (cont.)

'I do hereby consent and do hereby agree to serve as elector for President and Vice-President of the United States, if elected to that position, and do hereby agree that, if so elected, I shall cast my ballot as such for _____ for President and _____ for Vice-President of the United States'

(inserting in said blank spaces the respective names of the persons named as nominees for said respective offices in the certificate to which this statement is attached).

"(4) The State Board of Election Commissioners and any other official charged with the preparation of official ballots shall place on such official ballots the words

'PRESIDENTIAL ELECTORS FOR (here insert the name of the candidate for President, the word 'AND' and the name of the candidate for Vice-President)'

in lieu of placing the names of such presidential electors on such official ballots, and a vote cast therefore shall be counted and shall be in all respects effective as a vote for each of the presidential electors representing such candidates for President and Vice-President of the United States. In the case of unpledged electors, the State Board of Election Commissioners and any other official charged with the preparation of official ballots shall place on such official ballots the words 'UNPLEDGED ELECTOR(S) (here insert the name(s) of individual unpledged elector(s) if placed upon the ballot based upon a petition granted in the manner provided by law stating the individual name(s) of the elector(s) rather than a slate of electors).' "[68]

2.12 FAITHLESS PRESIDENTIAL ELECTORS

In the 1952 case of *Ray v. Blair*, U.S. Supreme Court Justice Robert H. Jackson summarized the history of presidential electors as follows:

"No one faithful to our history can deny that the plan originally contemplated, what is implicit in its text, that electors

---

[68] Mississippi election law. Section 23-15-785.

would be free agents, to exercise an independent and non-partisan judgment as to the men best qualified for the Nation's highest offices....

"This arrangement miscarried. Electors, although often personally eminent, independent, and respectable, officially become voluntary party lackeys and intellectual nonentities to whose memory we might justly paraphrase a tuneful satire:

'They always voted at their party's call

'And never thought of thinking for themselves at all' "[69]

Among the 21,915 electoral votes cast in the 55 presidential elections in the 217 years between 1789 and 2004, there have been 11 cases when a presidential elector has cast a vote for President in an unexpected way.[70,71,72]

- In 1796, Samuel Miles was one of the two Federalist presidential electors chosen in Pennsylvania; however, he voted for Thomas Jefferson (the Democratic-Republican candidate) instead of for Federalist John Adams (section 2.2.2).
- In the uncontested presidential election of 1820, a New Hampshire Democratic-Republican presidential elector who had been expected to vote for James Monroe instead voted for John Quincy Adams, thereby preventing Monroe from duplicating George Washington's 1789 and 1792 unanimous votes in the Electoral College.
- In 1948, a Truman elector (Preston Parks) in Tennessee voted for Strom Thurmond, the Dixiecrat presidential nominee.
- In 1956, a Stevenson elector (W. F. Turner) in Alabama voted for Walter B. Jones, a local judge.
- Nixon lost one electoral vote on each of the three occasions (1960, 1968, and 1972) when he ran for President. In 1960,

---

[69] *Ray v. Blair* 343 U.S. 214 at 232. 1952.

[70] Congressional Quarterly. 2002. *Presidential Elections 1789–2002*. Washington, DC: CQ Press. Page 159.

[71] Peirce, Neal R. 1968. *The People's President: The Electoral College in American History and Direct-Vote Alternative*. New York, NY: Simon and Schuster. Pages 122–127.

[72] Edwards, George C., III. 2004. *Why the Electoral College Is Bad for America*. New Haven, CT: Yale University Press. Pages 21–27.

an Oklahoma Republican elector (Henry D. Irwin) voted for United States Senator Harry F. Byrd (a Democrat). In 1968, a North Carolina Republican elector (Lloyd W. Bailey) voted for Governor George Wallace (that year's nominee of the American Independent Party). In 1972, a Virginia Republican elector (Roger L. MacBride) voted for John Hospers (a Libertarian).

- In 1976, one Ford elector from the state of Washington voted for Ronald Reagan (who had lost the presidential nomination to Ford at the closely contested 1976 Republican nominating convention).
- In 1988, a Democratic elector (Margaret Leach) from West Virginia voted for Lloyd Bentsen for President and Michael Dukakis for Vice President, saying that she thought that the Democratic ticket would have been better in opposite order.
- In 2000, a Democratic presidential elector from the District of Columbia (Barbara Lett-Simmons) did not vote for Al Gore, as a protest against the lack of representation in Congress for the District.
- In 2004, an unknown Democratic presidential elector from Minnesota accidentally voted for John Edwards for both President and Vice President (section 2.6).

These 11 cases can be divided into three categories:

- **Clear Case of a Faithless Elector:** In 1796, Samuel Miles cast his electoral vote in an unexpected way in an election in which the overall electoral vote was very close (71 for Adams and 68 for Jefferson). Given the slow communications of the day, Miles might have had reason to believe, at the time he voted, that his vote might affect the outcome of the election in the Electoral College (section 2.2.2).
- **Grand-Standing Votes:** There have been nine cases (one in 1820 and eight others between 1948 and 2000) of presidential electors who cast an unexpected vote; however, these nine electors knew, at the time they voted, that their vote would not affect the outcome of the election in the Electoral College.
- **Accidental Vote:** In 2004 in Minnesota, there was one accidentally miscast electoral vote for President (section 2.6).

Thus, after 55 presidential elections, the vote of Samuel Miles in 1796 was the only case when an electoral vote was cast in an unexpected way by a presidential elector who might have had reason to think, at the time he cast the vote, that his vote might have affected the outcome.

Table 2.3 shows the number of presidential electors voting in the 55 presidential elections between 1789 and 2004 (a total of 21,915 electoral votes), the number of electoral votes that were cast as expected (a total of 21,904 electoral votes), and the 11 electoral votes that were cast in an unexpected way (that is, one clear faithless elector, nine grand-standing votes, and one accidental vote).[73,74]

Most recently, Richie Robb, one of the candidates nominated by the Republican Party as presidential elector from West Virginia in 2004, threatened, prior to the November 2004 voting, not to vote for George W. Bush in the Electoral College. Ultimately, Robb changed his mind and voted for Bush when the Electoral College met on December 13, 2004.

The laws of a majority of the 51 jurisdictions that appoint presidential electors (including Minnesota) do not mention the way that a presidential elector should vote. Nineteen states have laws that assert that the presidential elector is obligated to vote for the nominee of his or her party, but contain no enforcement provision.[75,76] For example, Maine law provides:

> "The presidential electors at large shall cast their ballots for the presidential and vice-presidential candidates who received the largest number of votes in the State. The presidential electors of each congressional district shall cast their ballots for the presidential and vice-presidential candidates who received the largest number of votes in each respective congressional district."[77]

---

[73] Congressional Quarterly. 2002. *Presidential Elections 1789-2002*. Washington, DC: CQ Press. Page 159.

[74] There were, arguably, three additional faithless electors in the 1796 presidential election. As *Congressional Quarterly* notes, "Some historians and political scientists claim that three Democratic-Republican electors voted for Adams. However, the fluidity of political party lines at that early date, and the well-known personal friendship between Adams and at least one of the electors, makes the claim of their being 'faithless electors' one of continuing controversy." See Congressional Quarterly. 1979. *Presidential Elections Since 1789*. Second Edition. Washington, DC: CQ Press. Page 7.

[75] Berns, Walter (editor). *After the People Vote: A Guide to the Electoral College*. Washington, DC: The AEI Press. Pages 10–13 and 86–88.

[76] Concerning pledges by presidential electors, see *Ray v. Blair*. 343 U.S. 214. 1952.

[77] Maine 21-A M.R.S. section 805.

Table 2.3 FAITHLESS ELECTORS

ELECTION	ELECTORS VOTING	CAST AS EXPECTED	CLEAR FAITHLESS ELECTOR	GRAND-STANDING VOTE	ACCIDENTAL VOTE
1789	69	69			
1792	132	132			
1796	138	138			
1800	138	137	1		
1804	176	176			
1808	175	175			
1812	218	218			
1816	221	221			
1820	232	231		1	
1824	261	261			
1828	261	261			
1832	288	288			
1836	294	294			
1840	294	294			
1844	275	275			
1848	290	290			
1852	296	296			
1856	296	296			
1860	303	303			
1864	234	234			
1868	294	294			
1872	366	366			
1876	369	369			
1880	369	369			
1884	401	401			
1888	401	401			
1892	444	444			
1896	447	447			
1900	447	447			
1904	476	476			
1908	483	483			
1912	531	531			
1916	531	531			
1920	531	531			
1924	531	531			
1928	531	531			
1932	531	531			
1936	531	531			
1940	531	531			

Table 2.3 FAITHLESS ELECTORS (cont.)

ELECTION	ELECTORS VOTING	CAST AS EXPECTED	CLEAR FAITHLESS ELECTOR	GRAND- STANDING VOTE	ACCIDENTAL VOTE
1944	531	531			
1948	531	530		1	
1952	531	531			
1956	531	530		1	
1960	537	536		1	
1964	538	538			
1968	538	537		1	
1972	538	537		1	
1976	538	537		1	
1980	538	538			
1984	538	538			
1988	538	537		1	
1992	538	538			
1996	538	538			
2000	538	537		1	
2004	538	537			1
Total	**21,915**	**21,904**	**1**	**9**	**1**

Pennsylvania election law (section 2878) addresses the potential problem of faithless electors by providing that each party's presidential nominee shall have the power to nominate the entire slate of candidates for the position of presidential elector in Pennsylvania:

"The nominee of each political party for the office of President of the United States shall, within thirty days after his nomination by the National convention of such party, nominate as many persons to be the candidates of his party for the office of presidential elector as the State is then entitled to. If for any reason the nominee of any political party for President of the United States fails or is unable to make the said nominations within the time herein provided, then the nominee for such party for the office of Vice-President of the United States shall, as soon as may be possible after the expiration of thirty days, make the nominations. The names of such nominees, with their residences and post office addresses, shall be certified immediately to the Secretary of the Commonwealth by the nominee for the office of President or

Vice-President, as the case may be, making the nominations. Vacancies existing after the date of nomination of presidential electors shall be filled by the nominee for the office of President or Vice-President making the original nomination. Nominations made to fill vacancies shall be certified to the Secretary of the Commonwealth in the manner herein provided for in the case of original nominations."

Five states (New Mexico, North Carolina, Oklahoma, South Carolina, and Washington) have laws imposing penalties of up to $1,000 on faithless electors.

North Carolina's election law specifies that failure to vote as pledged constitutes resignation from the office of the elector, cancels the vote cast by the faithless elector, and provides for another person to be appointed to cast the vote by the remaining electors.[78] North Carolina law (section 163-212) provides:

"Any presidential elector having previously signified his consent to serve as such, who fails to attend and vote for the candidate of the political party which nominated such elector, for President and Vice-President of the United States at the time and place directed in G.S. 163-210 (except in case of sickness or other unavoidable accident) shall forfeit and pay to the State five hundred dollars ($500.00), to be recovered by the Attorney General in the Superior Court of Wake County. In addition to such forfeiture, refusal or failure to vote for the candidates of the political party which nominated such elector shall constitute a resignation from the office of elector, his vote shall not be recorded, and the remaining electors shall forthwith fill such vacancy as hereinbefore provided."

In short, the states have ample power to enact various preventive measures (e.g., Pennsylvania's system of empowering each presidential nominee to directly nominate the elector candidates who run under his name) as well as to provide remedies for faithless electors (e.g., North Carolina's approach).[79]

---

[78] Berns, Walter (editor). *After the People Vote: A Guide to the Electoral College.* Washington, DC: The AEI Press. Pages 12 and 87–88.

[79] Edwards, George C., III. 2004. *Why the Electoral College Is Bad for America.* New Haven, CT: Yale University Press. Pages 25–27.

In summary, faithless electors are a historical curiosity associated with the Electoral College, but they never have had any practical effect on any presidential election.

2.13 FIVE MAJOR CHANGES IN THE PRESIDENTIAL ELECTION SYSTEM THAT HAVE BEEN IMPLEMENTED WITHOUT A FEDERAL CONSTITUTIONAL AMENDMENT

Five of the most salient features of the present-day system of electing the President and Vice President of the United States are:

- popular voting for president,
- the statewide winner-take-all rule,
- nomination of candidates by nationwide political parties,
- the non-deliberative nature of the Electoral College, and
- the short presidential ballot.

Although some people today mistakenly believe that the current system of electing the President and Vice President of the United States was designed by the Founding Fathers, none of the above five features reflected a consensus of the Founding Fathers or is mentioned in the original U.S. Constitution. None of these features was implemented by means of a federal constitutional amendment. None was the creation of federal legislation.

Instead, three of these five features came into being by the piecemeal enactment of state laws over a period of years, and two resulted from actions taken by non-government entities—namely the political parties that emerged at the time of the nation's first competitive presidential election (1796).

- **Popular Vote:** As recounted in section 2.2, there was no consensus among the Founding Fathers as to whether the voters should be directly involved in process of choosing presidential electors. The Constitution left the manner of choosing presidential electors to the states. Popular election was not the norm in the nation's first presidential election (1789). In fact, the voters were allowed to choose presidential electors in only four states. However, state laws changed over years. By 1824, voters were allowed to choose presidential electors in three quarters of the states, and by 1832, voters were able to choose presidential electors in all but one state.[80] Since 1876, all presidential electors have been elected directly by the voters. In short, direct popular voting for presidential electors became the norm by virtue of the piecemeal enactment of state laws—not because the Founders advocated popular voting, not because the original Constitution required it, and not because of any federal constitutional amendment. The states used the built-in flexibility of the Constitution to change the system.

* **Statewide Winner-Take-All Rule:** The Founding Fathers certainly did not advocate that presidential electors be chosen on a statewide winner-take-all basis in a popular election. In fact, this approach was used by only three of the states participating in the nation's first presidential election. "Madison wrote that it was [the district system] which was contemplated by the framers of the constitution,"[81] and some states elected presidential electors by districts in the early years of the Republic. However, those states soon came to realize what Thomas Jefferson called the "folly"[82] of diminishing their influence by fragmenting their electoral votes, and the states gravitated to the winner-take-all rule. Since 1836, the presidential slate receiving the most popular votes statewide has won all of a state's presidential electors—with only occasional and isolated exceptions.[83] The statewide winner-take-all rule emerged over a period of years because of the piecemeal enactment of state laws—not because the Founders advocated the winner-take-all rule, not because the original Constitution required it, and not because of any federal constitutional amendment.

---

[80] The South Carolina legislature chose presidential electors up to 1860. There were two isolated instances of the election of presidential electors by the state legislature since then—Florida in 1868 and Colorado in 1876.

[81] *McPherson v. Blacker:* 146 U.S. 1 at 29. 1892.

[82] Letter from Thomas Jefferson to James Monroe on January 12, 1800. Ford, Paul Leicester. 1905. *The Works of Thomas Jefferson.* New York: G. P. Putnam's Sons. 9:90.

[83] The exceptions include the present-day use of the district system in Maine (since 1969) and Nebraska (since 1992) and the one-time use of a district system by Michigan in 1892.

- **Nomination of Presidential Candidates by Political Parties:** Since the nation's first competitive presidential election (1796), candidates for President and Vice President have been nominated on a nationwide basis by a central body of a political party (e.g., by the congressional caucus of each party starting in 1796 and by the national conventions of each party starting in the 1820s). This feature of the present-day system of electing the President emerged because of the actions taken by non-government entities— namely the political parties. This change did not come about because the Founders wanted it, because the original Constitution required it, or because of any federal constitutional amendment.

- **Non-Deliberative Nature of the Electoral College:** The Founding Fathers intended that the Electoral College would act as a deliberative body in which the presidential electors would exercise independent judgment as to the best persons to serve as President and Vice President. However, once political parties began nominating presidential and vice-presidential candidates on a centralized basis, and once political parties began actively campaigning for their nominees throughout the country (1796), the presidential elector necessarily became a rubberstamp. "[W]hether chosen by the legislatures or by popular suffrage on general ticket or in districts, [the presidential electors] were so chosen simply to register the will of the appointing power."[84] Thus, since 1796, presidential electors have been expected to vote for the candidates nominated by their party—that is, "to act, not to think."[85] Moreover, this expectation has been achieved with remarkable fidelity. Of the 21,915 electoral votes cast for President in the 55 presidential elections in the 217 years between 1789 and 2004, the vote of Samuel Miles for Thomas Jefferson in 1796 was the only instance when a presidential elector might

---

[84] *McPherson v. Blacker.* 146 U.S. 1 at 36. 1892.
[85] *United States Gazette.* December 15, 1796. Item signed "CANDOUR."

have thought, at the time he cast his unexpected vote, that his vote might affect the national outcome.[86] The change in character of the Electoral College—from the deliberative body envisioned by the Founding Fathers—to a rubberstamp came about because of the emergence of political parties. This change did not come into being because the Founders wanted it, because the original Constitution required it, or because of any federal constitutional amendment.

- **Short Presidential Ballot:** Since the later part of the 20th century, voters have not cast separate votes for individual candidates for presidential elector but, instead, have cast a single vote for a presidential slate consisting of a candidate for President and a candidate for Vice President. Moreover, in all but a few states, the names of the individual presidential electors have entirely disappeared from the ballot. The universal adoption of the short presidential ballot has almost entirely erased the presidential elector from the public's consciousness. This feature of modern-day presidential elections emerged over a period of years because of the piecemeal enactment of laws by the individual states—not because the Founders advocated it, not because the original Constitution required it, and not because of any federal constitutional amendment.

In short, the original U.S. Constitution did not specify in detail the manner of electing the President and Vice President. The flexibility built into the original U.S. Constitution permitted the development of a system that is very different from the one that the Founding Fathers originally envisioned. The built-in flexibility of the original U.S. Constitution concerning the manner of choosing presidential electors remains today.

---

[86] As discussed in greater detail in section 2.12, nine of the other instances of faithless electors are considered to have been grand-standing votes, and one electoral vote (in 2004) was cast by accident.

3 | Three Previously Proposed Federal Constitutional Amendments

There have been hundreds of proposals to change the current system of electing the President and Vice President over the years. This chapter examines the three most prominent approaches to presidential election reform that have been proposed as a federal constitutional amendment. The next chapter (chapter 4) will analyze two approaches that can be enacted entirely at the state level (without a federal constitutional amendment and without action by Congress). Later, chapter 6 will discuss this book's suggested approach for reform.

The three most discussed proposals for a federal constitutional amendment are:

- **Fractional Proportional Allocation of Electoral Votes** in which a state's electoral votes are divided proportionally according to the percentage—carried out to three decimal places—of votes received in that state by each presidential slate (section 3.1);

- **District Allocation of Electoral Votes** in which the people elect two presidential electors statewide and one presidential elector for each district (section 3.2); and

- **Direct Nationwide Popular Election** in which all the popular votes are added together on a nationwide basis (section 3.3).[1]

The chapter analyzes how each of these three approaches would operate in terms of the following criteria:

---

[1] Numerous variations on each of the three approaches presented in this chapter have been introduced in Congress over the years. The major differences include the extent to which the proposal empowers Congress to adopt uniform federal laws governing presidential elections, whether the casting of electoral votes is made automatic (i.e., the office of presidential elector is eliminated), the percentage of the vote required to trigger a contingent election, and the procedures for a contingent election (e.g., separate voting by the two houses of Congress, voting in a joint session of Congress, or a nationwide run-off popular election).

- Would it accurately reflect the nationwide popular vote?
- Would it improve upon the current situation in which most areas of the country are non-competitive?
- Would every vote be equal?

Interest in reform tends to follow troublesome presidential elections. Under the original Constitution, each presidential elector cast two votes. The candidate with the most electoral votes (provided that the candidate had a majority) became President, and the second-place candidate became Vice President (again, provided that the candidate had a majority). The nation's first two presidential elections (1789 and 1792) were unanimous in the sense that George Washington received a vote from each presidential elector who voted.[2]

The problems inherent with doubling voting surfaced as soon as political parties formed and presidential elections became competitive. In 1796, the Federalist members of Congress caucused and nominated John Adams of Massachusetts for President and Thomas Pinckney of South Carolina for Vice President. Meanwhile, the Republicans in Congress nominated Thomas Jefferson of Virginia for President and Aaron Burr of New York for Vice President. The Federalists were strongest in the north, and the Republicans were strongest in the south. Thus, each party had a presidential nominee from the part of the country where the party was strongest and a vice-presidential candidate from the other part of the county. Vice-presidential nominee Pinckney was, however, more highly regarded than Burr. In particular, Pinckney was expected to be able to win electoral votes from his Republican-leaning home state of South Carolina (where the state legislature chose the electors), whereas Burr was not expected to be able to make counter-balancing inroads in the New York legislature's solid support for the Federalist ticket of Adams and Pinckney. The Federalist Party thus faced the dilemma of whether to give its wholehearted support to its own ticket. If Federalist presidential electors were to uniformly cast one vote for Adams and one vote for Pinckney, and if Pinckney then won additional electoral votes in his home state of South Carolina, their own party's nominee for Vice President would end up as President. As Stanwood reports,

[2] In 1789, two Maryland electors and two Virginia electors did not vote. In 1796, two Maryland electors and one Vermont elector did not vote. Congressional Quarterly. 2002. *Presidential Elections 1789-2002.* Washington, DC: CQ Press. Pages 174–175.

"No less than eighteen [Federalist] electors in New England resolved that Pinckney's vote should not exceed Adam's, withheld their votes from the candidate for Vice president, and scattered them upon others.[3]

This "strategic voting" by the Federalists to ensure the Presidency to their own party's nominee for President enabled the Republican presidential nominee (Jefferson) to end up with the second-highest number of electoral votes. Thus, Federalist John Adams was elected President, and his chief critic, Thomas Jefferson, was elected Vice President.[4,5]

In 1800, Thomas Jefferson and Aaron Burr again ran together as candidates of the Anti-Federalist Party. Anti-Federalist presidential electors won a majority in the Electoral College. In 1800, all of the winning party's presidential electors cast one vote for each of their party's nominees. Thus, Jefferson and Burr each received an equal number of votes in the Electoral College, thereby creating a tie. Under the Constitution, such ties are resolved by a "contingent election" in which the House of Representatives elects the President and the Senate elects the Vice President. In the House, each state is entitled to cast one vote for President (with equally divided states being unable to cast a vote). In the Senate, each Senator is entitled to cast one vote for Vice President. After a bitter dispute in Congress, Thomas Jefferson emerged from the House of Representatives as President.[6]

Given the emergence of political parties that centrally nominated presidential and vice-presidential candidates and given that it was necessary for each presidential elector to vote for both of his party's nominees (to prevent a recurrence of the 1796 debacle), it was apparent that tied presidential elections would be the norm for future elections. Congress

---

[3] Stanwood, Edward. 1924. *A History of the Presidency from 1788 to 1897.* Boston, MA: Houghton Mifflin Company. Page 49.

[4] Peirce, Neal R. 1968. *The People's President: The Electoral College in American History and Direct-Vote Alternative.* New York, NY: Simon and Schuster. Pages 63–64.

[5] Stanwood, Edward. 1924. *A History of the Presidency from 1788 to 1897.* Boston: Houghton Mifflin Company. Pages 49-53. There is considerable historical controversy concerning Alexander Hamilton's possible motives and role in the "strategic voting" by Federalist presidential electors in the 1796 election. The main point, for the purposes of this chapter, is that the original Constitution's provision for double voting by presidential electors was unworkable in the context of political parties and competitive presidential elections.

[6] Dunn, Susan. 2004. Jefferson's Second Revolution: *The Elections Crisis of 1800 and the Triumph of Republicanism.* Boston, MA: Houghton Mifflin.

therefore passed the 12th Amendment specifying that each presidential elector would cast a separate vote for President and Vice President. Separate voting enables the winning political party to elect its nominees to both nationwide offices. The states quickly ratified the amendment, and it was in effect in time for the 1804 election.[7]

In 1824, there was a four-way race for President. The presidential election was again thrown into the U.S. House and Senate. This controversial election spotlighted various undemocratic practices, including the continued selection of presidential electors in many states by the state legislature.[8] After the 1824 election, the laws of many states were changed to empower the voters to choose the state's presidential electors directly. Within two presidential elections, the voters directly elected presidential electors in all but one state (South Carolina).

In 1876, Democrat Samuel J. Tilden received 254,694 more popular votes than the 4,033,497 votes received by Rutherford B. Hayes; however, Hayes led by one electoral vote by virtue of carrying a number of states by extremely small margins (e.g., South Carolina by 889 votes, Florida by 922 votes, Oregon by 1,050 votes, Nevada by 1,075 votes, and California by 2,798 votes).[9] Moreover, conflicting returns were submitted from three southern states that still had reconstruction governments (South Carolina, Florida, and Louisiana). A 15-member electoral commission eventually awarded the Presidency to Hayes.[10,11,12] The contested Tilden-Hayes 1876 election led to the passage of federal legislation governing the handling of controversies involving presidential elections.[13]

In the 1888 election, President Grover Cleveland received 5,539,118 popular votes to Benjamin Harrison's 5,449,825. Harrison won in the

---

[7] Kuroda, Tadahisa. 1994. *The Origins of the Twelfth Amendment: The Electoral College in the Early Republic, 1787–1804*. Westport, CT: Greenwood Press.

[8] Schlesinger, Arthur M., Jr. and Hewson, Martha S. 2002. Philadelphia, PA: Chelsea House Publishers. Pages 34–36.

[9] Congressional Quarterly. 2002. *Presidential Elections 1789–2002*. Washington, DC: CQ Press. Page 125.

[10] Morris, Roy B. 2003. *Fraud of the Century: Rutherford B. Hayes, Samuel Tilden, and the Stolen Election of 1876*. Waterville, ME: Thorndike Press.

[11] Robinson, Lloyd. 1996. *The Stolen Election: Hayes versus Tilden—1876*. New York, NY: Tom Doherty Associates Books.

[12] Rehnquist, William H. 2004. *Centennial Crisis: The Disputed Election of 1876*. New York, NY: Alfred A. Knopf.

[13] The federal election laws resulting from the 1876 election evolved into what is now Title 3 of the United States Code (found in appendix B).

Electoral College by a substantial margin—233 to 168 despite Cleveland's 89,293-vote lead in the popular vote. In the 1890 mid-term elections, the Democrats won control in Michigan (then regularly Republican). The Democrats passed a law switching Michigan from the statewide winner-take-all system to a system in which one presidential elector was to be elected from each of the state's congressional districts and in which the state's two senatorial electors were to be elected from two special districts, each comprising half of the state's congressional districts. Republicans contested the constitutionality of Michigan's change from the statewide winner-take-all system to the district system. In the 1892 case of *McPherson v. Blacker* (discussed in chapter 2), the U.S. Supreme Court upheld Michigan's right to change its law concerning the method of choosing its presidential electors.

The 1968 presidential election was held in the midst of continuing controversy over recently passed civil rights laws, urban rioting, and the war in Vietnam. Governor George Wallace of Alabama ran for President against Richard Nixon and Hubert Humphrey.[14] Wallace hoped to win enough electoral votes to prevent either major-party nominee from winning a majority of the electoral votes. His primary goal was not to throw the election into the Congress. Instead, he planned to negotiate with one of the major-party candidates before the meeting of the Electoral College in mid-December to extract policy concessions on civil rights and cabinet positions. To aid in these anticipated post-November negotiations, Wallace obtained affidavits from each of his presidential electors committing them to vote in the Electoral College for Wallace or "for whomsoever he may direct."[15]

Wallace won 45 electoral votes in 1968 by carrying Alabama, Arkansas, Georgia, Louisiana, and Mississippi. Richard Nixon ended up with 43.42% of the popular vote (compared to Hubert Humphrey's 42.72%) as well as a majority of the electoral votes. Although Nixon was elected President by a majority of the Electoral College, a shift of only 10,245 popular votes in Missouri and 67,481 popular votes in Illinois would have left Nixon without a majority of the electoral votes (while still leading Humphrey by more than 300,000 popular votes on a nationwide basis).

[14] Longley, Lawrence D. and Braun, Alan G. 1972. *The Politics of Electoral College Reform.* New Haven, CT: Yale University Press. Pages 7–21.

[15] Congressional Quarterly. 1979. *Presidential Elections Since 1789.* Second Edition. Washington, DC: CQ Press. Page 8.

Faithless presidential electors had begun to emerge as an irritant in presidential politics in several southern states during the period immediately before and after passage of the civil rights legislation of the mid-1960s. In the 1968 presidential election, George Wallace received one electoral vote from a faithless Republican presidential elector from North Carolina. This was one of three occasions when Nixon suffered the loss of an electoral vote because of a faithless Republican elector.

Thus, shortly after taking office as President in 1969, Nixon sent a message to Congress saying:

> "I have in the past supported the proportional plan. But I am not wedded to the details of this plan or any other specific plan. I will support any plan that moves toward ... the abolition of individual electors ... allocation of presidential candidates of the electoral vote of each state and the District of Columbia in a manner that may more closely approximate the popular vote than does the present system ... making a 40 percent electoral vote plurality sufficient to choose a President."[16]

President Nixon's message ignited a flurry of activity in the 91st Congress.

- Senator Howard Cannon (D–Nevada) introduced a proposed constitutional amendment for a fractional proportional allocation of each state's electoral votes (section 3.1).
- Senator Karl Mundt (R–South Dakota) introduced a proposed amendment for electing presidential electors by congressional district (section 3.2).
- Representative Emmanuel Celler (D–New York) and Senator Birch Bayh (D–Indiana) introduced amendments for nationwide popular election of the president (section 3.3).

Celler's proposal (House Joint Resolution 681 of the 91st Congress) passed in the House of Representatives by a 338–70 vote in 1969. After the strong bipartisan vote in the House, President Nixon urged the Senate to adopt the House bill. That bill, however, was filibustered and died in the Senate.[17]

---

[16] February 20, 1969.

[17] Congressional Quarterly. 2002. *Presidential Elections 1789-2002*. Washington, DC: CQ Press. Page 169.

Interest in electoral reform was rekindled after the 1976 presidential elections. A shift of 3,687 popular votes in Hawaii and 5,559 popular votes in Ohio would have elected Gerald Ford, even though Jimmy Carter led Ford by 1,682,970 popular votes nationwide.

President Carter, President Ford (the losing presidential candidate in 1976), and Senator Robert Dole (the losing vice-presidential candidate) publicly supported nationwide popular election of the President. In 1979, a majority of the Senate voted in favor a proposed constitutional amendment (Senate Joint Resolution 28) sponsored by Senator Birch Bayh that closely resembled the bill that had passed in the House in 1969. Lacking the required two-thirds support, the bill was defeated.

The 2000 election resulted in the election of a President who had not received the most popular votes nationwide. After the 2000 election, former Presidents Jimmy Carter and Gerald Ford created a bipartisan Commission to make recommendations for improving the nation's electoral system. Many of the reforms proposed by the Carter-Ford Commission became part of the Help America Vote Act (HAVA) of 2002.

If 59,393 Ohio votes had switched in the 2004 presidential election, Kerry would have been elected President despite George W. Bush's lead of about 3,500,000 votes in the nationwide popular vote. After the 2004 election, former President Jimmy Carter and former Secretary of State James Baker formed another bipartisan commission to review the implementation of HAVA in light of the nation's experience in the 2004 election and to make additional recommendations concerning election administration.

Potential problems with the current statewide winner-take-all system appear to be becoming increasingly common.[18] As shown in table 1.3, there have been six presidential elections—1948, 1960, 1968, 1976, 2000, and 2004—in the past six decades in which the shift of a relatively small number of votes in one or two states would have elected a presidential candidate who had not received the most popular votes nationwide.

Meanwhile, the 2004 presidential election made it clear that the number of battleground states is decreasing. Although voter turnout increased in the battleground states in 2004, it decreased in noncompetitive states.[19]

---

[18] Abbott, David W. and Levine, James P. 1991. *Wrong Winner: The Coming Debacle in the Electoral College.* Westport, CT: Praeger.

[19] Committee for the Study of the American Electorate (2004). "President Bush, Mobilization Drives Propel Turnout to Post-1968 High." November 4, 2004.

3.1 FRACTIONAL PROPORTIONAL ALLOCATION OF ELECTORAL VOTES

In the fractional proportional approach, a state's electoral votes are divided proportionally—carried out to three decimal places—according to the percentage of votes received in the state by each presidential slate.

Senator Howard Cannon (D–Nevada) introduced the following proposed federal constitutional amendment (Senate Joint Resolution 33 in the 91st Congress) to implement the fractional proportional approach:

"Resolved by the Senate and House of Representatives of the United States of America in Congress assembled (two-thirds of each House concurring therein),

That the following article is proposed as an amendment to the Constitution of the United States, which shall be valid to all intents and purposes as part of the Constitution if ratified by the legislatures of three-fourths of the several States:

'Article—
'SECTION 1. The Executive power shall be vested in a President of the United States of America. He shall hold his office during the term of four years, and, together with the Vice President, chosen for the same term, be elected as provided in this article. No person constitutionally ineligible for the office of President shall be eligible for the office of Vice President.

'SECTION 2. The President and Vice President shall be elected by the people of the several States and the District of Columbia. The electors in each State shall have the qualifications requisite for electors of the most numerous branch of the State legislature, except that the legislature of any State may prescribe lesser qualifications with respect to residence therein. The electors of the District of Columbia shall have such qualifications as the Congress may prescribe. The places and manner of holding such election in each State shall be prescribed by the legislature thereof, but the Congress may at any time by law make or alter such regulations.

The place and manner of holding such election in the District of Columbia shall be prescribed by the Congress. The Congress shall determine the time of such election, which shall be the same throughout the United States. Until otherwise determined by the Congress, such election shall be held on the Tuesday next after the first Monday in November of the year preceding the year in which the regular term of the President is to begin.

'**SECTION 3.** Each state shall be entitled to a number of electoral votes equal to the whole number of Senators and Representatives to which each State may be entitled in the Congress. The District of Columbia shall be entitled to a number of electoral votes equal to the whole number of Senators and Representatives in Congress to which such District would be entitled if it were a State, but in no event more than the least populous State.

'**SECTION 4.** Within forty-five days after such election, or at such time as Congress shall direct, the official custodian of the election returns of each State and the District of Columbia shall make distinct lists of all persons for whom votes were cast for President and the number of votes cast for each person, and the total vote cast by the electors of the State of the District for all persons for President, which lists he shall sign and certify and transmit sealed to the seat of Government of the United States, directed to the President of the Senate. On the 6th day of January following the election, unless the Congress by law appoints a different day not earlier than the 4th day of January and not later than the 10th day of January, the President of the Senate shall, in the presence of the Senate and House of Representatives, open all certificates and the votes shall then be counted. Each person for whom votes were cast shall be credited with such proportion of the electoral votes thereof as he received of the total vote cast by the electors therein for President. In making the computation, fractional numbers less than one one-thousandth shall be disregarded. The person having the greatest aggregate number of electoral votes of the States and the District of Columbia for President shall be President, if such number be at least 40 per centum of the whole number of such electoral votes, or if two persons have received an identical number of such electoral votes which is at least 40 per centum of the whole number of electoral votes, then from the persons having the two greatest number of such electoral votes for President, the Senate and the House of Representatives sitting in joint session shall choose immediately, by ballot, the President. A majority of the votes of the combined membership of the Senate and House of Representatives shall be necessary for a choice.

'**SECTION 5.** The Vice President shall be likewise elected, at the same time, in the same manner, and subject to the same provisions as the President.

'**SECTION 6.** The Congress may by law provide for the case of the death of any of the persons from whom the Senate and the House of Representatives may choose a President whenever the right of choice shall have devolved upon them, and for the case of death of any of the persons from whom the Senate and the House of Representatives may choose a Vice President whenever the right of choice shall have devolved upon them. The Congress shall have power to enforce this article by appropriate legislation.

'**SECTION 7.** The following provisions of the Constitution are hereby repealed: paragraphs 1, 2, 3, and 4 of section 1, Article II; the twelfth article of amendment; section 4 of the twentieth article of amendment; and the twenty-third article of amendment.

'**SECTION 8.** This article shall take effect on the 1st day of February following its ratification, except that this article shall be inoperative unless it shall have been ratified as an amendment to the Constitution by the legislatures of three-fourths of the States within seven years from the date of its submission to the States by the Congress.' "

The remainder of this section analyzes how the proposed fractional proportional approach would operate in terms of the following criteria:

- Would it accurately reflect the nationwide popular vote?
- Would it improve upon the current situation in which most areas of the country are non-competitive?
- Would every vote be equal?

Almost any electoral system will work well in a landslide. Thus, we start our analysis of the fractional proportional approach with data from a close recent presidential election—the 2000 election.

Table 3.1 shows how the fractional proportional approach would have operated in the 2000 presidential election. Columns 3, 4, and 5 of this table show, for each state, the number of population votes received by Al Gore, George W. Bush, and Ralph Nader. Column 6 shows, for each state, the number of electoral votes that Gore would have received under the fractional proportional approach (expressed as a fraction with three decimal places of precision, as specified by Senator Cannon's proposal). This number of electoral votes is obtained by dividing Gore's popular vote in the state by the total popular vote received by Gore, Bush, and Nader together, and then multiplying this quotient by the number of electoral votes possessed by the state. Columns 7 and 8 show the same information for Bush and Nader. For each state, the number of electoral votes for the three presidential candidates (columns 6, 7, and 8) adds up to the number of electoral votes possessed by the state (column 2). As can be seen from the bottom line of the table, Al Gore would have received 259.969 electoral votes; George W. Bush would have received 260.323 electoral votes; and Ralph Nader would have received 17.707 electoral votes if the 2000 presidential election had been run under the fractional proportional approach.[20]

---

[20] In this book, all analyses of the results of hypothetically using some alternative electoral system are based on the data available from the actual election using the current electoral system.

Table 3.1 2000 ELECTION UNDER THE FRACTIONAL PROPORTIONAL APPROACH (CONSIDERING THREE PARTIES)

STATE	ELECTORAL VOTES	GORE	BUSH	NADER	GORE	BUSH	NADER
Alabama	9	692,611	941,173	18,323	3.773	5.127	0.100
Alaska	3	79,004	167,398	28,747	0.861	1.825	0.313
Arizona	8	685,341	781,652	45,645	3.625	4.134	0.241
Arkansas	6	422,768	472,940	13,421	2.790	3.121	0.089
California	54	5,861,203	4,567,429	418,707	29.178	22.737	2.084
Colorado	8	738,227	883,748	91,434	3.447	4.126	0.427
Connecticut	8	816,015	561,094	64,452	4.529	3.114	0.358
Delaware	3	180,068	137,288	8,307	1.659	1.265	0.077
DC	3	171,923	18,073	10,576	2.571	0.270	0.158
Florida	25	2,912,253	2,912,790	97,488	12.293	12.295	0.412
Georgia	13	1,116,230	1,419,720	134,322	5.434	6.912	0.654
Hawaii	4	205,286	137,845	21,623	2.251	1.512	0.237
Idaho	4	138,637	336,937	122,922	0.927	2.252	0.822
Illinois	22	2,589,026	2,019,421	103,759	12.087	9.428	0.484
Indiana	12	901,980	1,245,836	185,312	4.639	6.408	0.953
Iowa	7	638,517	634,373	29,374	3.432	3.410	0.158
Kansas	6	399,276	622,332	36,086	2.265	3.530	0.205
Kentucky	8	638,898	872,492	23,192	3.331	4.548	0.121
Louisiana	9	792,344	927,871	20,473	4.097	4.797	0.106
Maine	4	319,951	286,616	37,127	1.988	1.781	0.231
Maryland	10	1,145,782	813,797	53,768	5.691	4.042	0.267
Massachusetts	12	1,616,487	878,502	173,564	7.269	3.950	0.780
Michigan	18	2,170,418	1,953,139	84,165	9.285	8.355	0.360
Minnesota	10	1,168,266	1,109,659	126,696	4.858	4.615	0.527
Mississippi	7	404,614	572,844	8,122	2.874	4.069	0.058
Missouri	11	1,111,138	1,189,924	38,515	5.224	5.595	0.181
Montana	3	137,126	240,178	24,437	1.024	1.794	0.182
Nebraska	5	231,780	433,862	24,540	1.679	3.143	0.178
Nevada	4	279,978	301,575	15,008	1.877	2.022	0.101
New Hampshire	4	266,348	273,559	22,198	1.895	1.947	0.158
New Jersey	15	1,788,850	1,284,173	94,554	8.471	6.081	0.448
New Mexico	5	286,783	286,417	21,251	2.412	2.409	0.179
New York	33	4,107,697	2,403,374	244,030	20.067	11.741	1.192
North Carolina	14	1,257,692	1,631,163	0	6.095	7.905	0.000
North Dakota	3	95,284	174,852	9,486	1.022	1.876	0.102
Ohio	21	2,186,190	2,351,209	117,857	9.862	10.606	0.532
Oklahoma	8	474,276	744,337	0	3.114	4.886	0.000
Oregon	7	720,342	713,577	77,357	3.337	3.305	0.358
Pennsylvania	23	2,485,967	2,281,127	103,392	11.740	10.772	0.488
Rhode Island	4	249,508	130,555	25,052	2.464	1.289	0.247

Table 3.1 2000 ELECTION UNDER THE FRACTIONAL PROPORTIONAL APPROACH (CONSIDERING THREE PARTIES) (cont.)

STATE	ELECTORAL VOTES	POPULAR VOTES			ELECTORAL VOTES		
		GORE	BUSH	NADER	GORE	BUSH	NADER
South Carolina	8	565,561	785,937	20,200	3.298	4.584	0.118
South Dakota	3	118,804	190,700	0	1.152	1.848	0.000
Tennessee	11	981,720	1,061,949	19,781	5.233	5.661	0.105
Texas	32	2,433,746	3,799,639	137,994	12.223	19.084	0.693
Utah	5	203,053	515,096	35,850	1.347	3.416	0.238
Vermont	3	149,022	119,775	20,374	1.546	1.243	0.211
Virginia	13	1,217,290	1,437,490	59,398	5.830	6.885	0.284
Washington	11	1,247,652	1,108,864	103,002	5.580	4.959	0.461
West Virginia	5	295,497	336,475	10,680	2.299	2.618	0.083
Wisconsin	11	1,242,987	1,237,279	94,070	5.311	5.287	0.402
Wyoming	3	60,481	147,947	46,252	0.712	1.743	0.545
Total	**538**	**50,999,897**	**50,456,002**	**2,882,955**	**259.969**	**260.323**	**17.707**

Concerning the accurate reflection of the nationwide popular vote, table 3.1 shows that, if the fractional proportional approach had been in use throughout the country in the 2000 presidential election, it would not have awarded the most electoral votes to the candidate receiving the most popular votes nationwide. Gore would have received 0.354 fewer electoral votes than George W. Bush even though Gore led by 537,179 popular votes nationwide. Because Bush would have received "the greatest aggregate number of electoral votes" and such number would have been "at least 40 per centum of the whole number of such electoral votes," Bush would have been elected under Senate Joint Resolution 33 as proposed by Senator Cannon in 1969.

Under some variants of the proposed fractional proportional approach, no electoral votes are awarded to a presidential slate receiving less than a specified "cut-off" percentage (e.g., 5%) of a state's popular vote (or the national popular vote). Table 3.2 shows how the fractional proportional approach would have operated in the 2000 presidential election if only the two major political parties are considered. Column 2 shows Gore's popular vote percentage for each state. Columns 3 and 4 show, for each state, the electoral votes (rounded off to three decimal places) that Gore and Bush, respectively, would have received under the fractional proportional approach with a cut-off. Columns 5 and 6 show the actual numbers of electoral votes that Gore and Bush, respectively, received in the 2000 presidential election.

Table 3.2 2000 ELECTION UNDER THE FRACTIONAL PROPORTIONAL APPROACH (CONSIDERING THE TWO MAJOR PARTIES)

STATE	GORE POPULAR VOTES	GORE FRACTIONAL ELECTORAL VOTES	BUSH FRACTIONAL ELECTORAL VOTES	GORE ACTUAL ELECTORAL VOTES	BUSH ACTUAL ELECTORAL VOTES
Alabama	42.393058%	3.815	5.185		9
Alaska	32.063051%	0.962	2.038		3
Arizona	46.717401%	3.737	4.263		8
Arkansas	47.199310%	2.832	3.168		6
California	56.202990%	30.350	23.650	54	
Colorado	45.514080%	3.641	4.359		8
Connecticut	59.255658%	4.740	3.260	8	
Delaware	56.740065%	1.702	1.298	3	
DC	90.487694%	2.715	0.285	3	
Florida	49.995391%	12.499	12.501		25
Georgia	44.016246%	5.722	7.278		13
Hawaii	59.827296%	2.393	1.607	4	
Idaho	29.151510%	1.166	2.834		4
Illinois	56.180010%	12.360	9.640	22	
Indiana	41.995217%	5.039	6.961		12
Iowa	50.162779%	3.511	3.489	7	
Kansas	39.083093%	2.345	3.655		6
Kentucky	42.272213%	3.382	4.618		8
Louisiana	46.060754%	4.145	4.855		9
Maine	52.747842%	2.110	1.890	4	
Maryland	58.470825%	5.847	4.153	10	
Massachusetts	64.789344%	7.775	4.225	12	
Michigan	52.634606%	9.474	8.526	18	
Minnesota	51.286412%	5.129	4.871	10	
Mississippi	41.394515%	2.898	4.102		7
Missouri	48.288051%	5.312	5.688		11
Montana	36.343638%	1.090	1.910		3
Nebraska	34.820519%	1.741	3.259		5
Nevada	48.143162%	1.926	2.074		4
New Hampshire	49.332200%	1.973	2.027		4
New Jersey	58.211409%	8.732	6.268	15	
New Mexico	50.031926%	2.502	2.498	5	
New York	63.087885%	20.819	12.181	33	
North Carolina	43.536003%	6.095	7.905		14
North Dakota	35.272603%	1.058	1.942		3
Ohio	48.181568%	10.118	10.882		21
Oklahoma	38.919329%	3.114	4.886		8
Oregon	50.235892%	3.517	3.483	7	

Table 3.2 2000 ELECTION UNDER THE FRACTIONAL PROPORTIONAL APPROACH (CONSIDERING THE TWO MAJOR PARTIES) (cont.)

STATE	GORE POPULAR VOTES	GORE FRACTIONAL ELECTORAL VOTES	BUSH FRACTIONAL ELECTORAL VOTES	GORE ACTUAL ELECTORAL VOTES	BUSH ACTUAL ELECTORAL VOTES
Pennsylvania	52.148479%	11.994	11.006	23	
Rhode Island	65.649116%	2.626	1.374	4	
South Carolina	41.846973%	3.348	4.652		8
South Dakota	38.385287%	1.152	1.848		3
Tennessee	48.037133%	5.284	5.716		11
Texas	39.043730%	12.494	19.506		32
Utah	28.274495%	1.414	3.586		5
Vermont	55.440351%	1.663	1.337	3	
Virginia	45.852764%	5.961	7.039		13
Washington	52.944771%	5.824	5.176	11	
West Virginia	46.757926%	2.338	2.662		5
Wisconsin	50.115068%	5.513	5.487	11	
Wyoming	29.017694%	0.871	2.129		3
	50.268045%	**268.766**	**269.234**	**267**	**271**

Table 3.2 shows that, if the fractional proportional approach had been used in the 2000 presidential election (with a cut-off percentage excluding all but the two major-party candidates), it would not have awarded the most electoral votes to the candidate receiving the most popular votes nationwide. Even though Al Gore led by 537,179 popular votes nationwide, he would have received only 268.766 electoral votes, whereas George W. Bush would have received 269.234 electoral votes. Since 269.234 is more than half of 538, George W. Bush would have been elected President.

Concerning competitiveness, the fractional proportional approach improves upon the current situation in which about three-quarters of states are non-competitive. Winning a few hundred more popular votes in any state will earn a presidential candidate an additional 0.001 electoral votes, thus giving some political importance to every vote, regardless of the state in which it is cast.

On the other hand, not every vote is equal under the fractional proportional approach. In fact, there are three different inequalities inherent in the fractional proportional approach as explained below. These inequalities (3.79-to-1, 1.76-to-1, and 1.27-to-1) are substantial and, in particular, are considerably larger than the small variations that are considered to be constitutionally tolerable nowadays when congressional and other types of districts are drawn within states.[21]

The inequalities under the fractional proportional approach arise from the

- two bonus electoral votes that each state receives regardless of its population,
- inequalities in the apportionment of the membership of the House of Representatives among the several states, and
- differences in voter turnout in various states.

First, a vote cast in a large state has less weight than a vote cast in a small state because of the two bonus in the Electoral College that each state receives regardless of its population. For example, in the 2000 presidential election, Wyoming (with a population of 453,588 in 1990) had three electoral votes, whereas California (with a population of 29,760,021 in 1990) had 54 electoral votes. As shown in table 3.3, in the presidential elections of 1992, 1996, and 2000, one electoral vote corresponded to 151,196 people in Wyoming but to 572,308 in California. The last column of this table shows the ratio of California's population per electoral vote compared to that of Wyoming—a 3.79-to-1 variation.

Table 3.3 DIFFERENCE IN WEIGHT OF A POPULAR VOTE ARISING FROM EACH STATE'S BONUS OF TWO ELECTORAL VOTES

STATE	POPULATION	REPRESENTATIVES	SENATORS	ELETORAL VOTES	POPULATION CORRESPONDING TO ONE ELECTORAL VOTE	RATIO TO LOWEST
California	29,760,021	52	2	54	572,308	3.79
Wyoming	453,588	1	2	3	151,196	1.00

Second, a vote cast in certain states has less weight than a vote cast in certain other states because of inequalities in the apportionment of membership of the House of Representatives among the several states. For example, Wyoming (with a population of 453,588 in 1990) and Montana (with a population of 799,065 in 1990) each had one member in the House of Representatives (and hence three electoral votes). As

---

[21] Of course, if the fractional proportional approach were enacted in the form of a federal constitutional amendment, it could not be successfully challenged in court on the grounds that it countenances inequalities that are greater than those constitutionally allowed for election districts for other offices.

shown in table 3.4, in the presidential elections of 1992, 1996, and 2000, one electoral vote corresponded to 151,196 people in Wyoming but to 266,355 in Montana. The last column of this table shows the ratio of Montana's population per electoral vote compared to the ratio for Wyoming—a 1.76-to-1 variation. There are numerous other pairs of states with similar variations.[22]

Table 3.4 I **DIFFERENCE IN WEIGHT OF A POPULAR VOTE ARISING FROM CONGRESSIONAL APPORTIONMENT**

STATE	POPULATION	POPULATION CORRESPONDING BY ONE ELECTORAL VOTE	RATIO TO LOWEST
Montana	799,065	266,355	1.76
Wyoming	453,588	151,196	1.00

Third, voter turnout within a voter's own state changes the weight of a given voter's vote. For example, a vote cast in a state with a low turnout has a greater weight than a vote cast in a state where more total votes are cast. Column 4 of table 3.5 shows the numbers of popular votes cast in the 2000 presidential election in the four states with five electoral votes (Nebraska, New Mexico, Utah, and West Virginia). As can be seen in column 5 of the table, one electoral vote corresponds to 118,900 popular votes in New Mexico but to 150,800 popular votes in Utah. Column 6 shows the ratio of the number of votes representing one electoral vote in each state compared to that of the lowest in the table (New Mexico). The greatest variation is between Utah and New Mexico—a 1.27-to-1 variation.

Table 3.5 COMPARISON OF WEIGHT OF A POPULAR VOTE CAST IN FOUR STATES WITH THE SAME NUMBER OF ELECTORAL VOTES

STATE	1990 POPULATION	2000 POPULATION	VOTES CAST IN 2000 PRESIDENTIAL ELECTION	POPULAR VOTES CORRESPONDING TO ONE ELECTORAL VOTE	RATIO TO LOWEST
Nebraska	1,578,385	1,711,263	690,182	138,000	1.16
New Mexico	1,515,069	1,819,046	594,451	118,900	1.00
Utah	1,722,850	2,233,169	753,999	150,800	1.27
West Virginia	1,793,477	1,808,344	642,652	128,600	1.08

---

[22] These include pairs of states with more than three electoral votes and pairs of states with different numbers of electoral votes.

The total number of votes cast in states with the same number of electoral votes varies for at least two reasons.

- First, the actual population of the state at the moment of the election might have increased or decreased since the last census.
- Second, the number of voters turning out for the particular election depends on the degree of civic participation in the state.

As to the first of these factors, a state's allocation of electoral votes depends on its number of Representatives and Senators. The number of Representatives to which a state is entitled changes every 10 years based on the federal census. For example, the 1992, 1996, and 2000 presidential elections were conducted under the apportionment that resulted from the 1990 census. This means that the 2000 presidential election was conducted using an allocation of electoral votes based on 10-year-old population data. Thus, the weight of a citizen's vote in a rapidly growing state is diminished. Column 2 of table 3.5 shows the population of each state according to the 1990 census. Column 3 shows the population of each state according to the 2000 census. The 2000 census was taken in the spring of 2000 but was not applicable to the 2000 presidential election. These numbers closely approximate each state's population in the 2000 presidential election held a few months later. As can be seen, Utah, a fast-growing state, had 510,319 more people in 2000 than it did in 1990, whereas West Virginia barely grew at all during the 10-year period (only 14,867 more people than in 1990). New Mexico also experienced rapid population growth during the 1990s. Because of the time lag in reallocating electoral votes (a full 10 years in the case of the 2000 election), Utah and New Mexico had the same number of electoral votes in the 2000 presidential election as West Virginia.

Concerning the second of the above factors, voter turnout within a state also affects the relative weight of a vote under the fractional proportional approach. A citizen's vote gets less weight if it happens to be cast in a state with a high degree of civic participation. For example, Utah consistently has high voter turnout in its elections.

In summary, if the fractional proportional approach had been in use throughout the country in the 2000 presidential election,

- it would not have more accurately reflected the nationwide popular vote;

- it would have made all states competitive; and
- not every vote would have been equal.

It should be noted that the fractional proportional approach discussed above differs significantly from the whole-number proportional approach (discussed in section 4.1). In the whole-number proportional approach, the office of presidential elector is not abolished and, therefore, the states continue to choose presidential electors. Because human presidential electors each have one indivisible vote, it is not possible to divide the electoral votes precisely (e.g., to three decimal places as specified in Senator Cannon's proposal). Thus, a state's electoral votes must necessarily be rounded off to the nearest whole number in the whole-number proportional approach. The counter-intuitive effects of this rounding-off, in the context of a system in which the average state has only 11 electoral votes, is discussed in detail in section 4.1.

3.2 DISTRICT ALLOCATION OF ELECTORAL VOTES

In the district approach, voters elect two presidential electors statewide and one presidential elector for each district.

Senator Karl Mundt (R–South Dakota) was the leading sponsor of a proposed federal constitutional amendment to implement the district system in 1969. Senate Joint Resolution 12 of the 91st Congress provided (in part):

> *"Resolved by the Senate and House of Representatives of the United States of America in Congress assembled (two-thirds of each House concurring therein),*

That the following article is proposed as an amendment to the Constitution of the United States, which shall be valid to all intents and purposes as part of the Constitution if ratified by the legislatures of three-fourths of the several States within seven years from the date of its submission by the Congress:

> **'Article—**
> **'SECTION 1.** Each State shall choose a number of electors of President and Vice President equal to the whole number of Senators and Representatives to which the State may be entitled in the Congress; but no Senator or Representative, or person holding an office of trust or profit under the United States shall be chosen elector.

'The electors assigned to each State with its Senators shall be elected by the people thereof. Each of the electors apportioned with its Representatives shall be elected by the people of a single-member electoral district formed by the legislature of the State. Electoral districts within each State shall be of compact and contiguous territory containing substantially equal numbers of inhabitants, and shall not be altered until another census of the United States has been taken. Each candidate for the office of elector of President and Vice President shall file in writing under oath a declaration of the identity of the persons for whom he will vote for President and Vice President, which declaration shall be binding on any successor to his office. In choosing electors the voters in each State have the qualifications requisite for electors of the most numerous branch of the State legislature.

'The electors shall meet in their respective States, fill any vacancies in their number as directed by the State legislature, and vote by signed ballot for President and Vice President, one of whom, at least, shall not be an inhabitant of the State with themselves....

"Any vote cast by an elector contrary to the declaration made by him shall be counted as a vote cast in accordance with his declaration.' "

Senate Joint Resolution 12 of the 91st Congress in 1969 was sponsored by the following Senators:

- Mundt (R–South Dakota),
- Boggs (R–Delaware),
- Byrd (D–West Virginia),
- Cotton (R–New Hampshire),
- Curtis (R–Nebraska),
- Dominick (R–Colorado),
- Fong (R–Hawaii),
- Goldwater (R–Arizona),
- Hansen (R–Wyoming),
- Hruska (R–Nebraska),
- Jordan (R–Idaho),
- Miller (R–Iowa),
- Sparkman (D–Alabama),
- Stennis (D–Mississippi),
- Thurmond (R–South Carolina),
- Tower (R–Texas),
- Williams (R–Delaware), and
- Young (R–North Dakota).

The characteristics of the congressional-district approach are analyzed in detail in section 4.2, where it is demonstrated that

- it would not accurately reflect the nationwide popular vote;
- it would not improve upon the current situation in which most areas of the country are non-competitive but, instead, would simply create a small set of battleground congressional districts (with most districts being non-competitive), and
- not every vote would be equal.

The Mundt proposal was noteworthy in that it retained the office of presidential elector while eliminating the possibility of a faithless presidential elector. First, Mundt's proposed amendment provided that each candidate for presidential elector must take an oath to vote in the Electoral College for particular persons for President and Vice President (and made the original candidate's oath binding on any replacement). Second, Mundt's proposal then stated that regardless of the way the presidential elector actually voted in the Electoral College, his or her vote would "be counted as a vote cast in accordance with his declaration."

3.3 DIRECT NATIONWIDE POPULAR ELECTION

In 1969, the House of Representatives approved, by a 338–70 vote, a federal constitutional amendment sponsored by Representative Emmanuel Celler for direct nationwide popular election. Celler's proposal (House Joint Resolution 681 of the 91st Congress) provided:

> *"Resolved by the Senate and House of Representatives of the United States of America in Congress assembled (two-thirds of each House concurring therein),*

That the following article is proposed as an amendment to the Constitution of the United States, which shall be valid to all intents and purposes as part of the Constitution when ratified by the legislatures of three-fourths of the several States within seven years from the date of its submission by the Congress:

'**Article—**
'**SECTION 1:** The people of the several States and the District constituting the seat of government of the United States shall elect the President and Vice President. Each elector shall cast a single vote for two persons who shall have consented to the joining of their names as candidates for the offices of President and Vice President. No candidate shall

consent to the joinder of his name with that of more than one other person.

'**SECTION 2:** The electors of President and Vice President in each State shall have the qualifications requisite for electors of the most numerous branch of the State legislature, except that for electors of President and Vice President, the legislature of any State may prescribe less restrictive residence qualifications and for electors of President and Vice President the Congress may establish uniform residence qualifications.

'**SECTION 3:** The pair of persons having the greatest number of votes for President and Vice President shall be elected, if such number be at least 40 per centum of the whole number of votes cast for such offices. If no pair of persons has such number, a runoff election shall be held in which the choice of President and Vice President shall be made from the two pairs of persons who received the highest number of votes.

'**SECTION 4:** The times, places, and manner of holding such elections and entitlement to inclusion on the ballot shall be prescribed in each State by the legislature thereof; but the Congress may at any time by law make or alter such regulations. The days for such elections shall be determined by Congress and shall be uniform throughout the United States. The Congress shall prescribe by law the time, place, and manner in which the results of such elections shall be ascertained and declared.

'**SECTION 5:** The Congress may by law provide for the case of the death or withdrawal of any candidate for President or Vice President before a President and Vice President have been elected, and for the case of the death of both the President-elect and Vice-President-elect.

'**SECTION 6:** The Congress shall have power to enforce this article by appropriate legislation.

'**SECTION 7:** This article shall take effect one year after the 21st day of January following ratification.' "

When it was first introduced, House Joint Resolution 681 was sponsored by the following Representatives:

- Biester (R–Pennsylvania),
- Cahill (R–New Jersey),
- Celler (D–New York),
- Conyers (D–Michigan),
- Donohue (D–Massachusetts),
- Edwards (D–California),
- Eilberg (D–Pennsylvania),
- Feighan (D–Ohio),
- Fish (R–New York),
- Hungate (D–Missouri),
- Jacobs (D–Indiana),
- Kastenmeier (D–Wisconsin),
- MacGregor (R–Minnesota),
- McClory (R–Illinois),
- McCulloch (R–Ohio),
- Meskill (R–Connecticut),
- Mikva (D–Illinois),
- St. Onge (D–Connecticut),
- Railsback (R–Illinois),
- Rodino (D–New Jersey),
- Rogers (D–Colorado),
- Ryan (D–New York),
- Sandman (R–New Jersey),
- Smith (R–New York), and
- Waldie (D–California).

Congressman George Herbert Walker Bush (R–Texas), like many of his colleagues in Congress, supported all three of the prominent approaches to abolish the present Electoral College system. He spoke in favor of nationwide direct popular election (House Joint Resolution 681) on September 18, 1969, saying:

"Frankly I think this legislation has a great deal to commend it. It will correct the wrongs of the present mechanism because by calling for direct election of the President and Vice President it will eliminate the formality of the electoral college and by providing for a runoff in case no candidate receives 40 percent of the vote it eliminates the unrealistic ballot casting in the House of Representatives. Yet, in spite of these drastic reforms, the bill is not, when viewed in the light of current practice, one that will be detrimental to our federal system or one that will change the departmentalized and local nature of voting in this country.

"In electing the President and Vice President, the Constitution establishes the principle that votes are cast by States. This legislation does not tamper with that principle. It only changes the manner in which the States vote. Instead of voting by intermediaries, the States will certify their popular vote count to the Congress. The states will maintain primary responsibility for the ballot and for the qualifications of voters. In other words, they will still designate the time, place, and manner in which elections will be held. Thus, there is a very good argument to be made that the basic nature of our federal system has not been disturbed.

"On the walls of the Jefferson Memorial are written these words that we might well consider today:

> 'I am not an advocate for frequent changes in laws and constitutions, but laws and constitutions must go hand in hand with the progress of the human mind as that becomes more developed, more enlightened, as new discoveries are made, new truths discovered, and manners and opinions change. With the change of circumstances institutions must advance also to keep pace with the times.'

"The world has changed a great deal since the 12th amendment was approved, and the system it perpetuates is one fraught with a history of fraud, leaves our country open to constitutional crisis, and is clearly unresponsive to the desires of the American people. I do support the proposal before us today because I believe it combines the best features of our current practice with the desirable goal of a simpler, more direct voting system."[23]

Senator Birch Bayh (D–Indiana) introduced Senate Joint Resolution 1 in the 91st Congress in 1969 (with substantially the same provisions as Representative Celler's House Joint Resolution 681). The sponsors of Senate Joint Resolution 1 included the following Senators:

- George D. Aiken (R–Vermont),
- Birch Bayh (D–Indiana),
- Henry Bellmon (R–Oklahoma),
- Alan Bible (D–Nevada),
- Quentin Burdick (D–North Dakota),
- Robert C. Byrd (D–West Virginia),
- Clifford P. Case (R–New Jersey),

---

[23] *Congressional Record.* September 18, 1969. Pages 25,990–25,991.

- Frank Church (D–Idaho),
- Marlow Cook (R–Kentucky),
- Alan Cranston (D–California),
- Thomas F. Eagleton (D–Missouri),
- Charles E. Goodell (R–New York),
- Mike Gravel (D–Alaska),
- Fred R. Harris (D–Oklahoma),
- Mark O. Hatfield (R–Oregon),
- Vance Hartke (D–Indiana),
- Daniel K. Inouye (D–Hawaii),
- Henry M. Jackson (D–Washington),
- Jacob K. Javits (R–New York),
- Warren G. Magnuson (D–Washington),
- Mike Mansfield (D–Montana),
- Charles McC. Mathias, Jr. (R–Maryland),
- George McGovern (D–South Dakota),
- Thomas J. McIntyre (D–New Hampshire),
- Lee Metcalf (D–Montana),
- Walter F. Mondale (D–Minnesota),
- Joseph M. Montoya (D–New Mexico),
- Edmund S. Muskie (D–Maine),
- Gaylord Nelson (D–Wisconsin),
- Robert W. Packwood (R–Oregon),
- John O. Pastore (D–Rhode Island),
- James B. Pearson (R–Kansas),
- Claiborne Pell (D–Rhode Island),
- William Proxmire (D–Wisconsin),
- Jennings Randolph (D–West Virginia),
- Abraham Ribicoff (D–Connecticut),
- Richard S. Schweiker (R–Pennsylvania),
- Joseph D. Tydings (D–Maryland),
- Harrison A. Williams, Jr. (D–New Jersey), and
- Stephen M. Young (D–Ohio).

After the 338–70 vote in the House of Representatives in favor of House Joint Resolution 681 in 1969, the House bill was filibustered and died in the Senate.

Throughout the 1970s, Senator Bayh repeatedly introduced constitutional amendments for nationwide popular election of the President. For example, the sponsors of Senate Joint Resolution 1 in the 95th Congress in 1977 included the following Senators:

- Abourezk (R–South Dakota),
- Anderson (D–Minnesota),
- Baker (R–Tennessee),
- Bartlett (R–Oklahoma),
- Bayh (D–Indiana),
- Bellmon(R–Oklahoma),
- Brooke (R–Massachusetts),
- Chafee (R–Rhode Island),
- Church (D–Idaho),
- Clark (D–Iowa),
- Cranston (D–California),
- Danforth (R–Missouri),
- DeConcini (D–Arizona),
- Dole (R–Kansas),
- Ford (D–Kentucky),
- Garn (R–Utah),
- Glenn (D–Ohio),
- Gravel (D–Alaska),
- Hart (D–Michigan),
- Haskell (D–Colorado),
- Hatfield (R–Oregon),
- Hathaway (D–Maine),
- Huddleston (D–Kentucky),
- Humphrey (D–Minnesota),
- Inouye (D–Hawaii),
- Jackson (D–Washington),
- Javits (R–New York),
- Kennedy (D–Massachusetts),
- Leahy (D–Vermont),
- Magnuson (D–Washington),
- Mathias (R–Maryland),
- Matsunaga (D–Hawaii),
- McIntyre (D–New Hampshire),
- Metzenbaum (D–Ohio),
- Packwood (R–Oregon),
- Randolph (D–West Virginia),
- Ribicoff (D–Connecticut),
- Riegle (D–Michigan),
- Schweiker (R–Pennsylvania),
- Stafford (R–Vermont),
- Stevenson (D–Illinois),
- Williams (D–New Jersey), and
- Zorinsky (D–Nebraska).

The sponsors of Senate Joint Resolution 28[24] in the 96th Congress in 1979 included the following Senators:

- Baker (R–Tennessee),
- Bayh (D–Indiana),
- Bellmon (R–Oklahoma),
- Burdick (D–North Dakota),
- Chafee (R–Rhode Island),
- Cranston (D–California),
- Danforth (R–Missouri),
- DeConcini (D–Arizona),
- Dole (R–Kansas),
- Kennedy (D–Massachusetts),
- Leahy (D–Vermont),
- Levin (D–Michigan),
- Magnuson (D–Washington),
- Mathias (R–Maryland),
- Matsunaga (D–Hawaii),
- Packwood (R–Oregon),
- Pell (D–Rhode Island),
- Proxmire (D–Wisconsin),

---

[24] Senate Joint Resolution 28 of the 96th Congress in 1979 was substantially the same as Celler's House Joint Resolution 681 that the House of Representatives passed in 1969.

- Durenberger (R–Minnesota),
- Ford (D–Kentucky),
- Garn (R–Utah),
- Gravel (D–Alaska),
- Hatfield (R–Oregon),
- Huddleston (D–Kentucky),
- Inouye (D–Hawaii),
- Jackson (D–Washington),
- Javits (R–New York),
- Johnston (D–Louisiana),
- Pryor (D–Arkansas),
- Randolph (D–West Virginia),
- Ribicoff (D–Connecticut),
- Riegle (D–Michigan),
- Stafford (R–Vermont),
- Stevenson (D–Illinois),
- Tsongas (D–Massachusetts),
- Williams (D–New Jersey), and
- Zorinsky (D–Nebraska).

Senator Robert E. Dole of Kansas, the Republican nominee for Vice President in 1976 and later Republican nominee for President in 1996, spoke in the Senate on January 14, 1979 on the subject of nationwide popular election of the President and Vice President, saying:

"That candidates for these two positions should be selected by direct election is an idea which I have long supported....

"The electoral college system was provided for in the Constitution because, at one time, it seemed the most fair way to select the President and Vice President. Alexander Hamilton apparently expressed the prevailing view when we wrote that a small number of persons selected from the general population would most likely have the ability and intelligence to select the best persons for the job. I have no doubt but that in the 18th century, the electoral college was well suited for our country. However, already by the early 19th century, misgivings were being voiced about the college.

"The skepticism seems to be related to the formation of political party candidates and the difference they made in the selection of the President and Vice President. In the years since then, the electoral college has remained in use. It has served us fairly well—except for three times when it allowed a candidate to gain the Presidency who did not have the most popular votes.

"There have been numerous other elections in which a shift of a few thousand votes would have changed the outcome of the electoral college vote, despite the fact that the would-be winner came in second place in popular votes. Mr. President, I think we are leaving a little too much to chance, and to hope, that we will not witness yet another unrepresentative election."[25] [Emphasis added]

Senator Dole then specifically addressed the question of the effect of the bonus of two electoral votes that each state receives regardless of its population.

"Many persons have the impression that the electoral college benefits those persons living in small states. I feel that this is somewhat of a misconception. Through my experience with the Republican National Committee and as a Vice Presidential candidate in 1976, it became very clear that the populous states with their large blocks of electoral votes were the crucial states. It was in these states that we focused our efforts.

"Were we to switch to a system of direct election, I think we would see a resulting change in the nature of campaigning. While urban areas will still be important campaigning centers, there will be a new emphasis given to smaller states. **Candidates will soon realize that all votes are important, and votes from small states carry the same import as votes from large states. That to me is one of the major attractions of direct election. Each vote carries equal importance.**

"Direct election would give candidates incentive to campaign in States that are perceived to be single party states. For no longer will minority votes be lost. Their accumulated total will be important, and in some instances perhaps even decisive.

"The objections raised to direct election are varied. When they are analyzed, I think many objections reflect not so much satisfaction with the electoral college, but rather a reluctance to change an established political system. While I could never advocate change simply for the sake of changing, neither should we defer action because we fear change.

---

[25] *Congressional Record.* January 14, 1979. Page 309.

"In this situation, I think the weaknesses in the current system have been demonstrated, and that the prudent move is to provide for direct election of the President and Vice President.

"I hope that the Senate will be able to move ahead on this resolution. As long as we continue with the electoral college system, we will be placing our trust in an institution which usually works according to design, but which sometimes does not. There are remedies available to us and I trust the Senate will act to correct this weakness in our political system."[26] [Emphasis added]

In a 1979 Senate speech, Senator Henry Bellmon (R–Oklahoma) described how his views on the Electoral College had changed while he had served as Governor, Senator, national campaign director for Richard Nixon, and a member of the American Bar Association's commission studying electoral reform.

"While the consideration of the electoral college began–and I am a little embarrassed to admit this–I was convinced, as are many residents of smaller States, that the present system is a considerable advantage to less populous States such as Oklahoma, and that it was to the advantage of the small States for the electoral college concept be preserved.

"I think if any Member of the State has that concept he would be greatly enlightened by the fact that the Members of the Senate from New York are now actively supporting the retention of the electoral college system....

"Mr. President, as the deliberations of the American Bar Association Commission proceeded and as more facts became known, I came to the realization that the present electoral system does not give an advantage to the voters from the less populous States. Rather, it works to the disadvantage of small State voters who are largely ignored in the general election for President.

---

[26] *Congressional Record.* January 14, 1979. Page 309.

"It is true that the smaller States which are allowed an elector for each U.S. Senator and for each Congressman do, on the surface, appear to be favored; but, in fact, the system gives the advantage to the voters in the populous States. The reason is simple as I think our friends from New York understand: A small State voter is, in effect, the means whereby a Presidential candidate may receive a half-dozen or so electoral votes. On the other hand, a vote in a large State is the means to 20 or 30 or 40 or more electoral votes. Therefore, Presidential candidates structure their campaigns to appeal to the States with large blocs of electors. This gives special and disproportionate importance to the special interest groups which may determine the electoral outcome in those few large States.

"Here, Mr. President, let me say parenthetically that during 1967 and part of 1968 I served as the national campaign director for Richard Nixon, and I know very well as we structured that campaign we did not worry about Alaska, about Wyoming, or about Nevada or about New Mexico or about Oklahoma or Kansas. We worried about New York, California, Pennsylvania, Texas, Michigan, Illinois, all of the populous States, where there are these big blocks of electors that we could appeal to, provided we chose our issues properly and provided we presented the candidates in an attractive way.

"The result, Mr. President, is that the executive branch of our National Government has grown and is continuing to become increasingly oriented toward populous States, to the disadvantage of the smaller, less populous areas. An examination of past campaign platforms and campaign schedules of the major party candidates will bear out this position. Therefore, it is obvious that any political party or any candidate for President or Vice President will spend his efforts primarily in the populous States. The parties draft their platforms with the view in mind of attracting the voters of the populous States and generally relegate the needs of the smaller States to secondary positions.

"This whole situation would change if we go for a direct election and, therefore, **make the voters of one State equally important with the voters of any other State.**"[27] [Emphasis added]

Senator Carl Levin (D–Michigan) spoke in the Senate on June 21, 1979, and said:

"Mr. President, the direct election of the President and the Vice President of the United States is an electoral reform which is long overdue. It is long overdue because of its basic fairness, democratic nature, and its inherent simplicity. There is no principle which is more basic to our concept of democracy than equal treatment under the law. And yet when this Nation goes to the polls every 4 years in the only truly national election that we have, that principle is abrogated. The effect of the electoral college system on our Presidential election is often drastically unequally treatment of individual voters and their votes. The discrepancies are real and widespread, and they defy our basic sense of fairness....

"Mr. President, we ask the wrong question when we ask who gains and who loses under the electoral college, and how will this group lose its advantage under direct election? The function of the President is to serve the interests of all persons, all citizens of this country, and, therefore, all citizens should have an equal say as to who the President will be. In the debate over who will gain and who will lose, there is only one real winner in implementing direct election, and that is the American people who will finally be able to participate in a democratic and fair national election where **each vote counts for as much as every other vote.**

"The American people will also win because we have eliminated the threat which the electoral college has always posed—that is the possibility that a candidate who has not won the popular vote will, through the mechanisms of the

---

[27] *Congressional Record.* July 10, 1979. Page 17748.

electoral college, be elevated to the Presidency."[28] [Emphasis added]

In a Senate speech on July 10, 1979, Senator Charles McC. Mathias, Jr. (R–Maryland) listed the faults of the existing system, including the "state-by-state winner-take-all" system and the possibility of electing the second-place candidate, saying:

"Direct election is the most effective method to remedy these faults. As the late Senator Hubert Humphrey noted, only direct election insures that

'the votes of the American people wherever cast [are] counted directly and equally in determining who shall be President of the United States.'

"Only by direct election can the fundamental principle of equal treatment under the law for all Americans be incorporated into our Presidential selection process."[29] [Emphasis added]

After discussing the ever-present possibility that the presidential candidate receiving the most popular votes nationwide might not win the Presidency, Senator David Durenberger (R-Minnesota) said:

"[T]he most damaging effect of the electoral system has already occurred, in **every** State and in **every** Presidential election. For with its 'winner take all' requirement, the electoral college effectively disenfranchises every man and woman supporting the candidate who fails to carry their State. Under that system, votes for the losing candidate have no significance whatsoever in the overall outcome of the election. And for this reason, candidates who either pull far ahead or fall far behind in a State have the incentive to 'write it off'— simply ignore it—in planning their campaign appearances. In contrast, **the proposed amendment would grant every vote the same degree of significance in determining the final outcome.** Candidates would be forced to consider their margins in every State, and the tendency to ignore a 'safe' or

---

[28] *Congressional Record.* June 21, 1979. Page 15095.
[29] *Congressional Record.* July 10, 1979. Page 17751.

'lost' State would be sharply diminished. By restoring the significance of every vote, Senate Joint Resolution 28 increases the incentive to vote, which in itself is a significant argument for passage."

"Had the Founding Fathers adopted a direct election system, it is inconceivable that anyone would be rising after 200 years to propose replacing that system with the electoral college."[30] [Emphasis added]

On July 20, 1979, 51 senators voted in favor of Senate Joint Resolution 28 (with one additional senator being announced in favor).

Appendix W contains the March 14, 1979, speech of Senator Birch Bayh on his proposed constitutional amendment.

In subsequent years, numerous other proposed federal constitutional amendments for nationwide popular election of the President have been introduced. For example, Senator J. James Exon of Nebraska introduced a proposed federal constitutional amendment in 1992. The sponsors included the following Senators:

- Exon (D–Nebraska),
- Murkowski (R–Alaska),
- Burdick (D–North Dakota),
- Boren. (D–Oklahoma),
- Adams (D–Washington),
- D'Amato (R–New York),
- Kennedy (D–Massachusetts),
- Coats (R–Indiana),
- Reid (D–Nevada),
- Dixon (D–Illinois),
- Durenberger (R–Minnesota),
- Glenn (D–Ohio),
- Lieberman (D–Connecticut), and
- Hollings (D–South Carolina).

The Exon proposal (Senate Joint Resolution 302) reads as follows:

"Resolved by the Senate and House of Representatives of the United States of America in Congress assembled,

"That the following article is proposed as an amendment to the Constitution of the United States, which shall be valid to all intents and purposes as part of the Constitution when ratified by the legislatures of three-fourths of the several States within seven years from the date of its submission by the Congress:

---

[30] *Congressional Record.* July 10, 1979. Pages 17706–17707.

'**Article—**
'**SECTION 1.** The people of the several States and the District constituting the seat of government of the United States shall elect the President and Vice President. Each elector shall cast a single vote for two persons who shall have consented to the joining of their names as candidates for the offices of President and Vice President.

'**SECTION 2.** The electors of President and Vice President in each State shall have the qualifications requisite for electors of the most numerous branch of the State legislature, except that for the electors of President and Vice President, any State may prescribe by law less restrictive residence qualifications and for electors of President and Vice President the Congress may by law establish uniform residence qualification.

'**SECTION 3.** The persons joined as candidates for President and Vice President having the greatest number of votes shall be elected President and Vice President, if such number be at least 50 per centum of the whole number of votes cast and such number be derived from a majority of the number of votes cast in each State comprising at least one-third of the several States. If, after any such election, none of the persons joined as candidates for President and Vice President is elected pursuant to the preceding paragraph, a runoff election shall be held within sixty days in which the choice of President and Vice President shall be made from the two pairs of persons joined as candidates for President and Vice President receiving the greatest number of votes in such runoff election shall be elected President and Vice President.

'**SECTION 4.** The times, places, and manner of holding such elections and entitlement to inclusion on the ballot shall be prescribed by law in each State; but the Congress may by law make or alter such regulations.

The days for such elections shall be determined by Congress and shall be uniform throughout the United States. The Congress shall prescribe by law the times, places, and manner in which the results of such elections shall be ascertained and declared. No such election, other than a runoff election, shall be held later than the first Tuesday after the first Monday in November, and the results thereof shall be declared no later than thirty days after the date on which the election occurs.

'**SECTION 5.** The Congress may by law provide for the case of the death, inability, or withdrawal of any candidate for President or Vice President before a President and Vice President have been elected, and for the case of the death of either the President-elect or the Vice President-elect.

'**SECTION 6.** Sections 1 through 4 of this article shall take effect two years after ratification of this article.

'**SECTION 7.** The Congress shall have power to enforce this article by appropriate legislation.' "

In 2005, Representatives Jesse Jackson Jr. (D–Illinois) and Barney Frank (D–Massachusetts) introduced a federal constitutional amendment for nationwide popular election of the President (House Joint Resolution 36). Like the Exon proposal of 1992, this proposal would have required that a candidate receive "a majority of the votes cast" in order to be elected.

In addition, Senator Dianne Feinstein (D–California) introduced Senate Joint Resolution 11 in March 2005 as follows:

"Resolved by the Senate and House of Representatives of the United States of America in Congress assembled (two-thirds of each House concurring therein),

That the following article is proposed as an amendment to the Constitution of the United States, which shall be valid to all intents and purposes as part of the Constitution when ratified by the legislatures of three-fourths of the several States within seven years after the date of its submission to the States for ratification:

'**Article—**

'**SECTION 1.** The President and Vice President shall be elected by the people of the several States and the district constituting the seat of government of the United States. The persons having the greatest number of votes for President and Vice President shall be elected.

'**SECTION 2.** The voters in each State shall have the qualifications requisite for electors of Representatives in Congress from that State, except that the legislature of any State may prescribe less restrictive qualifications with respect to residence and Congress may establish uniform residence and age qualifications. Congress may establish qualifications for voters in the district constituting the seat of government of the United States.

'**SECTION 3.** Congress may determine the time, place, and manner of holding the election, and the entitlement to inclusion on the ballot. Congress shall prescribe by law the time, place, and manner in which the results of the election shall be ascertained and declared.

'**SECTION 4.** Each voter shall cast a single vote jointly applicable to President and Vice President in any such election. Names of candidates shall not be joined unless both candidates have consented thereto, and no candidate shall consent to being joined with more than one other person.

'**SECTION 5.** Congress may by law provide for the case of the death of any candidate for President or Vice President before the day on which the President-elect or the Vice President-elect has been chosen, and for the case of a tie in any such election.

'**SECTION 6.** This article shall take effect one year after the twenty-first day of January following ratification.' "

The Exon proposal of 1992 provided that a run-off election would be held if no presidential slate were to receive at least 50% of the popular vote. In contrast, the constitutional amendment introduced by Senator

Feinstein in 2005 (Senate Joint Resolution 11) required only a plurality of the popular votes.

> "The persons having the greatest number of votes for President and Vice President shall be elected."

The 2005 Feinstein proposal also differed from the 1992 Exon proposal in that the Feinstein proposal provided that

> "Congress may determine the time, place, and manner of holding the election, and the entitlement to inclusion on the ballot ..."

The Exon proposal provided that

> "The times, places, and manner of holding such elections and entitlement to inclusion on the ballot shall be prescribed by law in each State; but the Congress may by law make or alter such regulations."

Appendix S shows, state by state, members of Congress who have sponsored proposed constitutional amendments for nationwide popular election of the President in recent years or who voted in favor of constitutional amendments in the 1969 roll call in the House of Representatives or the 1979 roll call in the Senate. As shown in appendix S, there has been at least one supporter in Congress from each of the 50 states.

In summary, in terms of the three criteria mentioned at the beginning of this chapter, nationwide popular voting for President would

- accurately reflect the nationwide popular vote,
- make every area of the country competitive, and
- make every vote equal.

4 | Two Previously Proposed Approaches for State-Level Action

Chapter 3 analyzed the three most discussed proposals for federal constitutional amendments for changing the current system of electing the President and Vice President. This chapter examines the two most prominent approaches to presidential election reform that can be unilaterally enacted at the state level (i.e., without a federal constitutional amendment and without action by Congress). Later, chapter 6 will discuss this book's suggested approach for reform.

The office of presidential elector is established by the Constitution (as discussed in section 2.1), and therefore cannot be eliminated without a federal constitutional amendment. However, the manner of choosing the presidential electors is determined on a state-by-state basis by means of state legislation. As the U.S. Supreme Court stated in *McPherson v. Blacker* in 1892:[1]

> "In short, the appointment and mode of appointment of electors belong **exclusively** to the states under the constitution of the United States." (Emphasis added).

Two proposals for changing the current system of electing the President and Vice President that can be enacted at the state level have received attention in recent years. Neither approach involves abolition of the office of presidential elector or of the Electoral College (and hence neither requires a federal constitutional amendment). Both proposals can be enacted at the state level without any involvement of Congress. Both approaches involve dividing a state's electoral votes in a manner that is different from the statewide winner-take-all system that is currently used by all states except Maine and Nebraska. The two approaches are the:

- **Whole-Number Proportional Approach** in which a state's electoral votes are divided proportionally—*rounded*

---

[1] *McPherson v Blacker.* 146 U.S. 1 at 35. 1892.

off to the nearest whole number—according to the percentage of votes received in the state by each presidential slate (section 4.1); and

- **Congressional-District Approach** in which one presidential elector is elected from each congressional district and two presidential electors are elected statewide (section 4.2).

4.1 WHOLE-NUMBER PROPORTIONAL APPROACH

The whole-number proportional approach was considered by Colorado voters in the November 2, 2004, election. The proposition, called Amendment 36, was placed on the ballot by initiative petition. It was defeated by the voters.

The *whole-number* proportional approach is distinctly different from the *fractional* proportional approach (discussed in section 3.1). The two approaches differ in that the whole-number proportional approach divides a state's electoral votes *to the nearest whole number*, whereas the fractional proportional approach carries out the division of a state's electoral votes *to three decimal places*. As will be seen below, the whole-number proportional approach operates in a highly counter-intuitive way because of this seemingly minor difference.

The voting in Colorado in the 2004 presidential election can be used to illustrate the difference between the two approaches. George W. Bush received 1,068,233 popular votes (52.6508712%), and John Kerry received 960,666 popular votes (47.3606128%) in Colorado. The state has nine electoral votes.

Under the fractional proportional approach, Bush would have received 4.739 electoral votes, and Kerry would have received 4.261 electoral votes. The fractional numbers from Colorado—4.739 and 4.261—would be added together with fractional numbers from all the other states (and the District of Columbia) in order to yield a nationwide grand total. It is possible for candidates to receive fractional numbers of electoral votes from each state because the fractional proportional approach would be implemented by a federal constitutional amendment that would abolish the office of presidential elector. Fractions (carried out to three decimal places) would be possible because the human electors (each casting one *indivisible* vote) would be eliminated under the fractional proportional approach.

As discussed in section 3.1, Senator Cannon's proposed federal constitutional amendment implementing the fractional proportional approach would definitely increase the competitiveness of presidential elections. Additional popular votes would matter in every state. A presidential candidate could, for example, earn an additional 0.001 electoral vote by winning an additional hundred or so popular votes in any state. Thus, no state would be written off by any presidential candidate. All states would be battleground states.

In contrast, the whole-number proportional approach (i.e., Colorado's Amendment 36) was proposed as a *state* constitutional amendment—not as a *federal* constitutional amendment. A state may not abolish the office of presidential elector or the Electoral College—it may simply choose the method by which it allocates its own electoral votes within the Electoral College. Any approach adopted unilaterally in Colorado must necessarily award 0, 1, 2, 3, 4, 5, 6, 7, 8, or 9 presidential electors to each presidential slate. Only whole numbers—not fractions— are allowed because Colorado must choose nine human presidential electors, each casting one *indivisible* vote in the Electoral College. Based on the fact that Bush received 52.6508712% of the popular vote in the November 2004 voting in Colorado, he would have received five of Colorado's nine electoral votes, and Kerry would have received four under the whole-number proportional approach. In other words, the whole-number proportional approach would have produced a 5–4 division of Colorado's electoral votes, compared to the 9–0 division produced by the current statewide winner-take-all rule.

The problem with the whole-number proportional approach stems from the fact that there are only 538 electoral votes in the Electoral College (i.e., one for each U.S. Representative and Senator). The average number of electoral votes per state is, therefore, about 11. As it happens, about three-quarters (36) of the states have a below-average number of electoral votes. The important difference between *whole numbers* and *fractions carried out to three decimal places* arises because the number of electoral votes possessed by a typical state is so small. For example, in an average-sized state with 11 electoral votes, one electoral vote corresponds to a 9.09% share of the state's popular vote under the whole-number proportional approach. In Colorado (a slightly below-average sized state), one electoral vote corresponds to an 11.11% share of the popular vote. In states with only three electoral votes, one electoral vote corresponds to a 33.3% share of the popular vote. Except for occasional landslides (e.g., Reagan's 60% in 1984, Nixon's 61% in 1972, and Johnson's 61% in 1964), most elections are decided by only a few percentage points. A system that requires a 33% share, an 11% share, or a 9% share of the popular vote in order to win one electoral vote is fundamentally out of sync with the small-percentage vote shifts that are encountered in non-landslide elections.

As will be shown in the detailed analysis below, if the whole-number proportional approach were adopted nationwide,

- it would not accurately reflect the nationwide popular vote; and
- it would not make every state competitive but, instead, would simply create a small new group of battleground states in presidential elections.

In fact, if the whole-number proportional approach were adopted nationwide,

- it would amount to a "winner-take-one" system in all states except California—that is, the presidential election would revolve around winning a single electoral vote, here and there, from a small group of battleground states; and
- it would retain the political importance of carrying a state only if the state happens to have an odd number of electoral votes, while eliminating that importance if the state happens to have an even number of electoral votes.

Of course, almost any electoral system will yield a reasonable outcome in a landslide election. The test of an electoral system is how it works in a close election. Therefore, our analysis here starts with data from a close recent presidential election (i.e., 2000).

Column 2 of table 4.1 shows the number of electoral votes possessed by each of the 50 states and the District of Columbia in the 2000 presidential election. The table is sorted in order of electoral votes, with the smallest states listed first. Columns 3 and 4 show the respective percentage of the two-party popular vote received by Al Gore and George W. Bush. Columns 5 and 6 show the number of electoral votes received respectively by Al Gore and George W. Bush under the existing statewide winner-take-all system.[2]

---

[2] Maine and Nebraska use the congressional-district approach for allocating their electoral votes. However, since the adoption of this system (1969 for Maine and 1992 for Nebraska), the candidate carrying the state has always also carried all the congressional districts.

Table 4.1 RESULTS OF 2000 PRESIDENTIAL ELECTION

STATE	ELECTORAL VOTES	GORE POPULAR VOTE	BUSH POPULAR VOTE	GORE ELECTORAL VOTES	BUSH ELECTORAL VOTES
Alaska	3	32%	68%		3
Delaware	3	57%	43%	3	
District of Columbia	3	90%	10%	3	
Montana	3	36%	64%		3
North Dakota	3	35%	65%		3
South Dakota	3	38%	62%		3
Vermont	3	55%	45%	3	
Wyoming	3	29%	71%		3
Hawaii	4	60%	40%	4	
Idaho	4	29%	71%		4
Maine	4	53%	47%	4	
Nevada	4	48%	52%		4
New Hampshire	4	49%	51%		4
Rhode Island	4	66%	34%	4	
Nebraska	5	35%	65%		5
New Mexico	5	50%	50%	5	
Utah	5	28%	72%		5
West Virginia	5	47%	53%		5
Arkansas	6	47%	53%		6
Kansas	6	39%	61%		6
Iowa	7	50%	50%	7	
Mississippi	7	41%	59%		7
Oregon	7	50%	50%	7	
Arizona	8	47%	53%		8
Colorado	8	46%	54%		8
Connecticut	8	59%	41%	8	
Kentucky	8	42%	58%		8
Oklahoma	8	39%	61%		8
South Carolina	8	42%	58%		8
Alabama	9	42%	58%		9
Louisiana	9	46%	54%		9
Maryland	10	58%	42%	10	
Minnesota	10	51%	49%	10	
Missouri	11	48%	52%		11
Tennessee	11	48%	52%		11
Washington	11	53%	47%	11	
Wisconsin	11	50%	50%	11	
Indiana	12	42%	58%		12
Massachusetts	12	65%	35%	12	

Table 4.1 RESULTS OF 2000 PRESIDENTIAL ELECTION (cont.)

STATE	ELECTORAL VOTES	GORE POPULAR VOTE	BUSH POPULAR VOTE	GORE ELECTORAL VOTES	BUSH ELECTORAL VOTES
Georgia	13	44%	56%		13
Virginia	13	46%	54%		13
North Carolina	14	44%	56%		14
New Jersey	15	58%	42%	15	
Michigan	18	53%	47%	18	
Ohio	21	48%	52%		21
Illinois	22	56%	44%	22	
Pennsylvania	23	52%	48%	23	
Florida	25	50%	50%		25
Texas	32	39%	61%		32
New York	33	63%	37%	33	
California	54	56%	44%	54	
Total	**538**			**267**	**271**

4.1.1 JURISDICTIONS WITH THREE ELECTORAL VOTES

There were eight jurisdictions with three electoral votes in the 2000 presidential election—Alaska, Delaware, the District of Columbia, Montana, North Dakota, South Dakota, Vermont, and Wyoming (as shown in the top eight rows of table 4.1).

Under the whole-number proportional approach, one electoral vote corresponds to a 33.3% share of the state's popular vote for the states with three electoral votes.

To implement the whole-number proportional approach, the number of popular votes that each presidential slate received statewide is divided by the total number of votes cast statewide in order to obtain that slate's percentage of the statewide popular vote. This percentage is then multiplied by the state's number of electoral votes. The number of electoral votes received by each presidential slate is then rounded off to the nearest whole number.

There are four possibilities in states with three electoral votes:[3]

   • If a presidential slate receives less than 16.66% of the popular

---

[3] If there are more than two presidential slates on the ballot in a state with three electoral votes and no minor-party slate receives at least 16.66% of the popular vote in the state, it may be necessary to repeat the calculation without the minor parties in order to allocate all of the state's electoral votes.

vote (that is, less than one half of the 33.3% share necessary to win one electoral vote), then it gets no electoral votes.

- If a presidential slate receives between 16.67% and 50.00% of the popular vote, then it gets one electoral vote.
- If a presidential slate receives between 50.01% and 83.33% of the popular vote, then it gets two electoral votes.
- Finally, at the high end of the scale, if a presidential slate receives more than 83.33% of the popular vote, then it gets all three of the state's electoral votes.

Table 4.2 summarizes the number of electoral votes (from zero to three) that a presidential slate receives for various ranges of percentages of the popular vote in the states with three electoral votes. Column 3 shows the *breakpoints* (i.e., 16.67%, 50.00%, and 83.33%) in the ranges of percentages of popular votes. These breakpoints are the spots, along the percentage scale, where the number of electoral votes changes. The breakpoints are the critical numbers that would dictate campaign strategy under the whole-number proportional approach.

Table 4.2 TABLE OF BREAKPOINTS FOR STATES WITH THREE ELECTORAL VOTES

PERCENT OF POPULAR VOTE	NUMBER OF ELECTORAL VOTES	BREAKPOINT
0.00% to 16.66%	0	16.67%
16.67% to 50.00%	1	50.00%
50.01% to 83.33%	2	83.33%
83.33% to 100.00%	3	NA

Figure 4.1 graphically presents the breakpoints (16.67%, 50.0%, and 83.33%) for states with three electoral votes. The horizontal line in the figure represents a presidential candidate's percentage share of the popular vote—from 0% to 100%. The vertical tick marks show the breakpoints (16.67%, 50.0%, and 83.33%) for states with three electoral votes. The small numbers (0, 1, 2, or 3) immediately under the horizontal line show the number of electoral votes that a candidate would receive by winning a particular share of the popular vote.

Figure 4.1 Scale showing the number of electoral votes that a candidate would receive under the whole-number proportional approach by winning a particular share of the popular vote in a state with three electoral votes

For example, a candidate receiving 58% of the popular vote would get two electoral votes under the whole-number proportional approach.

Table 4.3 shows the consequences of the whole-number proportional approach in the eight jurisdictions with three electoral votes in the 2000 presidential election.

Table 4.3 2000 ELECTION UNDER THE WHOLE-NUMBER PROPORTIONAL APPROACH IN JURISDICTIONS WITH THREE ELECTORAL VOTES

STATE	GORE VOTE	GORE EV UNDER WTA	BUSH EV UNDER WTA	GORE EV UNDER WNP	BUSH EV UNDER WNP	BREAKPOINT JUST BELOW GORE VOTE	BREAKPOINT JUST ABOVE GORE VOTE	CHANGE NEEDED TO GAIN OR LOSE 1 ELECTORAL VOTE UNDER WNP
AK	32.06%	0	3	1	2	16.67%	50.00%	-15.39%
DE	56.74%	3	0	2	1	50.00%	83.33%	-6.74%
DC	90.49%	3	0	3	0	83.33%	100.00%	-7.16%
MT	36.34%	0	3	1	2	16.67%	50.00%	+13.66%
ND	35.27%	0	3	1	2	16.67%	50.00%	+14.18%
SD	38.39%	0	3	1	2	16.67%	50.00%	+11.61%
VT	55.44%	3	0	2	1	50.00%	83.33%	-5.44%
WY	29.02%	0	3	1	2	16.67%	50.00%	-12.35%
Total		**9**	**15**	**12**	**12**			

Column 2 of table 4.3 shows Al Gore's percentage share of the two-party presidential vote for the 2000 presidential election for the eight jurisdictions with three electoral votes.

Columns 3 and 4 present the respective number of electoral votes (abbreviated "EV" in the table) that Al Gore and George W. Bush received under the existing statewide winner-take-all system (abbreviated "WTA" in the table) in the 2000 presidential election.

Columns 5 and 6 show the respective number of electoral votes that Gore and Bush would have received if the whole-number proportional approach (abbreviated "WNP") had been in effect for the 2000 presidential election.

Column 7 of table 4.3 shows the breakpoint (taken from table 4.2) that is just below the percentage that Gore actually received in the 2000 presidential election.

Column 8 shows the breakpoint that is just above the percentage that Gore actually received in the 2000 presidential election.

Column 9 of table 4.3 shows the percentage change in popular votes that Gore would have needed to change his electoral vote count in the state. That is, column 9 shows the difference between the percentage of the vote that Gore actually received (column 2) and the *nearer* of the two breakpoints in columns 7 and 8. The percentage in column 9 is the most important number in understanding how the whole-number proportional approach would work in practice in a particular state. It shows whether it is likely for a candidate to gain or lose one electoral vote in the state. Unless this percentage is reasonably small, it will prove very difficult for a candidate to gain or lose one electoral vote in that state in a non-landslide election. In other words, unless this percentage is small, candidates will simply write the state off (just as they now write states off under the statewide winner-take-all system).

In column 9 of table 4.3, an entry with a positive sign, such as +11.61% for South Dakota, means that if Gore had received an additional 11.61% share of the popular vote (i.e., 11.61% added to the 38.39% share of the popular vote that he actually received in South Dakota), he would have gained one electoral vote under the whole-number proportional approach. The reason why Gore would have gained one electoral vote is that he would have risen above the breakpoint of 50.00%—the breakpoint between one and two electoral votes in a state with three electoral votes. Gore would have received one fewer electoral vote (i.e., no electoral votes) in South Dakota under the whole-number proportional approach if his share of the popular vote had dropped below 16.67% (the breakpoint between one and zero electoral votes). This would occur by losing a 21.72% share of the popular vote (i.e., 21.72% subtracted from the 38.39%). Column 9 contains an entry of "+11.61%" because the breakpoint at 50.00% is closer to Gore's actual popular vote (38.39%) than the breakpoint at 16.67%.

Figure 4.2 presents, along a horizontal line, Gore's percentage share (38.39%) of the two-party popular vote in South Dakota in the 2000

Figure 4.2 2000 presidential vote in South Dakota (with the Democrat receiving 38% of the popular vote)

presidential election. As in figure 4.1, the figure contains tick marks along the horizontal line representing the breakpoints of 16.67%, 50.00%, and 83.33% applicable to states with three electoral votes under the whole-number proportional approach. The small numbers (0, 1, 2, or 3) immediately under the horizontal line show the number of electoral votes that a candidate would receive under the whole-number proportional approach by winning a particular share of the popular vote. The figure shows that Gore's vote share in South Dakota was not close to the 16.67% or 50.00% breakpoints. Because Gore's vote share was so distant from these breakpoints, it is unlikely that a Democratic presidential candidate could gain or lose even a single electoral vote in South Dakota under the whole-number proportional approach in a non-landslide election. In terms of practical politics, figure 4.2 shows that South Dakota would be written off by both the Democrats and Republicans because there would be no realistic possibility that either party could win or lose an electoral vote under the whole-number proportional approach in that state.

An entry with a negative sign in column 9 of table 4.3, such as -7.16% for the District of Columbia, means that if Gore's share of the popular votes had been 7.16% less than he actually received in the District of Columbia (that is, 7.16% subtracted from the 90.49%), he would have lost one electoral vote under the whole-number proportional approach. The reason why Gore would have lost one electoral vote is that he would have fallen below the breakpoint of 83.33%—the boundary between two and three electoral votes in the District of Columbia.

Table 4.3 shows the division of electoral votes for the eight jurisdictions with three electoral votes in the 2000 presidential election. The division was 9–15 under the existing statewide winner-take-all system (columns 4 and 5) and would be 12–12 under the whole-number proportional approach (columns 6 and 7).

Overall, table 4.3 shows that the effect of the whole-number proportional approach for awarding electoral votes in the states with three electoral votes is generally to convert the existing statewide winner-take-all system (yielding either three or zero electoral votes to each presidential slate) into a "statewide winner-take-one" system. Indeed, the discussion below will establish, for states of all sizes, that the whole-number proportional approach is, as a practical matter, a "statewide winner-take-one" system (except that two electoral votes might occasionally be in play in California).

Under the existing statewide winner-take-all system, Gore carried three of the eight jurisdictions with three electoral votes and, therefore, received nine of the 24 available electoral votes (column 3 of table 4.3). George W. Bush carried five of the eight jurisdictions and, therefore, received 15 of the 24 (column 4). Under the whole-number proportional approach, the 24 electoral votes available in these eight jurisdictions would have divided 12–12 (columns 5 and 6).

None of the eight jurisdictions with three electoral votes is politically competitive under the existing statewide winner-take-all system. Accordingly, none received any significant attention from any presidential campaign in 2000. Under the whole-number proportional approach, all eight jurisdictions would remain politically irrelevant. The reason for their non-competitiveness can be seen from the percentages in column 9 of table 4.3, namely -15.39%, -6.74%, -7.16%, +13.66%, +14.18%, +11.61%, -5.44%, and -12.35%. These percentages (averaging 10.8%) are so large that it is unlikely that a presidential slate could gain or lose even a single electoral vote in a non-landslide election in any of these eight jurisdictions under the whole-number proportional approach.

Figure 4.3 summarizes the information in table 4.3. The figure presents, along a horizontal line, Gore's percentage share of the two-party popular vote in the 2000 presidential election for the eight jurisdictions with three electoral votes (obtained from column 2 of table 4.3). As in figure 4.1, the figure contains tick marks along the horizontal line at 16.67%, 50.00%, and 83.33% representing the breakpoints applicable to jurisdictions with three electoral votes under the whole-number proportional approach. The small numbers (0, 1, 2, or 3) immediately under the horizontal line show the number of electoral votes that a candidate would receive under the whole-number proportional approach by winning a particular share of the popular vote. Figure 4.3 shows graphically that Gore's share of the vote is not close to 50.00% in any of the eight jurisdictions. Thus, none of the eight is competitive under the existing statewide winner-take-all system. The figure also shows that Gore's vote

Figure 4.3 2000 presidential vote in jurisdictions with three electoral votes

share is not close to any of the three breakpoints (16.67%, 50.00%, and 83.33%).

4.1.2 STATES WITH FOUR ELECTORAL VOTES

There were six states with four electoral votes in the 2000 presidential election—Hawaii, Idaho, Maine, Nevada, New Hampshire, and Rhode Island.

For the states with four electoral votes, one electoral vote corresponds to a 25.0% share of the state's popular vote under the whole-number proportional approach.

Table 4.4 shows the number of electoral votes that a presidential slate would receive for various ranges of percentages of the popular vote in the states with four electoral votes. Column 3 shows the breakpoints that are applicable to states with four electoral votes.

Table 4.6 is constructed in the same manner as table 4.2. The general rule for constructing this table (and others in the section) is that if x is the number of electoral votes,

- $\frac{1}{2x}$ is the breakpoint between 0 and 1 electoral vote (0.1250 when x is 4);
- $\frac{1}{2x}+\frac{1}{x}$ is the breakpoint between 1 and 2 electoral votes (0.3750 when x is 4);
- $\frac{1}{2x}+\frac{2}{x}$ is the breakpoint between 2 and 3 electoral votes (0.6250 when x is 4); and
- $\frac{1}{2x}+\frac{3}{x}$ is the breakpoint between 3 and 4 electoral votes (0.8750 when x is 4).

Thus, the breakpoints are 12.50%, 37.50%, 62.50%, and 87.50% for states with four electoral votes.

Table 4.4 TABLE OF BREAKPOINTS FOR STATES WITH FOUR ELECTORAL VOTES

PERCENT OF POPULAR VOTE	NUMBER OF ELECTORAL VOTES	BREAKPOINT
0.00% to 12.50%	0	12.50%
12.51% to 37.50%	1	37.50%
37.51 to 62.50%	2	62.50%
62.51% to 87.50%	3	87.50%
87.51% to 100.00%	4	NA

In table 4.4, there is no breakpoint at 50.00% for the states with four electoral votes under the whole-number proportional approach. In fact, this observation is true for every state with an even number of electoral votes under the whole-number proportional approach. Thus, it no longer would matter which presidential slate carries a state with an even number of electoral votes. The winner of the state would get no particular reward for carrying a state. This characteristic contrasts with the situation in the states with an odd number of electoral votes (where carrying the state would still matter). In other words, the whole-number proportional approach operates in a manner that is politically different in states with an even number of electoral votes from the manner it does in states with an odd number of electoral votes.

Table 4.5 is constructed in the same manner of table 4.3 and shows the consequences of the whole-number proportional approach in the six states with four electoral votes in the 2000 presidential election.

Table 4.5 2000 ELECTION UNDER THE WHOLE-NUMBER PROPORTIONAL APPROACH IN STATES WITH FOUR ELECTORAL VOTES

STATE	GORE VOTE	GORE EV UNDER WTA	BUSH EV UNDER WTA	GORE EV UNDER WNP	BUSH EV UNDER WNP	BREAKPOINT JUST BELOW GORE VOTE	BREAKPOINT JUST ABOVE GORE VOTE	CHANGE NEEDED TO GAIN OR LOSE 1 ELECTORAL VOTE UNDER WNP
HI	59.83%	4	0	2	2	37.50%	62.50%	+2.67%
ID	29.15%	0	4	1	3	12.50%	37.50%	+8.35%
ME	52.75%	4	0	2	2	37.50%	62.50%	+9.75%
NV	48.14%	0	4	2	2	37.50%	62.50%	-10.64%
NH	49.33%	0	4	2	2	37.50%	62.50%	-11.83%
RI	65.65%	4	0	3	1	62.50%	87.50%	-3.15%
Total		**12**	**12**	**12**	**12**			

Table 4.5 shows the division of electoral votes for the six states with four electoral votes in the 2000 presidential election. The division was 12–12 under the existing statewide winner-take-all system (columns 4 and 5) and would remain at 12–12 under the whole-number proportional approach (columns 6 and 7).

Despite not affecting the overall 12–12 allocation of electoral votes between the presidential candidates, the whole-number proportional approach has a dramatic effect on the particular states within this group of states in terms of their competitiveness.

Figure 4.4 presents, along a horizontal line, Gore's percentage share of the popular vote in the 2000 presidential election for the six states with four electoral votes (from column 2 of table 4.5). The figure contains tick marks along the horizontal line at 12.50%, 37.50%, 62.50%, and 87.50% representing the breakpoints (from table 4.4) that are applicable to states with four electoral votes under the whole-number proportional approach. The small numbers between zero and four immediately under the horizontal line show the number of electoral votes that a candidate would receive under the whole-number proportional approach by winning a particular share of the popular vote.

Figure 4.4 2000 presidential vote in states with four electoral votes

New Hampshire (where Gore received 49.33% of the popular vote) and Nevada (where Gore received 48.14%) were competitive under the existing statewide winner-take-all system. However, both New Hampshire and Nevada would become non-competitive under the whole-number proportional approach because there is no breakpoint at 50% for states with an even number of electoral votes. In states with four electoral votes, a candidate gets two electoral votes for receiving anywhere between 37.50% and 62.50% of the popular vote. The Democratic vote shares (49.33% and 48.14%) are almost in the middle of the band between 37.50% and 62.50%. Thus, in anything other than a landslide election, both the Democrats and Republicans would be virtually certain to win two electoral votes each in New Hampshire and Nevada. In New Hampshire, for example, it would take a downswing of 11.83% in the share of the Democratic vote (from 49.33%) for the Democratic candidate to lose one electoral vote. It would take an upswing of 13.19% by the Democrat to gain one electoral vote in New Hampshire. Neither is likely to happen in an ordinary election.

Similarly, Maine (where Gore received 52.75% of the popular vote) becomes distinctly non-competitive under the whole-number proportional approach because a presidential candidate gets two electoral votes for receiving anywhere between 37.50% and 62.50% of the popular vote. The Democratic vote in Maine (52.75%) is far from either 37.50% or 62.50%.

As will be seen in the sections below relating to other states with an even number of electoral votes, the whole-number proportional approach frequently converts current battleground states into non-competitive states.

On the other hand, Hawaii (which is non-competitive under the statewide winner-take-all system) becomes somewhat competitive under the whole-number proportional approach. In Hawaii, a change of +2.67% would result in a gain for the Democrats of one electoral vote.

Thus, the overall effect of the whole-number proportional approach in terms of competitiveness is to make New Hampshire, Nevada, and Maine non-competitive and to make Hawaii borderline competitive.

4.1.3 STATES WITH FIVE ELECTORAL VOTES

There were four states with five electoral votes in the 2000 presidential election—Nebraska, New Mexico, Utah, and West Virginia. For such states, one electoral vote corresponds to a 20% share of the state's popular vote under the whole-number proportional approach.

Table 4.6 shows the number of electoral votes that a presidential slate would receive for various ranges of percentages of the popular vote in the states with five electoral votes.

Table 4.6 TABLE OF BREAKPOINTS FOR STATES WITH FIVE ELECTORAL VOTES

PERCENT OF POPULAR VOTE	NUMBER OF ELECTORAL VOTES	BREAKPOINT
0.00% to 10.00%	0	10.00%
10.01 to 30.00%	1	30.00%
30.01% to 50.00%	2	50.00%
50.01% to 70.00%	3	70.00%
70.01% to 90.00%	4	90.00%
90.01% to 100.00%	5	NA

Table 4.7 shows the consequences of the whole-number proportional approach in the four states with five electoral votes in the 2000 presidential election.

Gore received five electoral votes in 2000 in the four states with five electoral votes but would have received eight under the whole-number proportional approach.

Figure 4.5 presents, along a horizontal line, Gore's percentage share (column 2 of table 4.7) of the popular vote in the 2000 presidential election for the four states with five electoral votes. The figure contains tick

Table 4.7 2000 ELECTION UNDER THE WHOLE-NUMBER PROPORTIONAL APPROACH IN STATES WITH FIVE ELECTORAL VOTES

STATE	GORE VOTE	GORE EV UNDER WTA	BUSH EV UNDER WTA	GORE EV UNDER WNP	BUSH EV UNDER WNP	BREAKPOINT JUST BELOW GORE VOTE	BREAKPOINT JUST ABOVE GORE VOTE	CHANGE NEEDED TO GAIN OR LOSE 1 ELECTORAL VOTE UNDER WNP
HI	59.83%	4	0	2	2	37.50%	62.50%	+2.67%
NB	34.82%	0	5	2	3	30.00%	50.00%	-4.82%
NM	50.03%	5	0	3	2	50.00%	70.00%	-0.03%
UT	28.27%	0	5	1	4	10.00%	30.00%	+1.73%
WV	46.76%	0	5	2	3	30.00%	50.00%	+3.24%
Total		**5**	**15**	**8**	**12**			

Figure 4.5 2000 presidential vote in states with five electoral votes

marks along the horizontal line at 10%, 30%, 50%, 70%, and 90% representing the breakpoints that are applicable to states with five electoral votes (from table 4.6). The small numbers from zero to five immediately under the horizontal line show the number of electoral votes that a candidate would receive under the whole-number proportional approach by winning a particular share of the popular vote.

As a general rule, states with an odd number of electoral votes always have a breakpoint at 50%. Thus, states that have an odd number of electoral votes and are competitive under the existing statewide winner-take-all system will remain competitive under the whole-number proportional approach. For instance, New Mexico is very competitive under the existing statewide winner-take-all system and would remain so under the whole-number proportional approach.

Utah is an example of a state that is non-competitive under the existing statewide winner-take-all system but that becomes competitive under the whole-number proportional approach. In a state with a lopsided partisan balance, the breakpoint at 30.00% can become politically important under the whole-number proportional approach. Specifically, Gore could have gone from one to two electoral votes by increasing his popular vote by 1.73% from 28.27% to 30.00%. This is an example of the phenomenon of a non-competitive state becoming a battleground state because of a breakpoint other than 50.00%.

4.1.4 STATES WITH SIX ELECTORAL VOTES

Arkansas and Kansas each had six electoral votes in the 2000 presidential election. For these states, one electoral vote corresponds to a 16.67% share of the state's popular vote under the whole-number proportional approach. Table 4.8 shows the number of electoral votes that a presidential slate would receive in states with six electoral votes for various ranges of percentages of the popular vote.

Table 4.8 TABLE OF BREAKPOINTS FOR STATES WITH SIX ELECTORAL VOTES

PERCENT OF POPULAR VOTE	NUMBER OF ELECTORAL VOTES	BREAKPOINT
0.00% to 8.33%	0	8.33%
8.34% to 25.00%	1	25.00%
25.01% to 41.66%	2	41.66%
41.67% to 58.33%	3	58.33%
58.34% to 75.00%	4	75.00%
75.00% to 91.677%	5	91.66%
91.67% to 100.00%	6	NA

Table 4.9 shows the consequences of the whole-number proportional approach in the two states with six electoral votes in the 2000 presidential election.

Table 4.9 2000 ELECTION UNDER THE WHOLE-NUMBER PROPORTIONAL APPROACH IN STATES WITH SIX ELECTORAL VOTES

STATE	GORE VOTE	GORE EV UNDER WTA	BUSH EV UNDER WTA	GORE EV UNDER WNP	BUSH EV UNDER WNP	BREAKPOINT JUST BELOW GORE VOTE	BREAKPOINT JUST ABOVE GORE VOTE	CHANGE NEEDED TO GAIN OR LOSE 1 ELECTORAL VOTE UNDER WNP
AR	47.20%	0	6	3	3	41.66%	58.33%	-5.54%
KS	39.08%	0	6	2	4	25.00%	41.66%	+2.58%
Total		**0**	**12**	**5**	**7**			

Gore received no electoral votes in 2000 in the two states with six electoral votes, but he would have received five under the whole-number proportional approach.

Figure 4.6 presents, along a horizontal line, Gore's percentage share of the popular vote in the 2000 presidential election for the two states with six electoral votes.

Figure 4.6 2000 presidential vote in states with six electoral votes

Arkansas is borderline competitive under the existing statewide winner-take-all system (requiring a change of 2.80% in the popular vote to switch its six electoral votes). The whole-number proportional approach would make Arkansas considerably less competitive because a change of 5.54% in the popular vote would be necessary to affect one electoral vote there. Meanwhile, Kansas (which is non-competitive under the existing statewide winner-take-all system) would become somewhat more competitive under the whole-number proportional approach.

4.1.5 STATES WITH SEVEN ELECTORAL VOTES

Iowa, Mississippi, and Oregon each had seven electoral votes in the 2000 presidential election. For states with seven electoral votes, one electoral vote corresponds to a 14.29% share of the state's popular vote under the whole-number proportional approach. Table 4.10 shows the number of electoral votes that a presidential slate would receive in states with seven electoral votes for various ranges of percentages of the popular vote.

Table 4.10 TABLE OF BREAKPOINTS FOR STATES WITH SEVEN ELECTORAL VOTES

PERCENT OF POPULAR VOTE	NUMBER OF ELECTORAL VOTES	BREAKPOINT
0.00% to 7.14%	0	7.14%
7.15% to 21.43%	1	21.43%
21.44% to 35.71%	2	35.71%
35.72% to 50.00 %	3	50.00%
50.01% to 64.28%	4	64.28%
64.29% to 78.57%	5	78.57%
78.58% to 92.86%	6	92.86%
92.87% to 100.00%	7	NA

Table 4.11 shows the consequences of the whole-number proportional approach in the three states with seven electoral votes.

Table 4.11 2000 ELECTION UNDER THE WHOLE-NUMBER PROPORTIONAL APPROACH IN STATES WITH SEVEN ELECTORAL VOTES

STATE	GORE VOTE	GORE EV UNDER WTA	BUSH EV UNDER WTA	GORE EV UNDER WNP	BUSH EV UNDER WNP	BREAKPOINT JUST BELOW GORE VOTE	BREAKPOINT JUST ABOVE GORE VOTE	CHANGE NEEDED TO GAIN OR LOSE 1 ELECTORAL VOTE UNDER WNP
IA	50.16%	7	0	4	3	50.00%	64.28%	-0.16%
MS	41.39%	0	7	3	4	35.71%	50.00%	-5.68%
OR	50.24%	7	0	4	3	50.00%	64.28%	-0.24%
Total		**14**	**7**	**11**	**10**			

Gore received 14 electoral votes in 2000 in the three states with seven electoral votes, but he would have received 11 under the whole-number proportional approach.

Figure 4.7 presents, along a horizontal line, Gore's percentage share of the popular vote in the 2000 presidential election for the two states with seven electoral votes.

Figure 4.7 2000 presidential vote in states with seven electoral votes

Iowa and Oregon are competitive under the existing statewide winner-take-all system. They would remain so under the whole-number proportional approach because Gore's popular vote in those states was near the breakpoint of 50.00%. Mississippi, however, would have been noncompetitive under both systems.

4.1.6 STATES WITH EIGHT ELECTORAL VOTES

Arizona, Colorado, Connecticut, Kentucky, Oklahoma, and South Carolina each had eight electoral votes in the 2000 presidential election. For those states, one electoral vote corresponds to a 12.5% share of the state's popular vote under the whole-number proportional approach.

Table 4.12 shows the number of electoral votes that a presidential slate would receive in states with eight electoral votes for various ranges of percentages of popular votes.

Table 4.12 TABLE OF BREAKPOINTS FOR STATES WITH EIGHT ELECTORAL VOTES

PERCENT OF POPULAR VOTE	NUMBER OF ELECTORAL VOTES	BREAKPOINT
0.00% to 6.25%	0	6.25%
6.26% to 18.75%	1	18.75%
18.76% to 31.25%	2	31.25%
31.26% to 43.75%	3	43.75%
43.76% to 56.25%	4	56.25%
56.26% to 68,75%	5	68.75%
68.76% to 81.25%	6	81.25%
81.26% to 93.75%	7	93.75%
92.9% to 100.0%	8	NA

Table 4.13 shows the consequences of the whole-number proportional approach in the six states with eight electoral votes in the 2000 presidential election.

Table 4.13 2000 ELECTION UNDER THE WHOLE-NUMBER PROPORTIONAL APPROACH IN STATES WITH EIGHT ELECTORAL VOTES

STATE	GORE VOTE	GORE EV UNDER WTA	BUSH EV UNDER WTA	GORE EV UNDER WNP	BUSH EV UNDER WNP	BREAKPOINT JUST BELOW GORE VOTE	BREAKPOINT JUST ABOVE GORE VOTE	CHANGE NEEDED TO GAIN OR LOSE 1 ELECTORAL VOTE UNDER WNP
AZ	46.72%	0	8	4	4	43.75%	56.25%	-2.97%
CO	45.51%	0	8	4	4	43.75%	56.25%	-1.76%
CT	59.26%	8	0	5	3	56.25%	68.75%	-3.01%
KY	42.27%	0	8	3	5	31.25%	43.75%	+1.48%
OK	38.92%	0	8	3	5	31.25%	43.75%	+4.83%
SC	41.85%	0	8	3	5	31.25%	43.75%	+1.90%
Total		8	40	22	26			

Among these six states, Gore carried only Connecticut in 2000. His popular vote was in the 40% range in the other five states of this group. Gore, therefore, received only eight electoral votes out of the 48 available from these six states. He would have received 22 under the whole-number proportional approach.

Figure 4.8 presents, along a horizontal line, Gore's percentage share of the popular vote in the 2000 presidential election for the six states with eight electoral votes.

Figure 4.8 2000 presidential vote in states with eight electoral votes

Only Arizona was even border-line competitive under the existing statewide winner-take-all system in the six states with eight electoral votes. Colorado, Kentucky, and South Carolina become competitive under the whole-number proportional approach.

4.1.7 STATES WITH NINE ELECTORAL VOTES

Alabama and Louisiana each had nine electoral votes in the 2000 presidential election. For these states with nine electoral votes, one electoral vote corresponds to an 11.11% share of the state's popular vote under the whole-number proportional approach.

Table 4.14 shows the consequences of the whole-number proportional approach in these states. The relevant breakpoints for this table are at 38.88% (the boundary between three and four electoral votes) and 50.00% (the boundary between four and five electoral votes).

Table 4.14 2000 ELECTION UNDER THE WHOLE-NUMBER PROPORTIONAL APPROACH IN STATES WITH NINE ELECTORAL VOTES

STATE	GORE VOTE	GORE EV UNDER WTA	BUSH EV UNDER WTA	GORE EV UNDER WNP	BUSH EV UNDER WNP	BREAKPOINT JUST BELOW GORE VOTE	BREAKPOINT JUST ABOVE GORE VOTE	CHANGE NEEDED TO GAIN OR LOSE 1 ELECTORAL VOTE UNDER WNP
AL	42.39%	0	9	4	5	38.88%	50.00%	-3.51%
LA	46.06%	0	9	4	5	38.88%	50.00%	+3.94%
Total		**0**	**18**	**8**	**10**			

Figure 4.9 presents, along a horizontal line, Gore's percentage share of the popular vote in the 2000 presidential election for the two states with nine electoral votes.

Figure 4.9 2000 presidential vote in states with nine electoral votes

4.1.8 STATES WITH 10 ELECTORAL VOTES

There were two states with 10 electoral votes in the 2000 presidential election—Maryland and Minnesota. For those states, one electoral vote corresponds to a 10% share of the state's popular vote under the whole-number proportional approach.

Table 4.15 shows the consequences of the whole-number proportional approach in these states. The relevant breakpoint for this table is at 55.00% (the boundary between five and six electoral votes).

Table 4.15 2000 ELECTION UNDER THE WHOLE-NUMBER PROPORTIONAL APPROACH IN STATES WITH 10 ELECTORAL VOTES

STATE	GORE VOTE	GORE EV UNDER WTA	BUSH EV UNDER WTA	GORE EV UNDER WNP	BUSH EV UNDER WNP	BREAKPOINT JUST BELOW GORE VOTE	BREAKPOINT JUST ABOVE GORE VOTE	CHANGE NEEDED TO GAIN OR LOSE 1 ELECTORAL VOTE UNDER WNP
MD	58.47%	10	0	6	4	55.00%	65.00%	-3.47%
MN	51.29%	10	0	5	5	45.00%	55.00%	+3.71%
Total		**20**	**0**	**11**	**9**			

Figure 4.10 presents, along a horizontal line, Gore's percentage share of the popular vote in the 2000 presidential election for the two states with 10 electoral votes.

Figure 4.10 2000 presidential vote in states with 10 electoral votes

4.1.9 STATES WITH 11 ELECTORAL VOTES

There were four states with 11 electoral votes in the 2000 presidential election—Missouri, Tennessee, Washington, and Wisconsin. For states with 11 electoral votes, one electoral vote corresponds to a 9.09% share of the state's popular vote under the whole-number proportional approach.

Table 4.16 shows the consequences of the whole-number proportional approach in these states. The relevant breakpoint for this table is at 50.00% (the boundary between five and six electoral votes).

Table 4.16 2000 ELECTION UNDER THE WHOLE-NUMBER PROPORTIONAL APPROACH IN STATES WITH 11 ELECTORAL VOTES

STATE	GORE VOTE	GORE EV UNDER WTA	BUSH EV UNDER WTA	GORE EV UNDER WNP	BUSH EV UNDER WNP	BREAKPOINT JUST BELOW GORE VOTE	BREAKPOINT JUST ABOVE GORE VOTE	CHANGE NEEDED TO GAIN OR LOSE 1 ELECTORAL VOTE UNDER WNP
MO	48.29%	0	11	5	6	40.91%	50.00%	+1.71%
TN	48.04%	0	11	5	6	40.91%	50.00%	+1.96%
WA	52.94%	11	0	6	5	50.00%	59.09%	-2.94%
WI	50.12%	11	0	6	5	50.00%	59.09%	-0.12%
Total		**22**	**22**	**22**	**22**			

Figure 4.11 presents, along a horizontal line, Gore's percentage share of the popular vote (column 2 of table 4.16) in the 2000 presidential election for the four states with 11 electoral votes.

Figure 4.11 2000 presidential vote in states with 11 electoral votes

Because Gore's percentage was reasonably close to 50.00% in all four of the states with 11 electoral votes in the 2000 presidential election (table 4.16), the whole-number proportional approach makes no difference in terms of the degree of competitiveness for these particular states.

4.1.10 STATES WITH 12 ELECTORAL VOTES

Indiana and Massachusetts each had 12 electoral votes in the 2000 presidential election. For these two states, one electoral vote corresponds to an 8.33% share of the state's popular vote under the whole-number proportional approach.

Table 4.17 shows the consequences of the whole-number proportional approach in states with 12 electoral votes. The relevant breakpoints for this table are at 45.83% (the boundary between five and six electoral votes) and 62.50% (the boundary between seven and eight electoral votes).

Table 4.17 2000 ELECTION UNDER THE WHOLE-NUMBER PROPORTIONAL APPROACH IN STATES WITH 12 ELECTORAL VOTES

STATE	GORE VOTE	GORE EV UNDER WTA	BUSH EV UNDER WTA	GORE EV UNDER WNP	BUSH EV UNDER WNP	BREAKPOINT JUST BELOW GORE VOTE	BREAKPOINT JUST ABOVE GORE VOTE	CHANGE NEEDED TO GAIN OR LOSE 1 ELECTORAL VOTE UNDER WNP
IN	42.00%	0	12	6	6	37.50%	45.83%	+3.83%
MA	64.79%	12	0	7	5	62.50%	70.83%	-2.29%
Total		**12**	**12**	**13**	**11**			

Figure 4.12 presents, along a horizontal line, Gore's percentage share of the popular vote in the 2000 presidential election for the two states with 12 electoral votes.

Figure 4.12 2000 presidential vote in states with 12 electoral votes

4.1.11 STATES WITH 13 ELECTORAL VOTES

There were two states with 13 electoral votes in the 2000 presidential election—Georgia and Virginia. For the states with 13 electoral votes, one electoral vote corresponds to a 7.69% share of the state's popular vote under the whole-number proportional approach.

Table 4.18 shows the consequences of the whole-number proportional approach in the states with 13 electoral votes. The relevant breakpoints for this table are at 42.31% (the boundary between five and six electoral votes) and 50.00% (the boundary between six and seven electoral votes).

Table 4.18 2000 ELECTION UNDER THE WHOLE-NUMBER PROPORTIONAL APPROACH IN STATES WITH 13 ELECTORAL VOTES

STATE	GORE VOTE	GORE EV UNDER WTA	BUSH EV UNDER WTA	GORE EV UNDER WNP	BUSH EV UNDER WNP	BREAKPOINT JUST BELOW GORE VOTE	BREAKPOINT JUST ABOVE GORE VOTE	CHANGE NEEDED TO GAIN OR LOSE 1 ELECTORAL VOTE UNDER WNP
GA	44.02%	0	13	6	7	42.31%	50.00%	-1.71%
VA	45.85%	0	13	6	7	42.31%	50.00%	-3.54%
Total		**0**	**26**	**12**	**14**			

Figure 4.13 presents, along a horizontal line, Gore's percentage share of the popular vote for the two states with 13 electoral votes in the 2000 presidential election.

Figure 4.13 2000 presidential vote in states with 13 electoral votes

Under the whole-number proportional approach, Gore would have received 12 of the 26 electoral votes available from these two states (compared to none under the statewide winner-take-all system).

One of Georgia's electoral votes would have been contested under the whole-number proportional approach.

4.1.12 THE 10 STATES WITH 14 OR MORE ELECTORAL VOTES

The remaining 10 states (North Carolina, New Jersey, Michigan, Ohio, Illinois, Pennsylvania, Florida, Texas, New York, and California) each had a different number of electoral votes (between 14 and 54) in the 2000 presidential election.

Table 4.19 shows the percentage share of the popular vote that corresponds to one electoral vote under the whole-number proportional approach for the 10 states with 14 or more electoral votes in the 2000 election.

Table 4.19 SHARE OF THE POPULAR VOTE CORRESPONDING TO ONE ELECTORAL VOTE FOR THE 10 LARGEST STATES

STATE	ELECTORAL VOTE	SHARE OF POPULAR VOTE CORRESPONDING TO 1 ELECTORAL VOTE
North Carolina	14	7.1%
New Jersey	15	6.7%
Michigan	18	5.6%
Ohio	21	4.8%
Illinois	22	4.5%
Pennsylvania	23	4.4%
Florida	25	4.0%
Texas	32	3.1%
New York	33	3.0%
California	54	1.9%
Total	**254**	

The breakpoints for the 10 states with 14 to 54 electoral votes were different because each of these states had a different number of electoral votes. Table 4.20 shows the consequences of the whole-number proportional approach for these 10 states for the 2000 presidential election.

Table 4.20 2000 ELECTION UNDER THE WHOLE-NUMBER PROPORTIONAL APPROACH FOR THE 10 STATES WITH 14 OR MORE ELECTORAL VOTES

STATE	GORE VOTE	GORE EV UNDER WTA	BUSH EV UNDER WTA	GORE EV UNDER WNP	BUSH EV UNDER WNP	BREAKPOINT JUST BELOW GORE VOTE	BREAKPOINT JUST ABOVE GORE VOTE	CHANGE NEEDED TO GAIN OR LOSE 1 ELECTORAL VOTE UNDER WNP
NC	43.54%	0	14	6	8	39.28%	46.42%	+2.88%
NJ	58.21%	15	0	9	6	56.66%	63.33%	-1.55%
MI	52.63%	18	0	10	8	47.22%	52.78%	+0.15%
OH	48.18%	0	21	10	11	45.23%	50.00%	+1.82%
IL	56.18%	22	0	12	10	52.27%	56.82%	+0.18%
PA	52.15%	23	0	12	11	50.00%	54.35%	-2.15%
FL	49.99%	0	25	12	13	46.00%	50.00%	+0.01%
TX	39.04%	0	32	12	20	35.94%	39.06%	+0.02%
NY	63.09%	33	0	20	13	62.12%	65.15%	-0.97%
CA	56.20%	54	0	30	24	54.63%	56.48%	+0.28%
Total		**165**	**92**	**133**	**124**			

Figure 4.14 presents, along a horizontal line, Gore's percentage share of the popular vote in the 2000 presidential election in North Carolina (14 electoral votes). As can be seen, the Democrats were within 2.88% of the breakpoint (46.42%) between getting six and seven electoral votes in North Carolina and therefore could have gained one electoral vote in North Carolina under favorable circumstances. This opportunity is, however, not symmetrical. There would have been little likelihood of the Republicans being able to reduce Gore's share of the electoral vote from six to five.

Figure 4.14 2000 presidential vote in North Carolina (14 electoral votes)

Figure 4.15 presents, along a horizontal line, Gore's percentage share of the popular vote in New Jersey (15 electoral votes) in the 2000 presidential election. As can be seen, the Democrats were within 1.55% of the breakpoint between getting nine and eight electoral votes. Thus, the Republicans could have gained one electoral vote in New Jersey under favorable circumstances. This opportunity to affect one electoral vote is not, however, symmetrical. There would have been little likelihood of the Democrats being able to increase their share of the electoral vote from nine to 10.

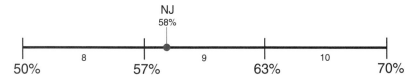

Figure 4.15 2000 presidential vote in New Jersey (15 electoral votes)

Figure 4.16 presents, along a horizontal line, Gore's percentage share of the popular vote in the 2000 presidential election in Michigan (18 electoral votes). The Democrats were within 0.15% of getting 11 (as compared to 10) electoral votes from Michigan. Neither party, however, has any realistic chance of gaining or losing as many as two electoral votes in Michigan in anything other than a landslide election.

Figure 4.16 2000 presidential vote in Michigan (18 electoral votes)

Figure 4.17 presents, along a horizontal line, Gore's percentage share of the popular vote in the 2000 presidential election in Ohio (which had 21 electoral votes in 2000). The Democrats were within 1.82% of the breakpoint between getting 10 and 11 electoral votes in Ohio and could have gained one electoral vote in the state under favorable circumstances. There would have been little likelihood, however, of the Republican's decreasing the Democrat's share of the electoral vote in Ohio from 10 to nine.

Figure 4.17 2000 presidential vote in Ohio (21 electoral votes)

Figure 4.18 presents, along a horizontal line, Gore's percentage share of the popular vote in the 2000 presidential election in Illinois (which had 22 electoral votes in 2000). The Democrats were within 0.18% of the breakpoint between getting 12 and 13 electoral votes in Illinois.

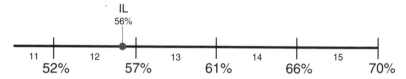

Figure 4.18 2000 presidential vote in Illinois (22 electoral votes)

Figure 4.19 presents, along a horizontal line, Gore's percentage share of the popular vote in the 2000 presidential election in Pennsylvania (23 electoral votes). The Democrats were within 2.15% of the nearest breakpoint, and the Republicans were within 2.20% of the nearest breakpoint. Thus, one electoral vote is potentially in play for both parties. Because both parties are more than 2% away from gaining or losing one electoral vote, it is entirely conceivable that Pennsylvania might be passed over in favor of states where less effort would be necessary to affect one electoral vote.

Figure 4.19 2000 presidential vote in Pennsylvania (23 electoral votes)

Figure 4.20 presents, along a horizontal line, Gore's percentage share of the popular vote in the 2000 presidential election in Florida (which had 25 electoral votes in 2000). The Democrats were within +0.01% of the breakpoint between getting 12 and 13 electoral votes in Florida.

Figure 4.20 2000 presidential vote in Florida (25 electoral votes)

Figure 4.21 presents, along a horizontal line, Gore's percentage share of the popular vote in the 2000 presidential election in Texas (32 electoral votes in 2000). The Democrats were within +0.02% of the breakpoint between getting 12 and 13 electoral votes in Texas.

Figure 4.21 2000 presidential vote in Texas (32 electoral votes)

Figure 4.22 presents, along a horizontal line, Gore's percentage share of the popular vote in the 2000 presidential election in New York (which had 33 electoral votes in 2000). The Democrats were within 0.97% of the breakpoint between getting 20 and 19 electoral votes in New York. Thus, the Republicans could possibly have gained one electoral vote in the state under favorable circumstances. The opportunity is not, however, symmetrical. It is less likely that the Democrats would have been able to increase their share of the electoral vote from 20 to 21.

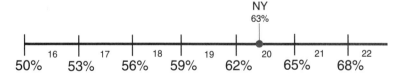

Figure 4.22 2000 presidential vote in New York (33 electoral votes)

Figure 4.23 presents, along a horizontal line, Gore's percentage share of the popular vote in California (which had 54 electoral votes in the 2000 presidential election). The Democrats were within 0.28% of getting 31 (as compared to 30) electoral votes from California. One electoral vote was in play in California for both parties. Moreover, two electoral votes might sometimes be in play in California because one electoral vote corresponds to a mere 1.85% share of the state's popular vote. For example, if the Democrats were to increase their share of the popular vote by 2.13% (0.28% plus 1.85%), they would pick up two electoral votes. That is, the whole-number proportional approach could operate as a "statewide winner-take-two" system for the Democrats in California. Note that this opportunity is not symmetric. A change of 3.43% in the popular vote would have been necessary for the Bush 2004 campaign to pick up two electoral votes in California.

Figure 4.23 2000 presidential vote in California (54 electoral votes)

In summary, table 4.20 shows that all of the 10 most populous states are competitive to some degree under the whole-number proportional approach.

In particular, the six biggest states (North Carolina, New Jersey, Illinois, Texas, New York, and California) that are spectator states under the statewide winner-take-all system become battleground states under the whole-number proportional approach. The "battle" would only be for one electoral vote ("winner-take-one") in five of these six states. In California, the battle would sometimes be for two electoral votes ("winner-take-two").

Michigan, Ohio, Pennsylvania, and Florida are battleground states under the current statewide winner-take-all system. These four states would remain competitive under the whole-number proportional approach. However, the battle would not be for 18, 21, 23, or 25 electoral votes but, instead, for only one electoral vote in each state.

4.1.13 NATIONWIDE ANALYSIS OF THE WHOLE-NUMBER PROPORTIONAL APPROACH

This section addresses two questions. The first is whether the whole-number proportional approach would, if adopted by every state, more accurately reflect the nationwide popular vote than the existing statewide winner-take-all system. The second question is whether the whole-number proportional approach would, if adopted by every state, improve the competitiveness of presidential elections on a nationwide basis.

Table 4.21 combines the information from 12 of the foregoing tables in order to show the overall consequences of the whole-number proportional approach for all 50 states and the District of Columbia for the 2000 presidential election. Table 4.21 is sorted in descending order according to the percentage change (column 9) in popular votes that Gore would have needed to change his electoral vote count by one electoral vote in each jurisdiction.

Table 4.21 shows that, if the whole-number proportional approach had been in use throughout the country in the 2000 presidential election, it would not have awarded the most electoral votes to the candidate receiving the most popular votes nationwide. Instead, the result would have been a tie of 269–269 in the electoral vote, even though Al Gore led by 537,179 popular votes across the nation.[4] That is, the whole-number proportional approach would not have accurately reflected the nationwide popular vote.

In order to analyze competitiveness, let us try to visualize how each political party might have approached the 2004 presidential election if all states had used the whole-number proportional approach.

The best starting point for planning a strategy in any election is the outcome of the previous election. Thus, under the whole-number proportional approach, the starting point for planning a strategy for the 2004 presidential election would have been the data in table 4.21 (showing both parties tied at 269 electoral votes). The central question for each party's campaign would have been focused on the way to win more than 269 electoral votes. Each party's campaign would have been aware that the whole-number proportional approach is predominantly a "statewide winner-take-one" system. Thus, the challenge to each party would be to

---

[4] If there had been a tie when the electoral votes for the 2000 presidential election were counted on January 6, 2001, the election for President would have been thrown into the House of Representatives (voting on a one-state-one-vote basis). Based on the party alignment of the newly elected House, George W. Bush would have been elected President. However, the newly elected Senate—responsible for electing the new Vice President—was equally divided after the 2000 elections. The U.S. Constitution is not entirely clear as to whether Vice President Gore (whose term of office ran until January 20, 2001) would have been entitled to vote to break the tie in the Senate in order to elect a new Vice President.

Table 4.21 2000 ELECTION UNDER THE WHOLE-NUMBER PROPORTIONAL APPROACH

STATE	GORE VOTE	GORE EV UNDER WTA	BUSH EV UNDER WTA	GORE EV UNDER WNP	BUSH EV UNDER WNP	BREAKPOINT JUST BELOW GORE VOTE	BREAKPOINT JUST ABOVE GORE VOTE	CHANGE NEEDED TO GAIN OR LOSE 1 ELECTORAL VOTE UNDER WNP
ND	35.27%	0	3	1	2	16.67%	50.00%	14.18%
MT	36.34%	0	3	1	2	16.67%	50.00%	13.66%
SD	38.39%	0	3	1	2	16.67%	50.00%	11.61%
ME	52.75%	4	0	2	2	37.50%	62.50%	9.75%
ID	29.15%	0	4	1	3	12.50%	37.50%	8.35%
OK	38.92%	0	8	3	5	31.25%	43.75%	4.83%
LA	46.06%	0	9	4	5	38.88%	50.00%	3.94%
IN	42.00%	0	12	6	6	37.50%	45.83%	3.83%
MN	51.29%	10	0	5	5	45.00%	55.00%	3.71%
WV	46.76%	0	5	2	3	30.00%	50.00%	3.24%
NC	43.54%	0	14	6	8	39.28%	46.42%	2.88%
HI	59.83%	4	0	2	2	37.50%	62.50%	2.67%
KS	39.08%	0	6	2	4	25.00%	41.66%	2.58%
TN	48.04%	0	11	5	6	40.91%	50.00%	1.96%
SC	41.85%	0	8	3	5	31.25%	43.75%	1.90%
OH	48.18%	0	21	10	11	45.23%	50.00%	1.82%
UT	28.27%	0	5	1	4	10.00%	30.00%	1.73%
MO	48.29%	0	11	5	6	40.91%	50.00%	1.71%
KY	42.27%	0	8	3	5	31.25%	43.75%	1.48%
CA	56.20%	54	0	30	24	54.63%	56.48%	0.28%
IL	56.18%	22	0	12	10	52.27%	56.82%	0.18%
MI	52.63%	18	0	10	8	47.22%	52.78%	0.15%
FL	49.99%	0	25	12	13	46.00%	50.00%	0.01%
TX	39.04%	0	32	12	20	35.94%	39.06%	-0.02%
NM	50.03%	5	0	3	2	50.00%	70.00%	-0.03%
WI	50.12%	11	0	6	5	50.00%	59.09%	-0.12%
IA	50.16%	7	0	4	3	50.00%	64.28%	-0.16%
OR	50.24%	7	0	4	3	50.00%	64.28%	-0.24%
NY	63.09%	33	0	20	13	62.12%	65.15%	-0.97%
NJ	58.21%	15	0	9	6	56.66%	63.33%	-1.55%
GA	44.02%	0	13	6	7	42.31%	50.00%	-1.71%
CO	45.51%	0	8	4	4	43.75%	56.25%	-1.76%
PA	52.15%	23	0	12	11	50.00%	54.35%	-2.15%
MA	64.79%	12	0	7	5	62.50%	70.83%	-2.29%
WA	52.94%	11	0	6	5	50.00%	59.09%	-2.94%

Table 4.21 2000 ELECTION UNDER THE WHOLE-NUMBER PROPORTIONAL APPROACH (cont.)

STATE	GORE VOTE	GORE EV UNDER WTA	BUSH EV UNDER WTA	GORE EV UNDER WNP	BUSH EV UNDER WNP	BREAKPOINT JUST BELOW GORE VOTE	BREAKPOINT JUST ABOVE GORE VOTE	CHANGE NEEDED TO GAIN OR LOSE 1 ELECTORAL VOTE UNDER WNP
AZ	46.72%	0	8	4	4	43.75%	56.25%	-2.97%
CT	59.26%	8	0	5	3	56.25%	68.75%	-3.01%
RI	65.65%	4	0	3	1	62.50%	87.50%	-3.15%
MD	58.47%	10	0	6	4	55.00%	65.00%	-3.47%
AL	42.39%	0	9	4	5	38.88%	50.00%	-3.51%
VA	45.85%	0	13	6	7	42.31%	50.00%	-3.54%
NB	34.82%	0	5	2	3	30.00%	50.00%	-4.82%
VT	55.44%	3	0	2	1	50.00%	83.33%	-5.44%
AR	47.20%	0	6	3	3	41.66%	58.33%	-5.54%
MS	41.39%	0	7	3	4	35.71%	50.00%	-5.68%
DE	56.74%	3	0	2	1	50.00%	83.33%	-6.74%
DC	90.49%	3	0	3	0	83.33%	100.00%	-7.16%
NV	48.14%	0	4	2	2	37.50%	62.50%	-10.64%
NH	49.33%	0	4	2	2	37.50%	62.50%	-11.83%
WY	29.02%	0	3	1	2	16.67%	50.00%	-12.35%
AK	32.06%	0	3	1	2	16.67%	50.00%	-15.39%
Total		**267**	**271**	**269**	**269**			

devise a strategy for accumulating additional electoral votes by targeting particular states.

Landslides take care of themselves. Thus, the planning process for a political campaign inevitably concentrates on what might happen if the upcoming election turns out to be close. Planners for the Bush 2004 campaign would have carefully considered what might happen if they were to improve their nationwide popular vote by various reasonably attainable percentages—1%, 2%, or 3%.

We *now* know that the Republicans increased their share of the two-party popular presidential vote by 1.98% (from 49.72% in 2000 to 51.71% in 2004). Hindsight of this sort is not, however, required for us to know that, at the beginning of the 2004 presidential campaign, it was imperative for each campaign to consider small percentage swings such as 1%, 2%, or 3%.

Referring to table 4.21, those involved in planning the Bush 2004 campaign would have immediately identified the nine battleground states where a gain of 2% or less in the popular vote could yield them one additional electoral vote under the whole-number proportional approach. These nine states (shown in table 4.22 and in figure 4.24) would have been the highest-priority "upside" battleground states for Bush in 2004.

Table 4.22 shows that the Bush 2004 campaign could have picked up nine electoral votes in the following way under the whole-number proportional approach:

- **Lowest-Hanging Fruit:** Pick up one electoral vote in Texas by reducing the Democratic share of the vote there by a mere 0.02% (from 39.04% to the breakpoint of 39.02%).

- **Easy Pickings:** Pick up one electoral vote in each of four states by reducing the Democratic share of the vote by 0.03% in New Mexico, 0.16% in Iowa, 0.12% in Wisconsin, and 0.24% in Oregon.

- **1% Neighborhood:** Pick up one electoral vote in New York by reducing the Democratic share of the vote by 0.97% (from 63.09% to the breakpoint of 62.12%).

- **2% Neighborhood:** Pick up one electoral vote by reducing the Democratic share of the vote by 1.55% in New Jersey, 1.71% in Georgia and 1.76% in Colorado.

Similarly, those involved in planning the Kerry 2004 campaign under the whole-number proportional approach would surely have considered the consequences of improving upon Gore's popular vote in 2000 by various attainable small percentages. Referring to table 4.21, planners for the Kerry 2004 campaign surely would have quickly identified the 10 battleground states where a gain of 2% or less could yield them one additional electoral vote. These 10 states (shown in table 4.23 and in figure 4.25) would have been the highest-priority "upside" battleground states for Kerry in 2004.

Table 4.23 shows that the Kerry 2004 campaign could have picked up 10 electoral votes in the following way under the whole-number proportional approach:

- **Lowest-Hanging Fruit:** Pick up one electoral vote in Florida by increasing the Democratic share of the vote in Florida by 0.01% (from 49.99% to the breakpoint of 50.00%).

- **Easy Pickings:** Pick up one electoral vote by increasing the Democratic share of the vote by 0.15% in Michigan, 0.18% in Illinois, and 0.28% in California.

Table 4.22 THE NINE "UPSIDE" BATTLEGROUND STATES FOR BUSH IN 2004 UNDER THE WHOLE-NUMBER PROPORTIONAL APPROACH

STATE	GORE VOTE	GORE EV UNDER WTA	BUSH EV UNDER WTA	GORE EV UNDER WNP	BUSH EV UNDER WNP	BREAKPOINT JUST BELOW GORE VOTE	BREAKPOINT JUST ABOVE GORE VOTE	CHANGE NEEDED TO GAIN OR LOSE 1 ELECTORAL VOTE UNDER WNP
TX	39.04%	0	32	12	20	35.94%	39.06%	-0.02%
NM	50.03%	5	0	3	2	50.00%	70.00%	-0.03%
WI	50.12%	11	0	6	5	50.00%	59.09%	-0.12%
IA	50.16%	7	0	4	3	50.00%	64.28%	-0.16%
OR	50.24%	7	0	4	3	50.00%	64.28%	-0.24%
NY	63.09%	33	0	20	13	62.12%	65.15%	-0.97%
NJ	58.21%	15	0	9	6	56.66%	63.33%	-1.55%
GA	44.02%	0	13	6	7	42.31%	50.00%	-1.71%
CO	45.51%	0	8	4	4	43.75%	56.25%	-1.76%
Total		**78**	**53**	**68**	**63**			

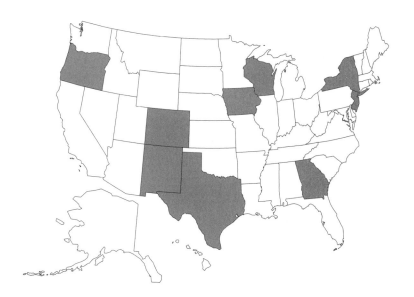

Figure 4.24 The nine "upside" battleground states for Bush in 2004 under the whole-number proportional approach

Table 4.23 THE 10 "UPSIDE" BATTLEGROUND STATES FOR KERRY IN 2004 UNDER THE WHOLE-NUMBER PROPORTIONAL APPROACH

STATE	GORE VOTE	GORE EV UNDER WTA	BUSH EV UNDER WTA	GORE EV UNDER WNP	BUSH EV UNDER WNP	BREAKPOINT JUST BELOW GORE VOTE	BREAKPOINT JUST ABOVE GORE VOTE	CHANGE NEEDED TO GAIN OR LOSE 1 ELECTORAL VOTE UNDER WNP
TN	48.04%	0	11	5	6	40.91%	50.00%	1.96%
SC	41.85%	0	8	3	5	31.25%	43.75%	1.90%
OH	48.18%	0	21	10	11	45.23%	50.00%	1.82%
UT	28.27%	0	5	1	4	10.00%	30.00%	1.73%
MO	48.29%	0	11	5	6	40.91%	50.00%	1.71%
KY	42.27%	0	8	3	5	31.25%	43.75%	1.48%
CA	56.20%	54	0	30	24	54.63%	56.48%	0.28%
IL	56.18%	22	0	12	10	52.27%	56.82%	0.18%
MI	52.63%	18	0	10	8	47.22%	52.78%	0.15%
FL	49.99%	0	25	12	13	46.00%	50.00%	0.01%
Total		94	89	91	92			

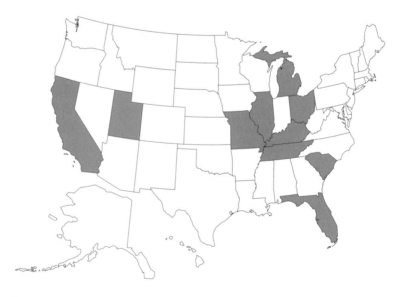

Figure 4.25 The 10 "upside" battleground states for Kerry in 2004 under the whole-number proportional approach

- **1% Neighborhood:** Pick up one electoral vote in Kentucky by increasing the Democratic share of the vote by 1.48% (from 42.27% to the breakpoint of 43.75%).
- **2% Neighborhood:** Pick up one electoral vote by increasing the Democratic share of the vote by 1.71% in Missouri, 1.73% in Utah, 1.82% in Ohio, 1.90% in South Carolina, and 1.96% in Tennessee.

Of course, the 10 "upside" states for the Kerry 2004 campaign would have been the same states where the Bush 2004 campaign would have had to play defense under the whole-number proportional approach. Conversely, the nine "upside" states for the Bush 2004 campaign are the states where Kerry would have been on the defensive.

Of course, those planning a campaign would have, in practice, added or deleted certain states from the above list of 19 battleground states for numerous reasons, including the following:

First, planners of both campaigns would have considered adding or deleting a state with various unusual local political factors, such as a noticeable shift in partisan alignment since the last election, significant demographic changes since the last election, the localized impact of a controversial existing or planned government policy, the effect of an unusually popular or unpopular state administration, the home states of the candidates, or other political considerations.

Second, those involved in planning the Bush 2004 campaign would have given some consideration to the three states where they could have picked up one electoral vote each by reducing the Democratic share of the popular vote by between 2% and 3% (e.g., 2.29% in Massachusetts, 2.94% in Washington, and 2.97% in Arizona). Similarly, planners for the Kerry 2004 campaign would have given some consideration to the four states where they could have picked up one electoral vote each by increasing the Democratic share of the popular vote by between 2% and 3% (e.g., 2.15% in Pennsylvania, 2.29% in Massachusetts, 2.94% in Washington, and 2.97% in Arizona). Both campaigns would have glanced briefly at states where they might conceivably pick up an electoral vote by increasing their popular vote by 4% or more.

Third, California is the one exception to the statement that, except in landslide elections, the whole-number proportional approach is a "winner-take-one" system. In California, one electoral vote corresponds to a

1.85% share of the state's popular vote. If, for example, the 2004 Kerry campaign could have increased the Democratic share of the vote by 2.13% (0.28% plus 1.85%), it would have picked up two electoral votes in California. It would have required a change of 3.43% in the popular vote for the Bush 2004 campaign to have gained two electoral votes in California. In states other than California, the share of popular vote corresponding to one electoral vote is considerably larger than 1.85%. For example, for the two next largest states (New York and Texas), the shares of the popular vote corresponding to one electoral vote were 3.0% and 3.1%, respectively. For the fourth largest state (Florida), the percentage was 4.0%. As mentioned earlier, 41 of the 51 jurisdictions that are entitled to appoint presidential electors had 13 or fewer electoral votes in 2000. The share of the popular vote corresponding to one electoral vote is 7.69% for states with 13 electoral votes. The share of the popular vote corresponding to one electoral vote is 33.33% for states with three electoral votes.

Notwithstanding the above caveats, the political reality is that campaign strategies in ordinary elections are based on trying to change a reasonably achievable small percentage of the votes—1%, 2%, or 3%. The bottom line is that the number of battleground states under the whole-number proportional approach would approximate the list of 19 states shown in tables 4.22 and 4.23. Something like 32 states would be non-competitive.

Table 4.24 presents the 19 battleground states in 2004 (based on a 2% swing) under the whole-number proportional approach. The states in this table are sorted in order of the absolute value of the percentage change that would have been needed in order to gain or lose one electoral vote under the whole-number proportional approach.

Figure 4.26 summarizes the information in table 4.24. The figure presents, along a horizontal line, Gore's percentage share of the popular vote in the 19 battleground states listed in table 4.24.

Several observations can be made by comparing the 19 battleground states under the whole-number proportional approach listed in table 4.24 with the 19 closest states in the 2000 presidential election (table 1.3) and the 16 closest states in the 2004 presidential election (table 1.4 and figure 1.1).

First, over half of the 19 battleground states under the whole-number proportional approach in table 4.24 are different from the actual battleground states of the 2004 election. The 19 battleground states under the

Table 4.24 THE 19 BATTLEGROUND STATES IN 2004 UNDER THE WHOLE-NUMBER PROPORTIONAL APPROACH

STATE	CHANGE NEEDED TO GAIN OR LOSE 1 ELECTORAL VOTE UNDER THE WHOLE-NUMBER PROPORTIONAL APPROACH
Florida	0.01%
Texas	-0.02%
New Mexico	-0.03%
Wisconsin	-0.12%
Michigan	0.15%
Iowa	-0.16%
Illinois	0.18%
Oregon	-0.24%
California	0.28%
New York	-0.97%
Kentucky	1.48%
New Jersey	-1.55%
Missouri	1.71%
Georgia	-1.71%
Utah	1.73%
Colorado	-1.76%
Ohio	1.82%
South Carolina	1.90%
Tennessee	1.96%

Figure 4.26 The 19 battleground states in 2004 under the whole-number proportional approach

whole-number proportional approach include states such as Texas, Illinois, California, New York, Kentucky, New Jersey, Georgia, Utah, South Carolina, and Tennessee. None of these 10 states was a battleground state in the actual 2004 presidential election. Five of these newcomers are among the nation's 10 largest states (i.e., states with 14 or more electoral votes). Kentucky, Georgia, Utah, South Carolina, and Tennessee are newcomers because of the accident of the numerical breakpoints.

Second, the biggest states are more likely to be battleground states under the whole-number proportional approach (subject to a caveat below concerning the difference between vote percentages and popular votes). The reason is that the share of the popular vote corresponding to one electoral vote is smaller for large states. Eight of the 10 states with 14 or more electoral votes are among the 19 battleground states under the whole-number proportional approach (table 4.24). Moreover, Pennsylvania and North Carolina would be included on the list of battleground states if the percentage window considered by a particular campaign were widened to 3%. In contrast, six of the nation's 10 largest states (California, Texas, New York, Illinois, New Jersey, and North Carolina) are decidedly non-competitive under the current statewide winner-take-all system.

Third, five states (Florida, New Mexico, Wisconsin, Iowa, and Oregon) are battleground states under both the existing statewide winner-take-all-system and the whole-number proportional approach. These states are on the list either because the major parties received close to 50% of the vote in those states in 2000 or because these states happen to have had an odd number of electoral votes in 2000 (and hence have a breakpoint at 50.00%). On the other hand, states with an even number of electoral votes that were battlegrounds under the existing statewide winner-take-all system, such as New Hampshire, would not be battlegrounds under the whole-number proportional approach because there is no breakpoint at 50.00%.

It is, of course, difficult to predict exactly how a new system, such as the whole-number proportional approach, would actually work in practice if all the states were to adopt it for a future presidential election. For one thing, the above discussion is based on *percentages* and therefore somewhat overstates the degree of competitiveness of the larger states under the whole-number proportional approach. Almost all of the 19 or so battleground states under the whole-number proportional approach offer a campaign the possibility of winning or losing only one electoral vote. Changing the statewide percentage of the popular vote in a large state is more costly (in terms of campaigning time, advertising, and organizational efforts) than generating the same percentage change in a small state. Thus, in practice, the largest of the 19 battleground states in table 4.24 might receive less attention because they would offer far less "bang for the buck" to the campaign managers who are responsible for prudently allocating limited resources. If we were to exclude the 10 largest states (i.e., the states with 14 or more electoral votes), the actual list of battleground states under the whole-number proportional approach might consist of the following 11 states (as shown in figure 4.27):

- New Mexico,
- Iowa,
- Wisconsin,
- Oregon,
- Kentucky,
- Missouri,
- Georgia,
- Utah,
- Colorado,
- South Carolina, and
- Tennessee.

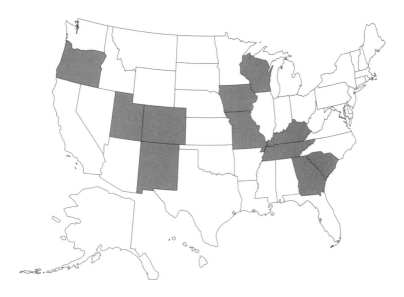

Figure 4.27 The 11 battleground states with greatest "bang for the buck" under the whole-number proportional approach

4.1.14 AMENDMENT 36 IN COLORADO IN 2004

The whole-number proportional approach was on the ballot in November 2, 2004, as a proposed amendment to the Colorado state constitution. It received 35% of the vote. There are three main reasons why the voters defeated Amendment 36 in 2004.

First, Amendment 36 was written so that it would take effect immediately and apply to the November 2004 presidential election. That is, the initiative would have applied to the very election in which the voters were deciding the initiative's fate. Many voters said that they would have approved the change for a subsequent election but that they were troubled by changing the rules of the game in the midst of a presidential campaign.

Second, Amendment 36's retroactivity provision interacted with the changing fortunes of the presidential candidates during the campaign. During the summer of 2004, Bush was expected to carry Colorado easily. Given that expectation, the political effect of Amendment 36 would have been to give four of Colorado's nine electoral votes in 2004 to the candidate who was expected to lose the state (Kerry). Part of the historical context of the 2004 presidential campaign was that Bush received only 271 votes in the Electoral College in 2000 (i.e., one more electoral vote than is necessary to win). In addition, it was widely (and correctly) predicted that the national vote in the Electoral College was likely to be very close in 2004. Therefore, Amendment 36 was perceived to have a strong possibility of affecting the outcome of the 2004 presidential election nationally. Indeed, Bush ultimately received only 16 more electoral votes than he needed in order to win in 2004. Thus, from the beginning, there was little Republican support for Amendment 36 because it was perceived to be a partisan issue. Bill Owens, Colorado's Republican Governor, made a decision to spend over a million dollars in opposition to Amendment 36. Then, as election day approached, some polls showed Kerry almost tied with Bush in Colorado. At that point, Democrats started believing that the measure could cost Kerry four electoral votes, and the proposition's remaining support evaporated.

Third, if Amendment 36 had been adopted, Colorado would have been the only state in the country dividing its electoral votes proportionally. Everyone agreed that the practical political effect of Amendment 36 would be to convert Colorado from a "winner-take-nine" state into a "winner-take-one" state. Many voters in Colorado felt that Colorado's influence would be greatly reduced if it were the only state in the nation to select its presidential electors proportionally. In his campaign against Amendment 36, Governor Owens argued that it did not make sense for just one state to adopt the whole-number proportional approach. The Governor's argument was, in essence, the same argument that Thomas Jefferson had made in his January 12, 1800, letter to James Monroe concerning the district system that had worked to Jefferson's disadvantage by dividing Virginia's electoral votes in the 1796 presidential election (quoted immediately below in the next section).

4.1.15 PRACTICAL POLITICAL IMPEDIMENT CONCERNING THE WHOLE-NUMBER PROPORTIONAL APPROACH

Whatever the merits of the whole-number proportional approach, there is a prohibitive practical impediment associated with the adoption of this approach on a piecemeal basis by individual states, namely the political disadvantage suffered by states that divide their electoral vote in a political environment in which other states do not divide their votes.

Thomas Jefferson summed up this objection in his January 12, 1800, letter to James Monroe arguing that Virginia should switch from its existing district system to the statewide winner-take-all system. As Jefferson wrote:

> "All agree that an election by districts would be best, if it could be general; but while 10. states chuse either by their legislatures or by a general ticket, **it is folly & worse than folly** for the other 6. not to do it."[5] (Emphasis added; spelling and punctuation as per original)

The now-prevailing statewide winner-take-all system became entrenched in the political landscape by the 1830s precisely because virtually all parties came to realize that any fragmentation of a state's electoral votes diminishes a state's political influence in comparison to states employing a statewide winner-take-all approach. Once even one state adopts the statewide winner-take-all approach, it is disadvantageous for any other state not to do so as well.

Suppose, for the purpose of argument, that 50 of the 51 jurisdictions entitled to appoint presidential electors decided to allocate their electoral votes using the whole-number proportional approach. Recall (from table 4.24) that there would be about 19 battleground states under the whole-number proportional approach where one electoral vote would be in play. If even one state with 19 or more electoral votes were to retain the statewide winner-take-all system, then that single state would immediately become the only state that would matter in presidential politics. Indeed, even a single state with 10 or 15 electoral votes would, as a practical matter, become the most important state in an environment in which

---

[5] The entire letter and citations appear in the text and footnotes of section 2.2.3 of this book.

all the other jurisdictions used the whole-number proportional approach. The same argument would apply *a fortiori* if 49, 48, 47, or 46 jurisdictions were to adopt the whole-number proportional approach.

Moreover, if states were to ever start adopting the whole-number proportional approach on a piecemeal basis, each additional state adopting the approach would increase the influence of the remaining states and thereby would decrease the remaining state's incentive to adopt it. Thus, a state-by-state process of adopting the whole-number proportional approach would quickly bring itself to a halt, leaving the states that adopted it without any influence in presidential elections.

Of course, the above impediment associated with piecemeal adoption by the states of the whole-number proportional approach would not apply if it were adopted on a uniform national basis in the form of a federal constitutional amendment. A federal constitutional amendment would, if ratified, take effect simultaneously in all 50 states and the District of Columbia.

4.2 CONGRESSIONAL-DISTRICT APPROACH

The congressional-district approach would retain the existing statewide winner-take-all approach for both of the state's senatorial electors; however, it would use a district-level winner-take-all rule for the state's remaining presidential electors.

Of the three approaches described in chapter 3 and the two approaches described in this chapter, the congressional-district approach is the only approach that has ever been used in the United States. In recent times, the district approach has been used in Maine since 1969 and in Nebraska since 1992. Maine has only two congressional districts, and Nebraska has only three. In the nine presidential elections in which the congressional-district approach has been used in Maine and in the four elections in which it has been used in Nebraska, the presidential candidate carrying the state has also carried all of the state's congressional districts. Thus, the congressional-district approach has had no practical effect in terms of affecting the ultimate disposition of electoral votes in either Maine or Nebraska.

In this section, we will analyze two questions. The first is whether the congressional-district approach, if adopted nationwide, would more accurately reflect the nationwide popular vote than the existing statewide winner-take-all system. The second is whether the approach, if adopted nationwide, would improve the competitiveness of presidential elections on a nationwide basis.

As will be seen in the analysis below, if the congressional-district approach were adopted nationwide,

- it would not accurately reflect the nationwide popular vote; and
- it would not make every state or district competitive, but, instead, would simply create a small group of battleground congressional districts and battleground states (with most districts and most states remaining non-competitive in presidential elections).

We again start our analysis with a close recent election (the 2000 election) because almost any electoral system will yield the desired outcome in a landslide.

In the 2000 presidential election:

- George W. Bush carried 228 of the 435 congressional districts, whereas Al Gore carried 207 districts.
- Bush carried 30 states (having 60 senatorial electors), whereas Gore carried 20 states (having 40 senatorial electors).
- Gore carried the District of Columbia, which has three electoral votes.

If the congressional-district approach were applied to the results of the 2000 presidential election, then Bush would have received 288 electoral votes (53.3% of the total number of electoral votes), and Gore would have received 250 electoral votes (46.5% of the total). That is, the congressional-district approach would have given Bush a 6.8% lead in electoral votes over Gore in 2000.

Gore received 50,992,335 popular votes (50.2% of the two-party popular vote), whereas Bush received 50,455,156 (49.7% of the two-party popular vote). Under the existing statewide winner-take-all system, Bush received 271 electoral votes in 2000 (50.4% of the total number of electoral votes)—a 0.8% lead in electoral votes over Gore.

In summary, the congressional-district approach would have been even less accurate than the existing statewide winner-take-all system in terms of mirroring the nationwide popular vote.

There are three reasons why the congressional-district approach would not accurately reflect the nationwide popular vote in presidential elections.

First, congressional districts are generally skewed in favor of the Republican Party because the Democratic vote is relatively more heavily concentrated in those geographic areas where Democrats are in the majority than is the case for the areas where Republicans are in the majority. This is one reason why Bush carried 228 of the 435 congressional districts, whereas Gore carried only 207 districts in 2000 despite the fact that Gore received 537,179 more popular votes nationwide than Bush.

The Republican geographical bias in congressional districts became more pronounced after the 2000 census. The congressional district boundaries that were in place at the time of the 2000 presidential election were, of course, the ones that were adopted in the early 1990s using data from the 1990 federal census. If the results of the 2000 presidential election are viewed from the perspective of the up-to-date congressional districts based on data from the 2000 federal census (i.e., those first used in the 2002 congressional elections), George W. Bush would have carried 241 (55%) of the 435 congressional districts.[6]

In the 2004 presidential election, George W. Bush carried 255 (59%) of the 435 congressional districts, whereas John Kerry carried 180.[7] Bush also carried 31 (61%) of the 51 jurisdictions entitled to appoint presidential electors. If the congressional-district approach had been in place nationwide for the 2004 presidential election, Bush would have won 317 (59%) of the 538 electoral votes in an election in which he received 51.5% of the two-party popular vote.

Second, the congressional-district approach retains the existing statewide winner-take-all approach for 100[8] of the 538 presidential electors (i.e., the two presidential electors to which each state is entitled regardless of its population). That is, the congressional-district approach overlays a "statewide winner-takes-two" system on top of a "district-wide winner-takes-one" system.

[6] Barone, Michael; Cohen, Michael; and Ujifusa, Grant. 2003. *The 2004 Almanac of American Politics*. Washington, DC: National Journal Group.

[7] America's choice in 2004: Votes by congressional district. *Cook Political Report*. 2005.

[8] This total would be 102 if one were to count the District of Columbia (which has three presidential electors) as a state. The District of Columbia, like the seven states with three electoral votes, employs the winner-take-all rule. The District does not have any representation in Congress.

The third, and most fundamental, reason why the congressional-district approach does not accurately reflect the nationwide popular vote is simply that it is a *district* system. At the end of the day, the congressional-district approach would merely replace one kind of district (the existing state boundaries) with another (the congressional district boundaries) for 435 of the 538 presidential electors. Whenever a single political office is filled by an electoral process in which the winner-take-all rule is applied to geographic areas that are smaller than the entire jurisdiction encompassed by the office, there will be significant differences in the political value of individual votes. The inequality arises because some geographic areas will be battlegrounds, whereas others will not. Inevitably, candidates will compete vigorously for votes in the closely divided areas, while ignoring the voters in non-competitive areas. In addition, there is always the possibility, in any district system, of electing a candidate who did not receive the most popular votes in the jurisdiction as a whole.

Turning now to competitiveness, table 4.25 lists the 55 congressional districts in which the difference between George W. Bush and Al Gore was 4% or less in the 2000 presidential election.[9] Column 2 shows Bush's percentage of the popular vote for President in the district, and column 3 shows Gore's percentage. Column 4 shows the difference.

Overall, table 4.25 shows that

- in 6.7% of the congressional districts (29 of 435), the difference in the presidential vote was 2% or less;
- in 10.8% of the congressional districts (47 of 435), the difference in the presidential vote was 3% or less; and
- in 12.6% of the congressional districts (55 of 435), the difference in the presidential vote was 4% or less.

In short, the vast majority of congressional districts are non-competitive in terms of a presidential election.[10]

One reason why the congressional-district approach is so much less competitive than the existing statewide winner-take-all approach is that congressional districts are gerrymandered in many states. Gerrymandering is most commonly done to give a partisan advantage to

---

[9] *The Cook Political Report.* April 10, 2001.

[10] Of course, the vast majority of congressional districts are also non-competitive in congressional elections.

Table 4.25 THE 55 CLOSEST CONGRESSIONAL DISTRICTS IN THE 2000 PRESIDENTIAL ELECTION

DISTRICT	BUSH	GORE	DIFFERENCE
California–22	49%	45%	4%
Florida–7	51%	47%	4%
Ohio–13	50%	46%	4%
Wisconsin–4	50%	46%	4%
Arizona–5	49%	46%	3%
California–11	50%	47%	3%
California–41	50%	47%	3%
New Hampshire–1	49%	46%	3%
Pennsylvania–4	50%	47%	3%
Pennsylvania–10	50%	47%	3%
Texas–10	46%	43%	3%
California–44	49%	47%	2%
Florida–8	50%	48%	2%
Iowa–4	50%	48%	2%
Minnesota–1	48%	46%	2%
Minnesota–6	48%	46%	2%
Oregon–5	48%	46%	2%
Arkansas–2	49%	48%	1%
Florida–2	49%	48%	1%
Iowa–3	49%	48%	1%
Pennsylvania–21	49%	48%	1%
Tennessee–8	50%	49%	1%
Washington–3	48%	47%	1%
Michigan–10	49%	49%	0%
California–22	49%	45%	4%
Michigan–11	49%	49%	0%
New York–24	48%	48%	0%
Texas–27	49%	49%	0%
Virginia–4	49%	49%	0%
California–23	47%	48%	-1%
New Hampshire–2	47%	48%	-1%
Wisconsin–7	47%	48%	-1%
California–20	48%	50%	-2%
California–28	47%	49%	-2%
New Mexico–1	47%	49%	-2%
Pennsylvania–15	47%	49%	-2%
Texas–25	48%	50%	-2%
Virginia–11	47%	49%	-2%
Washington–2	46%	48%	-2%
Washington–8	47%	49%	-2%

Table 4.25 THE 55 CLOSEST CONGRESSIONAL DISTRICTS IN THE 2000 PRESIDENTIAL ELECTION (cont.)

DISTRICT	BUSH	GORE	DIFFERENCE
Wisconsin–1	47%	49%	-2%
Arkansas–1	47%	50%	-3%
Arkansas–4	47%	50%	-3%
Florida–16	47%	50%	-3%
Michigan–8	47%	50%	-3%
North Carolina–4	48%	51%	-3%
Ohio–1	47%	50%	-3%
Ohio–3	47%	50%	-3%
Pennsylvania–7	47%	50%	-3%
Pennsylvania–8	47%	50%	-3%
Texas–24	48%	51%	-3%
Wisconsin–3	46%	49%	-3%
Florida–5	46%	50%	-4%
Ohio–19	46%	50%	-4%
Pennsylvania–20	47%	51%	-4%
West Virginia–3	47%	51%	-4%

one political party. It is sometimes done to protect congressional incumbents of both parties.

If the presidential election were based on congressional districts, then the incentive for politically motivated districting would be even greater than it is today.

Many current efforts to change the process of congressional districting require districts to be compact in shape and to adhere closely to existing city and county boundaries. Generally, geometrically compact districts that adhere closely to local government boundaries tend to yield non-competitive areas. In most cases, the only way to achieve competitiveness (in the context of the single-member districts) is to intentionally create irregularly shaped districts that make competitiveness the top priority (after population equality). Thus, to the extent that redistricting procedures are changed to favor compact districts adhering to local government boundaries, one can expect to see fewer (not more) competitive districts.

Table 4.26 shows that the congressional districts that are close in the presidential race are heavily concentrated in the 10 largest states. Specifically, 58% of the close congressional districts (32 of the 55) lie in eight of the 10 largest states. Thus, the congressional-district approach would not only focus presidential campaigns on a tiny fraction of the nation's congressional-districts, but it would also concentrate the presidential race on the 10 largest states to a degree that exceeds their share of the nation's population and that exceeds their prominence under the current winner-take-all system. Four of the eight large states in the table are currently competitive statewide in presidential elections (i.e., Pennsylvania, Florida, Ohio, and Michigan), whereas four are not (i.e., California, Texas, New York, and North Carolina).

Table 4.26 CONGRESSIONAL DISTRICTS IN THE 10 LARGEST STATES THAT ARE CLOSE IN THE PRESIDENTIAL ELECTION

STATE	NUMBER OF CONGRESSIONAL DISTRICTS THAT ARE CLOSE IN THE PRESIDENTIAL RACE
California	7
Pennsylvania	7
Florida	5
Ohio	4
Texas	4
Michigan	3
New York	1
North Carolina	1

Votes do not have equal weight under the congressional-district approach. In fact, there are four different inequalities inherent in the congressional-district approach, namely

- inequalities resulting from the fact that each state has two statewide (senatorial) presidential electors regardless of its population;
- inequalities stemming from the decennial apportionment of the membership of the House of Representatives among the states;
- inequalities caused by differences in voter turnout caused by the level of civic participation in the state or the state's rate of population growth; and
- inequalities caused by differences in voter turnout in particular congressional districts.

First, a vote cast in a large state for the two statewide (senatorial) presidential electors has less weight than a vote cast in a small state for its two statewide electors. For example, in the 2000 presidential election, Wyoming had two statewide presidential electors (with a 1990 population of 453,588), whereas California had two statewide presidential electors (with a 1990 population of 29,760,021). As shown in table 4.27 for the presidential elections of 1992, 1996, and 2000, each statewide presidential elector corresponded to 226,794 people in Wyoming but to 14,880,011 people in California. The last column of this table shows the ratio of California's population per electoral vote compared to that of Wyoming—a 65.6-to-1 variation.

Table 4.27 DIFFERENCE IN WEIGHT OF A VOTE CAST FOR THE TWO STATEWIDE PRESIDENTIAL ELECTORS UNDER THE CONGRESSIONAL-DISTRICT APPROACH

STATE	POPULATION	POPULATION CORRESPONDING TO EACH STATEWIDE PRESIDENTIAL ELECTOR	RATIO TO LOWEST
California	29,760,021	14,880,011	65.6
Wyoming	453,588	226,794	1.00

Second, a vote cast in certain states has less weight than a vote cast in certain other states because of inequalities in the apportionment of the membership of the House of Representatives among the several states. For example, in the 1990 census, Wyoming had a population of 453,588, and Montana had 799,065; however both states received one House seat. As shown in table 4.28, in the presidential elections of 1992, 1996, and 2000, each statewide presidential elector corresponded to 226,794 people in Wyoming but to 399,533 in Montana. The last column of this table shows the ratio of Montana's population per electoral vote to that of the lowest in the table (Wyoming)—a 1.76-to-1 variation.

Table 4.28 DIFFERENCE IN WEIGHT OF A VOTE CAST BECAUSE OF CONGRESSIONAL APPORTIONMENT UNDER THE CONGRESSIONAL-DISTRICT APPROACH

STATE	POPULATION	POPULATION CORRESPONDING TO EACH STATEWIDE PRESIDENTIAL ELECTOR	RATIO TO LOWEST
Montana	799,065	399,533	1.76
Wyoming	453,588	226,794	1.00

Numerous other such substantial variations could be cited between various pairs of states, including variations between states with differing numbers of electoral votes.

Third, among states with equal numbers of electoral votes, a vote cast in a state with a lower voter turnout has a greater weight than a vote cast in a state where more votes are cast. Voter turnout may be high in a particular state because of a high level of civic participation (e.g., Utah) or because the state is fast-growing (e.g., Nevada). See table 3.5.

Fourth, a vote cast in a congressional district where fewer total votes are cast has a greater weight than a vote cast in a congressional district where more total votes are cast. There are many congressional districts (typically those with lopsided majorities in favor of one party) where voter turnout is noticeably lower than that of other districts within the state.

Summarizing the above points, if the congressional-district approach were adopted nationwide,

- it would not more accurately reflect the nationwide popular vote than the existing statewide winner-take-all approach, and
- it would not produce greater competition.

4.2.1 PRACTICAL POLITICAL IMPEDIMENT CONCERNING THE CONGRESSIONAL-DISTRICT APPROACH

Whatever the merits of the congressional-district approach, there is a prohibitive practical impediment associated with the adoption of this approach on a piecemeal basis by individual states.

In his January 12, 1800, letter to James Monroe, Thomas Jefferson argued that Virginia should switch from its then-existing district system to the statewide winner-take-all system because of the political disadvantage suffered by states that divided their electoral votes by districts in a political environment in which other states use the winner-take-all approach:

> "All agree that an election by districts would be best, if it could be general; but while 10. states chuse either by their legislatures or by a general ticket, **it is folly & worse than folly** for the other 6. not to do it."[11] (Emphasis added; spelling and punctuation as per original)

---

[11] The entire letter and citations appear in the text and footnotes of section 2.2.3 of this book.

Indeed, the now-prevailing statewide winner-take-all system became entrenched in the political landscape in the 1830s precisely because dividing a state's electoral votes diminishes the state's political influence relative to states employing the statewide winner-take-all approach.

The Florida legislature considered adopting the congressional-district approach in the early 1990s. The proposal failed there largely because of concern that it would reduce the state's political importance in presidential elections. As it happened, George W. Bush carried 13 of Florida's 23 congressional districts in the 2000 presidential election, whereas Gore carried 10. If the congressional-district approach had been used in Florida in the 2000 presidential election (with the electoral system remaining unchanged in all other states), Gore would have been elected President because Bush would not have received all of Florida's 25 electoral votes.

The "folly" of individual states adopting the congressional-district approach on a *piecemeal* basis is shown by the listing of the 55 closest congressional districts in table 4.25. Suppose that 50 of the 51 jurisdictions entitled to appoint presidential electors were to allocate electoral votes by district but that California (with 55 electoral votes in the 2004 presidential election) did not. California would immediately become the only state that would matter in presidential politics. The same thing would happen if two or three medium-sized states were to retain the statewide winner-take-all system while the remaining states decided to employ the congressional-district approach. The congressional-district approach only makes sense if 100% of the states adopt it.

Moreover, if states started adopting the congressional-district approach on a piecemeal basis, each additional state adopting the approach would increase the influence of the remaining states and thereby would increase the disincentive for the remaining states to adopt it. Thus, a state-by-state process adopting the congressional-district approach would bring itself to a halt.

Of course, the above impediment associated with piecemeal adoption of the congressional-district approach would not apply if the system were adopted simultaneously on a nationwide basis as a federal constitutional amendment (such as Senator Mundt's proposed amendment described in section 3.2).

5 | Background on Interstate Compacts

An interstate compact is a contractual agreement between two or more states.

This chapter covers the

- constitutional basis for interstate compacts (section 5.1),
- legal standing of compacts (section 5.2),
- history of compacts (section 5.3),
- subjects covered by compacts (section 5.4),
- parties to compacts (section 5.5),
- formulation of compacts (section 5.6),
- methods by which a state enacts a compact (section 5.7),
- contingent nature of compacts (section 5.8),
- congressional consent and involvement in compacts (section 5.9),
- effect of congressional consent (section 5.10),
- compacts that are contingent on enactment of federal legislation at the time Congress grants its consent to the compact (section 5.11),
- compacts that do not require congressional consent (section 5.12),
- enforcement of compacts (section 5.13),
- amendments to compacts (section 5.14),
- duration, termination, and withdrawals from compacts (section 5.15),
- administration of compacts (section 5.16),
- style of compacts (section 5.17),
- comparison of treaties and interstate compacts (section 5.18),
- comparison of uniform state laws and interstate compacts (section 5.19),

- comparison of federal multi-state commissions and interstate compacts (section 5.20),
- future of interstate compacts (section 5.21), and
- proposals for compacts on elections (section 5.22).

5.1 CONSTITUTIONAL BASIS FOR INTERSTATE COMPACTS

Interstate compacts predate the U.S. Constitution. The Articles of Confederation[1] provided:

> "No two or more States shall enter into any treaty, confederation or alliance whatever between them, without the consent of the United States in Congress assembled, specifying accurately the purposes for which the same is to be entered into, and how long it shall continue."[2]

The Continental Congress consented to four interstate compacts under the Articles of Confederation. An interstate compact regulating fishing and navigation on the Chesapeake Bay and the Potomac River received congressional consent under the Articles of Confederation in 1785 and remained in force until 1958.

Article I, section 10, clause[3] of the U.S. Constitution provides:

> "No state shall, without the consent of Congress, ... enter into any agreement or compact with another state...."[4]

The terms "compact" and "agreement" are generally used interchangeably. As the U.S. Supreme Court wrote in the 1893 case of *Virginia v. Tennessee*:

> "Compacts or agreements ... we do not perceive any difference in the meaning...."[5]

The Supreme Court also wrote:

> "The terms 'agreement' or 'compact,' taken by themselves, are sufficiently comprehensive to embrace all forms of

---

[1] The Articles of Confederation were proposed by the Continental Congress in 1777 and ratified by the states by 1781.

[2] Articles of Confederation. Article VI, clause 2.

[3] The U.S. Constitution was proposed by the Constitutional Convention in 1787 and ratified by the requisite number of states by 1789.

[4] See appendix C for full wording of the compacts clause.

[5] *Virginia v. Tennessee*. 148 U.S. 503 at 520. 1893.

stipulation, written or verbal, and relating to all kinds of subjects...."[6]

The terms "compact" and "agreement" encompass arrangements that are enacted by statutory law as well as those entered into by a state's executive officers and commissions.

5.2 LEGAL STANDING OF INTERSTATE COMPACTS

An interstate compact is, first and foremost, a contract. As the Supreme Court wrote in the 1959 case of *Petty v. Tennessee-Missouri Bridge Commission*:

> "[a] compact is, after all, a contract."[7]

As contracts, compacts enjoy strong protection from the U.S. Constitution. Article I, section 10, clause 1 of the Constitution provides:

> "No State shall ... pass any ... Law impairing the Obligation of Contracts...."[8]

The Council of State Governments summarizes the nature of interstate compacts as follows:

> "Compacts are agreements between two or more states that bind them to the compacts' provisions, just as a contract binds two or more parties in a business deal. As such, compacts are subject to the substantive principles of contract law and are protected by the constitutional prohibition against laws that impair the obligations of contracts (U.S. Constitution, Article I, Section 10).

> "That means that compacting states are bound to observe the terms of their agreements, even if those terms are inconsistent with other state laws. In short, compacts between states are somewhat like treaties between nations. Compacts have the force and effect of statutory law (whether enacted by statute or not) and they take precedence over conflicting state laws, regardless of when those laws are enacted.

---

[6] *Id.* at 517–518.

[7] *Petty v. Tennessee-Missouri Bridge Commission.* 359 U.S. 275 at 285. 1959.

[8] See appendix C for the full wording of the impairments clause.

"However, unlike treaties, compacts are not dependent solely upon the good will of the parties. Once enacted, compacts may not be unilaterally renounced by a member state, except as provided by the compacts themselves. Moreover, Congress and the courts can compel compliance with the terms of interstate compacts. That's why compacts are considered the most effective means of ensuring interstate cooperation."[9]

Once a state enters into an interstate compact, the state—like an individual, corporation, or any other legal entity—is bound by the compact's terms. The contractual obligations undertaken by a state in an interstate compact bind all state officials. In addition, an interstate compact binds the state legislature because a legislature may not enact any law impairing a contract. Thus, after a state enters into an interstate compact, the state is bound by all the terms of the compact until the state withdraws from the compact in accordance with the compact's terms for withdrawal, until the compact is terminated in accordance with the compact's terms for termination, or until the compact ends in accordance with the compact's stated duration.

States generally enter into interstate compacts in order to obtain some benefit that can only be obtained by cooperative and coordinated action with one or more sister states. In most cases, it would make no sense for a state to agree to the terms of a compact unless certain desired other states simultaneously agreed to abide by the terms of the compact. For example, a state generally would not want to agree to limitations on its use of water in a river basin unless the other states in the basin agreed to limit their water use. When two states are involved in a boundary dispute, neither state would generally want to acknowledge a compromise boundary until the other state accepted the compromise.

When a state enters into an interstate compact (other than a purely advisory compact), it is typically agreeing to a constraint, to one degree or another, on its ability to exercise some power that it otherwise might independently exercise.

5.3 HISTORY OF INTERSTATE COMPACTS

There were four interstate compacts approved under the Articles of Confederation. Three of them were settlements of boundary disputes.

---

[9] Council of State Governments. 2003. *Interstate Compacts and Agencies 2003.* Lexington, KY: The Council of State Governments. Page 6.

The first regulatory compact was an agreement between Maryland and Virginia concerning fishing and navigation on the Chesapeake Bay and the Potomac River. This compact received congressional consent under the Articles of Confederation in 1785 and remained in force until it was replaced by the Potomac River Compact (which received congressional consent in 1958).

In their seminal 1925 article entitled "The Compact Clause of the Constitution," Felix Frankfurter (subsequently a Justice of the U.S. Supreme Court) and James Landis reported that the vast majority (25 of the 32) of interstate compacts prior to 1921 were for the purpose of resolving boundary disputes.[10]

Prior to 1921, pre-existing agencies of the compacting states administered all interstate compacts.

The modern era of interstate compacts began in 1921. The inadequacies of the port of New York became obvious during World War I. After the war, the states of New York and New Jersey decided that efficient operation and development of the port required closer cooperation and coordination between the two states. The result was the 1921 Port of New York Authority Compact. The 1921 compact broke new ground by establishing a bi-state governmental entity—the Port Authority. Under the compact, the Port Authority is administered by its own governing body—a commission appointed by the governors of the two states.

The compact's intended purposes are summarized in the compact's preamble:

> "Whereas, In the year eighteen hundred and thirty-four the states of New York and New Jersey did enter into an agreement fixing and determining the rights and obligations of the two states in and about the waters between the two states, especially in and about the bay of New York and the Hudson river; and

> "Whereas, Since that time the commerce of the port of New York has greatly developed and increased and the territory in and around the port has become commercially one center or district; and

---

[10] Frankfurter, Felix and Landis, James. 1925. The compact clause of the constitution—A study in interstate adjustments. 34 *Yale Law Journal* 692–693 and 730–732. May 1925.

"Whereas, It is confidently believed that a better co-ordination of the terminal, transportation and other facilities of commerce in, about and through the port of New York, will result in great economies, benefiting the nation, as well as the states of New York and New Jersey; and

"Whereas, The future development of such terminal, transportation and other facilities of commerce will require the expenditure of large sums of money and the cordial co-operation of the states of New York and New Jersey in the encouragement of the investment of capital, and in the formulation and execution of the necessary physical plans; and

"Whereas, Such result can best be accomplished through the co-operation of the two states by and through a joint or common agency."

After 1921, the number of compacts and the variety of topics covered by compacts increased dramatically. Nowadays, about one half of all interstate compacts establish a commission to administer the subject matter of the compact.[11] Compact commissions are generally composed of a specified number of representatives from each party state. Many modern-day compacts receive annual funding from each member state for the operation of the compact commission and its staff.

5.4 SUBJECT MATTER OF INTERSTATE COMPACTS

There are no constitutional restrictions on the subject matter of interstate compacts other than the implicit limitation that the compact's subject matter must be among the powers that the states are permitted to exercise. Thus, interstate compacts have been employed for a wide variety of purposes, including those listed below.

An *advisory compact* establishes a commission that is authorized only to conduct studies and to develop recommendations to solve interstate problems.

Examples of *agricultural compacts* include the Compact on Agricultural Grain Marketing and the Northeast Interstate Dairy Compact.

Two states may enter into a *boundary compact*. A freely negotiated settlement of a boundary dispute is often a desirable alternative to a trial

---

[11] Council of State Governments. 2003. *Interstate Compacts and Agencies 2003.* Lexington, KY: The Council of State Governments.

in the U.S. Supreme Court to establish the official boundaries between two states. The South Dakota–Nebraska Boundary Compact (which received congressional consent in 1990) settled a dispute arising from the fact that the Missouri River had changed its course with the passage of time.

Many *civil defense compacts* were adopted during the Cold War period when the Soviet Union was viewed as a potential aggressor nation. The Emergency Management Assistance Compact (found in appendix N), to which Congress consented in 1996, is a broad compact that effectively replaces the earlier Civil Defense Compact.

Crime-control and *corrections compacts* are traceable to 1910 when Congress gave its consent in advance to four states—Illinois, Indiana, Michigan, and Wisconsin—to enter into an agreement with respect to the exercise of jurisdiction "over offenses arising out of the violation of the laws" of these states on the waters of Lake Michigan.[12] The Interstate Agreement on Detainers is one of the best-known compacts concerning crime. This agreement facilitates speedy and proper disposition of detainers based on indictments, information, or complaints from the jurisdictions that are parties to the compact. The parties to this compact include 48 states, the District of Columbia, Puerto Rico, the Virgin Islands, and the federal government.

In 2000, Congress gave its consent to Kansas and Missouri to enter into the nation's first *cultural compact*. The compact established a metropolitan cultural district governed by a commission.

The first *education compact* pooled the resources of southern states by means of the Southern Regional Education Compact. The aim of the compact was to reduce each state's need to maintain expensive post-graduate and professional schools. There are two additional compacts of this nature: the New England Higher Education Compact and the Western Regional Education Compact. The New Hampshire–Vermont Interstate School Compact has been used to establish two interstate school districts, each involving a New Hampshire town and one or more Vermont towns.

Energy Compacts include the Interstate Compact to Conserve Oil and Gas, the Southern States Energy Compact (originally the Southern Interstate Nuclear Compact), the Midwest Energy Compact, and the Western Interstate Energy Compact (originally the Western Interstate Nuclear Compact).

---

[12] 36 Stat. 882.

Facilities compacts provide for the joint construction and operation of physical facilities—commonly bridges and tunnels. A compact entered into by Maine and New Hampshire dealt with the construction and maintenance of a single bridge over the Piscataqua River.[13] On the other hand, the Port Authority of New York and New Jersey operates extensive facilities, including the Holland and Lincoln Tunnels, the George Washington Bridge, three airports (Kennedy, LaGuardia, and Newark Liberty), the PATH rail system, ferries, industrial development projects, and marine facilities. The Port Authority's police force alone numbers over 1,600.

The four *fisheries compacts* are the Atlantic States Marine Fisheries Compact of 1942, the Pacific States Marine Fisheries Compact of 1947, the Gulf States Marine Fisheries Compact of 1949, and the Connecticut River Basin Atlantic Salmon Compact of 1983.

Flood-control compacts relate to the construction of projects to prevent flooding. A 1957 compact between Massachusetts and New Hampshire established the Merrimack Valley Flood Control Commission, which determines the annual amount of compensation that Massachusetts must pay New Hampshire for loss of tax revenue resulting from the construction of flood-control projects.

The Interstate Compact on Mental Health and New England Compact on Radiological Health Protection are examples of *health compacts.*

Congress encouraged the formation of *low-level radioactive waste compacts* to construct regional waste storage facilities as an alternative to the development of individual storage sites in each state. In particular, the federal Low Level Radioactive Waste Policy Act of 1980[14] (as amended in 1985) encourages the use of interstate compacts to establish and operate regional facilities for management of low-level radioactive waste. A total of 44 states have entered into 10 such compacts. One example is the Southwestern Low-Level Radioactive Waste Disposal Compact in which California agreed to serve, for 35 years, as the host state for the storage of radioactive waste for the states of Arizona, North Dakota, South Dakota, and California (and such other states to which the compact commission might later decide to grant membership).

Because of the sensitive subject matter, radioactive-waste compacts generally attract considerable public attention and generate fierce debate

---

[13] 50 Stat. 536.

[14] 94 Stat. 3347.

in state legislatures. Voters have often become directly involved in radioactive waste compacts by means of the citizen-initiative process, the protest-referendum process, and the legislative referral process.[15]

Marketing and development compacts address a variety of subjects and include the Agricultural Grain Marketing Compact, the Midwest Nuclear Compact promoting the use of nuclear energy, and the Mississippi River Parkway Compact.

The objective of each *metropolitan problems compact* is generally conveyed by in its title. For example, the Washington Metropolitan Area Transit Regulation Compact was entered into by the District of Columbia, Maryland, and Virginia and was granted congressional consent in 1960.[16]

The only *military compact* is the National Guard Mutual Assistance Compact. It provides for the sharing of military personnel and equipment among its member states.

There are 12 *motor vehicle compacts*, including ones that relate to driver's licenses, nonresident violators, equipment safety, and uniform vehicle registration prorogation.

Natural resources compacts are designed to settle disputes and to promote the conservation and development of resources. For example, in 1963, Maryland and Virginia established the Potomac River Fisheries Commission to settle a dispute that had originated during the colonial period. Ever since a royal charter made the river a part of Maryland, Maryland oyster fishermen have resented Virginia oyster fishermen intruding in Maryland's waters. The more recent Connecticut River Basin Atlantic Salmon Restoration Compact involves the return of salmon to the river.[17]

The Columbia River Gorge Compact and the 1900 Palisades Interstate Park Compact are two of the five *parks and recreation compacts*.

Economic interest groups often encourage the establishment of *regulatory compacts*. Such groups typically lobby Congress not to exercise its preemption powers in a particular area by arguing that coordinated action by the states, by means of an interstate compact, is sufficient to solve a problem.

---

[15] See sections 5.7 and 5.13 for discussion of the political controversies, spanning a 20-year period, concerning Nebraska's participation in the Central Interstate Low-Level Radioactive Waste Compact.

[16] 74 Stat. 1031.

[17] 97 Stat. 1983.

The Interstate Sanitation Compact, entered into by New Jersey and New York in 1935 and by Connecticut in 1941, created a commission with the power to abate and prevent pollution in tidal waters of the New York City metropolitan area. Subsequently, the compact was amended to allow the commission to monitor, but not to regulate, air quality. The commission (renamed the Interstate Environmental Commission) shares concurrent regulatory authority with the environmental protection departments of the member states.

The Atlantic States Marine Fisheries Compact does not grant its commission regulatory enforcement powers; however, the commission obtained indirect regulatory authority by a congressional act. In 1986, the Atlantic Striped Bass Conservation Act was amended to offer each concerned state the choice of complying with the management plan developed by the commission or being subject to a fishing moratorium on striped bass imposed by the U.S. Fish and Wildlife Service in the state's coastal waters.[18]

One of the greatest problems in southwestern states—the shortage of water—led to the filing of numerous lawsuits between states in the U.S. Supreme Court. *River basin compacts* provide an alternative to litigation. The first such compact was the Colorado River Compact apportioning waters of the river among various western states. More recently, various mid-Atlantic states have entered into river basin compacts.

A *federal-interstate compact* is an interstate compact to which the federal government is one of the parties.

A *service compact* seeks to eliminate social problems by committing each member state to provide services to legal residents of other member states. The Interstate Compact on the Placement of Children in Interstate Adoption, for example, facilitates the adoption of children by qualified foster parents in other compact states if there are too few families willing to adopt children in the home state. This compact has 50 members—49 states and the Virgin Islands.

In 1934, Congress enacted the Crime Control Consent Act authorizing states to enter into crime-control compacts.[19] The Interstate Compact for Supervision of Parolees and Probationers is based on this statute and is the first interstate compact to have been joined by all states. Puerto Rico

---

[18] 100 Stat. 989, 16 U.S.C. §1857.

[19] *Crime Control Consent Act of 1934.* 48 Stat. 909. 4 U.S.C. §112.

and the Virgin Island also are members. The importance of this compact is illustrated by the fact that more than 300,000 persons are on parole or probation in states other than those in which they committed their crimes. The Interstate Compact on Juveniles and the Interstate Corrections Compact authorize the return of delinquents and convicts, respectively, to their states of domicile to serve their sentences. Supporters of these compacts believe that rehabilitation of delinquents and convicts will be promoted if they are incarcerated in close proximity to their families.

The levying of state income and sales taxes and the growth of interstate commerce has encouraged states to enter into *tax compacts*. The Great Lakes Interstate Sales Compact was the first multi-state compact to focus on enforcement of state sales and use taxes. New Jersey and New York belong to an agreement providing for a mutual exchange of information relative to purchases by residents of the other state from in-state vendors. The states have also entered into numerous administrative agreements concerning taxation.

Twenty-three states and the District of Columbia are parties to the Multistate Tax Compact. Twenty-one additional states are associate members of the compact by virtue of their participation in, and their providing funding for, various programs established by the compact's commission. The impetus for the Multistate Tax Compact was the 1966 decision of the U.S. Supreme Court in *Northwestern States Portland Cement Company v. Minnesota*. The Court ruled that a state may tax the net income of a foreign corporation (i.e., one chartered in a sister state) if the tax is nondiscriminatory and is apportioned equitably on the basis of the corporation's activities with a nexus to the taxing state.[20]

Felix Frankfurter and James Landis anticipated the possibility of *federal-interstate compacts* in 1925 and wrote:

> "[T]he combined legislative powers of Congress and of the several states permit a wide range of permutations and combinations for governmental action. Until very recently these potentialities have been left largely unexplored.... Creativeness is called for to devise a great variety of legal alternatives to cope with the diverse forms of interstate interests."[21]

---

[20] *Northwestern States Portland Cement Company v. Minnesota.* 358 U.S. 450. 1966.

Frankfurter and Landis's call for creativity led to the first *federal-interstate compact* in 1961. After a prolonged drought in the 1950s made the careful management of Delaware River waters essential, four states and the federal government entered into the Delaware River Basin Compact. Congress enacted the compact into federal law with a provision that the United States be a member of the compact. That law created a commission with a national co-chairman and a state co-chairman. The commission also has additional members from the national and member state governments.

Additionally, the federal government, Maryland, New York, and Pennsylvania entered into the Susquehanna River Basin Compact, which became effective in 1971. This is another example of a federal-interstate compact. It is modeled on the Delaware River Basin Compact.

Federal-interstate compacts have also been employed to promote economic development in large regions of the nation. The Appalachian Regional Compact was the first such compact. It was enacted by Congress and thirteen states in 1965. This compact has a commission with a state co-chairman appointed by the governors involved and a federal co-chairman appointed by the President with the Senate's advice and consent.[22]

A unique federal-interstate agreement resulted from a 1980 congressional statute granting consent to an agreement entered into by the Bonneville Power Administration, a federal entity, with Idaho, Montana, Oregon, and Washington.[23] The term "interstate compact" does not appear in the act, and the agreement was not negotiated by the member states. Instead, the proposed compact was drafted by the Pacific Northwest Electric Power and Conservation Planning Council, which sent the proposal to the states. If the states had not enacted the proposed compact, a federal council would have been appointed by the U.S. Secretary of the Interior to perform the functions of the proposed federal-interstate council, namely preparing of a conservation and electric power plan and implementing a program to protect fish and wildlife. A second unique

---

[21] Frankfurter, Felix and Landis, James. 1925. The compact clause of the constitution—A study in interstate adjustments. 34 *Yale Law Journal* 692–693 and 730–732. May 1925.

[22] *Appalachian Regional Development Act of 1966,* 79 Stat. 5, 40 U.S.C. app. §1.

[23] *Pacific Northwest Electric Power and Conservation Planning Act of 1980.* 94 Stat. 2697. 16 U.S.C. §839b.

feature of this legislation was the provision for membership by a federal agency, rather than the federal government.[24]

In 1990, Congress created a similar temporary body—the Northern Forest Lands Council. The Northern Forest Lands Council Act[25] authorized each of the governors of Maine, New Hampshire, New York, and Vermont to appoint four council members charged with developing plans to maintain the "traditional patterns of land ownership and use" of the northern forest. The council was disbanded in 1994.

The National Criminal Prevention and Privacy Compact Act, enacted by Congress in 1998, established what may be termed a federal-interstate compact that

> "organizes an electronic information sharing system among the Federal Government and the States to exchange criminal history records for non-criminal justice purposes authorized by Federal or State law, such as background checks for governmental licensing and employment."[26]

Federal and state law enforcement officers were not involved in the negotiations leading to this compact. The compact is activated when entered into by two or more states. Article VI of the compact established a Compact Council with authority to promulgate rules and procedures pertaining to use of the Interstate Identification Index System for non-criminal justice purposes. The council is composed of fifteen members appointed by the Attorney General of the United States, including nine members selected from among the law enforcement officers of member states, two at-large members nominated by the Chairman of the Compact Council, two other at-large members, a member of the FBI's advisory policy board, and an FBI employee appointed by the FBI director. The Director of the FBI designates the federal "Compact Officer."

Indian tribe gaming compacts are a new type of compact. The origin of such compacts is the U.S. Supreme Court's 1987 decision in the case of *Cabazon Band of Mission Indians v. California*, which held that

---

[24] Olsen, Darryll and Butcher, Walter R. The Regional Power Act: A model for the nation? *Washington State Policy Notes 35.* Winter 1984. Pages 1–6.

[25] *Northern Forest Lands Council Act of 1990*, 104 Stat. 3359, 16 U.S.C. §2101.

[26] *National Crime Prevention and Privacy Compact Act of 1998.* 112 Stat. 1874. 42 U.S.C. §14611.

a state may not unduly restrict gaming on Indian lands.[27] This decision led to a sharp increase in gaming on Indian lands. Congress became concerned that tribal governments and their members were not actually profiting from the gaming and that organized crime might acquire a stake in such activity. The Indian Gaming Regulatory Act of 1988[28] therefore authorized tribe–state gaming compacts. The 1988 act established three classes of Indian gaming. Class I gaming—primarily social gaming for small prizes—is regulated totally by Indian tribes. Class II gaming—bingo and bingo-type games and non-banking card games—is regulated by tribes, but is subject to limited oversight by the National Indian Gaming Commission. Class III contains all other types of gaming. Class III gaming is prohibited in the absence of a tribal-state compact approved by the U.S. Secretary of the Interior. The compact device permits states to exercise their reserved powers without the need for direct congressional action.

Appendix M contains a listing of 196 active interstate compacts compiled by the National Center for Interstate Compacts (NCIC) of the Council of State Governments (CSG). The Center has also identified 62 defunct or inactive interstate compacts.[29]

5.5 PARTIES TO INTERSTATE COMPACTS

Although most early interstate compacts usually involved only two states, modern-day interstate compacts frequently involve numerous parties.

The parties to an interstate compact are often determined by geography (e.g., the Colorado River Compact and the Great Lakes Basin Compact). Membership in many compacts is defined by the activities in which the states engage. For example, the Interstate Oil Compact encompasses the 22 oil-producing states. The Multistate Lottery Agreement operates a quasi-national lotto game in geographically scattered states. In some cases, compacts are open to all states, and their actual membership is simply determined by whichever states decide to enact the compact. Examples include the Interstate Compact for Adult Offender Supervision (enacted by 38 states) and the Agreement on Detainers (enacted by 47 states).

---

[27] *Cabazon Band of Mission Indians v. California.* 480 U.S. 202. 1987.

[28] *Indian Gaming Regulatory Act of 1988.* 108 Stat. 2467. 25 U.S.C. §2701.

[29] Council of State Governments. 2003. *Interstate Compacts and Agencies 2003.* Lexington, KY: The Council of State Governments.

Today, there are interstate compacts that include as few as two states and compacts that involve all 50 states. Certain interstate compacts include the District of Columbia, the Commonwealth of Puerto Rico, the Virgin Islands, American Samoa, and provinces of Canada. The Interstate Compact for Education, for example, encompasses 48 states, the District of Columbia, American Samoa, Puerto Rico, and the Virgin Islands. In 1949, the Northeastern Interstate Forest Fire Compact became the first interstate compact to include a Canadian province. The Great Lakes Basin Compact (appendix K) includes Ontario and Quebec.

The federal government may be a party to an interstate compact. For example, the membership of the Agreement on Detainers (appendix L) includes 47 states, the District of Columbia, and the federal government as parties.

The Interstate Compact on the Placement of Children and the Interstate Compact on Juveniles are examples of compacts adhered to by all 50 states and the District of Columbia.

States belong to an average of 25.4 interstate compacts.[30] The numbers of compacts entered into range from a low of 16 for Hawaii and Wisconsin to a high of 32 for Colorado and Maryland.

5.6 FORMULATION OF INTERSTATE COMPACTS

Prior to 1930, gubernatorially appointed commissioners negotiated and drafted all interstate compacts. This method is especially appropriate when the contemplated compact requires lengthy negotiations among the prospective parties and frequent consultation with the governors and legislative leaders of the states involved.

Since the 1930s, some interstate compacts (e.g., the Interstate Compact on Parolees and Probationers) have been drafted by non-governmental organizations. Over the years, the National Conference of State Legislatures (NCSL) and the Council of State Governments (CSG) have proposed numerous interstate compacts to the states.[31] Compacts have occasionally been initiated by private citizens. As Marian E. Ridgeway describes in *Interstate Compacts: A Question of Federalism:*

---

[30] Bowman, Ann O'M. 2004. Trends and issues in interstate cooperation. In *The Book of the States 2004 Edition*. Chicago, IL: The Council of State Governments. Page 36.

[31] Hardy, Paul T. 1982. *Interstate Compacts: The Ties That Bind*. Athens, GA: Institute of Government, University of Georgia.

"The Compact on Education is largely the product of the zeal and energy of former governor Terry Sanford of North Carolina, acting on a suggestion of James B. Conant in his [1964 book] *Shaping Education Policy.*"[32]

Interstate compacts may also originate in state legislatures. A legislature may unilaterally enact a statute that serves as a prospective compact and invitation to other states to join by enacting identical statutes.

In recent years, various industry groups have promoted interstate regulatory compacts in attempts to discourage Congress from exercising its preemption powers over the subject matter involved. These groups argue that a compact obviates the need for federal regulation and that cooperative action by the states can adequately address the problem at hand.

Representatives of the federal government occasionally participate in the negotiation of interstate compacts. Such federal participation is usually at the invitation of the states themselves. Federal participation is, however, sometimes necessary, given the nature of the compact. For example, federal representatives participated from the beginning in the negotiation of the Potomac River Compact. Both the federal government and the District of Columbia are represented on the commission established by the compact.

In the case of the Colorado River Compact, Congress passed legislation[33] in 1921 calling on the seven western states in the Colorado River basin (Arizona, California, Colorado, Nevada, New Mexico, Utah and Wyoming) to enter negotiations to resolve their long-standing water dispute and to provide for the use of the water for agriculture and power generation. Under the terms of the federal legislation, the negotiations were headed by Secretary of Commerce Herbert Hoover. These negotiations led to the Colorado River Compact of 1922.[34,35]

There are no constitutional or statutory restrictions on the length of time for the negotiation of interstate compacts.

---

[32] Ridgeway, Marian E. 1971. *Interstate Compacts: A Question of Federalism.* Carbondale, IL: Southern Illinois University Press. Page 41.

[33] 42 Stat. 171.

[34] Barton, Weldon V. 1967. *Interstate Compacts in the Political Process.* Chapel Hill, NC: University of North Carolina Press.

[35] Zimmerman, Joseph F. 2002. *Interstate Cooperation: Compacts and Administrative Agreements.* Westport, CT: Praeger.

5.7 METHODS BY WHICH A STATE ENACTS AN INTERSTATE COMPACT

A state may enter an interstate compact in several ways. In certain circumstances, the Governor, the head of an administrative department, or a commission may have sufficient legal authority to enter into a compact on a particular subject on behalf of the state. For example, the Multi-State Lottery Agreement was adopted in many states merely by the action of state lottery commissions. The focus of this book is, however, on compacts that require explicit legislative action in order to come into effect.

Enactment of an interstate compact is generally accomplished in the same way that ordinary state laws are enacted. Enactment of a state statute typically requires a majority vote of the state legislature and submission of the legislative bill to the state's Governor for approval or disapproval. If the Governor approves a bill that has been passed by the legislature, then the bill becomes law. All Governors have the power to veto legislation passed by their state legislatures. If a Governor vetoes a bill, the bill may nonetheless become law if the legislature overrides the veto in the manner provided by the state's constitution. Overriding a gubernatorial veto typically requires a super-majority (e.g., a two-thirds vote of all houses of the state legislature). See *The Book of the States* for general information about vetoes in particular states.[36] The veto by the Governor of Vermont of the bill enacting the New England Water Pollution Compact is an example of a gubernatorial veto of a legislative bill enacting an interstate compact.

If a state allows the citizen-initiative process, an interstate compact may be enacted in that fashion. Each state constitution specifies the legislature's role, if any, in the initiative process. For example, in some states, the legislature has the option (sometimes the obligation) of voting on an initiative petition before the proposition is submitted to the voters. See *The Initiative: Citizen Law-Making*[37] for additional information on the citizen-initiative process. The citizen-initiative process may, in general, be used to repeal a state law. Thus, a state law enacting an interstate compact can be subjected to review and possible repeal by the voters. For example, an initiative petition was used in Nebraska in 1988 to force

---

[36] Council of State Governments. 2005. *The Book of the States.* Lexington, KY: The Council of State Governments. 2005 Edition. Volume 37. Pages 161–162.

[37] Zimmerman, Joseph F. 1999. *The Initiative: Citizen Law-Making.* Westport, CT: Praeger. See pages 24-25 for citations to the constitutional and statutory provisions governing the initiative processes in various states.

a statewide vote on the question of Nebraska's continued participation in the Central Interstate Low-Level Radioactive Waste Compact. The compact (which had been passed several years earlier by the Nebraska legislature) provided for the building of a nuclear waste site in Nebraska. In the statewide vote on Proposition 402 in 1988, Nebraska voters rejected the opportunity to repeal the state's participation in the compact. The compact nonetheless remained controversial, and, in 1999, the Nebraska legislature enacted a law withdrawing the state from the compact.[38]

The protest-referendum process, if available in a given state, provides another way to subject a law enacted by the legislature (including a law enacting an interstate compact) to review by the voters. The protest-referendum process usually must be invoked within a short and limited time after the law was originally passed by the legislature. See *The Referendum: The People Decide Public Policy*[39] for additional information on the protest-referendum process.

In some cases, the state legislature has referred enactment of an interstate compact to the state's voters. For example, the Maine legislature referred the question of enactment of the Texas Low-Level Radioactive Waste Disposal Compact to its voters in 1993. The question on the ballot was:

> "Do you approve of the interstate compact to be made with Texas, Maine and Vermont for the disposal of the State's low-level radioactive waste at a proposed facility in the State of Texas?"

The proposition received 170,411 "yes" votes and 63,672 "no" votes.

The statutory language required to enact an interstate compact at the state level is not complex. For example, the legislation by which the state of Ohio entered into the Great Lakes Basin Compact in 1963 consists of two parts. The first part consists of the following 43-word enacting clause:

> "The 'great lakes basin compact' is hereby ratified, enacted into law, and entered into by this state as a party thereto with

---

[38] See section 5.13 for additional discussion of the political controversies, spanning a 20-year period, concerning Nebraska's participation in the Central Interstate Low-Level Radioactive Waste Compact.

[39] Zimmerman, Joseph F. 1997. *The Referendum: The People Decide Public Policy.* Westport, CT: Praeger.

any other state or province which, pursuant to Article II of said compact, has legally joined in the compact as follows: ..."

The second part consists of the text of the compact (placed inside quotation marks). Appendix K contains the entire text of the Ohio legislation. Statutory language for enacting an interstate compact at the state level may, or may not, be self-executing. The above Ohio legislation is an example of self-executing legislation—that is, no further action is required by any official or body in Ohio with respect to the process of adopting the compact in Ohio. On the other hand, the statutory language enacting an interstate compact may require that the compact be subsequently executed by the state's Governor, Attorney General, or other official—perhaps at the discretion of the official involved, perhaps after some specified condition is satisfied, or perhaps merely after a certain number of other states have joined the compact. The Interstate Compact for the Supervision of Parolees and Probationers is an example of a non-self-executing compact. That particular compact was enacted in 1936 by the New York Legislature. Because of the opposition of Governor Herbert H. Lehman, the compact remained unexecuted for eight years.

An interstate compact may sometimes be adopted on a temporary basis by executive or administrative action. For example, the Compact for Education stipulates that it may be adopted

"either by enactment thereof or by adherence thereto by the Governor; provided that in the absence of enactment, adherence by the Governor shall be sufficient to make his state a party only until December 31, 1967."

The governor authorized participation by Kansas in the Interstate Compact for Supervision of Parolees and Probationers for a period of time prior to enactment of the compact by the legislature.

There are no constitutional or statutory restrictions on the length of time that potential parties to an interstate compact may take in deciding whether to join the compact.[40] Indeed, history is replete with examples of long delays prior to the enactment of interstate compacts. In 1955, the Great Lakes Basin Compact (appendix K) was enacted by the state legislatures in Illinois, Indiana, Michigan, Minnesota, and Wisconsin. It was

---

[40] Of course, a particular compact could explicitly contain a time limitation for its adoption by its prospective members.

enacted in 1956 by the Pennsylvania General Assembly. However, the New York Legislature did not enact the compact until 1960, and the Ohio General Assembly did not enact the compact until 1963. It took twelve years to gain approval from the California and Nevada legislatures for the California-Nevada Water Apportionment Interstate Compact. It took five years to secure the necessary enactments of the Atlantic States Marine Fisheries Compact (which became effective in 1942).

5.8 CONTINGENT NATURE OF COMPACTS

As a general rule, a state enters into an interstate compact in order to obtain some benefit that can only be obtained by mutually agreed coordinated action with its sister state(s). In most cases, it would make no sense for a state to agree to the terms of a compact unless certain desired other states agreed to the compact. Thus, an interstate compact generally does not come into effect until it is approved by a specified number or a specified combination of prospective parties.

A bi-state compact does come into effect until it is adopted by both of the states involved.

A compact involving three or more parties typically contains a specific provision specifying the conditions under which the compact will come into effect. If a compact is silent as to the number of parties necessary to bring it into effect, then, in accordance with standard contract law, it comes into effect only when adopted by all of its named parties.

The Gulf States Marine Fisheries Compact contemplated participation of five states but required only two states to enact the compact in order to bring it into effect.

> "This compact shall become operative immediately as to those states ratifying it whenever any two or more of the States of Florida, Alabama, Mississippi, Louisiana and Texas have ratified it."

The Tri-State Lotto Compact is an example of a multi-state compact that did not come into effect until it was enacted by all of its prospective parties (Maine, New Hampshire, and Vermont).

The Multistate Tax Compact is open to all states and provides:

> "This compact shall enter into force when enacted into law by any seven states. Thereafter, this compact shall become

effective as to any other state upon its enactment thereof."

The Great Lakes Basin Compact was intended to include eight states but came into effect when four states enacted it.

"This compact shall enter into force and become effective and binding when it has been enacted by the legislatures of any four of the states of Illinois, Indiana, Michigan, Minnesota, New York, Ohio, Pennsylvania, and Wisconsin and thereafter shall enter into force and become effective and binding as to any other of said states when enacted by the legislature thereof."

The Great Lakes Basin Compact is noteworthy because it permitted two Canadian provinces to join the Great Lakes Basin Compact. The Canadian provinces did not, however, count toward the threshold of four states necessary to bring the compact into effect.

"The province of Ontario and the province of Quebec, or either of them, may become states party to this compact by taking such action as their laws and the laws of the government of Canada may prescribe for adherence thereto. For the purpose of this compact the word 'state' shall be construed to include a province of Canada."

The Midwest Interstate Passenger Rail Compact came into effect when it was enacted by three states out of a pool of 12 named prospective members. The membership of this compact may be expanded by action of the commission established by the compact.

"The states of Illinois, Indiana, Iowa, Kansas, Michigan, Minnesota, Missouri, Nebraska, North Dakota, Ohio, South Dakota and Wisconsin are eligible to join this compact. Upon approval of the Commission, according to its bylaws, other states may also be declared eligible to join the compact. As to any eligible party state, this compact shall become effective when its legislature shall have enacted the same into law; provided that it shall not become initially effective until enacted into law by any three (3) party states incorporating the provisions of this compact into the laws of such states.

Amendments to the compact shall become effective upon their enactment by the legislatures of all compacting states."[41]

The Central Interstate Low-Level Radioactive Waste Compact named 10 states as eligible for membership. It specified that it would become effective when enacted by any three of the 10 prospective parties. The compact enabled the compact's commission to admit additional states by a unanimous vote.

Sometimes the requirements for bringing a compact into effect are of paramount importance. The original version of the Colorado River Compact was negotiated in 1922 by gubernatorially appointed commissioners from the seven western states involved (Arizona, California, Colorado, Nevada, New Mexico, Utah, and Wyoming). The negotiations were headed by Herbert Hoover, and the compact was signed, amid considerable fanfare, on November 24, 1922, in Santa Fe, New Mexico. The 1922 version provided:

"This compact shall become binding and obligatory when it shall have been approved by the legislatures of each of the signatory states."[42]

The Arizona legislature, however, did not enact a statute approving the 1922 compact. Congress then initiated a revised version of the compact—the Boulder Canyon Project Act of 1928. The 1928 version specified that the compact would come into effect when enacted by six of the seven western states involved, provided that California was one of the six.[43] Arizona, the seventh prospective member, did not approve the 1928 version of compact until 1944.

5.9 CONGRESSIONAL CONSENT AND INVOLVEMENT IN INTERSTATE COMPACTS

Congress may become involved with an interstate compact in one of several different ways:
- consenting to a compact,
- consenting to a compact on behalf of the District of Columbia,

---

[41] Midwest Interstate Passenger Rail Compact. Section 1 of Article X.

[42] See http://ssl.csg.org/compactlaws/coloradoriver.html

[43] 45 Stat.1057.

- making the federal government a party to a compact,
- granting implied consent to a compact,
- consenting in advance to a broad category of compacts, and
- consenting in advance to a particular compact.

The statutory language necessary for congressional consent to an interstate compact is straight-forward.

A joint resolution is generally used if Congress is simply granting its consent. For example, House Joint Resolution 193 (Public Law 104-321)[44] of the 104th Congress entitled "Joint Resolution Granting the consent of Congress to the Emergency Management Assistance Compact" was used to grant consent to the Emergency Management Assistance Compact in 1996. The joint resolution consists of three major parts. In the first part, Congress grants its consent.

> *"Resolved by the Senate and House of Representatives of the United States in Congress assembled,*
>
> "SECTION 1: CONGRESSIONAL CONSENT.
> "The Congress consents to the Emergency Management Assistance Compact entered into by Delaware, Florida, Georgia, Louisiana, Maryland, Mississippi, Missouri, Oklahoma, South Carolina, South Dakota, Tennessee, Virginia and West Virginia. The compact reads substantially as follows ..."

The second part of this joint resolution consists of the entire wording of the Emergency Management Assistance Compact (which is inserted in the joint resolution inside quotation marks).

The third part of a joint resolution consenting to a compact generally contains several sections that qualify the grant of consent.

> "SECTION 2. RIGHT TO ALTER, AMEND, OR REPEAL.
> "The right to alter, amend, or repeal this joint resolution is hereby expressly reserved. The consent granted by this joint resolution shall
>
> (1) not be construed as impairing or in any manner affecting any right or jurisdiction of the United States in and over the subject of the compact;

---

[44] Appendix N contains Public Law 104-321 of 1996 entitled "Joint Resolution Granting the consent of Congress to the Emergency Management Assistance Compact."

(2) not be construed as consent to the National Guard Mutual Assistance Compact;

(3) be construed as understanding that the first paragraph of Article II of the compact provides that emergencies will require procedures to provide immediate access to existing resources to make a prompt and effective response;

(4) not be construed as providing authority in Article IIIA.7 that does not otherwise exist for the suspension of statutes or ordinances;

(5) be construed as understanding that Article IIIC does not impose any affirmative obligation to exchange information, plans, and resource records on the United States or any party which has not entered into the compact; and

(6) be construed as understanding that Article XIII does not affect the authority of the President over the National Guard provided by article I of the Constitution and title 10 of the United States Code.

"SECTION 3. CONSTRUCTION AND SEVERABILITY.

"It is intended that the provisions of this compact shall be reasonably and liberally construed to effectuate the purposes thereof. If any part or application of this compact, or legislation enabling the compact, is held invalid, the remainder of the compact or its application to other situations or persons shall not be affected.

"SECTION 4. INCONSISTENCY OF LANGUAGE.

"The validity of this compact shall not be affected by any insubstantial difference in its form or language as adopted by the States."

When the District of Columbia is a party to a compact, Congress may consent to the compact on behalf of the District. When the federal government is a party to a compact, Congress enters into the compact on behalf of the United States. Thus, when Congress acted on the Interstate Agreement on Detainers, it simultaneously consented to the compact on behalf of the District of Columbia, made the federal government a party to the compact, and enacted some additional permanent statutory language (sections 5 and 6). Appendix L contains Public Law 91-538 of 1970 entitled "An Act to enact the Interstate Agreement on Detainers into law." This law begins:

> *"Be it enacted by the Senate and House of Representatives of the United States of America in Congress assembled,*
>
> "[Sec. 1.] That this Act may be cited as the 'Interstate Agreement on Detainers Act.'
>
> "Sec. 2. The Interstate Agreement on Detainers is hereby enacted into law and entered into by the United States on its own behalf and on behalf of the District of Columbia with all jurisdictions legally joining in substantially the following form: …"

At this point, Public Law 91-538 incorporates the entire Interstate Agreement on Detainers (inside quotation marks).

Public Law 91-538 then concludes with several additional sections:

> "Sec. 3. The term 'Governor' as used in the agreement on detainers shall mean with respect to the United States, the Attorney General, and with respect to the District of Columbia, the Commissioner of the District of Columbia.
>
> "Sec. 4. The term 'appropriate court' as used in the agreement on detainers shall mean with respect to the United States, the courts of the United States, and with respect to the District of Columbia, the courts of the District of Columbia, in which indictments, informations, or complaints, for which disposition is sought, are pending.
>
> "Sec. 5. All courts, departments, agencies, officers, and employees of the United States and of the District of Columbia are hereby directed to enforce the agreement on detainers and to cooperate with one another and with all party States in enforcing the agreement and effectuating its purpose.

"Sec. 6. For the United States, the Attorney General, and for the District of Columbia, the Commissioner of the District of Columbia, shall establish such regulations, prescribe such forms, issue such instructions, and perform such other acts as he deems necessary for carrying out the provisions of this Act.

"Sec. 7. The right to alter, amend, or repeal this Act is expressly reserved.

"Sec. 8. This Act shall take effect on the ninetieth day after the date of its enactment."

Congressional consent to an interstate compact need not be explicit. For example, there is nothing in Public Law 91-538 (quoted above) that specifically mentions that Congress is consenting to the Interstate Agreement on Detainers. The reason is that congressional consent is *implied* by its consent to the compact on behalf of the District of Columbia and by its action making the federal government a party to the compact. As the U.S. Supreme Court observed in the 1893 case of *Virginia v. Tennessee:*

> **The constitution does not state when the consent of congress shall be given, whether it shall precede or may follow the compact made, or whether it shall be express or may be implied.** In many cases the consent will usually precede the compact or agreement.... But where the agreement relates to a matter which could not well be considered until its nature is fully developed, it is not perceived why the consent may not be subsequently given. [Justice] Story says that **the consent may be implied, and is always to be implied when congress adopts the particular act by sanctioning its objects and aiding in enforcing them;** and observes that where a state is admitted into the Union, notoriously upon a compact made between it and the state of which it previously composed a part, there the act of congress admitting such state into the Union is an implied consent to the terms of the compact. Knowledge by congress of the boundaries of a state and of its political subdivisions may reasonably be presumed, as much of its legislation is affected by them, such as relate to the territorial jurisdiction of the

courts of the United States, the extent of their collection districts, and of districts in which process, civil and criminal, of their courts may be served and enforced."[45] [Emphasis added]

Congressional consent is given in the same way that Congress enacts an ordinary statute. That is, such legislation requires a majority vote of both houses of Congress and approval of the President. As part of the legislative process, the President may veto such legislation. Congress has the power to override a presidential veto by a two-thirds vote in both houses. For example, in 1941, Franklin D. Roosevelt vetoed the bill granting consent to the Republican River Compact (perhaps preferring a Democratic river); however, two years later he signed a bill consenting to a modified version of the compact. Congress's failure to grant its consent for the Connecticut River and Merrimack River Flood Control Compacts in the 1930s has been attributed to the threat of a presidential veto.

There is no constitutional limitation on the amount of time that Congress may take in considering a compact. Maryland, New York, and Pennsylvania enacted the Susquehanna River Basin Compact in 1967 and 1968, but Congress did not grant its consent until 1970. The Washington Metropolitan Area Transit Regulation Compact was approved by Maryland, Virginia, and the District of Columbia in 1958; however, the compact did not receive the consent of Congress until 1960.

Congress is free to grant its unrestricted consent in advance for all compacts pertaining to a particular subject. For example, Congress consented in advance to interstate crime control compacts in the Crime Control Consent Act of 1934.

"Be it enacted by the Senate and House of Representatives of the United States of America in congress assembled,

"[Sec. 1.] That the consent of Congress is hereby given to any two or more States to enter into agreements or compacts for cooperative effort and mutual assistance in the prevention of crime and in the enforcement of their respective criminal laws and policies, and to establish such agencies, joint or otherwise, as they deem desirable for making effective such agreement and compacts.

---

[45] *Virginia v. Tennessee.* 148 U.S. 503 at 521. 1893.

"Sec. 2. The right to alter, amend, or repeal this Act is hereby expressly reserved."

In the Weeks Act of 1911, Congress granted unrestricted consent in advance to interstate compacts formed

"for the purpose of conserving the forests and water supply...."[46]

In the Tobacco Control Act of 1936, Congress authorized tobacco-producing states to enter into interstate compacts

"to enable growers to receive a fair price for such tobacco."[47]

Another example of congressional consent in advance involved the development and operation of airports.[48]

In 1939, President Franklin D. Roosevelt vetoed a bill that would have granted consent in advance to states to enter into compacts relating to fishing in the Atlantic Ocean because he considered the advance authorization to be overly vague.

On rare occasions, Congress has combined consent and advance permission in the same statute. For example, in 1921, it granted its consent to a Minnesota–South Dakota compact relating to criminal jurisdiction over boundary waters and simultaneously granted its consent in advance for a similar compact among Iowa, Minnesota, Nebraska, North Dakota, South Dakota, and Wisconsin.[49]

In 1951, Congress authorized states to enter into interstate civil defense compacts that, upon enactment, were required to be filed with the U.S. House of Representatives and Senate. These compacts were all deemed to have the consent of Congress unless disapproved by a concurrent resolution within 60 days of filing.[50]

Generally, a congressional grant of consent to an interstate compact is for an indefinite period of time. However, Congress originally subjected the Interstate Oil and Gas Compact of 1935 and the Atlantic States Marine Fisheries Compact to sunset provisions. Later, Congress removed the time restrictions on its consent.[51] The 10 compacts (involving a total

---

[46] 36 Stat. 961.
[47] 49 Stat. 1239.
[48] 73 Stat. 333.
[49] 41 Stat. 1447.
[50] 64 Stat. 1249.
[51] 86 Stat. 383 and 64 Stat. 467.

of 44 states) authorized by the Low Level Radioactive Waste Policy Act of 1980 were each approved for a period of five years.[52] Of course, Congress is not obligated to renew its consent. The controversial Northeast Interstate Dairy Compact established a commission with authority to fix the price of fluid or drinking milk above the minimum prices set by the New England federal milk-marketing order. This compact was enacted by each state legislature in New England. Congress granted its consent to this particular compact for a limited period of time. In the meantime, the compact attracted considerable opposition from consumer groups and mid-western and western dairy states. Consumer advocates opposed the compact because it would increase the retail price of milk, thereby adversely impacting low-income citizens. Representatives of mid-western and western dairy states argued that their farmers suffered from low milk prices because of the compact. Wisconsin dairy farmers, in particular, argued that the compact prevented them from selling their products in New England. The compact became inactive in 2001 when Congress failed to grant an extension of its consent.

Congress may impose conditions in granting its consent. For example, Congress granted its consent to the Wabash Valley Compact in 1959[53] and the Washington Metropolitan Area Transit Regulation Compact in 1960[54] with the proviso that each compact authority was to publish specified data and information. Congress always reserves its authority over navigable waters. It almost always reserves its right to "alter, amend, or repeal" its consent. The Boulder Canyon Project Act of 1928[55] granted congressional consent to the Colorado River Compact subject to several stipulated conditions, including approval of the modified compact by California and five of the other six states involved (it being understood, at the time, that Arizona was unlikely to join immediately).

In the 1962 case of *Tobin v. United States*, the United States Court of Appeals for the District of Columbia Circuit upheld the authority of Congress to attach conditions to a compact.[56] The U.S. Supreme Court declined to review the decision.

---

[52] 94 Stat. 3347.

[53] 73 Stat. 694.

[54] 74 Stat. 1031.

[55] 45 Stat.1057.

[56] *Tobin v. United States.* 306 F.2d 270 at 272–74. 1962.

The Constitution does not detail the specific form or manner by which congressional consent is to be granted. In 1823, the U.S. Supreme Court in *Green v. Biddle* noted this fact in a case involving a congressional statute that granted consent to the admission of Kentucky to the Union and simultaneously referred to the Virginia–Kentucky Interstate Compact of 1789.[57] Kentucky unsuccessfully challenged the compact on the ground that Congress had not explicitly consented to the compact.

The Central Interstate Low-Level Radioactive Waste Compact enabled the commission established by the compact to accept additional states as members by a unanimous vote. The compact (which was submitted to Congress for its consent) contained a provision granting advance congressional consent to any additional new states:

> "The consent given to this compact by the Congress shall extend to any future admittance of new party states under subsections B and C of Article VII of the compact."

5.10 EFFECT OF CONGRESSIONAL CONSENT

The question arises as to whether an interstate compact is converted into federal law when Congress grants its consent. This question is important because it may determine which court has the power to interpret the compact and whether the compact is interpreted under the state or federal law.

The Supreme Court's answer to this question has changed over the years. In 1938, the Court held in the case of *Hinderlider v. La Plata River and Cherry Creek Ditch Company* that congressional consent does not make a compact the equivalent of a United States statute or treaty.[58] The Court modified its *Hinderlider* ruling in *Delaware River Joint Toll Bridge Commission v. Colburn*. The Court expanded the authority of a compact that had been granted consent by Congress and involved

> "a federal 'title, right, privilege, or immunity' which when explicitly identified and claimed in a state court may be reviewed here on certiorari...."[59]

---

[57] *Green v. Biddle.* 21 U.S. 1. 1823.

[58] *Hinderlider v. La Plata River and Cherry Creek Ditch Company.* 304 U.S. 92. 1938.

[59] *Delaware River Joint Toll Bridge Commission v. Colburn.* 320 U.S. 419. 1940.

In 1874, the Supreme Court held in *Murdock v. City of Memphis* that federal courts are required to apply the interpretation of state law by the highest state court in the state.[60] In 1981, however, the Court overturned *Murdock* in *Cuyler v. Adams*. The Court held that congressional consent converts an interstate compact into federal law provided that the compact's subject matter was

"an appropriate subject for congressional legislation."[61]

By overturning *Murdock*, the Court was free to reject the interpretation provided by the Pennsylvania Supreme Court and to interpret the statute on its own.[62,63]

The question repeatedly arises as to whether the grant of congressional consent to an interstate compact invalidates other federal statutes containing inconsistent provisions. Courts could interpret congressional consent as repealing, relative to the interstate compact, conflicting federal statutes. The question also arises as to the effect of a new federal statute whose provisions conflict with an interstate compact previously approved by Congress. Apparently, the consent would be repealed relative to the conflicting provisions with the exception of any vested rights protected by the Fifth Amendment to the Constitution.

5.11 COMPACTS CONTINGENT ON ENACTMENT OF FEDERAL LEGISLATION

An interstate compact may contain terms specifying that it is contingent on the enactment of federal legislation at the time Congress grants its consent to the compact.

For example, the Belle Fourche River Compact between South Dakota and Wyoming stipulated that it would not become effective unless congressional consent were accompanied by congressional legislation satisfactorily addressing three enumerated points that the compact's parties desired. The compact provided:

---

[60] *Murdock v. City of Memphis*. 87 U.S. 590. 1874.

[61] *Cuyler v. Adams*. 449 U.S. 433. 1981.

[62] Hardy, Paul T. 1982. *Interstate Compacts: The Ties That Bind*. Athens, GA: Institute of Government, University of Georgia.

[63] Zimmerman, Joseph F. 2002. *Interstate Cooperation: Compacts and Administrative Agreements*. Westport, CT: Praeger.

"This compact shall become operative when approved by the legislature of each of the states, and when consented to by the congress of the United States by legislation providing, among other things, that:

"(i) Any beneficial uses hereafter made by the United States, or those acting by or under its authority, within a state, of the waters allocated by this compact, shall be within the allocations hereinabove made for use in that state and shall be taken into account in determining the extent of use within that state;

"(ii) The United States, or those acting by or under its authority, in the exercise of rights or powers arising from whatever jurisdiction the United States has in, over and to the waters of the Belle Fourche River and all its tributaries, shall recognize, to the extent consistent with the best utilization of the waters for multiple purposes, that beneficial use of the waters within the basin is of paramount importance to development of the basin, and no exercise of such power or right thereby that would interfere with the full beneficial use of the waters shall be made except upon a determination, giving due consideration to the objectives of this compact and after consultation with all interested federal agencies and the state officials charged with the administration of this compact, that such exercise is in the interest of the best utilization of such waters for multiple purposes;

"(iii) The United States, or those acting by or under its authority, will recognize any established use, for domestic and irrigation purposes, of the apportioned waters which may be impaired by the exercise of federal jurisdiction in, over, and to such waters; provided, that such use is being exercised beneficially, is valid under the laws of the appropriate state and in conformity with this compact at the time of the impairment thereof, and was validly initiated under state law prior to the initiation or authorization of the federal program or project which causes such impairment."

Congress agreed to the states' request in its legislation granting consent to the Belle Fourche River Compact.

Similarly, the Republican River Compact contained a description of congressional legislation desired by the compact's parties. Again, Congress agreed to the states' request at the time of granting its consent to the compact.

5.12 COMPACTS NOT REQUIRING CONGRESSIONAL CONSENT

Two reasons are generally given as to why the U.S. Constitution requires congressional consent for interstate compacts.

First, congressional consent provides a means of protecting the federal government from efforts by the states to encroach upon its delegated powers and federal supremacy.

Second, congressional consent provides a means of safeguarding the interests of states that are not parties to the compact. For example, absent congressional supervision, upstream states in a river basin might enter into a compact to use water to the extreme disadvantage of downstream states that do not belong to the compact.

At first glance, the Constitution seems to be unambiguous as to the necessity for congressional consent to interstate compacts. Article I, section 10, clause 3 provides:

> "No state shall, without the consent of Congress, … enter into any agreement or compact with another state...."

The Supreme Court has interpreted this clause to allow states to enter into compacts without Congressional consent. In deciding the 1978 case of *U.S. Steel Corporation v. Multistate Tax Commission,*[64] the Court wrote:

> "Read literally, the Compact Clause would require the States to obtain congressional approval before entering into any agreement among themselves, irrespective of form, subject, duration, or interest to the United States. The difficulties with such an interpretation were identified by Mr. Justice Field in his opinion for the Court in *Virginia v. Tennessee,* supra.[65] His conclusion that the Clause could not be read literally was approved in subsequent dicta, … but this Court did not have

---

[64] *U.S. Steel Corporation v. Multistate Tax Commission.* 434 U.S. 452. 1978.

[65] *Virginia v. Tennessee.* 148 U.S. 503. 1893.

occasion expressly to apply it in a holding until our recent [1976] decision in *New Hampshire v. Maine*[66] ....."[67]

Litigation started in the early 19th century over whether congressional consent to interstate compacts is necessary in all circumstances. In the 1833 case of *Barron v. Baltimore*, Chief Justice John Marshall wrote:

> "If these compacts are with foreign nations, they interfere with the treaty-making power, which is conferred entirely on the general government; if with each other, for political purposes, they can scarcely fail to interfere with the general purpose and intent of the constitution."[68]

In 1845, the New Hampshire Supreme Court in *Dover v. Portsmouth Bridge* dismissed the contention that an 1819 New Hampshire statute and an 1821 Maine statute that authorized construction of a bridge over navigable waters (the Piscataqua River) without congressional consent violated the U.S. Constitution.[69] The court held that there is no constitutional provision precluding each of the two states from granting authority for the erection of a bridge to the middle of the river.

In 1854, the U.S. Supreme Court held in *Florida v. Georgia* that a boundary compact enacted by the two states would be invalid unless Congress were to grant its consent.[70]

The seminal case on the issue of the necessity for congressional consent to interstate compacts is the 1893 case of *Virginia v. Tennessee*.[71] The two states involved never obtained congressional consent for a boundary agreement that they had reached earlier in the 19th century. The U.S. Supreme Court framed the issue in the case as follows:

> "Is the agreement, made without the consent of congress, between Virginia and Tennessee, to appoint commissioners to run and mark the boundary line between them, within the prohibition of this clause? The terms 'agreement' or

---

[66] *New Hampshire v. Maine.* 426 U.S. 363. 1976.

[67] *U.S. Steel Corporation v. Multistate Tax Commission.* 434 U.S. 452. at 459. 1978.

[68] *Barron v. Baltimore.* 32 U.S. 243. 1833.

[69] *Dover v. Portsmouth Bridge.* 17 N.H. 200. 1845.

[70] *Florida v. Georgia.* 55 U.S. 478. 1854.

[71] *Virginia v. Tennessee.* 148 U.S. 503. 1893.

'compact,' taken by themselves, are sufficiently comprehensive to embrace all forms of stipulation, written or verbal, and relating to all kinds of subjects; to those to which the United States can have no possible objection or have any interest in interfering with, as well as to those which may tend to increase and build up the political influence of the contracting states, so as to encroach upon or impair the supremacy of the United States, or interfere with their rightful management of particular subjects placed under their entire control."[72]

The Court observed:

"**There are many matters upon which different states may agree that can in no respect concern the United States.** If, for instance, Virginia should come into possession and ownership of a small parcel of land in New York, which the latter state might desire to acquire as a site for a public building, it would hardly be deemed essential for the latter state to obtain the consent of congress before it could make a valid agreement with Virginia for the purchase of the land."[73] [Emphasis added]

The Court continued:

"If Massachusetts, in forwarding its exhibits to the World's Fair at Chicago, should desire to transport them a part of the distance over the Erie canal, it would hardly be deemed essential for that state to obtain the consent of congress before it could contract with New York for the transportation of the exhibits through that state in that way."[74]

Further, the Court stated:

"If the bordering line of two states should cross some malarious and disease-producing district, there could be no possible reason, on any conceivable public grounds, to obtain the consent of congress for the bordering states to agree to unite

---

[72] *Id.* at 517–518.

[73] *Id.* at 518.

[74] *Id.*

in draining the district, and thus removing the cause of disease. So, in case of threatened invasion of cholera, plague, or other causes of sickness and death, it would be the height of absurdity to hold that the threatened states could not unite in providing means to prevent and repel the invasion of the pestilence without obtaining the consent of congress, which might not be at the time in session."[75]

Having established that the requirement for congressional consent is not universal, the Court then recast the issue in the case:

"If, then, the terms 'compact' or 'agreement' in the constitution do not apply to every possible compact or agreement between one state and another, for the validity of which the consent of congress must be obtained, to what compacts or agreements does the constitution apply?"[76]

The Court then answered the question as follows:

"We can only reply by looking at the object of the constitutional provision, and construing the terms 'agreement' and 'compact' by reference to it. It is a familiar rule in the construction of terms to apply to them the meaning naturally attaching to them from their context. 'Noscitur a sociis' is a rule of construction applicable to all written instruments. Where any particular word is obscure or of doubtful meaning, taken by itself, its obscurity or doubt may be removed by reference to associated words; and the meaning of a term may be enlarged or restrained by reference to the object of the whole clause in which it is used.

"Looking at the clause in which the terms 'compact' or 'agreement' appear, it is evident that **the prohibition is directed to the formation of any combination tending to the increase of political power in the states, which may encroach upon or interfere with the just supremacy of the United States**."[77] [Emphasis added]

---

[75] *Id.*
[76] *Id.*
[77] *Id.* at 519.

The Court continued:

"[Justice] Story, in his Commentaries, (section 1403,) referring
to a previous part of the same section of the constitution in
which the clause in question appears, observes that its language

'may be more plausibly interpreted from the terms used,
'treaty, alliance, or confederation,' and upon the ground
that the sense of each is best known by its association
(*'noscitur a sociis'*) to apply to treaties of a political
character; such as treaties of alliance for purposes of
peace and war, and treaties of confederation, in which
the parties are leagued for mutual government, political
co-operation, and the exercise of political sovereignty,
and treaties of cession of sovereignty, or conferring
internal political jurisdiction, or external political
dependence, or general commercial privileges;'

"and that

'the latter clause, 'compacts and agreement,' might then
very properly apply to such as regarded what might be
deemed mere private rights of sovereignty; such as
questions of boundary, interests in land situate in the
territory of each other, and other internal regulations
for the mutual comfort and convenience of states bordering on each other.'

"And he [Story] adds:

'In such cases the consent of congress may be properly required, in order to check any infringement of
the rights of the national government; and, at the
same time, a total prohibition to enter into any compact or agreement might be attended with permanent
inconvenience or public mischief.' "[78]

The Court continued:

"Compacts or agreements—and we do not perceive any difference in the meaning, except that the word 'compact' is

---

[78] *Id.* at 520–521.

generally used with reference to more formal and serious engagements than is usually implied in the term 'agreement'— cover all stipulations affecting the conduct or claims of the parties. The mere selection of parties to run and designate the boundary line between two states, or to designate what line should be run, of itself imports no agreement to accept the line run by them, and such action of itself does not come within the prohibition. Nor does a legislative declaration, following such line, that is correct, and shall thereafter be deemed the true and established line, import by itself a contract or agreement with the adjoining state. It is a legislative declaration which the state and individuals affected by the recognized boundary line may invoke against the state as an admission, but not as a compact or agreement. The legislative declaration will take the form of an agreement or compact when it recites some consideration for it from the other party affected by it; for example, as made upon a similar declaration of the border or contracting state. The mutual declarations may then be reasonably treated as made upon mutual considerations. The compact or agreement will then be within the prohibition of the constitution, or without it, according as the establishment of the boundary line **may lead or not to the increase of the political power or influence of the states affected, and thus encroach or not upon the full and free exercise of federal authority.**"[79] [Emphasis added]

The Court continued:

"If the boundary established is so run as to cut off an important and valuable portion of a state, the political power of the state enlarged would be affected by the settlement of the boundary; and to an agreement for the running of such a boundary, or rather for its adoption afterwards, the consent of congress may well be required. But the running of a boundary may have no effect upon the political influence of either state; it may simply serve to mark and define that which actually existed before, but was undefined and unmarked. In that

---

[79] *Id.*

case the agreement for the running of the line, or its actual survey, would in no respect displace the relation of either of the states to the general government. There was, therefore, no compact or agreement between the states in this case which required, for its validity, the consent of congress, within the meaning of the constitution, until they had passed upon the report of the commissioners, ratified their action, and mutually declared the boundary established by them to be the true and real boundary between the states. Such ratification was mutually made by each state in consideration of the ratification of the other.

"The constitution does not state when the consent of congress shall be given, whether it shall precede or may follow the compact made, or whether it shall be express or may be implied. In many cases the consent will usually precede the compact or agreement, as where it is to lay a duty of tonnage, to keep troops or ships of war in time of peace, or to engage in war. But where the agreement relates to a matter which could not well be considered until its nature is fully developed, it is not perceived why the consent may not be subsequently given. [Justice] Story says that the consent may be implied, and is always to be implied when congress adopts the particular act by sanctioning its objects and aiding in enforcing them; and observes that where a state is admitted into the Union, notoriously upon a compact made between it and the state of which it previously composed a part, there the act of congress admitting such state into the Union is an implied consent to the terms of the compact. Knowledge by congress of the boundaries of a state and of its political subdivisions may reasonably be presumed, as much of its legislation is affected by them, such as relate to the territorial jurisdiction of the courts of the United States, the extent of their collection districts, and of districts in which process, civil and criminal, of their courts may be served and enforced.

"In the present case the consent of congress could not have preceded the execution of the compact, for until the line was run it could not be known where it would lie, and whether or

not it would receive the approval of the states. The preliminary agreement was not to accept a line run, whatever it
might be, but to receive from the commissioners designated
a report as to the line which might be run and established by
them. After its consideration each state was free to take such
action as it might judge expedient upon their report. The
approval by congress of the compact entered into between
the states upon their ratification of the action of their commissioners is fairly implied from its subsequent legislation
and proceedings. The line established was treated by that
body as the true boundary between the states in the assignment of territory north of it as a portion of districts set apart
for judicial and revenue purposes in Virginia, and as included
in territory in which federal elections were to be held, and for
which appointments were to be made by federal authority in
that state, and in the assignment of territory south of it as a
portion of districts set apart for judicial and revenue purposes in Tennessee, and as included in territory in which federal
elections were to be held, and for which federal appointments were to be made for that state. Such use of the territory on different sides of the boundary designated in a single
instance would not, perhaps, be considered as absolute proof
of the assent or approval of congress to the boundary line; but
the exercise of jurisdiction by congress over the country as a
part of Tennessee on one side, and as a part of Virginia on the
other, for a long succession of years, without question or dispute from any quarter, furnishes as conclusive proof of assent
to it by that body as can usually be obtained from its most formal proceedings."[80]

In summary, despite the absence of congressional consent, the U.S.
Supreme Court upheld the interstate compact between Virginia and
Tennessee because the compact did not

- increase "the political power of influence" of the party
  states, or

---

[80] *Id.*

- encroach "upon the full and free exercise of federal authority."

In deciding *Virginia v. Tennessee*, the Court also noted that Congress had relied, over the years, upon the compact's terms for judicial and revenue purposes, thereby implying the grant of consent.

Relying on *Virginia v. Tennessee*, the legislatures of New York and New Jersey did not submit the Palisades Interstate Park Agreement of 1900 to Congress for its consent.

In the same vein, the legislatures of New Jersey and New York initially had no intention of submitting the 1921 Port of New York Authority Compact to Congress, despite the compact's many novel and unique features. The compact simply specified that it would become effective

> "when signed and sealed by the Commissioners of each State as hereinbefore provided and the Attorney General of the State of New York and the Attorney General of New Jersey...."[81]

After the newly created Authority's bankers and bond counsels advised the Authority that potential investors might be hesitant to purchase bonds of such an unusual governmental entity in the absence of congressional consent, the two states sought, and quickly obtained, congressional consent for the compact.[82]

Note that, as a matter of convention, many compacts do not explicitly mention congressional consent, even when it is the intent of the compacting parties to seek it.

In the 1976 case of *New Hampshire v. Maine*, the U.S. Supreme Court reaffirmed the 1893 case of *Virginia v. Tennessee* and decided that an interstate agreement locating an ancient boundary did not require congressional consent.[83]

The 1978 case of *U.S. Steel Corporation v. Multistate Tax Commission*[84] is the most important recent case on the issue of whether

---

[81] *New York Laws of 1921*. Chapter 154.

[82] Zimmerman, Joseph F. 1996. *Interstate Relations: The Neglected Dimension of Federalism*. Westport, CT: Praeger.

[83] *New Hampshire v. Maine*. 426 U.S. 363. 1976.

[84] *U.S. Steel Corporation v. Multistate Tax Commission*. 434 U.S. 454. 1978. Justice Powell wrote the opinion of the Court, joined by Chief Justice Burger and Justices Brennan, Stewart, Marshall, Rehnquist, and Stevens.

congressional consent is necessary for interstate compacts. In that case, the U.S. Supreme Court reaffirmed its 1893 holding in *Virginia v. Tennessee.*[85] The Multistate Tax Compact addresses issues relating to multistate taxpayers and uniformity among state tax systems. Like many compacts, the compact itself is silent as to congressional consent, saying only:

> "This compact shall enter into force when enacted into law by any seven states."[86]

The Multistate Tax Compact was submitted to Congress for its consent. However, the compact languished there because of fierce political opposition from various business interests that were concerned about multi-million-dollar tax audits. The compacting states decided to proceed with the implementation of the compact without congressional consent. Predictably, the opponents of the compact, led by U.S. Steel, challenged the constitutionality of their action.

In upholding the constitutionality of the Multistate Tax Compact, despite the lack of congressional consent, the Supreme Court noted that the compact did not

> "authorize the member states to exercise any powers they could not exercise in its absence...."[87]

The Court again applied the interpretation of the Compact Clause from its 1893 holding in *Virginia v. Tennessee*, writing that:

> "the test is whether the Compact enhances state power *quaod* the National Government."[88]

The dissent of Justice Byron White (joined by Justice Harry Blackmun) in *U.S. Steel Corporation v. Multistate Tax Commission* is noteworthy because it suggests that the Court's majority opinion may have implicitly recognized a second test, namely whether a compact possibly encroaches on non-party states.

> "A proper understanding of what would encroach upon federal authority, however, must also incorporate encroach-

---

[85] *Virginia v. Tennessee.* 148 U.S. 503. 1893.

[86] Multistate Tax Compact. Section 1 of Article X.

[87] *U.S. Steel Corporation v. Multistate Tax Commission.* 434 U.S. 454 at 473. 1978. Justice Powell wrote the opinion of the Court, joined by Chief Justice Burger and Justices Brennan, Stewart, Marshall, Rehnquist and Stevens.

[88] *Id.* at 473. 1978.

ments on the authority and power of non-Compact States."[89]

Accordingly, it might be necessary to analyze the impact of a disputed compact on the power of the federal government and on the power of non-member states in order to determine whether Congressional consent is required for a particular compact.

As the Supreme Court noted in *U.S. Steel Corporation v. Multistate Tax Commission:*

> "most multilateral compacts have been submitted for Congressional approval."[90]

Recognizing the historical precedent of submitting compacts to Congress for approval, we have been unable to locate a single case where a court invalidated a compact for lack of consent on the grounds that it impermissibly encroached on federal supremacy.[91]

In analyzing the diverse range of issues on which courts have allowed states to enter into interstate compacts, it is hard to predict circumstances under which a court will invalidate an interstate compact that has not received Congressional approval, except in the rare cases where the compact clearly encroaches on federal supremacy.[92] As Michael S. Greve wrote in 2003:

> "After *U.S. Steel* one can hardly imagine a state compact that would run afoul of the Compact Clause without first, or at

---

[89] *Id.* at 494.

[90] *Id.* at 471.

[91] See *Star Scientific, Inc. v. Beales*, 278 F.3d 339 (4th Cir. 2002) involving the Master Settlement Agreement that resolved the lawsuit between states and major companies in the tobacco industry and established an administrative body to determine compliance with the agreement; *McComb v. Wambaugh*, 934 F.2d 474 (3rd Cir. 1991) involving the Interstate Compact on Placement of Children focusing on adoption and foster care of children; *New York v. Trans World Airlines*, Inc., 728 F.Supp. 162 (S.D.N.Y. 1990) involving a compact among several states to regulate airline advertising; *Breest v. Moran*, 571 F.Supp. 343 (D.R.I. 1983) involving the New England Interstate Corrections Compact allowing for the transfer of prisoners among detention facilities in the New England states.

[92] Even where encroachment arguably occurs, Congressional consent might not be required. For example, encroachment on federal powers arguably occurred in both the Multistate Tax Compact involved in *U.S. Steel Corporation v. Multistate Tax Commission* (434 U.S. 454, 1978) which sought to short-circuit a federal statutory solution to the allocation of interstate taxes and the compact involved in *Star Scientific, Inc. v. Beales*, 278 F.3d 339 (4th Cir. 2002) that resolved the lawsuit between states and major tobacco companies concerning the regulation of national cigarette advertising. Yet, both were held to be valid despite not receiving Congressional consent.

least also, running afoul of other independent constitutional obstacles."[93]

Moreover, in the 1991 case of *McComb v. Wambaugh*, the U.S. Court of Appeals for the Third Circuit held that no encroachment occurs where the subject of the compact concerns

"areas of jurisdiction historically retained by the states."[94]

In *The Law and Use of Interstate Compacts*, Frederick L. Zimmermann[95] and Mitchell Wendell point out:

"Consent bills for interstate compacts dealing with issues in the realm of state activity, law, and administration, with interstate jurisdictional problems and with the settlement of interstate equities, normally serve only to clutter congressional calendars and complicate and obstruct interstate cooperation."[96]

A number of compacts involving the concerned states' constitutionally reserved powers have been submitted to Congress for its consent. On one occasion, one house of Congress declined to grant consent on the grounds that congressional consent was unnecessary. The House of Representatives approved a bill granting consent to the Southern Regional Education Compact; however, the Senate did not concur because it concluded that the subject matter of the compact—education—was entirely a state prerogative.[97]

5.13 ENFORCEMENT OF INTERSTATE COMPACTS

The granting of consent suggests that Congress may enforce compact provisions; however, in practice, enforcement of interstate compacts is usually left to courts.

Party states have, on numerous occasions, filed suits in the U.S. Supreme Court requesting its interpretation of the provisions of interstate compacts. For example, the Court granted a request by Kansas in 2001 to

---

[93] Compacts, Cartels, and Congressional Consent. 68 Mo. L. Rev. 285 at 308. 2003.

[94] 934 F.2d at 479 (3rd Cir. 1991).

[95] Not to be confused with Joseph F. Zimmerman, co-author of this book.

[96] Zimmermann, Frederick. Lloyd and Wendell, Mitchell. 1976. *The Law and Use of Interstate Compacts*. Lexington, KY: Council of State Governments.

[97] Barton, Weldon V. 1967. *Interstate Compacts in the Political Process*. Chapel Hill, NC: University of North Carolina Press. Pages 132–133.

file a bill of complaint in equity against Colorado in an attempt to resolve disputes pertaining to the Arkansas River Compact. In *Kansas v. Colorado*, the Court rejected Colorado's argument that the 11th Amendment barred a damages award for Colorado's violation of the compact because the damages were losses suffered by individual farmers in Kansas and not by the State of Kansas.[98]

An individual or a state may challenge the validity of a compact in state or federal court. Similarly, an individual or a state may bring suit to have provisions of a compact enforced. In general, the 11th Amendment forbids a federal court from considering a suit in law or equity against a state brought by a citizen of a sister state or a foreign nation. Notwithstanding the 11th Amendment, a citizen can challenge a compact or its execution in a state or federal court in a proceeding to prevent a public officer from enforcing a compact. If brought in a state court, the suit can potentially be removed to a United States District Court under provisions of the Removal of Causes Act of 1920 on the ground the state court

"... might conceivably be interested in the outcome of the case...."[99]

Nebraska's participation in the Central Interstate Low-Level Radioactive Waste Compact created controversy over a 20-year period starting in the 1980s. As discussed in section 5.7, an initiative petition was used in Nebraska in 1988 in an unsuccessful attempt to repeal the law authorizing Nebraska's participation in the compact. Then, in 1999, the legislature decided to withdraw from the compact. Nebraska's change of heart proved costly. The Central Interstate Low-Level Radioactive Waste Commission filed a federal lawsuit resulting from Nebraska's withdrawal from the compact and its alleged refusal to meet its contractual obligations to store the radioactive waste. Waste generators and the compact commission's contractor filed a suit in the U.S. District Court for the District of Nebraska, alleging that the state of Nebraska had deliberately delayed review of their license application for eight years and that it had always intended to deny it. The court ruled in 1999 that Nebraska had waived its 11th Amendment immunity when it joined the

---

[98] *Kansas v. Colorado.* 533 U.S. 1. 2001.

[99] 41 Stat. 554.

compact.[100] In 2001, the U.S. Court of Appeals for the Eighth Circuit affirmed the lower court's decision.[101] In 2004, Nebraska agreed to settle the lawsuit for $141,000,000.[102]

5.14 AMENDMENTS TO INTERSTATE COMPACTS

Party states may amend an interstate compact. Proposed amendments to an interstate compact typically follow the same process employed in the enactment of the original compact by each party (e.g., approval of a bill by the legislature and Governor). For example, the Tri-States Lotto Compact provides:

> "Amendments and supplements to this compact may be adopted by concurrent legislation of the party states."

In addition, the consent of Congress is necessary for an amendment of an interstate compact if the original compact received such consent.

As a matter of practical politics, an objection by a member of Congress who represents an area affected by a compact will often be able to halt congressional consideration of consent. This fact is illustrated by the experience of the New Jersey Legislature and the New York Legislature, which each enacted an amendment to the Port Authority of New York and New Jersey Compact (signed by the two Governors) allowing the Port Authority to initiate industrial development projects. In 1967, Representative Elizabeth Holtzman of New York placed a hold on the consent bill on the grounds that the Port Authority had failed to solve the port's transportation problems. Holtzman argued that the Port Authority should construct a railroad freight tunnel under the Hudson River to obviate the need of trains to travel 125 miles to the north to a rail bridge over the river. She removed the hold upon reaching an agreement with the Authority. The Port Authority agreed that it would finance an independent study of the economic feasibility of constructing such a tunnel. The study ultimately reached the conclusion that a rail freight tunnel would not be economically viable.

The Constitution (section 10 of Article I) authorizes Congress to revise state statutes levying import and export duties; however, it does

---

[100] *Entergy, Arkansas, Incorporated v. Nebraska*, 68 F.Supp.2d 1093 at 1100 (D.Neb.1999).

[101] *Entergy, Arkansas, Incorporated v. Nebraska*, 241 F.3d 979 at 991–992 (8th Cir. 2001).

[102] *Lincoln Journal Star.* July 15, 2005.

not grant similar authority to revise interstate compacts. Congress withdrew its consent to a Kentucky–Pennsylvania Interstate Compact that stipulated that the Ohio River should be kept free of obstructions. In 1855, the U.S. Supreme Court ruled in *Pennsylvania v. Wheeling and Belmont Bridge Company* that the compact was constitutional under the Constitution's Supremacy Clause (Article VI) and that a compact approved by Congress did not restrict Congress's power to regulate an interstate compact.[103] In the 1917 case of *Louisville Bridge Company v. United States*, the Court ruled that Congress may amend a compact even in the absence of a specific provision reserving to Congress the authority to alter, amend, or repeal the compact.[104] A federal statute terminating a compact is not subject to the due process guarantee of the 5th Amendment to the Constitution on the ground that this protection extends only to persons.

5.15 DURATION, TERMINATION, AND WITHDRAWALS

The duration of an interstate compact, the method of terminating a compact, and the method by which a party may withdraw from a compact are generally specified by the compact itself.

5.15.1 DURATION OF AN INTERSTATE COMPACT

The U.S. Constitution does not address the question of the permissible duration of interstate compacts. The 1785 Maryland–Virginia compact regulating fishing and navigation on the Chesapeake Bay and the Potomac was ratified under the Articles of Confederation and remained in effect until 1958 (when it was replaced by the Potomac River Compact).

Some compacts contain a sunset provision specifying the compact's duration. For example, California agreed to serve, for 35 years, as the host state for the storage of radioactive waste for the states of Arizona, North Dakota, South Dakota, and California in the Southwestern Low-Level Radioactive Waste Disposal Compact.

5.15.2 TERMINATION OF AN INTERSTATE COMPACT

Many compacts contain a termination provision. For example, the Colorado River Compact stipulates that termination may be authorized only by a unanimous vote of all party states.

---

[103] *Pennsylvania v. Wheeling and Belmont Bridge Company.* 50 U.S. 647. 1855.

[104] *Louisville Bridge Company v. United States.* 242 U.S. 409. 1917.

The Central Interstate Low-Level Radioactive Waste Compact permits states to withdraw, but that the compact shall not be terminated until all parties leave the compact.

> "G. The withdrawal of a party state from this compact under subsection D of Article VII of the compact or the revocation of a state's membership in this compact under subsection E of Article VII of the compact shall not affect the applicability of this compact to the remaining party states.

> "H. This compact shall be terminated when all party states have withdrawn pursuant to subsection D of Article VII of the compact."

5.15.3 WITHDRAWAL FROM AN INTERSTATE COMPACT

Most compacts (other than those settling boundary disputes) have a provision permitting a party state to withdraw. If a state originally joined a compact by enacting a statute, withdrawal is usually accomplished by enacting a new statute withdrawing from the compact.

Examples of withdrawals include the action of the Maryland General Assembly withdrawing from the Interstate Bus Motor Fuel Tax Compact in 1967 and its action withdrawing from the National Guard Mutual Assistance Compact in 1981. In 1995, the Virginia General Assembly enacted a statute withdrawing from the Atlantic States Marine Fisheries Compact, complaining that Virginia's fishing quotas were too low.

States may withdraw from a compact and then rejoin it. For example, Florida withdrew from the Atlantic States Marine Fisheries Compact and then subsequently rejoined the compact.

Although some compacts allow instantaneous withdrawal, most require a party to provide a specified amount of advance notice before its withdrawal becomes effective. For example, the Interstate Mining Compact authorizes a party state to withdraw its membership one year after the Governor of the withdrawing state notifies the Governors of all the other compacting states.

The Delaware River Basin Compact requires advance notice of at least 20 years for withdrawal, with such notice being allowed only during a five-year window every 100 years.

Section 8.6 contains a considerably more detailed discussion of withdrawals from interstate compacts.

5.16 ADMINISTRATION OF INTERSTATE COMPACTS

About one half of all modern-day interstate compacts establish a commission to administer the subject matter of the compact. The remaining compacts are generally administered by departments and agencies of the party states.

For example, the Driver License Compact (to which 45 states adhere) requires a party state to report each conviction of a driver from another party state for a motor vehicle violation to the licensing authority of the driver's home state. The compact requires the home state to treat the reported violation as if it had occurred in the home state. The compact also requires the licensing authority of each member state to determine whether an applicant for a driver license has held or currently holds a driver's license issued by another party state.

Similarly, the Nonresident Violator Compact (enacted by 44 states) ensures that nonresident drivers answer summonses or appearance tickets for moving violations. This compact (like the Driver License Compact) requires each member state to report each conviction of a driver from another party state for a motor vehicle violation to the licensing authority of the driver's home state. This compact is designed to ensure that nonresident motorists are treated in the same manner as resident motorists and that their due process rights are protected. A driver who fails to respond to an appearance ticket or summons will have his or her license suspended by the issuing state.

5.17 STYLE OF INTERSTATE COMPACTS

As a matter convention, modern interstate compacts are typically organized into articles, with unnumbered sections. After each member state enacts the compact, the various articles of the compact are given numbers and letters in the state's compiled code in accordance with the state's style. Similarly, after Congress consents to a compact, the various articles of the compact may be assigned different letters and numbers. Thus, compacts (and congressional legislation consenting to compacts) typically make reference to enactment of "substantially" the same agreement by other member states.

5.18 COMPARISON OF TREATIES AND COMPACTS

Although interstate compacts bear many similarities to international treaties among nations, they differ in three important respects.

First, Congress may enact a statute that conflicts with an international treaty, whereas a state legislature lacks the authority to enact a statute conflicting with any provision of an interstate compact.

Second, a compact is a contract that is enforceable by courts. In contrast, the procedure for enforcement of an international treaty is specified within the treaty itself. In practice, many treaties contain no specific provision for enforcement and merely rely on the goodwill of the parties.

Third, under the Constitution, the President is granted the sole authority to negotiate a treaty with another nation. In contrast, no provision in the Constitution stipulates the manner of negotiation of interstate compacts. Moreover, Congress has never enacted any general statute specifying procedures to be followed by a state that is contemplating entry into an interstate compact.

There is no international law provision authorizing citizens of a signatory to a treaty to be involved in its termination. In 1838, the U.S. Supreme Court applied this principle of international law to interstate compacts. The Court ruled, in the case of *Georgetown v. Alexander Canal Company*, that citizens whose rights would be affected adversely by a compact are not parties to a compact and that they consequently can have no direct involvement in a compact's termination.[105]

5.19 COMPARISON OF UNIFORM STATE LAWS AND INTERSTATE COMPACTS

The term "uniform state law" usually refers to a law drafted and recommended by the National Conference of Commissioners on Uniform State Laws (NCCUSL), although the term is occasionally used to refer to laws originating elsewhere. The Conference, formed in 1892 upon the recommendation of the American Bar Association, is a non-governmental body. The Conference primarily works on private civil law and is most widely known for its work on the Uniform Commercial Code. Since 1892, the Conference has produced more than 200 recommended laws in areas such as commercial law, family or domestic relations law, estates, probate and trusts, real estate, implementation of full faith and credit, interstate enforcement of judgments, and alternative dispute resolution. There are numerous uniform acts that have been adopted by large

---

[105] *Georgetown v. Alexander Canal Company.* 37 U.S. 91 at 95–96. 1838.

numbers of states, including the Uniform Anatomical Gift Act, the Uniform Fraudulent Transfer Act, the Uniform Interstate Family Support Act, the Uniform Enforcement of Foreign Judgments Act, and the Uniform Transfers to Minors Act.

There is some resemblance between an interstate compact and a uniform state law. Both, for example, entail enactment of identical statutes by a group of states. An interstate compact encompassing all 50 states and the District of Columbia and a uniform state law enacted by the same 51 jurisdictions each has the effect of establishing national policy. There are, however, a number of important differences.

First, the goal of a uniform state law is, almost always, enactment of the identical statute by all states. Many interstate compacts are inherently limited to particular geographic areas (e.g., the Port of New York Authority Compact, the Arkansas River Compact, and the Great Lakes Basin Compact) or to states that are engaged in particular activities (e.g., the Interstate Oil Compact and the Multistate Lottery Agreement).

Second, the effective date of a uniform state law is typically not contingent on identical legislation being passed in any other state. A uniform state law generally takes effect in each state as soon as each state enacts it. That is, a uniform state law stands alone and is not coordinated with the identical laws that other states may, or may not, pass. If it happens that all 50 states enact a particular uniform state law, then the goal of establishing a uniform policy for the entire country is achieved. If a substantial fraction of the states enact a uniform state law, then the goal of uniformity is partially achieved. If only one state enacts a uniform state law, that particular statute serves as the law of that state on the subject matter involved. In contrast, the effective date of a compact is almost always contingent on the enactment by some specified number or some specified combination of states. The reason for this is that states are apt to enter into interstate compacts in order to obtain some benefit that can be obtained only by cooperative and coordinated action with one or more sister states.

Third, although the goal of the National Conference of Commissioners on Uniform State Laws is that identical laws be adopted in all states, it is very common for individual states to amend the Conference's recommended statute in response to local pressures. If the changes are not major, the Conference's goal of uniformity may nonetheless be substantially (albeit not perfectly) achieved. In contrast, adoption of a compact requires a meeting of minds. Because an interstate compact is a contract, each party that desires to adhere to an interstate compact must enact identical wording (except for insubstantial differences such as numbering and punctuation). Variations in substance are not allowed.

Fourth, and most importantly, a uniform state law does not establish a contractual relationship among the states involved. When a state enacts a uniform state law, it undertakes no obligations to other states. The enacting state merely seeks the benefits associated with uniform treatment of the subject matter at hand. Each state's legislature may repeal or amend a uniform state law at any time, at its own pleasure and convenience. There is no procedure for withdrawal (or advance notice for withdrawal) in a uniform state law. A uniform state law does not create any new legal entity, and therefore there is no legal entity from which to withdraw. In contrast, an interstate compact establishes a contractual relationship among its party states. Once a state enters into a compact, it is legally bound to the compact's terms, including the compact's specified restrictions and procedures for withdrawal and the compact's specified procedure for termination of the compact as a whole.

5.20 COMPARISON OF FEDERAL MULTI-STATE COMMISSIONS AND INTERSTATE COMPACTS

Federal multi-state commissions bear some resemblance to the commissions that are established by some interstate compacts. There are, however, a number of important differences between federally created multi-state commissions and interstate compacts.

In 1879, Congress first recognized the need for a governmental body in a multi-state region by establishing the Mississippi River Commission. The enabling statute directed the Commission to deepen channels; improve navigation safety; prevent destructive floods; and promote commerce, the postal system, and trade. The Commission's original members were three officers of the U.S. Army Corps of Engineers, one member of the U.S. Coast and Geodetic Survey, and three citizen members, including two civil engineers. Commission members are nominated by the President, subject to the Senate's advice and consent.

In a similar vein, the Water Resources Planning Act of 1965

authorizes the President, at the request of the concerned governors, to establish other river basin commissions. Such commissions have been created for the Ohio River and Upper Mississippi River basin.

The most well-known multi-state commission—the Tennessee Valley Authority—was created by Congress in 1933. The TVA operates in an area encompassing parts of seven states. Its purposes are to promote agricultural and industrial development, control floods, and improve navigation on the Tennessee River. The President appoints, with the Senate's advice and consent, three TVA commissioners for nine-year terms. The creation of the TVA is credited to populist Senator George Norris of Nebraska, who conducted a crusade for many years against the high rates charged by electric utility companies. Aside from the benefits to the states in the Tennessee Valley, Norris and his supporters argued that the cost of TVA-generated electricity would serve as a yardstick for evaluating the rates charged by private power companies elsewhere in the country.

Although the TVA possesses broad powers to develop the river basin, the authority has largely concentrated its efforts on dams and channels, fertilizer research, and production of electricity. The TVA is generally credited with achieving considerable success in its flood control, land and forest conservation, and river-management activities. At the same time, the TVA has engendered considerable controversy over the years in a number of areas.

There are several differences between federal multi-state commissions and the commissions that are established by interstate compacts.

First, federal multi-state commissions are entirely creatures of the federal government. The states play no official role in enacting the enabling legislation establishing such bodies. In contrast, each state makes its own decision as to whether to enact an interstate compact.

Second, although state officials often provide advice on appointments to federal multi-state commissions, the appointing authority for members of a federal multi-state commissions is entirely federal (i.e., the President). In contrast, the members of a commission established by an interstate compact are typically appointed by the states (e.g., by the Governors).

5.21 FUTURE OF INTERSTATE COMPACTS

In recent years, Congress has, with increasing frequency, exercised its preemption powers to remove regulatory authority totally or partially from the states. This tendency is responsible for the decrease in the number of new regulatory compacts since the mid 1960s.[106] For example, the Mid-Atlantic States Air Pollution Control Compact was entered into by Connecticut, New Jersey, and New York; however, Congress did not consent to the compact and instead enacted the Air Quality Act of 1967,[107] preempting state regulatory authority over air pollution abatement.

There are countervailing tendencies. Economic interest groups frequently lobby for the establishment of regulatory compacts among states, arguing that coordinated action by the states is sufficient to solve a particular problem.

It is reasonable to predict that increasing urban sprawl may someday lead to an interstate compact that establishes an interstate city encompassing an urban area spread over two or more states. Although no such interstate city has been created to date, the New Hampshire–Vermont Interstate School Compact has been used to establish two interstate school districts, each including a New Hampshire town and one or more Vermont towns. In the same vein, Kansas and Missouri have entered into a compact establishing a metropolitan cultural district governed by a commission. The commission's membership is determined by the number of counties that decide to join the district. Eligible counties include one with a population exceeding 300,000 that is adjacent to the state line, one that contains a part of a city with a population exceeding 400,000, and one that is contiguous to one of these.[108]

5.22 PROPOSALS FOR INTERSTATE COMPACTS ON ELECTIONS

There have been suggestions, over the years, for using interstate compacts in the field of elections.

The 1970 U.S. Supreme Court case of *Oregon v. Mitchell* was concerned with congressional legislation to bring about uniformity among state durational residency requirements for voters in presidential elections. In his opinion (partially concurring and partially dissenting), Justice Potter Stewart pointed out that if Congress had not acted, the states could have adopted an interstate compact to accomplish the same

---

[106] Zimmerman, Joseph F. 2005. *Congressional Preemption: Regulatory Federalism* Albany, NY: State University of New York Press.

[107] 81 Stat. 485.

[108] 114 Stat. 909.

objective. Justice Stewart pointed out that a compact involving all the states would, in effect, establish a nationwide policy on residency for election purposes.[109]

In the 1990s, Senator Charles Schumer of New York proposed a bi-state interstate compact in which New York and Texas would pool their electoral votes in presidential elections. Both states were (and still are) non-competitive in presidential politics. Schumer observed that the two states have almost the same number of electoral votes (currently 34 for Texas and 31 for New York) and regularly produce majorities of approximately the same magnitude in favor of each state's respective dominant political party. The Democrats typically carry New York by about 60%, and the Republicans typically carry Texas by about 60%. The purpose of the proposed compact was to create a large super-state (slightly larger than California) that would attract the attention of the presidential candidates during presidential campaigns.

---

[109] *Oregon v. Mitchell.* 400 U.S. 112 at 286–287. 1970.

6 The Agreement Among the States to Elect the President by National Popular Vote

This chapter

- summarizes the motivation for the authors' proposal to employ an interstate compact to change the system for electing the President and Vice President of the United States (section 6.1),
- presents the text of the authors' proposal, namely the "Agreement Among the States to Elect the President by National Popular Vote" (section 6.2),
- explains the authors' proposed compact (section 6.3),
- mentions federal legislation that might be enacted by Congress in connection with the proposed interstate compact (section 6.4), and
- discusses previous proposals for multi-state electoral legislation (section 6.5).

6.1 MOTIVATION FOR THE PROPOSED INTERSTATE COMPACT

Chapter 1 of this book made the following points:

- Under the winner-take-all rule that is in nearly universal use in the United States, all of a state's electoral votes are controlled by a statewide plurality of the popular votes. Under this rule, a person's vote is nearly worthless unless the voter happens to live in a closely divided battleground state.
- Because only about 18 states are competitive in presidential elections, voters in two-thirds of the states are ignored in presidential elections.
- The existing winner-take-all system divides the nation's 122,000,000 popular votes into 51 separate pools, thereby

regularly manufacturing artificial electoral crises even when the nationwide popular vote is not particularly close. In the past six decades, there have been six presidential elections in which a shift of a small number of votes in one or two states would have elected (and in 2000, did elect) a presidential candidate who lost the popular vote nationwide.

- In about one election in 14, the existing system elects a candidate to the Presidency who did not win the nationwide popular vote.
- The statewide winner-take-all system is the reason why presidential voting does not matter in two thirds of the states, artificial crises are regularly manufactured, and second-place candidates are sometimes elected to the Presidency.

Chapter 2 established the following facts:

- The statewide winner-take-all system is established by state law—not the U.S. Constitution or federal law.
- The U.S. Constitution gives each state the exclusive power to choose the manner of choosing its presidential electors. Unlike the states' power to choose the manner of electing U.S. Representatives and Senators, the states' power to choose the manner of allocating its electoral votes is not subject to Congressional oversight.
- The Founding Fathers did not design or advocate the current system of electing the President. Instead, the current system evolved over a period of decades as a result of political considerations. The statewide winner-take-all rule was used by only three states in the nation's first presidential election (1789). Because each state realized that it diminished its voice by dividing its electoral votes, the statewide winner-take-all rule for the popular election of presidential electors became the norm in the first five decades after the Constitution's ratification.
- Because the power to allocate electoral votes is exclusively a state power and the statewide winner-take-all rule is contained only in state statutes, a federal constitutional

amendment is not necessary to change the existing state laws specifying use of the statewide winner-take-all system. The states have the constitutional power to change the current system.

Chapter 3 analyzed the three most prominent approaches to presidential election reform that have been proposed in the form of a federal constitutional amendment, namely the fractional proportional allocation of electoral votes, allocation of electoral votes by congressional district, and direct nationwide popular election. Each of these three approaches is analyzed in terms of three criteria:

- **Accuracy:** Would it ensure the election to the Presidency of the candidate with the most popular votes nationwide?
- **Competitiveness:** Would it improve upon the current situation in which voters in two-thirds of the states are ignored because they live in presidentially non-competitive states?
- **Equality:** Would every vote be equal?

Chapter 4 analyzed the two most prominent approaches to presidential election reform that can be unilaterally enacted without a federal constitutional amendment and without action by Congress, namely the whole-number proportional approach and the congressional-district approach.

Chapters 3 and 4 reached the conclusion that nationwide popular election of the President is the only approach that satisfies the criteria of accuracy, competitiveness, and equality.

Chapter 5 provided background on interstate compacts and made the following points:

- Interstate compacts are specifically authorized by the U.S. Constitution as a means by which the states may act in concert to address a problem.
- There are several hundred interstate compacts in existence, covering a wide variety of topics.
- An interstate compact is enacted in the same manner as a state law—that is, by a legislative bill receiving gubernatorial approval (or sufficient legislative support to override a gubernatorial veto) or by the citizen-initiative process (in states having this process).

- Interstate compacts typically address problems that cannot be solved unilaterally, but that can be solved by coordinated action. Accordingly, a compact almost always takes effect on a contingent basis—that is, the compact does not take effect until it is enacted by a specified number or combination of states that are sufficient to achieve the compact's goals.

- There are no constitutional restrictions on the subject matter of interstate compacts (other than the implicit limitation that the compact's subject matter must be among the powers that the states are permitted to exercise).

- An interstate compact has the force and effect of statutory law in the states belonging to the compact. The provisions of an interstate compact bind all state officials with the same force as all other state laws. The provisions of a compact are enforceable in court in the same way that any other state law is enforceable—that is, a court may compel a state official to execute the provisions of a compact (by mandamus), and a court may enjoin a state official from violating a compact's provisions (by injunction).

- An interstate compact is a binding contractual arrangement among states involved. The U.S. Constitution prohibits states from impairing the obligations of any contract, including interstate compacts. Thus, each state belonging to an interstate compact is assured that its sister states will perform their obligations under the compact.

- Because a compact is a contract, the provisions of an interstate compact take precedence over any conflicting law of any state belonging to the compact. As long as a state remains a party to a compact, it may not enact a law in conflict with its obligations under the compact. That is, the provisions of an interstate compact take precedence over a conflicting law—even if the conflicting law is enacted after the state enters into the compact.

- A state may withdraw from an interstate compact in accordance with the provisions for withdrawal contained in the compact.

The authors' proposal, namely an interstate compact entitled the "Agreement Among the States to Elect the President by National Popular Vote," would not become effective in any state until it is enacted by states collectively possessing a majority of the electoral votes (that is, 270 of the 538 electoral votes).

The proposed compact does not change a state's internal procedures for operating a presidential election. After the 50 states and the District of Columbia certify their popular vote counts for President in the usual way, a grand total of popular votes would be calculated by adding up the popular vote count from all 51 jurisdictions.

The Electoral College would remain intact under the proposed compact. The compact would simply change the Electoral College from an institution that reflects the voters' state-by-state choices (or, in the case of Maine and Nebraska, district-wide choices) into a body that reflects the voters' nationwide choice. Specifically, the proposed compact would require that each member state award its electoral votes to the presidential candidate who received the largest number of popular votes in all 50 states and the District of Columbia. Because the compact would become effective only when it encompasses states collectively possessing a majority of the electoral votes, the presidential candidate receiving the most popular votes in all 50 states and the District of Columbia would be guaranteed enough electoral votes in the Electoral College to be elected to the Presidency.

Note that every state's popular vote is included in the nationwide total regardless of whether it is a member of the compact. Membership in the compact is not required for the popular votes of a state to count.

Note also that the political complexion of the particular states belonging to the compact does not affect the outcome—that is, the presidential candidate receiving the most popular votes in all 50 states and the District of Columbia is assured sufficient electoral votes to be elected to the Presidency.

6.2 TEXT OF THE PROPOSED COMPACT

This section presents the entire text (888 words) of the proposed "Agreement Among the States to Elect the President by National Popular Vote."

	ARTICLE I—MEMBERSHIP
I-1	Any State of the United States and the District of Columbia may become a member of this agreement by enacting this agreement.
	ARTICLE II—RIGHT OF THE PEOPLE IN MEMBER STATES TO VOTE FOR PRESIDENT AND VICE PRESIDENT
II-1	Each member state shall conduct a statewide popular election for President and Vice President of the United States.
	ARTICLE III—MANNER OF APPOINTING PRESIDENTIAL ELECTORS IN MEMBER STATES
III-1	Prior to the time set by law for the meeting and voting by the presidential electors, the chief election official of each member state shall determine the number of votes for each presidential slate in each State of the United States and in the District of Columbia in which votes have been cast in a statewide popular election and shall add such votes together to produce a "national popular vote total" for each presidential slate.
III-2	The chief election official of each member state shall designate the presidential slate with the largest national popular vote total as the "national popular vote winner."
III-3	The presidential elector certifying official of each member state shall certify the appointment in that official's own state of the elector slate nominated in that state in association with the national popular vote winner.
III-4	At least six days before the day fixed by law for the meeting and voting by the presidential electors, each member state shall make a final determination of the number of popular votes cast in the state for each presidential slate and shall communicate an official statement of such determination within 24 hours to the chief election official of each other member state.
III-5	The chief election official of each member state shall treat as conclusive an official statement containing the number of popular votes in a state for each presidential slate made by the day established by federal law for making a state's final determination conclusive as to the counting of electoral votes by Congress.
III-6	In event of a tie for the national popular vote winner, the presidential elector certifying official of each member state shall certify the appointment of the elector slate nominated in association with the presidential slate receiving the largest number of popular votes within that official's own state.
III-7	If, for any reason, the number of presidential electors nominated in a member state in association with the national popular vote winner is less than or greater than that state's number of electoral votes, the presidential candidate on the presidential slate that has been designated as the national popular vote winner shall have the power to nominate the presidential electors for that state and that state's presidential elector certifying official shall certify the appointment of such nominees.
III-8	The chief election official of each member state shall immediately release to the public all vote counts or statements of votes as they are determined or obtained.

III-9   This article shall govern the appointment of presidential electors in each member state in any year in which this agreement is, on July 20, in effect in states cumulatively possessing a majority of the electoral votes.

ARTICLE IV—OTHER PROVISIONS

IV-1   This agreement shall take effect when states cumulatively possessing a majority of the electoral votes have enacted this agreement in substantially the same form and the enactments by such states have taken effect in each state.

IV-2   Any member state may withdraw from this agreement, except that a withdrawal occurring six months or less before the end of a President's term shall not become effective until a President or Vice President shall have been qualified to serve the next term.

IV-3   The chief executive of each member state shall promptly notify the chief executive of all other states of when this agreement has been enacted and has taken effect in that official's state, when the state has withdrawn from this agreement, and when this agreement takes effect generally.

IV-4   This agreement shall terminate if the electoral college is abolished.

IV-5   If any provision of this agreement is held invalid, the remaining provisions shall not be affected.

ARTICLE V—DEFINITIONS

V-1   For purposes of this agreement,
"chief executive" shall mean the Governor of a State of the United States or the Mayor of the District of Columbia;

V-2   "elector slate" shall mean a slate of candidates who have been nominated in a state for the position of presidential elector in association with a presidential slate;

V-3   "chief election official" shall mean the state official or body that is authorized to certify the total number of popular votes for each presidential slate;

V-4   "presidential elector" shall mean an elector for President and Vice President of the United States;

V-5   "presidential elector certifying official" shall mean the state official or body that is authorized to certify the appointment of the state's presidential electors;

V-6   "presidential slate" shall mean a slate of two persons, the first of whom has been nominated as a candidate for President of the United States and the second of whom has been nominated as a candidate for Vice President of the United States, or any legal successors to such persons, regardless of whether both names appear on the ballot presented to the voter in a particular state;

V-7   "state" shall mean a State of the United States and the District of Columbia; and

V-8   "statewide popular election" shall mean a general election in which votes are cast for presidential slates by individual voters and counted on a statewide basis.

6.3 EXPLANATION OF THE PROPOSED COMPACT

6.3.1 Explanation of Article I—Membership

Article I of the compact identifies the compact's prospective parties, namely the 51 jurisdictions that are currently entitled to appoint presidential electors under the U.S. Constitution. These 51 jurisdictions include the 50 states and the District of Columbia (which acquired the right to appoint presidential electors under terms of the 23rd Amendment). Elsewhere in the compact, the uncapitalized word "state" (defined in article V of the compact) refers to any of these 51 jurisdictions. The term "member state" refers to a jurisdiction where the compact has been enacted into law and is in effect.

6.3.2 Explanation of Article II—Right of the People in Member States to Vote for President and Vice President

Article II of the compact mandates a popular election for President and Vice President in each member state.

> "Each member state shall conduct a statewide popular election for President and Vice President of the United States."

The term "statewide popular election" is defined in article V of the compact as

> "a general election at which votes are cast for presidential slates by individual voters and counted on a statewide basis."

From the perspective of the operation of the compact, this clause establishes an essential precondition for a nationwide popular vote for President and Vice President, namely that there will be popular votes to count. As discussed in detail in section 2.2, the people of the United States have no federal constitutional right to vote for President and Vice President. The people have acquired the privilege to vote for President and Vice President as a consequence of legislative action by their respective states. Moreover, except in Colorado, the people have no state constitutional right to vote for President and Vice President, and the existing privilege may be withdrawn at any time merely by passage of a state law. Indeed, state legislatures chose the presidential electors in a majority of the states participating in the nation's first presidential election (1789). Moreover, state legislatures have changed the rules for voting for President for purely political reasons. For example, just prior to the 1800 presidential election, the Federalist-controlled legislatures of Massachusetts and New Hampshire—fearing Jeffersonian victories in the popular votes in their states—repealed existing state statutes allowing the people to vote for presidential electors and vested that power in themselves. Article II of the compact precludes the state legislature of a member state from doing this.

Because an interstate compact is a contractual obligation among the member states, the provisions of a compact take precedence over any conflicting law of any member state. This principle applies regardless of when the conflicting law may have been enacted.[1] Thus, once a state enters into an interstate compact and the compact takes effect, the state is bound by the terms of the compact as long as the state remains in the compact. Because a compact is a contract, a state must remain in an interstate compact until the state withdraws from the compact in accordance with the compact's terms for withdrawal. Thus, in reading each provision of a compact, the reader may find it useful to imagine that every section of the compact is preceded by the words

> "Notwithstanding any other provision of law in the member state, whether enacted before or after the effective date of this compact, ..."

Thus, as long as a state remains in the compact, article II of the compact establishes the right of the people in each member state to vote for President and Vice President.

Article II of the compact also requires continued use by member states of another feature of presidential voting that is an essential precondition for a nationwide popular vote for President and Vice President (and that is currently in universal use by the states). Specifically, article II of the compact requires that member states continue to use the short presidential ballot (section 2.2.6) in which the voter is presented with a choice among "presidential slates" containing a specifically named presidential nominee and a vice-presidential nominee.[2] The term "presidential

---

[1] Council of State Governments. 2003. *Interstate Compacts and Agencies 2003.* Lexington, KY: The Council of State Governments. Page 6.

[2] This clause does not prevent a presidential candidate from running with more than one vice-presidential nominee. In 2004, for example, Ralph Nader appeared on the ballot in New York as the presidential nominee of the Independence Party with Jan D. Pierce as his vice-presidential nominee. He simultaneously appeared on the New York ballot as the presidential nominee of the Peace and Justice Party with Peter Miguel Camejo as his

slate" is defined in article V of the compact as

> "a slate of two persons, the first of whom has been nominated as a candidate for President of the United States and the second of whom has been nominated as a candidate for Vice President of the United States, or any legal successors to such persons ...."

The continued use of the short presidential ballot is an essential precondition for a nationwide popular vote because it permits the aggregation, from state to state, of the popular votes that have been cast for various presidential slates. If, for example, the voters in a particular state cast separate votes for individual presidential electors (say, in the manner shown in the 1964 Vermont ballot shown in figure 2.1 and discussed in section 2.2.6 or the 1960 Alabama ballot shown in figure 2.13 and discussed in section 2.11), the winning presidential electors from that state would each inevitably have a different vote count. Thus, there would not be any single number available to add into the nationwide tally being accumulated by the presidential slates running in the remainder of the country.

6.3.3 Explanation of Article III—Manner of Appointing Presidential Electors in Member States

Article III of the compact prescribes the manner by which each state would appoint its presidential electors under the compact. Article III establishes the mechanics for a nationwide popular election. The first three clauses of article III are the main clauses for implementing nationwide popular election of the President and Vice President.

The first clause of article III of the compact provides:

> "Prior to the time set by law for the meeting and voting by the presidential electors, the chief election official of each member state shall determine the number of votes for each presidential slate in each State of the United States and in the District of Columbia in which votes have been cast in a statewide popular election and shall add such votes together

vice-presidential nominee. There were, necessarily, two different lists of 31 nominees for presidential elector associated with each of the two Nader "presidential slates" in New York in 2004. Existing New York law treated and counted Nader's Independence Party votes separately from Nader's Peace and Justice Party votes. That is, there were two different Nader "presidential slates" in New York in 2004.

to produce a 'national popular vote total' for each presidential slate."

The phrase "the time set by law for the meeting and voting by the presidential electors" refers to the federal law (title 3, chapter 1, section 7 of the United States Code) providing:

> "The electors of President and Vice President of each State shall meet and give their votes on the first Monday after the second Wednesday in December next following their appointment at such place in each State as the legislature of such State shall direct."

In 2004, the federally designated day for the meeting of the Electoral College was Monday, December 13.

The term "chief election official" used throughout the compact is defined in article V of the compact as

> "the state official or board that is authorized to certify the total number of popular votes cast for each presidential slate."

In most states, the "chief election official" is the Secretary of State or the state canvassing board.

The first clause of article III of the compact requires that the chief election official obtain statements showing the number of popular votes cast for each presidential slate in each state. Then, this clause requires that the popular votes for each presidential slate from all the states be added together to yield a "national popular vote total" for each presidential slate.

Because the purpose of the compact is to achieve a nationwide popular vote for President and Vice President, the popular vote counts from all 50 states and the District of Columbia are included in the "national popular vote total" regardless of whether the jurisdiction is a member of the compact. That is, the compact counts the popular votes from member states on an equal footing with those from non-member states.

Popular votes can, however, only be counted from non-member states if there are popular votes available to count. As already mentioned, Article II of the compact guarantees that each member state will produce a popular vote count because it requires member states to allow their voters to vote for President and Vice President in a "statewide popular election." Even though all states currently permit their voters to vote for presidential electors in a "statewide popular election," non-member states are, of course, not bound by the compact. In the unlikely event that a non-member state were to take the presidential vote away from its own people (as Massachusetts and New Hampshire did, for partisan political reasons, prior to the 1800 presidential election), there would be no popular vote count available from such a state.

Similarly, in the unlikely event that a non-member state were to remove the names of the presidential nominees and vice-presidential nominees from the ballot and present the voters only with names of unpledged candidates for presidential elector (such as the 1960 Alabama ballot shown in figure 2.13 and discussed in section 2.11), there would be no way to associate the vote counts of the various unpledged presidential electors with the nationwide tally being accumulated by any regular "presidential slate" running in the rest of the country.

The compact addresses the above two unlikely possibilities by specifying that the popular votes that are to be aggregated to produce the "national popular vote total" are those that are

" ... cast for each presidential slate in each State of the United States and in the District of Columbia **in which votes have been cast in a statewide popular election....**" [Emphasis added]

The purpose of the second clause of article III of the compact is to identify the winner of the presidential election:

"The chief election official of each member state shall designate the presidential slate with the largest national popular vote total as the 'national popular vote winner.' "

The third clause of article III of the compact guarantees that the "national popular vote winner" will end up with a majority of the electoral votes in the Electoral College.

"The presidential elector certifying official of each member state shall certify the appointment in that official's own state of the elector slate nominated in that state in association with the national popular vote winner."

The third clause of article III of the compact refers to the "presidential elector certifying official" rather than the "chief election official" because these two officials are not the same in every state. For example, in some states, the "presidential elector certifying official" is an official or entity that is not otherwise involved in the administration of elections (e.g., the Governor or the Superior Court). The term "presidential elector certifying official" is defined in article V of the compact.

For purposes of illustration, suppose that the compact was in effect in 2004, and that Colorado was a member of the compact in 2004, and that the Republican presidential slate received the most popular votes in all 50 States and the District of Columbia (as was the case in the 2004 presidential election). In that event, the Colorado Secretary of State would declare the nine presidential electors who had been nominated by the Colorado Republican Party to be elected as Colorado's members of the Electoral College.

Because the purpose of the compact is to implement a nationwide popular election of the President and Vice President, it is the *national* vote total—not each state's separate statewide vote count—that would determine the national winner. Under the compact, the Electoral College would reflect the *nationwide* will of the voters—not the voters' separate statewide wills. Thus, the presidential electors nominated by the Republican Party in *all* states belonging to the compact would have won election as members of the Electoral College in their states. If Colorado voters had favored the Kerry-Edwards slate in 2004, the presidential electors nominated by the Republican Party in Colorado, for example, still would have won election as members of the Electoral College in Colorado in 2004 because the specific purpose of the compact is to award enough electoral votes to win the Presidency to the presidential candidate with the most votes nationwide.

Because the compact becomes effective only when it encompasses states collectively possessing a majority of the electoral votes (i.e., 270 or more of the 538 electoral votes), the presidential slate receiving the most popular votes in all 50 States and the District of Columbia is guaranteed at least 270 electoral votes when the Electoral College meets in mid-December. Given the fact that the Bush-Cheney presidential slate received about 3,500,000 more popular votes in the 50 States and the District of Columbia in 2004 than the Kerry-Edwards slate, the compact would have guaranteed the Bush-Cheney slate a majority of the electoral votes in the Electoral College. Under the compact, the Bush-Cheney slate would have received a majority of the electoral votes even if 59,393 Bush voters in Ohio had switched to Kerry in 2004 thereby giving Kerry a plurality of the popular votes in Ohio. In contrast, under the present system, if Kerry had carried Ohio, Kerry would have received all of Ohio's 20 electoral votes and Kerry would have been elected to the Presidency with 272 electoral votes (to Bush's 266).

The first three clauses of article III of the compact are the main clauses for implementing nationwide popular election of the President and Vice President. The remaining clauses of article III of the compact deal with administrative matters and technical issues.

The fourth clause of article III of the compact requires the timely issuance by each of the compact's member states of an "official statement" of the state's "final determination" of its presidential vote.

> "At least six days before the day fixed by law for the meeting and voting by the presidential electors, each member state shall make a final determination of the number of popular votes cast in the state for each presidential slate and shall communicate an official statement of such determination within 24 hours to the chief election official of each other member state."

The particular deadline in this clause corresponds to the deadline contained in the "safe harbor" provision of federal law (section 5 of title 3, chapter 1 of the United States Code). The phrase "final determination" in this clause corresponds to the term used in the "safe harbor" provision. Section 5 provides:

> "If any State shall have provided, by laws enacted prior to the day fixed for the appointment of the electors, for its final determination of any controversy or contest concerning the appointment of all or any of the electors of such State, by judicial or other methods or procedures, and such determination shall have been made at least six days before the time fixed for the meeting of the electors, such determination made pursuant to such law so existing on said day, and made at least six days prior to said time of meeting of the electors, shall be conclusive, and shall govern in the counting of the electoral votes as provided in the Constitution, and as hereinafter regulated, so far as the ascertainment of the electors appointed by such State is concerned."

The federally established "safe harbor" date for the 2004 presidential election was Monday December 6, 2004.

The fourth clause of article III of the compact, in effect, mandates each member state to comply with the "safe harbor" deadline. As a practical matter, this clause is merely a backstop because the vast majority of states already have specific state statutory deadlines for certifying the results of presidential elections, and these existing statutory deadlines come earlier than the federal "safe harbor" date (appendix T). This clause is a backstop for the additional reason that the U.S. Supreme Court in *Bush v. Gore* effectively treated the "safe harbor" date as a deadline for a state's "final determination" of its presidential election results.[3]

The word "communicated" in the fourth clause of article III of the compact is intended to permit transmission of the "official statement" by secure electronic means that may become available in the future (rather than, say, physical delivery of the official statement by an overnight courier service).

The fifth clause of article III of the compact provides:

> "The chief election official of each member state shall treat as conclusive an official statement containing the number of popular votes in a state for each presidential slate made by the day established by federal law for making a state's final determination conclusive as to the counting of electoral votes by Congress."

When the joint session of Congress counts the electoral votes on January 6th as provided in title 3, chapter 1, section 15 of the United States Code, each state's own "final determination" of its vote is considered "conclusive" as to the counting of electoral votes by Congress if it was finalized by the date established in the "safe harbor" provision of federal law (title 3, chapter 1, section 5). This section makes each state's (and, in particular, each *non-member* state's) final determination of its popular vote similarly "conclusive" when the chief election officials of the compact's member states add up the national popular vote under the terms of the compact.

The sixth clause of article III of the compact deals with the highly unlikely event of a tie in the national popular vote count:

---

[3] *Bush v. Gore.* 531 U.S. 98. 2000.

"In event of a tie for the national popular vote winner, the presidential elector certifying official of each member state shall certify the appointment of the elector slate nominated in association with the presidential slate receiving the largest number of popular votes within that official's own state."

The purpose of the seventh clause of article III of the compact is to ensure that the presidential slate receiving the most popular votes nationwide gets what it is entitled to—namely 100% of the electoral votes of each member state.

"If, for any reason, the number of presidential electors nominated in a member state in association with the national popular vote winner is less than or greater than that state's number of electoral votes, the presidential candidate on the presidential slate that has been designated as the national popular vote winner shall have the power to nominate the presidential electors for that state and that state's presidential elector certifying official shall certify the appointment of such nominees."

The seventh clause of article III of the compact addresses six potential situations that might prevent the national popular vote winner from receiving all of the electoral votes from a member state. These situations arise because of gaps and ambiguities in the widely varying language of state election laws concerning presidential elections.

First, the winning presidential slate might not be on the ballot in a particular member state. Presidential candidates (particularly third-party candidates) frequently fail to get on the ballot in a particular state because they did not comply with the state's ballot-access requirements (or perhaps did not even attempt to be on the ballot in a particular state). If a presidential candidate were to win the popular vote nationally without having qualified to be the ballot in a particular state belonging to the compact, there would no official slate of presidential electors "nominated in association with" the "national popular vote winner" in that particular member state. The remedy for this situation (and each of the other situations described below) is to employ the concept behind the current law for choosing presidential electors in Pennsylvania. Under current Pennsylvania law, each presidential nominee directly nominates the presidential electors who will run in association with the nominee's presidential slate in Pennsylvania.[4] Thus, under the seventh clause of article III of the compact, the unrepresented presidential candidate would have the power to nominate the presidential electors for the state involved. The state's presidential elector certifying official would then certify the appointment of the candidate's choices for presidential elector. Note that the nomination of the presidential electors would, in this situation, come after the November voting (i.e., after the presidential slate involved had won the nationwide popular vote and had been declared to be the "national popular vote winner").

Second, no presidential electors may be "nominated in association with" the winning presidential slate in a particular member state because of some unforeseen situation that might arise under the language of state election codes. The Republican National Committee scheduled the 2004 Republican National Convention somewhat later than usual. In particular, the convention was scheduled to be held after Alabama's statutory deadline for each political party to file the name of its presidential and vice-presidential nominees with state officials. The scheduling of the convention created the possibility that there would be no Republican presidential slate on the Alabama ballot in 2004. The problem was satisfactorily resolved when the Alabama legislature agreed to pass special legislation in early 2004 to change the state law.

Third, a full slate of presidential electors may not be nominated in association with the winning presidential slate in a particular member state. For example, in 2004, Congressman Sherrod Brown was nominated as a Democratic presidential elector in Ohio. Brown was ineligible to be a presidential elector because the U.S. Constitution provides:

> "No Senator or Representative, or Person holding an Office of Trust or Profit under the United States, shall be appointed an Elector."[5]

---

[4] The method of direct appointment of presidential electors by the presidential nominee is regularly used in Pennsylvania. Section 2878 of the Pennsylvania election code provides: "The nominee of each political party for the office of President of the United States shall, within thirty days after his nomination by the National convention of such party, nominate as many persons to be the candidates of his party for the office of presidential elector as the State is then entitled to."

[5] U.S. Constitution. Article II, section 1, clause 2.

Although Brown submitted his resignation and the Ohio Democratic Party nominated a replacement, some contended that Ohio's procedure for filling a vacancy among the list of nominees for presidential elector did not permit naming a replacement in this case because there had been no legal nomination for Brown's position in the first place and hence no vacancy to fill. This contention remained unresolved because Kerry did not carry Ohio in 2004.

Fourth, the possibility exists that more presidential electors might be nominated in association with a presidential candidate than the state is entitled to send to the Electoral College. Fusion voting (section 2.10) creates the possibility that two or more competing slates of presidential electors could be nominated in association with the same presidential slate.

At the present time, fusion voting is routinely and widely used in only one state—New York. Because fusion voting is so routinely used in New York, the procedures for handling fusion voting in connection with presidential elector slates are well established. In 2004, for example, voters in New York had the opportunity to vote for the Bush-Cheney presidential slate on either the Republican Party line or the Conservative Party line (as shown by the voting machine face in figure 2.11). The political parties sharing a presidential nominee in New York nominate a common slate of presidential electors. Thus, the Republican and Conservative parties nominated the same slate of 31 presidential electors for the 2004 presidential election. The popular votes cast for Bush-Cheney on the Republican and Conservative lines were added together and treated as votes for all 31 Republican-Conservative candidates for the position of presidential elector. The popular votes cast for Kerry-Edwards on the Democratic Party line and the Working Families Party line were similarly aggregated and attributed to the common Kerry-Edwards slate of presidential electors. In 2004, the Kerry-Edwards presidential slate received the most popular votes in New York and therefore became entitled to all of New York's 31 electoral votes. The common Kerry-Edwards slate of 31 presidential electors was therefore declared to be elected to the Electoral College in New York. New York's 2004 Certificate of Ascertainment (appendix H) shows this aggregation.

Fusion voting is, however, permissible at the present time under the laws of a dozen and a half other states under various circumstances. Moreover, fusion voting proposals are currently under active consideration in several other states.[6] The laws of states where fusion is not routinely used would almost certainly lead to situations in which two competing elector slates are nominated under the banner of the same presidential slate.

Fifth, there is another way in which more presidential electors might be nominated in association with a particular presidential candidate than the state is entitled to send to the Electoral College. In states permitting presidential write-ins (section 2.8), it is possible for different slates of presidential electors to be written in by the voters in association with the same write-in presidential slate. Thus, a situation akin to fusion might arise in those states in connection with presidential write-ins.

Sixth, in some states permitting presidential write-ins, it is possible that an insufficient number of presidential electors may be nominated in association with a particular presidential slate. For example, the Minnesota election code does not specifically require that a full slate of presidential electors be identified at the time of the advance filing of write-in slates (section 2.8). In fact, it requires advance filing of the name of only one presidential elector even though Minnesota has 10 electoral votes.[7] Moreover, voters in Minnesota may cast write-in votes for President without advance filing.

The eighth clause of article III of the compact enables the public, the press, and political parties to closely monitor the implementation of the compact within each member state:

> "The chief election official of each member state shall imme-
> diately release to the public all vote counts or statements of
> votes as they are determined or obtained."

The unmodified term "statements" is intended to refer to both "official statements" of a state's "final determination" of its presidential vote (the fourth clause of article III of the compact) and any intermediate statements that the chief election official may obtain or consider at any time during the process of determining a state's presidential vote. The unmodified term "statement" is also intended to encompass the variety of types of documentation that may arise under the various practices and

---

[6] There was a statewide ballot proposition in 2002 in Alaska on fusion voting. The proposition was defeated.

[7] Minnesota election law. Section 204B.09, subdivision 3.

procedures of the states for officially recording and reporting their presidential votes. The Certificate of Ascertainment issued by the state in accordance with federal law,[8] for example, would be considered to be a "statement."

Because time is severely limited prior to the constitutionally mandated meeting of the Electoral College in mid-December, the term "immediately" is intended to eliminate any delays that might otherwise apply to the release of information by a public official under general public-disclosure laws.

The ninth clause of article III of the compact provides:

> "This article shall govern the appointment of presidential electors in each member state in any year in which this agreement is, on July 20, in effect in states cumulatively possessing a majority of the electoral votes."

This "governing" clause operates in conjunction with the first clause of article IV of the compact relating to the date when the compact as a whole first comes into effect:

> "This agreement shall take effect when states cumulatively possessing a majority of the electoral votes have enacted this agreement in substantially the same form and the enactments by such states have taken effect in each state."

The ninth clause of article III—the "governing" clause—employs the date of July 20 of a presidential election year because the six-month period starting on this date contains the following six important events relating to presidential elections:

- the national nominating conventions,[9]
- the fall general election campaign period,
- election day on the Tuesday after the first Monday in November,
- the meeting of the Electoral College on the first Monday after the second Wednesday in December,

---

[8] Title 3, chapter 1, section 6 of the United States Code deals with issuance of Certificates of Ascertainment by the states (and is discussed in section 2.4). See appendix A for the provisions of the U.S. Constitution and appendix B for provisions of federal law relating to presidential elections.

[9] All recent national nominating conventions of the major parties have met after July 20.

- the counting of the electoral votes by Congress on January 6, and
- the scheduled inauguration of the President and Vice President for the new term on January 20.

The ninth clause of article III of the compact addresses the question of whether article III governs the conduct of the presidential election in a particular year whereas the first clause of article V specifies when the compact as a whole initially comes into effect. The importance of this distinction is that it is theoretically possible that the compact could come into effect by virtue of enactment by states possessing a majority of the votes in the Electoral College (i.e., 270 or more of the 538 electoral votes), but that, at some future time, the compacting states might no longer possess a majority of the electoral votes. The situation could arise in any of four ways.

First, a future federal census might reduce the number of electoral votes possessed by the compacting states so that they no longer account for a majority of the electoral votes. This could occur if the compacting states happened to lose population relative to the remainder of the country. In that event, the compact provides that the compact as a whole would remain in effect (because the compact would have come into initial effect under the first clause of article IV of the compact); however, article III (the operative article in the compact) would then not "govern" the next presidential election. If additional state(s) subsequently enacted the compact—thereby raising the number of electoral votes possessed by the compacting states above 270 by July 20 of a subsequent presidential election year—article III of the compact would then again govern presidential elections.[10]

As a second example, if one or more states withdrew from the compact and thereby reduced the number of electoral votes possessed by the remaining compacting states below 270 by July 20 of a presidential election year, the compact as a whole would remain in effect, but article III (the operative article in the compact) would not govern the next presidential election.

As a third example, if a new state were admitted to the Union and if the total number of seats in the U.S. House of Representatives (and hence the total number of electoral votes) were permanently or temporarily

---

[10] As a practical matter, the scenario can only arise if the number of electoral votes possessed by states belonging to the compact hovers close to 270.

adjusted upwards, it is conceivable that the compacting states might no longer possess a majority of the new number of electoral votes. If the newly admitted state and/or some combination of other pre-existing state(s) subsequently enacted the compact—thereby raising the number of electoral votes possessed by the compacting states above a majority of the new number of electoral votes—article III of the compact would again govern.

As a fourth example, if the number of U.S. Representatives (set by federal statute) were changed so that the number of electoral votes possessed by the compacting states no longer accounted for a majority of the new number of electoral votes, article III of the compact would not govern the next presidential election. Proposals to change the number of members of the House are periodically floated for a variety of reasons. For example, Representative Tom Davis (R–Virginia) recently proposed increasing the number of Representatives from 435 to 437 on a temporary basis in connection with his bill to give the District of Columbia voting representation in Congress.[11]

As long as the compacting states possess a majority of the electoral votes on July 20 of a presidential election year, article III of the compact would govern the presidential election. In practice, the question as to whether the compact would govern a particular presidential election would be known long before July 20 of the presidential election year. Changes resulting from the census are no surprise because the census does not affect congressional reapportionment until two years after the census.[12] A new state enters the Union only after a time-consuming congressional process. Moreover, no territories are likely to be admitted as a new state in the near future. Enactment of a state law withdrawing from an interstate compact is a time-consuming, multi-step legislative process

---

[11] H.R. 2043—The D.C. Fairness in Representation Act. Introduced May 3, 2005. Based on the 2000 census, Utah is the state that would become entitled, under the existing formula for distributing U.S. Representatives among the states, to the second temporary additional congressional seat. As a matter of practical politics, the two additional seats would be expected to divide equally among the Democrats and Republicans. If the Davis bill were to pass in, say, 2006, there would be 540 electoral votes in the 2008 presidential election. The Davis bill provides that the number of seats in the House would revert to 435 after the 2010 census.

[12] For example, the 2000 federal census did not affect the 2000 presidential election. The results of the 2000 census affected the 2002 congressional election and the 2004 presidential election.

involving the introduction of a bill, action on the bill in a committee in each house of the state legislature, debate and voting on the bill on the floor of each house, and presentation of the bill to the state's Governor for approval or disapproval.[13] In addition, new state laws generally do not take immediate effect but, instead, take effect at a particular future time.[14] Moreover, a withdrawal from the proposed compact cannot take effect during the six-month period between July 20 of a presidential election year and the subsequent January 20 inauguration date (as discussed below). Finally, enactment of any federal statutory change in the number of U.S. Representatives is a time-consuming, multi-step legislative process.

6.3.4 Explanation of Article IV—Additional Provisions

The first clause of article IV of the compact (quoted above) specifies the time when the compact initially would take effect. A state is not counted for purposes of this clause until the compact is "in effect" in the state in accordance with the terms of the state's constitution schedule specifying when state laws take effect.

The same version of a compact must, of course, be enacted by each member state. The phrase "substantially the same form" is found in many interstate compacts and is intended to permit minor variations (e.g., differences in punctuation and numbering or inconsequential typographical errors) that sometimes occur when the same law is enacted by various states.

The second clause of article IV of the compact permits a state to withdraw from the compact but provides for a "blackout" period (of approximately six months) restricting withdrawals:

> "Any member state may withdraw from this agreement, except that a withdrawal occurring six months or less before the end of a President's term shall not become effective until a President or Vice President shall have been qualified to serve the next term."

---

[13] Similarly, the citizen-initiative process is a time-consuming, multi-step process that typically involves an initial filing and review by a designated state official (e.g., the Attorney General), circulation of the petition, and voting in a statewide election (usually a November general election).

[14] State constitutions generally specify when new state laws take effect. A super-majority vote is typically required to give immediate effect to a legislative bill. The details vary from state to state.

The purpose for the delay in the effective date of a withdrawal is to ensure that a withdrawal will not be undertaken—perhaps for partisan political purposes—in the midst of a presidential campaign or in the period between the popular voting in early November and the meeting of the Electoral College in mid-December. This restriction on withdrawals is warranted in light of the subject matter of the proposed interstate compact.[15] The blackout period starts on July 20 of a presidential election year and would normally end on January 20 of the following year (the scheduled inauguration date). Thus, if a statute repealing the compact in a particular state were enacted and came into effect in the midst of the presidential election process, that state's withdrawal from the compact would not take effect until completion of the entire current presidential election cycle. The language used in the compact tracks the wording of the 20th Amendment. The date for the end of the present President's term is fixed by the 20th Amendment as January 20th; however, the 20th Amendment recognizes the possibility that a new President might, under certain circumstances, not have been "qualified" by that date. The blackout period in the compact ends when the entire presidential election cycle is completed under terms of the 20th Amendment.

The third clause of article IV of the compact concerns the process by which each state notifies all the other states of the status of the compact. Notices are required on three occasions—namely when the compact has taken effect in a particular state, when the compact has taken effect generally (that is, when it has been enacted and taken effect in states cumulatively possessing a majority of the electoral votes), and when a state's withdrawal has taken effect.

The fourth clause of article IV provides that the compact would automatically terminate if the Electoral College were to be abolished.

The fifth clause of article IV is a severability clause.

6.3.5 Explanation of Article V—Definitions

Article V of the compact contains definitions.

There are separate definitions for the "chief election official" and the "presidential elector certifying official" because these terms may, in some states, refer to a different official or body.

---

[15] Delays in the effective date of withdrawals are commonplace in interstate compacts (and, indeed, in contracts in general). See section 5.15.3 for additional discussion on withdrawals from interstate compacts in general and section 8.6 for additional discussion on withdrawals from the proposed compact in particular.

The definition of "presidential slate" in Article V of the compact is important because voters cast votes for a team consisting of a presidential and vice-presidential candidate and because the votes for each distinct team are aggregated separately in the national count under the terms of the compact. "Presidential slate" is defined as

> "a slate of two persons, the first of whom has been nominated as a candidate for President of the United States and the second of whom has been nominated as a candidate for Vice President of the United States, or any legal successors to such persons, regardless of whether both names appear on the ballot presented to the voter in a particular state."

The above definition permits the substitution of nominees on a given presidential slate if, for example, a nominee were to die during the presidential election cycle,[16] resign from a slate,[17] or become disqualified.[18]

Because North Dakota's ballot lists only the name of the presidential candidate (figure 2.3), the definition of "presidential slate" in the proposed compact contains a savings clause for North Dakota.

Note that this definition comports with present practice in that it treats a slate as a unit containing two particular candidates in a specified order. As discussed in section 2.10 and shown in figure 2.11, Ralph Nader appeared on the ballot in New York in 2004 as the presidential nominee of both the Independence Party and the Peace and Justice Party. Nader ran with Jan D. Pierce for Vice President on the Independence Party line in New York in 2004, but with Peter Miguel Camejo for Vice President on the Peace and Justice Party line. Thus, there were two different "Nader" presidential slates in New York in 2004. Each "Nader" slate had a different slate of presidential electors in New York in 2004. The votes for these two distinct "presidential slates" were counted separately (as shown on the sixth page of New York's Certificate of Ascertainment in appendix H). There was no fusion of votes between the Independence Party and the Peace and Justice Party in this situation because there were

---

[16] Horace Greeley, the (losing) Democratic presidential nominee in 1872, died between the time of the November voting and the counting of the electoral votes.

[17] Senator Thomas F. Eagleton of Missouri resigned from the 1972 Democratic presidential slate.

[18] A presidential candidate must be a natural-born citizen.

two distinct presidential slates and two distinct slates of presidential electors.

The definition of "statewide popular election" in article V is important. At the present time, all states conduct a "statewide popular election" for President and Vice President. However, if a state were to withdraw from its voters the power to vote for President (as Massachusetts and New Hampshire did in the 1800 presidential election, as described in section 2.2.3), there would be no popular votes available to count from that state. If there is no popular vote to count from a particular state, the "national popular vote total" would necessarily not include that state.

6.4 POSSIBLE FEDERAL LEGISLATION

The enactment of the proposed "Agreement Among the States to Elect the President by National Popular Vote" would provide an excellent opportunity for Congress to review existing federal laws concerning presidential elections.

The proposed "Agreement Among the States to Elect the President by National Popular Vote" is intended to be entirely self-executing. To this end, the compact identifies officials in each member state to perform the necessary tasks of obtaining the popular vote counts from all the states, adding up the votes from all the states to yield the "national popular vote total," and designating the "national popular vote winner." These tasks could be simplified by the establishment of an administrative clearinghouse for these functions. Such a clearinghouse might be established by federal law. Alternatively, the officials of the compacting states might themselves establish such a clearinghouse.

Numerous problems have been identified concerning the existing schedule of events involving the November general election, the "safe harbor" date, the timing of the meeting of the Electoral College in mid-December, the counting of the votes by Congress in early January, and the presidential inauguration scheduled for January 20.

Leonard M. Shambon, an assistant to the co-chairman of the Ford-Carter Commission on Election Reform in 2001 and a member of the advisory board to the Carter-Baker Commission in 2005, described some of the problems associated with the current schedule in a 2004 article entitled "Electoral-College Reform Requires Change of Timing."[19] Many of

---

[19] Shambon, Leonard M. 2004. Electoral-College Reform Requires Change of Timing. *Roll Call*. June 15, 2004.

problems identified in the Shambon article are incorporated in H.R. 1579, introduced by Representative David Price (D–North Carolina) on April 12, 2005.[20] They are discussed further by Suzanne Nelson in an article entitled "Three-Month Period Imperils Presidency."[21]

In addition, Norman Ornstein, a resident scholar at the American Enterprise Institute, described additional potential problems concerning presidential elections in a 2004 article entitled "Want a Scary Scenario for Presidential Chaos? Here Are a Few."[22]

Additional issues have been raised by John C. Fortier, a resident fellow of the American Enterprise Institute and Norman Ornstein in a 2004 article entitled "If Terrorists Attack Our Presidential Elections"[23] and by Jerry H. Goldfeder, an elections law attorney in New York and Adjunct Professor at Fordham University School of Law, in an article entitled "Could Terrorists Derail a Presidential Election?"[24]

6.5 PREVIOUS PROPOSALS FOR MULTI-STATE ELECTORAL LEGISLATION

Several previous proposals contained elements of the proposed "Agreement Among the States to Elect the President by National Popular Vote."[25]

In *Oregon v. Mitchell*, U.S. Supreme Court Justice Potter Stewart pointed out in 1970 that an interstate compact could be employed by the states for electoral purposes. This case concerned congressional legislation establishing uniformity among the states for durational residency requirements for voters in presidential elections. In his opinion (partially concurring and partially dissenting), Justice Potter Stewart observed that if Congress had not enacted federal legislation concerning residency

---

[20] H.R. 1579—To amend title 3, United States Code, to extend the date provided for the meeting of electors of the President and Vice President in the States and the date provided for the joint session of Congress held for the counting of electoral votes, and for other purposes. Introduced April 12, 2005.

[21] Nelson, Suzanne. Three-Month Period Imperils Presidency. *Roll Call.* November 2, 2004.

[22] Ornstein, Norman. 2004. Want a Scary Scenario for Presidential Chaos? Here Are a Few. *Roll Call.* October 21, 2004

[23] Fortier, John C. and Ornstein, Norman. 2004. If Terrorists Attack Our Presidential Elections. 3 *Election Law Journal* 4. Pages 597–612.

[24] Goldfeder, Jerry H. 2005. Could Terrorists Derail a Presidential Election. 32 *Fordham Urban Law Journal* 3. May 2005. Pages 523–566.

[25] None of the proposals discussed in this section was known to the authors of this book at the time when the authors developed their proposed interstate compact in 2004.

requirements, the states could have adopted an interstate compact to accomplish the same objective.[26]

In the 1990s, Senator Charles Schumer (D–New York) proposed a bi-state compact in which New York and Texas would pool their electoral votes in presidential elections. Both states were then (and still are) non-competitive in presidential politics and receive little attention in presidential campaigns except for fund raising. Schumer observed that the two states have almost the same number of electoral votes (at the time, 33 for New York and 32 for Texas)[27] and the two states regularly produce majorities of approximately the same magnitude in favor of the state's dominant political party. The Democrats typically carry New York by about 60%, and the Republicans typically carry Texas by about 60%. The purpose of the proposed compact was to create a presidentially competitive super-state (slightly larger than California) that would attract the attention of the presidential candidates during presidential campaigns.

After the 2000 election in which George W. Bush was elected to the Presidency without receiving a majority of the popular votes, Robert W. Bennett, Northwestern University Law Professor and former Dean of the Northwestern University School of Law, published a highly creative and innovative idea concerning the Electoral College. At a January 2001 conference and in an April 2001 publication, Bennett observed that that a federal constitutional amendment was not necessary to achieve the goal of nationwide popular election of the President because the states could use their power under Article II of the U.S. Constitution to allocate their electoral votes based on the nationwide popular vote.[28] Bennett expanded his thoughts in subsequent publications suggesting several variations on his basic idea.[29,30] In December 2001, Akhil Reed Amar and Vikram David

---

[26] *Oregon v. Mitchell.* 400 U.S. 112 at 286–287. 1970.

[27] In the 2004 presidential election, New York had 31 electoral votes, and Texas had 34.

[28] Bennett, Robert W. 2001. Popular election of the president without a constitutional amendment. 4 *Green Bag.* Spring 2001. Posted on April 19, 2001. The January 11–12, 2001, presentation was contained in *Conference Report, Election 2000: The Role of the Courts, The Role of the Media; The Roll of the Dice* (Northwestern University).

[29] Bennett, Robert W. 2002. Popular election of the president without a constitutional amendment. In Jacobson, Arthur J. and Rosenfeld, Michel (editors). *The Longest Night: Polemics and Perspectives on Election 2000.* Berkeley, CA: University of California Press. Pages 391–396.

[30] Bennett, Robert W. 2002. Popular election of the president II: State coordination in popular election of the president without a constitutional amendment. *Green Bag.* Winter 2002.

Amar, citing Bennett, continued the discussion about the fact that the states could allocate their electoral votes to the nationwide winner of the popular vote.[31,32]

In one variation on these proposals, a single state would enact a law that would award its electoral votes to the nationwide winner without regard to whether any other state enacted similar legislation. In another variation, the state laws would be made contingent on the enactment of identical laws by other states. It was further argued the resulting arrangement would not constitute an interstate compact and therefore would not require congressional consent.[33]

These earlier proposals differ from the authors' proposed "Agreement Among the States to Elect the President by National Popular Vote" in several respects.

First, the earlier proposals were not framed as an interstate compact. Interstate compacts are specifically authorized by the U.S. Constitution as a means by which the states may act in concert to address a problem. An arrangement that takes effect only when a specified combination of states agree to participate, that no state would enact without the offer and assurance of complementary action by other states, and that ultimately involves the states acting in concert would probably be regarded by the courts as a contract and hence an "agreement or compact" as that phrase is used in the U.S. Constitution.[34]

Compacts have the specific advantage of making the states' contemplated joint actions into a legally enforceable contractual obligation on all the participating states. This assurance is particularly salient concerning the provision preventing a state from unilaterally withdrawing from the agreed arrangement for partisan political reasons in the midst of a

---

[31] Amar, Akhil Reed and Amar, Vikram David. 2001. How to achieve direct national election of the president without amending the constitution: Part three of a three-part series on the 2000 election and the electoral college. *Findlaw's Writ*. December 28, 2001. http://writ.news.findlaw.com/amar/20011228.html

[32] Amar, Akhil Reed and Amar, Vikram David Amar. 2001. Rethinking the electoral college debate: The Framers, federalism, and one person, one vote. 114 *Harvard Law Review* 2526 at 2549, n. 112.

[33] The question of whether such an arrangement requires congressional consent is separate from the question of whether the arrangement is an interstate compact. As discussed in section 5.12, many interstate compacts do not require congressional consent.

[34] Article I, section 10, clause 3 of the U.S. Constitution states, "No state shall, without the consent of Congress, ... enter into any agreement or compact with another state...."

presidential election campaign or, even more egregiously, after the election results become known in early November but before the Electoral College meets in mid-December. Enforceability is most relevant in the event that the winner of the nationwide popular vote did not carry states having a majority of the electoral votes (as occurred in 1824, 1876, 1892, and 2000). A state whose legislature and Governor are controlled by a political party whose presidential candidate did not win the nationwide popular vote could, in the absence of an enforceable restriction on withdrawal, abandon its obligations at the precise moment when they would matter. Once a state enters into an interstate compact, it may not unilaterally nullify the compact because the Impairments Clause of the U.S. Constitution provides:

> "No State shall ... pass any ... Law impairing the Obligation of Contracts...."[35]

Instead, a party to a contract must withdraw from the agreement in accordance with the agreement's provisions for withdrawal. Most interstate compacts contain provisions that delay the effective date of a state's withdrawal by a certain amount of time that is appropriate given the nature of the compact. As described in sections 6.2.3 and discussed in section 8.6, the proposed "Agreement Among the States to Elect the President by National Popular Vote" has a "blackout" period (of approximately six months) starting on July 20 of a presidential election year and continuing until a President or Vice President shall have been qualified to serve the next term (normally on January 20 of the following year).

Second, earlier proposals did not contain a provision making the effective date of the system contingent on the enactment of substantially identical laws in states that collectively possess a majority of the electoral votes (i.e., 270 of the 538 electoral votes). No single state would be likely to alone enact a law awarding its electoral votes to the nationwide winner. For one thing, such an action would give the voters of all the other states a voice in the selection of the state's own presidential electors, while not giving the state a voice in the selection of presidential electors in other states and would not alone guarantee achievement of the goal of nationwide popular election of the President. Moreover, enactment of such a law in a single state would encourage the presidential can-

---

[35] See appendix C for the full wording of the Impairments Clause.

didates to ignore that state. The effect of such a law in a single state would be to negate the voice of the enacting state in the presidential election, except in the unlikely event that the electoral votes of the other states are so nearly equally divided that the lone enacting state could weigh in on the side of the winner of the nationwide popular vote.

Moreover, the earlier proposals do not work in a even-handed and non-partisan way when the arrangement contains states possessing fewer than a majority of the electoral votes. Suppose, for example, that a group of states that consistently voted Democratic in presidential elections were to participate in an arrangement to award their electoral votes to the nationwide popular vote winner without the electoral-majority threshold. Then, if the Republican presidential candidate won the most popular votes nationwide (but did not carry states with a majority of the electoral votes), the participating (Democratic) states would award their electoral votes to the Republican candidate—thereby helping to achieve the desired result of electing the presidential candidate with the most popular votes nationwide. On the other hand, if the Democratic presidential candidate won the most popular votes nationwide (but did not carry states with a majority of the electoral votes), the similarly situated Democratic presidential candidate would not receive a symmetric benefit. Instead, the Republican candidate would be elected because the Democratic candidate could not receive any additional electoral votes from the group of states involved because the Democratic candidate would already be getting all of the electoral votes from that group of states. In short, a Republican presidential nominee would be the only beneficiary if only Democratic states participated in such an arrangement, and vice versa. In fact, an arrangement without a electoral majority threshold would operate in an even-handed and non-partisan way only in the unlikely that the participating states were equally divided (in terms of electoral votes) among reliably Republican and reliably Democratic states. In contrast, if the states participating in the arrangement possess a majority of the electoral votes, the system operates in an even-handed and non-partisan way without regard to the political complexion of the states that happen to be members of the compact.

If the earlier proposals were altered so that the participating states awarded all of their electoral votes to the popular vote winner calculated only within the group of participating states, then a candidate with a bare majority of the popular votes in that group of states would negate the popular votes of the losing candidate in that group of states—thereby again permitting the Presidency to be won by a candidate who did not receive a nationwide majority of the popular vote.

Third, the statutory language and the operational details were not specified in the earlier proposals.

The authors submit that the proposed "Agreement Among the States to Elect the President by National Popular Vote" does not have the above-mentioned problems of the earlier proposals.

7 | Strategy for Enacting the Proposed Interstate Compact

Public opinion has supported nationwide popular election of the President for over six decades. For example, the Gallup poll in 1944 asked:

> "It has been suggested that the electoral vote system be discontinued and Presidents of the United States be elected by total popular vote alone. Do you favor or oppose this proposal?"[1]

In 1977 and 1980, the Gallup poll asked:

> "Would you approve or disapprove of an amendment to the Constitution which would do away with the electoral college and base the election of a President on the total vote cast throughout the nation?"[2]

Table 7.1 shows the results for these public opinion polls in 1944, 1977, and 1980.

TABLE 7.1 PUBLIC SUPPORT FOR NATIONWIDE POPULAR ELECTION OF THE PRESIDENT

	APPROVE	DISAPPROVE	NO OPINION
June 22-27, 1944	65%	23%	13%
June 14-17, 1977	73%	15%	12%
November 7-10, 1980	67%	19%	15%

The Gallup News Service has also reported:

> "The greatest level of support, 81%, was recorded after the 1968 election when Richard Nixon defeated Hubert Humphrey in another extremely close election."[3]

---

[1] Gallup News Service. 2000. Americans Have Historically Favored Changing Way Presidents Are Elected. November 10, 2000. Page 1.

[2] *Id.* at 2.

[3] *Id.* at 2.

Nationwide, the Washington Post, Kaiser Family Foundation, and Harvard University poll in 2007 showed 72% support for direct nationwide election of the President.

Recent polls show high levels of public support for a national popular vote for President in battleground states, small states, southern and border states, and elsewhere.

High support for a national popular vote exists in recent battleground states such as Colorado (68%), Florida (78%), Iowa (75%), Michigan (73%), Missouri (70%), New Hampshire (69%), Nevada (72%), New Mexico (76%), North Carolina (74%), Ohio (70%), Pennsylvania (78%), Virginia (74%), and Wisconsin (71%).

In Southern and border states, support is strong in Arkansas (80%), Florida (78%), Kentucky (80%), Mississippi (77%), Missouri (70%), North Carolina (74%), South Carolina (71%), and Virginia (74%).

In low-population states, support is strong in Delaware (75%), Maine (71%), Montana (72%), Rhode Island (74%), and Vermont (75%).

Support is also strong in California (70%), Connecticut (73%), Massachusetts (73%), Minnesota (75%), Nebraska (74%), New York (78%), Oregon (76%), and Washington (77%).

Public opinion plays only an indirect and muted role in the top-down process of amending the federal constitution. Proposed amendments require a two-thirds vote by both houses of Congress, followed by favorable votes in three-quarters of the state legislatures.[4]

The authors of this book envision a bottom-up strategy for securing enactment of the proposed "Agreement Among the States to Elect the President by National Popular Vote" (presented in chapter 6). The contemplated process would start where support for this proposal is strongest—the voters. The three-part process would include the following:

(1) **Citizen-Initiative Process:** The citizen-initiative process could be used to place the proposed compact on the ballot in various states. Each ballot measure would enable a state's voters to vote directly on a state law enacting the proposed interstate compact in that state (section 7.1).

---

[4] For a detailed discussion of various alternative modes of amending the federal constitution, see Orfield, Lester Bernhardt. 1942. *The Amending of the Federal Constitution.* Ann Arbor, MI: The University of Michigan Press.

(2) **State Legislative Action:** The proposed compact has been introduced into all 50 state legislatures. As of 2010, the National Popular Vote bill has been enacted by jurisdictions possessing over a quarter of the electoral votes needed to bring it into effect (Hawaii, Illinois, Maryland, Massachusetts, New Jersey, Washington state, and the District of Columbia) (section 7.2).

(3) **Action by Congress:** After enactment of the compact by numerous states, Congress might take action on the compact (section 7.3) by granting consent (expressed or implied) to the proposed compact.

TABLE 7.2 THE 25 JURISDICTIONS WITH THE CITIZEN-INITIATIVE PROCESS

STATE	STATUTORY	CONSTITUTIONAL	ELECTORAL VOTES
Alaska	Yes	No	3
Arizona	Yes	Yes	10
Arkansas	Yes	Yes	6
California	Yes	Yes	55
Colorado	Yes	Yes	9
District of Columbia	Yes	No	3
Florida	No	Yes	27
Idaho	Yes	Very Limited	4
Illinois	Advisory Only	Very Limited	21
Maine	Yes	Yes	4
Massachusetts	Yes	Yes	12
Michigan	Yes	Yes	17
Mississippi	No	Yes	6
Missouri	Yes	Yes	11
Montana	Yes	Yes	3
Nebraska	Yes	Yes	5
Nevada	Yes	Yes	5
North Dakota	Yes	Yes	3
Ohio	Yes	Yes	20
Oklahoma	Yes	Yes	7
Oregon	Yes	Yes	7
South Dakota	Yes	Yes	3
Utah	Yes	No	5
Washington	Yes	No	11
Wyoming	Yes	No	3
TOTAL			**260**

7.1 DIRECTLY INVOLVING THE PEOPLE

The people in 22 states have reserved to themselves the power to enact state statutes through the citizen-initiative process. In addition, the people in 19 states have reserved to themselves the power to adopt state constitutional amendments through the citizen-initiative process. These 19 states include two states (Florida and Mississippi) that are not among the previously mentioned 22 states with the statutory initiative process. Also, the District of Columbia has a citizen-initiative process for statutes. Thus, 25 jurisdictions permit either statutory or constitutional initiatives. As can be seen in table 7.2, these 25 jurisdictions collectively possess 260 electoral votes based on the 2000 census (i.e., just short of the 270 electoral votes necessary to elect a President in the Electoral College and to bring the National Popular Vote compact into effect). See *The Initiative: Citizen Law-Making* for citations to the constitutional and statutory provisions governing the initiative processes in various states.[5]

The effort to secure adoption of the proposed compact could involve the use of the citizen-initiative process.

The citizen initiative process is, however, problematic in several of the 25 jurisdictions listed in table 7.2. For example, in Illinois, the statutory initiative is advisory only. Moreover, the constitutional initiative in Illinois is limited to matters relating to legislative procedure. Fortuitously, the National Popular Vote bill has been enacted in Illinois.

Because there is no statutory initiative in Florida or Mississippi, the constitutional initiative process would have to be invoked in those states in order to adopt the proposed interstate compact. The initiative process for constitutional amendments in Florida is time-consuming and uncertain. The procedure generally includes a preliminary review of the proposition by the Florida Supreme Court. The initiative process for constitutional amendments in Mississippi is somewhat difficult to use.

The first step in invoking the citizen-initiative process in a typical state is to file the proposed legislation with a state official (usually the Attorney General). Ohio, Maine, Massachusetts, Mississippi, Nevada, Florida, and Missouri have deadlines for starting the citizen-initiative

---

[5] Zimmerman, Joseph F. 1999. *The Initiative: Citizen Law-Making.* Westport, CT: Praeger. Pages 24–25.

process that come early in each two-year election cycle.

In some states, there are significant legal limitations (including both statutory law and case law) concerning the circulation of petitions on private property. In some states (such as Alaska and Arizona), weather conditions shorten the time window during which it is practical to circulate initiative petitions. Signature gathering is difficult in Michigan because of a combination of the weather and relatively tight legal limitations on petition circulation on private property. In some states, election administrators and the courts are not favorably disposed to the citizen-initiative process, and it is common for ballot measures to be disqualified in pre-election or post-election challenges. Finally, in some states, state constitutional provisions and existing judicial interpretations do not make it clear whether the citizen initiative process is co-extensive with the powers of the state legislature.

On the other hand, in numerous states (including many western states), the citizen-initiative process is an accepted part of the overall political process.

7.2 STATE LEGISLATIVE ACTION

Even if there were no practical or legal obstacles to the effective use of the citizen-initiative process, the 25 jurisdictions listed in table 7.2 do not possess a majority of the electoral votes. Thus, at least some state legislatures must enact the proposed interstate compact in order to bring it into effect. In practice, the authors of this book believe that a significant fraction of the 270 electoral votes would, as a practical matter, come from state legislatures.

As of 2010, the National Popular Vote bill has been enacted in seven jurisdictions possessing 74 electoral votes (according to the 2010 census)—that is, about 27% of the 270 electoral votes needed to bring the compact into effect. The seven jurisdictions are Hawaii, Illinois, Maryland, Massachusetts, New Jersey, Washington state, and the District of Columbia. A state legislature enacts an interstate compact in the same way that it enacts an ordinary statute. Enactment of a statute typically requires a majority vote of the legislature and gubernatorial approval. All governors have the power to veto legislation passed by their state legislatures. If a governor vetoes a bill, the legislation may nonetheless become law if the legislature overrides the veto in the manner provided by the state's constitution. Overriding a gubernatorial veto typically requires a super-majority (e.g., two-thirds vote of all houses of the state legislature). See *The Book of the States* for general information about vetoes in particular states.[6]

In the District of Columbia, interstate compacts may be enacted by the District of Columbia Council. The Mayor has veto power. Legislation enacted by the District of Columbia Council is subject to congressional review under the District of Columbia Home Rule Act of 1973.

7.3 CONGRESSIONAL ACTION

The appropriate time to seek congressional action on the proposed interstate compact would be after the compact has been adopted by states possessing a majority of the electoral votes. At that time, the group of states supporting the compact might include states that had enacted the compact by means of the citizen-initiative process as well as states where the legislature enacted the compact.

Congress has the option of explicitly consenting to the compact (section 5.10). However, as the U.S. Supreme Court wrote in the 1893 case of *Virginia v. Tennessee,*

"… consent may be implied, and is always to be implied when congress adopts the particular act by sanctioning its objects and aiding in enforcing them.…"[7]

Federal legislation concerning the compact could be adopted by a majority vote of both houses of Congress and approval by the President. The President could veto such legislation. If the President vetoes the bill, the Congress could override the veto by a two-thirds vote of both houses.

In the event that all of the above steps are completed by July 20, 2012, the compact would govern the 2012 presidential election, and the President would, for the first time in American history, be elected by all of the people in an election in which every vote is equal.

If, on the other hand, the compact is not effective by July 20, 2012, the debate on the issue of nationwide popular election of the President would inevitably become a part of the 2012 campaign. Candidates for

---

[6] Council of State Governments. 2005. *The Book of the States.* Lexington, KY: The Council of State Governments. 2005 Edition. Volume 37. Pages 161–162.

[7] *Virginia v. Tennessee.* 148 U.S. 503 at 521. 1893.

Senator, Representative, and President would be asked for their position on the issue. Newspapers and television stations would editorialize on the question of how the President should be elected. The travel, advertising, and "on the ground" activity of the presidential candidates would be scrutinized in terms of whether the candidates are, in fact, ignoring voters in two-thirds of the states. In addition, the citizen-initiative process could be used in the November 2012 elections to further demonstrate voter support for nationwide popular election of the President (and to increase the number of states that have enacted the proposed compact). The authors of this book believe that a robust debate on the issue will inevitably lead to a nationwide decision to embrace nationwide popular election of the President in time for the 2016 presidential election.

8 | Legal Issues Concerning the Proposed Interstate Compact

The proposed interstate compact entitled the "Agreement Among the States to Elect the President by National Popular Vote" (presented in chapter 6) would change the laws by which presidential electors are appointed in the states belonging to the compact. This chapter addresses the following legal questions in connection with the proposed compact:

- Is the subject matter of the proposed compact appropriate for an interstate compact (section 8.1)?
- May the citizen-initiative process be used to enact interstate compacts in general (section 8.2)?
- May the citizen-initiative process be used to enact a state law concerning the manner of choosing presidential electors (section 8.3)?
- Does the proposed compact encroach on the powers or rights of non-member states (section 8.4)?
- Does the proposed compact impermissibly delegate a state's sovereign power (section 8.5)?
- Is the six-month blackout period for withdrawals from the proposed compact enforceable (section 8.6)?

8.1 IS THE SUBJECT MATTER OF THE PROPOSED COMPACT APPROPRIATE FOR AN INTERSTATE COMPACT?

The U.S. Constitution authorizes states to enter into interstate compacts:

> "No state shall, without the consent of Congress, ... enter into any agreement or compact with another state or with a foreign power."[1]

---

[1] U.S. Constitution. Article I, section 10, clause 3.

The U.S. Constitution places no restriction on the subject matter of an interstate compact other than the implicit limitation that a compact's subject matter must be among the powers that the states are permitted to exercise.

The subject matter of existing interstate compacts varies widely and has included such topics as agriculture, boundaries, bridges, building construction and safety, child welfare, civil defense, conservation, corrections, crime control, cultural issues, education, emergency management, energy, facilities, flood control, gambling and lotteries, health, insurance, interstate school districts, low-level radioactive wastes, metropolitan problems, motor vehicles, national guard, natural resources, navigation, parks and recreation, pest control, planning and development, ports, property, public safety, river basins, taxation, transportation, and water (section 5.4).

Beginning in the 1920s, the states have used interstate compacts in increasingly creative ways. The judiciary has been repeatedly asked to consider the validity of various novel compacts; however, we are aware of no case in which the courts have invalidated an interstate compact.[2]

The subject matter of the proposed "Agreement Among the States to Elect the President by National Popular Vote" concerns the manner of appointment of a state's presidential electors. The U.S. Constitution gives each state the power to select the manner of appointing its presidential electors.[3] As the Supreme Court stated in *McPherson v. Blacker* in 1892:

> "In short, **the appointment and mode of appointment of electors belong exclusively to the states** under the constitution of the United States.... Congress is empowered to determine the time of choosing the electors and the day on which they are to give their votes, which is required to be the same day throughout the United States; but otherwise **the power and jurisdiction of the state is exclusive,** with the exception of the provisions as to the number of electors and the ineligibility of certain persons, so framed that

---

[2] There are cases where a higher court invalidated a ruling by a lower court invalidating an interstate compact. See, for example, *West Virginia ex rel. Dyer v. Sims.* 341 U.S. 22. 1950.

[3] U.S. Constitution. Article II, section 1, clause 2.

congressional and federal influence might be excluded."⁴ [Emphasis added]

Thus, the subject matter of the proposed interstate compact is a state power and an appropriate subject for an interstate compact. Although there is currently no interstate compact concerned with presidential elections, Justice Potter Stewart noted the possibility of compacts involving elections in his concurring and dissenting opinion in *Oregon v. Mitchell* in 1970. In that case, the U.S. Supreme Court examined the constitutionality of the Voting Rights Act Amendments of 1970 that removed state-imposed durational residency requirements on voters casting ballots in presidential elections. Justice Stewart concurred with the majority that Congress had the power to make durational residency requirements uniform in presidential elections, and observed:

> "Congress could rationally conclude that the imposition of durational residency requirements unreasonably burdens and sanctions the privilege of taking up residence in another State. The objective of § 202 is clearly a legitimate one. Federal action is required if the privilege to change residence is not to be undercut by parochial local sanctions. No State could undertake to guarantee this privilege to its citizens. At most a single State could take steps to resolve that its own laws would not unreasonably discriminate against the newly arrived resident. Even this resolve might not remain firm in the face of discriminations perceived as unfair against those of its own citizens who moved to other States. Thus, the problem could not be wholly solved by a single State, or even by several States, since every State of new residence and every State of prior residence would have a necessary role to play. **In the absence of a unanimous interstate compact, the problem could only be solved by Congress.**"⁵ [Emphasis added]

In summary, the states are constitutionally permitted to use an interstate compact to specify the manner in which they choose their presidential electors.

---

⁴ *McPherson v. Blacker.* 146 U.S. 1 at 35. 1892.

⁵ *Oregon v. Mitchell.* 400 U.S. 112 at 286–287. 1970.

8.2 MAY THE CITIZEN-INITIATIVE PROCESS BE USED TO ENACT AN INTERSTATE COMPACT?

A state may enact an interstate compact in the same manner as it enacts a state law.

The legislative process at the state level generally entails adoption of a proposed legislative bill by a majority vote of each house of the state legislature. All state governors currently have the power to veto bills passed by their legislatures, so bills are presented to the governor for approval or disapproval.[6] If a governor vetoes a bill, the legislation may nonetheless become law if the legislature overrides the veto in the manner specified by the state's constitution. Overriding a gubernatorial veto typically requires a super-majority (typically a two-thirds vote) of both houses of the legislature.[7]

In 22 states, an alternative method, called the *citizen-initiative process*, may be used to enact a state law. In those states (listed in table 7.2), the voters have reserved to themselves the power to enact statutes through the citizen-initiative process.[8] The initiative process is invoked by filing a petition signed by a constitutionally specified number of voters. The voters then decide whether to enact the proposed law in a statewide vote.[9]

In many of these same states, the voters have also reserved to themselves the power to suspend temporarily a law enacted by the legislature and subsequently to vote on whether to retain the law in a statewide referendum—a process called the *protest-referendum*.[10]

The Michigan Constitution (article II, section 9) provides a good description of both the citizen-initiative process and the protest-referendum process:

---

[6] Council of State Governments. 2005. *The Book of the States*. Lexington, KY: The Council of State Governments. 2005 Edition. Volume 37. Pages 161–162.

[7] For simplicity, we refer to the two houses of a state legislature, even though Nebraska has a unicameral state legislature.

[8] Zimmerman, Joseph F. 1999. *The Initiative: Citizen Law-Making*. Westport, CT: Praeger.

[9] In addition, the voters in 19 states may use the citizen-initiative process to propose and enact amendments to the state constitution. These 19 states include two states (Florida and Mississippi) that are not among the group of 22 states with the statutory initiative process. Also, the District of Columbia has a citizen-initiative process for statutes. Thus, there are 25 jurisdictions with the process. See table 7.2 for details.

[10] Zimmerman, Joseph F. 1997. *The Referendum: The People Decide Public Policy*. Westport, CT: Praeger.

"The people reserve to themselves the power to propose laws and to enact and reject laws, called the initiative, and the power to approve or reject laws enacted by the legislature, called the referendum. The power of initiative extends only to laws which the legislature may enact under this constitution. The power of referendum does not extend to acts making appropriations for state institutions or to meet deficiencies in state funds and must be invoked in the manner prescribed by law within 90 days following the final adjournment of the legislative session at which the law was enacted. To invoke the initiative or referendum, petitions signed by a number of registered electors, not less than eight percent for initiative and five percent for referendum of the total vote cast for all candidates for governor at the last preceding general election at which a governor was elected shall be required.

"No law as to which the power of referendum properly has been invoked shall be effective thereafter unless approved by a majority of the electors voting thereon at the next general election.

"Any law proposed by initiative petition shall be either enacted or rejected by the legislature without change or amendment within 40 session days from the time such petition is received by the legislature. If any law proposed by such petition shall be enacted by the legislature it shall be subject to referendum, as hereinafter provided.

"If the law so proposed is not enacted by the legislature within the 40 days, the state officer authorized by law shall submit such proposed law to the people for approval or rejection at the next general election. The legislature may reject any measure so proposed by initiative petition and propose a different measure upon the same subject by a yea and nay vote upon separate roll calls, and in such event both measures shall be submitted by such state officer to the electors for approval or rejection at the next general election.

"Any law submitted to the people by either initiative or referendum petition and approved by a majority of the votes cast thereon at any election shall take effect 10 days after the date of the official declaration of the vote. No law initiated or adopted by the people shall be subject to the veto power of the governor, and no law adopted by the people at the polls under the initiative provisions of this section shall be amended or repealed, except by a vote of the electors unless otherwise provided in the initiative measure or by three-fourths of the members elected to and serving in each house of the legislature. Laws approved by the people under the referendum provision of this section may be amended by the legislature at any subsequent session thereof. If two or more measures approved by the electors at the same election conflict, that receiving the highest affirmative vote shall prevail."[11]

The Arizona Constitution provides:

"The legislative authority of the state shall be vested in the legislature, consisting of a senate and a house of representatives, but the people reserve the power to propose laws and amendments to the constitution and to enact or reject such laws and amendments at the polls, independently of the legislature; and they also reserve, for use at their own option, the power to approve or reject at the polls any act, or item, section, or part of any act, of the legislature."[12]

The Ohio Constitution provides:

"The legislative power of the state shall be vested in a General Assembly consisting of a Senate and House of Representatives, but the people reserve to themselves the power to propose to the General Assembly laws and amendments to the Constitution, and to adopt or reject the same at the polls on a referendum vote as hereinafter provided."[13]

The origin of the citizen-initiative process is generally attributed to various Swiss cantons in the early 19th century.[14] In 1898, the state

---

[11] Michigan Constitution. Article II, section 9.

[12] Arizona Constitution. Article I, section 1.

[13] Ohio Constitution. Article II, section 1.

constitution of South Dakota was amended to permit the citizen-initiative process. Oregon adopted the process in 1902. In 1904, Oregon voters became the first in the United States to use the citizen-initiative process to enact legislation when they enacted a direct primary statute and a local-option liquor statute.[15]

The initiative process spread rapidly to additional states as part of the Progressive movement in the early decades of the 20th century. Maine adopted the initiative and referendum in 1908. In California, the voters adopted the initiative process in the belief that it would reduce the dominance of the state legislature by the railroads and other corporations and that it would reduce the power of political machines. By 1918, 19 states had adopted the initiative. All were west of the Mississippi River, except for Maine, Massachusetts, and Ohio. The initiative process was included in Alaska's original constitution at the time of that state's admission to the Union in 1959.[16]

The question arises as to whether an interstate compact may be enacted by means of the citizen-initiative process.

The scope of the statutory initiative process and the scope of protest-referendum process varies considerably from state to state. Thus, an examination of the provisions of each state constitution is necessary to answer this question.

There is no provision of any state constitution that specifically singles out interstate compacts as being ineligible for enactment by the voters by means of the citizen-initiative process. Likewise, there is no provision of any state constitution that specifically states that interstate compacts are ineligible for temporary suspension and subsequent repeal by the voters by means of the protest-referendum process.

Having said that, there are significant limitations as to subject matter of the citizen-initiative and protest-referendum processes in about half of the states having these processes.[17] The limitations are so severe in Illinois that it would not be possible to enact an interstate compact using

---

[14] Zimmerman, Joseph F. 1999. *The Initiative: Citizen Law-Making.* Westport, CT: Praeger.

[15] *Id.*

[16] *Id.*

[17] Alaska, California, Illinois, Massachusetts, Michigan, Mississippi, Missouri, Montana, Nebraska, Nevada, North Dakota, Ohio, South Dakota, and Wyoming.

the citizen-initiative process in that state.[18] In general, the restraints on the protest-referendum process are more severe than those applying to the initiative process.[19] The constitutional limitations typically relate to appropriations, the judiciary, measures involving the support of governmental operations, and emergency measures.[20]

In short, unless an interstate compact deals with a subject that is outside a state's constitutional power, there is no state with the citizen-initiative process (other than Illinois) where an interstate compact could not, in principle, be adopted by the citizen-initiative process.

There are, in fact, precedents for the use of the citizen-initiative process and protest-referendum processes in connection with interstate compacts.

In 1988, an initiative petition forced a statewide vote on the question of repealing the law providing for Nebraska's participation in the Central Interstate Low-Level Radioactive Waste Compact (enacted several years earlier by the legislature).[21] In the statewide vote on Proposition 402, voters rejected the initiative proposition to repeal the compact.

In South Dakota in 1984, there was a statewide vote on an initiated law to require the approval of the voters of the state on the state's participation in any nuclear-waste-disposal compact. The measure passed 182,952 to 112,161.

In addition, legislatures have occasionally referred enactment of an interstate compact to the state's voters.[22] For example, the Maine legislature referred the question of enactment of the Texas Low-Level Radioactive Waste Disposal Compact to its voters in 1993. The question on the ballot was:

"Do you approve of the interstate compact to be made with Texas, Maine and Vermont for the disposal of the State's low-

---

[18] In Illinois, the statutory initiative process is advisory only, and the constitutional initiative process is limited to matters relating to legislative procedure.

[19] Zimmerman, Joseph F. 1997. *The Referendum: The People Decide Public Policy.* Westport, CT: Praeger.

[20] Zimmerman, Joseph F. 1999. *The Initiative: Citizen Law-Making.* Westport, CT: Praeger.

[21] The protest-referendum process is typically available only for a relatively short period after a state legislature enacts a particular law. After expiration of that period, the citizen-initiative process may be used to repeal an existing law.

[22] State legislatures generally have the power to refer questions to the state's voters.

level radioactive waste at a proposed facility in the State of Texas?"

The proposition received 170,411 "yes" votes and 63,672 "no" votes.

8.3 MAY THE CITIZEN-INITIATIVE PROCESS BE USED TO ENACT THE PROPOSED COMPACT?

The proposed "Agreement Among the States to Elect the President by National Popular Vote" could be brought into effect solely by the collective action of state legislatures. Nonetheless, in order to demonstrate public support for the concept of nationwide popular election of the President, the authors of this book suggest (in chapter 7) that the citizen-initiative process might be used to enact the proposed compact in an initial group of states.

Article II, section 1, clause 2 of the U.S. Constitution (which we will frequently refer to as "Article II" in the remainder of this section) provides:

> "Each State shall appoint, in such Manner as the **Legislature** thereof may direct, a Number of Electors, equal to the whole Number of Senators and Representatives to which the State may be entitled in the Congress...." [Emphasis added]

The use of the word "legislature" in Article II raises the question of whether the citizen-initiative process may be used to enact legislation specifying the manner of choosing presidential electors.

An answer to this question requires an examination of the way that the word "legislature" is used in the U.S. Constitution.

The word "legislature" appears in 15 places in the U.S. Constitution— 13 of which relate to the powers of state legislatures.[23] As will become clear later in this section, the word "legislature" is used with two distinct meanings in the U.S. Constitution, namely

- **the state's two legislative chambers**—that is, the state house of representatives and the state senate agreeing on a

---

[23] Two of the 15 occurrences of the word "legislature" in the U.S. Constitution are unrelated to the powers of state legislatures and will therefore not be discussed further in this chapter. The first such provision is the requirement in Article I, section 2, clause 1 that voters for U.S. Representatives have "the Qualifications requisite for Electors of the most numerous Branch of the State Legislature." The second is the requirement in Article VI, clause 2 that "Members of the several State Legislatures" take an oath or affirmation to support the U.S. Constitution.

common action—either by sitting together in a joint convention or adopting a concurrent resolution while sitting
separately;[24] or
* **the state's law-making process**—that is, the process of
enacting a state law.

These 13 occurrences of the word "legislature" appear in the following 11 provisions of the U.S. Constitution:

* electing United States Senators in the state legislature
(prior to ratification in 1913 of the 17th Amendment providing for popular election of Senators);
* filling a U.S. Senate vacancy (prior to the 17th
Amendment);
* ratifying a proposed federal constitutional amendment;
* making an application to Congress for a federal constitutional convention;
* choosing the manner of electing U.S. Representatives and
U.S. Senators;
* choosing the manner of appointing presidential electors;
* choosing the manner of conducting a popular election to
fill a U.S. Senate vacancy (under the 17th Amendment);
* empowering the state's Governor to fill a U.S. Senate
vacancy temporarily until the voters fill the vacancy in a
popular election (under the 17th Amendment);
* consenting to the purchase of enclaves by the federal government for "forts, magazines, arsenals, dock-yards, and
other needful buildings;"
* consenting to the formation of new states from territory of
existing state(s); and
* requesting federal assistance to quell domestic violence.

Table 8.1 displays these 11 provisions of the U.S. Constitution referring to the powers of the state "legislature."

8.3.1 Electing U.S. Senators

Under the original Constitution, each state legislature elected the state's
two U.S. Senators. Two methods were commonly used by the states. In
some states, the two houses of the state legislature met in a joint con-

---

[24] For simplicity, we frequently refer to the "two houses" of a state legislature, even though
Nebraska has a unicameral state legislature.

TABLE 8.1 PROVISIONS OF THE U.S. CONSTITUTION REFERRING TO POWERS OF THE STATE "LEGISLATURE"

	POWER	PROVISION OF THE U.S. CONSTITUTION
1	**Electing U.S. Senators** (prior to the 17th Amendment)	"The Senate of the United States shall be composed of two Senators from each State, **chosen by the Legislature thereof,** for six Years; and each Senator shall have one Vote."[25] [Emphasis added]
2	**Filling a U.S. Senate vacancy** (prior to the 17th Amendment)	"… if Vacancies happen by Resignation, or otherwise, during the Recess of the **Legislature** of any State, the Executive thereof may make temporary Appointments until the next Meeting of the **Legislature, which shall then fill such Vacancies.**"[26] [Emphasis added]
3	**Ratifying a proposed federal constitutional amendment**	"The Congress, whenever two thirds of both Houses shall deem it necessary, shall propose Amendments to this Constitution, or, on the Application of the Legislatures of two thirds of the several States, shall call a Convention for proposing Amendments, which, in either Case, shall be valid to all Intents and Purposes, as Part of this Constitution, **when ratified by the Legislatures** of three fourths of the several States, or by Conventions in three fourths thereof, as the one or the other Mode of Ratification may be proposed by the Congress … "[27] [Emphasis added]
4	**Making an application to Congress for a federal constitutional convention**	"The Congress, whenever two thirds of both Houses shall deem it necessary, shall propose Amendments to this Constitution, or, **on the Application of the Legislatures** of two thirds of the several States, shall call a Convention for proposing Amendments, which, in either Case, shall be valid to all Intents and Purposes, as Part of this Constitution, when ratified by the Legislatures of three fourths of the several States, or by Conventions in three fourths thereof, as the one or the other Mode of Ratification may be proposed by the Congress … "[28] [Emphasis added]

[25] U.S. Constitution. Article I, section 3, clause 1. Superseded by the 17th Amendment.

[26] U.S. Constitution. Article I, section 3, clause 2. Superseded by the 17th Amendment.

[27] U.S. Constitution. Article V.

[28] U.S. Constitution. Article V.

[29] U.S. Constitution. Article I, section 4, clause 1.

TABLE 8.1 PROVISIONS OF THE U.S. CONSTITUTION REFERRING TO POWERS OF THE STATE "LEGISLATURE" (cont.)

	POWER	PROVISION OF THE U.S. CONSTITUTION
5	**Choosing the manner of electing U.S. Representatives and Senators**	"The Times, Places and Manner of holding Elections for Senators and Representatives, shall be **prescribed in each State by the Legislature** thereof; but the Congress may at any time by Law make or alter such Regulations, except as to the Places of chusing Senators."[29] [Emphasis added]
6	**Choosing the manner of appointing presidential electors**	"Each State shall appoint, in such Manner **as the Legislature thereof may direct,** a Number of Electors, equal to the whole Number of Senators and Representatives to which the State may be entitled in the Congress ...."[30] [Emphasis added]
7	**Choosing the manner of conducting a popular election to fill a U.S. Senate vacancy** (under the 17th Amendment)	"When vacancies happen in the representation of any State in the Senate, the executive authority of such State shall issue writs of election to fill such vacancies: Provided, That the legislature of any State may empower the executive thereof to make temporary appointments until the people fill the vacancies by election **as the legislature may direct.**"[31] [Emphasis added]
8	**Empowering the Governor to fill a U.S. Senate vacancy temporarily until a popular election is held** (under the 17th Amendment)	"When vacancies happen in the representation of any State in the Senate, the executive authority of such State shall issue writs of election to fill such vacancies: Provided, That **the legislature of any State may empower** the executive thereof to make temporary appointments until the people fill the vacancies by election as the legislature may direct."[32] [Emphasis added]
9	**Consenting to the purchase of enclaves by the federal government**	"To exercise exclusive Legislation in all Cases whatsoever, over such District (not exceeding ten Miles square) as may, by Cession of particular States, and the Acceptance of Congress, become the Seat of the Government of the United States, and to exercise like Authority over all Places purchased by the **Consent of the Legislature** of the State in which the Same shall be, for the Erection of Forts, Magazines, Arsenals, dock-Yards, and other needful Buildings."[33] [Emphasis added]

[29] U.S. Constitution. Article I, section 4, clause 1.
[30] U.S. Constitution. Article II, section 1, clause 2.
[31] U.S. Constitution. 17th Amendment, section 2.
[32] U.S. Constitution. 17th Amendment, section 2.
[33] U.S. Constitution. Article I, section 9, clause 17.

TABLE 8.1 PROVISIONS OF THE U.S. CONSTITUTION REFERRING TO POWERS OF THE STATE "LEGISLATURE" (cont.)

	POWER	PROVISION OF THE U.S. CONSTITUTION
10	**Consenting to the formation of new states from territory of existing state(s)**	"New States may be admitted by the Congress into this Union; but no new State shall be formed or erected within the Jurisdiction of any other State; nor any State be formed by the Junction of two or more States, or Parts of States, without the **Consent of the Legislatures** of the States concerned as well as of the Congress."[34] [Emphasis added]
11	**Requesting federal military assistance to quell domestic violence**	"The United States shall guarantee to every State in this Union a Republican Form of Government, and shall protect each of them against Invasion; and on **Application of the Legislature,** or of the Executive (when the **Legislature** cannot be convened) against domestic Violence."[35] [Emphasis added]

vention in which each state representative and each state senator cast one vote in the election for the state's U.S. Senator. In other states, the state house of representatives and the state senate voted separately on a concurrent resolution expressing their choice for the state's U.S. Senator.[36] Regardless of which method was used, the state's Governor was *not* part of the constitutional process of electing U.S. Senators. Neither the decision of a joint convention of the two houses nor the concurrent resolution agreed to by both houses of the legislature was presented to the Governor for approval or disapproval. In other words, the word "legislature" in the U.S. Constitution, in connection with the election of U.S. Senators (the first entry in table 8.1), refers to the state's two legislative chambers—not to the state's usual process for making laws.

---

[34] U.S. Constitution. Article IV, section 3, clause 1.

[35] U.S. Constitution. Article IV, section 4.

[35] Separate voting for U.S. Senators by the two houses of the state legislature, of course, created the possibility of a deadlock between the two houses. Thus, it became common for U.S. Senate seats to remain vacant for prolonged periods. Article I, section 4, clause 1 of the U.S. Constitution provides that "The Times, Places and Manner of holding Elections for Senators and Representatives, shall be prescribed in each State by the Legislature thereof; but the Congress may at any time by Law make or alter such Regulations, except as to the Places of chusing Senators." In 1866, Congress exercised its power under this constitutional provision to change the "manner" by which state legislatures conducted their Senate elections and to specify the "time" of such elections. Congress required the two houses of each state legislature to meet in a joint convention on a specified day and to meet every day thereafter until a Senator was selected (14 Stat. 243).

8.3.2 Filling a U.S. Senate Vacancy

Similarly, under the original Constitution, a vacancy in the U.S. Senate was filled by action of the state's two legislative chambers (either voting in a joint convention or acting separately by concurrent resolution). That is, the word "legislature" in the U.S. Constitution, in connection with the filling of U.S. Senate vacancies (the second entry in table 8.1), refers to the state's two legislative chambers.

8.3.3 Ratifying a Proposed Federal Constitutional Amendment

The meaning of the word "legislature" in connection with the ratification of amendments to the federal Constitution (the third entry in table 8.1) was decided by the U.S. Supreme Court in *Hawke v. Smith* in 1920.[37] Article V of the U.S. Constitution provides that proposed amendments

> "… shall be valid to all Intents and Purposes, as Part of this Constitution, when ratified by the **Legislatures** of three fourths of the several States.…" [Emphasis added]

Before deciding the specific issue in the Hawke case in 1920, the U.S. Supreme Court reviewed the Court's decision in 1798 in *Hollingsworth et al. v. Virginia.*[38] The *Hollingsworth* case explored the two distinct meanings of the word "Congress" in the U.S. Constitution (the analog of the issue concerning the two meanings of the word "legislature").

The U.S. Constitution frequently uses the word "Congress" to refer to the national government's law-making process—that is, the process by which the legislative bills are passed by the two houses of Congress and presented to the President for approval or disapproval. The word "Congress" appears with this meaning in numerous places in the Constitution, including

> "The **Congress** shall have Power To lay and collect Taxes, Duties, Imposts and Excises, to pay the Debts and provide for the common Defence and general Welfare of the United States.…"[39] [Emphasis added]

---

[37] *Hawke v. Smith.* 253 U.S. 221. 1920.

[38] *Hollingsworth et al. v. Virginia.* 3 Dall. 378. 1798.

[39] U.S. Constitution. Article I, section 8, clause 1.

The word "Congress" also appears in Article V:

> "The **Congress,** whenever two thirds of both Houses shall deem it necessary, shall propose Amendments to this Constitution...." [Emphasis added]

The *Hollingsworth* case addressed the question of whether the word "Congress" in the U.S. Constitution meant

- **the national government's legislative chambers**—that is, the U.S. House of Representatives and U.S. Senate sitting separately and agreeing to a concurrent resolution, or
- **the national government's law-making process.**

In 1798, the U.S. Supreme Court ruled that when the Congress proposes an amendment to the U.S. Constitution, the resolution of ratification need not be submitted to the President for approval or disapproval. Referring to the 1798 *Hollingsworth* case, the Court noted in the 1920 *Hawke* case:

> "At an early day this court settled that the submission of a constitutional amendment did not require the action of the President. The question arose over the adoption of the Eleventh Amendment. *Hollingsworth et al. v. Virginia,* 3 Dall. 378. In that case it was contended that the amendment had not been proposed in the manner provided in the Constitution as an inspection of the original roll showed that it had never been submitted to the President for his approval in accordance with article 1, section 7, of the Constitution. The Attorney General answered that **the case of amendments is a substantive act, unconnected with the ordinary business of legislation,** and not within the policy or terms of the Constitution investing the President with a qualified negative [veto] on the acts and resolutions of Congress. In a footnote to this argument of the Attorney General, Justice Chase said:
>
> > 'There can, surely, be no necessity to answer that argument. **The negative of the President applies only to the ordinary cases of legislation. He has nothing to do with the proposition, or adoption, of amendments to the Constitution.'**

"The court by a unanimous judgment held that the amendment was constitutionally adopted."[40] [Emphasis added]

In other words, the 1798 *Hollingsworth* case concluded that a federal constitutional amendment was *not* the "ordinary business of legislation." The U.S. Supreme Court then addressed the specific issue in the 1920 *Hawke* case, namely the constitutionality of a 1918 amendment to the Ohio Constitution. This state constitutional amendment extended the protest-referendum process to resolutions of ratification by the Ohio legislature of proposed federal constitutional amendments. Specifically, the 1918 amendment to the Ohio Constitution provided:

> "The people also reserve to themselves the legislative power of the referendum on the action of the General Assembly ratifying any proposed amendment to the Constitution of the United States."

The *Hawke* case arose as a result of the Ohio Legislature's ratification of the 18th Amendment prohibiting the manufacture, sale, and transportation of intoxicating liquors for beverage purposes. On January 7, 1919, the Ohio Legislature passed a concurrent resolution[41] ratifying the Amendment.[42] Ohio's ratification was crucial because the U.S. Secretary of State was in possession of resolutions of ratification from 35 other states, and 36 ratifications were sufficient, at the time, to make a pending amendment part of the U.S. Constitution. A protest-referendum petition was quickly circulated in Ohio. Supporters of the 18th Amendment challenged the petition's validity in state court. The Ohio Supreme Court decided that the legislature's ratification of the 18th Amendment should be temporarily suspended and submitted to the state's voters for approval or disapproval in a statewide referendum. The U.S. Supreme Court, however, decided otherwise.

> "The argument to support the power of the state to require the approval by the people of the state of the ratification of

---

[40] *Hawke v. Smith.* 253 U.S. 221 at 229–230. 1920.

[41] A concurrent resolution is a type of resolution that is passed by both houses of the legislature but not submitted to the Governor for approval or disapproval.

[42] The resolution of ratification for the 18th Amendment was adopted by the Ohio Legislature in accordance with the long-standing practice in Ohio (and other states) of not submitting the legislature's resolution to the state's Governor for approval or disapproval.

amendments to the federal Constitution through the medium of a referendum rests upon the proposition that the federal Constitution requires ratification by the legislative action of the states through the medium provided at the time of the proposed approval of an amendment. This argument is fallacious in this—**ratification by a state of a constitutional amendment is not an act of legislation** within the proper sense of the word. **It is but the expression of the assent of the state to a proposed amendment.**"[43] [Emphasis added]

In short, in connection with ratification of amendments to the U.S. Constitution (the third entry in table 8.1), the word "legislature" in the U.S. Constitution refers to the state's two legislative chambers. Ratification is

- "unconnected with the ordinary business of legislation,"[44] and
- "not an act of legislation."[45]

Appendix U contains the full text of the Supreme Court's 1920 decision in *Hawke v. Smith.*

8.3.4 Making an Application to Congress for a Federal Constitutional Convention

The word "legislature" appears in the U.S. Constitution in connection with one of the two ways by which amendments to the Constitution may be proposed to the states. Article V provides:

"The Congress, whenever two thirds of both Houses shall deem it necessary, shall propose Amendments to this Constitution, or, on the **Application of the Legislatures** of two thirds of the several States, shall call a Convention for proposing Amendments...." [Emphasis added]

State legislatures sometimes call on Congress to convene a federal Constitutional Convention. For example, prior to congressional passage of the 17th Amendment, 26 states had petitioned Congress for a federal Constitutional Convention to consider the specific question of the

---

[43] *Hawke v. Smith.* 253 U.S. 221 at 229–230. 1920.

[44] *Id.* at 230.

[45] *Id.*

popular election of U.S. Senators. In addition, two additional states had, during the period immediately prior to congressional action on the 17th Amendment, issued requests for a federal Constitutional Convention without mentioning the topic to be considered by the Convention. Similarly, by the time Congress acted on the 21st Amendment, almost two-thirds of the states had petitioned Congress for a federal Constitutional Convention to repeal the 18th Amendment.

According to Orfield's *The Amending of the Federal Constitution*, when state legislatures apply to Congress for a federal Constitutional Convention, the long-standing practice of the states has been that the action of the legislature is not presented to the state's Governor for approval or disapproval.[46] Instead, the two houses of the state legislature pass a concurrent resolution. Thus, in connection with applications to Congress for a federal Constitutional Convention (the fourth entry in table 8.1), historical practice indicates that the word "legislature" in the U.S. Constitution refers to the state's two legislative chambers.

8.3.5 Choosing the Manner of Electing U.S. Representatives and Senators

As demonstrated in the previous four sections, judicial precedent and long-standing practice by the states indicate that the word "legislature" in the U.S. Constitution refers, in connection with the first, second, third, and fourth entries in table 8.1, to the state's two legislative chambers—not to the state's Governor or the state's citizen-initiative or protest-referendum processes.

In many other parts of the U.S. Constitution, however, the word "legislature" has a different meaning—namely, the state's law-making process. In these parts of the Constitution, "legislature" includes the state's Governor—an official who is manifestly not part of the state legislature. Moreover, in these parts of the U.S. Constitution, "legislature" may also include the state's voters—who, like the Governor, are plainly not members of the two chambers of the state legislature.

An example of this second meaning of the word "legislature" is found in Article I, section 4, clause 1 of the U.S. Constitution concerning the manner of holding elections for U.S. Representatives and Senators (the fifth entry in table 8.1).

---

[46] Orfield, Lester Bernhardt. 1942. *The Amending of the Federal Constitution*. Ann Arbor: The University of Michigan Press.

"The Times, Places and **Manner** of holding Elections for Senators and Representatives, shall be prescribed in each State by the **Legislature** thereof; but the Congress may at any time by Law make or alter such Regulations, except as to the Places of chusing Senators." [Emphasis added]

The U.S. Supreme Court addressed the meaning of "legislature" in Article I, section 4, clause 1 in *Smiley v. Holm* in 1932.[47] The issue in *Smiley* was whether the Minnesota Governor could veto a law passed by the legislature redrawing the state's congressional districts after the 1930 census. In other words, the question in *Smiley* was whether the word "legislature" refers to the state's two legislative chambers or the state's law-making process which, in Minnesota in 1932, included the Governor.

The question of whether the word "legislature" includes a state's Governor depends, in large part, on the answer to the following question:

"When a state exercises authority pursuant to powers granted to it by the U.S. Constitution in connection with deciding on the manner of electing its U.S. Representatives,

(1) does it derive the power to act solely from the U.S. Constitution, or

(2) does it enact the legislation in accordance with the procedures specified in the state's constitution?"

The 1932 *Smiley* case involving the meaning of the word "legislature" in the U.S. Constitution came to the U.S. Supreme Court over a decade after various cases arising from the adoption of the initiative and referendum processes in the early years of the 20th century. These earlier cases included the 1920 *Hawke* case (discussed above) and the 1916 case of *State of Ohio ex rel. Davis v. Hildebrant* (discussed below). *Smiley* thus provided the Court with the opportunity to put all of these related cases into perspective. The U.S. Supreme Court wrote in *Smiley* in 1932:

"[W]henever the term 'legislature' is used in the Constitution, it is necessary to consider the nature of the particular action in view."[48] [Emphasis added]

---

[47] *Smiley v. Holm.* 285 U.S. 355. 1932.

[48] *Id.* at 366.

Applying this test, the Court found that the term "legislature" in Article I, section 4, clause 1 referred to "making laws"[49] and therefore included the Governor.

> "[I]t follows, in the absence of an indication of a contrary intent, that **the exercise of the authority must be in accordance with the method which the State has prescribed for legislative enactments. We find no suggestion in the Federal constitutional provision of an attempt to endow the legislature of the State with power to enact laws in any manner other than that in which the constitution of the State has provided that laws shall be enacted.**"[50] [Emphasis added]

Thus, the word "legislature" in the U.S. Constitution, in connection with the state's deciding on the "manner of holding Elections" for U.S. Representatives" (the fifth entry in table 8.1), refers to the state's process of making laws—not just to the two chambers of the state legislature.

Appendix V contains the full text of the Supreme Court's 1932 decision in *Smiley v. Holm*.

In 1916, the U.S. Supreme Court addressed the specific question of whether the word "legislature" in Article I, section 4, clause 1 of the U.S. Constitution included the voters acting through the processes of direct democracy. The Supreme Court described the origins of *State of Ohio ex rel. Davis v. Hildebrant* as follows:

> "By an amendment to the Constitution of Ohio, adopted September 3d, 1912, the **legislative power was expressly declared to be vested** not only in the senate and house of representatives of the state, constituting the general assembly, but **in the people,** in whom a right was reserved by way of referendum to approve or disapprove by popular vote any law enacted by the general assembly." [51] [Emphasis added]

The Supreme Court continued:

> "In May, 1915, the general assembly of Ohio passed an act redistricting the state for the purpose of congressional

---

[49] *Id.* at 365.

[50] *Id.* at 368.

[51] *State of Ohio ex rel. Davis v. Hildebrant.* 241 U.S. 565 at 566. 1916.

elections, by which act twenty-two congressional districts were created, in some respects differing from the previously established districts, and this act, after approval by the governor, was filed in the office of the secretary of state. The requisite number of electors under the referendum provision having petitioned for a submission of the law to a popular vote, such vote was taken and the law was disapproved.

"Thereupon, in the supreme court of the state, the suit before us was begun against state election officers for the purpose of procuring a mandamus, directing them to disregard the vote of the people on the referendum, disapproving the law, and to proceed to discharge their duties as such officers in the next congressional election, upon the assumption that the action by way of referendum was void, and that the law which was disapproved was subsisting and valid."[52]

Summarizing the issue, the Supreme Court wrote:

"The right to this relief was based upon the charge that the referendum vote was not and could not be a part of the legislative authority of the state, and therefore could have no influence on the subject of the law creating congressional districts for the purpose of representation in Congress. Indeed, it was in substance charged that both from the point of view of the state Constitution and laws and from that of the Constitution of the United States, especially [clause] 4 of article 1, providing that

'the times, places and manner of holding elections for Senators and Representatives, shall be prescribed in each state by the legislature thereof; but the Congress may at any time by law, make or alter such regulations, except as to the places of choosing Senators;'

and also from that of the provisions of the controlling act of Congress of August 8, 1911 (chap. 5, 37 Stat. at L. 13, Comp. Stat. 1913, 15), apportioning representation among the states, the attempt to make the referendum a component part of the

---

[52] *Id.* at 566–567.

legislative authority empowered to deal with the election of members of Congress was absolutely void. **The court below adversely disposed of these contentions, and held that the provisions as to referendum were a part of the legislative power of the state, made so by the Constitution, and that nothing in the act of Congress of 1911, or in the constitutional provision, operated to the contrary,** and that therefore the disapproved law had no existence and was not entitled to be enforced by mandamus."[53] [Emphasis added]

The U.S. Supreme Court then upheld the Ohio Supreme Court and rejected the argument that the word "legislature" in Article I, section 4, clause 1 of the U.S. Constitution excluded the referendum process. The popular vote rejecting Ohio's redistricting statute was allowed to stand.

Additionally, the Court noted:

"Congress recognize[d] the referendum as part of the legislative authority of a state."[54]

Appendix P contains the full text of the Supreme Court's 1916 decision in *State of Ohio ex rel. Davis v. Hildebrant*.

In 1920, the U.S. Supreme Court distinguished its decision in *Hawke* from its decision in *State of Ohio ex rel. Davis v. Hildebrant* by saying in *Hawke:*

"But it is said this view runs counter to the decision of this court in *Davis v. Hildebrant* (241 U.S. 565) 36 S. Ct. 708. But that case is inapposite. It dealt with article 1 section 4, of the Constitution, which provides that the times, places, and manners of holding elections for Senators and Representatives in each state shall be determined by the respective Legislatures thereof, but that Congress may at any time make or alter such regulations, except as to the place for choosing Senators. As shown in the opinion in that case, Congress had itself recognized the referendum as part of the legislative authority of the state for the purpose stated. It was held, affirming the

---

[53] *Id.* at 568.
[54] *Id.* at 569.

judgment of the Supreme Court of Ohio, that the referendum provision of the state Constitution, when applied to a law redistricting the state with a view to representation in Congress, was not unconstitutional. **Article 1, section 4, plainly gives authority to the state to legislate within the limitations therein named. Such legislative action is entirely different from the requirement of the Constitution as to the expression of assent or dissent to a proposed amendment to the Constitution. In such expression no legislative action is authorized or required."**[55] [Emphasis added]

Relying on *Smiley v. Holm*[56] and *State of Ohio ex rel. Davis v. Hildebrant*,[57] the Colorado Supreme Court wrote in *Colorado, ex rel. Salazar v. Davidson* in 2003:

"[T]he United States Supreme Court has interpreted the word 'legislature' in Article I to broadly encompass any means permitted by state law [including] citizen referenda and initiatives, mandatory gubernatorial approval, and any other procedures defined by the state." [58,59]

Chief Justice Rehnquist, joined by Justices Thomas and Scalia, affirmed this view in a dissenting opinion when the U.S. Supreme Court denied review of the *Colorado, ex rel. Salazar v. Davidson* decision. Rehnquist stated that the Court had

"explained that the focus of our inquiry was **not on the 'body' but the function performed** [and that] the function referred to by Article I, §4, was **the lawmaking process,** which is defined by state law."[60] [Emphasis added]

[55] *Hawke v. Smith.* 253 U.S. 221 at 230–231. 1920.

[56] *Smiley v. Holm.* 285 U.S. 355. 1932.

[57] *State of Ohio ex rel. Davis v. Hildebrant.* 241 U.S. 565. 1916.

[58] *Colorado, ex rel. Salazar v. Davidson.* 79 P.3d 1221, 1232 (Colorado 2003).

[59] In *Cook v. Gralike*, 531 U.S. 510, 526 n.20 (2001), the Court declined to consider whether the Elections Clause of Art. 1, §4, which is a grant of power to "each State by the Legislature thereof," could be invoked to protect to a statute adopted by referendum. The Court reaffirmed, however, the notion in *Smiley* that "[w]herever the term 'legislature' is used in the Constitution, it is necessary to consider the nature of the particular action in view." *Id.*

[60] *Colorado General Assembly v. Salazar,* 124 S. Ct. 2228 at 2230. 2004.

The distinction between "the lawmaking process" and the two chambers of the state legislature is not new. In fact, this distinction has been made since the earliest days of the U.S. Constitution. When the U.S. Constitution took effect in 1788, two states had the gubernatorial veto.[61,62]

The provisions of the Massachusetts Constitution at the time when the U.S. Constitution took effect were substantially the same as the procedures for gubernatorial approval, veto, and legislative override found in most state constitutions today (and substantially the same as the procedures for presidential veto in the U.S. constitution).

> "No bill or resolve of the senate or house of representatives shall become a law, and have force as such, until it shall have been laid before the governor for his revisal; and if he, upon such revision, approve thereof, he shall signify his approbation by signing the same. But if he have any objection to the passing of such bill or resolve, he shall return the same, together with his objections thereto, in writing, to the senate or house of representatives, in whichsoever the same shall have originated, who shall enter the objections sent down by the governor, at large, on their records, and proceed to reconsider the said bill or resolve; but if, after such reconsideration, two-thirds of the said senate or house of representatives shall, notwithstanding the said objections, agree to pass the same, it shall, together with the objections, be sent to the other branch of the legislature, where it shall also be reconsidered, and if approved by two-thirds of the members present, shall have the force of law; but in all such cases, the vote of both houses shall be determined by yeas and nays; and the names of the persons voting for or against the said bill or resolve shall be entered upon the public records of the commonwealth."[63]

---

[61] Kole, Edward A. 1999. *The First 13 Constitutions of the First American States.* Haverford, PA: Infinity Publishing.

[62] Kole, Edward A. *The True Intent of the First American Constitutions of 1776–1791.* Haverford, PA: Infinity Publishing.

[63] Massachusetts Constitution of 1780. Chapter I, Section I, Article II.

On November 20, 1788, both chambers of the Massachusetts legislature approved legislation specifying the manner for electing U.S. representatives. This legislation was forwarded to Governor John Hancock, and he approved it.[64]

The New York Constitution of 1777 was in effect when the U.S. Constitution took effect. The New York Constitution (like many state constitutions of the colonial era and immediate post-independence era) had a Governor's Council.[65] In particular, the New York Constitution required that all bills passed by the legislature be submitted to a Council of Revision composed of the Governor, the Chancellor, and judges of the state supreme court. A two-thirds vote of both houses of the legislature was necessary to override a veto by the Council. On January 23, 1789, the New York legislature approved legislation specifying the manner for electing U.S. representatives. The bill was presented to the Council; the Council approved the bill; and the bill became law.

Article I, section 4, clause 1 of the U.S. Constitution covers the manner of electing U.S. Senators as well as the manner of electing U.S. Representatives.

> "The Times, Places and **Manner** of holding Elections for **Senators** and Representatives, shall be prescribed in each State by the **Legislature** thereof...." [Emphasis added]

The two meanings of the word "legislature" in the U.S. Constitution are dramatically illustrated by the actions of the first New York legislature that met under the U.S. Constitution. As mentioned in section 8.3.1, the state's Governor was not part of the constitutional process of electing U.S. Senators under the original Constitution. The two chambers of the state legislature elected the state's U.S. Senators. The Governor of New York was, however, part of the law-making process that decided the *manner* of electing U.S. Senators. For example, in 1789, both houses of the New York legislature passed a bill providing for the manner of electing U.S. Senators. This bill was presented to the Council composed of the Governor, the Chancellor, and the judges of the state supreme court. The

---

[64] Smith, Hayward H. 2001. *Symposium, Law of Presidential Elections: Issues in the Wake of Florida 2000.* History of the Article II Independent State legislature Doctrine. 29 *Florida State University Law Review* 731-785 at 760. Issue 2.

[65] Currently, Massachusetts has a Governor's Council and New Hampshire has an Executive Council.

Council vetoed the bill.[66] That bill did not become law. In short, when a state chose the "manner" of electing its U.S. Senators, the word "legislature" in the U.S. Constitution meant "the lawmaking process" (which included the Governor and Council); however, when the state elected its U.S. Senators, the same word "legislature" meant only the two legislative chambers (which did not include the Governor or the Council).

Congressional districting is arguably the most important aspect of the "manner" of electing U.S. Representatives. In recent years, the voters have used the processes of direct democracy not only to review congressional districting plans enacted by the state legislature (as they did in Ohio in the 1916 case of *State of Ohio ex rel. Davis v. Hildebrant*), but also to entirely exclude the state legislature from the process of congressional districting. For example, Arizona voters recently approved an initiative establishing a non-partisan commission to draw the state's congressional districts. The voters' decision to exclude the state legislature power from the redistricting process was taken by the voters unilaterally through the citizen-initiative process—without the involvement, much less the consent, of the state legislature. The power of congressional redistricting in Arizona now resides in the non-partisan commission. Similar initiative measures were on the ballot in the November 2005 elections in California and Ohio (but were defeated). Initiative petitions were in circulation in 2005 in Florida and Massachusetts for similar measures.

In summary, present-day practice, practice at the time of ratification of the U.S. Constitution, and court decisions consistently support the interpretation that the word "legislature" in article I, section 4, clause 1 of the U.S. Constitution (the fifth entry in table 8.1) does not refer to the two chambers of the state legislature but, instead, refers to the "lawmaking process" that includes

- the state's Governor, an official who is manifestly not a member of the two chambers of the state legislature, and
- in states having the citizen-initiative process and protest-referendum process, the state's voters, who, like the Governor, are manifestly not members of the two chambers of the state legislature.

---

[66] DenBoer, Gordon; Brown, Lucy Trumbull; and Hagermann, Charles D. (editors). 1986. *The Documentary History of the First Federal Elections 1788–1790*. Madison, WI: University of Wisconsin Press. Volume III.

8.3.6 Choosing the Manner of Appointing Presidential Electors

The word "legislature" appears in Article II of the U.S. Constitution (the sixth entry in table 8.1).

> "Each State shall appoint, in such Manner **as the Legislature thereof may direct,** a Number of Electors, equal to the whole Number of Senators and Representatives to which the State may be entitled in the Congress...."[67] [Emphasis added]

In *U.S. Term Limits v. Thornton*, the U.S. Supreme Court in 1995 noted the parallelism between the use of the word "legislature" in Article I, section 4, clause 1 (relating to the "manner" of electing U.S. Representatives) and the word "legislature" in Article II. The Court wrote,

> "... the provisions governing elections reveal the Framers' understanding that powers over the election of federal officers had to be delegated to, rather than reserved by, the States. It is surely no coincidence that **the context of federal elections provides one of the few areas in which the Constitution expressly requires action by the States,** namely that
>
> > '[t]he Times, Places and **Manner** of holding Elections for Senators and Representatives, shall be prescribed in each State by the **legislature** thereof.' [Art I., §4, cl. 4.]
>
> **"This duty parallels the duty under Article II** that
>
> > 'Each State shall appoint, in such **Manner** as the **Legislature** thereof may direct, a Number of Electors.' Art II., §1, cl. 2.
>
> "These Clauses are express delegations of power to the States to act with respect to federal elections."[68] [Emphasis added]

The parallelism noted by the Court supports the power of the people to act legislatively through the citizen-initiative process concerning the manner of electing presidential electors.

---

[67] U.S. Constitution. Article II, section 1, clause 2.

[68] *U.S. Term Limits v. Thornton.* 514 U.S. 779 at 805. 1995.

The question of whether the word "legislature" includes the state's initiative and referendum processes depends, in large part, on the answer to the following question:

> "When a state exercises authority pursuant to powers granted to it by the U.S. Constitution in connection with deciding on the manner of choosing its presidential electors,
>
> > (1) does it derive the power to act solely from the U.S. Constitution, or
> >
> > (2) does it enact the legislation in accordance with the procedures specified in the state's constitution?"

The leading U.S. Supreme Court case interpreting Article II, section 1, clause 2 of the U.S. Constitution is the 1892 case of *McPherson v. Blacker*.[69] In *Blacker*, the U.S. Supreme Court rejected a challenge to Michigan legislation providing for selection of presidential electors by district, as opposed to the statewide winner-take-all method that Michigan had been using prior to 1892 and that had become the national norm. In that case, the Court analyzed the meaning of the word "legislature" as used in Article II and noted that the interpretation of this word was governed by fundamental law of the state. The U.S. Supreme Court wrote:

> "The state does not act by its people in their collective capacity, but through such political agencies as are duly constituted and established. The legislative power is the supreme authority, **except as limited by the constitution of the state,** and the sovereignty of the people is exercised through their representatives in the legislature, **unless by the fundamental law power is elsewhere reposed.** The constitution of the United States frequently refers to the state as a political community, and also in terms to the people of the several states and the citizens of each state. What is forbidden or required to be done by a state is forbidden or required of the legislative power under state constitutions as they exist."[70]
> [Emphasis added]

---

[69] *McPherson v. Blacker.* 146 U.S. 1. 1892.
[70] *Id.* at 27.

The possibility that a state's legislative power might be "reposed" in a place other than the state legislature is noteworthy, given that the case was decided when the idea of the citizen-initiative process was an active topic of public debate (just before South Dakota became the first state to adopt the citizen-initiative process in 1898).

Given that the citizen-initiative process is generally considered to be a co-equal grant of authority to that given to the state's legislature, the treatment of the initiative process as a legislative power is consistent with the fundamental law of states that have the initiative process.

There are two cases that have specifically involved the question of whether the word "legislature" in Article II of the U.S. Constitution includes the initiative and referendum processes.[71]

The first case arose as a result of a 1919 law entitled "An act granting to women the right to vote for presidential electors." This law was passed by the two houses of the Maine legislature and presented to the state's Governor. The Governor signed the law. Under the protest-referendum provisions of the Maine Constitution, if a petition protesting a just-enacted law is filed with the signatures of at least 10,000 voters, the new law is temporarily suspended and referred to the voters for their approval or disapproval in a statewide referendum. A petition was circulated and duly filed with the Governor's office concerning this statute. Before proceeding with the referendum, the Governor raised the question of whether the referendum provision of the Maine Constitution applied to legislation involving the manner of appointing the state's presidential electors. Specifically, he propounded the following question to the Justices of the Maine Supreme Judicial Court:

> "Is the effect of the act of the Legislature of Maine of 1919, entitled 'An act granting to women the right to vote for presidential electors,' approved by the Governor on March 28, 1919, suspended by valid written petitions of not less than

---

[71] Court cases specifically interpreting the word "legislature" in Article II in relation to the initiative or referendum process are necessarily rare for several reasons. First, the initiative and referendum processes are only slightly more than 100 years old. Second, the initiative or referendum processes are available in fewer than one half of the states. Third, only a handful of the laws that a state enacts in a typical year involve the conduct of elections. Fourth, few new state laws involve the manner of conducting congressional and senatorial elections, and even fewer relate to presidential elections. Fifth, the vast majority of new state laws each year are enacted without the use of either the initiative or referendum processes.

10,000 electors, addressed to the Governor and filed in the office of the secretary of state within 90 days after the recess of the Legislature, requesting that it be referred to the people, and should the act be referred to the people as provided in article 4 of the Constitution of Maine, as amended by Amendment 31, adopted September 14, 1908?"

On August 28, 1919, the Maine Supreme Judicial Court unanimously answered this question in the affirmative. Relying extensively on the 1892 decision of the U.S. Supreme Court in *McPherson v. Blacker*,[72] the Maine Supreme Judicial Court wrote:

"The language of section 1, subd. 2, is clear and unambiguous. It admits of no doubt as to where the constitutional power of appointment is vested, namely, in the several states.

'Each state shall appoint in such manner as the Legislature thereof may direct'

are the significant words of the section, and their plain meaning is that **each state is thereby clothed with the absolute power to appoint electors in such manner as it may see fit, without any interference or control on the part of the federal government,** except, of course, in case of attempted discrimination as to race, color, or previous condition of servitude under the fifteenth amendment. The clause,

'in such manner as the Legislature thereof may direct,'

means, simply that **the state shall give expression to its will, as it must, of necessity, through its law-making body, the Legislature.** The will of the state in this respect must be voiced in legislative acts or resolves, which shall prescribe in detail the manner of choosing electors, the qualifications of voters therefor, and the proceedings on the part of the electors when chosen.

---

[72] *McPherson v. Blacker.* 146 U.S. 1. 1892. The *Blacker* case is also discussed in section 2.2.5 and later in this section. The complete opinion of the U.S. Supreme Court in the *Blacker* case is found in appendix O.

"**But these acts and resolves must be passed and become effective in accordance with and in subjection to the Constitution of the state, like all other acts** and resolves having the force of law. **The Legislature was not given in this respect any superiority over or independence from the organic law of the state in force at the time when a given law is passed.** Nor was it designated by the federal Constitution as a mere agency or representative of the people to perform a certain act, as it was under article 5 in ratifying a federal amendment, a point more fully discussed in the answer to the question concerning the federal prohibitory amendment. 107 Atl. 673. **It is simply the ordinary instrumentality of the state, the legislative branch of the government, the law-making power, to put into words the will of the state in connection with the choice of presidential electors. The distinction between the function and power of the Legislature in the case under consideration and its function and power as a particular body designated by the federal Constitution to ratify or reject a federal amendment is sharp and clear and must be borne in mind.**

"It follows, therefore, that under the provisions of the federal Constitution the state by its legislative direction may establish such a method of choosing its presidential electors as it may see fit, and may change that method from time to time as it may deem advisable; but **the legislative acts both of establishment and of change must always be subject to the provisions of the Constitution of the state in force at the time such acts are passed** and can be valid and effective only when enacted in compliance therewith."[73] [Emphasis added]

The Court continued:

"It is clear that this act, extending this privilege to women, constitutes a change in the method of electing presidential electors....

---

[73] *In re Opinion of the Justices.* 107 A. 705. 1919.

"... this state during the century of its existence prior to 1919, had by appropriate legislative act or resolve directed that only male citizens were qualified to vote for presidential electors. By the act of 1919 it has attempted to change that direction, by extending the privilege of suffrage, so far as presidential electors are concerned, to women. Had this act been passed prior to the adoption of the initiative and referendum amendment in 1908, it would have become effective, so far as legal enactment is concerned, without being referred to the people; but now under Amendment 31 such reference must be had, if the necessary steps therefor are taken."

"... **This is the public statute of a law-making body, and is as fully within the control of the referendum amendment as is any other of the 239 public acts passed at the last session of the Legislature,** excepting, of course, emergency acts. **It is shielded from the jurisdiction of that referendum neither by the state nor by the federal Constitution.** In short, the state, through its Legislature, has taken merely the first step toward effecting a change in the appointment of presidential electors; but, because of the petitions filed, it must await the second step which is the vote of the people. The legislative attempt in this case cannot be fully effective until

> 'thirty days after the Governor shall have announced by public proclamation that the same has been ratified by a majority of the electors voting thereon at a general or special election.'"[74] [Emphasis added]

Appendix Q contains the entire text of the Court's opinion in *In re Opinion of the Justices.*

---

[74] *Id.*

[75] There was a flurry of activity concerning women's suffrage at the time. The Maine legislature adopted its contested law on women's suffrage in presidential elections on March 28, 1919. Congress proposed the women's suffrage amendment to the U.S. Constitution on June 4, 1919 and sent it to the states for ratification. The Maine Supreme Judicial Court announced its decision on August 28, 1919. The Maine Legislature ratified the proposed federal constitutional amendment on November 5, 1919. Tennessee's ratification on August 18, 1920, brought the 19th Amendment to the U.S. Constitution into effect.

When the voters of Maine voted on the suspended law, it was passed by a vote of 88,080 to 30,462.[75]

The second case involving an interpretation of the word "legislature" in Article II of the U.S. Constitution came just prior to the November 2, 2004, presidential election. *Napolitano v. Davidson* involved a federal court challenge to an initiative petition proposing an amendment to the Colorado Constitution to adopt the whole-number proportional approach for choosing the state's presidential electors (section 4.1.14). In that case, a Colorado voter asked that the Colorado Secretary of State be enjoined from holding the election on the proposed amendment. The plaintiff alleged that Amendment 36 violated Article II of the U.S. Constitution in that the voters were attempting to unconstitutionally preempt the role of the "legislature" in connection with the manner of appointing presidential electors.

The Colorado Attorney General defended the Secretary of State. Two representatives of those who had signed initiative petitions to place Amendment 36 on the ballot (the "proponents") were granted the right to intervene in the litigation. Additionally, one Democratic and one Republican candidate for presidential elector in the November 2004 election attempted to intervene.[76]

The Colorado Attorney General unqualifiedly defended the substantive provisions of Amendment 36. In response to the claim that the voters' exercise of the initiative power to allocate presidential electors infringed upon Article II, the Attorney General stated that, when the people of Colorado use the initiative process, they act as the "legislature." Specifically, the State of Colorado took the position that its voters were fully empowered to act, pursuant to Article II, to allocate presidential electors.

> "Article II, §1 authorizes each state to act in a lawmaking capacity to select the manner in which it appoints its presidential electors.... For example, the lawmaking authority conferred by Article II, §1 encompasses the people's power of referendum when such power is provided by the state constitution. *Cf. Hildebrant*, 241 U.S. at 569.[77] It follows that **the**

---

[76] The Elector-Intervenors were permitted to brief each of their legal arguments. After addressing the substance of their arguments, however, Judge Babcock ruled from the bench that their attempted intervention was not authorized, as they lacked standing to participate in the litigation.

[77] Appendix P contains the opinion of the U.S. Supreme Court in the case of *State of Ohio ex rel. Davis v. Hildebrant* cited by the Colorado Attorney General.

> **lawmaking authority conferred by Article II, §1 also encompasses the people's power of initiative where the people are empowered by the state constitution to legislate via initiative**....
>
> **"The Proposal (to proportionally allocate presidential electors based on the state's popular vote)** is an initiative by the people of Colorado as authorized by the Colorado Constitution. As such, it **is an exercise of legislative power** for the purpose of appointing presidential electors. **The Proposal, therefore, is authorized by Article II, §1.**"[78] [Emphasis added]

By the time the matter was fully briefed for the court, early voting had commenced in Colorado. Most absentee ballots had been sent to voters. A little more than one week remained until election day. On October 26, 2004, Judge Lewis Babcock heard the motions for preliminary injunction, filed by the plaintiff and the elector-intervenors, as well as the motions to dismiss filed by the Colorado Attorney General and the petition's proponents. Judge Babcock denied the former and granted the latter, clearing the way for a vote by the people on Amendment 36 on November 2, 2004.

From the bench, Judge Babcock noted that the matter was not ripe for adjudication, as an actual controversy could be said to exist only if the election were held and a majority of voters approved the proposed change in the method of allocating Colorado's presidential electors. Until that time, any opinion would only be advisory in nature.

Judge Babcock also noted that the issues involved in this case should be resolved in the first instance by the Colorado state courts and, therefore, that it was proper for the federal courts to abstain from intervening in this matter. Indeed, the Colorado challenge to the initiative petition on Amendment 36 was unusual in that it started in federal court. Most challenges to initiative and referendum petitions start in state courts.

In his oral ruling, Judge Babcock noted that the elector-intervenors had argued that Amendment 36 was "patently unconstitutional." The judge expressly stated that this was not the case, but he added that

---

[78] The Secretary of State's Combined Motion to Dismiss and Response to Motion for Preliminary Injunction at 21–22, filed in *Napolitano v. Davidson*, Civil Action No. 04-B-2114, D.Colo. (2004).

because he did not have to reach the merits of the case, his ruling should not be taken as a judicial imprimatur concerning the constitutionality of Amendment 36.

In order to obtain a preliminary injunction, one generally must establish (among other things) that there is a substantial likelihood of prevailing on the merits when the matter goes to trial. This standard generally applies when one seeks to enjoin an election or any part of the election process.[79] The federal district court, in evaluating the motions for preliminary injunction, did not find that either the plaintiff or the elector-intervenors had a substantial likelihood of success on the merits with regard to their argument that Amendment 36 violated Article II.

On November 2, 2004, Amendment 36 was rejected by the voters (section 4.1.14), so none of the legal issues raised by the pre-election lawsuit was subsequently addressed in court. Nonetheless, the voters' right to use the initiative process to change the manner of appointing presidential electors in Colorado was not disturbed by the judiciary.

Long-standing historical practice by the states is consistent with the 1920 decision by the Maine Supreme Judicial Court and the outcome of the 2004 litigation in Colorado concerning the meaning of the word "legislature" in Article II of the U.S. Constitution.

When the U.S. Constitution took effect in 1788, the gubernatorial veto existed in Massachusetts and New York.[80,81]

On November 20, 1788, both chambers of the Massachusetts legislature approved legislation specifying the manner for appointing the state's presidential electors. This legislation was presented to Governor John Hancock—an official who was manifestly not part of the two chambers of the state legislature. Governor Hancock approved the legislation.[82]

In New York, a comprehensive bill was introduced in the Senate on December 13, 1788, for electing presidential electors, U.S. Representatives, and U.S. Senators. The Federalists controlled the state

---

[79] *Libertarian Party v. Buckley.* 938 F.Supp. 687, 690 (D. Colo. 1997). See also *Chandler v. Miller.* 520 U.S. 305, 311. 1997.

[80] Kole, Edward A. 1999. *The First 13 Constitutions of the First American States.* Haverford, PA: Infinity Publishing.

[81] Kole, Edward A. *The True Intent of the First American Constitutions of 1776–1791.* Haverford, PA: Infinity Publishing.

[82] Smith, Hayward H. 2001. Symposium, Law of Presidential Elections: Issues in the Wake of Florida 2000, History of the Article II Independent State legislature Doctrine, 29 *Florida State University Law Review* 731 at 760.

Senate, and the Anti-Federalists controlled the Assembly. The two houses could not agree on the method by which the legislature would elect
presidential electors or U.S. Senators because each house wanted to
enhance its own power in the process. The three issues were therefore
considered separately.

As previously mentioned (section 8.3.5), the legislature passed legislation on January 27, 1789, providing the "manner" of electing U.S.
Representatives (including the districts to be used). That bill was submitted to the Council of Revision composed of the Governor, the
Chancellor, and the judges of the state supreme court. The Council
approved the bill; the bill became law; and the elections of U.S.
Representatives were held on March 3, 1789, in accordance with that law.

In addition (section 8.3.5), the legislature passed a bill in 1789 providing for the manner of electing U.S. Senators. This bill was presented to
the Council, but the Council vetoed the bill, and the bill did not become
law.

The legislature also debated a bill entitled "An act for regulating the
manner of appointing electors who are to elect the President, and Vice-
President of the United States of America."[83] That is, the legislation specifying the manner of appointing presidential electors was in the same
form as the vetoed bill specifying the manner of electing U.S.
Representatives and U.S. Senators. That is, the legislature debated the bill
concerning the manner of appointing presidential electors as an ordinary
legislative bill—not as a concurrent resolution to be voted upon only by
the two houses.

As it happened the two chambers of the New York legislature did not
reach an agreement on the manner of appointing presidential electors in
time for the first presidential election. Consequently, New York did not
cast any electoral votes in the 1789 presidential election. Later, a bill was
passed by both chambers of the legislature and submitted to the Council
in time for the 1792 presidential election. It took effect.

Thus, actual practice in the two states that had the gubernatorial veto
at the time when the U.S. Constitution first took effect indicates that, in
connection with the state's decision on the manner of appointing

[83] DenBoer, Gordon; Brown, Lucy Trumbull; and Hagermann, Charles D. (editors). 1986.
The Documentary History of the First Federal Elections 1788–1790. Madison, WI:
University of Wisconsin Press. Volume III. Pages 217–435.

presidential electors, the word "legislature" in Article II meant the state's lawmaking process—not just the two chambers of the state legislature.

Present-day practice by the states is consistent with practice from the time when the U.S. Constitution first took effect. Table 8.2 shows the section of each state's current law specifying the manner of appointing

Table 8.2 PRESENT-DAY PRACTICE BY THE STATES CONCERNING THE MEANING OF THE WORD "LEGISLATURE" IN CONNECTION WITH STATE LAWS SPECIFYING THE MANNER OF APPOINTING PRESIDENTIAL ELECTORS

STATE	SECTION	WAS THE LEGISLATURE'S BILL PRESENTED TO THE STATE'S GOVERNOR?
Alabama	Ala.Code § 17-19-4	Yes
	Ala.Code § 17-19-5	Yes
	Ala. Code § 17-19-6	Yes
Alaska	AK ST § 15.15.450	Yes
Arizona	A.R.S. § 16-650	Yes
Arkansas	Ar. Code §7-8-304	Yes
California	Cal.Elec.Code § 15505	Yes
Colorado	C.R.S. § 1-11-106	Yes
	Section. 20 of Schedule to	No—Provision of 1876
	Colorado Constitution	Colorado Constitution
Connecticut	C.G.S. § 9-315	Yes
Delaware	15 Del. C. § 5703	Yes
	15 Del. C. § 5711	Yes
District of Columbia	D.C. Code, Sect. 1-1001.10	Yes
Florida	F.S.A. § 9.103.011	Yes
Georgia	Ga. Code Ann., § 21-2-499	Yes
Hawaii	H.R.S. § 2-14-24	Yes
Idaho	ID ST § 34-1215	Yes
Illinois	10 ILCS 5/21-2	Yes
	10 ILCS 5/21-3	Yes
Indiana	IC 3-12-5-7	Yes
Iowa	I.C.A. § 50.45	Yes
Kansas	KS ST § 25-702	Yes
Kentucky	KRS § 118.425	Yes
Louisiana	LSA-R.S. 18:1261	Yes
Maine	21-A M.R.S. § 723	Yes
	21-A M.R.S. § 802	Yes
Maryland	MD Code § 11-601	Yes
Massachusetts	M.G.L.A. 54 § 118	Yes
Michigan	M.C.L.A. 168.42	Yes
Minnesota	M.S.A. § 208.05	Yes
Mississippi	Miss. Code Ann. § 23-15-605	Yes
Missouri	V.A.M.S. 128.070	Yes

Table 8.2 PRESENT-DAY PRACTICE BY THE STATES CONCERNING THE MEANING OF THE WORD "LEGISLATURE" IN CONNECTION WITH STATE LAWS SPECIFYING THE MANNER OF APPOINTING PRESIDENTIAL ELECTORS (cont.)

STATE	SECTION	WAS THE LEGISLATURE'S BILL PRESENTED TO THE STATE'S GOVERNOR?
Montana	Mt. St. §13-25-103	Yes
	Mt. St. §13-1-103	Yes
Nebraska	NE ST § 32-710	Yes
	NE ST § 32-1040	Yes
Nevada	N.R.S. 293.395	Yes
New Hampshire	N.H. Rev. Stat. § 659:81	Yes
New Jersey	§19:3-26	Yes
New Mexico	N. M. S. A. 1978, § 1-15-14	Yes
New York	§ 12-102	Yes
North Carolina	N.C.G.S.A. § 163-210	Yes
North Dakota	ND ST 16.1-14-01	Yes
Ohio	R.C. § 3505.33	Yes
Oklahoma	26 Okl.St.Ann. § 7-136	Yes
	26 Okl.St.Ann. § 10-103	Yes
Oregon	O.R.S. § 254.065	Yes
Pennsylvania	25 P.S. § 3166	Yes
Rhode Island	§ 17-4-10	Yes
South Carolina	Code 1976 § 7-19-70	Yes
South Dakota	SDCL. § 12-20-35	Yes
Tennessee	T. C. A. § 2-8-110	Yes
Texas	§ 192.005	Yes
Utah	Utah Code 20A-4-304	Yes
	Utah Code 20A-13-302	Yes
Vermont	VT ST T. 17 § 2731	Yes
	VT ST T. 17 § 2592	Yes
Virginia	§ 24.2-675	Yes
	§ 24.2-673	Yes
Washington	Rev. Code Wash. (ARCW) § 29A.56.320[84]	Yes
West Virginia	Article VII, Section 3 of West Virginia constitution[85]	No
Wisconsin	W.S.A. 5.01	Yes
Wyoming	WY ST § 22-17-117	Yes
	WY ST § 22-19-103	Yes

[84] Article III, section 4 of the Washington State Constitution specifies that, in all elections, the candidate "having the highest number of votes shall be declared duly elected."

[85] Article VII, section 3 (ratified November 4, 1902) specifies that, in all elections, the candidate with "the highest number of votes for either of said offices, shall be declared duly elected thereto."

presidential electors.[86] In every state, the law was not enacted merely by action of the two chambers of the state legislature but, instead, was presented to the state's Governor for approval or disapproval.

None of the state laws in table 8.2 was enacted by means of the citizen-initiative process; however, there have been numerous initiatives and referenda over the years on provisions of state election laws involving the manner of electing presidential electors.

On February 23, 1917, Maine voted on a "Proposed Constitutional Amendment Granting Suffrage to Women upon Equal Terms with Men." The proposition received 20,604 "yes" vote and 38,838 "no" votes.

In 1919, the Maine Supreme Judicial Court upheld a statewide referendum on a state statute entitled "An act granting to women the right to vote for presidential electors."[87]

In the late 1950s and early 1960s, there was considerable controversy in Michigan (and other states) concerning the coattail effect of votes cast for President on races for lower offices. In particular, Republican county and township officeholders in Michigan sought to eliminate the voter's option to vote for all nominees of one party by casting a single so-called *straight-party* vote. When the Republicans ended 14 years of Democratic control of the Governor's office in 1962, the new Republican Governor and the Republican legislature enacted a statute requiring that voters cast a separate vote for President and a separate vote for each other office on the ballot (the so-called *Massachusetts ballot*).[88] A protest-referendum petition was circulated and filed, thereby suspending the statute. The voters rejected the statute in the November 1964 elections. Thus, presidential electors remained tethered in Michigan to the party's candidates for other offices (if the voter so desired).

Similarly, in 1972, an initiative petition was filed in Maine proposing to change the form of the ballot from party columns to individual offices (the Massachusetts ballot). This proposition passed by a vote of 110,867 to 64,506.

In 1976, an Oklahoma court wrote the following in *McClendon v. Slater* about state legislation concerning the manner of appointing presidential electors:

---

[86] That is, the statewide winner-take-all rule in 48 states and the District of Columbia and the congressional district system in Maine and Nebraska.

[87] *In re Opinion of the Justices.* 107 Atl. 705. 1919.

[88] Michigan Public Act 240 of 1964.

"It is fundamental that each state and its Legislature, under a
Republican form of government possess all power to protect
and promote the peace, welfare and safety of its citizens. The
only restraints placed thereon are those withdrawn by the
United States Constitution and the state's fundamental law.
Art. V, ss 1 and 2 express that these reservations **or withdrawals in the people under the Constitution of the
State of Oklahoma are two in nature and as explicitly
set out in Art. V, s 2 to be the 'initiative' and the 'referendum' processes.** For our purpose, **no other withdrawal
or restraint is placed upon the broad fundamental powers of this state's Legislature** by Art. V of the State
Constitution."[89] [Emphasis added]

More recently, voters have considered initiatives for instant run-off
voting for presidential electors and other offices in Alaska in 2002,
requirements for voter identification in Arizona in 2004, and voting by
convicted felons in Massachusetts in 2000.

In *Commonwealth ex rel. Dummit v. O'Connell*, the Kentucky Court
of Appeals wrote the following in 1944 in connection with a state law permitting soldiers to vote by absentee ballot for U.S. Representatives, U.S.
Senators, and presidential electors:

"[T]he legislative process must be completed in the manner
prescribed by the State Constitution in order to result in a
valid enactment, even though that enactment be one which
the Legislature is authorized by the Federal Constitution to
make."[90]

It is important to note that the decision of the U.S. Supreme Court in
Bush v. Gore in 2000 did nothing to change the meaning of the word "legislature" in the U.S. Constitution in Article II. In that case, the Court settled the dispute over Florida's 2000 presidential vote by halting the manual recount of ballots that the Florida Supreme Court had ordered.

Referring to the 1892 case of *McPherson v. Blacker*, the U.S. Supreme
Court wrote in *Bush v. Gore:*[91]

---

[89] *McClendon v. Slater.* 554 P.2d 774, 776 (Ok. 1976).

[90] *Commonwealth ex rel. Dummit v. O'Connell.* 181 S.W.2d 691, 694 (Ky. Ct. App. 1944).

[91] *McPherson v. Blacker.* 146 U.S. 1 at 27. 1892.

"The individual citizen has no federal constitutional right to vote for electors for the President of the United States unless and until the state legislature chooses a statewide election as the means to implement its power to appoint members of the Electoral College. U.S. Const., Art. II, §1. **This is the source for the statement in *McPherson v. Blacker*, 146 U.S. 1, 35 (1892), that the State legislature's power to select the manner for appointing electors is plenary;** it may, if it so chooses, select the electors itself, which indeed was the manner used by State legislatures in several States for many years after the Framing of our Constitution. *Id.*, at 28-33. History has now favored the voter, and in each of the several States the citizens themselves vote for Presidential electors. When the state legislature vests the right to vote for President in its people, the right to vote as the legislature has prescribed is fundamental; and one source of its fundamental nature lies in the equal weight accorded to each vote and the equal dignity owed to each voter. The State, of course, after granting the franchise in the special context of Article II, can take back the power to appoint electors. See *id.*, at 35."[92] [Emphasis added]

The U.S. Supreme Court did not change the prevailing definition of the word "legislature" in *Bush v. Gore* but, instead, identified the source (i.e., *McPherson v. Blacker*) of the undisputed statement that the "legislature" is indeed supreme in matters of choosing the manner of appointing a state's presidential electors. The issues in *Bush v. Gore* did not concern the way that Florida's election code was originally enacted (e.g., whether the election code was presented to the Governor for approval or disapproval or whether the voters had perhaps enacted the election code through the citizen-initiative process). Indeed, the Florida election code at issue in *Bush v. Gore* was not enacted by the legislature alone but, instead, was enacted as part by the ordinary lawmaking process involving presentation of the bill to the Governor for approval or disapproval (as shown in table 8.2).

Rather, *Bush v. Gore* was concerned with the breadth of authority of the Florida Supreme Court to establish a recount process *not found in*

---

[92] *Bush v. Gore.* 531 U.S. 98 at 104. 2000.

Florida's pre-existing legislation after the voters had cast their votes on November 7, 2000. The U.S. Supreme Court specifically identified two issues to be decided in *Bush v. Gore,* namely

(1) "whether the Florida Supreme Court established new standards for resolving Presidential election contests, thereby violating Art. II, §1, cl. 2, of the United States Constitution and failing to comply with 3 U.S.C. §5, ..."[93] and

(2) "whether the use of standardless manual recounts violates the Equal Protection and Due Process Clauses."[94]

In reaching its decision in *Bush v. Gore,* the Court referred to the "safe harbor" provision (3 U.S.C. §5).

"If any State shall have provided, **by laws enacted prior to the day fixed for the appointment of the electors,** for its final determination of any controversy or contest concerning the appointment of all or any of the electors of such State, by judicial or other methods or procedures, and such determination shall have been made at least six days before the time fixed for the meeting of the electors, such determination made pursuant to such law so existing on said day, and made at least six days prior to said time of meeting of the electors, shall be conclusive, and shall govern in the counting of the electoral votes as provided in the Constitution, and as hereinafter regulated, so far as the ascertainment of the electors appointed by such State is concerned."[95] [Emphasis added]

The Court ruled (on December 12, 2000) that insufficient time remained to conduct a constitutional recount before the meeting of the Electoral College scheduled for December 18, 2000. Because there was insufficient time for a constitutional recount, Bush's 537-vote plurality that had already been certified under terms of the Florida election code was allowed to stand.[96]

---

[93] *Bush v. Gore.* 531 U.S. 98 at 103. 2000. See Appendix B for the complete wording of the so-called "safe harbor" provision—Title 3, Chapter 1, section 5 of the United States Code.

[94] *Bush v. Gore.* 531 U.S. 98 at 103. 2000.

[95] Title 3, chapter 1, section 5 of the United States Code.

[96] *Bush v. Gore.* 531 U.S. 98 at 110. 2000.

In *Bush v. Gore*, the Supreme Court did not address the issue of whether the Florida voters could substitute themselves for the legislature, through the citizen-initiative process or the protest-referendum process, concerning the manner of choosing presidential electors in Florida. In fact, the 1892 case *(McPherson v. Blacker)* cited by the Court in *Bush v. Gore* specifically mentioned the possibility that a state's legislative power might be "reposed" in a place other than the state legislature.

> **"The legislative power is the supreme authority, except as limited by the constitution of the state,** and the sovereignty of the people is exercised through their representatives in the legislature, **unless by the fundamental law power is elsewhere reposed."**[97] [Emphasis added]

The citizen-initiative process—representing the authority of the citizens of a state to make their own laws—is consistent with the two exceptions contained in *McPherson v. Blacker*; namely that the legislature's power is supreme "except as limited by the constitution of the state" and except when "power is elsewhere reposed" "by the [state's] fundamental law." Initiatives are limitations on the power of the legislature because they enable the voters to displace the legislature by enacting laws of their own design. The initiative process is established by the state's fundamental law (i.e., constitution). Indeed, initiatives are the obvious alternative place where the state's legislative power might be "elsewhere reposed."

The citizen-initiative process has consistently been viewed as a limitation on the state legislature. For example, in 1964, *Lucas v. Forty-Fourth General Assembly*[98] approved the use of the initiative to "obtain relief against alleged malapportionment" of state legislative seats. In 1975, *Chapman v. Meier*[99] concerned the adoption of an initiative substituting the voters' will for the legislature's unwillingness to act. As a reservation of legislative power by the voters, the initiative process is necessarily an element of the fundamental law. In *Eastlake v. Forest City Enterprises, Inc.*, the U.S. Supreme Court wrote in 1976:

> "Under our constitutional assumptions, all power derives from the people, who can delegate it to representative instru-

---

[97] *McPherson v. Blacker.* 146 U.S. 1 at 25. 1892.

[98] *Lucas v. Forty-Fourth General Assembly.* 377 U.S. 713 at 732–733. 1964.

[99] *Chapman v. Meier.* 420 U.S. 1 at 21. 1975.

ments which they create. See e.g., *The Federalist*, No. 39 (J. Madison). **In establishing legislative bodies, the people can reserve to themselves power to deal directly with matters which might otherwise be assigned to the legislature.**"[100],[101] [Emphasis added]

In commenting on *Bush v. Gore* in *Breaking the Deadlock*, Judge Richard Posner wrote:

> "[I]t is important that the approach be understood, and not rejected out of hand as meaning, for example, that the governor of a state cannot veto a proposed law on the appointment of the state's Presidential electors or that the state's supreme court cannot invalidate an election law as unconstitutional. **Article II does not regulate the process by which state legislation is enacted and validated,** any more than it precludes interpretation. **But once the law governing appointment of the state's presidential electors is duly enacted,** upheld, and interpreted, (so far as interpretation is necessary to fill gaps and dispel ambiguities), the legislature has spoken and **the other branches of the state government must back off**...."[102] [Emphasis added]

Bush v. Gore was not about "the process by which state legislation is enacted" but, instead, was about the extent to which the Florida Supreme should "back off."

In summary, present-day practice by the states, actual practice by the states at the time that the U.S. Constitution took effect, legal commentary, and court decisions are consistent in supporting the view that the word "legislature" in Article II, section 1, clause 2 of the U.S. Constitution (the sixth entry in table 8.1) means the state's lawmaking process—a process that includes the state's Governor and the state's voters in states having citizen-initiative and protest-referendum procedures.

---

[100] *Eastlake v. Forest City Enterprises, Inc.* 426 U.S. 668 at 672. 1976.

[101] *Cf. James v. Valtierra*, 401 U.S. 137, 141 (1971) "[p]rovisions for referendums demonstrate devotion to democracy."

[102] Posner, Richard A. 2001. *Breaking the Deadlock: The 2000 Election, the Constitution, and the Courts.* Princeton, NJ: Princeton University Press. Page 111.

As Kirby stated in 1962,

> "it is safe to assume that state legislatures are limited by constitutional provisions for veto, referendum, and initiative in prescribing the manner of choosing presidential electors."[103]

8.3.7 Choosing the Manner of Conducting a Popular Election to Fill a U.S. Senate Vacancy

The 17th Amendment (providing for popular election of U.S. Senators) was ratified in 1913—in the midst of the period (1898–1918) when 19 states were adopting the initiative and referendum processes.[104,105] The 17th Amendment provides:

> "When vacancies happen in the representation of any State in the Senate, the executive authority of such State shall issue writs of election to fill such vacancies: Provided, That the legislature of any State may empower the executive thereof to make temporary appointments until the people fill the vacancies by election **as the legislature may direct.**" [Emphasis added]

The phrase "as the legislature may direct" in the 17th Amendment parallels the wording of Article II of the U.S. Constitution concerning presidential electors, namely

> "Each State shall appoint, in such Manner **as the Legislature thereof may direct,** a Number of Electors, equal to the whole Number of Senators and Representatives to which the State may be entitled in the Congress...."[106] [Emphasis added]

Moreover, the phrase "as the legislature may direct" in the 17th Amendment and Article II parallels the wording of Article I, section 4,

---

[103] Kirby, J. 1962. Limitations on the powers of the state legislatures over presidential elections. 27 *Law and Contemporary Problems* 495 at 504.

[104] Zimmerman, Joseph F. 1999. *The Initiative: Citizen Law-Making.* Westport, CT: Praeger.

[105] Zimmerman, Joseph F. 1997. *The Referendum: The People Decide Public Policy.* Westport, CT: Praeger.

[106] U.S. Constitution. Article II, section 1, clause 2.

clause 1 of the U.S. Constitution concerning the "manner" of holding elections for U.S. Representatives and Senators, namely

> "The Times, Places and Manner of holding Elections for Senators and Representatives, shall be **prescribed in each State by the Legislature thereof;** but the Congress may at any time by Law make or alter such Regulations, except as to the Places of chusing Senators." [Emphasis added]

The practice of the states in enacting laws to implement the 17th Amendment is shown in table 8.3. This table shows the section of each state's law that specifies the manner of holding the popular election to fill a vacancy in the U.S. Senate under the 17th Amendment and the section that specifies whether the Governor is empowered to make temporary appointments to the U.S. Senate prior to the vacancy-filling election. As can be seen, in no state was the enactment of implementing legislation for the 17th Amendment accomplished merely by action of the two chambers of the legislature. Instead, the actual practice of all states has been to treat the word "legislature" in the 17th Amendment to mean the "lawmaking process." The "lawmaking process" concerning the 17th Amendment has involved legislative bills that have been presented to the state's Governor for approval or disapproval and the use of the citizen-initiative process (in the cases of Arkansas in 1938 and Alaska in 2004).

Arkansas's implementation of the 17th Amendment is noteworthy for two reasons. First, its current implementation was proposed by a citizen-initiative petition that was adopted by the voters in the November 8, 1938, general election. Second, Arkansas's implementation was in the form of an amendment to the state constitution as distinguished from a statutory enactment.[107] In other words, neither the "legislature" nor "legislation" was involved in implementing the 17th Amendment in Arkansas.

The November 2004 elections provided two additional examples of the interpretation given to the word "legislature" by the states in connection with the 17th Amendment.

When U.S. Senator John Kerry was running for President in 2004, the Democratic-controlled legislature in Massachusetts passed a bill changing the procedure for filling U.S. Senate vacancies in Massachusetts. Under the pre-existing Massachusetts law, the Governor had the power to

---

[107] Section 1 Amendment 29 adopted November 8, 1938.

Table 8.3 PRACTICE BY THE STATES CONCERNING THE MEANING OF THE WORD "LEGISLATURE" IN CONNECTION WITH STATE LAWS SPECIFYING THE IMPLEMENTATION OF THE 17TH AMENDMENT

STATE	SECTION	WAS THE LEGISLATURE'S BILL PRESENTED TO THE STATE'S GOVERNOR?
Alabama	Ala.Code § 36-9-7	Yes
	Ala.Code § 36-9-8	Yes
Alaska	AK ST § 15.40.140	No–Citizen-initiative process
	AK ST § 15.40.145	
Arizona	A.R.S. § 16-222	Yes
Arkansas	Const. Am. 29, § 1	No–Citizen-initiative process
California	Cal.Elec.Code § 10720	Yes
Colorado	C.R.S.A. § 1-12-201	Yes
Connecticut	C.G.S.A. § 9-211	Yes
Delaware	DE ST TI 15 § 7321	Yes
Florida	F.S.A. § 100.161	Yes
Georgia	Ga. Code Ann., § 21-2-542	Yes
Hawaii	HI ST § 17-1	Yes
Idaho	ID ST § 59-910	Yes
Illinois	10 ILCS 5/25-8	Yes
Indiana	IC 3-13-3-1	Yes
Iowa	I.C.A. § 69.8	Yes
Kansas	KS ST § 25-318	Yes
Kentucky	KRS § 63.200	Yes
Louisiana	LSA-R.S. 18:1278	Yes
Maine	21-A M.R.S.A. § 391	Yes
Maryland	MD Code, Election Law, § 8-602	Yes
Massachusetts	M.G.L.A. 54 § 140	Yes
Michigan	M.C.L.A. 168.105	Yes
Minnesota	M.S.A. § 204D.28	Yes
Mississippi	Miss. Code Ann. § 23-15-855	Yes
Missouri	V.A.M.S. 105.040	Yes
Montana	Mt. St. 13-25-202	Yes
Nebraska	NE ST § 32-565	Yes
Nevada	N.R.S. 304.030	Yes
New Hampshire	N.H. Rev. Stat. § 661:5	Yes
New Jersey	§19:3-26	Yes
New Mexico	N. M. S. A. 1978, § 1-15-14	Yes
New York	Mckinney's Consolidated Laws of New York, Chapter 47, Article 3	Yes
North Carolina	N.C.G.S.A. § 163-12	Yes
North Dakota	ND ST 16.1-13-08	Yes
Ohio	R.C. § 3521.02	Yes

Table 8.3 PRACTICE BY THE STATES CONCERNING THE MEANING OF THE WORD "LEGISLATURE" IN CONNECTION WITH STATE LAWS SPECIFYING THE IMPLEMENTATION OF THE 17TH AMENDMENT (cont.)

STATE	SECTION	WAS THE LEGISLATURE'S BILL PRESENTED TO THE STATE'S GOVERNOR?
Oregon	O.R.S. § 188.120	Yes
Pennsylvania	25 P.S. § 2776	Yes
Rhode Island	§ 17-4-9	Yes
South Carolina	Code 1976 § 7-19-20	Yes
South Dakota	SDCL. § 12-11-4	Yes
	SDCL. § 12-11-5	Yes
Tennessee	T. C. A. § 2-16-101	Yes
Texas	§ 204.001	Yes
	§ 204.002	Yes
	§ 204.003	Yes
	§ 204.004	Yes
Utah	§ 20A-1-502	Yes
Vermont	VT ST T. 17 § 2621	Yes
	VT ST T. 17 § 2622	Yes
Virginia	§ 24.2-207	Yes
Washington	RCW 29A.28.030	Yes
	RCW 29A.28.041	Yes
West Virginia	W. Va. Code, § 3-10-3	Yes
Wisconsin	W.S.A. 17.18	Yes
	W.S.A. 8.50	Yes
Wyoming	WY ST § 22-18-111	Yes

appoint a temporary replacement who would serve until the next general election. In other words, if Democrat Kerry had won the Presidency in November 2004, then the Republican Governor of Massachusetts would have been able to appoint a Republican to serve in the then-closely-divided U.S. Senate until November 2006 (almost two full years). Under the bill that the legislature passed, the Senate seat would remain vacant until a special election could be held (between 145 and 160 days after the creation of the vacancy). Thus, a special Senate election would have been held in Massachusetts in the spring of 2005 if Kerry had been elected President. The legislative bill was presented to Governor Mitt Romney for his approval or disapproval. That is, the constitutional phrase "as the Legislature thereof may direct" was interpreted to mean the law-making process. Predictably, the Republican Governor vetoed the bill passed by the Democratic legislature. As it happened, the legislature overrode the Governor's veto, and the bill became law.

The election of U.S. Senator Frank Murkowski as Governor of Alaska in 2002 created a vacancy in the U.S. Senate. Murkowski appointed his daughter Lisa to serve the last two years of his Senate term, thereby focusing public attention on the operation of the 17th Amendment in Alaska. An initiative petition was circulated and filed to require that, in the future, a vacancy in the U.S. Senate would remain vacant until a special election could be called. The Alaska Constitution enables the legislature to keep an initiative proposition off the ballot if the legislature responds to the petition by enacting a "substantially" similar law. The legislature's bill resembled the proposal in the petition in that it required a special election to fill a Senate vacancy; however, the legislature's bill differed from the petition in that it authorized the Governor to appoint a temporary Senator prior to the popular election. This legislature's bill was presented to the Governor for his approval or disapproval, and he signed it. The petition's sponsors protested that the legislature's alternative approach was not substantially the same as the initiative proposition because it gave the Governor's appointee the advantage of incumbency in the special election.

On August 20, 2004, the Alaska Supreme Court decided that the legislature's alternative was not substantially the same as the proposition in the initiative petition.[108] At the same time, the Court refused to consider a pre-election challenge to the use of the citizen-initiative process to change the manner of filling a vacancy in the U.S. Senate on the grounds that the U.S. Constitution required the "legislature" to make the decision. The Alaska Supreme Court allowed the voters to vote on the proposition in the petition in the November 2004 election. The voters then enacted the proposition in the petition (Ballot Measure 4) in the November 2004 election by a margin of 165,017 to 131,821.[109]

That is, the phrase "as the Legislature thereof may direct" in the 17th Amendment (the seventh entry in table 8.1) has been interpreted as the state's entire law-making process—not action by the two chambers of state's legislature.

---

[108] *State of Alaska et al. v. Trust the People Initiative Committee.* Supreme Court Order No. S-11288.

[109] In the same election, the voters elected Lisa Murkowski to a full six-year term in the Senate by a margin of 149,446 to 139,878.

8.3.8 Empowering the Governor to Temporarily Fill a U.S. Senate Vacancy Until a Popular Election Is Held

The word "legislature" also appears in the 17th Amendment in connection with temporary appointments to the U.S. Senate.

> "When vacancies happen in the representation of any State in the Senate, the executive authority of such State shall issue writs of election to fill such vacancies: Provided, That **the legislature of any State may empower the executive thereof to make temporary appointments until the people fill the vacancies by election** as the legislature may direct." [Emphasis added]

As shown in table 8.3, the word "legislature" in the 17th Amendment (the eighth entry in table 8.1) has meant the state's entire law-making process—not action by the two chambers of state's legislature.

8.3.9 Consenting to the Federal Purchase of Enclaves

The U.S. Constitution empowers Congress to exercise exclusive

> "… Authority over all Places purchased by the **Consent of the Legislature** of the State in which the Same shall be, for the Erection of Forts, Magazines, Arsenals, dock-Yards, and other needful Buildings."[110] [Emphasis added]

Prior to ratification of the U.S. Constitution, the states had been paying for the operation and maintenance of 13 lighthouses. Moreover, in 1789, several additional lighthouses were under construction. When the first Congress met in 1789, it offered to fund the operation and maintenance of all the lighthouses; however, Congress insisted that the sites become federal enclaves. Accordingly, Congress passed the Lighthouse Act on August 7, 1789, offering permanent funding for lighthouses on the condition that the state "legislatures" consented to the creation of the federal enclaves by August 15, 1790.[111] The Constitution required consent from the state "legislatures" and thus set the stage for a contemporary

---

[110] U.S. Constitution. Article I, section 9, clause 17.

[111] Grace, Adam S. 2005. *Federal-State "Negotiations" over Federal Enclaves in the Early Republic: Finding Solutions to Constitutional Problems at the Birth of the Lighthouse System.* Berkeley, CA: Berkeley Electronic Press. Working Paper 509. http://law.bepress.com/expresso/eps/509. Pages 1–11.

interpretation of the word "legislature" in the Enclaves Clause of the U.S. Constitution. The question was whether the word "legislature" referred to the two chambers of the state legislature or "the lawmaking process."

At the time when the U.S. Constitution took effect, the gubernatorial veto existed in Massachusetts and New York.[112] Both chambers of the legislatures of Massachusetts and New York approved legislation consenting to the cession of their lighthouses. These legislative bills were then presented, respectively, to the Governor of Massachusetts (an official who was manifestly not part of the state legislature) and the New York Council of Revision (a body composed of the Governor and other officials who were manifestly not part of the state legislature). The Massachusetts legislation became law on June 10, 1790,[113] and the New York legislation became law on February 3, 1790.[114] Cession legislation was similarly enacted in New York in connection with the construction of a new lighthouse at Montauk in 1792—with the legislative bill again being presented to the Governor and the Council.[115]

Thus, practice by the states in connection with the ninth entry in table 8.1 has interpreted the word "legislature" to mean the state's lawmaking process in connection with the consent by a state to the acquisition of enclaves by the federal government (the ninth entry in Table 8.1).

8.3.10 Consenting to the Formation of New States from Territory of Existing States

The U.S. Constitution provides:

"... No new State shall be formed or erected within the Jurisdiction of any other State; nor any State be formed by the Junction of two or more States, or Parts of States, without the **Consent of the Legislatures** of the States concerned as well as of the Congress."[116] [Emphasis added]

As of the time of the writing of this edition, the authors believe that this usage of the word "legislature" refers to the state's law-making

---

[112] Kole, Edward A. 1999. *The First 13 Constitutions of the First American States.* Haverford, PA: Infinity Publishing.

[113] Ch. 4, 1790 Massachusetts Laws 77.

[114] New York, Ch. 3, February 3, 1790.

[115] New York, Ch. 4, December 18, 1792.

[116] U.S. Constitution. Article IV, section 3, clause 1.

process in connection with the consent of a state to the formation of a new state from its territory (the 10th entry in table 8.1).

8.3.11 Requesting Federal Military Assistance to Quell Domestic Violence

The U.S. Constitution provides:

> "The United States shall guarantee to every State in this Union a Republican Form of Government, and shall protect each of them against Invasion; and on **Application of the Legislature,** or of the Executive (when the Legislature cannot be convened) against domestic Violence."[117] [Emphasis added]

This provision of the U.S. Constitution (the Guarantee Clause) specifically creates a contrast between the state's "executive" and the "legislature."

The Guarantee Clause has been only rarely invoked. On April 4, 1842, Rhode Island Governor Samuel Ward King requested that President John Tyler provide federal military aid to quell a potential insurrection, known as the Dorr Rebellion, in which an alternative government for Rhode Island was attempting to gain recognition and legitimacy. The Governor's request was not accompanied by any action by the state legislature. President Tyler took no action in response to the Governor's request.[118]

Then, in 1844, the Freeholders' legislature of Rhode Island passed a resolution requested that President John Tyler provide federal military aid to quell the Dorrites. Again, President Tyler took no action in response to the Legislature's resolution.[119]

The Guarantee Clause of the U.S. Constitution distinguishes the state's "legislature" from the state's Governor. These two requests concerning the Dorr Rebellion in Rhode Island suggest that the word "legislature" Article IV, section 4 of the U.S. Constitution (the 11th entry in table 8.1) was interpreted, in Rhode Island in the 1840s, to mean the two chambers of the state legislature.

---

[117] U.S. Constitution. Article IV, section 4.

[118] Wiecek, William M. 1972. *The Guarantee Clause of the U.S. Constitution.* Ithaca, NY: Cornell University Press. Page 105.

[119] Gettleman, Marvin E. 1973. *The Dorr Rebellion: A Study in American Radicalism 1833–1849.* New York, NY: Random House. Page 105.

8.3.12 Pre-Election Challenges Versus Post-Election Litigation

The use of the citizen-initiative process to enact the proposed interstate compact can be challenged either before or after the statewide vote on the statute proposed by a petition.

Both state and federal courts have been reluctant, as a general principle, to intervene in the citizen-initiative process prior to enactment of a proposition by the voters. In "Pre-Election Judicial Review of Initiatives and Referendums," James Gordon and David Magleby wrote:

> "Most courts will not entertain a challenge to a measure's substantive validity before the election. A minority of courts, however, are willing to conduct such review. Arguably, pre-election review of a measure's substantive validity involves issuing an advisory opinion, violates ripeness requirements and the policy of avoiding unnecessary constitutional questions, and is an unwarranted judicial intrusion into a legislative process." [120]

The numerous practical difficulties with pre-election judicial challenges to ballot propositions partly explain judicial reluctance to such challenges. As Justice William O. Douglas wrote in his concurring opinion in *Ely v. Klahr* in 1971:

> "We are plagued with election cases coming here on the eve of election, with the remaining time so short we do not have the days needed for oral argument and for reflection on the serious problems that are usually presented." [121]

The practical difficulties associated with pre-election challenges have been compounded in recent years by the increasing use of absentee voting and early voting (where walk-in polling places are operated at designated locations, such as government buildings, for several weeks prior to election day).

The general reluctance of courts to prevent a vote on ballot measures proposed by the citizen-initiative process is illustrated by the efforts in the early 1990s to enact state constitutional amendments imposing term

---

[120] Gordon, James D. and Magleby, David B. 1989. Pre-Election Judicial Review of Initiatives and Referendums. 64 *Notre Dame Law Review* 298–320 at 303.

[121] *Ely v. Klahr.* 403 U.S. 103 at 120–121. 1971.

limits on members of the U.S. House of Representatives and U.S. Senate. Many questioned whether the proposed state constitutional amendments were consistent with the specific federal constitutional provisions establishing qualifications for these federal offices. Despite pre-election legal challenges to the initiative petitions in some states, in no instance did the courts prevent a vote by the people on the grounds that congressional term limits violated the U.S. Constitution. It was only after these propositions had been enacted by the voters in a number of states that the courts examined the constitutional validity of the ballot propositions. In 1995, the U.S. Supreme Court held that term limits on members of the U.S. House of Representatives and U.S. Senate could not be imposed at the state level.[122]

More recently, the California Supreme Court refused, on July 26, 2005, to remove an initiated proposition from the ballot in California's November 8, 2005, statewide election. The court order stated:

> "The stay issued by the Court of Appeal as part of its July 22, 2005, decision, restraining the Secretary of State from taking any steps, pending the finality of the Court of Appeal's decision, to place Proposition 80 in the ballot pamphlet or on the ballot of the special election to be held on November 8, 2005, is vacated. As the Court of Appeal recognized, California authorities establish that
>
>> 'it is usually more appropriate to review constitutional and other challenges to ballot propositions or initiative measures after an election rather than to disrupt the electoral process by preventing the exercise of the people's franchise, in the absence of some clear showing of invalidity.' (*Brosnahan v. Eu* (1982) 31 Cal.3d 1, 4.)
>
> "Because, unlike the Court of Appeal, at this point we cannot say that it is clear that article XII, section 5, of the California Constitution precludes the enactment of Proposition 80 as an initiative measure, we conclude that the validity of Proposition 80 need not and should not be determined prior to the November 8, 2005 election. Accordingly, the Secretary

---

[122] *U.S. Term Limits v. Thornton.* 514 U.S. 779. 1995.

of State and other public officials are directed to proceed with all the required steps to place Proposition 80 in the ballot pamphlet and on the ballot of the special election to be held on November 8, 2005. After that election, we shall determine whether to retain jurisdiction in this matter and resolve the issues raised in the petition."[123]

8.3.13 Curability of the Potential Invalidity of Popular Voting

Were a court decision to invalidate a popular vote in favor of the proposed interstate compact on state constitutional grounds applicable to one particular state or on federal constitutional grounds applicable to all states, the fact would remain that the people would have spoken in favor of nationwide popular election of the President in those states where the people had voted on the invalidated ballot measures. The favorable public vote would remain as a political fact. In that event, practical political considerations suggest that legislators in any affected state would probably be willing to correct the technical defect concerning the method of enactment of the compact in their state by re-enacting the compact in the legislature. The proposed compact is not inherently adverse to the interests of state legislators, and there is no reason that state legislators are, as a group, any less likely to favor the concept of nationwide popular election of the President than the public at large. It should, therefore, be possible to re-enact the proposed compact in the legislatures of many or all states where the voters spoke in favor of the compact. Regardless of the extent to which the citizen-initiative process may be used to spotlight the issue of the nationwide popular election of the President, state legislatures must necessarily provide most of the support needed to bring the proposed compact into effect.

8.4 DOES THE PROPOSED COMPACT ENCROACH ON THE POWERS OF NON-MEMBER STATES?

An interstate compact may potentially affect non-member states. For example, upstream states in a river basin might enter into a compact to use water to the extreme disadvantage of downstream states that do not belong to the compact.

---

[123] *Independent Energy Producers Association et al., Petitioners, v. Bruce McPherson, as Secretary of State, etc., Respondent; Robert Finkelstein et al., Real Parties in Interest.* Case number S135819. July 26, 2005.

Justice White's dissent in *U.S. Steel Corp. v. Multistate Tax Commission* in 1978 raises the possibility that a court would consider the question of whether a particular interstate compact adversely encroaches on the powers of non-member states.

> "A proper understanding of what would encroach upon federal authority, however, must also incorporate encroachments on the authority and power of non-Compact States."[124]

The U.S. Supreme Court has twice considered, but rejected, arguments that an interstate compact was unconstitutional because it impaired the sovereign rights of non-member states or enhanced the political power of the member states at the expense of other states. For example, in *U.S. Steel Corp. v. Multistate Tax Commission*, the Supreme Court wrote in 1978:

> "Appellants' final Compact Clause argument charges that the Compact impairs the sovereign rights of nonmember States. Appellants declare, without explanation, that if the use of the unitary business and combination methods continues to spread among the Western States, unfairness in taxation—presumably the risks of multiple taxation—will be avoidable only through the efforts of some coordinating body. Appellants cite the belief of the Commission's Executive Director that the Commission represents the only available vehicle for effective coordination, and conclude that **the Compact exerts undue pressure to join upon nonmember States in violation of their "sovereign right" to refuse.**
>
> "We find no support for this conclusion. It has not been shown that any unfair taxation of multistate business resulting from the disparate use of combination and other methods will redound to the benefit of any particular group of States or to the harm of others. Even if the existence of such a situation were demonstrated, it could not be ascribed to the existence of the Compact. **Each member State is free to adopt**

---

[124] *U.S. Steel Corp. v. Multistate Tax Commission.* 434 U.S. at 494. 1978.

the auditing procedures it thinks best, just as it could if the Compact did not exist. Risks of unfairness and double taxation, then, are independent of the Compact.

"Moreover, **it is not explained how any economic pressure that does exist is an affront to the sovereignty of nonmember States.** Any time a State adopts a fiscal or administrative policy that affects the programs of a sister State, pressure to modify those programs may result. Unless that pressure transgresses the bounds of the Commerce Clause or the Privileges and Immunities Clause of Art. IV, 2, see, e.g., *Austin v. New Hampshire*, 420 U.S. 656 (1975), it is not clear how our federal structure is implicated. Appellants do not argue that an individual State's decision to apportion nonbusiness income—or to define business income broadly, as the regulations of the Commission actually do—touches upon constitutional strictures. This being so, we are not persuaded that the same decision becomes a threat to the sovereignty of other States if a member State makes this decision upon the Commission's recommendation."[125] [Emphasis added]

In *Northeast Bancorp, Inc. v. Board of Governors of the Federal Reserve System*, the U.S. Supreme Court wrote in 1985 that it

"do[es] not see how the statutes in question ... enhance the *political* power of the New England states at the expense of other States...."[126]

Justice White's criterion has never been embraced to invalidate any compact. In any event, it is unlikely that the courts would apply his criterion to the proposed "Agreement Among the States to Elect the President by National Popular Vote" because both member and non-member states would be treated equally in that the popular votes of all 50 states and the District of Columbia would be added together to obtain a nationwide popular vote total for each presidential slate.

---

[125] *Id.* at 477–478.

[126] *Northeast Bancorp, Inc. v. Board of Governors of the Federal Reserve System.* 472 U.S. 159 at 176. 1985.

8.5 DOES THE PROPOSED COMPACT IMPERMISSIBLY DELEGATE A STATE'S SOVEREIGN POWER?

No court has invalidated an interstate compact on the grounds that the compact impermissibly has delegated a state's sovereign power. Indeed, the purpose of almost every interstate compact[127] is, as Marian Ridgeway put it in *Interstate Compacts: A Question of Federalism,*

> "[to] shift a part of a state's authority to another state or states."[128]

Nonetheless, the question arises as to whether the proposed "Agreement Among the States to Elect the President by National Popular Vote" would be an impermissible delegation of a state's sovereign power. In particular, the following question might be raised:

> May a state delegate, under the auspices of an interstate compact, the choice of its presidential electors to the collective choice of the voters of a group of states?

This inquiry requires an examination of whether the appointment of a state's presidential electors is one of its sovereign powers and, if so, whether that power can be shared with voters throughout the United States.

8.5.1 A State's "Sovereign Powers" May Be Delegated by an Interstate Compact

The sovereign authority of a state is not easily defined. The federal courts have not defined sovereignty, although they have attempted to describe it on various occasions. In *Hinderlider v. La Plata River and Cherry Creek Ditch Co.* in 1938, the U.S. Supreme Court traced the history of compacts during the colonial period and immediately thereafter and viewed compacts as a corollary to the ability of independent nations to enter into treaties with one another.

> "The compact—the legislative means [for resolving conflicting claims]—adapts to our Union of sovereign States the age-old treaty making power of sovereign nations."[129]

---

[127] Except for purely advisory compacts.

[128] Ridgeway, Marian E. 1971. *Interstate Compacts: A Question of Federalism.* Carbondale, IL: Southern Illinois University Press. Page 300.

[129] *Hinderlider v. La Plata River & Cherry Creek Ditch Co.* 304 U.S. 92 at 104. 1938.

In the 1992 case of *Texas Learning Technology Group v. Commissioner of Internal Revenue*, the Fifth Circuit wrote:

"The power to tax, the power of eminent domain, and the police power are the generally acknowledged sovereign powers."[130]

The appropriation power is another example of a power that is viewed as fundamental to a state.

The filling of public positions that are central to the operation of state government (including legislative, executive, or judicial positions and the position of delegate to a state constitutional convention) is regarded as a sovereign state power.[131,132]

The historical practice of the states, the long history of approvals of interstate compacts by Congress, and court decisions all support the view that a state's sovereign powers may be granted to a group of states acting through an interstate compact. For example, New York and New Jersey delegated certain sovereign powers to the Port Authority of New York and New Jersey, including the power of eminent domain and the power to exempt property from taxation. New York and New Jersey granted the power to tax to the commission created by the 1953 New York–New Jersey Waterfront Compact. Such delegation was upheld in 1944 in *Commissioner of Internal Revenue v. Shamberg's Estate.*[133]

The Ohio River Valley Water Sanitation Compact provided:

"The signatory states agree to appropriate for the salaries, office and other administrative expenses, their proper proportion of the annual budget as determined by the Commission and approved by the governors of the signatory states...."

---

[130] *Texas Learning Technology Group v. Commissioner of Internal Revenue.* 958 F.2d 122 at 124 (5th Cir. 1992).

[131] See, e.g., *Kingston Associates Inc. v. LaGuardia*, 281 N.Y.S. 390, 398 (S.Ct. 1935) (the exercise of public offices within the legislative, executive, or judicial branches of government); *People v. Brady*, 135 N.E. 87, 89 (Ill. 1922) (same); *People v. Hardin*, 356 N.E.2d 4 (Ill. 1976) (the power to appoint officials to commissions or agencies within the three branches of state government); *State v. Schorr*, 65 A.2d 810, 813 (Del. 1948) (same); and *Forty-Second Legislative Assembly v. Lennon*, 481 P.2d 330, 330 (Mont. 1971) (the role of a delegate to a state constitutional convention).

[132] Engdahl. 1965. Characterization of Interstate Arrangements: When Is a Compact Not a Compact? 64 *Michigan Law Review* 63 at 64–66.

[133] *Commissioner of Internal Revenue v. Shamberg's Estate* 144 F.2d 998 at 1005–1006. (2nd Cir. 1944).

In *West Virginia ex rel. Dyer v. Sims* (discussed at greater length in section 8.6.2), the U.S. Supreme Court upheld the delegation of West Virginia's appropriation power and wrote in 1950:

> "The issue before us is whether the West Virginia Legislature had authority, under her Constitution, to enter into a compact which involves delegation of power to an interstate agency and an agreement to appropriate funds for the administrative expenses of the agency.

> "That a legislature may delegate to an administrative body the power to make rules and decide particular cases is one of the axioms of modern government. The West Virginia court does not challenge the general proposition but objects to the delegation here involved because it is to a body outside the State and because its Legislature may not be free, at any time, to withdraw the power delegated.... **What is involved is the conventional grant of legislative power. We find nothing in that to indicate that West Virginia may not solve a problem such as the control of river pollution by compact and by the delegation, if such it be, necessary to effectuate such solution by compact.**... Here, the State has bound itself to control pollution by the more effective means of an agreement with other States. The Compact involves a reasonable and carefully limited delegation of power to an interstate agency."[134] [Emphasis added]

In the 1970 U.S. Supreme Court case of *Oregon v. Mitchell*, Justice Potter Stewart (concurring in part and dissenting in part) pointed out that if Congress had not acted to bring about uniformity among state durational residency requirements for voters casting ballots in presidential elections, then the states could have adopted an interstate compact to do so.[135] The right to vote for a presidential elector is not beyond the reach of an interstate compact.

In short, there is nothing about the nature of an interstate compact that fundamentally prevents the delegation of a state's sovereign power to a group of compacting states.

---

[134] *West Virginia ex rel. Dyer v. Sims.* 341 U.S. 22 at 30–31. 1950.
[135] *Oregon v. Mitchell.* 400 U.S. 112 at 286–287.

As Ridgeway wrote:

"If the state chooses to inaugurate some new pattern of local government [by means of an interstate compact] that is not in conflict with the state's constitution, it can do so, as long as the people lose none of their **ultimate power to control the state itself.**"[136] [Emphasis added]

This statement reflects various court decisions that emphasize the ability of a sovereign entity to operate independently of any other.[137]

8.5.2 The Proposed Compact Does Not Delegate a Sovereign State Power

There is no authority from any court regarding whether presidential electors exercise a sovereign power of their state. Given the temporary nature of the function of presidential electors, it is doubtful that a court would rule that presidential electors exercise inherent governmental authority. In contrast to members of the legislative, executive, or judicial branches of state government or members of a state constitutional convention, the function that presidential electors perform is not one that addresses the sovereign governance of the state. Instead, presidential electors decide the identity of the chief executive of the federal government. That is, the selection of electors is not in any way a manifestation of the way in which the state itself is governed.

If the power to determine a state's electors is deemed not to be a sovereign power of the state, then the ability to delegate it is unquestioned. No court has invalidated an interstate compact for delegating a power that is not central to the organic ability of a state to operate independently as a political and legal entity, no matter how broad the delegation. In *Hinderlider v. La Plata River and Cherry Creek Ditch Co.*, the U.S. Supreme Court ruled that a compact to administer an interstate stream was

"binding upon the citizens of each State and all water claimants, even where the State had granted the water rights before it entered into the compact."[138]

---

[136] Ridgeway, Marian E. 1971. *Interstate Compacts: A Question of Federalism.* Carbondale, IL: Southern Illinois University Press.

[137] See, for example, the 1793 case of *Chisholm v. Georgia* for a discussion of the historic origins of state sovereignty.

[138] *Hinderlider v. La Plata River and Cherry Creek Ditch Company.* 304 U.S. 92 at 106. 1938.

Given the states' exclusive role under the Constitution to determine the manner of appointing its presidential electors,[139] if the determination of a state's electors is a sovereign power and its delegation would shift political power to the group of compacting states, the proposed compact will not be deemed to compromise federal supremacy.[140] The fact of the delegation would not, in and of itself, violate the U.S. Constitution.

8.6 IS THE SIX-MONTH BLACKOUT PERIOD FOR WITHDRAWALS FROM THE COMPACT ENFORCEABLE?

This section begins by discussing the importance of the withdrawal provisions of the proposed "Agreement Among the States to Elect the President by National Popular Vote" and then considers the

- withdrawal provisions of typical interstate compacts (section 8.6.1),
- legal enforceability of withdrawal provisions of the proposed compact (section 8.6.2), and
- additional state and federal limitations on withdrawals from the proposed compact (section 8.3.3).

The proposed "Agreement Among the States to Elect the President by National Popular Vote" permits any member state to withdraw, subject to the limitation that a withdrawal cannot take effect during a six-month period between July 20 of a presidential election year and January 20 of the following year. This blackout period contains the following six events relating to presidential elections:

(1) national nominating conventions,[141]

(2) the fall campaign period,

(3) election day in early November,

(4) the meeting of the Electoral College in mid-December,

(5) the counting of the electoral votes by Congress on January 6, and

(6) the inauguration of the President and Vice President for the new term on January 20.

The blackout period in the proposed compact is aimed at preventing a withdrawal, for partisan political reasons, in the midst of the

---

[139] *McPherson v. Blacker.* 146 U.S. 1. 1892.

[140] See *Northeast Bancorp, Inc. v. Board of Governors of the Federal Reserve System.* 472 U.S. 159 at 176. 1985.

[141] All recent national nominating conventions of the major parties have occurred after July 20 of the presidential election year.

presidential election process and, in particular, during the especially sensitive 35-day period between election day in early November and the meeting of the Electoral College in mid-December. Withdrawal from the proposed compact requires passage of legislation to repeal the compact. Because most state legislatures are not in session in November and December, it would be necessary to call the legislature into special session for this purpose. Governors generally have the power to call their state legislatures into special session. In some cases, legislative leaders have an independent power to convene a special session. All Governors have the power to veto legislative bills.[142] Thus, unless the legislative leadership possesses the power to convene a special session and has a veto-proof majority, the Governor's support would, as a practical matter, be required for any politically motivated effort to repeal the compact. An additional obstacle to a politically motivated repeal of the compact arises from the fact that most state constitutions specify that new state laws do not take immediate effect—that is, the effective date for new legislation is automatically delayed by a designated amount of time. Immediate effect would be required for a politically motivated withdrawal from the compact because such an effort would necessarily occur during the 35-day window between election day in early November and the meeting of the Electoral College in mid-December. Most constitutions require a super-majority (typically two-thirds) in both houses of the legislature to give immediate effect to new legislation. In addition, many state constitutions impose significant state-specific constitutional limitations applicable to the repeal or amendment of legislation enacted by the citizen-initiative process (section 8.6.3).

Having said all that, at any given time, a certain small number of states would inevitably have the lopsided political control that could, in theory, permit the proposed compact to be repealed during the 35-day period between election day in early November and the meeting of the Electoral College in mid-December. Even then, such a repeal would be politically relevant only if

- the number of electoral votes cast in favor of the nationwide popular vote winner by the compacting states remain-

---

[142] In North Carolina, a gubernatorial veto can be overridden by a majority vote of both houses. In other states, a super-majority vote of both houses is necessary to override a veto.

ing after the withdrawal, when added to the electoral votes cast in favor of the nationwide winner by all non-compacting states, were less than 270; and

- the winner of the nationwide popular vote is different from the winner of the electoral vote (computed using the statewide winner-take-all rule).

If all of the above conditions were to converge, then it would be possible—absent the compact's six-month blackout period—for a state to escape its obligation to award its electoral votes to the nationwide popular vote winner at the very moment when it would matter. Such a result would be unfair to voters, candidates, political parties, and the states that entered the compact in reliance on each member state fulfilling its obligations under the compact.

The question therefore arises as to the enforceability of the blackout period for withdrawals contained in the proposed compact.

8.6.1 Withdrawal Provisions of Typical Interstate Compacts

An interstate compact is, first of all, a contract. Consequently, the general principles of contract law apply to interstate compacts. Unless a contract provides otherwise, a contract may be amended or terminated only by unanimous consent of its signatories. In particular, unless a contract provides otherwise, a party cannot unilaterally renounce a contract.

With the exception of compacts that are presumed to be permanent (for example, those settling boundary disputes), almost all interstate compacts permit a party state to withdraw. Moreover, almost all compacts specify the procedures that a party state must follow in order to withdraw.

A small number of interstate compacts permit any party state to withdrawal instantaneously. For example, the Boating Offense Compact provides:

> "Any party state may withdraw from this compact by enacting a statute repealing the same."

The Interstate Compact on Licensure of Participants in Horse Racing with Parimutuel Wagering permits instantaneous withdrawal as soon as the Governor of the withdrawing state performs the task of notifying the other compacting states.

"Any party state may withdraw from this compact by enacting a statute repealing this compact, but no such withdrawal shall become effective until the head of the executive branch of the withdrawing state has given notice in writing of such withdrawal to the head of the executive branch of all other party states."

In contrast, the vast majority of interstate compacts impose both a notification requirement for withdrawal and a delay before a withdrawal becomes effective. The length of the delay is typically calibrated based on the nature of the compact. Compacts frequently specify that a withdrawal does not interrupt, in midstream, any process that began while the withdrawing state was part of the compact and that a withdrawal does not cancel obligations that a withdrawing state incurred while it was part of the compact.

For example, the compact on the Interstate Taxation of Motor Fuels Consumed by Interstate Buses permits withdrawal after one year's notice.

"This compact shall enter into force when enacted into law by any 2 states. Thereafter it shall enter into force and become binding upon any state subsequently joining when such state has enacted the compact into law. Withdrawal from the compact shall be by act of the legislature of a party state, but shall not take effect until one year after the governor of the withdrawing state has notified the governor of each other party state, in writing, of the withdrawal."

The Interstate Mining Compact contains similar provisions.

The delay is generally based on the subject matter of the compact. The delay is typically lengthy when the compact's remaining parties may need time to make alternative arrangements or to adjust economically to a withdrawal. For example, the Rhode Island–Massachusetts Interstate Low-Level Radioactive Waste Management Compact requires that a withdrawing state give notice five years in advance.

"Any party state may withdraw from this compact by repealing its authorizing legislation, and such rights of access to regional facilities enjoyed by generators in that party state shall thereby terminate. However, no such withdrawal shall

take effect until five years after the governor of the withdrawing state has given notice in writing of such withdrawal
to the Commission and to the governor of each party state."

Some compacts impose a longer withdrawal period for a member
having a special obligations under the compact. For example, the
Southwestern Low-Level Radioactive Waste Disposal Compact imposes a
five-year delay for withdrawal on the state that receives and stores the
radioactive waste (California in this case), but only a two-year delay on
the non-host states (Arizona, North Dakota, and South Dakota). A host
state withdrawal would require that all of the non-host states scramble to
find an alternative place to store their radioactive waste, whereas a withdrawal by a non-host state would merely necessitate economic readjust-
ment at the facility operated by the host state.

"A party state, other than the host state, may withdraw from
the compact by repealing the enactment of this compact, but
this withdrawal shall not become effective until two years
after the effective date of the repealing legislation....

"If the host state withdraws from the compact, the withdrawal shall not become effective until five years after the effective date of the repealing legislation."

The Texas Low-Level Radioactive Waste Disposal Compact similarly
imposes a longer time delay for withdrawal by hosts than non-hosts.

The Delaware River Basin Compact requires advance notice of at
least 20 years for withdrawal, with such notice being allowed only during
a five-year window every 100 years.

"The duration of this compact shall be for an initial period of
100 years from its effective date, and it shall be continued for
additional periods of 100 years if not later than 20 years nor
sooner than 25 years prior to the termination of the initial
period or any succeeding period none of the signatory States,
by authority of an act of its Legislature, notifies the commission of intention to terminate the compact at the end of the
then current 100-year period."

Some compacts provide that a state's withdrawal will not affect any
legal action or process that was undertaken while the withdrawing party

was still part of the compact. For example, the Agreement on Detainers provides:

> "This agreement shall enter into full force and effect as to a party state when such state has enacted the same into law. A state party to this agreement may withdraw herefrom by enacting a statute repealing the same. However, the withdrawal of any state shall not affect the status of any proceedings already initiated by inmates or by state officers at the time such withdrawal takes effect, nor shall it affect their rights in respect thereof."

The Interstate Compact on the Placement of Children (one of the compacts to which all 50 states and the District of Columbia belong) provides:

> "This compact shall be open to joinder by any state, territory or possession of the United States, the District of Columbia, the Commonwealth of Puerto Rico, and, with the consent of Congress, the Government of Canada or any province thereof. It shall become effective with respect to any such jurisdiction when such jurisdiction has enacted the same into law. Withdrawal from this compact shall be by the enactment of a statute repealing the same, but shall not take effect until two years after the effective date of such statute and until written notice of the withdrawal has been given by the withdrawing state to the Governor of each other party jurisdiction. Withdrawal of a party state shall not affect the rights, duties and obligations under this compact of any sending agency therein with respect to a placement made prior to the effective date of withdrawal."

The Interstate Compact on Juveniles (another compact to which all 50 states and the District of Columbia adhere) provides:

> "That this compact shall continue in force and remain binding upon each executing state until renounced by it. Renunciation of this compact shall be by the same authority which executed it, by sending six months' notice in writing of its intention to withdraw from the compact to the other states

party hereto. The duties and obligations of a renouncing state under Article VII hereof shall continue as to parolees and probationers residing therein at the time of withdrawal until retaken or finally discharged. Supplementary agreements entered into under Article X hereof shall be subject to renunciation as provided by such supplementary agreements, and shall not be subject to the six months' renunciation notice of the present Article."

The Multistate Tax Compact provides:

"Any party state may withdraw from this compact by enacting a statute repealing the same. No withdrawal shall affect any liability already incurred by or chargeable to a party state prior to the time of such withdrawal.

"No proceeding commenced before an arbitration board prior to the withdrawal of a state and to which the withdrawing state or any subdivision thereof is a party shall be discontinued or terminated by the withdrawal, nor shall the board thereby lose jurisdiction over any of the parties to the proceeding necessary to make a binding determination therein."

The Interstate Agreement Creating a Multistate Lottery (MUSL) delays return of the departing lottery's share of the prize reserve fund until the expiration of the period for winners to claim their lotto prizes.

"That MUSL shall continue in existence until this agreement is revoked by all of the party lotteries. The withdrawal of one or more party lotteries shall not terminate this agreement among the remaining lotteries....

"A party lottery wishing to withdraw from this agreement shall give the board a six months notice of its intention to withdraw....

"In the event that a party lottery terminates, voluntarily or involuntarily, or MUSL is terminated by agreement of the parties, the prize reserve fund share of the party lottery or lotteries shall not be returned to the party lottery or lotteries until the later of one year from and after the date of termination or final resolution of any pending unresolved liabilities arising from transactions processed during the tenure of the departing lottery or lotteries. The voluntary or involuntary termination of a party lottery or lotteries does not cancel any obligation to MUSL which the party lottery or lotteries incurred before the withdrawal date."

Many compacts specifically provide that a state's withdrawal will not affect any obligations that the withdrawing state incurred while it was part of the compact. For example, the Multistate Tax Compact provides:

"No withdrawal shall affect any liability already incurred by or chargeable to a party state prior to the time of such withdrawal."

The Rhode Island–Massachusetts Interstate Low-Level Radioactive Waste Management Compact and Central Interstate Low-Level Radioactive Waste Compact have a similar provision.

Occasionally, a compact permits a member state to withdraw selectively from its obligations under the compact—that is, to withdraw from the compact with respect to some states, but to remain in the compact with respect to other states. For example, the Interpleader Compact provides:

"This compact shall continue in force and remain binding on a party state until such state shall withdraw therefrom. To be valid and effective, any withdrawal must be preceded by a formal notice in writing of one year from the appropriate authority of that state. Such notice shall be communicated to the same officer or agency in each party state with which the notice of adoption was deposited pursuant to Article VI. In the event that a state wishes to withdraw with respect to one or more states, but wishes to remain a party to this compact with other states party thereto, its notice of withdrawal shall be communicated only to those states with respect to which withdrawal is contemplated."

Although withdrawals from interstate compacts are relatively rare, they do occur. For example, Florida withdrew from the Atlantic States Marine Fisheries Compact in 1995. Maryland withdrew from the Interstate Bus Motor Fuel Tax Compact in 1967 and from the National Guard Mutual Assistance Compact in 1981.

8.6.2 Enforceability of Compact Provisions

The Impairments Clause of the U.S. Constitution restricts the action of all state legislatures concerning contracts:

> "No State shall ... pass any ... Law impairing the Obligation of Contracts...."[143]

The courts have long held that a state belonging to an interstate compact may not unilaterally renounce the agreement. The U.S. Supreme Court addressed this issue in a 1950 case involving the Ohio River Valley Water Sanitation Compact. The parties to this compact included eight states and the federal government. The compact established a commission consisting of representatives from each of the governmental units. It provided that each party state would pay a specified share of the operating expenses of the compact's commission.

> "The signatory states agree to appropriate for the salaries, office and other administrative expenses, their proper proportion of the annual budget as determined by the Commission and approved by the governors of the signatory states, one half of such amount to be prorated among the several states in proportion of their population within the district at the last preceding federal census, the other half to be prorated in proportion to their land area within the district."

There was considerable political division in West Virginia over the desirability of the compact. The legislature ratified the compact and, in 1949, appropriated $12,250 as West Virginia's initial contribution to the expenses of the compact's commission. The state Auditor, however, refused to make the payment from the state treasury. He argued that the legislature's approval of the compact violated the state constitution in two respects. First, the Auditor argued that the compact was unconstitutional because it delegated the state's police power to an interstate agency involving other states and the federal government. Second, the Auditor argued that the compact was invalid because it bound the West Virginia Legislature to make appropriations for the state's share of the commission's operating expenses in violation of a general provision of

---

[143] U.S. Constitution. Article I, section 10, clause 3. See appendix C for the full wording of the Impairments Clause.

the state constitution concerning the incurring of "debts." The West Virginia State Water Commission supported the compact and went to court requesting a mandamus order to compel the Auditor to make the payment from the state treasury. The Supreme Court of Appeals of West Virginia invalidated the legislature's ratification of the compact on the grounds that the compact violated the state constitution.

In 1950, the U.S. Supreme Court reversed the state ruling and prevented West Virginia from avoiding its obligations under the compact. The Court wrote in *West Virginia ex rel. Dyer v. Sims:*

> "But a compact is after all a legal document.... **It requires no elaborate argument to reject the suggestion that an agreement** solemnly entered into between States by those who alone have political authority to speak for a State **can be unilaterally nullified,** or given final meaning by an organ of one of the contracting States. **A State cannot be its own ultimate judge in a controversy with a sister State."**[144] [Emphasis added]

The U.S. Supreme Court continued:

> "That a legislature may delegate to an administrative body the power to make rules and decide particular cases is one of the axioms of modern government. The West Virginia court does not challenge the general proposition but objects to the delegation here involved **because it is to a body outside the State and because its Legislature may not be free, at any time, to withdraw the power delegated....** What is involved is the conventional grant of legislative power. We find nothing in that to indicate that West Virginia may not solve a problem such as the control of river pollution by compact and by the delegation, if such it be, necessary to effectuate such solution by compact.... Here, the State has bound itself to control pollution by the more effective means of an agreement with other States. **The Compact involves a reasonable and carefully limited delegation of power to an interstate agency."**[145] [Emphasis added]

---

[144] *West Virginia ex rel. Dyer v. Sims.* 341 U.S. 22 at 28. 1950.
[145] *Id.* at 30–31.

Justice Robert Jackson's concurring opinion set forth an additional justification for Court's decision. Justice Jackson suggested that the Supreme Court did not need to interpret the West Virginia state constitution in order to conclude that the compact bound West Virginia. Instead, he stated that West Virginia was estopped from changing its position after each of the other governmental entities relied upon, and changed their position because of, the compact.

> "**West Virginia assumed a contractual obligation** with equals by permission of another government that is sovereign in its field (the federal government). After Congress and **sister states had been induced to alter their positions and bind themselves to terms of a covenant,** West Virginia should be estopped from repudiating her act. For this reason, I consider that whatever interpretation she put on the generalities of her Constitution, **she is bound by the Compact.**"[146] [Emphasis added]

The pre-ratification expectations of states joining a compact are especially important whenever there is a post-ratification dispute among compacting parties concerning voting rights within the compact. In one case, Nebraska (which was obligated to store radioactive waste under the terms of a compact) sought additional voting power on the compact's commission after the compact had gone into effect. A majority (but not all) of the compact's other members consented to Nebraska's request. Nebraska's request was, however, judicially voided in 1995 in *State of Nebraska v. Central Interstate Low-Level Radioactive Waste Commission*

> "because changes in 'voting power' substantially alter the original expectations of the majority of states which comprise the compact."[147]

Amplifying the principle of *West Virginia ex rel. Dyer v. Sims*, the courts have noted that a single state cannot obstruct the workings of a compact. In *Hess v. Port Authority Trans-Hudson Corp.*, the U.S. Supreme Court held in 1994 that a compact is

---

[146] *Id.* at 36.

[147] *State of Nebraska v. Central Interstate Low-Level Radioactive Waste Commission.* 902 F.Supp. 1046, 1049 (D.Neb. 1995).

"... not subject to the unilateral control of any one of the States...."[148]

Similarly, in *Lake Country Estates, Inc. v. Tahoe Regional Planning Agency,* the U.S. Supreme Court in 1979 held that a member state may not unilaterally veto the actions of a compact's commission. Instead, the remedy of an aggrieved state consists of withdrawing from the compact in accordance with the compact's terms for withdrawal.[149]

In *Kansas City Area Transportation Authority v. Missouri,* the Eighth Circuit in 1981 held that a member state may not legislatively burden the other member states unless they concur.[150]

Moreover, a compacting state, motivated by politics, may be prevented from undermining the workings of that compact. In the 1993 case of *Alcorn v. Wolfe,* the removal of an appointee to a compact commission, initiated by a Governor to inject his political influence into the operations of the commission, was invalidated because it

"clearly frustrate[d] one of the most important objectives of the compact."[151]

In *State of Nebraska v. Central Interstate Low-Level Radioactive Waste Commission,* Nebraska was estopped in 1993 from seeking equitable relief to prevent a compact, of which it was a member, from pursuing its central mission.[152] In *New York v. United States,* the U.S. Supreme Court held that the estoppel doctrine was applicable only to the states that have adopted the interstate compact.[153]

In short, a state may be estopped from withdrawing from a compact in any manner not permitted by the terms of the compact.

The six-month blackout period for withdrawing from the proposed "Agreement Among the States to Elect the President by National Popular Vote" is reasonable and appropriate in order to ensure that a politically

---

[148] *Hess v. Port Authority Trans-Hudson Corp.* 513 U.S. 30 at 42. 1994.

[149] *Lake Country Estates, Inc. v. Tahoe Regional Planning Agency.* 440 U.S. 391 at 399 and 402. 1979.

[150] *Kansas City Area Transportation Authority v. Missouri.* 640 F.2d 173 at 174 (8th Cir.). 1979.

[151] *Alcorn v. Wolfe.* 827 F.Supp. 47, 53 (D.D.C. 1993).

[152] *State of Nebraska v. Central Interstate Low-Level Radioactive Waste Commission.* 834 F.Supp. 1205 at 1215 (D.Neb. 1993).

[153] *New York v. United States.* 505 U.S. 144 at 183. 1992.

motivated member state does not change its position after the candidates, the political parties, the voters, and the other compacting states have proceeded through the presidential campaign and presidential election cycle in reliance on each compacting state fulfilling its obligations under the compact.

8.6.3 Additional State and Federal Constraints on Withdrawal

There are two additional potential constraints on a withdrawal from the "Agreement Among the States to Elect the President by National Popular Vote" that are applicable to the 35-day period between election day in November and the meeting of the Electoral College in mid-December.

The first constraint is applicable if the compact were to be enacted in a particular state using the citizen-initiative process. In 11 states, there are state constitutional limitations concerning the repeal or amendment of a statute originally enacted by the voters by means of the citizen-initiative process.[154] In seven of these states, the constraint on the legislature runs for a specific period of time. In four of the 11 states, the constraint is permanent—that is, the voters must be consulted in a subsequent ref-

Table 8.4 STATE CONSTITUTIONAL LIMITATIONS ON THE REPEAL OR AMENDMENT OF STATUTES ORIGINALLY ENACTED BY THE VOTERS THROUGH THE CITIZEN-INITIATIVE PROCESS

STATE	LIMITATION
Alaska	No repeal within two years; amendment by majority vote anytime
Arizona	Three-quarters vote to amend; amending legislation must "further the purpose" of the measure
Arkansas	Two-thirds vote to amend or repeal
California	No amendment or repeal of an initiative statute by the legislature unless the initiative specifically permits it
Michigan	Three-quarters vote to amend or repeal
Nebraska	Two-thirds vote to amend or repeal
Nevada	No amendment or repeal within three years of enactment
North Dakota	Two-thirds vote to amend or repeal within seven years of effective date
Oregon	Two-thirds vote to amend or repeal within two years of enactment
Washington	Two-thirds vote to amend or repeal within two years of enactment
Wyoming	No repeal within two years of effective date; amendment by majority vote any time

---

[154] National Conference on State Legislatures.

erendum about any proposed repeal or amendment. Table 8.4 briefly describes these constitutional limitations. Appendix R contains the complete constitutional provisions.

In addition to the above constitutional limitations, public opinion acts as an inhibition against legislative repeal of, or substantive amendments to, a statute that the voters originally enacted by means of the citizen-initiative process. This political inhibition is particularly forceful in western states that have the citizen-initiative process.

Second, there is a federal law that would likely be interpreted to constrain repeal of the proposed compact withdrawal during the 35-day period between "the day fixed for the appointment of the electors" (that is, election day in early November) and the meeting of the Electoral College in mid-December. The federal "safe harbor" provision (quoted in full in section 8.3.6) gives preference to presidential election returns that are in accord with

> "laws enacted prior to the day fixed for the appointment of the electors...."[155]

In the 1960 presidential election, for example, John F. Kennedy won the nationwide popular vote by 114,673 votes. However, his electoral-vote majority depended on the fact that he had carried Illinois by 4,430 popular votes and South Carolina by 4,732 votes. Some members of the South Carolina legislature suggested that the legislature ignore the popular vote count in the state, change the rules for awarding the state's electoral votes after election day, and appoint all the state's presidential electors themselves. One reason that nothing came of this suggestion was that the "safe harbor" provision requires that an ascertainment of a state's votes based on the laws that existed prior to election day be treated as "conclusive" in the national count of the electoral votes. Nothing came of similar post-election suggestions that the Florida Legislature appoint all of the state's presidential electors in 2000.

---

[155] See section 8.3.6 for the complete wording of this provision (title 3, chapter 1, section 6 of the United States Code).

9 | Administrative Issues Concerning the Proposed Interstate Compact

The proposed "Agreement Among the States to Elect the President by National Popular Vote" (presented in chapter 6) raises several issues concerning the administration of elections, including the following:

- Does the proposed compact impose any significant additional financial cost or administrative burden on state election officials (section 9.1)?
- How would recounts be handled (section 9.2)?

9.1 DOES THE PROPOSED COMPACT IMPOSE ANY SIGNIFICANT FINANCIAL COST OR ADMINISTRATIVE BURDEN ON STATE ELECTION OFFICIALS?

Under the proposed interstate compact, a presidential election would be conducted by each state in the same way that it is now conducted. The proposed compact makes no changes in a state's laws or procedures for preparing ballots; administering polling places; counting votes at the precinct level; or aggregating the vote counts from the precincts to determine the total number of popular votes cast for each presidential slate in the state.

Under the statewide winner-take-all system currently used by 48 states and the District of Columbia, the state's chief election official (or state canvassing board) certifies the election of the entire list of presidential electors that is affiliated with the presidential slate that received the most votes in the state. For example, if the Republican presidential slate carries the state, the state's chief election official certifies the election of the entire slate of Republican presidential electors for the state. These presidential electors collectively represent the will of their state's voters.

The system currently used in Maine and Nebraska is different. The state's chief election official certifies the election of a presidential elector affiliated with the presidential slate that carried each separate congressional district in the state. Each district-level presidential elector represents the will of the voters in the district involved. In addition, the chief election official certifies two presidential electors affiliated with the presidential slate that carried the state. These two senatorial presidential electors collectively represent the will of the voters in their state. For example, if the Democratic presidential slate carries the state and the 1st congressional district, the state's chief election official certifies the election of three Democratic presidential electors (two senatorial electors and one district elector from the 1st district). If the Republican presidential slate carries the 2nd congressional district, the state's chief election official certifies the election of one Republican presidential elector for that district. In this example, two senatorial presidential electors collectively represent the will of their state's voters; the Democratic elector from the 1st district represents the will of that district's voters; and the Republican elector from the 2nd district represents the will of that district's voters.

The only change introduced by the proposed compact occurs *after* a state has finished tallying the statewide total number of popular votes cast for each presidential slate. At that point, there is one additional step under the proposed compact. The votes cast for each presidential slate in all 50 states and the District of Columbia would be added together to produce a national grand total for each presidential slate (section 6.3.3). This is, of course, the same adding-up process that the media, the political parties, and various watchdog groups already do on election night and in the days following each presidential election. Under the proposed compact, the presidential slate with the largest national grand total from all 50 states and the District of Columbia would be designated as the "national popular vote winner." The chief election official of each state belonging to the compact would then certify the election of the entire slate of presidential electors that is affiliated with the presidential slate that has been designated as the "national popular vote winner." For example, if the Democratic presidential slate is the "national popular vote winner," the state's chief election official in every state belonging to the compact would certify the election of the slate of Democratic presidential electors.

The effect of the proposed compact would be that all the presidential electors of all states belonging to the compact would be affiliated with the presidential slate that received the largest total number of popular votes in all 50 states and the District of Columbia. These presidential electors from the states belonging to the compact will collectively represent the nationwide will of the voters. Under the proposed compact, the presidential electors will meet in mid-December and cast their electoral votes. Because the proposed compact only goes into effect when it has been enacted by states possessing a majority of the electoral votes, the presidential slate receiving the most popular votes from all 50 states and the District of Columbia will receive a majority of the electoral votes in the Electoral College.

As can be seen, there is no significant additional administrative burden or financial cost associated with the proposed interstate compact.

9.2 HOW WOULD RECOUNTS BE HANDLED?

Before discussing the mechanics of recounts, let us recognize that there would be less opportunity for a close election under nationwide popular election of the President than under the prevailing statewide winner-take-all system. A close outcome is considerably less likely in an election with a single pool of votes than in an election in which there are 51 separate pools and hence 51 separate opportunities for a close outcome. Moreover, a close outcome is considerably less likely in larger pool than in a smaller one. Thus, a close outcome is less likely in a single pool of 122,000,000 popular votes than in 51 separate pools each averaging 2,392,159 votes (1/51 of 122,000,000).

The 2000 presidential election is remembered as being close because George W. Bush's total of 2,912,790 popular votes in Florida was a mere 537 more than Gore's statewide total of 2,912,353. Under the statewide winner-take-all rule used in Florida (and almost all other states), the 537-vote lead entitled Bush to all 25 of Florida's electoral votes. There was, however, nothing particularly close about the 2000 presidential election on a nationwide basis. Al Gore had a nationwide lead of 537,179 popular votes. Gore's nationwide lead was larger than, for example, Nixon's lead of 510,314 in 1968 and Kennedy's lead of 118,574 in 1960.[1] The closeness of the 2000 presidential election was an artificial crisis manufactured by Florida's use of the statewide winner-take-all system.

---

[1] Congressional Quarterly. 2002. *Presidential Elections 1789–2002*. Washington, DC: CQ Press. Pages 146 and 148.

No one would even have considered a recount in 2000 if the nationwide popular vote had controlled the outcome. No one would have cared whether Bush did, or did not, carry Florida by 537 popular votes. Similarly, the 2004 election was also not close in terms of the nationwide popular vote. President George W. Bush had a nationwide lead of about 3,500,000 popular votes. However, people had to wait until the morning of Wednesday November 3, 2004, to find out the outcome of the popular vote in Ohio. A switch of 59,388 popular votes in Ohio would have given Kerry all of Ohio's 20 electoral votes and the Presidency. Again, the illusion of closeness resulted from the statewide winner-take-all system used in Ohio—not because the election was genuinely close on a nationwide basis.

In fact, no presidential election since the 19th century has been won by fewer than 100,000 votes on a nationwide basis. The closest presidential election since 1900 was the 1960 election in which John F. Kennedy led Richard M. Nixon by 118,574 popular votes nationwide. A margin of 118,574 popular votes is not particularly close on a nationwide basis. Such a margin would have been unlikely to be questioned. No margin of that size is likely to be overturned by any recount. The 1960 election is remembered as being close because a switch of 4,430 votes in Illinois and a switch 4,782 votes in South Carolina would have given Nixon a majority of the electoral votes. If Nixon had carried both of those states, Kennedy still would have been ahead nationwide by almost 110,000 popular votes, but Nixon would have won the Presidency. The 1960 election then would have become yet another election in which the winner of the nationwide popular vote did not win the Presidency. In any case, the perceived closeness of the 1960 election was an illusion manufactured by the statewide winner-take-all system used in Illinois and South Carolina—not because the nationwide margin of 118,574 was ever likely to be overturned by any recount.

Table 9.1 shows the popular vote count for the Democratic and Republican presidential candidates in each presidential election since 1900 (except that Theodore Roosevelt's vote is shown for the 1912 presidential election because he polled more votes as nominee of the Progressive Party than did the Republican nominee, William Howard Taft). Column 4 shows the difference between the first- and second-place candidates. None of these elections was particularly close in terms of the nationwide popular vote. This is true even though the number of votes cast nationwide in the early years of the 20th century was only about 10%

Table 9.1 WINNING MARGINS IN PRESIDENTIAL ELECTIONS BETWEEN 1900 AND 2004

ELECTION	DEMOCRAT	REPUBLICAN	DIFFERENCE
1900	6,357,698	7,219,193	861,495
1904	5,083,501	7,625,599	2,542,098
1908	6,406,874	7,676,598	1,269,724
1912	6,294,326	4,120,207	2,174,119
1916	9,126,063	8,547,039	579,024
1920	9,134,074	16,151,916	7,017,842
1924	8,386,532	15,724,310	7,337,778
1928	15,004,336	21,432,823	6,428,487
1932	22,818,740	15,760,426	7,058,314
1936	27,750,866	16,679,683	11,071,183
1940	27,343,218	22,334,940	5,008,278
1944	25,612,610	22,021,053	3,591,557
1948	24,105,810	21,970,064	2,135,746
1952	27,314,992	33,777,945	6,462,953
1956	26,022,752	35,590,472	9,567,720
1960	34,226,731	34,108,157	118,574
1964	43,129,566	27,178,188	15,951,378
1968	31,275,166	31,785,480	510,314
1972	29,170,383	47,169,911	17,999,528
1976	40,830,763	39,147,793	1,682,970
1980	35,483,883	43,904,153	8,420,270
1984	37,577,185	54,455,075	16,877,890
1988	41,809,074	48,886,097	7,077,023
1992	44,909,326	39,103,882	5,805,444
1996	47,402,357	39,198,755	8,203,602
2000	50,992,335	50,455,156	537,179
2004	59,028,111	62,040,610	3,012,499

of the present-day turnout of 122,000,000 votes.

Even the highly controversial 1876 presidential election was not close in terms of the nationwide popular vote. Democrat Samuel J. Tilden received 4,288,191 popular votes—254,694 more than the 4,033,497 popular votes received by Rutherford B. Hayes. Tilden's percentage lead of 3.05% was greater than George W. Bush's 2004 lead of 2.8%. The 1876 election is remembered as having been close because Hayes had extremely narrow popular-vote leads in several states, namely

  • 889 votes in South Carolina,
  • 922 votes in Florida,

- 1,050 votes in Oregon,
- 1,075 votes in Nevada, and
- 2,798 votes in California.[2,3,4,5]

Again, the closeness of the 1876 presidential election was an artificial crisis created by the statewide winner-take-all system.

Having said that, even with a single pool of 122,000,000 votes, it is conceivable that the nationwide popular vote could some day be extremely close (say, a few hundred or a few thousand votes out of 122,000,000). In that event, the vote count and the inevitable recount would be handled in the same way as it is currently handled—that is, under the generally serviceable laws that govern all elections. An extremely close election will almost inevitably engender controversy. The guiding principle in such circumstances should be that all votes should be counted fairly and expeditiously. Of course, if the nationwide popular vote count were extremely close on a nationwide basis, it would be very likely that the vote count would, simultaneously, be close in a number of states.

In terms of logistics, the personnel and procedures for a nationwide recount are already in place because every state is always prepared to conduct a statewide recount after any election. Indeed, there are statewide recounts for certain statewide offices and ballot propositions in virtually every election cycle. As Senator David Durenberger (R-Minnesota) said in the Senate in 1979:

> "There is no reason to doubt the ability of the States and localities to manage a recount, and nothing to suggest that a candidate would frivolously incur the expense of requesting one. And even if this were not the case, the potential danger in selecting a President rejected by a majority of the voters far outweighs the potential inconvenience in administering a recount."[6]

---

[2] Congressional Quarterly. 2002. *Presidential Elections 1789–2002*. Washington, DC: CQ Press. Page 125.

[3] Morris, Roy B. 2003. *Fraud of the Century: Rutherford B. Hayes, Samuel Tilden, and the Stolen Election of 1876*. Waterville, ME: Thorndike Press.

[4] Robinson, Lloyd. 1996. *The Stolen Election: Hayes versus Tilden—1876*. New York, NY: Tom Doherty Associates Books.

[5] Rehnquist, William H. 2004. *Centennial Crisis: The Disputed Election of 1876*. New York, NY: Alfred A. Knopf.

[6] *Congressional Record.* July 10, 1979. Pages 17706–17707.

Senator Birch Bayh (D-Indiana) summed up the concerns about extremely close elections and recounts in a Senate speech by saying:

"Fraud is an ever present possibility in the electoral college system, even if it rarely has become a proven reality. With the electoral college, relatively few irregular votes can reap a healthy reward in the form of a bloc of electoral votes, because of the unit rule or winner take all rule. Under the present system, fraudulent popular votes are much more likely to have a great impact by swinging enough blocs of electoral votes to reverse the election. A like number of fraudulent popular votes under direct election would likely have little effect on the national vote totals.

"I have said repeatedly in previous debates that there is no way in which anyone would want to excuse fraud. We have to do everything we can to find it, to punish those who participate in it; but **one of the things we can do to limit fraud is to limit the benefits to be gained by fraud.**

"Under a direct popular vote system, one fraudulent vote wins one vote in the return. In the electoral college system, one fraudulent vote could mean 45 electoral votes, 28 electoral votes.

"So the incentive to participate in 'a little bit of fraud,' if I may use that phrase advisedly, can have the impact of turning a whole electoral block, a whole State operating under the unit rule. Therefore, so the incentive to participate in fraud is significantly greater than it would be under the direct popular vote system."[7] [Emphasis added]

---

[7] *Congressional Record.* March 14, 1979. Page 5000.

10 | Responses to Myths about the National Popular Vote Plan

This chapter responds to concerns that have been raised during the debate about the National Popular Vote bill.

The 91 myths discussed in this chapter are organized into 34 sections as follows:

- Myths about the U.S. Constitution (section 10.1),
- Myth that Candidates Reach Out to All the States under the Current System (section 10.2),
- Myth that "Wrong Winner" Elections are Rare (section 10.3),
- Myths about the Low-Population States and Rural States (section 10.4),
- Myths about High-Population States and Big Cities (section 10.5),
- Myth about State Identity (section 10.6),
- Myths about Absolute Majority Requirement, Proliferation of Candidates, and Breakdown of the Two-Party System (section 10.7),
- Myths about Extremist and Regional Candidates (section 10.8),
- Myths about Logistical Nightmares Arising from Differences in State Laws (section 10.9),
- Myths about Faithless Electors (section 10.10),
- Myths about Post-Election Changes in the Rules of the Game, Withdrawal, and Enforceability (section 10.11),
- Myth about Campaign Spending (section 10.12),
- Myths about Election Administration (section 10.13),
- Myths about Lack of an Official National Count for Presidential Elections and Secret Elections (section 10.14),
- Myths about Recounts (section 10.15),

- Myths about Federalism (section 10.16),
- Myths about Interstate Compacts and Congressional Consent (section 10.17),
- Myths about Encroaching on Federal Sovereignty and State Sovereignty (section 10.18),
- Myth about Our Republican Form of Government (section 10.19),
- Myths about Mob Rule (section 10.20),
- Myth about an Incoming President's Mandate (section 10.21),
- Myth about Presidential Power (section 10.22),
- Myth about the 12th Amendment (section 10.23),
- Myths about the 14th Amendment (section 10.24),
- Myths about the Voting Rights Act (section 10.25),
- Myth about a Federal Election Bureaucracy (section 10.26),
- Myths about the District of Columbia (section 10.27),
- Myths about Congressional or Proportional Allocation of Electoral Votes (section 10.28),
- Myth That One State Can Derail the National Popular Vote Compact (section 10.29),
- Myth about Decline in Voter Turnout (section 10.30),
- Myth that the National Popular Vote Compact is a Conspiracy (section 10.31),
- Myth that our Nation's Freedom, Security, and Prosperity Are Protected by the Winner-Take-All Rule (section 10.32),
- Myth about the Replacement of a Dead, Disabled, or Discredited Presidential Candidate (section 10.33),
- Myth That the Winner-Take-All Rule Produces Good Presidents (section 10.34).

The 91 myths discussed in this chapter are organized into 34 sections and 91 subsections as follows:

- **Myths about the U.S. Constitution**
  - MYTH: A federal constitutional amendment is required to change the method of electing the President (section 10.1.1).

- MYTH: The "traditional," "appropriate," and "normal" way of changing the method of electing the President is by means of a federal constitutional amendment (section 10.1.2).
- MYTH: The current system of electing the President was created and favored by the Founding Fathers (section 10.1.3).
- MYTH: Seeking change by means of a federal constitutional amendment shows respect for the Founding Fathers (section 10.1.4).
- MYTH: A federal constitutional amendment is the most democratic approach for considering a change in the manner of electing the President (section 10.1.5).
- MYTH: "Eleven colluding states" are trying to impose a national popular vote on the country (section 10.1.6).
- MYTH: A federal constitutional amendment is the superior way to change the system (section 10.1.7).
- MYTH: It is inappropriate for state legislatures and governors to consider changing the method of electing the President (section 10.1.8).
- MYTH: The National Popular Vote bill is unconstitutional (section 10.1.9).
- **Myth that Candidates Reach Out to All the States under the Current System**
  - MYTH: The current system ensures that presidential candidates reach out to all states (section 10.2.1).
  - MYTH: A national popular vote will simply make a different group of states irrelevant in presidential elections (section 10.2.2).
- **Myth that "Wrong Winner" Elections are Rare**
  - MYTH: "Wrong winner" elections are rare, and therefore not a problem (section 10.3.1).
- **Myths about the Low-Population States and Rural States**
  - MYTH: The low-population states would be disadvantaged by a national popular vote (section 10.4.1).
  - MYTH: The low-population states are so small that they will not attract any attention under any system (section

10.4.2).

- MYTH: The least populous states are opposed to a national popular vote for President (section 10.4.3).
- MYTH: Equal representation of the states in the U.S. Senate is threatened by the National Popular Vote plan (section 10.4.4).
- MYTH: The Republican Party enjoys a partisan advantage from the low-population states in presidential elections (section 10.4.5).
- MYTH: The distribution of political influence envisioned by the Great Compromise would be upset by a national popular vote (section 10.4.6).
- MYTH: The rural states would lose their electoral advantage under a national popular vote (section 10.4.7).
- **Myths about High-Population States and Big Cities**
  - MYTH: Only the 11 most populous states would matter under a national popular vote (section 10.5.1).
  - MYTH: California would swamp the low-population western states under a national popular vote (section 10.5.2).
  - MYTH: The South would be swamped by high-population Democratic states under a national popular vote (section 10.5.3).
  - MYTH: Big cities, such as Los Angeles, would control the election under a national popular vote (section 10.5.4).
  - MYTH: Candidates would only campaign in media markets, while ignoring the rest of the country (section 10.5.5).
  - MYTH: Under a national popular vote, candidates would concentrate on major metropolitan markets because the cost per advertising impression is lower there (section 10.5.6).
  - MYTH: The current system prevents 11 states from electing the President (section 10.5.7).

- **Myth about State Identity**
  - MYTH: The public strongly desires that electoral votes be cast on a state-by-state basis because it provides a sense of "state identity" (section 10.6.1).
- **Myths about Absolute Majority Requirement, Proliferation of Candidates, and Breakdown of the Two-Party System**
  - MYTH: The National Popular Vote plan is defective because it does not require an absolute majority of the popular vote to win (section 10.7.1).
  - MYTH: The National Popular Vote plan is defective because it does not provide for a run-off (section 10.7.2).
  - MYTH: A national popular vote will result in a proliferation of candidates, Presidents being elected with 15% of the vote, and a breakdown of the two-party system (section 10.7.3).
- **Myths about Extremist and Regional Candidates**
  - MYTH: Extremist candidates will proliferate under a national popular vote (section 10.8.1).
  - MYTH: Regional candidates will proliferate under a national popular vote (section 10.8.2).
- **Myths about Logistical Nightmares Arising from Differences in State Laws**
  - MYTH: Logistical nightmares would plague a national popular vote because of differences among the states concerning ballot access requirements, ex-felon eligibility requirements, and poll closing times (section 10.9.1).
  - MYTH: A state's electoral votes could be awarded to a candidate not on a state's own ballot, and out-of-state persons could become presidential electors (section 10.9.2).
- **Myths about Faithless Electors**
  - MYTH: Faithless presidential electors would be a problem under the National Popular Vote compact (section 10.10.1).
  - MYTH: It might be difficult to coerce presidential electors to vote for the national popular vote winner (sec-

tion 10.10.2).

- MYTH: Presidential electors might succumb to outside pressure and abandon the national popular vote in favor of the winner of the popular vote in the state (section 10.10.3).
- **Myths about Post-Election Changes in the Rules of the Game, Withdrawal, and Enforceability**
  - MYTH: A state legislature might change a state's method of awarding electoral votes after the people vote in November, but before the Electoral College meets in December (section 10.11.1).
  - MYTH: A Secretary of State might change a state's method of awarding electoral votes after the people vote in November, but before the Electoral College meets in December (section 10.11.2).
- **Myth about Campaign Spending**
  - MYTH:Campaign spending would skyrocket if candidates had to campaign throughout the country (section 10.12.1).
- **Myths about Election Administration**
  - MYTH: Local election officials would be burdened by the National Popular Vote compact (section 10.13.1).
  - MYTH: The state's chief election official would be burdened by the National Popular Vote compact (section 10.13.2).
  - MYTH: The National Popular Vote compact would burden the state's chief elections official with the need to evaluate the election returns of other states (section 10.13.3).
  - MYTH: The National Popular Vote compact would be costly (section 10.13.4).
  - MYTH: Post-election audits cannot be conducted under a national popular vote (section 10.13.5).
- **Myths about Lack of an Official National Count for Presidential Elections and Secret Elections**
  - MYTH: There is no official count of the national popular vote (section 10.14.1).
  - MYTH: A single state could frustrate the National

Popular Vote compact by making its election returns a state secret (section 10.14.2).

- **Myths about Recounts**
  - MYTH: The current system typically produces undisputed outcomes, and problems are rare (section 10.15.1).
  - MYTH: The current system acts as a firewall that helpfully isolates recounts to particular states (section 10.15.2).
  - MYTH: Resolution of a presidential election could be prolonged beyond the inauguration date because of recounts (section 10.15.3).
  - MYTH: Conducting a recount would be a logistical impossibility under a national popular vote (section 10.15.4).
  - MYTH: States would be put in the uncomfortable position of judging election returns from other states under a national popular vote (section 10.15.5).
  - MYTH: Fraud and mischief would be magnified under a national popular vote (section 10.15.6).
  - MYTH: A recount might be warranted, but unobtainable, under the National Popular Vote compact (section 10.15.7).
- **Myths about Federalism**
  - MYTH: Federalism would be undermined by a national popular vote (section 10.16.1).
- **Myths about Interstate Compacts and Congressional Consent**
  - MYTH: Interstate compacts are exotic and fishy (section 10.17.1).
  - MYTH: The National Popular Vote compact is defective because Congress did not consent to the compact prior to its consideration by state legislatures (section 10.17.2).
  - MYTH: The National Popular Vote compact is defective because it fails to mention Congress in its text (section 10.17.3).
  - MYTH: The National Popular Vote compact requires congressional consent to become effective (section

10.17.4).

• **Myths about Encroaching on Federal Sovereignty and State Sovereignty**

  ▪ MYTH: The National Popular Vote compact encroaches on federal sovereignty (section 10.18.1).

  ▪ MYTH: The National Popular Vote compact encroaches on state sovereignty (section 10.18.2).

• **Myth about Our Republican Form of Government**

  ▪ MYTH: A national popular vote violates the concept that the United States is a republic, not a democracy (section 10.19.1).

• **Myths about Mob Rule**

  ▪ MYTH: A national popular vote would be mob rule (section 10.20.1).

  ▪ MYTH: The Electoral College acts as a buffer and damper against popular passions (section 10.20.2).

• **Myth about an Incoming President's Mandate**

  ▪ MYTH: The current winner-take-all system gives the incoming President a "mandate" in the form of an exaggerated lead in the Electoral College (section 10.21.1).

• **Myth about Presidential Power**

  ▪ MYTH: The President's powers would be changed by a national popular vote (section 10. 22.1).

• **Myth about the 12th Amendment**

  ▪ MYTH: The Meeting Clause of the 12th Amendment precludes the National Popular Vote compact (section 10.23.1).

• **Myths about the 14th Amendment**

  ▪ MYTH: Section 2 of the 14th Amendment precludes the National Popular Vote compact (section 10.24.1).

  ▪ MYTH: The Privileges and Immunities Clause of the 14th Amendment precludes the National Popular Vote compact (section 10.24.2).

  ▪ MYTH: The Due Process Clause of the 14th Amendment precludes the National Popular Vote compact (section 10.24.3).

  ▪ MYTH: The Equal Protection Clause of the 14th Amendment precludes the National Popular Vote compact (section 10.24.4).

- **Myths about the Voting Rights Act**
  - MYTH: Section 2 of the Voting Rights Act precludes the National Popular Vote compact (section 10.25.1).
  - MYTH: The political influence of racial and ethnic minorities would be diminished by a national popular vote (section 10.25.2).
- **Myth about a Federal Election Bureaucracy**
  - MYTH: A federal election bureaucracy would be created by the National Popular Vote compact (section 10.26.1)
- **Myths about the District of Columbia**
  - MYTH: The National Popular Vote compact would permit the District of Columbia to vote for President, even though it is not a state (section 10.27.1).
  - MYTH: Because it is not a state, the District of Columbia may not enter into interstate compacts (section 10.27.2).
  - MYTH: Only Congress may enter into interstate compacts on behalf of the District of Columbia (section 10.27.3).
  - MYTH: Only Congress may change the winner-take-all rule for the District of Columbia (section 10.27.4).
  - MYTH: Because it is not a state, the District of Columbia cannot bind itself by means of an interstate compact (section 10.27.5).
  - MYTH: The enactment of the National Popular Vote compact by the District of Columbia Council is incomplete because Congress has not approved the Council's action (section 10.27.6).
- **Myths about Congressional or Proportional Allocation of Electoral Votes**
  - MYTH: It would be better to allocate electoral votes by congressional district (section 10.28.1).
  - MYTH: It would be better to allocate electoral votes proportionally (section 10.28.2).
- **Myth That One State Can Derail the National Popular Vote Compact**
  - MYTH: There is an "Achilles' heel" that enables one discordant state to derail the National Popular Vote compact (section 10.29.1).

- **Myth about Decline in Voter Turnout**
  - MYTH: A national popular vote will decrease turnout (section 10.30.1).
- **Myth that the National Popular Vote Compact Is a Conspiracy**
  - MYTH: The National Popular Vote compact is a conspiracy (section 10.31.1).
- **Myth that our Nation's Freedom, Security, and Prosperity Are Protected by the Winner-Take-All Rule**
  - MYTH: Our nation's freedom, security, and prosperity are protected by the current winner-take-all method of awarding electoral votes (section 10.32.1).
- **Myth About the Replacement of a Dead, Disabled, or Discredited Presidential Candidate**
  - MYTH: The Electoral College provides a way to replace a dead, disabled, or discredited President-Elect after the people vote in November, but before the Electoral College meets in December (section 10.33.1).
- **Myth That the Winner-Take-All Rule Produces Good Presidents**
  - MYTH: The winner-take-all method for awarding electoral votes produces good Presidents (section 10.34.1).

10.1 MYTHS ABOUT THE U.S. CONSTITUTION

10.1.1 MYTH: A federal constitutional amendment is required to change the current method of electing the President.

QUICK ANSWER:

- The U.S. Constitution gives states the "exclusive" and "plenary" power to choose the method for awarding their electoral votes.
- The shortcomings of the current system of electing the President stem from state winner-take-all statutes that award all of a state's electoral votes to the candidate who receives the most popular votes within each separate state.
- The winner-take-all method of awarding electoral votes is not in the U.S. Constitution and, in fact, was used by only three states in the nation's first presidential election in 1789.
- Maine and Nebraska currently award electoral votes by

congressional district—a reminder that the method of awarding electoral votes is a matter of state law.

• The winner-take-all rule is used today in 48 of the 50 states because it was enacted as a state statute in those states, under the same provision of the U.S. Constitution (empowering the states to choose the method of awarding their electoral votes) being used to enact the National Popular Vote plan.

• Winner-take-all statutes may be repealed in the same way they were enacted—namely, through each state's process for enacting and repealing state laws. Therefore, a federal constitutional amendment is not necessary to change the state-by-state winner-take-all method of awarding electoral votes.

• The Constitution's grant of exclusive power to the states to decide how presidential elections are conducted was not a historical accident or mistake, but was intended as a "check and balance" on a sitting President who, with a compliant Congress, might be inclined to manipulate election rules to perpetuate himself in office.

MORE DETAILED ANSWER:

It is important to recognize what the U.S. Constitution says—and does not say—about electing the President.

Section 1 of article II of the U.S. Constitution says:

"Each State shall appoint, in such Manner as **the Legislature thereof may direct**, a Number of Electors...."[1] [Emphasis added]

Those 17 words are the only guidance that the Constitution gives states about how they may award their electoral votes.

In 1787, the delegates to the Constitutional Convention debated the method of electing the President on 22 separate days and held 30 separate votes on the topic.

One of the major points of contention at the Convention was whether the people should be allowed to vote for President.

---

[1] U.S. Constitution. Article II, section 1, clause 2.

On four separate occasions, the Convention voted (and then reversed its decision) that Congress should choose the President—that is, the people would not be allowed to vote for President. On another occasion, the delegates voted that the state legislatures would choose the President. At one point, the delegates considered empowering state governors to choose the President.[2]

Even when the delegates eventually decided—toward the end of the Constitutional Convention—that the President would be elected by presidential electors (collectively called the "Electoral College"), the Founders were still unable to agree on how the presidential electors would be chosen.

- Should the presidential electors be chosen directly by the people—analogous to the method of electing members of the U.S. House of Representatives?
- Should the presidential electors be chosen by the state legislatures—analogous to the appointment of U.S. Senators by state legislatures that was specified in the original Constitution?[3]
- Should the presidential electors be chosen by some other method (perhaps by the governors)?

In the end—unable to agree upon any particular method—the Founding Fathers adopted the language now contained in section 1 of Article II, leaving the choice of method for selecting presidential electors to the states.

The eventual wording in section 1 of Article II ("as the Legislature … may direct") is unqualified. It does not encourage, discourage, require, or prohibit the use of any particular method for awarding a state's electoral votes.

- If the legislature decides to give the people a vote for President, the Constitution does not specify whether the presidential electors should be elected statewide, in single-member districts, in multi-member districts, or otherwise.

---

[2] Edwards, George C. III. 2004. *Why the Electoral College Is Bad for America*. New Haven, CT: Yale University Press.

[3] The 17th Amendment (ratified in 1913) provided that U.S. Senators would be elected by the people.

- If the legislature decides against giving the people a vote for President, the Constitution does not specify whether the presidential electors should be appointed by the governor and his cabinet, selected by both houses of the legislature sitting together in a joint convention, selected by passage by both legislative houses of a resolution containing a common list of names, or selected by some other method.

Indeed, over the years, all of the above methods have been used.

But the most salient feature of our nation's current method of electing the President namely, the winner-take-all method of awarding electoral votes, was never debated at the Constitutional Convention. It was never voted upon at the Constitutional Convention, and it appears nowhere in the U.S. Constitution.

Under the winner-take-all rule (also known as the "unit rule" or "general ticket"), a plurality of a state's voters are capable of electing all of a state's presidential electors.

When the Founding Fathers returned from the Constitutional Convention in Philadelphia to organize the nation's first presidential election in 1789, only three states chose to employ the winner-take-all method for awarding their electoral votes.[4]

Today, the winner-take-all method of awarding electoral votes is used in 48 of the 50 states.

The U.S. Supreme Court has repeatedly characterized the authority of the states over the manner of awarding their electoral votes as "exclusive" and "plenary."

---

[4] In the version of the winner-take-all rule that was used in 1789 (and, indeed, until the middle of the 20th century in most states), each voter was allowed to cast as many votes as the state's number of presidential electors. This at-large approach permits a disciplined majority or plurality of a state's voters to elect all of a state's presidential electors—hence, the name "winner-take-all." Voting for individual presidential electors remained in use as late as 1980 in Vermont. Today, all states use the so-called "short presidential ballot" which enables a voter to conveniently cast a single vote for a slate composed of the name of a candidate for President and the name of a candidate for Vice President. Under the short presidential ballot, a vote for the presidential and vice-presidential candidate whose names appear on the ballot is deemed to be a vote for all of the individual presidential electors nominated in association with those candidates. For example, when a voter chose John McCain in California in 2008, the voter was actually casting a vote for each of 55 individual candidates for the position of presidential elector nominated by the California Republican Party. See section 2.2.6.

The leading case on the awarding of electoral votes is the 1892 case of *McPherson v. Blacker*. As the U.S. Supreme Court stated in that case:

> **"The constitution does not provide that the appointment of electors** shall be by popular vote, nor that the electors **shall be voted for upon a general ticket [the winner-take-all rule]** nor that the majority of those who exercise the elective franchise can alone choose the electors. It recognizes that the people act through their representatives in the legislature, and **leaves it to the legislature exclusively to define the method** of effecting the object. The framers of the constitution employed words in their natural sense; and, where they are plain and clear, resort to collateral aids to interpretation is unnecessary, and cannot be indulged in to narrow or enlarge the text....

> "In short, **the appointment and mode of appointment of electors belong exclusively to the states** under the constitution of the United States."[5] [Emphasis added]

In *Bush v. Gore* in 2000, the Court approvingly referred to the characterization in *McPherson v. Blacker* of the state's power under section 1 of article II of the Constitution.

> "The individual citizen has no federal constitutional right to vote for electors for the President of the United States unless and until the state legislature chooses a statewide election as the means to implement its power to appoint members of the Electoral College. U.S. Const., Art. II, §1. **This is the source for the statement in *McPherson v. Blacker*,** 146 U.S. 1, 35 (1892), that the State legislature's power to select the manner for appointing electors is **plenary**; it may, if it so chooses, select the electors itself, which indeed was the manner used by State legislatures in several States for many years after the Framing of our Constitution. Id., at 28-33....

> **"There is no difference between the two sides of the present controversy on these basic propositions."**[6] [Emphasis added]

---

[5] *McPherson v. Blacker.* 146 U.S. 1 at 29. 1892.

[6] *Bush v. Gore.* 531 U.S. 98. 2000.

In short, states may exercise their power to choose the manner of appointing their presidential electors in any way they see fit (provided, of course, that they do not violate any specific restriction contained elsewhere in the U.S. Constitution).[7]

There is good reason to give the states the power to control the conduct of presidential elections. State control over presidential elections thwarts the possibility of over-reaching Presidents, in conjunction with a compliant Congress, manipulating the manner of conducting the presidential election (and, in particular, their own re-election) in a politically advantageous way. The delegation of control over presidential elections was intended to guard against the establishment of a self-perpetuating President (that is, a restoration of a monarchy in the United States). Thus, neither the sitting President nor Congress has any role in the choice of method for choosing any state's presidential electors. Under the U.S. Constitution, control over presidential elections is an exclusive state power.

The winner-take-all statutes are state law. This method of awarding electoral votes was adopted piece-meal on a state-by-state basis. During the lives of the Founding Fathers, the winner-take-all rule was never the prevailing method of awarding electoral votes. Instead, winner-take-all statutes became prevalent decades later, in the period prior to the Civil War, with the emergence of strong political parties aiming to maximize their own political power within their states to stifle the minority party.

More importantly, these winner-take-all statutes did not come into use by means of an amendment to the U.S. Constitution. Accordingly, changing the winner-take-all rule does not require an amendment to the Constitution. Winner-take-all statutes may be repealed in the same way they were enacted—namely, through each state's process for enacting and repealing state laws.

---

[7] All powers delegated to Congress and the states are subject to general restrictions found elsewhere in the Constitution. For example, in *Bush v. Gore* (531 U.S. 98), the Court observed that "Having once granted the right to vote on equal terms, the State may not, by later arbitrary and disparate treatment, value one person's vote over that of another. See, e.g., *Harper v. Virginia Bd. of Elections*, 383 U.S. 663, 665 (1966) ('[O]nce the franchise is granted to the electorate, lines may not be drawn which are inconsistent with the Equal Protection Clause of the Fourteenth Amendment'). It must be remembered that 'the right of suffrage can be denied by a debasement or dilution of the weight of a citizen's vote just as effectively as by wholly prohibiting the free exercise of the franchise.' *Reynolds v. Sims*, 377 U.S. 533, 555 (1964). There is no difference between the two sides of the present controversy on these basic propositions."

Indeed, the winner-take-all method of awarding electoral votes has been adopted and repealed by various states on numerous occasions. All three of the states that used the winner-take-all rule in the first presidential election in 1789 abandoned it by 1800. As recently as 1992, Nebraska replaced its winner-take-all statute with a congressional-district system of awarding electoral votes. Maine did so in 1969. After the 2008 presidential election (when Barack Obama won one electoral vote in Nebraska), the Nebraska legislature conducted hearings on the possibility of repealing the congressional-district system and returning to the statewide winner-take-all approach. Within the past decade, a Republican-controlled New York Senate and a Democratic-controlled North Carolina House and Senate passed bills switching to the congressional-district system (although none of these bills became law).

Massachusetts has changed its method of awarding its electoral votes on 11 different occasions.

- In 1789, Massachusetts had a two-step system in which the voters cast ballots indicating their preference for presidential elector, and the legislature chose from the top two vote-getters in each district.[8]
- In 1792, the voters were allowed to elect presidential electors in four multi-member regional districts.
- In 1796, the voters picked electors by congressional districts (with the legislature choosing the state's remaining two electors).
- In 1800, the legislature took back the power to pick all of the state's presidential electors (excluding the voters entirely).
- Later, the voters were allowed to elect presidential electors on a statewide basis using the winner-take-all method.
- Then, the legislature again decided to pick the electors itself.
- This was followed by election by the voters at the district level.
- Then, Massachusetts returned to state legislative choice.
- This was followed by the voters using districts.
- Then, Massachusetts adopted the present-day statewide winner-take-all rule.

---

[8] The state legislature alone chose the state's two senatorial electors.

- Finally, in 2010, Massachusetts made the 11th change to its method of appointing its presidential electors by enacting the National Popular Vote compact.

None of these 11 changes required an amendment to the U.S. Constitution. These changes were accomplished using the Constitution's built-in method for changing the method of electing the President—namely, section 1 of Article II. That constitutional provision gives Massachusetts (and all the other states) exclusive and plenary power to choose the manner of awarding their electoral votes.

In the nation's first presidential election in 1789, the New Jersey legislature passed a law empowering the Governor and his Council to appoint the state's presidential electors.[9] In 1804, the legislature permitted the people to vote for presidential electors by enacting a statewide winner-take-all statute.

Delaware has used three different methods. In 1789, it used a quasi-proportional "limited" vote system. Candidates for presidential elector ran statewide for the state's three available positions. However, each voter was limited to casting just one vote. Then, between 1792 and 1828, the Delaware legislature decided to exclude the voters and appointed all of the state's presidential electors itself. Starting in 1832, Delaware allowed each voter to cast three votes for the state's three presidential electors (i.e., the statewide winner-take-all method).

The North Carolina legislature has exercised its power to change the method of awarding the state's electoral votes on four occasions. In 1792, the legislature chose the presidential electors. The people then voted for electors from presidential-elector districts between 1796 and 1808. Then, the legislature chose the electors in 1812. In 1816, the legislature changed to the statewide winner-take-all method.[10]

In short, there is nothing in the U.S. Constitution that needs to be amended in order to repeal the existing winner-take-all statutes for awarding a state's electoral votes. Under the U.S. Constitution, the states already have the power to make this change. States are free to replace their winner-take-all statutes with a different system—in particular, a

---

[9] DenBoer, Gordon (editor). 1986. *The Documentary History of the First Federal Elections.* Madison, WI: The University of Wisconsin Press. Volume III. Page 29.

[10] Since 2000, both the North Carolina Senate and House have voted, in different years, to change from the statewide winner-take-all rule to a congressional-district system for awarding electoral votes.

system in which the states award their electoral votes to the candidate who receives the most popular votes in all 50 states and the District of Columbia.

For additional information, see section 1.1 and chapter 2.

10.1.2 MYTH: The "appropriate," "traditional," and "normal" way of changing the method of electing the President is by means of a federal constitutional amendment.

QUICK ANSWER:

- Nearly all the major reforms in the method of conducting U.S. presidential elections have been initiated at the state level—not by action at the federal level.
- State-level action is the historically precedented, "appropriate," "traditional," and "normal" way of changing the method of electing the President.
- None of the most politically important characteristics of our nation's current system of electing the President (namely, voting by the people for President, expecting presidential electors to support their political party's nominees faithfully, and the winner-take-all method) were established by a federal constitutional amendment.
- The winner-take-all method of awarding electoral votes was not established by a constitutional amendment. It may be repealed by any state in the same manner as it was originally adopted, namely by an ordinary state statute.
- State action is the right way to change the method of awarding electoral votes because this is the mechanism that is built into the U.S. Constitution for this specific purpose.

MORE DETAILED ANSWER:

The most significant change that has ever been made in the way the President of the United States is elected was to allow the people to vote for President. This change was not implemented by means of a federal constitutional amendment but, instead, by state statutes.

There is nothing in the U.S. Constitution that gives the people the right to vote for President or presidential electors.

As the U.S. Supreme Court stated in the 1892 case of *McPherson v. Blacker*:

"The constitution does not provide that the appointment of electors shall be by popular vote, nor that the electors shall be voted for upon a general ticket, nor that the majority of those who exercise the elective franchise can alone choose the electors. **It recognizes that the people act through their representatives in the legislature, and leaves it to the legislature exclusively to define the method of effecting the object."**[11] [Emphasis added]

As the U.S. Supreme Court wrote in 2000:

"The individual citizen has no federal constitutional right to vote for electors for the President of the United States unless and until the state legislature chooses a statewide election as the means to implement its power to appoint members of the Electoral College."[12] [Emphasis added]

In fact, the people were not permitted to vote for presidential electors in the nation's first presidential election in 1789 *in a majority of states*. In most states, the state legislature appointed the presidential electors. In New Jersey, the Governor and his 13-member Legislative Council (Privy Council) appointed the state's presidential electors.[13]

The Founding Fathers were divided on whether the people should be allowed to vote for President.

The *Federalist Papers* made it clear that the choice of method for appointing presidential electors is a state power, but skirted the question of exactly what choice the states would likely make.

Federalist No. 45 (presumably written by James Madison) says:

"Without the intervention of the State legislatures, the President of the United States cannot be elected at all. They must in all cases have a great share in his appointment, and will, perhaps, **in most cases, of themselves determine it."** [Emphasis added]

---

[11] *McPherson v. Blacker*. 146 U.S. 1 at 27. 1892.

[12] *Bush v. Gore*. 531 U.S. 98. 2000.

[13] DenBoer, Gordon; Brown, Lucy Trumbull; and Hagermann, Charles D. (editors). 1986. *The Documentary History of the First Federal Elections 1788–1790*. Madison, WI: University of Wisconsin Press. Volume III.

Federalist No. 44 (said to be written by James Madison) says:

> "The members and officers of the State governments ...
> will have an essential agency in giving effect to the federal
> Constitution. **The election of the President and Senate
> will depend, in all cases, on the legislatures of the sev-
> eral States.**" [Emphasis added]

In any event, section 1 of Article II gives the states flexibility in the manner of appointing their presidential electors, and in the nation's first presidential election, five states—New Hampshire, Pennsylvania, Maryland, Virginia, and Massachusetts—permitted the people to vote for presidential electors.[14]

In giving the people the right to vote for President, the states exercised their role, under the U.S. Constitution, as the "laboratories of democracy."[15]

With the passage of time, more and more states observed that permitting the people to vote for President did not produce disastrous consequences. In fact, popular elections became popular.

By 1824, three-quarters of the states had embraced the idea of permitting the people to vote for the state's presidential electors. The state-by-state process of empowering the people to vote for President was not completed until the 1880 election—almost a century after the Constitutional Convention.[16]

This fundamental change in the manner of electing the President was not accomplished by means of a federal constitutional amendment. It was instituted through state-by-state piecemeal changes in state laws.

Today, this feature of presidential elections is so widely regarded as a fixed feature of American politics that virtually no one even suggests that it might be done another way.

Permitting the people to vote for President was not an "end run"

---

[14] New Hampshire, Pennsylvania, and Maryland used the winner-take-all method, whereas Virginia and Massachusetts used districts to elect presidential electors.

[15] Justice Louis Brandeis wrote in the 1932 case of *New State Ice Co. v. Liebmann* (285 U.S. 262), "It is one of the happy incidents of the federal system that a single courageous state may, if its citizens choose, serve as a laboratory; and try novel social and economic experiments without risk to the rest of the country."

[16] The appointment of presidential electors by the legislature of the newly admitted state of Colorado in 1876 was the last occasion when presidential electors were not chosen by a direct vote of the people.

around the U.S. Constitution but, instead, an exercise of a power that the Founding Fathers explicitly assigned to state legislatures in the Constitution. We have not encountered a single person who argues that state legislatures did anything improper, inappropriate, or unconstitutional when they made this fundamental change in the way the President is elected.

When the U.S. Constitution came into effect in 1789, only wealthy white male property holders were entitled to vote in most states. At that time, there were only about 100,000 eligible voters in a nation of over 3,000,000 people. By 1800, three states permitted universal white male suffrage. By 1830, this number had increased to 10 (of the 24 states at the time).

Today, there are no property qualifications for voting in any state. The elimination of property qualifications was not accomplished by means of a federal constitutional amendment. The elimination of property qualifications for voting by the states was not improper, inappropriate, or unconstitutional. It was not an "end run" around the U.S. Constitution. This very substantial expansion of the electorate was an example of the use by state legislatures of a power that rightfully belongs to them.

In several instances, a major reform initiated at the state level led to a subsequent federal constitutional amendment after a particular reform had become established in a substantial number of states.

For example, women did not have the right to vote when the U.S. Constitution came into effect in 1789 (except in New Jersey, where that right was withdrawn in 1807). Wyoming gave women the right to vote in 1869. By the time the 19th Amendment was passed by Congress (50 years later), women already had the vote in 30 of the then-48 states. The main effect of the 19th Amendment was to impose women's suffrage on the minority of states (18) that had not already adopted it at the state level.[17]

The decision by 30 separate states to permit women to vote in the 50-year period between 1869 and 1919 was not an "end run" around the U.S. Constitution. We have not encountered a single person who argues that state legislatures did anything improper, inappropriate, or unconstitutional when they made this very substantial expansion of their

---

[17] The amendment also served to extend women's suffrage to all offices in those states where women only had the right to vote for certain specified offices (e.g., just President, just local offices). In addition, the constitutional amendment made it more difficult to ever reverse the granting of the vote to women.

electorates. Women's suffrage is another example of state legislatures collectively using the authority granted to them by the U.S. Constitution to institute a major change concerning the conduct of elections. Women's suffrage was achieved because 30 states exercised their power as the "laboratories of democracy" to change the manner of conducting their own elections.[18]

The direct election of U.S. Senators is another example of a major change initiated at the state level (and later enshrined in the Constitution by means of a constitutional amendment). The original U.S. Constitution was explicit in specifying that U.S. Senators were to be elected by state legislatures. There was enormous public support for the idea of electing Senators through a popular vote. Consequently, starting with the "Oregon Plan" in 1907, states passed laws establishing "advisory" elections for U.S. Senator. Under the Oregon plan, the people cast their votes for U.S. Senator in a statewide "advisory" election, and the state legislature then dutifully rubberstamped the people's choice by actually electing the winner of the "advisory" election. By the time the 17th Amendment passed the U.S. Senate in 1912, the voters were, for all practical purposes, electing U.S. Senators in a majority of the states.

States took the lead in granting suffrage to African Americans and 18-year-olds.

African Americans were given the right to vote in New York in the 1820s and in five states by the 1850s. Black suffrage was later extended to all states by the 15th Amendment (ratified in 1870).

Persons under the age of 21 first acquired the right to vote in various states (e.g., Georgia, Kentucky, Alaska, Hawaii, and New Hampshire). Later, the 26th Amendment extended this practice to all states in 1971.

In terms of electing the President, state control is precisely what the Founding Fathers intended, and it is precisely what the U.S. Constitution specifies. The Founding Fathers created an open-ended system with built-in flexibility concerning the manner of electing the President.

Indeed, the 12th Amendment (ratified in 1804) was the only time when a federal constitutional amendment was used to initiate a change

---

[18] One of the reasons that the 19th Amendment passed Congress in 1919 was that women already constituted half the electorate in 30 states and because the members of Congress from the remaining states knew that it was only a matter of time before women would obtain the right to vote in the remaining states—with or without a federal constitutional amendment.

in the manner of voting for the President. The original Constitution specified that each presidential elector would vote for two persons (with the candidate receiving the most votes becoming President and the second-place candidate becoming Vice President). The 12th Amendment changed that procedure and specified that each presidential elector would cast a separate vote for President and a separate vote for Vice President.[19]

In referring to the National Popular Vote plan, Professor Joseph Pika (author of *The Politics of the Presidency*) pointed out:

> "This effort would represent **amendment-free constitutional reform, the way that most other changes have been made in the selection process since 1804.**"[20]
> [Emphasis added]

It is worth noting that while the states have exclusive control over the awarding of electoral votes, the Constitution treats state power over congressional elections differently. Article I, section 4, clause 1 of the U.S. Constitution states:

> "The Times, Places and Manner of holding Elections for Senators and Representatives, shall be prescribed in each State by the Legislature thereof; **but the Congress may at any time by Law make or alter such Regulations**, except as to the Places of chusing Senators." [Emphasis added]

Thus, the U.S. Constitution gives *primary*—but not *exclusive*—con-

---

[19] The 12th Amendment acknowledged the reality of the emergence of political parties. When political parties emerged in the 1796 election, each party centrally nominated its candidate for President and Vice President (through the party's congressional caucus). Once there were national nominees, presidential electors were expected to vote for their party's nominee for President in the Electoral College. The emergence of political parties extinguished the vision of the Founding Fathers that the Electoral College would act as a deliberative body. In the 1800 presidential election, the winning party's electors each dutifully cast one vote for their party's presidential and vice-presidential nominees—thus creating a tie in the Electoral College and throwing the election of the President and Vice President into Congress. The 1800 election made it clear that ties in the Electoral College would be a continuing occurrence if political parties continued to exist. Thus, a constitutional amendment was necessary. See Ferling, John. 2004. *Adams vs. Jefferson: The Tumultuous Election of 1800.* Oxford: Oxford University Press. Also see Kuroda, Tadahisa. 1994. *The Origins of the Twelfth Amendment: The Electoral College in the Early Republic, 1787–1804.* Westport, CT: Greenwood Press.

[20] Pika, Joseph. Improving on a doubly indirect selection system. *Delaware On-Line.* September 16, 2008. http://www.delawareonline.com/apps/pbcs.dll/article?AID=/20080916/OPINION09/809160318/1004/OPINION.

trol over the manner of electing Congress to the states. In the case of congressional elections, the U.S. Constitution gave Congress the power to review and override state decisions. This override power has been used on only rare and minor occasions.

In contrast, state power to choose the manner of electing the President is "exclusive" and "plenary" (i.e., complete)—that is, Congress does not have the power to override a state's decision concerning the manner of awarding its electoral votes.

10.1.3 MYTH: The Electoral College would be abolished by the National Popular Vote compact.

QUICK ANSWER:

- The National Popular Vote compact would preserve the Electoral College. It would not abolish it. It would not affect the structure of the Electoral College contained in the U.S. Constitution.

- The National Popular Vote plan is based on the power of the states to choose the method of awarding their electoral votes. The compact would replace state winner-take-all statutes with a different state statute, namely one that guarantees the Presidency to the candidate who receives the most popular votes in all 50 states.

- Under the National Popular Vote plan, the states would retain their exclusive and plenary power to choose the method of awarding their electoral votes, including the option to make other changes in the future.

MORE DETAILED ANSWER:

The National Popular Vote bill is state legislation—not a federal constitutional amendment. As such, it would not (and could not) change the structure of the Electoral College as specified in the U.S. Constitution.

Instead, the National Popular Vote bill would accomplish its objective by changing the method by which the states award their electoral votes in the Electoral College.

The National Popular Vote bill uses the Constitution's built-in state-based method for changing the method of awarding electoral votes namely, section 1 of Article II of the U.S. Constitution:

"Each State shall appoint, in such Manner **as the Legislature thereof may direct**, a Number of Electors...."[21] [Emphasis added]

The "manner" of appointment of presidential electors is specified by clause 3 of article III of the National Popular Vote compact.

"The presidential elector certifying official of each member state shall certify the appointment in that official's own state of the elector slate nominated in that state in association with the national popular vote winner."

Because the compact takes effect only when enacted by states possessing a majority of the electoral votes (i.e., 270 of 538), the compact guarantees that presidential electors supporting the "national popular vote winner" will have enough votes to choose the President.

The National Popular Vote compact would not abolish the Electoral College. Instead, it would reform the Electoral College so that it would reflect the choice of the voters in all 50 states and the District of Columbia.

10.1.4 MYTH: The Founding Fathers designed and favored our nation's current system of electing the President.

QUICK ANSWER:

- The Founding Fathers never agreed on how presidential electors should be chosen but, instead, left the matter entirely to the states.
- Despite the Founding Fathers' expectations that the Electoral College would be a deliberative body, presidential electors became a rubberstamp for their political party's nominees at the time of the nation's first competitive presidential election in 1796.
- The Electoral College further deviated from the Founders' vision when state winner-take-all statutes became prevalent (decades after the 1787 Constitutional Convention).
- The winner-take-all method of awarding electoral votes was not debated (much less voted upon or adopted) at the 1787 Constitutional Convention.
- The winner-take-all method was not the choice of the

---

[21] U.S. Constitution. Article II, section 1, clause 2.

Founders and was, in fact, used by only three states in the nation's first presidential election in 1789.

- The electoral system that we have today was not designed, anticipated, or favored by the Founding Fathers but, instead, is the product of decades of evolutionary change precipitated by the emergence of political parties and the enactment by most states of winner-take-all statutes.

MORE DETAILED ANSWER:

The Founding Fathers did not design nor anticipate—much less favor— the most salient feature of our nation's present-day system of electing the President namely, state winner-take-all statutes (i.e., awarding all of a state's electoral votes to the presidential candidate who receives the most popular votes within each separate state).

The Founding Fathers never intended that all of a state's presidential electors would mindlessly vote, in lockstep, for the candidate nominated at an extra-constitutional meeting (the party's nominating meeting).

In the debates of the Constitutional Convention and in the *Federalist Papers*, there is no mention of the winner-take-all method of awarding electoral votes. When the Founding Fathers went back to their states in 1789 to organize the nation's first presidential election, only three state legislatures chose to employ the winner-take-all method. Each of the three states that used the winner-take-all method in 1789 repealed it by 1800.

Instead, the Founding Fathers envisioned an Electoral College composed of "wise men" who would act as a deliberative body and exercise independent and detached judgment as to the best person to serve as President.

As Alexander Hamilton (presumed author of *Federalist No. 64*) wrote:

> "As the **select assemblies** for choosing the President ... will in general be composed of **the most enlightened and respectable citizens**, there is reason to presume that their attention and their votes will be directed to those men only who have become the most distinguished by their abilities and virtues." [Emphasis added]

In this regard, the Electoral College was patterned after ecclesiastical and royal elections. For example, the College of Cardinals in the Roman

Catholic Church constitutes the world's oldest and longest-running Electoral College. Cardinals (with lifetime appointments) deliberate to choose the Pope. The Holy Roman Emperor was elected by a similar small and distinguished group of "electors." In many kingdoms in Europe, a small group of "electors" would, upon the death of the king, choose the person best suited to be king from a pool consisting of certain members of the royal family or nobility.

The Founding Fathers' expectations that the Electoral College would be a deliberative and contemplative body were dashed by the political realities of the nation's first competitive presidential election in 1796 and the emergence of political parties.

After George Washington declined to run for a third term in 1796, the congressional caucuses of the Federalist and anti-Federalist parties nominated candidates for President and Vice President.

As soon as there were national nominees designated by a central nominating body, each party immediately nominated candidates for presidential elector who made it known that they would serve as willing "rubberstamps" in the Electoral College for their party's nominee.

As the Supreme Court observed in its opinion in the 1892 case of *McPherson v. Blacker*:

> "Doubtless it was supposed that the electors would exercise a reasonable independence and fair judgment in the selection of the chief executive, but experience soon demonstrated that, **whether chosen by the legislatures or by popular suffrage on general ticket or in districts, they were so chosen simply to register the will of the appointing power** in respect of a particular candidate. In relation, then, to the independence of the electors, the original expectation may be said to have been frustrated."[22] [Emphasis added]

In 1796, there was no hint of independent judgment by any of the presidential electors from the nine states where the legislatures appointed presidential electors. All 66 presidential electors from these nine states voted, in lockstep, for Jefferson or Adams in accordance with "the will of the appointing power"—that is, the will of the legislative majority that appointed them in their respective states.

---

[22] *McPherson v. Blacker.* 146 U.S. 1 at 36. 1892.

Similarly, all but one of the 73 presidential electors chosen by the people voted, in lockstep, in accordance with "the will of the appointing power"—that is, the will of the people in each respective state or district.

Moreover, the unexpected vote cast by Samuel Miles (a Federalist presidential elector) for Thomas Jefferson (the Anti-Federalist candidate) was "the exception that proved the rule." The reaction to Miles's unexpected vote cemented the presumption that presidential electors should vote for their party's nominees.

As a Federalist supporter notably complained in the December 15, 1796, issue of *United States Gazette*:

> "What, do I chufe Samuel Miles to determine for me whether John Adams or Thomas Jefferfon is the fittest man to be President of the United States? No, I chufe him to act, not to think." [Emphasis added] [Spelling per original]

Of the 22,453 electoral votes cast for President in the nation's 56 presidential elections, only 11 votes were cast in an unexpected way. Moreover, among these 11 cases, the vote of Samuel Miles for Thomas Jefferson in 1796 remains the only instance when the elector may have thought, at the time he cast his vote, that it might possibly affect the national outcome.[23]

The expectation that presidential electors should faithfully support their party's nominees has persisted to this day.[24]

In short, the Electoral College that we have today was not designed, anticipated, or favored by the Founding Fathers but, instead, is the product of decades of evolutionary change precipitated by the emergence of political parties and the enactment by most states of winner-take-all statutes.

10.1.5 MYTH: The Founding Fathers considered our nation's current system of electing the President to be "excellent."

QUICK ANSWER:

- Alexander Hamilton's statement in *Federalist No. 68* saying

---

[23] All but one of the other 10 instances of faithless electors were grand-standing and publicity-seeking votes (that is, votes cast after the presidential elector knew that his vote would not affect the national outcome). One electoral vote (in 2004) was cast by accident. See section 2.12.

[24] In 2010, the National Conference of Commissioners on Uniform State Laws drafted a "Uniform Faithful Presidential Electors Act" and recommended it for enactment by all the states.

that the Electoral College is "excellent" is frequently quoted out-of-context in order to suggest that Hamilton would have favored our current system of electing the President. In fact, Hamilton's statement does not refer to our current system but, instead, to the never-achieved vision of the Founding Fathers for an elite "judicious" and "deliberative" Electoral College possessing "discernment."

MORE DETAILED ANSWER:

Tara Ross, an opponent of the National Popular Vote plan, has asserted:

> "[The National Popular Vote compact] … tears apart a well-established institution that was admired by the Founding generation and that has **served America successfully for centuries**. Alexander Hamilton described its reception by the Founding generation, noting that

>> 'the mode of appointment of the Chief Magistrate of the United States is almost the only part of the system…which has escaped without severe censure.… I venture somewhat further, and hesitate not to affirm that **if the manner of it be not perfect, it is at least excellent.**'" [Emphasis added]

Trent England, another opponent, says:

> "**An 'excellent' system** Alexander Hamilton wrote in *The Federalist* (No. 68) that, if the Electoral College is not perfect, 'it is at least excellent.' **The system probably works even better than the American Founders expected, considering the addition of 37 states … since Hamilton's original judgment.**"[25] [Emphasis added]

This out-of-context quotation about the excellence of the Electoral College does not refer to the way that the Electoral College has actually operated "for centuries" or how it operates today in a nation with 37 states in addition to the original 13. As is made clear a few sentences later in *Federalist No. 68*, Hamilton was referring to the Founding Fathers'

---

[25] England, Trent. Op-Ed: Bypass the Electoral College? *Christian Science Monitor.* August 12, 2010.

never-achieved vision of a "deliberative" Electoral College:

> [The] election should be made by **men most capable of analyzing the qualities** adapted to the station, and **acting under circumstances favorable to deliberation, and to a judicious combination** of all the reasons and inducements which were proper to govern their choice. **A small number of persons**, selected by their fellow-citizens from the general mass, will be most **likely to possess the information and discernment requisite to such complicated investigations**. [Emphasis added]

As discussed in greater detail in section 10.1.4, the Electoral College never operated in this "deliberative" fashion because the Founding Fathers did not anticipate the emergence of political parties (which occurred at the time of the nation's first competitive presidential election in 1796).

The political reality that presidential electors act as rubberstamps became firmly established in the nation's first competitive election in 1796. All but one presidential elector in 1796 cast his vote in support of his party's nominee. The one exception was Samuel Miles (a Federalist elector from Pennsylvania), who unexpectedly cast his vote in the Electoral College for Thomas Jefferson—instead of John Adams (the nominee of the Federalist Party).[26]

Of the 22,453 electoral votes cast for President in the nation's 56 presidential elections (between 1789 and 2008), only 11 were cast in an unexpected way.[27] Moreover, the unexpected vote of Samuel Miles in 1796 remains the only instance (among these 11 cases) when the elector might have thought, at the time he cast his unexpected vote, that his vote might possibly affect the national outcome.[28]

---

[26] A Federalist supporter famously complained in the December 15, 1796, issue of *United States Gazette* that Samuel Miles, a Federalist presidential elector, had voted for Thomas Jefferson, instead of John Adams, by saying, "What, do I chufe Samuel Miles to determine for me whether John Adams or Thomas Jefferfon is the fittest man to be President of the United States? No, I chufe him to act, not to think."

[27] See section 2.12.

[28] As discussed in greater detail in section 2.12, all but one of the other 10 instances of faithless electors are considered grand-standing votes. One electoral vote (in 2004) was cast by accident.

10.1.6 MYTH: The National Popular Vote plan should be rejected because it is opposite to what the Founders wanted, and only their "failure of imagination" prevented them from explicitly prohibiting it.

QUICK ANSWER:

- The Constitutional Convention voted against a number of different methods for selecting the President, including having state legislatures choose the President, having governors make the choice, and a national popular vote.
- However, the wording that actually ended up in the Constitution is unqualified and does not prohibit any of the methods that were previously debated.
- A majority of the states employed two of the specifically rejected methods in the nation's first presidential election in 1789 (namely, appointment by the legislature and appointment by the governor and his cabinet).

MORE DETAILED ANSWER:

In 1787, the delegates to the Constitutional Convention debated the method of electing the President on 22 separate days and held 30 votes on the matter.

Even when the delegates eventually decided—toward the end of the Constitutional Convention—that the President would be elected by presidential electors (collectively called the "Electoral College"), the Founders were unable to agree on the method for choosing the presidential electors.

Unable to agree on any particular method, the Founding Fathers adopted the language contained in section 1 of Article II—leaving the choice of method for selecting presidential electors exclusively to the states.

> "Each State shall appoint, in such Manner as **the Legislature thereof may direct**, a Number of Electors...."[29] [Emphasis added]

Section 1 of article II does not prohibit, require, encourage, or discourage the use of any particular method for awarding the state's elec-

---

[29] U.S. Constitution. Article II, section 1, clause 2.

toral votes. This wording is unqualified and permits the states to exercise their power to choose the manner of appointing their presidential electors in any way they see fit—subject only to the implicit limitation on all grants of power in the Constitution namely, that the states not violate any specific restriction on state action contained elsewhere in the Constitution.

Prior to arriving at the eventual wording of section 1 of Article II, the Constitutional Convention specifically voted against a number of different methods for selecting the President, including

- having state legislatures choose the President,
- having governors choose the President, and
- a direct national popular vote.[30]

After these (and other) methods were debated and rejected, the Constitutional Convention agreed to leave the entire matter exclusively to the states.

The constitutional provision that was eventually adopted does not prohibit any of the methods that were debated and rejected. Indeed, a majority of the states appointed their presidential electors using two of the rejected methods in the nation's first presidential election in 1789 (i.e., appointment by the legislature and appointment by the governor and his cabinet). Presidential electors were appointed by state legislatures for almost a century (1876 being the last such occasion).

The report of the Senate Committee on Privileges and Elections in 1876 reviewed the history of the appointment of presidential electors by state legislatures and governors:

> "The appointment of these electors is thus placed absolutely and wholly with the Legislatures of the several states. **They may be chosen by the Legislature**, or the Legislature may provide that they shall be elected by the people of the State at large, or in districts, as are members of Congress, which was the case formerly in many States, and **it is no doubt competent for the Legislature to authorize the governor, or the Supreme Court of the State, or any other agent of its will, to appoint these electors**."[31] [Emphasis added]

---

[30] Edwards, George C. III. 2004. *Why the Electoral College Is Bad for America*. New Haven, CT: Yale University Press.

[31] Senate Report 395. Forty-Third Congress.

Tara Ross describes the Founding Fathers in glowing terms throughout her book *Enlightened Democracy: The Case for the Electoral College.*

"The Electoral College is ... a **carefully considered and thought-out solution.**"[32] [Emphasis added]

Ross extols the "finely wrought procedures found in the Constitution" and reminds us that:

"The Founders spent months debating the appropriate presidential election process for the new American nation." [33]

Ross then writes:

"The [U.S. Supreme] Court has held that 'the State legislature's power to select the manner for appointing electors is plenary.' ...

"Is this power of state legislators completely unrestricted? If it is, then Rhode Island could decide to allocate its electors to the winner of the Vermont election. In a more extreme move, New York could allocate its electors to the United Nations. **Florida could decide that Fidel Castro always appoints its electors....**

"NPV is the opposite of what the Founders wanted, but **failure of imagination prevented the Founders from explicitly prohibiting this particular manner of allocating electors.**"[34] [Emphasis added]

A glance at the U.S. Constitution shows that the Founders displayed no shortage of "imagination" or legal talent in placing restrictions on the exercise of power in the Constitution when they thought restrictions were required.

Section 8 of Article I provides:

"The Congress shall have Power To lay and collect Taxes,

---

[32] Ross, Tara. 2004. *Enlightened Democracy: The Case for the Electoral College.* Los Angeles, CA: World Ahead Publishing Company.

[33] Ross, Tara. 2010. Federalism & Separation of Powers: Legal and Logistical Ramifications of the National Popular Vote Plan. *Engage.* Volume 11. Number 2. September 2010.

[34] Ross, Tara. 2010. Federalism & Separation of Powers: Legal and Logistical Ramifications of the National Popular Vote Plan. *Engage.* Volume 11. Number 2. September 2010.

Duties, Imposts and Excises ... **but all Duties, Imposts and Excises shall be uniform throughout the United States.**" [Emphasis added]

For example, section 10 of Article I provides:

"No State shall ... make any Thing **but gold and silver Coin a Tender in Payment of Debts.**" [Emphasis added]

The Founders even limited the scope of constitutional amendments in Article V:

"**No Amendment which may be made prior to the Year One thousand eight hundred and eight shall in any Manner affect the first**[35] **and fourth**[36] **Clauses** in the Ninth Section of the first Article; and that no State, without its Consent, shall be deprived of its equal Suffrage in the Senate." [Emphasis added]

There are numerous other restrictions placed on grants of power throughout in the Constitution.

Indeed, Section 1 of Article II itself contains a specific restriction on the power of the states to appoint their presidential electors:

"Each State shall appoint, in such Manner as the Legislature thereof may direct, a Number of Electors, equal to the whole Number of Senators and Representatives to which the State may be entitled in the Congress: **but no Senator or Representative, or Person holding an Office of Trust or Profit under the United States, shall be appointed an Elector.**" [Emphasis added]

Ross's argument that a "failure of imagination prevented the Founders from explicitly prohibiting" the Florida legislature from authorizing Fidel Castro to appoint Florida's presidential electors echoes the argument made in 1892 before the U.S. Supreme Court by the losing attorney in

---

[35] Clause 1 of section 9 of Article I states, "The Migration or Importation of such Persons as any of the States now existing shall think proper to admit, shall not be prohibited by the Congress prior to the Year one thousand eight hundred and eight, but a Tax or duty may be imposed on such Importation, not exceeding ten dollars for each Person."

[36] Clause 4 of section 9 of article I of the Constitution states, "No Capitation, or other direct, Tax shall be laid, unless in Proportion to the Census or Enumeration herein before directed to be taken."

McPherson v. Blacker. Referring to villainous Great Britain (no doubt, the 1890s analog of Castro), F.A. Baker argued:

> "The crown in England is hereditary, the succession being regulated by act of parliament.

> "Would it be competent for a State legislature to pass a similar act, and provide that A. B. and his heirs at law forever, or some one or more of them, should appoint the presidential electors of that State?"[37]

In their unanimous ruling in *McPherson v. Blacker*, the U.S. Supreme Court answered Baker's argument about unstated constitutional restrictions on the power of the states to award their electoral votes:

> "The constitution does not provide that the appointment of electors shall be by popular vote, nor that the electors shall be voted for upon a general ticket, nor that the majority of those who exercise the elective franchise can alone choose the electors. It recognizes that the people act through their representatives in the legislature, and **leaves it to the legislature exclusively to define the method** of effecting the object. The framers of the constitution employed words in their natural sense; and, where they are plain and clear, **resort to collateral aids to interpretation is unnecessary, and cannot be indulged in to narrow or enlarge the text**."[38] [Emphasis added]

The Court continued:

> "In short, the appointment and mode of appointment of electors belong **exclusively** to the states under the constitution of the United States"[39] [Emphasis added]

The losing attorney also urged the Court to adopt a "more elastic system of government." He argued that the widespread use of state winner-take-all statutes, over a period of time, extinguished the power of the states to change methods.

---

[37] *Brief of F.A. Baker for Plaintiffs in Error in McPherson v. Blacker.* 1892. Page 73.

[38] *McPherson v. Blacker.* 146 U.S. 1 at 27. 1892.

[39] *Id.* at 29.

402 | Chapter 10

> "There is no rule of constitutional interpretation, or
> of judicial duty, which requires the court ... to adhere
> to the obsolete design of the constitution, and to dis-
> regard the plan of the electoral college as it actually exists,
> after a century of practical experience and development."[40]

[Emphasis added]

In his appeal for judicial activism, Baker further complained about
the earlier loss at the Michigan Supreme Court:

> "There can be no such thing as an absolutely rigid constitu-
> tion. It is an impossibility, although the supreme court in
> Michigan in its wisdom most solemnly declares, that it will
> recognize no other."[41]

The U.S. Supreme Court answered attorney Baker in its ruling in
McPherson v. Blacker:

> "The question before us is not one of policy, but of power
> .... The prescription of the written law cannot be over-
> thrown because the states have laterally exercised, in
> a particular way, a power which they might have exer-
> cised in some other way."[42] [Emphasis added]

The 10th Amendment independently addresses the question of
whether the states are prohibited from exercising a particular power
when the Constitution contains no specific prohibition against it (and
the question of whether there are unstated additional restrictions on the
allowable methods for appointing presidential electors).

> "The powers not delegated to the United States by the
> Constitution, nor prohibited by it to the States, are
> reserved to the States respectively, or to the people."
> [Emphasis added]

Finally, if it were the case that the states were precluded from using
any method of awarding electoral votes that was not specifically "imagined" by the Founders, then the winner-take-all method would itself be
unconstitutional. No historian, or anyone else of whom we are aware,

---

[40] *Brief of F.A. Baker for Plaintiffs in Error in McPherson v. Blacker.* 1892. Page 80.

[41] *Id.* At 80.

[42] *McPherson v. Blacker.* 146 U.S. 1 at 36. 1892.

has ever argued that the Founders expected, or wanted, 100% of a state's presidential electors to vote slavishly, in lockstep, for the choice for President made by an extra-constitutional meeting (namely, a political party's national nominating meeting). The winner-take-all rule was never debated or voted upon by the 1787 Constitutional Convention. There is unanimous agreement among historians that the Founding Fathers intended and expected that the Electoral College would operate as a deliberative body.

10.1.7 MYTH: Respect for the Constitution demands that we go through the formal constitutional amendment process.

QUICK ANSWER:

- The Constitution contains a built-in provision for changing the method of awarding a state's electoral votes.
- One does not show respect for the Constitution by unnecessarily amending it.
- The method that is built into the Constitution should be attempted first. Amending the Constitution should be the last resort.
- One does not show respect for the Founding Fathers and the Constitution by ignoring the procedures that the Constitution provides. Section 1 of Article II specifically empowers the states to change the method of awarding their electoral votes.
- One does not show respect for the judgment of the Founding Fathers by passing a constitutional amendment that eliminates the states' existing power to make future changes in the method of electing the President.

MORE DETAILED ANSWER:

Tara Ross, an opponent of the National Popular Vote plan, has argued:

> "Even assuming that the Electoral College should be eliminated, respect for the Constitution demands that we go through the formal amendment process."[43]

---

[43] Ross, Tara. 2010. The Electoral College Takes Another Hit. September 22, 2010. http://www.nationalreview.com/corner/247368/electoral-college-takes-another-hit-tara-ross

The National Popular Vote bill does not eliminate the Electoral College. It replaces state winner-take-all statutes (enacted on a piecemeal basis by the states over a period of decades after the 1787 Constitutional Convention) with a system that guarantees the Presidency to the candidate who receives the most popular votes in all 50 states and the District of Columbia.

The Founding Fathers did not anticipate—much less favor—the current winner-take-all method of awarding electoral votes (as discussed in detail in section 10.1.4).

The winner-take-all method is not in the U.S. Constitution and was never ratified as a federal constitutional amendment.

The winner-take-all method may be modified or replaced in the same manner it was originally adopted namely, passage of state-level legislation under the authority of section 1 of Article II.

> "Each State shall appoint, in such Manner as **the Legislature thereof may direct**, a Number of Electors...."[44] [Emphasis added]

One does not show respect for the Founding Fathers by ignoring the specific method that they built into the U.S. Constitution for changing the method of electing the President—that is, state-level action under section 1 of Article II. The Founding Fathers gave the states exclusive and plenary control over the manner of awarding their electoral votes.

There is nothing in the Constitution that needs to be amended in order for states to switch from their current practice of awarding their electoral votes to the candidate who receives the most popular votes inside their individual states (the winner-take-all method) to a system in which they award their electoral votes to the candidate who receives the most popular votes in all 50 states and the District of Columbia (the National Popular Vote plan).

One does not show respect for the Constitution by unnecessarily amending it. Before contemplating a change in the U.S. Constitution, states should be given the chance to exercise the specific authority that the Founding Fathers gave to the states in the Constitution to change the electoral system.

The method that is built into the Constitution should be attempted

---

[44] U.S. Constitution. Article II, section 1, clause 2.

first. Amending the Constitution should be the last resort.

Moreover, one does not show respect for the judgment of the Founding Fathers by passing a constitutional amendment that removes the states' existing power to make changes in the method of electing the President.

10.1.8 MYTH: The most democratic approach for making a change in the manner of electing the President is a federal constitutional amendment.

QUICK ANSWER:

- A federal constitutional amendment favored by states representing 97% of the nation's population can be blocked by states representing only 3% of the population.

MORE DETAILED ANSWER:

In her book *Enlightened Democracy: The Case for the Electoral College*, Tara Ross characterizes a federal constitutional amendment as being a fairer and more democratic means for replacing state winner-take-all statutes with the National Popular Vote compact because it turns the question of how to elect the President over to "the people."

A federal constitutional amendment must be ratified by 38 of the 50 states. Thus, an amendment favored by states representing 97% of the nation's population can be blocked by states representing only 3% of the population (i.e., the 13 least populous states).

Of course, existing winner-take-all statutes were not put into place by means of a federal constitutional amendment.

10.1.9 MYTH: "Eleven colluding states" are trying to impose a national popular vote on the country.

QUICK ANSWER:

- The theoretical possibility that the 11 largest states (possessing a majority of the electoral votes) would get together to adopt the National Popular Vote compact is as unlikely as the possibility that these same 11 politically disparate states would be able to get together and choose the President in a presidential election under the current system.
- Based on the current mix of states that have enacted the National Popular Vote compact, it will take about 25 states to

reach the 270 electoral votes needed to activate the compact.

MORE DETAILED ANSWER:

Tara Ross, an opponent of the National Popular Vote plan, has criticized it on the grounds that "11 colluding states" could, if they acted in concert, impose a national popular vote on the country.

The 11 most populous states do, indeed, contain 56% of the U.S. population and a majority of the electoral votes. Theoretically, these 11 states could, under the current system, get together and impose their choice of President on the country in every presidential election. In reality, the 11 largest states have little in common with one another politically, and they rarely act in concert on any issue.

In the nation's most recent reasonably close presidential elections (2000 and 2004), five of the 11 largest states (Texas, Florida, Ohio, Georgia, and North Carolina) voted Republican, and six (California, New York, Illinois, Pennsylvania, Michigan, and New Jersey) voted Democratic.

The 11 largest states are no more likely to get together on enactment of the National Popular Vote compact than they are to get together on the choice of a President or the level of state sales taxes.

Tara Ross's hypothesized scenario of collusion among the nation's 11 largest states has already been demonstrated to be false by the actual history of adoption by the states of the National Popular Vote compact.

As of 2010, the National Popular Vote compact has been enacted by seven jurisdictions, including low-population, medium-population, and high-population states:

- Hawaii (a low-population state),
- District of Columbia (low-population),
- Maryland (an average-sized state),
- Massachusetts (an averaged sized state),
- Washington (an average-sized state),
- New Jersey (a fairly large state), and
- Illinois (a high-population state).

Using the 2010 census figures, these seven jurisdictions possess 74 electoral votes (that is, 27% of the 270 electoral votes needed to bring the compact into effect). An extrapolation from this 27% suggests that about 25 states (that is, half of the states) will be needed to reach the 270 electoral votes needed to bring the National Popular Vote compact into force.

That is, the projected number of states needed, in practice, is not 11 but 25. Such a group of states would essentially represent a majority of the American people.

Ross's argument concerning the 11 largest states is apparently premised on the incorrect belief that support for the National Popular Vote plan is limited to large states. However, the National Popular Vote plan has considerable support in less-populous states.

As of 2010, the National Popular Vote bill has been enacted by Hawaii and the District of Columbia and approved by a total of nine legislative chambers in low-population jurisdictions, including the Maine Senate, Delaware House, and both houses in Vermont and Rhode Island (as well as two chambers in Hawaii and one in the District of Columbia).

Public opinion polls show a high level of support for a nationwide popular election for President in low-population states such as

- Alaska (70%),
- Delaware (75%),
- District of Columbia (76%),
- Idaho (77%),
- Maine (77%),
- Montana (72%),
- New Hampshire (69%),
- Rhode Island (74%),
- South Dakota (75%),
- Vermont (75%), and
- Wyoming (69%).[45]

In fact, public support for a national popular vote runs slightly higher than the national average in most of the low-population states. The reason may be that low-population states are the most disadvantaged group of states under the current system (as discussed in section 10.4.1).

10.1.10 MYTH: A federal constitutional amendment is the superior way to change the system.

QUICK ANSWER:
- State action is the right way to change the method of awarding electoral votes because the U.S. Constitution provides a built-in mechanism for this specific purpose.

---

[45] These polls (and many others) are available on National Popular Vote's web site at http://www.nationalpopularvote.com/pages/polls.

- Under the National Popular Vote plan, states would retain their exclusive and plenary power to choose the method of awarding their electoral votes, including the option to make other changes in the future.

MORE DETAILED ANSWER:

State action offers several advantages over a federal constitutional amendment.

First, it is far easier to amend state legislation than to amend or repeal a constitutional amendment if some "unintended consequence" materializes or some adjustment becomes advisable.

Second, the National Popular Vote compact leaves untouched the states' existing power to control presidential elections. Most of the constitutional amendments concerning the Electoral College that have been introduced and debated in Congress over the years were written so as to take away state control over presidential elections and give it to Congress. The Founders were suspicious of a sitting President who might, in conjunction with a compliant legislative branch, try to manipulate the method of conducting presidential elections in a politically advantageous manner.[46] As a "check and balance" on the central government, the Founders dispersed the power to control presidential elections among the states, knowing that no single "faction" would simultaneously be in power in all the states. Section 1 of Article II is not a historical accident or mistake, but was intended as a "check and balance" on a sitting President who, with a compliant Congress, might be inclined to manipulate election rules to perpetuate himself in office.

Third, passing a constitutional amendment requires an enormous head of steam at the front-end of the process (i.e., getting a two-thirds vote in both houses of Congress). There have been only 17 amendments since passage of the Bill of Rights. The last time that Congress successfully launched a federal constitutional amendment (voting by 18-year-olds) was in 1971. In contrast, state action permits support to bubble up from the people through the state legislative process. The genius of the U.S. Constitution is that it provides a way for both the central government and state governments to initiate action. Thus, experience indicates that

---

[46] In October 2008, the Mayor of New York City, in conjunction with the City Council, amended the City's term-limits law to permit the Mayor to run for a third term.

building support locally is more likely to yield success.

Fourth, state action is the right way to make the change. The U.S. Constitution provides a built-in mechanism for changing the method of electing the President. Section 1 of article II permits the states to choose the manner of awarding their electoral votes. The right way to make a change is the way already contained in the Constitution.

Debates over the process to be employed to achieve a particular objective have frequently delayed achievement of that objective. The passage of women's suffrage, for example, was delayed by decades as a result of a long-running argument within the women's suffrage movement over whether to pursue changes at the state level versus a federal constitutional amendment. Women's suffrage was first adopted by individual states using the state's power, under the U.S. Constitution, to conduct elections. It was 50 years between the time when the first state permitted women to vote (Wyoming in 1869) and the passage of the 19th Amendment by Congress (1919). By the time Congress finally passed the 19th Amendment, women had already won the right to vote in 30 of the then-48 states.

10.1.11 MYTH: It is inappropriate for state legislatures to consider changing the method of electing the President.

QUICK ANSWER:

- The U.S. Constitution specifically gives state legislatures control over the awarding of electoral votes.

MORE DETAILED ANSWER:

The Founding Fathers specifically gave the state legislatures the exclusive power to choose the manner of awarding their state's electoral votes. Article II of the U.S. Constitution provides:

> "Each State shall appoint, in such Manner as the Legislature thereof may direct, a Number of Electors...."[47] [Emphasis added]

The Founding Fathers had good reason to give the states the power to control the conduct of presidential elections. They specifically wanted to thwart the possibility that a sitting President, in conjunction with a

---

[47] U.S. Constitution. Article II, section 1, clause 2.

possibly compliant Congress, could manipulate the manner of conducting presidential elections in a politically advantageous way.

For similar reasons, the U.S. Constitution gives the states the primary power over the manner of conducting congressional elections. [48]

Control over elections is a state power under the U.S. Constitution. For additional information, see section 1.1 and chapter 2.

10.1.12 MYTH: The National Popular Vote compact is unconstitutional because it would prevent a tie in the Electoral College and thereby deprive the U.S. House of Representatives of its rightful opportunity to choose the President.

QUICK ANSWER:

* Most historians do not subscribe to the view that the Founding Fathers expected the U.S. House of Representatives to routinely choose the President, and most Americans would oppose that practice.

* If it were unconstitutional for a statute to have the effect, in practice, of preventing a tie in the Electoral College (thereby depriving the U.S. House of Representatives of the opportunity to choose the President), then federal statutes establishing the size of the U.S. House of Representatives created a constitutionally impermissible structure for approximately half of American history.

MORE DETAILED ANSWER:

In a 2007 article in the *Akron Law Review*, Adam Schleifer stated:

"The Framers assumed that the election of the President would often require resort to the House of Representatives; in the absence of a stable two-party system, it did not seem inevitable that all presidential elections would result in a majority vote total for any single candidate. Under the [National Popular Vote] plan, there could never be a situation where the House selected the President, as the electoral vote is guaranteed to constitute a majority of the total as a precon-

---

[48] U.S. Constitution. Article I, section 4, clause 1. State power over congressional elections in Article I (unlike state power over presidential elections in Article II) is subject to oversight by Congress.

dition of enactment of [the National Popular Vote plan]." [49]

Tara Ross, an opponent of the National Popular Vote plan, has stated:

"NPV affects the balance of power between federal and state governments because the House's role in presidential elections will be effectively removed."[50] [Emphasis added]

It is true that the National Popular Vote compact would guarantee an absolute majority of the electoral votes to the presidential candidate who receives the most popular votes in all 50 states and the District of Columbia.

Of course, most people would consider the elimination of the possibility that the House of Representatives might elect the President as a highly desirable collateral benefit of the National Popular Vote plan.

Nonetheless, let us consider this argument in detail.

A candidate can fail to win an absolute majority in the Electoral College either because of a tie (which occurred in 1800) or because, as Alexander Hamilton (the presumed author of *Federalist No. 68*) noted:

"A majority of the votes might not always happen to centre in one man, and as it might be unsafe to permit less than a majority to be conclusive, it is provided that . . . the House of Representatives shall [elect the President]."

In the 1824 election, four candidates received substantial numbers of electoral votes (99, 84, 41, and 37) and, as a result, no presidential candidate received an absolute majority in the Electoral College.

In the context of present-day politics, there are numerous scenarios for a 269–269 tie in the Electoral College as described in an article entitled "16 Plausible Ways the Electoral College Could Tie in 2012" by Dan Amira.[51]

In the event that no candidate wins an absolute majority in the Electoral College, the U.S. Constitution provides for a "contingent election" in which the Congress chooses the President and Vice President.

[49] Schleifer, Adam. 2007. Interstate agreement for electoral reform. 40 *Akron Law Review* 717 at 739–40.

[50] Ross, Tara. 2010. Federalism & Separation of Powers: Legal and Logistical Ramifications of the National Popular Vote Plan. *Engage.* Volume 11. Number 2. September 2010.

[51] Amira, Dan. 2010. 16 Plausible ways the electoral college could tie in 2012. *New York.* December 23, 2010.

The procedures for the contingent election were specified in Article II of the original Constitution and restated in the 12th Amendment.

In the contingent election, the U.S. House of Representatives would choose the President (with each state having one vote), and the U.S. Senate would choose the Vice President (with each Senator having one vote).

The House must make its choice from among the three presidential candidates who received the most electoral votes. The Senate must make its choice from among the two vice-presidential candidates with the most electoral votes.

In a contingent election, if a state's delegation in the House is divided, the state loses its vote for President. Nonetheless, an absolute majority of the states (currently 26 of 50) is required for the House to elect a President. Given that many states have divided congressional delegations, it is entirely possible that no presidential candidate could win the required absolute majority of 26. If the House is unable to make a choice, the Vice President chosen by the Senate becomes the acting President. Because the Senate's choice is limited to choosing between the two vice-presidential candidates with the most electoral votes, the candidates who had just campaigned for President would be precluded from being chosen as the acting President.

The choice is made by the newly elected Congress. It is entirely possible that the House and Senate would be controlled by different political parties at the time of the contingent election.

Some have argued that the Founding Fathers did not intend or expect that the Electoral College would elect the President in most elections. Instead, it is suggested that the Founders anticipated that, after George Washington, no candidate would win a majority of the Electoral College, and the choice for President would routinely devolve on the U.S. House of Representatives. Under this interpretation of history, the Electoral College is cast as a body that ordinarily would only nominate a number of candidates for President, and the U.S. House of Representatives is viewed as the body that would ordinarily make the final decision.

Based on this interpretation of the Founders' intentions, it is then argued that the National Popular Vote compact is unconstitutional because, by effectively preventing a tie in the Electoral College and guaranteeing an absolute majority of the electoral votes to the candidate receiving the most popular votes in all 50 states and the District of Columbia, the compact would have the practical political effect of depriving the U.S. House of Representatives of its rightful opportunity to choose the President.

The number of votes in the Electoral College is the sum of the number of members of the U.S. House of Representatives and the U.S. Senate. The size of the U.S. Senate is twice the number of states (and, hence, always an even number). Thus, the size of the Electoral College is odd or even, depending whether the size of the House of Representatives is odd or even.

The original size of the U.S. House of Representatives was established in the U.S. Constitution for the nation's first election (at 65 members). Since the 1790 census, the size of the House has been set by federal statute. The statute has been changed on numerous occasions.

It is difficult to sustain the argument that preserving the opportunity for the U.S. House of Representatives to choose the President was ever a significant guiding factor (much less a constitutional mandate) in the choice of the size of the House. Since ratification of the 12th Amendment in 1804, the size of the House has been an even number in exactly half (26 of 52) of the years in which presidential elections were held.

The Solicitor General's brief to the U.S. Supreme Court in 2010 in the case of *John Tyler Clemons et al. v. United States Department of Commerce* traces the history of the various statutes that set the size of the U.S. House of Representatives. The plaintiff in that case argued that the present-day size of the U.S. House of Representatives is unconstitutionally small because it creates unconstitutionally large differences in the number of people represented by congressmen from different states.[52]

The Solicitor General's brief shows that Congress did not view protection of its own prerogative to elect the President and Vice President as a factor in setting the size of the House.

> "After each decennial census from 1790 to 1910, Congress reconsidered the number of Representatives, enacting new apportionment legislation 'within two years after the taking of the census.' H.R. Rep. No. 2010, 70th Cong., 2d Sess.

---

[52] The lower courts rejected the argument advanced by Clemons, and the U.S. Supreme Court declined to hear the case.

1 (1929) (1929 House Report). Until 1850, Congress first determined the number of persons that would be represented by each Representative, then divided that number into the population of each State, assigned the resulting number of Representatives (less any fractional remainder) to each State, **and summed those numbers to arrive at the overall size of the House of Representatives.** *See United States Dep't of Commerce v. Montana,* 503 U.S. 442, 449-451 (1992). Although Congress repeatedly increased the number of persons represented by each Member of the House, the size of the House continued to grow steadily, rising from 105 Members in 1790 to 243 Members by 1850." [Emphasis added]

If Congress thought that the opportunity to break a tie in the Electoral College was a constitutional imperative—or even a worthy secondary objective—it could have easily accommodated that factor when it periodically adjusted the size of the House.

If it were unconstitutional to enact an electoral arrangement (e.g., an odd number of electoral votes) that has the practical effect of depriving the U.S. House of Representatives of the opportunity to choose the President, then the House has been operating with a constitutionally impermissible structure for approximately half of U.S. history.

Of course, no statute is unconstitutional because it has the practical political effect of preventing a contingent procedure from coming into play. The contingent election procedure exists in order to resolve a deadlock should it become necessary to do so. The existence of a backup procedure does not create a constitutional mandate to ensure that the contingent procedure can be used.

If the U.S. House of Representatives was intended to be a routine part of the procedure for electing the President, the Founding Fathers could have easily structured the size of the House accordingly.

Moreover, if it were important to protect the opportunity of the U.S. House of Representatives to play a routine part in most presidential elections, the country had two convenient opportunities shortly after ratification of the original Constitution to increase the likelihood of House participation.

The first Congress in 1789 debated the issue of the size of the House of Representatives and approved a constitutional amendment on that topic.[53] That amendment (part of a package of 12 amendments that included the Bill of Rights) was never ratified by the states. That proposed amendment did not require that the size of the House (and hence the Electoral College) be an even number.

Second, the 1800 presidential election (which produced a tie in the Electoral College) led to a reexamination of the procedure of electing the President. Congress then approved, and the states then ratified, the 12th Amendment in time for the 1804 election. Congress could easily have included, in the amendment, a requirement that the size of the House of Representatives always be an even number.[54] [55] [56]

10.1.13 MYTH: The National Popular Vote bill is unconstitutional because it circumvents the Constitution's amendment procedures.

QUICK ANSWER:

- Observing that a statute was enacted without employing the Constitution's amendment procedure cannot serve as a substitute for a specific legal argument as to why the statute in question violates the Constitution.
- Observing that a statute was enacted without employing the Constitution's amendment procedure merely establishes that the legislative body believed that it had authority to enact that statute and that a constitutional amendment was not necessary.

MORE DETAILED ANSWER:

John Samples (an economist) argues that the National Popular Vote compact

> "circumvent[s] the Constitution's amendment procedures."[57]

---

[53] Res. 3, 1st Cong., 1st Sess., Art. I, 1 Stat. 97.

[54] Dunn, Susan. 2004. *Jefferson's Second Revolution: The Elections Crisis of 1800 and the Triumph of Republicanism.* Boston, MA: Houghton Mifflin.

[55] Ferling, John. 2004. *Adams vs. Jefferson: The Tumultuous Election of 1800.* Oxford, UK: Oxford University Press.

[56] Kuroda, Tadahisa. 1994. *The Origins of the Twelfth Amendment: The Electoral College in the Early Republic, 1787–1804.* Westport, CT: Greenwood Press.

[57] Samples, John. *A Critique of the National Popular Vote Plan for Electing the President.* Cato Institute Policy Analysis No. 622. October 13, 2008.

It is a truism that every statute enacted by Congress and the state legislatures circumvents the Constitution's amendment procedures.

If a piece of legislation is a valid exercise of powers granted by the Constitution, there is no reason for it to be enacted using the Constitution's amendment procedures.

If the piece of legislation is not a valid exercise of powers granted by the Constitution (that is, if it is unconstitutional), then everyone would agree that the Constitution's amendment procedure is the only way to achieve that particular objective.

Observing that a statute was enacted without employing the Constitution's amendment procedure cannot serve as a substitute for a specific legal argument as to why the statute violates the Constitution.

The fact that a legislative body decided to implement a particular policy by means of a statute is evidence that the legislative body believed that it had authority to enact that statute and that it believed that it is not necessary to implement the policy by means of a constitutional amendment.

The state legislatures that have enacted the National Popular Vote compact believed that section 1 of article II of the U.S. Constitution provided them with authority to act:

> "Each State shall appoint, in such Manner **as the Legislature thereof may direct**, a Number of Electors...."[58] [Emphasis added]

That belief is supported by the decision of the U.S. Supreme Court in the leading case on the awarding of electoral votes:

> "**The constitution does not provide that the appointment of electors** shall be by popular vote, nor that the electors **shall be voted for upon a general ticket [the winner-take-all rule]** nor that the majority of those who exercise the elective franchise can alone choose the electors. It recognizes that the people act through their representatives in the legislature, and **leaves it to the legislature exclusively to define the method** of effecting the object. The framers of the constitution employed words in their natural sense; and, where they are plain and clear, resort to collateral

---

[58] U.S. Constitution. Article II, section 1, clause 2.

aids to interpretation is unnecessary, and cannot be indulged in to narrow or enlarge the text....

"In short, **the appointment and mode of appointment of electors belong exclusively to the states** under the constitution of the United States."[59] [Emphasis added]

If Samples has a specific legal argument as to why state legislatures that enacted the National Popular Vote compact are violating the Constitution, he should step forward and articulate it. He has yet to do so.

10.1.14 MYTH: The National Popular Vote bill is unconstitutional.

QUICK ANSWER:

- A legal challenge to the National Popular Vote compact on constitutional grounds is unlikely to be successful, given the fact that constitutional law concerning interstate compacts is well settled and given the fact that the National Popular Vote compact is based on the U.S. Constitution's built-in procedure empowering the states to choose the manner in which they award their electoral votes.

MORE DETAILED ANSWER:

A legal challenge to the National Popular Vote compact on constitutional grounds is unlikely to be successful for a number of reasons.

First, the U.S. Supreme Court has repeatedly characterized the authority of the states over the manner of awarding their electoral votes as "plenary" and "exclusive."

Section 1 of Article II of the U.S. Constitution says:

"Each State shall appoint, in such Manner as **the Legislature thereof may direct**, a Number of Electors...."[60] [Emphasis added]

The wording "as the Legislature … may direct" in the Constitution is an unqualified grant of power to the states. This constitutional provision does not encourage, discourage, require, or prohibit the use of any particular method for awarding a state's electoral votes. States may

---

[59] *McPherson v. Blacker.* 146 U.S. 1 at 29. 1892.

[60] U.S. Constitution. Article II, section 1, clause 2.

exercise this grant of power in any way they see fit, provided only that they do not violate other specific restrictions contained elsewhere in the Constitution.

As the U.S. Supreme Court stated in the 1892 case of *McPherson v. Blacker*:

> "The constitution does not provide that the appointment of electors shall be by popular vote, nor that the electors shall be voted for upon a general ticket, nor that the majority of those who exercise the elective franchise can alone choose the electors. It recognizes that the people act through their representatives in the legislature, and **leaves it to the legislature exclusively to define the method** of effecting the object. **The framers of the constitution employed words in their natural sense; and, where they are plain and clear, resort to collateral aids to interpretation is unnecessary, and cannot be indulged in to narrow or enlarge the text.**"[61] [Emphasis added]

The Court continued:

> "In short, the appointment and mode of appointment of electors belong **exclusively** to the states under the constitution of the United States" [62] [Emphasis added]

In *Bush v. Gore* in 2000, the Court characterized article II, section 1, clause 2 as:

> "The source for the statement in *McPherson v. Blacker* ... that the State legislature's power to select the manner for appointing electors is **plenary**."[63] [Emphasis added]

Second, there are no restrictions in the U.S. Constitution as to the subject matter of interstate compacts—other than the implicit limitation that a compact's subject matter must be among the powers that the states are permitted to exercise. That implicit limitation does not apply to the subject matter of the National Popular Vote compact because the U.S. Supreme Court has ruled that states possess *exclusive* power to

---

[61] *McPherson v. Blacker.* 146 U.S. 1 at 27. 1892.

[62] *McPherson v. Blacker.* 146 U.S. 1 at 29. 1892.

[63] *Bush v. Gore.* 531 U.S. 98. 2000.

choose the method of awarding their electoral votes. In addition, the 10th Amendment independently addresses the question of whether the states are prohibited from exercising a particular power when the Constitution contains no specific prohibition against it.

> "**The powers** not delegated to the United States by the Constitution, **nor prohibited by it to the States, are reserved to the States** respectively, or to the people." [Emphasis added]

Third, we are not aware of any case in which the courts have invalidated any interstate compact.[64] Given the recent tendencies of the courts to accord even greater deference to states' rights and even wider and freer use of interstate compacts by the states, it is unlikely that the courts would invalidate the National Popular Vote compact. The National Popular Vote compact is an example of federalism in action and of states exercising their rightful powers.

Fourth, there is no argument that the winner-take-all method of awarding electoral votes is entitled to any special deference based on history or the historical meaning of the words in the U.S. Constitution. The winner-take-all method (i.e., awarding all of a state's electoral votes to the candidate who receives the most popular votes in a particular state) is not mentioned in the U.S. Constitution, the debates of the Constitutional Convention, or the *Federalist Papers*. The actions taken by the Founding Fathers in organizing the nation's first presidential election in 1789 (in particular, the fact that only three states used the winner-take-all method) make it clear that the Founding Fathers never gave their imprimatur to the winner-take-all method.

Fifth, there is no validity to the argument that the National Popular Vote compact is unconstitutional because it prevents creation of a tie (or lack of an absolute majority) in the Electoral College and thereby deprives the U.S. House of Representatives of the opportunity to choose the President. See section 10.1.12.

Sixth, virtually all of the possible "creative" legal arguments about possible limitations on the states' exercise of their exclusive and plenary power to award their electoral votes have already been considered, and

---

[64] There have been cases where a higher court corrected a ruling by a lower court invalidating an interstate compact. See, for example, *West Virginia ex rel. Dyer v. Sims*. 341 U.S. 22. 1950.

unanimously rejected, by the U.S. Supreme Court in the 1892 case of *McPherson v. Blacker.* These arguments include:

- **The Non-Use Argument** that the widespread use of the winner-take-all method over a period of years has extinguished the power of the states to modify state winner-take-all statutes;[65]

- **The Judicial Activism Argument** that the Constitution is "obsolete" and therefore should be considered "elastic;"[66] and

- **The "Lack of Imagination" Argument** that there are constitutionally unstated restrictions on the states as to how they appoint presidential electors "but failure of imagination prevented the Founders from explicitly prohibiting them."[67] If states were precluded from using any method of awarding electoral votes that was not specifically "imagined" by the Founders, then the winner-take-all rule itself would be unconstitutional. Indeed, no one would dispute that the Founding Fathers expected that the Electoral College would be a deliberative body. The Founders neither expected nor wanted 100% of a state's presidential electors to vote slavishly, in lockstep, in the Electoral College for the choice made by an extra-constitutional body (namely, the national nominating meeting of a political party).

The 10th Amendment independently provides a rule for constitutional interpretation concerning the question of whether there are unstated prohibitions on the states restricting their choice of methods for appointing presidential electors.

"**The powers** not delegated to the United States by the Constitution, **nor prohibited by it to the States, are reserved to the States** respectively, or to the people." [Emphasis added]

---

[65] *Brief of F.A. Baker for Plaintiffs in Error* in *McPherson v. Blacker.* 1892. Page 73.

[66] See section 10.6.1 for a detailed discussion.

[67] See section 10.6.1 for a detailed discussion.

10.2 MYTH THAT CANDIDATES REACH OUT TO ALL THE STATES UNDER THE CURRENT SYSTEM

10.2.1 MYTH: The current system ensures that presidential candidates reach out to all states.

QUICK ANSWER:

- Far from ensuring that presidential candidates reach out to all states, winner-take-all statutes regularly result in two-thirds of the states being ignored in the general election campaign for President.

- In the 2008 post-convention general election campaign, candidates concentrated over two-thirds of their campaign events and ad money in just six states, and 98% in just 15 states.

MORE DETAILED ANSWER:

Tara Ross, an opponent of the National Popular Vote plan, has asserted in testimony at various state legislative hearings:

> "[Under the current system] candidates can't win unless they build nationwide support."[68]

> "Ultimately, the Electoral College ensures that the political parties must reach out to all the states."[69]

Nothing could be further from the truth.

Current state winner-take-all statutes (i.e., awarding all of a state's electoral votes to the candidate who receives the most popular votes in each separate state) are the reason that two-thirds of the states and two-thirds of the voters in the United States are systematically ignored in the general election campaign for President.

Because of the winner-take-all rule, presidential candidates have no reason to visit, advertise in, organize in, poll in, or pay attention to the voters in states where they are safely ahead or hopelessly behind.

There is simply no benefit to a presidential candidate to ascertain and address the issues of concern to the voters of a particular state and then

---

[68] Written testimony submitted by Tara Ross to Delaware Senate in June 2010.

[69] Oral and written testimony presented by Tara Ross at Nevada Senate Committee on Legislative Operations and Elections on May 7, 2009.

spend time and money visiting, advertising in, and organizing in that state in order to win that state by 60% (as compared to, say, 55%). Similarly, it does not help a presidential candidate to lose the state with 45% of the vote (as compared to, say, 40%).

As an approximate general rule, a state needs to be in the 46%–54% range to be worth contesting in the general election campaign for President.[70]

Because of the harsh political reality dictated by state winner-take-all statutes, candidates concentrate their attention on a small handful of closely divided battleground states.

In 2004, the presidential candidates concentrated two-thirds of their campaign events and money in the post-convention general election campaign in just five states, 80% in just nine states, and 99% in just 16 states.

In the spring of 2008—even before the nominating process was completed—the major political parties acknowledged that there would be only about 14 battleground states in 2008.[71]

In the 2008 post-convention general election campaign, candidates concentrated over two-thirds of their campaign events and ad money in just six states, and 98% in just 15 states.[72] All of the campaign events occurred in just 19 states.

Because of the winner-take-all method of awarding electoral votes, candidates do not even bother to conduct public opinion polls in spectator states because issues of concern to voters in these states are simply not relevant to the goal of winning the White House. If candidates (and sitting Presidents contemplating reelection) are not even aware of what issues are of concern to voters in two-thirds of the states, they are making policy based on the desires of a few at the expense of the many.

As Charlie Cook reported in 2004:

> "Senior Bush campaign strategist Matthew Dowd pointed out yesterday that the Bush campaign hadn't taken a national poll in almost two years; instead, it has been polling 18 battleground states."[73]

---

[70] Virtually all of the states that are considered "battleground states" (e.g., the states in table 10.1 that receive campaign events and the states in table 10.2 that receive substantial amounts of advertising money) lie in this range.

[71] Already, Obama and McCain Map Fall Strategies. *New York Times*. May 11, 2008.

[72] http://fairvote.org/tracker/?page=27&pressmode=showspecific&showarticle=230.

As Former White House Press Secretary Ari Fleischer said in 2009:

"If people don't like it, they can move from a safe state to a swing state and see their president more."[74] [Emphasis added]

A mere four weeks after the November 2010 congressional elections, a televised debate on C-SPAN among candidates for the chairmanship of the Republican National Committee focused on the question of how the party would conduct the 2012 presidential campaign in the 14 states that were expected to matter.[75]

Table 10.1 shows the states in which the presidential and vice-presidential candidates held their 300 post-convention general election campaign events in 2008. The table is organized according to the size of the jurisdiction, starting with the least populous state (Wyoming) at the top.

Fourteen states received seven or more of the 300 post-convention general election campaign events in 2008.

- Ohio—62 events,
- Florida—46 events,
- Pennsylvania—40 events,
- Virginia—23 events,
- Missouri—21 events,
- Colorado—20 events,
- North Carolina—15 events,
- Nevada—12 events,
- New Hampshire—12 events,
- Michigan—10 events,[76]
- Indiana—9 events,
- New Mexico—8 events,
- Wisconsin—8 events, and
- Iowa—7 events.

---

[73] John Kerry's 2004 campaign similarly concentrated on a small handful of states in the general election campaign.

[74] *Washington Post.* June 21, 2009.

[75] Freedomworks debate on December 1, 2010, available at http://www.freedomworks.org/rnc.

[76] On October 2, 2010, the McCain campaign abruptly pulled out of Michigan after it concluded that McCain could not win Michigan. Thus, Michigan appears on this list even though it was a "jilted battleground" state.

TABLE 10.1 DISTRIBUTION OF POST-CONVENTION CAMPAIGN EVENTS IN THE 2008 PRESIDENTIAL ELECTION (SORTED BY STATE POPULATION)

RANK	STATE	ELECTORAL VOTES	CAMPAIGN EVENTS
51	Wyoming	3	
50	District of Columbia	3	1
49	Vermont	3	
48	North Dakota	3	
47	Alaska	3	
46	South Dakota	3	
45	Delaware	3	
44	Montana	3	
43	Rhode Island	4	
42	Hawaii	4	
41	New Hampshire	4	12
40	Maine	4	2
39	Idaho	4	
38	Nebraska	5	
37	West Virginia	5	1
36	New Mexico	5	8
35	Nevada	5	12
34	Utah	5	
33	Kansas	6	
32	Arkansas	6	
31	Mississippi	6	
30	Iowa	7	7
29	Connecticut	7	
28	Oklahoma	7	
27	Oregon	7	
26	Kentucky	8	
25	Louisiana	9	

These 14 closely divided battleground states accounted for 97.7% of the 300 post-convention campaign events in the 2008 general election campaign for President (that is, 293 of the 300 events).[77]

Half of the 300 post-convention campaign events (148 of 300) were in the states of Ohio (62 events), Florida (46 events), and Pennsylvania (40 events).

---

[77] The remaining six of the 300 post-convention events (representing 2% of the events) occurred in five additional places namely, Maine (2 events), Minnesota (2 events), the District of Columbia (1 event), Tennessee (1 event), and West Virginia (1 event).

TABLE 10.1 DISTRIBUTION OF POST-CONVENTION CAMPAIGN EVENTS IN THE 2008 PRESIDENTIAL ELECTION (SORTED BY STATE POPULATION) (cont.)

RANK	STATE	ELECTORAL VOTES	CAMPAIGN EVENTS
24	South Carolina	8	
23	Alabama	9	
22	**Colorado**	**9**	**20**
21	**Minnesota**	**10**	**2**
20	**Wisconsin**	**10**	**8**
19	Maryland	10	
18	**Missouri**	**11**	**21**
17	**Tennessee**	**11**	**1**
16	**Indiana**	**11**	**9**
15	Massachusetts	12	
14	Arizona	10	
13	Washington	11	
12	**Virginia**	**13**	**23**
11	New Jersey	15	
10	**North Carolina**	**15**	**15**
9	Georgia	15	
8	**Michigan**	**17**	**10**
7	**Ohio**	**20**	**62**
6	**Pennsylvania**	**21**	**40**
5	Illinois	21	
4	**Florida**	**27**	**46**
3	New York	31	
2	Texas	34	
1	California	55	
	Total	**538**	**300**

Ninety-eight percent of the 300 post-convention events were conducted in just 15 states. That is, under the current system, two-thirds of the states, and two-thirds of the people of the United States, are irrelevant spectators in presidential elections.

Campaign events were held in only six of the 26 least populous states (the first half of the table). These events were heavily concentrated in four closely divided battleground states, namely, New Hampshire (12 events), New Mexico (8), Nevada (12), and Iowa (7).

Overall, campaign events were held in only 12 of the 25 largest states (the second half of the table).

Despite the evidence of what happens in actual presidential campaigns, Tara Ross and other defenders of the current state-by-state winner-take-all system make statements such as:

"Ultimately, **the Electoral College ensures that the political parties must reach out to all the states.**"[78] [Emphasis added]

As one might expect, the money that presidential candidates spend in the various states closely parallels the distribution of campaign events.

Table 10.2 shows the states ranked in order of their total contributions (column 2) to the 2008 presidential campaign (using data from Federal Elections Commission records compiled by FairVote).[79] Column 3 shows the percentage of total national donations for each state. Column 4 shows the peak-season candidate advertising expenses (using data compiled by CNN) covering the period from September 24, 2008 (two days before the first debate) to Election Day. Column 5 shows the percentage of total national peak-season candidate advertising expenses for each state.

As the table shows, 32 states received a combined total of ¼% of the advertising money.

The table also shows that 99.75% of all advertising spending was in just 18 states. This allocation parallels the allocation of 100% of all 300 post-convention campaign visits to just 19 states.

The 18 net importers of campaign money received 99.75% of all advertising (while providing only 27.70% of all donations). The top six donating states (California, New York, Illinois, Texas, Virginia, and the District of Columbia) made 60% of the donations but received only 0.06% of the advertising. California, for example, contributed $151,127,483, but received a mere $28,288 in advertising.

State winner-take-all statutes are the reason why two-thirds of the states and two-thirds of the voters are ignored in presidential elections. Under the current winner-take-all system, a non-battleground state receives no attention from either political party because neither party has anything to gain or lose in the state.

The time that candidates spend in various states, as well as the amount of money that they spend, indicates the value that candidates place on the

---

[78] Oral and written testimony presented by Tara Ross at Nevada Senate Committee on Legislative Operations and Elections on May 7, 2009.

[79] http://www.fairvote.org/following-the-money-campaign-donations-and-spending-in-the-2008-presidential-race.

issues of concern to the voters of those states. Policy issues important to the battleground states are more important to a presidential campaign than policy issues important to any of the 35-or-so spectator states. When a sitting President is governing (and contemplating re-election or the election of his preferred successor), policy issues important to the battleground states are more important than policy issues important to spectator states.

Consider the reliably Republican state of Idaho as an example of a spectator state. Given George W. Bush's 68% margin of victory of 228,000 in 2004, no amount of campaigning will alter the fact that the Republican nominee for President is virtually certain to win Idaho's four electoral votes in the politically foreseeable future under the current system. Therefore, the Republican candidate for President has nothing to lose in Idaho by taking Idaho for granted. Similarly, the Democratic candidate has nothing to gain in Idaho and can simply write it off. The result of not being a closely divided battleground state is that issues of concern to Idaho voters are made irrelevant to *both* parties.

Under a national popular vote for President, every vote in Idaho would matter to both the Democratic and Republican nominee in every election. A vote in Idaho would become as valuable as a vote anywhere else in the country.

Under the National Popular Vote plan, it would be foolish for Republican nominees to take Idaho for granted, because they would want to expand their margin or, failing that, at least maintain their party's historically large margin. Similarly, it would be folly for Democratic nominees to write off Idaho, because they would want to decrease the magnitude of their loss or, at a minimum, avoid losing by an even larger margin. Idaho's reliably large Republican margin would no longer be "wasted," and the votes of Idaho Democrats would no longer be counted as if they had voted for the Republican candidate for President.

Note that Idaho is not ignored in presidential elections because it is a low-population state—it is ignored because it is not a closely divided battleground state. In 2008, the battleground state of New Hampshire (with the same four electoral votes as Idaho) received 12 of the 300 campaign events in the post-convention general election campaign.

Presidential candidates are not hostile or indifferent to low-population states. They simply do not waste their time (or money) with non-battle-ground states in the general election campaign—whether they are low-

428 | *Chapter 10*

TABLE 10.2 CAMPAIGN DONATIONS COMPARED TO ADVERTISING SPENDING, BY STATE, FOR 2008 ELECTION

STATE	TOTAL DONATIONS	PERCENTAGE OF NATIONAL DONATIONS	PEAK-SEASON ADVERTISING EXPENDITURES	PERCENTAGE OF NATIONAL PEAK-SEASON ADVERTISING EXPENDITURES
California	$151,127,483	17.76%	$28,288	0.02%
New York	$89,538,628	10.52%	$2,235	0%
Illinois	$50,900,675	5.98%	$53,896	0.03%
Texas	$46,327,287	5.44%	$4,641	0%
Virginia	$44,845,304	5.27%	$16,634,262	10.34%
D.C.	$44,275,246	5.20%	$0	0%
Florida	$41,770,516	4.91%	$29,249,985	18.18%
Massachusetts	$36,230,225	4.26%	$20	0%
Maryland	$28,723,600	3.37%	$0	0%
Washington	$24,666,430	2.90%	$5,062	0%
Pennsylvania	$23,929,821	2.81%	$24,903,675	0%
New Jersey	$22,756,469	2.67%	$0	15.48%
Colorado	$18,800,854	2.21%	$7,944,875	0%
Connecticut	$16,526,530	1.94%	$0	4.94%
Georgia	$16,507,714	1.94%	$177,805	0.11%
Ohio	$15,984,435	1.88%	$ 16,845,415	10.47%
Arizona	$15,334,618	1.80%	$75,042	0.05%
Michigan	$15,007,118	1.76%	$5,780,198	3.59%
North Carolina	$14,337,669	1.68%	$9,556,598	5.94%
Minnesota	$10,894,627	1.28%	$4,262,784	2.65%
Oregon	$10,155,182	1.19%	$2,754	0%
Missouri	$9,997,747	1.17%	$7,970,313	4.95%
Wisconsin	$8,133,046	0.96%	$8,936,200	5.56%
Tennessee	$7,934,886	0.93%	$9,955	0.01%
New Mexico	$6,418,313	0.75%	$3,134,146	1.95%
Indiana	$6,225,848	0.73%	$8,964,817	5.57%

population, medium-population, or high-population.

Idaho voters are ignored because the winner-take-all rule makes it pointless for either party's presidential candidates to pay any attention to the state.

The above observations about Idaho apply equally to the five other low-population states (i.e., those with three or four electoral votes) that regularly vote Republican in presidential elections namely, Alaska,

TABLE 10.2 CAMPAIGN DONATIONS COMPARED TO ADVERTISING SPENDING, BY STATE, FOR 2008 ELECTION (cont.)

STATE	TOTAL DONATIONS	PERCENTAGE OF NATIONAL DONATIONS	PEAK-SEASON ADVERTISING EXPENDITURES	PERCENTAGE OF NATIONAL PEAK-SEASON ADVERTISING EXPENDITURES
South Carolina	$5,744,471	0.67%	$910	0%
Nevada	$5,273,523	0.62%	$7,108,542	4.42%
Hawaii	$5,045,151	0.59%	$0	0%
Oklahoma	$4,359,169	0.51%	$4,170	0%
Kentucky	$4,338,611	0.51%	$635	0%
Alabama	$4,333,420	0.51%	$1,385	0%
Louisiana	$4,330,756	0.51%	$2,279	0%
New Hampshire	$4,045,877	0.48%	$2,924,839	1.82%
Iowa	$3,649,836	0.43%	$3,713,223	2.31%
Maine	$3,344,447	0.39%	$832,204	0.52%
Kansas	$3,333,235	0.39%	$3,141	0%
Utah	$3,287,184	0.39%	$66	0%
Vermont	$2,852,896	0.34%	$0	0%
Arkansas	$2,446,323	0.29%	$1,897	0%
Mississippi	$2,400,625	0.28%	$1,731	0%
Rhode Island	$2,343,926	0.28%	$0	0%
Montana	$1,882,200	0.22%	$971,040	0.60%
Nebraska	$1,867,197	0.22%	$807	0%
Delaware	$1,745,123	0.21%	$0	0%
Alaska	$1,611,031	0.19%	$310	0%
Idaho	$1,610,072	0.19%	$368	0%
Wyoming	$1,488,479	0.17%	$0	0%
West Virginia	$1,236,993	0.15%	$733,025	0.46%
South Dakota	$758,626	0.09%	$980	0%
North Dakota	$442,998	0.05%	$18,635	0.01%
Total	**$851,122,440**	**100.00%**	**$160,862,883**	**100.00%**

Montana, Wyoming, North Dakota, and South Dakota. Like Idaho, they receive no campaign events or money in presidential campaigns. The observations also apply to the six low-population states that regularly vote Democratic (Hawaii, Vermont, Maine, Rhode Island, Delaware, and the District of Columbia). Indeed, the above observations apply equally to two-thirds of the states.

10.2.2 MYTH: A national popular vote will simply make a different group of states irrelevant in presidential elections.

QUICK ANSWER:

- Candidates must solicit every potential voter in an election in which the winner is the candidate who receives the most popular votes. Every vote, regardless of location, would matter equally under a national popular vote.

- The best predictor of how campaigns would be run under a national popular vote is to look at how campaigns are currently conducted for offices where the winner is the candidate who receives the most votes. For example, in serious gubernatorial campaigns, the candidates campaign throughout the entire constituency.

- When it is suggested that a national popular vote will make a different group of states irrelevant in presidential elections, the obvious question is "Which two-thirds of the United States would a presidential candidate totally ignore in an election in which the winner is the candidate who receives the most popular votes?" Which 200,000,000 Americans would a presidential candidate totally ignore under a national popular vote?

MORE DETAILED ANSWER:

We do not have to speculate on how a campaign would be conducted in an election in which the winner is the candidate who receives the most popular votes, because there is ample evidence available to answer this question.

We know, from actual experience, that in serious campaigns for governor or U.S. Senator, candidates pay attention to their entire constituency. The reason is that every vote is equal in winning an election in which the winner is the candidate who receives the most popular votes.

Focus, for a moment, on a state's congressional districts (because congressional districts within a state contain approximately equal numbers of people). Serious candidates for governor do not limit their campaigns to just one-third of the state's congressional districts while totally ignoring two-thirds of the districts. Taking Missouri as a specific example, it would be inconceivable for a serious candidate for governor to campaign only in the 1st, 2nd, and 3rd congressional districts, while totally ignoring the 4th, 5th, 6th, 7th, 8th, and 9th districts.

Yet, two-thirds of the voters of the United States are ignored in every presidential election. In the 2008 post-convention general election campaign, candidates concentrated over two-thirds of their campaign events and ad money in just six states, and 98% in 15 states.[80]

When it is suggested that a national popular vote will make a different group of states irrelevant in presidential elections, the obvious question is "Which two-thirds of the United States would a presidential candidate totally ignore?" Under the National Popular Vote plan, the winner would be the candidate who receives the most popular votes in the entire country. Every vote would be equally important. Which 200,000,000 Americans (in a nation of 308,000,000 people) would a presidential candidate totally ignore?

10.3 MYTH THAT "WRONG WINNER" ELECTIONS ARE RARE

10.3.1 MYTH: "Wrong winner" elections are rare, and therefore not a problem.

QUICK ANSWER:

- Far from being rare, there have been four elections out of the nation's 56 presidential election in which a candidate has won the Presidency without winning the most popular votes nationwide—a failure rate of 1 in 14.
- The failure rate is 1 in 7 among non-landslide presidential elections (i.e., elections where the margin is less than 10%).
- The country has experienced a string of six consecutive non-landslide elections since 1988. Because we appear to be in an era of non-landslide presidential elections, additional "wrong winner" elections can be expected in the future.

MORE DETAILED ANSWER:

There have been four "wrong winner" elections out of the nation's 56 presidential elections—a failure rate of 1 in 14.

Moreover, about half of American presidential elections are popular-vote landslides (i.e., those in which the winner's margin is greater than

---

[80] http://fairvote.org/tracker/?page=27&pressmode=showspecific&showarticle=230.

10%). Of course, almost any counting system will produce the correct winner in a popular-vote landslide. Among the non-landslide elections, the failure rate for the current system is 1 in 7.

Although landslide presidential elections were common for much of the 20th century, the nation is currently in an era of consecutive non-landslide presidential elections (1988, 1992, 1996, 2000, 2004, and 2008). Therefore, it should not be surprising that we have already had one "wrong winner" election in this recent string of six non-landslide presidential elections. If the country continues to experience non-landslide presidential elections, we can expect additional "wrong winner" elections.

The precariousness of the current state-by-state winner-take-all system is further highlighted by the fact that a shift of a handful of votes in one or two states would have elected the second-place candidate in five of the 13 presidential elections since World War II.

For example, in 1976, Jimmy Carter led Gerald Ford by 1,682,970 votes nationwide; however, a shift of 3,687 votes in Hawaii and 5,559 votes in Ohio would have elected Ford.

In 2004, President George W. Bush was ahead by over 3,000,000 popular votes nationwide on election night; however, the outcome of the election remained in doubt until Wednesday morning because it was not clear which candidate was going to win Ohio's 20 electoral votes. In the end, Bush received 118,785 more popular votes than John Kerry in Ohio—thus winning all of Ohio's 20 electoral votes and ensuring his re-election. However, if 59,393 voters in Ohio had switched in 2004, Kerry would have become President (thereby nullifying Bush's lead of 3,000,000 popular votes nationwide).

10.4 MYTHS ABOUT THE LOW-POPULATION STATES AND RURAL STATES

10.4.1 MYTH: The low-population states would be disadvantaged by a national popular vote.

QUICK ANSWER:

- The low-population states are the most disadvantaged group of states under the current state-by-state winner-take-all method of awarding electoral votes. The reason is that political power in presidential elections comes from being a closely divided battleground state, and almost all low-population states are one-party states in presidential elections.

- The 12 least-populous non-battleground states have about the same population (12 million) as the closely divided battleground state of Pennsylvania. The 12 least-populous states have 40 electoral votes compared to Pennsylvania's 20 electoral votes. However, Pennsylvania received 40 post-convention campaign events in 2008, while the 12 least-populous non-battleground states received almost no attention.

- The least-populous states are not ignored because of their low population, but because they are not closely divided battleground states.

- Under the current winner-take-all method for awarding electoral votes, a vote for President in Wyoming is equal to a vote in California—both are politically worthless.

MORE DETAILED ANSWER:

Tara Ross, an opponent of the National Popular Vote plan, writes:

"NPV will lessen the need of presidential candidates to obtain the support of voters in rural areas and in small states."[81]

A brochure published in 2010 by the Evergreen Freedom Foundation of Olympia, Washington states:

"The seven smallest states (Alaska, Delaware, Montana, North Dakota, South Dakota, Vermont, and Wyoming) and the District of Columbia each have three electoral votes. **A national popular vote would render all low-population states almost permanently irrelevant in presidential political strategy.**"[82] [Emphasis added]

Ross has also stated:

"Minority political interests, particularly the **small states, are protected** [by the current system]."[83] [Emphasis added]

---

[81] Written testimony submitted by Tara Ross to Delaware Senate in June 2010.

[82] Evergreen Freedom Foundation. 2010. Brochure. Olympia, Washington.

[83] Oral and written testimony presented by Tara Ross at Nevada Senate Committee on Legislative Operations and Elections on May 7, 2009.

"Ultimately, **the Electoral College ensures that the political parties must reach out to all the states.**"[84] [Emphasis added]

Far from being "protected," the least-populous states are the most disadvantaged group of states under the current system of electing the President.

Although the least-populous states theoretically benefit from receiving two extra electoral votes (corresponding to their two U.S. Senators), this "bonus" does not, in practice, translate into political power. Political power in presidential elections comes from being a closely divided battleground state—not from the two-vote bonus conferred on all states in the Electoral College.

Under the winner-take-all rule (i.e., awarding all of a state's electoral votes to the candidate who receives the most popular votes in each separate state), candidates have no reason to visit, advertise in, organize in, poll in, or pay attention to the concerns of voters in states where they are comfortably ahead or hopelessly behind. Instead, candidates concentrate their attention on a small handful of closely divided battleground states.

This means that voters in the vast majority of the states are ignored in presidential elections. In 2004, candidates concentrated over two-thirds of their money and campaign visits in five states; over 80% in nine states; and over 99% of their money in 16 states. In 2008, candidates concentrated over two-thirds of their campaign events and ad money in just six states, and 98% in 15 states.[85]

The reason that the least-populous states are the most disadvantaged group of states under the current system is that almost all of them are reliably Democratic or Republican in presidential races. Presidential candidates have nothing to lose, and nothing to gain, by paying attention to the least-populous states. The least-populous states are not ignored because of their low population, but because they are not closely divided battleground states.

In the last six presidential elections (1988 through 2008), six of the 13 least-populous states (i.e., those with three or four electoral votes) have regularly gone Republican:

---

[84] *Id.*

[85] http://fairvote.org/tracker/?page=27&pressmode=showspecific&showarticle=230.

- Alaska,
- Idaho,
- Montana,
- North Dakota,
- South Dakota, and
- Wyoming.

Six others have regularly gone Democratic:
- Delaware,
- District of Columbia,
- Hawaii,
- Maine,
- Rhode Island, and
- Vermont.

The exceptions to this currently prevailing 6–6 split were minor and occurred years ago.[86]

New Hampshire has been the only closely divided battleground state among the 13 least-populous states in the last six presidential elections (1988 through 2008).[87]

The 12 least-populous non-battleground states (named above) have a combined population of 11.5 million. Coincidentally, Pennsylvania has almost the same number of people (12.6 million) as these 12 states. Because of the bonus of two electoral votes that every state receives, the 12 least-populous non-battleground states have 40 electoral votes, whereas Pennsylvania has only about half as many (20 after the 2010 census).

However, political power does not arise from the number of electoral votes that a state possesses, but, instead, from whether the state is a closely divided battleground state. There were 40 post-convention campaign events in 2008 in the closely divided battleground state of Pennsylvania,[88] whereas the 12 least-populous non-battleground states

---

[86] There were only four exceptions to this 6–6 split in the 48 statewide presidential elections conducted in these 12 states between 1988 and 2008. In 1992, Bill Clinton carried Montana (presumably due to Ross Perot's presence on the ballot). In 1988, George H.W. Bush carried Delaware, Maine, and Vermont. Since then, these states have become reliably Democratic in presidential elections.

[87] New Hampshire went Democratic in 1992 and 1996, Republican in 2000, and Democratic in 2004 and 2008.

[88] There were a total of 300 post-convention campaign events in the 2008 presidential campaign, as shown in table 10.1.

received only three (which were "exceptions that prove the rule").[89]

In short, the 12 least-populous non-battleground states receive almost no visits, advertising, polling, or policy consideration by presidential candidates because the outcomes in those states are foregone conclusions. In contrast, the winner-take-all method of awarding electoral votes makes the 12 million people in Pennsylvania the center of attention.

Note that the 12 least-populous non-battleground states are not ignored because they are sparsely populated. Indeed, presidential candidates pay considerable attention to the only closely divided low-population state. New Hampshire (with four electoral votes) received 12 of the 300 post-convention campaign general election campaign events in 2008. Note that we are talking here about the *post-convention* campaign—not New Hampshire's influential early presidential primary.

Meanwhile, the voters of the 12 other least-populous states were ignored because the political division of their voters was outside the 46%–54% range that determines (more or less) whether presidential candidates consider a state to be worth contesting.[90] The 12 least-populous non-battleground states were not ignored because they have low population, but because they are safely Democratic or Republican in the general election campaign.

A national popular vote would make a voter in each of the 12 least-populous non-battleground states as important as a voter in New Hampshire.

A national popular vote would make a vote cast in a low-population state as important as a vote cast in Pennsylvania. The National Popular Vote plan would make every vote important in every state and every presidential election. In short, a national popular vote would force candidates to pay attention to the issues important broadly to Americans, not

---

[89] The two campaign events in Maine in 2008 were the "exceptions that prove the rule." Maine awards two of its electoral votes by congressional district. The two events in Maine in 2008 were in the state's 2nd congressional district. That particular district was closely divided—that is, it was a "battleground district." When there is even one electoral vote to be won or lost, candidates pay attention. The presidential candidates ignored Maine's other congressional district because it was reliably Democratic. Therefore neither party had anything to gain or lose by paying any attention to it. The third campaign event in a low-population jurisdiction in 2008 was another "exception that proves the rule." This event occurred in the District of Columbia (which occasionally receives campaign events because it is convenient to the candidates).

[90] See table 1.2.

just to those in battleground states.

Of course, battleground status is fleeting. Prior to 1992, New Hampshire was not a closely divided battleground state in the general election for President. Although New Hampshire has received enormous attention for about half a century because of its early presidential primary, it received virtually no attention during general election campaigns, because it was reliably Republican. New Hampshire's demographics and politics started changing in the last two decades. Today, it is a closely divided battleground state in the general election campaign period.

In 2004, Missouri was ignored (although it was a hotly contested state in 2000 and 2008).

Battleground status is so fleeting that a state can be jilted in the midst of a campaign. On October 2, 2008, the McCain campaign decided it could not win Michigan and abruptly pulled out of the state.

Ohio was ignored ("dark" in the parlance of presidential campaign consultants) as recently as the 2000 election. Al Gore and George W. Bush stopped campaigning there early in the post-convention campaign.

Most of the states with five or six electoral votes are similarly non-competitive in presidential elections (and therefore disadvantaged in the same way as almost all of the 13 least-populous states).

In fact, only four of the 25 least-populous states have been battleground states in recent elections namely:

- New Hampshire (4 electoral votes),
- New Mexico (5 electoral votes),
- Nevada (5 electoral votes), and
- Iowa (7 electoral votes).

The fact that the low-population states are disadvantaged by the current system has long been recognized by prominent officials from those states.

In a 1979 Senate speech, Senator Henry Bellmon (R–Oklahoma) described how his views on the Electoral College had changed as a result of serving as national campaign director for Richard Nixon and a member of the American Bar Association's commission studying electoral reform.

"While the consideration of the electoral college began—and I am a little embarrassed to admit this—I was convinced, as are many residents of smaller States, that the present system is a considerable advantage to less-populous States such as Oklahoma. ... As the deliberations of the American Bar Association Commission proceeded and as more facts became known, **I came to the realization that the present electoral system does not give an advantage to the voters from the less-populous States. Rather, it works to the disadvantage of small State voters who are largely ignored in the general election for President.**"[91] [Emphasis added]

Senator Robert E. Dole of Kansas, the Republican nominee for President in 1996 and Republican nominee for Vice President in 1976, stated in a 1979 floor speech:

"Many persons have the impression that the electoral college benefits those persons living in small states. I feel that this is somewhat of a misconception. Through my experience with the Republican National Committee and as a Vice Presidential candidate in 1976, it became very clear that the populous states with their large blocks of electoral votes were the crucial states. It was in these states that we focused our efforts.

"Were we to switch to a system of direct election, I think we would see a resulting change in the nature of campaigning. While urban areas will still be important campaigning centers, there will be a new emphasis given to smaller states. **Candidates will soon realize that all votes are important, and votes from small states carry the same import as votes from large states. That to me is one of the major attractions of direct election. Each vote carries equal importance**.

"Direct election would give candidates incentive to campaign in States that are perceived to be single party states."[92] [Emphasis added]

Because so few of the least-populous states are, or have ever been, closely divided battleground states in presidential elections, the current

---

[91] *Congressional Record*. July 10, 1979. Page 17748.

[92] *Congressional Record*. January 14, 1979. Page 309.

state-by-state winner-take-all system actually shifts power from voters in the low-population and medium-population states to voters in the hand-ful of high-population states that happen to be battleground states in a particular presidential election.

In 1966, the state of Delaware led a group of 12 predominantly low-population states (including North Dakota, South Dakota, Wyoming, Utah, Arkansas, Kansas, Oklahoma, Iowa, Kentucky, Florida, and Pennsylvania) in suing New York in the U.S. Supreme Court.[93]

David P. Buckson (Republican Attorney General of Delaware at the time) led the effort. Delaware's brief argued:

> "The state unit-vote system [the 'winner-take-all' rule] **debases the national voting rights and political status of Plaintiff's citizens and those of other small states** by discriminating against them in favor of citizens of the larger states. A citizen of a small state is in a position to influence fewer electoral votes than a citizen of a larger state, and therefore his popular vote is less sought after by major candidates. **He receives less attention in campaign efforts and in consideration of his interests.**" [Emphasis added]

In their brief, Delaware and the other plaintiffs stated:

> "This is an original action by the State of Delaware as *parens patriae* for its citizens, against the State of New York, all other states, and the District of Columbia under authority of Article III, Section 2 of the United States Constitution and 28 U.S. Code sec. 1251. The suit challenges the constitutionality of the respective state statutes employing the 'general ticket' or 'state unit-vote' system, by which the total number of presidential electoral votes of a state is arbitrarily misappropriated for the candidate receiving a bare plurality of the total number of citizens' votes cast within the state.

> "The Complaint alleges that, although the states, pursuant to Article II, Section 1, Par. 2 of the Constitution, have some discretion as to the manner of appointment of presidential

---

[93] In the 1960s, New York was a battleground state and also the state with the most electoral votes (43).

electors, they are nevertheless bound by constitutional limitations of due process and equal protections of the laws and
by the intention of the Constitution that all states' electors
would have equal weight. Further, general use of the state
unit system by the states is a collective unconstitutional
abridgment of all citizens' reserved political rights to associate meaningfully across state lines in national elections."[94]

The plaintiff's brief argued that the votes of the citizens of Delaware
and the other plaintiff states are

"diluted, debased, and misappropriated through the state unit
system."

The U.S. Supreme Court declined to hear the case (presumably
because of the well-established constitutional provision that the manner
of awarding electoral votes is exclusively a state decision). Ironically,
the defendant (New York) is no longer an influential closely divided
battleground state (as it was in the 1960s). Today, New York suffers the
very same disadvantage as the plaintiff states because it, too, has become
politically non-competitive in presidential elections. Today, a vote in New
York in a presidential election is equal to a vote in Delaware—both are
equally worthless.

The Electoral College is not the bulwark of influence for the less-
populous states in the U.S. Constitution. The bulwark of influence for
the less-populous states is the equal representation of the states in the
U.S. Senate. The 13 least-populous states (with 3% of the nation's population) have 25% of the votes in the U.S. Senate—a very significant source
of political clout. However, the 13 least-populous states (i.e., those with
three or four electoral votes) have only 26 extra votes in the Electoral
College by virtue of the two-vote bonus—not a large number in relation
to the overall total of 538 electoral votes. Although the 13 least-populous
states cast 3% of the nation's popular vote while possessing 6% of the
electoral votes, the extra 3% is a minor numerical factor in the context
of a presidential election. More importantly, this small theoretical advantage is negated by the fact that the least-populous states are equally divid-

---

[94] Information about *State of Delaware v. State of New York* (and links to Delaware's brief,
New York's brief, and Delaware's request for a re-hearing) may be found at http://www.
nationalpopularvote.com/pages/misc/de_lawsuit.php.

ed between the two major political parties and because the one-party character of 12 of the 13 least-populous states makes them irrelevant in presidential elections.

The states that are important in the presidential election can usually be identified very early in each election cycle—even before the party nominations are settled. In the spring of 2008, both major political parties acknowledged that there would be 14 battleground states (involving only 166 of the nation's 538 electoral votes) in the 2008 presidential election.[95] In other words, two-thirds of the states were regarded as irrelevant even before the national nominating conventions were held. New Hampshire (with 4 electoral votes) was the only less-populous state that was identified as being in this group of battleground states. The net result is that the current system shifts power from voters in the low-population states to voters in a handful of closely divided battleground states (almost all of which are more populous states).

A mere four weeks after the November 2010 congressional elections, a debate was televised on C-SPAN among candidates for chair of the Republican National Committee. The debate touched on the question of how the party would conduct the presidential campaign in the 14 states that were expected to matter in 2012.[96] Thus, two years before the 2012 presidential election, 36 states have been written off.

Tara Ross claims that

> "NPV will lessen the need of presidential candidates to obtain the support of voters in rural areas and in small states." [97]

The political reality is that the National Popular Vote plan cannot possibly "lessen the need" of candidates to win the support of low-population states because candidates have no need whatsoever to solicit support of the low-population states under the current system. In fact, it is the current state-by-state winner-take-all system that renders these states "almost permanently irrelevant in presidential political strategy."[98]

A national popular vote is the *only* way to give voters in the nation's less-populous states a voice in presidential elections. Under a national

[95] Already, Obama and McCain Map Fall Strategies. *New York Times*. May 11, 2008.

[96] Freedomworks debate on December 1, 2010, available at http://www.freedomworks.org/rnc.

[97] Written testimony submitted by Tara Ross to Delaware Senate in June 2010.

[98] Evergreen Freedom Foundation. 2010. Brochure. Olympia, Washington.

popular vote, a voter in a reliably one-party low-population state would be as important as a voter anywhere else in the country.

10.4.2 MYTH: The low-population states are so small that they will not attract any attention under any system.

QUICK ANSWER:

* Under a national popular vote, a voter in a low-population state would become as important as any other voter in the United States.
* The 13 least-populous states together have approximately the same population as Pennsylvania, and no one would suggest that Pennsylvania's 12 million people would be ignored in a national popular vote for President.
* The low-population states are not currently ignored because of their low population, but because they are not closely divided battleground states. The battleground state of New Hampshire received 12 campaign events in the post-convention general election campaign in 2008, while 10 other low-population non-battleground states received none.
* Serious candidates for office solicit every vote *that matters*. Every vote in every state will matter in every presidential election under the National Popular Vote plan.
* In most cases, low-population states offer presidential candidates the attraction of considerably lower per-impression media costs.

MORE DETAILED ANSWER:

Some argue that the least-populous states have so few people that they will not attract any attention from presidential candidates under any system. However, the fact is that serious candidates for office solicit every vote *that matters*.

This fact is demonstrated by the 2nd congressional district of Nebraska (the Omaha area). Even though this district contains less than 1/5% of the country's 538 electoral votes, the Obama campaign in 2008 operated three separate campaign offices staffed by 16 people there. The reason was that Nebraska is one of two states that awards electoral votes by congressional district. Both political parties spent a considerable amount of money and effort trying to win the 2nd district. Sarah Palin, the Republican vice-presidential candidate, visited the district during the post-convention general election campaign. Both parties paid attention to the 2nd district because it was a closely divided battleground district where one electoral vote was at stake. The outcome was that Barack Obama carried the 2nd district by 3,378 votes and won one electoral vote in Nebraska.

One Nebraska state senator whose district lies partially in the 2nd congressional district reported a heavy concentration of lawn signs, mailers, precinct walking, telephone calls to voters, and other campaign activity related to the presidential race in the portion of his state senate district that was inside the 2nd congressional district, but no such activity in the remainder of his state senate district. Indeed, the Obama and McCain presidential campaigns did not pay the slightest attention to the people of Nebraska's reliably Republican 1st and 3rd congressional districts, because it was a foregone conclusion that McCain would win the most popular votes in both of those districts. The issues relevant to voters of the 2nd district (the Omaha area) mattered, while the (very different) issues relevant to the remaining (mostly rural) two-thirds of the state were irrelevant.

Similarly, in Maine (which also awards electoral votes by congressional district), the closely divided 2nd congressional district received campaign events in 2008 (whereas Maine's reliably Democratic 1st district was ignored).

When votes matter, presidential candidates vigorously solicit those voters. When votes don't matter, they ignore those areas.

Table 10.3 addresses the argument that less-populous states are too small to attract the attention of presidential candidates. For the 13 least-populous states (i.e., those with three or four electoral votes), the table shows the distribution of presidential and vice-presidential campaign events during the post-convention general election campaign for 2008.

The table shows that the determinant of whether a state receives attention is whether it is a closely divided battleground area. Because it was a closely divided battleground state, New Hampshire received 12 post-convention general election campaign events (out of a total of 300). Because Maine awards electoral votes by congressional district, and its 2nd congressional district is a closely divided district, Maine received two post-convention campaign events in that district. Aside from one campaign event in the District of Columbia, all of the other least-populous states received no attention whatsoever. Wyoming, Vermont, North Dakota, Alaska, South Dakota, Delaware, Montana, Rhode Island, Hawaii, and Idaho were all ignored not because they were low-population states, but because presidential candidates had nothing to gain or lose by paying any attention to them because of the state-by-state winner-take-all system.

TABLE 10.3 DISTRIBUTION OF CAMPAIGN EVENTS IN THE 2008 PRESIDENTIAL ELECTION IN THE 13 LEAST-POPULOUS STATES

STATE	CAMPAIGN EVENTS
Wyoming	—
District of Columbia	1
Vermont	—
North Dakota	—
Alaska	—
South Dakota	—
Delaware	—
Montana	—
Rhode Island	—
Hawaii	—
New Hampshire	**12**
Maine	2
Idaho	—

In many cases, low-population states offer presidential candidates the attraction of considerably lower per-impression media costs.

Although no one can predict exactly how a presidential campaign would be run under the National Popular Vote plan, we do know how candidates conduct campaigns when running for other offices in elections in which the winner is the candidate who receives the most popular votes in the entire jurisdiction. In campaigns for governor, U.S. Senator, mayor, and state legislator, candidates pay attention to their entire constituency.

It would be inconceivable for a serious candidate for governor to ignore two-thirds of the voters in the state.

Similarly, it would be inconceivable, under a national popular vote for President, that a serious presidential campaign would allocate 12 of their 15 campaign events in the low-population states to just three of these states, while ignoring the other 10.

Any candidate ignoring a state would suffer a political penalty there. Most likely, the 15 campaign events that presidential candidates spent in 2008 (mostly in New Hampshire) would be reallocated among the 13 least-populous states, with each state receiving, more or less, one event each. The 13 least-populous states have approximately the same population as Pennsylvania (about 12 million people). No one would suggest that Pennsylvania's people would be ignored in a national popular vote for President. Therefore, there is no reason to expect that the 12 million people in the 13 least-populous states would be ignored.

10.4.3 MYTH: The least-populous states are opposed to a national popular vote for President.

QUICK ANSWER:

- The National Popular Vote bill has been enacted by Hawaii and the District of Columbia. As of 2010, the bill has been approved by a total of nine legislative chambers in the 13 least-populous states.
- In a 1966 lawsuit, the state of Delaware and a group of 12 predominantly low-population states argued that the winner-take-all rule "debases the national voting rights and political status of Plaintiff's citizens and those of other small states."
- Public support for a national popular vote runs slightly higher than the national average in most of the least-populous states.

MORE DETAILED ANSWER:

The facts speak for themselves. As of 2010, the National Popular Vote bill has been approved by a total of nine legislative chambers in low-population states, including the Maine Senate, Delaware House, and both houses in Vermont and Rhode Island (as well as two chambers in Hawaii and one in the District of Columbia).

The concept of a national popular vote for President is far from politically "radioactive" in the less-populous states. In fact, public opinion polls show a high level of support for a nationwide election for President in:

- Alaska (70%),
- Delaware (75%),

- District of Columbia (76%),
- Idaho (77%),
- Maine (77%),
- Montana (72%),
- New Hampshire (69%),
- Rhode Island (74%),
- South Dakota (75%),
- Vermont (75%), and
- Wyoming (69%).[99]

In fact, public support for a national popular vote runs slightly higher than the national average in most of the low-population states. *The Washington Post*, Kaiser Family Foundation, and Harvard University poll in 2007 showed 72% support for direct nationwide election of the President. The reason may be that less-populous states are the most disadvantaged group of states under the current system (as discussed in section 10.2).

As discussed in greater detail in section 10.4.1, the state of Delaware and a group of 12 predominantly low-population states argued in a 1966 lawsuit before the U.S. Supreme Court that the winner-take-all rule

> "debases the national voting rights and political status of Plaintiff's citizens and those of other small states."

10.4.4 MYTH: Equal representation of the states in the U.S. Senate is threatened by the National Popular Vote plan.

QUICK ANSWER:

- The equal representation of the states in the U.S. Senate is explicitly established and protected in the U.S. Constitution and cannot be affected by passage of any state statute.
- The National Popular Vote plan does not affect the equal representation of the states in the U.S. Senate.

MORE DETAILED ANSWER:

Equal representation of the states in the U.S. Senate is explicitly established in the U.S. Constitution. This feature cannot be changed by state law or an interstate compact.

---

[99] These polls (and many others) are available on National Popular Vote's web site at http://www.nationalpopularvote.com/pages/polls.

In fact, equal representation of the states in the U.S. Senate may not even be amended by an ordinary federal constitutional amendment. Article V of the U.S. Constitution provides:

> "No State, without its Consent, shall be deprived of its equal Suffrage in the Senate."

Thus, this feature of the U.S. Constitution may only be changed by a constitutional amendment approved by unanimous consent of all 50 states.

In contrast, the U.S. Constitution explicitly assigns the power of selecting the manner of appointing presidential electors to the states. The enactment by a state legislature of the National Popular Vote bill is an exercise of a legislature's existing powers under the U.S. Constitution.

In short, enactment of the National Popular Vote compact has no bearing on the federal constitutional provisions establishing equal representation of the states in the U.S. Senate.

10.4.5 MYTH: The Republican Party enjoys a partisan advantage from the low-population states in presidential elections.

QUICK ANSWER:

- The political reality is that the Republican Party receives no partisan advantage from the 13 least-populous states (i.e., those with three or four electoral votes) under the current state-by-state winner-take-all system because they have been divided 6–6 for the last six presidential elections (with New Hampshire being a battleground state).
- The 25 least-populous states (i.e., those with seven or fewer electoral votes) divided 13–12 in the 2008 presidential race (with their electoral votes divided 58–57).

MORE DETAILED ANSWER:

The misconception that the least-populous states confer a partisan advantage in favor of the Republican Party probably stems from the fact that most of these states did indeed regularly vote Republican in most presidential elections in the 1960s and 1970s. During that period, Rhode Island and the District of Columbia were often the only Democratic bastions among the less-populous states.

However, the political situation of the 1960s and 1970s does not reflect the political reality for the past quarter century. In the last six presidential elections (1988 through 2008), six of the 13 least-populous states (i.e., those with three or four electoral votes) have regularly gone Republican (Alaska, Idaho, Montana, Wyoming, North Dakota, and South Dakota), while six others (Hawaii, Vermont, Maine, Rhode Island, Delaware, and the District of Columbia) have regularly gone Democratic.[100]

In recent years, New Hampshire has been the only closely divided battleground state among the 13 least-populous states (having supported the Democrat in 1992 and 1996, the Republican in 2000, and the Democrat in 2004 and 2008).

Interestingly, under the current state-by-state winner-take-all system, the Democratic presidential candidate actually enjoys a slight political advantage in the 12 least-populous non-battleground states.

Table 10.4 shows the presidential election results in the six reliably Republican low-population states for the most recent reasonably close presidential election (2004). The table shows that George W. Bush's 650,421-vote lead in the six reliably Republican low-population states yielded him 19 electoral votes.

TABLE 10.4 BUSH'S 650,421-VOTE LEAD IN THE SIX RELIABLY REPUBLICAN LOW-POPULATION STATES YIELDED 19 ELECTORAL VOTES

STATE	BUSH	KERRY	BUSH LEAD	ELECTORAL VOTES
Alaska	151,876	86,064	65,812	3
Idaho	408,254	180,920	227,334	4
Montana	265,473	173,363	92,110	3
North Dakota	195,998	110,662	85,336	3
South Dakota	232,545	149,225	83,320	3
Wyoming	167,129	70,620	96,509	3
Total	**1,421,275**	**770,854**	**650,421**	**19**

Table 10.5 shows the 2004 presidential election results in the six reliably Democratic low-population states. The table shows that John Kerry's 444,115-vote lead in the six reliably Democratic low-population states yielded him 21 electoral votes. In other words, Kerry won more

[100] Among the six reliably Republican states with three or four electoral votes, Bill Clinton carried Montana in 1992 (almost certainly because of Ross Perot's presence on the ballot). Among the six Democratic-leaning small states, George H.W. Bush carried Delaware, Maine, and Vermont in 1988; however, these states have been reliably Democratic in presidential elections since then.

electoral votes than Bush with a lead that was only about two-thirds the size of Bush's lead.[101]

TABLE 10.5 KERRY'S 444,115-VOTE LEAD IN THE SIX RELIABLY DEMOCRATIC LOW-POPULATION STATES YIELDED 21 ELECTORAL VOTES

STATE	BUSH	KERRY	KERRY LEAD	ELECTORAL VOTES
Delaware	171,531	199,887	28,356	3
D.C.	19,007	183,876	164,869	3
Hawaii	194,109	231,318	37,209	4
Maine	330,374	395,391	65,017	4
Rhode Island	161,654	161,654	247,407	4
Vermont	120,710	183,621	62,911	3
Total	**997,385**	**1,441,500**	**444,115**	**21**

In other words, Kerry won more electoral votes than Bush did in the 12 least-populous non-battleground states despite the fact that Bush won 650,421 popular votes compared to Kerry's 444,115 votes.

The reason for this Democratic partisan advantage in the least-populous states under the current winner-take-all system is that the low-population red states are redder than the low-population blue states are blue.

Specifically, the Republican popular-vote margins in the reliably Republican six low-population states were

- Alaska–64%,
- Idaho–69%,
- Montana–61%,
- North Dakota–64%,
- South Dakota–61%, and
- Wyoming–70%.

In contrast, the Democrats carried three of their reliable low-population states (Delaware, Hawaii, and Maine) with just 54% of the vote and effortlessly harvested their electoral votes. A 46%–54% margin is generally viewed as the boundary that places a state safely out of reach for the opposition during a typical presidential campaign. [102]

In addition, the Democrats carried two more of their low-population

---

[101] In 2004, Kerry also won the swing state of New Hampshire, giving him a total of 25 electoral votes for an overall margin of 453,286 votes for the seven states that he carried.

[102] Although there is no universally accepted definition, a "battleground" state is (more or less) one in which the spread between the top two candidates is outside the range of 46%–54%. See table 1.2.

states (Vermont and Rhode Island) with only 60% of the vote (that is, a smaller margin than any of the six reliably Republican low-population states). The District of Columbia is the only low-population jurisdiction where the Democrats regularly win presidential races with a high margin.

A large number of Republican votes were left on the table because of the high margins of victory in the six reliably Republican low-population states, compared to the relatively modest winning margins in the six regularly Democratic low-population states. Under a national popular vote in which every vote would be equal, this wastage would not occur.

- Wyoming's 96,509-vote margin exceeded Vermont's 62,911-vote margin.
- Alaska's 65,812-vote margin exceeded Delaware's 28,356-vote margin.
- North Dakota's 85,336-vote margin exceeded Hawaii's 37,209-vote margin.
- Montana's 92,110-vote margin exceeded Rhode Island's 85,753-vote margin.
- South Dakota's 83,320-vote margin exceeded Maine's 65,017-vote margin.
- Idaho's 227,334-vote Republican margin exceeded the District of Columbia's 164,869-vote margin.

In the typical partisan gerrymander, the map-drawing party creates districts so that the minority party wins its districts by enormous margins, while the map-drawing party wins most of its districts by a percentage in the mid-50% range. If the boundaries of the 13 least-populous states had been drawn recently, there would be accusations that they were a Democratic gerrymander.

Similarly, there is no significant partisan advantage in favor of the Republican Party even if one considers the 25 least-populous states (i.e., those with seven or fewer electoral votes).

Table 10.6 shows that the Republicans won 13 of the 25 least-populous states in 2008 while the Democrats won 12. The Republicans won 58 electoral votes in the 25 least-populous states while the Democrats won 57.[103]

---

[103] Nebraska awards three of its five electoral votes by congressional district. In 2008, Barack Obama won one electoral vote by carrying the 2nd congressional district of Nebraska. Thus, Nebraska's electoral votes in 2008 were divided 4–1 in favor of McCain.

TABLE 10.6 THE 25 LEAST-POPULOUS STATES DIVIDED 13-12 IN FAVOR OF THE REPUBLICANS IN 2008, AND THEIR ELECTORAL VOTES DIVIDED 58-57.

ELECTORAL VOTES	STATE	DEMOCRATIC	REPUBLICAN
3	District of Columbia	3	
3	Wyoming		3
3	Vermont	3	
3	North Dakota		3
3	Alaska		3
3	South Dakota		3
3	Delaware	3	
3	Montana		3
4	Rhode Island	4	
4	Hawaii	4	
4	Idaho		4
4	Maine	4	
4	New Hampshire	4	
5	Nebraska	1	4
5	West Virginia		5
5	New Mexico	5	
5	Nevada	5	
5	Utah		5
6	Kansas		6
6	Arkansas		6
6	Mississippi		6
7	Iowa	7	
7	Connecticut	7	
7	Oklahoma		7
7	Oregon	7	
115	**Total Electoral Votes**	**57**	**58**

10.4.6 MYTH: The distribution of political influence envisioned by the Great Compromise would be upset by a national popular vote.

QUICK ANSWER:

- The distribution of political influence among the states in the Electoral College changed dramatically once political parties emerged in 1796, once most states started permitting the people to vote for President (completed by 1880), and once state winner-take-all statutes became widespread (by the 1830s).

• Political influence in the Electoral College today is not based on the distribution of electoral votes among the states, but instead on whether a state is a closely divided battleground state.

MORE DETAILED ANSWER:

The "Great Compromise" (also known as the "Connecticut Compromise" and "Sherman's Compromise") was adopted by the Constitutional Convention in July 1787. It was one of the most important compromises that permitted the Constitutional Convention to proceed to a successful conclusion.

The Great Compromise established a bicameral national legislature in which the U.S. House of Representatives was apportioned on the basis of population, and the U.S. Senate was structured on the basis of equal representation of the states (i.e., two U.S. Senators per state).

The National Popular Vote compact is state legislation. It would, therefore, have no effect on the structure of the nation's national legislature (that is, Congress). Changing the structure of Congress would require a federal constitutional amendment.

The delegates to the Constitutional Convention did not reach a compromise on the method of electing the President until the end of the Convention in September.[104] By that time, all of the other major issues had been settled. In particular, the notion of having a bicameral national legislature was settled at that time.

When the Convention finally agreed that the President would be elected by an Electoral College, each state was allocated as many presidential electors as it had members in the two houses of Congress. That is, the allocation of electoral votes mirrored the combined allocation of members in the two houses of Congress.

The National Popular Vote bill is state legislation and therefore would have no effect on the formula in the U.S. Constitution for allocating electoral votes among the states. Changing the formula for allocating electoral votes among the states would require a federal constitutional amendment.

---

[104] Edwards, George C. III. 2004. *Why the Electoral College Is Bad for America.* New Haven, CT: Yale University Press.

The important point is that the distribution of electoral votes in the Electoral College sheds little light on the distribution of political influence in the Electoral College.

The distribution of political influence among the states changed dramatically once political parties emerged, once most states started permitting the people to vote for President, and once state winner-take-all statutes became widespread. All three of these changes were, of course, legally permitted under the U.S. Constitution.

Once these three changes took place (and, in particular, the widespread adoption of winner-take-all statutes by the states), the determinant of a state's political influence in presidential elections became primarily a matter of whether the state is a closely divided battleground state.

Despite the Great Compromise, low-population states (with three and four electoral votes) such as Wyoming, Vermont, North Dakota, Alaska, South Dakota, Delaware, Montana, Rhode Island, Hawaii, and Idaho have no political influence in presidential elections.

Prior to 1992, New Hampshire was of no consequence in the post-convention general election campaign for President because it was safely Republican. However, since 1992, New Hampshire (with four electoral votes) has been a battleground in the post-convention general election campaign for President. Despite its small population, New Hampshire received 12 campaign events (out of a total of 300) in 2008.

Similarly, the "Great Compromise" resulted in Illinois and Pennsylvania each possessing 21 electoral votes in the 2008 presidential election. However, Illinois has not been consequential in recent presidential elections, because it has been safely Democratic, whereas closely divided Pennsylvania has been an extremely important battleground state. In 2008, Pennsylvania received 40 campaign events (out of a total of 300) and tens of millions of dollars in campaign spending, whereas Illinois received none. The issues of concern to Pennsylvania voters were foremost in the minds of the presidential candidates, whereas those of Illinois were not.

In short, the Great Compromise relates to the formal structure and numerical allocation of electoral votes among the states. It is not, however, the determinant of a state's political influence in presidential elections.

Of course, the Great Compromise still governs a state's relative political influence in terms of the process of bringing the National Popular Vote compact into effect. Less-populous states have relatively greater political influence in this process than their population alone would warrant because of the "Great Compromise."

10.4.7 MYTH: The rural states would lose their electoral advantage under a national popular vote.

QUICK ANSWER:

- The current state-by-state winner-take-all method of awarding electoral votes does not enhance the influence of rural states, because the most rural states are not battleground states.

MORE DETAILED ANSWER:

Tara Ross, an opponent of the National Popular Vote plan, writes:

> "NPV will lessen the need of presidential candidates to obtain the support of voters in rural areas and in small states."[105] [Emphasis added]

Table 10.7 shows, for each state, the rural population (column 2 using the 2000 definition found in the *Statistical Abstract of the United States*), the state's total population (column 3), the rural percentage (column 2 divided by column 3), and the rural index (obtained by dividing the state's rural percentage by the overall national rural percentage of 20.11%). An index above 100 indicates that the state is more rural than the nation as a whole, whereas an index below 100 indicates that the state is less rural. Thirty-three states have an index above 100 (meaning that more than 20.11% of their population is rural), whereas 18 jurisdictions have an index below 100 (that is, they are less rural than the nation as a whole).

Fourteen states received seven or more of the 300 post-convention general election campaign events in 2008.

- Ohio—62 events,
- Florida—46 events,
- Pennsylvania—40 events,
- Virginia—23 events,
- Missouri—21 events,

---

[105] Written testimony submitted by Tara Ross to Delaware Senate in June 2010.

- Colorado—20 events,
- North Carolina—15 events,
- Nevada—12 events,
- New Hampshire—12 events,
- Michigan—10 events,[106]
- Indiana—9 events,
- New Mexico—8 events,
- Wisconsin—8 events, and
- Iowa—7 events.

These 14 closely divided battleground states accounted for 97.7% of the 300 post-convention campaign events in the 2008 general election campaign for President (that is, 293 of the 300 events).[107] In the table, these 14 battleground states are shown in bold. Half of the 300 post-convention campaign events (148 of 300) are in the states of Ohio (62 events), Florida (46 events), and Pennsylvania (40 events).

As can be seen from the table, the 10 most rural states are

- Vermont (60.61% rural),
- Maine (57.86% rural),
- West Virginia (53.75% rural),
- Mississippi (50.20% rural),
- South Dakota (47.14% rural),
- Arkansas (46.10% rural),
- Montana (44.69% rural),
- North Dakota (44.68% rural),
- Alabama (43.74% rural), and
- Kentucky (43.13% rural).

Political influence in the Electoral College is not based on the distribution of electoral votes among the states, but instead on whether the state is a closely divided battleground state.

None of the 10 most rural states is a battleground state.

The current state-by-state winner-take-all method of awarding electoral votes does not enhance the influence of rural states, because the most rural states are not battleground states.

---

[106] On October 2, 2010, the McCain campaign abruptly pulled out of Michigan after it concluded that it could not win Michigan.

[107] The remaining six of the 300 post-convention events (that is, 2% of the events) occurred in Maine (2 events), Minnesota (2 events), the District of Columbia (1 event), Tennessee (1 event), and West Virginia (1 event).

TABLE 10.7 RURAL POPULATION OF THE UNITED STATES

STATE	RURAL POPULATION	TOTAL POPULATION	RURAL PERCENT	RURAL INDEX
Vermont	376,379	621,000	60.61%	301
Maine	762,045	1,317,000	57.86%	288
West Virginia	975,564	1,815,000	53.75%	267
Mississippi	1,457,307	2,903,000	50.20%	250
South Dakota	363,417	771,000	47.14%	234
Arkansas	1,269,221	2,753,000	46.10%	229
Montana	414,317	927,000	44.69%	222
North Dakota	283,242	634,000	44.68%	222
Alabama	1,981,427	4,530,000	43.74%	218
Kentucky	1,787,969	414,6000	43.13%	214
New Hampshire	**503,451**	**1,300,000**	**38.73%**	**193**
Iowa	**1,138,892**	**2,954,000**	**38.55%**	**192**
South Carolina	1,584,888	4,198,000	37.75%	188
North Carolina	**3,199,831**	**8,541,000**	**37.46%**	**186**
Tennessee	2,069,265	5,901,000	35.07%	174
Wyoming	172,438	507,000	34.01%	169
Oklahoma	1,196,091	3,524,000	33.94%	169
Alaska	215,675	655,000	32.93%	164
Idaho	434,456	1,393,000	31.19%	155
Wisconsin	**1,700,032**	**5,509,000**	**30.86%**	**153**
Missouri	**1,711,769**	**5,755,000**	**29.74%**	**148**
Nebraska	517,538	1,747,000	29.62%	147
Indiana	**1,776,474**	**6,238,000**	**28.48%**	**142**
Kansas	767,749	2,736,000	28.06%	140
Minnesota	1,429,420	5,101,000	28.02%	139
Louisiana	1,223,311	4,516,000	27.09%	135

10.5 MYTHS ABOUT HIGH-POPULATION STATES AND BIG CITIES

10.5.1 MYTH: Only the 11 most populous states would matter under a national popular vote.

QUICK ANSWER:

- Under the National Popular Vote compact, every vote would be equal throughout the United States. A vote cast in a more populous state is no more, or less, valuable than a vote cast anywhere else.
- The more populous states do not vote in concert.

Responses to Myths about the National Popular Vote Plan | **457**

TABLE 10.7 RURAL POPULATION OF THE UNITED STATES (CONT.)

STATE	RURAL POPULATION	TOTAL POPULATION	RURAL PERCENT	RURAL INDEX
Georgia	2,322,290	8,829,000	26.30%	131
Virginia	1,908,560	7,460,000	25.58%	127
Michigan	2,518,987	10,113,000	24.91%	124
New Mexico	455,545	1,903,000	23.94%	119
Pennsylvania	2,816,811	12,406,000	22.71%	113
Ohio	2,570,811	11,459,000	22.43%	112
Oregon	727,255	3,595,000	20.23%	101
Delaware	155,842	830,000	18.78%	93
Washington	1,063,015	6,204,000	17.13%	85
Texas	3,647,539	22,490,000	16.22%	81
Colorado	668,076	4,601,000	14.52%	72
Maryland	737,818	5,558,000	13.27%	66
New York	2,373,875	19,227,000	12.35%	61
Connecticut	417,506	3,504,000	11.92%	59
Illinois	1,509,773	12,714,000	11.87%	59
Utah	262,825	2,389,000	11.00%	55
Arizona	607,097	5,744,000	10.57%	53
Florida	1,712,358	17,397,000	9.84%	49
Rhode Island	95,173	1,081,000	8.80%	44
Massachusetts	547,730	6,417,000	8.54%	42
Hawaii	103,312	1,263,000	8.18%	41
Nevada	169,611	2,335,000	7.26%	36
New Jersey	475,263	8,699,000	5.46%	27
California	1,881,985	35,894,000	5.24%	26
D.C.	0	554,000	0.00%	0
Total	59,061,367	293,658,000	20.11%	100

- In the most recent reasonably close presidential election (2004), no candidate received more than 61% of the vote in any of the 11 most populous states.

MORE DETAILED ANSWER:

Under the National Popular Vote compact, every vote would be equal throughout the United States. A vote cast in a more populous state would be no more, or less, valuable than a vote cast anywhere else.

It is sometimes argued that only the 11 most populous states would matter under the National Popular Vote compact. In this hypothetical scenario, the least-populous 39 states (i.e., those with seven or fewer electoral votes) would be ignored because candidates would win the White House by winning 100% of the popular vote in the 11 largest states (and 0% in the 39 least-populous states).

This hypothetical scenario is not consistent with political reality in several respects.

First, although it is true that the 11 most populous states do contain 56% of the population of the United States, these states rarely act in concert concerning any political candidate.

In terms of the most recent reasonably close presidential election (namely, the 2004 election in which George W. Bush, the nationwide winner, had a 2.4% lead nationwide), the following five of the 11 most populous states voted Republican:

- Texas,
- Florida,
- Ohio,
- North Carolina, and
- Georgia.

Meanwhile, six of the 11 most populous states voted Democratic:

- California,
- New York,
- Illinois,
- Pennsylvania,
- Michigan, and
- New Jersey.

Second, even if the 11 largest states were to vote in concert in favor of the same presidential candidate, the notion that any candidate could win 100% (or 90% or 80% or even 70%) of the vote in these states is not consistent with political reality. In the most recent reasonably close presidential election (2004), George W. Bush's 61% share of the vote in Texas was the highest percentage level of popular support for any presidential candidate among the 11 most populous states.

The percentages that the winning candidates received in the 11 largest states were (in descending order):

- 61%—Texas—Republican,
- 58%—New York—Democratic,
- 58%—Georgia—Republican,
- 56%—North Carolina—Republican,

- 55%—Illinois—Democratic,
- 54%—California—Democratic,
- 53%—New Jersey—Democratic,
- 52%—Florida—Republican,
- 51%—Michigan—Democratic,
- 51%—Pennsylvania—Democratic, and
- 51%—Ohio—Republican).

The winner's margin in more than half of the 11 most populous states was below 55% (the number frequently used to define a "landslide"). In fact, far from voting heavily in favor of one candidate, four of the 11 most populous states were closely divided battleground states.

Third, if anyone were genuinely concerned about the hypothetical scenario that a candidate could win the Presidency under a national popular vote by winning 100% of the popular vote in the 11 largest states, they should be even more concerned about this same scenario under the current system. Under the current state-by-state winner-take-all system, a candidate could theoretically win the Presidency by winning a mere 50.01% of the popular vote in the 11 largest states. That is, under the current system, it is possible for a candidate to win the Presidency with less than 25% of the nation's popular votes.

Fourth, the hypothetical scenario is unrealistic for the additional reason that the margins generated in the nation's largest states are not overwhelming in relation to the 122,000,000 votes cast nationally in 2004. Among the 11 most populous states, the largest margins in the most recent reasonably close presidential election (2004) were generated by the following seven non-battleground states:

- Texas—1,694,213 Republican,
- New York—1,351,713 Democratic,
- California—1,235,659 Democratic,
- Georgia—548,105 Republican,
- North Carolina—435,317 Republican,
- Illinois—545,604 Democratic, and
- New Jersey—241,428 Democratic.

Significantly, the largest popular vote margins are not necessarily generated by the largest states. For example:

- Utah (with only 5 electoral votes) generated a margin of 385,000 votes for Bush in 2004—larger than the margin gen-

erated for Kerry by New Jersey (then the ninth largest state
with 15 electoral votes).

- Oklahoma (with only 7 electoral votes) generated a margin of 455,000 votes for Bush in 2004—almost the margin
  generated by Illinois (a state with about three times more
  people).

Although no one can predict exactly how a presidential campaign
would be run if every vote were equal throughout the United States, it is
clear that candidates would not ignore voters in any state, because every
vote would be as important as every other.

Fifth, under the current state-by-state winner-take-all system, it would
have been theoretically possible to win the Presidency with between 16%
and 22% of the popular vote in the 15 elections between 1948 and 2004.
Professor Alexander S. Belenky has computed (table 10.8) the percentage of voters who could have elected a President in the Electoral College
based on the numbers of votes cast in the election in each state (including
the District of Columbia starting in 1964).[108]

TABLE 10.8 PERCENTAGE OF VOTERS WHO COULD HAVE ELECTED A PRESIDENT IN THE ELECTORAL COLLEGE

YEAR	PERCENTAGE OF VOTERS WHO COULD HAVE ELECTED A PRESIDENT IN THE ELECTORAL COLLEGE
1948	16.072%
1952	17.547%
1956	17.455%
1960	17.544%
1964	18.875%
1968	19.97%
1972	20.101%
1976	21.202%
1980	21.348%
1984	21.53%
1988	21.506%
1992	21.944%
1996	22.103%
2000	21.107%
2004	21.666%

[108] Belenky, Alexander S. 2008. A 0-1 knapsack model for evaluating the possible
Electoral College performance in two-party U.S. presidential elections. *Mathematical
and Computer Modelling*. Volume 48. Pages 665–676.

10.5.2 MYTH: California would swamp the low-population western states under a national popular vote.

QUICK ANSWER:

- California's capacity to generate votes is greatly exaggerated in political mythology. In the most recent reasonably close presidential election (2004), eight small western states (with less than a third of California's population) provided George W. Bush with a bigger margin (1,283,076) than the margin that California provided John Kerry (1,235,659).

- Under the National Popular Vote compact, every vote would be equal throughout the United States. A vote cast in California would be no more, or less, valuable or powerful than a vote cast anywhere else.

MORE DETAILED ANSWER:

Under the National Popular Vote compact, every vote would be equal throughout the United States. A vote cast in California would be no more, or less, valuable than a vote cast anywhere else.

California has been a reliably Democratic state in recent presidential elections. Although safely Democratic, California is not as overwhelmingly Democratic as is generally thought. In the last 60 years, only four presidential candidates received more than 55% of the vote in California (2008, 1984, 1064, and 1956) and that candidate was a Democrat on only two of those four occasions (2008 and 1964).

Table 10.9 shows that in the most recent reasonably close presidential election (2004), eight low-population western states (with less than a third of California's population) provided George W. Bush with a bigger margin (1,347,175) than the margin that California provided John Kerry (1,235,659).

Although no one can predict exactly how a presidential campaign would be run if every vote were equal throughout the United States, it is clear that candidates would not ignore voters in any state, because every vote would be as important as every other.

TABLE 10.9 MARGINS PRODUCED IN EIGHT LOW-POPULATION WESTERN STATES, COMPARED TO CALIFORNIA, FOR BUSH AND KERRY IN 2004

STATE	BUSH MARGIN	KERRY MARGIN	BUSH ELECTORAL VOTES	KERRY ELECTORAL VOTES
Alaska	79,864		3	
California		1,235,659		55
Idaho	228,137		4	
Montana	92,353		3	
Nebraska	258,486		5	
North Dakota	85,599		3	
South Dakota	83,340		3	
Utah	422,543		5	
Wyoming	96,853		3	
Total	**1,347,175**	**1,235,659**	**28**	**55**

10.5.3 MYTH: The South would be swamped by high-population Democratic states under a national popular vote.

QUICK ANSWER:

- The capacity of the high-population states that are safely Democratic to generate votes is greatly exaggerated in political mythology. In the most recent reasonably close presidential election (2004), the 11 southern states provided George W. Bush with a bigger margin (5.1 million) than the margin (4.4 million) provided by the six states that generated John Kerry's largest margins (and that have about the same number of electoral votes as the South).

- Under the National Popular Vote compact, every vote would be equal throughout the United States. A vote cast in one place would be no more, or less, valuable or powerful than a vote cast anywhere else.

MORE DETAILED ANSWER:

Under the National Popular Vote compact, every vote would be equal throughout the United States.

Table 10.10 shows that the 11 southern states provided George W. Bush with a bigger margin (5,136,019) than the margin (4,428,268) provided by the six states that generated John Kerry's largest margins. In 2004, the six states that provided Kerry with his largest vote margins were California, Illinois, Maryland, Massachusetts, New Jersey, and New York. All 11 of the Southern states voted for Bush. The six Democratic states had a total of 154 electoral votes, whereas the 11 southern (solidly Republican) states had 154 electoral votes. The 11 southern states had a somewhat smaller combined population than the six Democratic states.

TABLE 10.10 MARGINS PRODUCED FOR BUSH IN THE 11 SOUTHERN STATES IN 2004, COMPARED TO MARGINS PRODUCED FOR KERRY IN THE SIX STATES THAT GENERATED THE LARGEST DEMOCRATIC MARGINS

STATE	BUSH MARGIN	KERRY MARGIN	BUSH ELECTORAL VOTES	KERRY ELECTORAL VOTES
Alabama	482,461		9	
Arkansas	102,945		6	
California		**1,235,659**		**55**
Florida	380,978		27	
Georgia	548,105		15	
Illinois		**545,604**		**21**
Louisiana	281,870		9	
Maryland		**309,790**		**10**
Massachusetts		**732,691**		**12**
Mississippi	226,887		6	
New Jersey		**241,427**		**15**
New York		**1,351,713**		**31**
North Carolina	435,317		15	
South Carolina	276,275		8	
Tennessee	347,898		11	
Texas	1,694,213		34	
Total	**5,136,019**	**4,428,268**	**156**	**154**

In an article in *Southern Political Report* entitled "The Electoral College is stacked against the South," Professor John A. Tures writes: "The South is largely disenfranchised by the Electoral College."[109]

10.5.4 MYTH: Big cities, such as Los Angeles, would control the election under a national popular vote.

QUICK ANSWER:

- Under a national popular vote, every vote would be equal throughout the United States. A vote cast in a big city would

---

[109] Tures, John A. 2009. The Electoral College is stacked against the South. *South Political Report*. November 30, 2009.

be no more, or less, valuable or powerful than a vote cast anywhere else.

- The fact is that Los Angeles cannot control the outcome of a statewide election in California, as evidenced by recent Republican governors such as Ronald Reagan, George Deukmejian, Pete Wilson, and Arnold Schwarzenegger—none of whom ever carried Los Angeles. If big cities cannot control the statewide elections in their own state, they can hardly control a nationwide election.

- 81% of the population of the United States lives in places with a population of less than 363,000 (the population of the nation's 50th largest city, Arlington, Texas).

MORE DETAILED ANSWER:

The fact is that there is nothing special about a vote cast in a big city. When every vote is equal, candidates of both parties know that they need to solicit voters everywhere in order to win.

A vote cast in a big city, under the National Popular Vote plan, would be no more (or less) valuable or powerful than a vote cast in the suburbs, exurbs, small towns, and rural parts of the state.

The fact is that a candidate cannot win a statewide election in California by concentrating on Los Angeles. When Ronald Reagan, George Deukmejian, Pete Wilson, and Arnold Schwarzenegger ran for governor, Los Angeles did not receive all the attention; these four recent Republican governors did not carry Los Angeles; and Los Angeles certainly did not control the election's outcome. If Los Angeles cannot control statewide elections in California, it can hardly control a nationwide election.

In fact, Los Angeles, San Francisco, San Jose, and Oakland together cannot control a statewide election in California.

Similarly, Republicans dominate Texas politics without carrying big cities such as Dallas and Houston.

There are numerous other examples of Republicans who won races for governor and U.S. Senator in other states that have big cities (e.g., New York, Illinois, Michigan, Pennsylvania, and Massachusetts) without ever carrying the big cities of their respective states. It is certainly true that the biggest cities in those states typically vote Democratic. However, the suburbs, exurbs, small towns, and rural parts of the states often voted

Republican. If big cities controlled the outcome of elections, the governors and U.S. Senators would be Democratic in virtually every state with a significant city.

When presidential candidates campaign to win the electoral votes of a closely divided battleground state, the big cities do not receive all the attention, much less control the outcome. Cleveland and Miami certainly did not receive all the attention and manifestly did not control the outcomes in Ohio and Florida in 2000 and 2004. The Democrats carried both cities, but the Republicans carried both states. In fact, John Kerry won the five largest cities in Ohio in 2004 but did not win the state.

The origins of the myth about big cities stem from the belief that big cities are bigger than they actually are, and that big cities account for much more of the nation's population than they actually do.

The populations of the nation's five biggest cities (New York, Los Angeles, Chicago, Houston, and Philadelphia) together constitute only 6% of the nation's population of approximately 300 million. Even if one makes the far-fetched assumption that a candidate could win 100% of the votes in the nation's top-five cities, that candidate would have won only 6% of the national popular vote.

The populations of the nation's 25 largest cities together constitute only 12% of the nation's population. To put this group of 25 cities in perspective, Denver is the nation's 25th largest city (with an estimated population of 558,000 in 2005).

The populations of the 50 largest cities together constitute only 19% of the nation's population. Arlington, Texas is the nation's 50th largest city (with an estimated population of 363,000 in 2005).

To put it another way, 81% of the population of the United States lives in places with a population of less than 363,000 (the population of Arlington, Texas).

The reason for the confusion underlying this myth is a lack of appreciation of the country's actual demographics.

An additional indication of the way a nationwide presidential campaign would be run comes from the way that national advertisers conduct nationwide sales campaigns. National advertisers (e.g., Ford, Coca-Cola) seek out customers in small, medium-sized, and large towns in every low-population, medium-sized, and high-population state. National advertisers do not advertise only in big cities. Instead, they go after every potential customer, regardless of where the customer is located. National advertisers do not write off a particular state merely because a competitor has an 8% lead in sales. Furthermore, a national advertiser with an 8% edge in a particular state does not stop trying to make additional sales in the state.

10.5.5 MYTH: Candidates would only campaign in media markets, while ignoring the rest of the country.

QUICK ANSWER:

* Every person in the United States lives in a media market, including the media markets for television, radio, newspapers, magazines, direct mail, billboards, and the Internet.

MORE DETAILED ANSWER:

This myth appears to be a carry-over from the long-past early days of over-the-air television when significant parts of the country were not reachable by television.

Today, every person in the United States lives in a media market, including the media markets for television, radio, newspapers, direct mail, billboards, magazines, and the Internet.

Focusing specifically on television (the largest single component of spending in presidential campaigns), virtually everyone in the United States has access to television. This has been true for decades. No one in the United States will be left out of a presidential campaign because they do not live in a media market.

People are, however, left out of presidential campaigns, under the current system, because of the state-by-state winner-take-all method of awarding electoral votes. Candidates have no reason to pay any attention to voters who do not live in closely divided battleground states. Under a national popular vote, every vote would be equal.

Under the National Popular Vote plan, every person's vote in every state would matter in every presidential election.

10.5.6 MYTH: Under a national popular vote, candidates would concentrate on major metropolitan markets because the cost per advertising impression is lower there.

QUICK ANSWER:

* The cost per advertising impression is higher (not lower)

in major metropolitan media markets. Therefore, this criticism is exactly backwards.

MORE DETAILED ANSWER:

Economist John Samples has predicted that:

> "NPV will encourage presidential campaigns to focus their efforts in dense **media markets where costs per vote are lowest....**

> "In general, because of the relative costs of attracting votes, the NPV proposal seems likely at the margin to attract candidate attention to populous states."[110] [Emphasis added]

The defect in this argument is that costs are *not* lower in the major metropolitan media markets. In fact, television advertising (the largest component of presidential campaigns) is premium-priced in the major metropolitan areas.

Television time is far less expensive, on a per-impression basis, in small towns and rural media markets than in larger media markets. It is, for example, considerably more expensive to buy television or radio time to reach Ohio's 11 million people than to buy television or radio time to reach the 11 million people who live in the 12 least-populous non-competitive states (i.e., the six "red" states of Alaska, Montana, Idaho, Wyoming, North Dakota, and South Dakota and the six "blue" states of Hawaii, Maine, Vermont, Rhode Island, Delaware, and the District of Columbia).

These facts explain why some Republicans have argued that a national popular vote for President would be good for the Republican Party because it would operate as a tax on the Democrats. This argument (unlike John Sample's argument) is at least consistent with the economic reality that television advertising is premium-priced in heavily Democratic big cities. However, Democrats needs not worry about the conjectured "big city tax" because they could easily evade this "tax" by purchasing media time on a nationwide basis. In fact, both parties could avoid this "tax" by campaigning more in the smaller media markets where the per-impression cost is lower and by campaigning nationwide on net-

---

[110]   Samples, John. *A Critique of the National Popular Vote Plan for Electing the President.* Cato Institute Policy Analysis No. 622. October 13, 2008.

work television.

10.5.7 MYTH: The current system prevents 11 states from electing the President.

QUICK ANSWER:

- There is nothing in the U.S. Constitution that currently prevents any group of states that possess a majority of the electoral votes (whether that groups consists of the 11 most populous states, the 40 least-populous states, or any other combination of states) from electing a President.

MORE DETAILED ANSWER:

Bert Sanders of Toney, Alabama wrote to *Parade* magazine on September 12, 2010 (in response to an article by Marilyn vos Savant on September 5, 2010) saying:

> "Marilyn: When people ask you a stupid question, you should tell them that it is a stupid question, and tell them why it is stupid. You should have explained why we have the electoral-college vote.

> "Apparently, a generation has evolved that has no understanding of why we have that system. **The electoral college gives voting representation to all fifty states. If it were abolished, ten to twelve of the largest states could elect the president, and everyone else could stay at home.**

> "The larger states vote differently than the smaller states do. Just look at the sea of red on your television on election night and then be told that the Democrat won the election. Fairness and decency dictate that we retain the Electoral College vote. [Emphasis added]

There is nothing in the U.S. Constitution that prevents any group of states that possess a majority of the electoral votes (whether that group consists of the 11 most populous states, the 40 least-populous states, or any other combination of states) from electing a President.

Although it is true that the 11 most populous states do contain 56% of the population of the United States and a majority of the electoral votes, these states rarely act in concert concerning any political candidate.

In terms of the most recent reasonably close presidential election (namely, the 2004 election in which George W. Bush, the nationwide winner, had a 2.4% lead nationwide), the following five of the 11 most populous states voted Republican:

- Texas,
- Florida,
- Ohio,
- North Carolina, and
- Georgia.

Meanwhile, six of the 11 most populous states voted Democratic

- California,
- New York,
- Illinois,
- Pennsylvania,
- Michigan, and
- New Jersey.

Under the National Popular Vote compact, every vote would be equal throughout the United States. A vote cast in a populous state is no more, or less, valuable than a vote cast anywhere else.

10.6   Myth about State Identity

10.6.1   MYTH: The public strongly desires that electoral votes be cast on a state-by-state basis because it provides a sense of "state identity."

QUICK ANSWER:

- The choice presented by the National Popular Vote plan is whether it is more important for the winner of the popular vote in a particular state to receive that state's electoral votes or for the winner of the most popular votes in the entire country to become President.
- The purpose of a presidential election is to elect someone to serve for four years as the nation's chief executive—not to permit a group of largely unknown loyal party activists to meet for a half hour in mid-December for the ceremonial purpose of casting electoral votes.
- A state's political "identity" is based on how all its citizens voted—not just how a plurality voted. The National Popular

Vote plan would give voice to every voter in every state, as opposed to stifling the voice of the minority within each state.

- State-level election returns would continue to be published under the National Popular Vote plan, so there will would no lack of information as how a particular state voted.

- In public opinion polls since the 1940s and recent state-level polls, the public has strongly favored the idea that the President should be the candidate who receives the most popular votes in the entire country. Support remains strong when the public is pointedly asked whether it is more important that a state's electoral votes be cast for the presidential candidate who receives the most popular votes in their own particular state, or whether it is more important to guarantee that the candidate who receives the most popular votes in all 50 states becomes President.

MORE DETAILED ANSWER:

The choice presented by the National Popular Vote plan is whether it is more important for the winner in a particular state to receive the state's electoral votes or for the winner of the most popular votes in the entire country to become President.

It is sometimes asserted that "the voters will rebel" when they discover, after the first election conducted under the National Popular Vote plan, that their state's electoral votes were awarded to a candidate who did not carry their own state.

This conjectured voter rebellion is based on the incorrect assumptions that

- the voters care more about which political party won their state than who is going to occupy the White House for four years,

- the voters will be surprised and shocked when the National Popular Vote compact results in the election of the presidential candidate who receives the most popular votes nationwide, and

- the voters are devoted and attached to the current state-by-state winner-take-all method of electing the President and will be unhappy that it is gone.

First, the conjectured voter rebellion is based on an incorrect assumption that voters care more about which political party won their state's presidential electors than who is going to occupy the White House for four years.

When voters watch presidential election returns on election night, they are—first and foremost—interested in finding out which candidate won the Presidency. The question of whether their preferred candidate won their state, county, city, congressional district, or precinct is a secondary concern. If a voter's preferred candidate loses the White House, it is no consolation that this losing candidate happened to win the voter's own state. Certainly, McCain supporters in Texas were not celebrating in 2008 because McCain carried Texas.

Also, ordinary voters are not concerned about the ceremonial position of presidential elector. Certainly, the average voter does not derive any satisfaction, on election night, from knowing that some little-known person associated with his or her own political party won the honorary position of presidential elector. It is the rare voter who knows the names of any presidential elector in the state.

Under the National Popular Vote plan, the focus of the media in the months prior to a presidential election would be on polls of the national popular vote—not just on the state-by-state polls from a small handful of closely divided battleground states. In fact, the concept of a battleground state would become obsolete under the National Popular Vote compact, because every vote would matter in every state in every presidential election.

Tellingly, there was no voter rebellion in reaction to the enactment by Maine (in 1969) and Nebraska (in 1992) of state laws that permit the potential awarding of electoral votes to a candidate who did not carry the state. In particular, there was no voter rebellion in Nebraska after Barack Obama carried the 2nd congressional district (the Omaha area) in the 2008 presidential election. The district system was the choice of the people's elected representatives in Nebraska, and it was the law that governed the conduct of the 2008 presidential election in Nebraska. Nebraska's law operated exactly as advertised in that it delivered one of the state's five electoral votes to the winner of the 2nd district (Barack Obama), despite the fact that another candidate (John McCain) carried the state as a whole.

Second, the voters would not be surprised or shocked when the national popular vote winner becomes President under the National Popular Vote plan. The environment of a future presidential election under the National Popular Vote plan would consist of the following elements:

- About 70% of the voters believe that the presidential candidate receiving the most votes in all 50 states and the District of Columbia should win the Presidency.
- The state legislature and governor of the state responded to the voters' wishes and enacted the National Popular Vote law in their state.
- The legislatures and governors of states possessing a majority of the electoral votes similarly responded to their voters and, as a result, the National Popular Vote compact had sufficient support to take effect nationally.
- A nationwide presidential campaign will have been conducted, over a period of many months, with everyone in the United States knowing that the presidential candidate receiving the most votes in all 50 states and the District of Columbia is going to win the Presidency.
- The public noticed that presidential candidates are, for the first time, paying attention to voters in every state and every part of the country.
- On Election Day in November, the National Popular Vote compact operates exactly as advertised and delivers a majority of the electoral votes to the presidential candidate who received the most popular votes in all 50 states and the District of Columbia.

Third, the conjectured voter rebellion would not occur, because most voters are simply not attached to the current state-by-state winner-take-all method of electing the President. To the contrary—most voters favor a national popular vote for President.

For example, a survey of 800 Utah voters conducted on May 19–20, 2009, showed 70% overall support for the idea that the President of the United States should be the candidate who receives the most popular votes in all 50 states. Voters were asked:

"How do you think we should elect the President: Should it be the candidate who gets the most votes in all 50 states, or the current Electoral College system?"

By political affiliation, support for a national popular vote on the first question was 82% among Democrats, 66% among Republicans, and 75% among others. By gender, support was 78% among women and 60% among men. By age, support was 70% among 18–29 year-olds, 70% among 30–45 year-olds, 70% among 46–65 year-olds, and 68% for those older than 65.

Then, voters were pointedly asked a "push" question that specifically highlighted the fact that Utah's electoral votes would be awarded to the winner of the national popular vote in all 50 states.

"Do you think it more important that a state's electoral votes be cast for the presidential candidate who receives the most popular votes in that state, or is it more important to guarantee that the candidate who receives the most popular votes in all 50 states becomes President?"

Support for a national popular vote did drop in this "push" question, but only from 70% to 66%.

On this second question, the results by political affiliation were as follows: 77% among Democrats, 63% among Republicans, and 62% among others. By gender, support was 72% among women and 58% among men. By age, support was 61% among 18–29 year-olds, 64% among 30–45 year-olds, 68% among 46–65 year-olds, and 66% for those older than 65. [111]

Similarly, a survey of 800 South Dakota voters conducted on May19–20, 2009, showed 75% overall support for a national popular vote for President for the first question and 67% for the "push" question.

A survey of 800 Connecticut voters conducted on May 14–15, 2009, showed 74% overall support for a national popular vote for President on the first question. The results of the first question, by political affiliation, were 80% support among Democrats, 67% among Republicans, and 71% among others.

Then, voters were asked the following "push" question that specifically highlighted the fact that Connecticut's electoral votes would be

[111] The Utah survey (and the others cited in this section) was conducted by Public Policy Polling, and had a margin of error of plus or minus 3 1/2%. See http://www.nationalpopularvote.com/pages/polls.

awarded to the winner of the national popular vote in all 50 states.

"Do you think it more important that Connecticut's electoral votes be cast for the presidential candidate who receives the most popular votes in Connecticut, or is it more important to guarantee that the candidate who receives the most popular votes in all 50 states becomes President?"

Support for a national popular vote did drop in this "push" question, but only from 74% to 68%.

The results of the second question, by political affiliation, was 74% among Democrats, 62% among Republicans, and 63% among others.

In Gallup polls since 1944, only about 20% of the public have supported the current system of awarding all of a state's electoral votes to the presidential candidate who receives the most votes in each separate state (with about 70% opposed and about 10% undecided). The 2007 *Washington Post*, Kaiser Family Foundation, and Harvard University poll showed 72% support for direct nationwide election of the President.

For those concerned about "state identity," official election returns showing the popular vote for President would continue to be certified and documented (as required by existing federal law and state laws), so the information as to which presidential candidate carried a particular state would be known to all.

The essence of a nationwide popular vote for President is that the winner would be determined by the nationwide popular vote—not by separate state-by-state outcomes. The National Popular Vote law would be a legally binding agreement among the compacting states to award their electoral votes to the presidential candidate who receives the most popular votes in all 50 states and the District of Columbia. It is a method to reform the Electoral College so that it reflects the nationwide will of the people.

The purpose of the National Popular Vote bill is to repeal the state-by-state approach of awarding of electoral votes and replace it with a system based on the national popular vote. It is the current state-by-state awarding of electoral votes that permits a second-place candidate to win the White House. It is the current state-by-state system that makes votes unequal in presidential elections. It is the current state-by-state system that makes two-thirds of the states politically irrelevant in presidential elections. Under the winner-take-all method, candidates have no reason to poll in, visit, advertise in, organize in, or pay attention to the concerns of states where they are comfortably ahead or hopelessly behind. Instead, candidates concentrate their attention on a small handful of closely divided battleground states. This means that voters in two-thirds of the states are ignored in presidential elections. In 2004, candidates concentrated over two-thirds of their money and campaign visits in five states; over 80% in nine states; and over 99% of their money in 16 states. In 2008, candidates concentrated over two-thirds of their campaign events and ad money in just six states, and 98% in just 15 states. [112]

The purpose of a presidential election is to elect someone to serve for four years as the nation's chief executive—not to permit a group of largely unknown loyal party activists to meet for a half hour in mid-December in the state capital for the ceremonial purpose of casting electoral votes. The concern that a state's electoral votes might be cast, in some elections, in favor of a candidate who did not carry a particular state is a matter of form over substance.

The choice presented by the National Popular Vote plan is whether it is more important for the winner in a particular state to receive the state's electoral votes or for the winner of the entire country to receive enough electoral votes to become President. You can't have it both ways.

10.7 Myths about Absolute Majority Requirement, Proliferation of Candidates, and the Breakdown of the Two-Party System

10.7.1 MYTH: The National Popular Vote plan is defective because it does not require an absolute majority of the popular vote to win.

QUICK ANSWER:

- Under the current system, there is no requirement that the winner receive an absolute majority of the national popular vote to win the Presidency—as evidenced by the non-majority elections of Presidents Lincoln, Wilson, Truman, Kennedy, Nixon, and Clinton.
- Under the current system, an absolute majority of the statewide popular vote is not required to win any state's

---

[112] http://fairvote.org/tracker/?page=27&pressmode=showspecific&showarticle=230.

electoral votes.

- The National Popular Vote plan reflects the nation's consensus that the winner of an election should be the candidate who receives the most popular votes. That is how virtually all elections, except for President, are run in the United States.

MORE DETAILED ANSWER:

Tara Ross objects to the National Popular Vote bill by saying:

> "The compact contemplated by [the National Popular Vote bill] would give the presidency to the candidate winning the 'largest national popular vote total.' Note that it says the 'largest' total. It is not looking for a majority winner." [113]

Of course, Ross's criticism applies equally to the current system. There is no requirement in current law that a candidate receive an absolute majority of the national popular vote in order to become President—as evidenced by Presidents Lincoln, Wilson, Truman, Kennedy, Nixon, and Clinton.

Moreover, there is no legal requirement in any state today that a candidate receive an absolute majority of the state's popular vote in order to win that state's electoral votes. In fact, it is common, under existing state laws, for a presidential candidate to win all of a state's electoral votes without receiving an absolute majority of the state's popular vote. For example, in 2008, no candidate received an absolute majority of the popular vote in four states.

The public seems content with elections that are conducted on the basis that the candidate who receives the most popular votes wins the office. That is how the vast majority of elections are conducted in the United States.

The National Popular Vote plan reflects the nation's consensus that the winner of an election should be the candidate who receives the most popular votes. There was certainly no outcry from the public, the media, Congress, or state legislators when Truman (1948), Kennedy (1960), Nixon (1968), or Clinton (1992 and 1996) were elected with less than an absolute majority of the national popular vote.

If, at some time in the future, the public demands that an absolute

---

[113] Written testimony submitted by Tara Ross to Delaware Senate in June 2010.

majority of the popular votes be required for election to office, that desire can be accommodated at that time.

10.7.2 MYTH: The National Popular Vote plan is defective because it does not provide for a run-off.

QUICK ANSWER:

- Under the current system, there is no procedure for a run-off. No run-off was conducted when Presidents Lincoln, Wilson, Truman, Kennedy, Nixon, or Clinton failed to receive an absolute majority of the national popular vote.

- Under the current system, there is no procedure for a run-off in states where no candidate receives an absolute majority of the statewide popular vote.

- The National Popular Vote plan reflects the nation's consensus that the winner of an election should be the candidate who receives the most popular votes. That is how virtually all elections, except for President, are run in the United States. There is no national consensus in favor of run-offs.

MORE DETAILED ANSWER:

Tara Ross complains that the National Popular Vote plan does not require an absolute majority of the national popular vote to win, and that

> "This problem is exacerbated by the fact that [the National Popular Vote compact] does not include a run-off provision."[114]

Ross's criticism applies equally to the current system. There is no provision in current law for a run-off when no presidential candidate receives an absolute majority of the national popular vote.

There is no provision in any state today for a run-off when no presidential candidate receives an absolute majority of the state's popular vote. In fact, it is common, under existing state laws, for a presidential candidate to win all of a state's electoral votes without receiving an absolute majority of the state's popular vote. For example, in 2008, no candidate received an absolute majority of the popular vote in four states.

If, at some time in the future, the public demands run-offs, that change can be implemented at that time.

---

[114] Written testimony submitted by Tara Ross to Delaware Senate in June 2010.

Note that traditional run-off elections present a number of difficulties. A run-off election would be expensive to administer. It is already difficult to recruit the required mass of citizen volunteers needed to operate elections. Given that the President has to be inaugurated in January and that the Electoral College meets in mid-December, it is already difficult to finish the initial counting of votes (and also conduct recounts, litigate disputes, and conduct required audits) in the limited amount of time available after Election Day in November. Turnout in run-off elections is typically low, so there is no evidence that a run-off would necessarily promote democracy. Perhaps most importantly, a run-off election would significantly alter the dynamics of financing of presidential campaigns because it would tilt the playing field in favor of candidates who are in a position to raise large amounts of additional money on very short notice.[115]

In any event, the National Popular Vote compact operates in a manner consistent with the widely held view in the United States today that the winner of an election should be the candidate who receives the most popular votes (that is, a plurality).

10.7.3 MYTH: A national popular vote will result in a proliferation of candidates, Presidents being elected with 15% of the vote, and a breakdown of the two-party system.

QUICK ANSWER:

- If an Electoral College type of arrangement were essential for avoiding a proliferation of candidates (and 15% winners), we should see evidence of these conjectured outcomes in elections that do not employ such an arrangement.

---

[115] If, at some time in the future, the public decides that it wants the benefits of a run-off election without the problems of a traditional run-off system, instant run-off voting (also called "ranked voting") offers a method for combining a run-off into the original election. In instant run-off voting, voters have the option of indicating their second choice for the office involved (and, in some variations of the system, additional choices). If no candidate receives an absolute majority of the first-place votes, the votes of the candidate receiving the fewest votes are distributed according to the second choices of those voters. This process of redistributing the votes received by the lowest candidate continues until one candidate receives an absolute majority of the voters expressing a choice. Instant run-off voting is currently used in a number of municipalities around the country. It is also used in many elections conducted among delegates at conventions of various organizations. Information about instant run-off voting is available from www.FairVote.org.

- Historical experience in over 5,000 elections for state chief executive shows no evidence of the conjectured proliferation of candidates or the conjectured 15% winners in elections in which the winner is the candidate who receives the most popular votes.
- Duverger's law (which is based on worldwide studies of elections) asserts that plurality-vote elections do not result in a proliferation of candidates or candidates being elected with tiny percentages of the vote.
- The two-party system is, in fact, sustained by the plurality-vote rule.

MORE DETAILED ANSWER:

Tara Ross, an opponent of the National Popular Vote plan, complains that a national popular vote would lead to a proliferation of candidates and a fracturing of the electorate, and that Presidents would be elected with only 15% of the vote:

> "[The National Popular Vote plan] is not even looking for a minimum plurality. Thus, a candidate could win with only 15 percent of votes nationwide."[116]

We can easily test Ross's conjectured outcome against actual historical experience and facts.

If an Electoral College type of arrangement were essential for avoiding Ross's conjectured outcome, we should see evidence of this outcome in elections that do not employ an Electoral College.

When elections are conducted in which the winner is the candidate who receives the most popular votes, candidates do not, in actual practice, win the office with low percentages of the vote (and certainly not percentages such as 15%).

In a study of the 918 elections for governor in the United States between 1948 and 2009 conducted by FairVote:[117]

- The winning candidate received more than 50% of the vote in 91% of the elections.
- The winning candidate received more than 45% of the vote

---

[116] Written testimony submitted by Tara Ross to Delaware Senate in June 2010.

[117] http://www.fairvote.org/majority-and-plurality-in-u-s-gubernatorial-elections.

in 98% of the elections.

* The winning candidate received more than 40% of the vote in 99% of the elections.
* No winning candidate received less than 35% of the popular vote.

In the real world, there aren't any 15% winners in elections in which the winner is the candidate with the most votes. There isn't any proliferation of candidates. There isn't any fracturing of the electorate. Elections for U.S. Senate, other statewide offices, and other offices confirm this pattern.

Moreover, elections in established democracies around the world show a similar pattern.

In political science, Duverger's law asserts that a plurality-rule election system tends to favor a two-party system. Maurice Duverger, the French sociologist who observed this tendency in election systems around the world, suggests that plurality voting favors a two-party system because political groups with broadly similar platforms tend to form alliances because it increases their chances of winning office. Voters generally desert weak parties or candidates on the grounds that they have no chance of winning. In practice, ordinary plurality voting discourages the formation of niche parties and candidacies by rewarding the formation of broad coalitions in which various groups and interests join together in order to win the most votes (and thereby win office).

The reason that ordinary plurality voting has this effect is that a vote cast for a splinter candidate frequently produces the politically counterproductive effect of helping the major-party candidate whose views are diametrically opposite of those of the voter. For example, votes cast for Bob Barr (the Libertarian Party candidate for President in 2008) made it easier for Barack Obama to win the electoral votes of North Carolina,[118] and votes cast for Ralph Nader (the Green Party candidate) in 2000 made it easier for George W. Bush to win the electoral votes of Florida and New Hampshire.[119]

---

[118] In North Carolina in 2008, Bob Barr (the Libertarian candidate) received considerably more votes than the margin between Barack Obama (the winner of the state) and John McCain (the second-place candidate).

[119] In Florida and New Hampshire in 2000, Ralph Nader received considerably more votes than the margin between George W. Bush (the winner of these two states) and Al Gore (the second-place candidate).

Ross's criticism of the National Popular Vote plan concerning third-party candidates is an example of a criticism that actually applies to the current state-by-state winner-take-all system far more than the National Popular Vote plan.

Under the current system of electing the President, minor-party candidates have significantly affected the outcome in 38% (six out of 16) of the presidential elections since World War II. Specifically, minor-party candidates affected the outcomes in the 1948, 1968, 1980, 1992, 1996, and 2000 presidential elections.

Segregationists such as Strom Thurmond (1948) or George Wallace (1968) won electoral votes in various Southern states. Candidates such as John Anderson (1980), Ross Perot (1992 and 1996), and Ralph Nader (2000) managed to affect the national outcome by switching electoral votes in numerous individual states.

None of these third-party candidates had any reasonable expectation of winning the most popular votes nationwide. The reason that the current system has encouraged so many minor-party candidacies is that a third-party candidate has 51 separate opportunities to find particular states that he might win outright or where he might be able to shift electoral votes from one major party to another.

Tara Ross writes:

> "The most likely consequence of a change to a direct popular vote is the breakdown of the two-party system."[120]

Ross's conjectured outcome can be tested against actual historical facts.

In 1789, only two states (Connecticut and Rhode Island) elected their governors.

Today, 100% of the states conduct a direct popular vote for governor. Yet, after over 5,000 direct popular elections for governor in over 220 years, the two-party system has not broken down.

The absence of a breakdown of the two-party system in gubernatorial races is especially noteworthy because about three-quarters of these elections occur in non-presidential years (that is, they stand apart from the presidential election cycle).

Returning to the history of presidential elections, only three states

---

[120] Written testimony submitted by Tara Ross to Delaware Senate in June 2010.

had winner-take-all statutes in the nation's first presidential election in 1789. Only three states used the winner-take-all rule in 1792 and 1796. Given that political parties came into full bloom in the 1796 election, it can hardly be argued that the existence of the state-by-state winner-take-all rule in just three states was the force that created the two-party system in the United States.

The two-party system in the United States (which dominates the electoral landscape for the vast majority of elective offices in the country) is not sustained by the existence of the winner-take-all rule for filling the single office of the Presidency.

Instead, the two-party system is the consequence of the plurality voting system in which the candidate who receives the most popular votes wins the office.

There is no reason to expect the emergence of some unique, new political dynamic that would promote multiple candidacies if the President were elected in the same manner as every other elected official in the United States.

What can be said about third-party candidacies in presidential elections is that the current system perversely discriminates in favor of regional third-party candidates, while discriminating against third-party candidates who have a broad national base of support. In 1948, Henry Wallace (a leftist candidate for President) and Strom Thurmond (a pro-segregation candidate for President) each received 1.2 million popular votes. However, Strom Thurmond (whose support was concentrated in the South) won 39 electoral votes in 1948, whereas Henry Wallace (whose support was distributed throughout the county) received no electoral votes.

Although Ross Perot's percentage of the national popular vote in 1992 was twice the percentage received in 1968 by George Wallace (a pro-segregation candidate), Perot won no electoral votes in 1992, whereas George Wallace won 46 in 1968. Although Perot received eight times Strom Thurmond's percentage of the popular vote in 1948, Perot won no electoral votes in 1992, while Thurmond won 39.[121] The current state-by-state winner-take-all system does not prevent the proliferation of candi-

---

[121] A simulation conducted by FairVote suggests that if Ross Perot had doubled his national popular vote from 19% to 38%, he probably would have won a majority of the electoral votes. http://www.fairvote.org/the-perot-simulator. But with 19% of the national popular vote broadly spread out over the entire country, Perot won no electoral votes.

dates; however, it does reward certain types of third-party candidacies while punishing others.

Some argue that third parties are inherently undesirable and that the election system should be skewed so as to strengthen and favor the two-party system. Even if one subscribes to this viewpoint, it is difficult to see what public purpose is served by the current system's perverse discrimination in favor of regionally divisive third parties and against broad-based third parties.

10.8 Myths about Extremist and Regional Candidates

10.8.1 MYTH: Extremist candidates will proliferate under a national popular vote.

QUICK ANSWER:

- If an Electoral College type of arrangement were essential for avoiding extremist candidates, we should see evidence of the occurrence of this conjectured apocalyptic outcome in elections (such as gubernatorial elections) that do not employ an Electoral College type of arrangement.

- However, the fact is that extremist candidates are rarely elected in elections in which the winner is the candidate who receives the most votes.

MORE DETAILED ANSWER:

Tara Ross has asserted that under a national popular vote:

> "Extremist candidates could more easily sway an election, because no candidate is required to obtain majority support.... Electoral votes are given to the winner of any plurality—even a very small one."[122]

On another occasion, Ross wrote:

> "Multi-party races have rather nasty side effects, including a deeply fractured populace and the possibility that an extremist candidate could win with a small plurality.... The Electoral College ... creates incentives for moderation and compromise."[123]

---

[122] Written testimony submitted by Tara Ross to Delaware Senate in June 2010.

[123] Ross, Tara. *Flash Report*, September 11, 2006.

If an Electoral College type of arrangement were essential for avoiding extremist candidates, we should see evidence of the occurrence of this conjectured apocalyptic outcome in elections (such as gubernatorial elections) that do not employ an Electoral College type of arrangement.

Ross provides no evidence suggesting that extremism results from elections in which the winner is the candidate who receives the most popular votes. However, there is considerable evidence to the contrary.

At the time the U.S. Constitution came into effect in 1789, governors were elected in only Rhode Island and Connecticut. The idea of popularly electing the governor was adopted piecemeal, on a state-by-state basis. Today, all governors are elected. After 220 years of actual experience in over 5,000 statewide elections for state chief executive, there has not been any widespread lack of moderation in political discourse. Extremist candidates are rarely elected in elections in which the winner is the candidate who receives the most popular votes.

How many of the winners in over 5,000 gubernatorial elections in the United States have been extremists?

How many of the U.S. Senators elected in almost 100 years of actual experience under the 17th Amendment have been extremists?

Given this historical record, there is no reason to expect the emergence of some new and currently unknown political dynamic if the President were elected in the same manner as virtually every other public official in the United States.

Candidates attempting to win any election have a strong incentive to capture "the middle" of the electorate. Counting the votes on a nationwide basis (instead of a statewide basis) would not make presidential candidates extreme.

Criticism of the National Popular Vote plan in connection with extremism is yet another example of a criticism that actually applies to the current state-by-state winner-take-all system more than the National Popular Vote plan.

Segregationists such as Strom Thurmond (1948) or George Wallace (1968) won electoral votes in various Southern states. Neither Strom Thurmond nor George Wallace had any reasonable expectation of winning a plurality of the popular votes nationwide. The reason that the current system has encouraged so many minor-party candidacies is that third-party candidates have 51 separate opportunities to find particular states that they might win outright or where they might be able to shift electoral votes from one major party to another.

The current state-by-state winner-take-all system encourages third-party candidates (such as Strom Thurmond and George Wallace) who hope to deny a majority of the Electoral College to the major-party candidates and thereby throw the election of the President to the U.S. House of Representatives or, alternatively, to bargain with the major-party candidates prior to the meeting of the Electoral College.

10.8.2 MYTH: Regional candidates will proliferate under a national popular vote.

QUICK ANSWER:

- If an Electoral College type of arrangement were essential for avoiding regional candidates, we should see evidence of this conjectured outcome in elections (such as gubernatorial elections) that do not employ an Electoral College type of arrangement.
- There is no evidence of the emergence of regional candidates or regional parties in statewide elections in which the winner is the candidate who receives the most popular votes.

MORE DETAILED ANSWER:

Tara Ross, an opponent of the National Popular Vote plan, raises the following question:

"What if voters in New York and Massachusetts throw all their weight behind one regional candidate?"[124]

We can easily test Ross's hypothetical scenario about regional candidates against actual historical experience and facts.

If an Electoral College type of arrangement were essential for avoiding Ross's conjectured outcome, we should see evidence of regional parties and regional candidates in elections that do not employ an Electoral College.

However, when elections for governor are conducted in which the winner is the candidate who receives the most popular votes, we do not

---

[124] Oral and written testimony presented by Tara Ross at Nevada Senate Committee on Legislative Operations and Elections on May 7, 2009.

see a Philadelphia Party and a Pittsburgh Party nominating regional candidates for governor of Pennsylvania. We do not see an Eastern Shore Party in Maryland opposing the Western Shore Party for statewide office in Maryland. We do not see an Upper Peninsula Party in Michigan or a Northern California Party in California.

Similarly, we do not see regional parties or candidates running for the U.S. Senate.

In the real world, ordinary plurality voting discourages the formation of niche parties and, instead, rewards the formation of broad coalitions in which various groups and interests join together in order to win the most votes (and thereby win office).

The reason that ordinary plurality voting has this effect is that a vote cast for a splinter candidate generally produces the politically counterproductive effect of helping the major-party candidate whose views are diametrically opposite to those of the voter.

For example, votes cast for Bob Barr (the Libertarian Party candidate for President in 2008) made it easier for Barack Obama to win North Carolina.[125] Votes cast in 2000 for Ralph Nader (the Green Party candidate) made it easier for George W. Bush to win Florida and New Hampshire.[126]

Based on historical evidence, regional candidates are far more common under the state-by-state winner-take-all system of electing the President than in elections in which the winner is the candidate who receives the most popular votes in the jurisdiction involved.

Under the current system of electing the President (in which all of a state's electoral votes are awarded to the candidate who receives a plurality of the popular vote in each separate state), regional segregationist candidates such as Strom Thurmond (1948) and George Wallace (1968) won electoral votes in various Southern states.

None of these third-party candidates had any reasonable expectation of winning a plurality of the popular votes nationwide. The reason that the current system has encouraged so many regional candidacies is that

---

[125] In North Carolina in 2008, Bob Barr (the Libertarian candidate) received considerably more votes than the margin between Barack Obama (the winner of the state) and John McCain (the second-place candidate).

[126] In Florida and New Hampshire in 2000, Ralph Nader received considerably more votes than the margin between George W. Bush (the winner of these two states) and Al Gore (the second-place candidate).

such candidates can win certain states outright or can affect the national outcome by shifting electoral votes from one major party to another.

Strom Thurmond (1948) and George Wallace (1968) sought to throw the presidential election into the U.S. House of Representatives or to bargain with the major-party candidates before the meeting of the Electoral College in mid-December.

10.9 Myths about Logistical Nightmares Arising from Differences in State Laws

10.9.1 MYTH: Logistical nightmares would plague a national popular vote because of differences among the states concerning ballot access requirements, ex-felon eligibility requirements, and poll closing times.

QUICK ANSWER:

- There is nothing incompatible between state control over elections and a national popular vote for President.
- Differences in election laws are inherent in our federalist system, which gives the states control over elections.
- Adding up the popular votes that are cast in each state to obtain the national popular vote total for each presidential candidate is not a difficult task, much less a "logistical nightmare."
- The National Popular Vote plan is based on the constitutional system that actually exists in the United States and on the political reality that there is widespread public and legislative support for federalism and state control of elections.

MORE DETAILED ANSWER:

Tara Ross predicts that the National Popular Vote plan would create "logistical nightmares [that] could haunt the country."[127]

Ross also notes:

> "There are ... inconsistencies among states' ballots that would skew the election results.... States differ in their requirements for ballot qualification." [128]

---

[127] Written testimony submitted by Tara Ross to Delaware Senate in June 2010.

[128] *Id.*

Differences in election laws are inherent in our federalist system which gives the states control over elections.

The Founders gave the states exclusive control over the manner of electing the President so as to provide a check on a sitting President who might try to manipulate the rules for his own reelection in conjunction with a possibly compliant Congress.

There is nothing incompatible between state control over elections and a national popular vote for President. That was certainly the mainstream view when the U.S. House of Representatives passed a constitutional amendment in 1969 for a national popular vote by a 338–70 margin. That amendment retained state control over elections. That amendment was endorsed by Richard Nixon, Gerald Ford, George H.W. Bush, Jimmy Carter, and contemporary vice-presidential candidates such as Bob Dole and Walter Mondale.

No "logistical nightmare" was perceived in simply adding up the certified popular vote total for each candidate from each state.

Concerning the differences in ballot-access requirements among the states, it is true that it is easier to get on the ballot in some states than others. Nonetheless, serious third-party candidates for President do manage to get on the ballot in virtually every state. For example, Ross Perot was on the ballot in all 50 states in 1992 and 1996. John Anderson was on the ballot in all 50 states. Even less viable third-party candidates usually manage to get on the ballot in almost every state. For example, Ralph Nader got onto the ballot in 45 states in 2008 and received about ½% of the vote.

The consequence to a candidate of not being on the ballot in a particular state is identical under both the current system and the National Popular Vote plan namely, that the candidate is unlikely to receive a substantial number of votes in that particular state (barring the remote possibility of a successful write-in campaign in that state). There is no "logistical nightmare."

If Ralph Nader had won electoral votes in any of the states where he was on the ballot, his absence from the ballot in other states would not have caused him to forfeit those electoral votes, much less have created a "logistical nightmare."

In terms of election administration, the absence from the ballot of a particular candidate in a particular state does not create any problem because election officials in each state simply report whatever votes are cast in their state for whatever candidates actually receive votes in their state. The states report the vote total for each presidential candidate on the "certificate of ascertainment" required by section 6 of title 3 of the United States Code. If a particular candidate does not receive any votes in a particular state, there is simply no vote total reported for that candidate from the state. The fact that Ralph Nader did not receive any popular votes from certain states (and therefore did not appear on the certificates of ascertainment from those states) hardly created a "logistical nightmare."

The National Popular Vote compact provides that the results from each state would be added up—the very same process of adding up of 51 sets of numbers that would have occurred under the constitutional amendment that was approved by the U.S. House of Representatives in 1969.

Tara Ross doesn't identify how the adding up of 51 sets of numbers would create a "logistical nightmare"—much less how it "would skew the election results."

It is true that some state election laws vary in many ways.

For example, some states have early poll closing times (e.g., 6:00 P.M. in Kentucky and Indiana), whereas the polls stay open until 9:00 P.M. in other states. In addition, polls close at different times due to the nation's numerous time zones. Differences in poll-closing times would be handled under the National Popular Vote in the same way they are handled now—that is, the polls would open and close in each state in accordance with state or federal law. [129]

Tara Ross cites the differences among the states in eligibility of ex-felons to vote. Under the National Popular Vote plan, each state would conduct the election under its own laws—the same thing that would have occurred under the constitutional amendment that was approved by the U.S. House of Representatives in 1969. The certified popular vote totals from each state for each candidate would be added up to produce nationwide totals—the same thing that would have occurred under the constitutional amendment that was approved by the U.S. House of Representatives in 1969.

---

[129] Clause 4 of section 1 of article II of the U.S. Constitution provides, "The Congress may determine the Time of chusing the Electors." Under existing federal law, Congress has chosen a uniform national day for choosing electors (namely, the Tuesday after the first Monday in November). However, Congress could specify the time of day as well.

Tara Ross further observes:

"Inevitably, [a state] would have to abide by national election results derived from policies with which it disagrees."[130]

Of course, this is precisely what happens now under the current U.S. Constitution because it empowers the states to control elections. All of the people of the United States are impacted by the election policies of other states. No one can dispute that the procedures governing presidential elections in battleground states (e.g., Florida and Ohio) have significantly affected the entire country.

The fact that Oregon conducts its elections 100% by mail arguably contributed to the defeat of the sitting Republican U.S. Senator in 2008, thereby giving the Democrats 60 votes in the U.S. Senate and thereby affecting numerous laws that were enacted immediately thereafter. The decision of the Massachusetts legislature to change its vacancy-filling procedure for the late U.S. Senator Ted Kennedy's seat (from a gubernatorial appointment to an early special election in which Republican Scott Brown was ultimately elected) significantly impacted the course of politics in the entire United States in early 2010.

The genius of the federalist approach (as specified in the U.S. Constitution) is that no single political party is ever in a position to impose politically advantageous voting procedures on the entire country and thereby lock in a self-perpetuating advantage on the national level.

The real question for opponents of state control over elections is whether they would have been comfortable under *all* of the following scenarios:

- Suppose in 2003 (just prior to the 2004 presidential election), the then-Republican-controlled Congress and a then-sitting Republican President enacted uniform national voting procedures, including photo identification; vigorous purging of the voter rolls of those who did not vote in the immediately preceding election; and closing the polls at 6:00 P.M. in every state.
- Suppose in 2009, the then-Democratic-controlled Congress and the then-sitting Democratic President enacted uniform national voting procedures, including automatic permanent

---

[130] Written testimony submitted by Tara Ross to Delaware Senate in June 2010.

voter registration based on the census; advance voting several weeks before Election Day in every state; no-excuse absentee voting in every state; and universal voting by mail in every state.

- Suppose at some future time (such as 2013), one political party controls both houses of Congress and the White House.

In short, there is a trade-off between the advantages of uniformity and the goal of preventing a single political party from imposing uniform national election rules that would enable it to perpetuate itself in office.

The Founders chose the federalist approach that gives state control over elections. Differences in state election laws resulting from our federalist system are not "logistical nightmares [that] could haunt the country" but a strength of our nation's Constitution.

Of course, if a national consensus emerges in favor of uniform federal control of elections at some time in the future, the U.S. Constitution can be so amended to eliminate state control over elections at that time.

Meanwhile, the National Popular Vote plan is based on the constitutional system that actually exists in the United States and on the reality that there is widespread public and legislative support for state control of elections.

10.9.2 MYTH: A state's electoral votes could be awarded to a candidate not on a state's own ballot, and out-of-state persons could become presidential electors.

QUICK ANSWER:

- This hypothesized scenario is politically implausible because a presidential candidate winning the most popular votes throughout the entire United States would, almost certainly, have been on the ballot in all 50 states.
- Even if the hypothesized national popular vote winner were not on a particular state's ballot, it would be politically preposterous for such a candidate to insult a state gratuitously by appointing out-of-state persons to become presidential electors on the eve of assuming the Presidency.
- If anyone considers the hypothesized scenario to be a real problem, the states have ample constitutional authority to prevent it.

- Even if the hypothesized scenario were to occur, the National Popular Vote compact would deliver precisely its advertised result namely, the election of the presidential candidate who received the most popular votes in all 50 states and the District of Columbia.

MORE DETAILED ANSWER:

Tara Ross, an opponent of the National Popular Vote compact, has raised the possibility that a Texas regional candidate (say, Ron Paul) might not be on the ballot in Delaware but nonetheless win the national popular vote. She then raises the possibility that

"Delaware could be required to cast its electoral votes for a candidate who did not qualify for the ballot in Delaware."[131]

It is most unlikely that a serious candidate for President would run without qualifying for the ballot in all 50 states.

- Ross Perot was on the ballot in all 50 states in both 1992 and 1996.
- John Anderson was on the ballot in all 50 states in 1980.
- Ralph Nader (who received only about ½% of the national popular vote in 2008) was on the ballot in 45 states.

Given that a new political party can qualify for the ballot in Delaware with 650 signatures, it would be unlikely that Tara Ross's hypothetical Texas regional candidate would have been unable to qualify in Delaware.

It is certainly not likely that the hypothesized Texas regional candidate would have received the most popular votes in all 50 states and the District of Columbia without being on the ballot in every state (or virtually every state).

However, even in this politically implausible scenario, the National Popular Vote compact would deliver precisely its promised result namely, the election of the presidential candidate who received the most popular votes in all 50 states and the District of Columbia.

Tara Ross further hypothesizes that Ron Paul might win the national popular vote and then appoint Texans to represent Delaware in the Electoral College.

---

[131] Written testimony submitted by Tara Ross to Delaware Senate in June 2010.

"Delaware probably did not nominate a slate of electors for Paul because he was not on its ballot. NPV's compact offers a solution, but it is doubtful that voters in Delaware will like it. Paul would be entitled to personally appoint the three electors who will represent Delaware in the Electoral College vote. In all likelihood, he would select Texans to represent Delaware in the presidential election...."[132]

First, under the National Popular Vote compact, nominees for the position of presidential elector would be chosen in exactly the same way as they currently are (that is, by local political parties in accordance with existing state law). The provision of the National Popular Vote compact cited in Ross's hypothetical scenario applies *only if* a local political party in a state fails to nominate the exact number of candidates for the position of presidential elector to which the state is entitled. In this unlikely contingency, the compact permits the winning presidential candidate to decisively and quickly untangle any problem that might prevent him or her from receiving the full number of electoral votes to which he or she is entitled. This back-up procedure is designed to ensure that the compact guarantees the election of the presidential candidate who receives the most popular votes in all 50 states and the District of Columbia. Clause 7 of article III of the compact states:

> "**If, for any reason, the number of presidential electors** nominated in a member state in association with the national popular vote winner **is less than or greater than that state's number of electoral votes**, the presidential candidate on the presidential slate that has been designated as the national popular vote winner shall have the power to nominate the presidential electors for that state and that state's presidential elector certifying official shall certify the appointment of such nominees." [Emphasis added]

Second, there is historical evidence about how real-world politicians would behave in this situation. Under existing law in Pennsylvania, *every* presidential candidate, in *every* election, directly chooses *every* presidential elector in Pennsylvania. Needless to say, no presidential candidate has ever chosen a Texan or any other out-of-state person for the position

---

[132] Written testimony submitted by Tara Ross to Delaware Senate in June 2010.

of presidential elector in Pennsylvania. Indeed, it would be politically pre-posterous for a presidential candidate to insult Pennsylvania gratuitously by selecting out-of-staters to the totally ceremonial position of presidential elector. It would be even more preposterous for someone who had just won the national popular vote (and was about to become President and face the task of unifying the country) to insult a state gratuitously.

Third, it would be extraordinary that Ron Paul (whom Ross hypothesizes just won the most popular votes across the entire United States) would not have three supporters in Delaware.

Fourth, if any state believes that Ross's hypothetical scenario is politically plausible and potentially harmful, every state has the power, under the U.S. Constitution, to adopt residency qualifications for the position of presidential elector. Indeed, Delaware is an example of a state that has enacted additional qualifications for the position of presidential elector (albeit not to disqualify Texans).

10.10   Myths about Faithless Electors

10.10.1 MYTH: Faithless presidential electors would be a problem under the National Popular Vote compact.

QUICK ANSWER:
- In the first place, there is no practical problem with faithless presidential electors (i.e., presidential electors who unexpectedly cast their vote in the Electoral College for someone other than the nominee of the political party under whose banner the elector was chosen). There have only been 11 such votes cast out of 22,453 electoral votes in the nation's 56 presidential elections (with only one, in 1796, being a true faithless elector).
- To the extent that any state believes that there is a problem, the states already have ample constitutional authority to remedy it.
- Moreover, one of the collateral benefits of the National Popular Vote plan is that it would virtually eliminate the possibility of faithless electors actually affecting the outcome of a presidential election because it would typically generate an exaggerated margin of victory in the Electoral College of about 75% for the national popular vote winner

(namely, an absolute majority of the electoral votes from the compacting states plus about half of the votes from the non-compacting states).

MORE DETAILED ANSWER:

The myth about faithless electors is yet another example of a situation that the National Popular Vote plan handles in a manner that is superior to the current system.

In the first place, faithless electors (i.e., presidential electors who unexpectedly cast their vote in the Electoral College for someone other than the nominee of the political party under whose banner the elector was chosen) are not a practical problem.

Questions about the possibility of faithless electors often stem from the incorrect belief that presidential electors are a lofty group of independent-minded people who sit in judgment of the people's choice for President, and then graciously accede to the people's choice. It is true that the Founding Fathers envisioned that the presidential electors would be outstanding citizens who would meet and debate and exercise independent judgment in choosing the best person to become President. However, that expectation was dashed with the emergence of political parties in the nation's first competitive presidential election in 1796.

Since 1796, presidential electors have been committed party activists who are nominated by their political party to cast their vote in the Electoral College for their party's nominee. That is, presidential electors have simply been willing "rubberstamps" for their party's nominee for President.

Of the 22,453 electoral votes cast for President in the nation's 56 presidential elections between 1789 and 2008, only 11 were cast in an unexpected way.[133] Moreover, among these 11 cases, the unexpected vote of Samuel Miles for Thomas Jefferson in 1796 was the only instance of a true faithless elector (that is, a situation where the elector might have thought, at the time he voted, that his vote might affect the national outcome).

Nine of the other 11 cases were simply post-election grand-standing votes cast by publicity-seeking electors who knew, at the time they voted, that their vote would not affect the outcome in the Electoral College.

---

[133] This count does not include 62 electors who did not vote in 1872 for Horace Greeley who died after he lost the election (but before the Electoral College met).

One electoral vote was accidentally and unintentionally cast by an unknown presidential elector in Minnesota who absentmindedly voted for his party's vice-presidential candidate for both President and Vice President.[134]

Second, if anyone perceives faithless presidential electors to be a real problem, the states already have ample constitutional authority to remedy the situation by means of state law.

In most states, each political party nominates candidates for the position of presidential elector (typically at a combination of party conventions at the congressional district level and state level).

About half of the states have laws involving pledges, penalties, or other procedures to ensure that presidential electors vote for their party's nominees. About half of the states do not address the problem at all.

Existing Pennsylvania law is noteworthy in that it empowers each presidential nominee to nominate all elector candidates directly. The presidential nominee is, after all, the person whose name actually appears on the ballot on Election Day and who has the greatest and most immediate interest in faithful voting by presidential electors.

Existing North Carolina law declares vacant the position of any contrary-voting elector, voids that elector's vote, and empowers the state's remaining electors to replace the contrary-voting elector immediately with an elector loyal to the party's nominee.

In the 1952 case of *Ray v. Blair*, The U.S. Supreme Court upheld the constitutionality of a pledge guaranteeing faithful voting by presidential electors. Justice Robert H. Jackson summarized the history of presidential electors as follows:

> "No one faithful to our history can deny that the plan originally contemplated, what is implicit in its text, that electors would be free agents, to exercise an independent and nonpartisan judgment as to the men best qualified for the Nation's highest offices. …
>
> "This arrangement miscarried. **Electors**, although often personally eminent, independent, and respectable, **officially become**

---

[134] The accidental vote was cast in Minnesota in 2004. After the ballots were counted, all 10 electors said that they intended to vote for John Kerry for President and John Edwards for Vice President. However, one of the 10 accidentally voted for John Edwards for both President and Vice President.

voluntary party lackeys and intellectual nonentities to whose memory we might justly paraphrase a tuneful satire:

'They always voted at their party's call 'And never thought of thinking for themselves at all.'" [135]

At its 119th annual meeting in 2010, the Uniform Law Commission (also known as the National Conference of Commissioners on Uniform State Laws) approved a "Uniform Faithless Presidential Electors Act" and submitted this model legislation to the state legislatures for their consideration. The proposed uniform law calls for the election of both electors and alternate electors. There is a pledge of faithfulness by both the candidates for position of elector and alternate electors. The proposed uniform law employs the removal and replacement concept similar to that contained in the current North Carolina law. The National Popular Vote organization has endorsed this proposed uniform law.

Third, if anyone views faithless presidential electors to be a real problem, the National Popular Vote plan is actually superior to the current system in ensuring that a wayward elector would not impact the ultimate choice of the President. Under the National Popular Vote compact, the national popular vote winner would generally receive an exaggerated margin (roughly 75%) of the votes in the Electoral College in any given presidential election. The reason is that the National Popular Vote compact guarantees that the presidential candidate receiving the most popular votes in all 50 states and the District of Columbia would receive at least 270 (of the 538) electoral votes from the states belonging to the compact. Then, beyond the guaranteed bloc of at least 270 electoral votes, the national popular vote winner would receive additional electoral votes from whichever non-compacting states he or she happened to carry (under the prevailing laws of those states). Because the non-compacting states would likely be divided approximately equally between the candidates, the nationwide winning candidate would generally receive an exaggerated margin (totaling roughly 75%) of the votes in the Electoral College (that is, about 404 of the 538 electoral votes). This cushion would make it even less likely for faithless electors to affect the outcome of a presidential election.

For additional information about faithless electors, see section 2.12.

---

[135] *Ray v. Blair* 343 U.S. 214 at 232. 1952.

10.10.2 MYTH: It might be difficult to coerce presidential electors to vote for the national popular vote winner.

QUICK ANSWER:

- No coercion would be required to force presidential electors to vote for the national popular vote winner, because the National Popular Vote plan would result in the election to the Electoral College of at least 270 presidential electors who are avid supporters of the national popular vote winner.

MORE DETAILED ANSWER:

No coercion is required to force presidential electors to vote as intended under either the current system or the National Popular Vote system.

Under both systems, each political party nominates strongly opinionated party activists for the ceremonial position of presidential elector. Each party's nominees for the position of presidential elector are selected precisely because they are passionate supporters of their political party and its candidate and because they can be relied upon to act as willing "rubberstamps" for their party's nominee.

When voters go to the polls on Election Day in November, they are, in reality, voting for a slate of presidential electors belonging to one party or the other. Under the winner-take-all system (currently used in 48 of the 50 states and the District of Columbia), the entire slate of elector candidates associated with the presidential candidate receiving the most popular votes within each separate state is elected to the position of presidential elector.[136]

Under the National Popular Vote compact, the state's presidential electors would be the elector candidates associated with the presidential candidate who won the most popular votes in all 50 states and the District of Columbia. This bloc of 270 (or more) presidential electors would reflect the will of the voters nationwide. All of these 270 or more presidential electors would be loyal and avid supporters of the national

---

[136] In two states (Maine and Nebraska), the elector candidates associated with the presidential candidate who receives the most popular votes in each of the state's congressional districts are elected (along with the two additional at-large elector candidates associated with the presidential candidate who receives the most popular votes in the state as a whole).

popular vote winner. These presidential electors would come from the political party that won the election nationally. Thus, no one in this bloc of 270 (or more) presidential electors would be asked to vote contrary to his or her own political inclinations or conscience. Instead, these electors would vote for their own strongly held personal choice namely, the nominee of their own political party.

Under the National Popular Vote plan, these 270 (or more) presidential electors would operate as willing "rubberstamps" for the nationwide choice of the voters, just as presidential electors currently act as willing "rubberstamps" for the statewide choice of the voters (or district-wide choice, in the cases of Maine and Nebraska).

10.10.3 MYTH: Presidential electors might succumb to outside pressure and abandon the national popular vote in favor of the winner of the popular vote in the state.

QUICK ANSWER:

- Presidential electors are very loyal party activists who are selected precisely because they can be relied upon to act as willing "rubberstamps" for their party's nominee.
- The low probability of presidential electors succumbing to outside pressure is illustrated by the fact that no Republican presidential elector voted for Al Gore in 2000 despite the fact that Gore received the most popular vote nationwide and that the fact the American public overwhelmingly believes that the President should be the candidate who receives the most popular vote in all 50 states and the District of Columbia. Instead, all 271 Republican presidential electors dutifully voted for their party's nominee in accordance with the virtually universal view of how the system that was legally in effect at the time should operate.

MORE DETAILED ANSWER:

Some have suggested that, under the National Popular Vote compact, presidential electors might, after the people vote in November, succumb to outside pressure and abandon the national popular vote in favor of the winner of the popular vote in the state.

This hypothetical scenario is based on the incorrect assumptions that
- there is any substantial pool of people who would support

the notion of changing the rules after the public has voted on Election Day,

- the public favors the current state-by-state winner-take-all approach to electing the President and hence there would be a vast pool of people to apply such pressure on presidential electors, and
- the supporters of the presidential candidate who just won the national popular vote, under laws that were in place on Election Day, would care about—much less succumb to—extra-legal pressure from people representing the losing party.

The reality is that there would be no substantial amount of pressure in the first place. The public simply does not favor the current system of awarding all of a state's electoral votes to the presidential candidate who receives the most popular votes in each separate state (the winner-take-all-rule). In polls since 1944, at least 70% (usually more) of the American people have said that they believed that the presidential candidate receiving the most votes throughout the United States should win the Presidency. A mere 20% of the public supports the current state-by-state winner-take-all system (with 10% undecided). Far from being attached to the state-by-state winner-take-all system of awarding electoral votes, the public strongly opposes it.

The environment in which this hypothetical scenario would arise consists of the following five elements:

(1) About 70% of the voters of any given state believe that the presidential candidate receiving the most votes in all 50 states and the District of Columbia should win the Presidency;

(2) The state legislature and governor of the state have responded to the wishes of its own voters and enacted the National Popular Vote law in their state;

(3) States possessing a majority of the electoral votes (essentially more than half the population of the country) have similarly enacted the National Popular Vote law and the law has taken effect nationally;

(4) A nationwide presidential campaign has been conducted, over a period of many months, with everyone in the

United States knowing that the National Popular Vote plan is the law that is in place and will govern the presidential election; and

(5) On Election Day in November, one presidential candidate emerged with the most popular votes in all 50 states and the District of Columbia.

The hypothetical scenario then conjectures that, when the time comes for the Electoral College to meet in mid-December, the 270 (or more) presidential electors (who are avid supporters of their own party's presidential candidate who just won the national popular vote) would respond to pressure from supporters of the political party that just lost the election.

In fact, there would be little inclination for party activists to vote against their own strongly held personal preferences, against their own party's presidential nominee, against their own state's law, and against the desires of an overwhelming majority of their state's voters (who favor a national popular vote for President).

Of course, the country has actual experience that relates to the hypothesized kind of scenario. In 2000, Al Gore won the national popular vote by a margin of over 537,000 votes. However, under the laws in place at the time, there were 271 Republican presidential electors (one more than the 270 required to elect a President) who were chosen for that position by their party on the presumption that they would vote for George W. Bush. About 70% of the American people believed (then and now) that the Presidency should go to the candidate who receives the most popular votes in all 50 states and the District of Columbia. Nevertheless, none of the 271 Republican presidential electors succumbed to public pressure and voted in favor of the winner of the national popular vote.

10.11 Myths about Post-Election Changes in the Rules of the Game, Withdrawal, and Enforceability

10.11.1 MYTH: A state legislature might change a state's method of awarding electoral votes after the people vote in November, but before the Electoral College meets in December.

QUICK ANSWER:

- There are seven *independent* reasons why there should be

no concern about the hypothetical scenario in which a governor and legislature attempt, for partisan political advantage, to change a state's method of awarding electoral votes after the people vote in November, but before the Electoral College meets in December.

- The National Popular Vote compact delays the effective date of a withdrawal until after the inauguration of the new President if the withdrawal occurred in the six-month period between July 20 of a presidential election year and the inauguration. Any law attempting to repeal the compact after the people vote in November, but before the Electoral College meets in December, would violate the Impairments Clause of the U.S. Constitution and be void.

- Any attempt to appoint presidential electors after the people vote in November would violate existing federal law requiring that presidential electors be appointed on a single designated day in every four-year period namely, the Tuesday after the first Monday in November (i.e., Election Day).

- Any attempt to appoint presidential electors after the people vote in November would invalidate the "conclusiveness" of that state's results under existing federal law specifying that presidential electors must be appointed under "laws enacted *prior*" to the Tuesday after the first Monday in November (Election Day).

- Any attempt to appoint presidential electors after the people vote in November would probably not matter anyway under the National Popular Vote compact because the national popular vote winner would typically receive about 75% of electoral votes in the Electoral College, thereby producing a cushion of about 135 electoral votes above the 270 needed to win the Presidency.

- Any attempt to appoint presidential electors after the people vote in November could only be contemplated, as a practical matter, in about three states because of the partisan division of most state governments, the significant time delay before new state laws take effect in most states, quorum requirements, and numerous opportunities for delay built into the legislative process by state constitutional provisions and legislative rules.

- Any attempt to appoint presidential electors after the people vote in November would be politically implausible in the real world.

MORE DETAILED ANSWER:

This section discusses the hypothetical scenario in which a governor and state legislature might try, for partisan political advantage, to change the "rules of the game" for electing the President by withdrawing from the National Popular Vote compact (say, after Election Day in November but before the mid-December meeting of the Electoral College) and enacting an alternative method of awarding their state's electoral votes (say, legislative appointment of the state's presidential electors).

There are seven *independent* reasons why there should be no concern about this hypothetical scenario.

THE IMPAIRMENTS CLAUSE OF THE U.S. CONSTITUTION PROHIBITS WITHDRAWAL FROM INTERSTATE COMPACTS IN ANY MANNER OTHER THAN THAT SPECIFIED IN THE COMPACT.

An interstate compact is a contract. Withdrawal from any contract may only be made in accordance with the contract's own terms.

Like most interstate compacts, the National Popular Vote compact permits states to withdraw from the compact (by passing a repeal statute).

However, like most other interstate compacts, the National Popular Vote compact delays the effectiveness of any withdrawal for a certain amount of time appropriate to the subject matter of the compact.

Clause 2 of Article IV of the National Popular Vote compact provides:

> "Any member state may withdraw from this agreement, except that a withdrawal occurring six months or less before the end of a President's term shall not become effective until a President or Vice President shall have been qualified to serve the next term."

This six-month "blackout" period includes six important events relating to presidential elections namely, the

- national nominating conventions,
- fall general election campaign period,
- Election Day on Tuesday after the first Monday in November,
- meeting of the Electoral College on the first Monday after the second Wednesday in December,
- counting of the electoral votes by Congress on January 6, and
- scheduled inauguration of the President and Vice President for the new term on January 20.

The Impairments Clause of the U.S. Constitution (Article I, section 10, clause 1) provides:

> "No State shall ... pass any ... Law impairing the Obligation of Contracts."

Because of the Impairments Clause, the courts have never allowed a state to withdraw from any interstate compact without following the procedure for withdrawal specified by the compact.

The U.S. Supreme Court dismissed the possibility succinctly in *Petty v. Tennessee-Missouri Bridge Commission* in 1952:

> "A compact, is after all, a contract." [137]

Federal and state courts have implemented the U.S. Supreme Court's interpretation of the Impairments Clause and rebuffed the occasional (sometimes creative) attempts by states to evade their obligations under interstate compacts.

The U.S. District Court for the District of Maryland in 1976 in *Hellmuth and Associates v. Washington Metropolitan Area Transit Authority* stated:

> "Further, when enacted, **a compact constitutes not only law, but a contract which may not be amended, modified, or otherwise altered** without the consent of all parties."[138] [Emphasis added]

---

[137] *Petty v. Tennessee-Missouri Bridge Commission.* 359 U.S. 275 at 285. 79 S.Ct. 785 at 792. 1952.

[138] *Hellmuth and Associates v. Washington Metropolitan Area Transit Authority* (414 F.Supp. 408 at 409).

The Commonwealth Court of Pennsylvania in *Aveline v. Pennsylvania Board of Probation and Parole* in 1999 stated:

> **"A compact takes precedence over the subsequent statutes of signatory states** and, as such, **a state may not unilaterally nullify, revoke, or amend one of its compacts if the compact does not so provide."**[139] [Emphasis added]

The Council of State Governments summarizes the nature of interstate compacts as follows:

> "Compacts are agreements between two or more states that bind them to the compacts' provisions, just as a contract binds two or more parties in a business deal. As such, compacts are subject to the substantive principles of contract law and are protected by the constitutional prohibition against laws that impair the obligations of contracts ("U.S. Constitution," Article I, Section 10).

> **"That means that compacting states are bound to observe the terms of their agreements, even if those terms are inconsistent with other state laws.** In short, compacts between states are somewhat like treaties between nations. Compacts have the force and effect of statutory law (whether enacted by statute or not) and **they take precedence over conflicting state laws, regardless of when those laws are enacted**.

> "However, unlike treaties, **compacts are not dependent solely upon the good will of the parties. Once enacted, compacts may not be unilaterally renounced by a member state, except as provided by the compacts themselves.** Moreover, Congress and the courts can compel compliance with the terms of interstate compacts. That's why **compacts are considered the most effective means of ensuring interstate cooperation."**[140] [Emphasis added]

---

[139] *Aveline v. Pennsylvania Board of Probation and Parole* (729 A.2d. 1254 at 1257, note 10).

[140] Council of State Governments. 2003. *Interstate Compacts and Agencies 2003.* Lexington, KY: The Council of State Governments. Page 6.

It should be remembered that most interstate compacts contain obligations that a member state would never have agreed to unless it could rely on the enforceability of the obligations undertaken by its sister states. Consequently, most interstate compacts impose a delay on withdrawal because each member state must be able to rely on each contracting party to fulfill its obligations and must have time (and sometimes compensation) to adjust if another state desires to withdraw.

The enforceability of interstate compacts under the Impairments Clause is precisely the reason why sovereign states enter into interstate compacts. If a state were willing to merely rely on the goodwill and graciousness of other states to undertake certain actions, it could unilaterally enact its own independent law on the subject matter involved (unconnected with the actions of other states), unilaterally enact a uniform state law (and hope that other states did the same), or unilaterally enact a contingent state law (if permitted by the state constitution). If a state wants an agreement that is legally binding on other states, it enters into an interstate compact.

Thus, if a governor and state legislature enacted legislation purporting to withdraw from the National Popular Vote compact in the six-month period between July 20 of a presidential election year and Inauguration Day (January 20), that legislation would be unconstitutional because of the Impairments Clause.

> "No State shall ... pass any ... Law impairing the Obligation of Contracts."[141]

The argument has been raised on an election blog that the state legislature's plenary power to choose the manner of appointing presidential electors is not subject to any specific provisions in the Constitution restricting the exercise of legislative power. (In order to promote free-flowing debate of speculative ideas, the blog involved does not permit attribution.)

According to this line of reasoning, specific restrictions in the Constitution, such as the Impairments Clause, cannot not restrict the exercise of a plenary legislative power.

This argument ignores the fact that the vast majority of interstate compacts involve state plenary powers. States voluntarily enter into

---

[141] U.S. Constitution. Article I, section 10, clause 1.

interstate compacts precisely because compacts, in conjunction with the Impairments Clause, provide a way to create and enforce restrictions on plenary state powers. The restrictions are agreed to mutually because each participating state believes that the restrictions are mutually beneficial.

The wording "in such manner as the ... may direct" that appears in the U.S. Constitution is a grant of power, but it does not create a power that stands above the rest of the Constitution or outside the Constitution. Section 1 of article II of the U.S. Constitution provides:

> "Each State shall appoint, **in such Manner as the Legislature thereof may direct**, a Number of Electors...."[142] [Emphasis added]

Section 1 does *not* say:

> "**Notwithstanding any other provision of this Constitution**, each State shall appoint, in such Manner as the Legislature thereof may direct, a Number of Electors...."

The wording "in such manner as the ... may direct" appears elsewhere in the Constitution in connection with the specific subject of selecting the manner of appointing presidential electors. The 23rd Amendment to U.S. Constitution (ratified in 1961) provides:

> "The District constituting the seat of government of the United States shall appoint **in such manner as the Congress may direct** a number of electors of President and Vice President...."

Surely no one would argue that "in such manner as the ... may direct" (the exact parallel of the wording of section 1 of Article II) means that Congress is not subject to specific provisions of the Constitution restricting the exercise of a plenary legislative power, and that Congress could therefore, for example, exclude women and blacks from voting in the selection of presidential electors in the District of Columbia, notwithstanding the specific requirements of the 19th Amendment (ratified in 1920) and the 15th Amendment (ratified in 1870).

The 17th Amendment of the Constitution (ratified in 1913) permits temporary appointments to fill U.S. Senate vacancies

---

[142] U.S. Constitution. Article II, section 1, clause 2.

"…until the people fill the vacancies by election **as the legislature may direct**." [Emphasis added]

Certainly no one would argue that the "may direct" wording means that a state legislature is not subject to other specific provisions in the Constitution restricting the exercise of this plenary legislative power such as, say, the Equal Protection clause of the 14th Amendment (ratified in 1868). A state legislature could not, for example, give two votes each to voters of a certain county in filling vacancies for the U.S. Senate.

In fact, both the U.S. Constitution and state constitutions are replete with plenary powers possessed by their respective legislative bodies. Congress, for example, has plenary power over counterfeiting, the District of Columbia, federal taxation, and numerous other "enumerated" areas, but no one would argue that these plenary powers are not subject to specific provisions of the Constitution restricting the exercise of all legislative power, such as, say, the specific constitutional prohibition against *ex post facto* laws (article I, section 9, clause 3). Congress surely cannot pass *ex post facto* laws for the District of Columbia under its plenary powers in Article I, section 8, clause 17:

> "The Congress shall have Power … to exercise exclusive Legislation in all Cases whatsoever, over such District."

Similarly, state legislatures have plenary power over innumerable matters, but no one would argue that these plenary powers are not subject to the specific provisions of their state constitution and the U.S. Constitution restricting the exercise of legislative power.

EXISTING FEDERAL LAW REQUIRES THAT PRESIDENTIAL ELECTORS BE APPOINTED ON A SINGLE DESIGNATED DAY IN EVERY FOUR-YEAR PERIOD NAMELY, THE TUESDAY AFTER THE FIRST MONDAY IN NOVEMBER.

An attempt by a governor and legislature to change the "rules of the game" between Election Day in November and the mid-December meeting of the Electoral College would involve several steps.

First, the rebellious state legislature and governor would have to enact a statute repealing (withdrawing from) the National Popular Vote compact in that state.

Second, the rebellious legislature would have to provide for the appointment of the state's presidential electors in some alternative way. For example, the legislature might enact a statute empowering the legislature or the governor to appoint the state's presidential electors. Third, the presidential electors would have to be appointed under the newly enacted procedure.

In addition to violating the Impairments Clause, an attempt by a governor and legislature to change the "rules of the game" between Election Day in early November and the mid-December meeting of the Electoral College would be invalid because it would violate existing federal law. The U.S. Constitution (Article II, section 1, clause 4) grants Congress the power to choose the time for appointing presidential electors:

> "**The Congress may determine the Time of chusing the Electors**, and the Day on which they shall give their Votes; which Day shall be the same throughout the United States." [Spelling as per original] [Emphasis added]

Existing federal law (section 1 of title 3 of the United States Code) specifies that presidential electors may only be appointed on one specific day in every four-year period namely, the Tuesday after the first Monday in November (Election Day).

> "**The electors** of President and Vice President **shall be appointed, in each State, on the Tuesday next after the first Monday in November**, in every fourth year succeeding every election of a President and Vice President." [Emphasis added]

Note that the U.S. Constitution does not require the states to permit their own voters to vote for President. State legislatures have always had the power to appoint presidential electors themselves, without consulting the voters. Indeed, the people participated in choosing presidential electors in only five states in the nation's first presidential election in 1789. One state legislature (Colorado) appointed the state's presidential electors as recently as 1876. However, if a state legislature decides that it is going to appoint presidential electors, it must do so on the specific single day authorized by Congress (the Tuesday next after the first Monday in November). In particular, the legislature cannot appoint presidential electors after Election Day (i.e., after seeing the election results in its own state or other states).

Section 1 of title 3 of the United States Code played a role after the people voted in November 1960. John F. Kennedy won the nationwide popular vote by 114,673 votes. However, his majority in the Electoral College depended on the fact that he had carried Illinois by a slender 4,430 popular votes and South Carolina by 4,732 votes. Some members of the South Carolina legislature suggested that the legislature ignore the popular vote count in the state in favor of Kennedy, change the rules for awarding the state's electoral votes after Election Day, and appoint non-Kennedy presidential electors themselves. Nothing came of this suggestion in South Carolina because of existing federal law (section 1 of title 3 of the United States Code) specifying that Election Day is the only day in the four-year cycle on which presidential electors may be appointed. If a legislature wants to appoint presidential electors itself, it must act on Election Day.

There is only one exception permitted by Congress to section 1's requirement of appointing presidential electors on Election Day. Section 2 of title 3 of the United States Code provides:

> "Whenever any State has held an election for the purpose of choosing electors, **and has failed to make a choice on the day prescribed by law**, the electors may be appointed on a subsequent day in such a manner as the legislature of such State may direct." [Emphasis added]

Section 2 covers the contingencies such as the occurrence of a tie in a state s popular vote.

The "failure to make a choice" exception in section 2 played a role in the debate over the disputed presidential election count in Florida in 2000. Because of section 1 of the United States Code, there was no possibility that the Florida legislature could meet after Election Day, retroactively cancel the popular vote, and appoint Republican presidential electors favorable to George W. Bush. However, the argument was advanced at the time that if a recount were ordered by a court that voided the initial count, and if the court-ordered recount were not completed by the "safe harbor" date (i.e., six days prior to the meeting of the Electoral College), then there would have been a "failure to make a choice" in Florida. Because of this potential "failure to make a choice," Florida could then have been left with no presidential electors by the "safe harbor" day. Al Gore would have been elected if Florida had failed to cast its 27 electoral votes.[143] To forestall that possibility, a resolution *reaffirming* the initial already-certified vote count (which certified the election of 27 Republican presidential electors) was passed by the Republican-controlled Florida House of Representatives. Nothing came of this "reaffirming" motion in the Republican-controlled state Senate because of subsequent action in the courts.

The "failure to make a choice" exception offered by section 2 would not, of course, be applicable to the hypothetical scenario involving the National Popular Vote compact, because the voters would have already made a choice on Election Day—simply a choice that the governor and legislature didn't like.

The important point is that section 1 of the United States Code prevents a governor and state legislature from appointing presidential electors after Election Day but before the mid-December meeting of the Electoral College.

THE SAFE HARBOR PROVISION OF FEDERAL LAW ONLY CONFERS CONCLUSIVENESS ON APPOINTMENTS OF PRESIDENTIAL ELECTORS MADE UNDER "LAWS ENACTED PRIOR TO ELECTION DAY."

The "safe harbor" section of federal law (Title 3, section 5) treats a state's appointment of presidential electors as "conclusive" only if the appointment is based on

> "**laws enacted prior to the day** fixed for the appointment
> of the electors." [Emphasis added]

The day fixed by law for appointment of presidential electors is the Tuesday after the first Monday in November (i.e., Election Day).

Under the hypothetical scenario, the law that would have been in effect "prior to" Election Day would have been the National Popular Vote compact.

That is, the presidential electors appointed under the law in effect "prior to" Election Day (that is, the National Popular Vote compact) would be the electors appointed on Election Day.

---

[143] The Constitution does not require an absolute majority of the electoral votes to become President but only a "majority of the whole number of Electors *appointed*." There have been occasional cases when a state failed to appoint its presidential electors. For example, New York did not in 1789 because the legislature could not agree on how to appoint them. Notably, the southern states did not appoint presidential electors in 1864.

THE HYPOTHETICAL SCENARIO WOULD PROBABLY NOT MATTER BECAUSE THE NATIONAL POPULAR VOTE WINNER WOULD TYPICALLY RECEIVE ABOUT 75% OF THE ELECTORAL VOTES IN THE ELECTORAL COLLEGE, THEREBY PRODUCING A CUSHION OF ABOUT 135 ELECTORAL VOTES ABOVE THE 270 NEEDED TO WIN THE PRESIDENCY.
Even if the Impairments Clause of the U.S. Constitution and sections 1 and 5 of Title 3 of the United States Code did not exist, the hypothetical scenario would probably not matter because the national popular vote winner would typically receive about 75% of the votes in the Electoral College under the National Popular vote compact.

The reason is that the compact guarantees that the presidential candidate receiving the most popular votes in all 50 states and the District of Columbia will receive at least 270 electoral votes from the states belonging to the compact. Then, in addition to this minimum guaranteed bloc of 270 or more electoral votes from the compacting states, the nationwide winning candidate would receive a certain number of additional electoral votes from whichever non-compacting states he or she happened to carry (under existing laws for awarding electoral votes in those states). Because the non-compacting states would likely be divided more or less equally between the candidates, the nationwide winning candidate would generally expect to receive a highly exaggerated percentage (about 75%) of the votes in the Electoral College. That is, there would be a substantial cushion equal to about 25% of the 538 electoral votes—that is, a cushion of about 135 of the 538 electoral votes. Thus, the hypothesized partisan maneuver in one state (or even several states) would almost certainly not actually affect who became President.

THE HYPOTHETICAL SCENARIO WOULD NOT WORK BECAUSE OF PRACTICAL REASONS, INCLUDING THE PARTISAN DIVISION IN MOST STATE GOVERNMENTS, THE TIME DELAY BEFORE NEW STATE LAWS TAKE EFFECT IN MOST STATES, QUORUM REQUIREMENTS, AND THE NUMEROUS TIME-DELAYING TACTICS AVAILABLE IN THE SHORT PERIOD OF TIME BEFORE THE ELECTORAL COLLEGE MEETS IN MID-DECEMBER.
Even if the Impairments Clause of the U.S. Constitution and sections 1 and 5 of Title 3 of the United States Code did not exist, there are practical timing reasons that would prevent the hypothetical scenario in which a state legislature and governor might try, for partisan political advantage, to change the "rules of the game" between Election Day in early November and meeting of the Electoral College in mid-December.

A state belonging to the National Popular Vote compact can only change the way it chooses its presidential electors by enacting two new state statutes. The first new statute would attempt to withdraw from the compact (i.e., repeal it) in violation of the compact's terms, and the second new statute would create a new procedure for choosing presidential electors (presumably the legislature designating itself as the body to appoint presidential electors).

A politically motivated change in the manner of appointing a state's presidential electors after the state's voters cast their votes on Election Day would be a partisan maneuver of the most extreme and extraordinary nature. It would elicit automatic and fierce opposition from the to-be-disadvantaged political party.

The hypothetical scenario could not even be contemplated in most states because of the

- partisan division in most state governments,
- time delay before new state laws take effect in most states,
- quorum requirements, and
- numerous time-delaying tactics that would be invoked by the minority in the very short period of time before the Electoral College meets in mid-December.

These practical difficulties can be appreciated by visualizing what would have happened if the hypothesized partisan maneuver had been attempted immediately after the nation's most recent presidential election (2008).

In four states (Texas, Oregon, Tennessee, and Indiana), there is a two-thirds quorum requirement for a meeting of the legislature. Although partisan control changes from year to year in particular states, in 2008, no political party had two-thirds control of both houses of the legislature in any of these states. Thus, it would be impossible even to contemplate executing the hypothetical partisan maneuver in these states because the minority party would simply have boycotted the legislative session. There would have been no possibility of repealing the compact and enacting an alternative procedure for appointing presidential electors.

As a general rule, no political party is in control of the governorship and both houses of the legislature in about half of the states at any given moment.[144] In 2008, for example, no political party controlled a majority

---

[144] Dubin, Michael J. 2007. *Party Affiliations in the State Legislatures: A Year by Year Summary 1796–2006.* Jefferson, NC: McFarland & Company Inc.

of both houses of the legislature plus the governorship (or had a veto-proof legislative majority in both houses) in 20 states (in addition to the above group of four). Thus, it would be impossible even to contemplate this kind of partisan maneuver in this additional group of 20 states (i.e., a total of 24 states in 2008) because partisan deadlock would have prevented repealing the National Popular Vote compact and enacting an alternative procedure.

In 13 additional states, there are state constitutional provisions that significantly delay the time before a newly passed state law takes effect. In these 13 additional states, a new state law does not take effect for 60 days (and, in most cases, considerably more than 60 days) after the governor's signature. There are only about 35 days between Election Day in November and the mid-December meeting of the Electoral College. Thus, the Electoral College would have met and voted under pre-existing state law (that is, the National Popular Vote compact) long before the politically motivated repeal law could even take effect. In fact, the new President would have been inaugurated before the politically motivated repeal law could take effect in most of these states. The only available exception to these constitutionally specified delays is to pass the new law as an "emergency bill." However, emergency bills require super-majorities (two-thirds, three-quarters, or four-fifths, depending on the state) in these states. In 2008, no political party had the super-majorities required to pass an emergency bill in this group of states. A statute repealing the compact could simply not take effect prior to the mid-December meeting of the Electoral College. Accordingly, it would be impossible to even contemplate the hypothetical scenario in this group of states.

Summarizing the above three points, the hypothetical partisan maneuver could not even be contemplated in 39 states. There would not be any special session of the legislature, because it would be self-evident that there would be no possibility of action in the brief period of time available between Election Day in November and the meeting of the Electoral College in mid-December.

That leaves 13 states where the hypothetical partisan maneuver would have been theoretically possible in 2008 (Arkansas, Colorado, Connecticut, Florida, Georgia, Hawaii, Iowa, New Hampshire, North Carolina, Rhode Island, South Carolina, West Virginia, and Wyoming). These are states without high quorums, without significant delays before new laws take effect, and where one political party was in total control of the law-making process (either by controlling both houses of the legislature and the governorship or by enjoying veto-proof super-majorities in both houses of the legislature).

However, this remaining group of 13 states is illusory because it would be immediately winnowed down to about three states because of two independent factors:

- The hypothetical scenario would be irrelevant if the state were not a member of the National Popular Vote compact in the first place. Making the reasonable assumption that about half of the states will be in the compact when it takes effect, this second factor would eliminate about half of this group of 13 states.

- The hypothetical scenario would be irrelevant in states where the political party in control happened to coincide with the national popular vote winner. In any given year, this factor would independently eliminate about half of the remaining half.

Half of a half of 13 is about three states.

Even then, the hypothetical scenario in this winnowed-down group of about three states would probably not work in practice, in the limited time involved, for several additional reasons.

First, the minority in most state legislatures can delay the enactment of new legislation through various parliamentary tactics (e.g., offering endless amendments, insisting that no action occur until pending amendments are printed, refusing to waive various notice and scheduling requirements that are ordinarily waived routinely, or filibusters).

Second, this winnowed-down group of states probably would not possess enough electoral votes to affect the outcome in the Electoral College. One reason (previously mentioned) is that, in a typical future presidential election under the National Popular Vote compact, the candidate winning the national popular vote would generally receive about 75% of the electoral votes. A second reason is that the compact might well be enacted by a sufficiently large number of states so that the compacting states would possess more than 270 electoral votes even without one, two, or even three rebellious states.

Third, in some states in this winnowed-down group (such as Colorado and Wyoming), a protest referendum petition could be circulated to suspend the action of the state legislature. The filing of a protest referendum petition automatically and unconditionally suspends the effectiveness of any new state law passed by the legislature until a subsequent statewide election. Protest referendum petitions generally require only a modest number of signatures. The aggrieved political party could, almost certainly, quickly acquire the requisite number of signatures. There would, of course, be no time to hold the referendum in the short five-week period between Election Day in early November and the meeting of the Electoral College in mid-December.

Thus, even if the Impairments Clause of the U.S. Constitution and sections 1 and 5 of Title 3 of the United States Code did not exist to prevent the hypothetical partisan maneuver, mechanical difficulties would make it unlikely that rebellious state legislatures and governors could possibly affect the outcome of the presidential election.

ANY ATTEMPT TO APPOINT PRESIDENTIAL ELECTORS AFTER THE PEOPLE VOTE IN NOVEMBER WOULD BE POLITICALLY IMPROBABLE IN THE REAL WORLD.

The hypothetical maneuver would be unprecedented and politically improbable in the real world. There would be virtually no public support for changing the "rules of the game" after the people voted in November.

It should be remembered that the political context of the hypothetical maneuver at some future time when the National Popular Vote compact is in effect would be that

- more than 70% of the American public favors a nationwide vote for President,
- more than 70% of the public in the state involved favors a nationwide vote for President,
- the legislature and governor of the state involved have responded to their own voters and enacted the National Popular Vote bill,
- the National Popular Vote compact has been enacted by (25 or so) states representing a majority of the people of the United States, and
- a nationwide presidential campaign had already been conducted in which the candidates and the voters acted in accordance with the expectation that the national popular

vote will determine who will become President.

The hypothetical scenario of a rebellious state legislature and governor assumes that the public strongly and enthusiastically supports the state-by-state winner-take-all system and would blindly support a high-handed, last-ditch maneuver to restore it (in a state whose governor and legislature had already enacted the National Popular Vote bill).

In reality, there is no significant public support for the current system, either at the national or state level. Seventy percent of the American people support the idea that the candidate who receives the most votes in all 50 states and the District of Columbia should win the Presidency (with 20% opposed and 10% undecided). Virtually identical percentages have been registered in polls in more populous states (California), less-populous states (Maine), battleground states (Michigan), mid-western states (Missouri), and southern states (Arkansas).

Given the citizen nature of most state legislatures, it would require an extraordinary degree of control to whip a party's state legislators into line for such an unprecedented maneuver.

To execute the proposed partisan maneuver, the governor and both houses of the legislature would have to convene on Election Day (i.e., the Tuesday after the first Monday in November) because this is the only day in every four-year period when it is legal to choose presidential electors. This is, of course, the very same day when most state legislators are usually out campaigning in their precincts (where, in most states, they are up for reelection). Election Day in presidential election years is also the day when about a quarter of the nation's governors are elected. This is also the very same day when the voters would be going to the polls to cast their ballots for President in accordance with pre-existing state law (i.e., the National Popular Vote compact). Thus, the governor and his supporters in the legislature would be holed up in the state Capitol Building on Election Day, telling the voters that they intended to ignore the choice the people were in the process of making on that very day (while simultaneously urging the voters to reelect them).

The fact is that there would be no public support for this hypothetical maneuver.

In short, the hypothetical partisan maneuver involving an illegal attempt to withdraw from the National Popular Vote compact is a parlor game having no connection to the real world.

Tellingly, in 2000, the American people accepted the ascendancy of the second-place candidate to the White House because everyone understood that the 2000 election had been conducted under the established "rules of the game" (i.e., the state-by-state winner-take-all method). This was the case even though 70% of the public disapproves of the current state-by-state winner-take-all system and favors a national popular vote for President.

Significantly, we did not see, in 2000, the Democratic governors and Democratic-controlled state legislatures of North Carolina or West Virginia convening special sessions to repeal their existing laws awarding their states' presidential electors to the candidate who received the most popular votes in their respective states (George W. Bush), but, instead, awarding their states' electoral votes to the candidate who received the most popular votes nationwide (Al Gore). Similarly, we did not see the North Carolina Legislature, for example, switching to an allocation of electoral votes based on congressional districts or proportionally. Either of those alternative methods would have given Al Gore enough electoral votes to win a majority of the Electoral College.

ANY ATTEMPT TO APPOINT PRESIDENTIAL ELECTORS AFTER THE PEOPLE VOTE IN NOVEMBER WOULD BE LESS LIKELY TO OCCUR UNDER THE NATIONAL POPULAR VOTE COMPACT THAN UNDER THE CURRENT SYSTEM.

For the reasons stated above, we contend there is no problem in the first place. However, if there is a problem, the current system is even worse.

The hypothetical scenario is an inappropriate criticism of the National Popular Vote compact because an interstate compact (relying on the Impairments Clause and existing federal law) handles the situation of a rebellious state legislature and governor in a way superior to the current system (which relies only on existing federal law).

Under the current system, if a governor and a state legislature were to attempt to appoint presidential electors themselves, the Impairments Clause would be unavailable to challenge that maneuver. In contrast, if a governor and legislature were to attempt such a maneuver under the National Popular Vote compact, two centuries of settled law concerning the enforceability of interstate compacts under the Impairments Clause would be available to rebuff the attempt.

10.11.2 MYTH: A Secretary of State might change a state's method of awarding electoral votes after the people vote in November, but before the Electoral College meets in December.

QUICK ANSWER:

- No Secretary of State has the power to change a state's method of awarding electoral votes.

MORE DETAILED ANSWER:

The following concern has been raised on an election blog regarding the National Popular Vote bill:

> "In 2004 George Bush won a majority of the votes nationwide, but John Kerry came within something like 60,000 votes in Ohio of winning the Electoral College while losing the popular vote. Say Kerry won those 60,000 votes in Ohio, and the NPV program was in place with California a signer. In that entirely plausible scenario, does anyone think California's (Democratic) Secretary of State, representing a state that Kerry won by a 10% margin (54%–44%), would actually certify George Bush's slate of electors and personally put George Bush over the top for re-election, as the NPV agreement would have required?"[145]

Section 1 of article II of the U.S. Constitution provides:

> "Each State shall appoint, in such Manner **as the Legislature thereof may direct,** a Number of Electors...."[146] [Emphasis added]

No legislature has delegated its power to select the manner of appointing the state's presidential electors to the Secretary of State. Instead, the method of awarding electoral votes in each state is controlled by the state's election law—not the personal political preferences of the Secretary of State. It does not matter whether the Secretary of State personally thinks that electoral votes should be allocated by congressional district, in a proportional manner, by the winner-take-all rule,

---

[145] In order to promote free-flowing debate of speculative ideas, the blog involved does not permit attribution.

[146] U.S. Constitution. Article II, section 1, clause 2.

or by a national popular vote. The role of the Secretary of State in certifying the winning slate of presidential electors is entirely ministerial—that is, the role of the Secretary of State is to execute existing state law.

A Secretary of State may not ignore or override the National Popular Vote law any more than he or she may ignore or override the winner-take-all rule that is currently the law in 48 states.

In the unlikely and unprecedented event that a Secretary of State were to attempt to certify an election using a method of awarding electoral votes different from the one specified by state law, a state court would immediately prevent the Secretary of State from violating a law's provisions (by injunction) and compel the Secretary of State to execute the provisions of the law (by mandamus).

There were 10 states[147] that George W. Bush carried in the 2000 presidential election with a Democratic Secretary of State (or chief elections official).[148] The electoral votes of *any one* of these 10 states would have been sufficient to give Al Gore enough electoral votes to become President (even after Bush received all 25 of Florida's electoral votes).[149] Seventy percent or more of voters in each of these 10 states (and, indeed, the rest of the country) supported the proposition that the candidate who receives the most popular votes in all 50 states and the District of Columbia should become President. Nonetheless, it can be safely stated that it did not even occur to any of these 10 Democratic Secretaries of State to attempt to ignore and override their states' laws by certifying the election of Democratic presidential electors in their states. Such a post-election change in the rules of the game would not have been supported by the public, would immediately have been nullified by a state court, and almost certainly would have led to the subsequent impeachment of any official attempting it.

Moreover, in any one of nine[150] of these states, awarding electoral votes proportionally would have been sufficient to give Al Gore enough electoral votes to become President. A proportional allocation of elec-

---

[147] Al Gore's home state of Tennessee, Alaska, Arkansas, Georgia, Kentucky, Mississippi, Missouri, New Hampshire, North Carolina, and West Virginia.

[148] In Alaska, there is no Secretary of State, and the Lieutenant Governor is the state's chief elections official.

[149] George W. Bush received 271 electoral votes in 2000 (including Florida's 25 electoral votes), and 270 electoral votes are required for election.

[150] All of those previously mentioned except Alaska.

toral votes would have, indisputably, represented the will of the people of each of these nine states more accurately than the state-level winner-take-all rule.

In addition, in any one of three[151] (of these same nine states), awarding electoral votes by congressional districts would have been sufficient to give Al Gore enough electoral votes to become President. A district allocation of electoral votes arguably would have represented the will of the people of each of these three states more closely than the winner-take-all rule.

There has also been speculation that a Secretary of State might be "vilified" by certifying the election of the national popular vote winner. Under the National Popular Vote legislation, a dilemma has been hypothesized as to

> "whether the Secretary of State would really certify the losing panel of electors from the state in question, or find some justification to send the panel actually elected by the voters in the state. That's a very tough call and near-certain political vilification, either way, for the Secretary of State."[152]

This is not a "tough call" at all. In fact, there is no call to make. The Secretary of State is a ministerial official whose actions are directed and controlled by state law.

If 70% of the voters in a state prefer that the President be elected by a national popular vote, and if a state legislature enacts the National Popular Vote bill in response to the strong desires of the state's voters, and if the presidential campaign is then conducted with both voters and candidates knowing that the National Popular Vote bill is going to govern the election in that state, then the voters are not going to complain about a Secretary of State who faithfully executes the state's law.

Aside from the legal issues, the hypothesized scenario presupposes that the people heavily support the currently prevailing winner-take-all rule. In fact, public support for the current system of electing the President is at the level of Nixon's approval rating when he resigned.

In short, the hypothesized scenario has no basis in law and certainly no basis in political reality.

---

[151] Georgia, Missouri, and North Carolina.

[152] *Election Law Blog*, November 13, 2007.

10.12 Myth about Campaign Spending

10.12.1 MYTH: Campaign spending would skyrocket if candidates had to campaign throughout the country.

QUICK ANSWER:

* The total amount of money that a presidential campaign can spend is determined by the amount of money that it can raise. It is controlled by available money—not by the number of opportunities to spend money.

* Under a national popular vote, the total amount of money available to run a campaign would have to be allocated throughout the country differently than is currently the case because every vote in every state would matter.

MORE DETAILED ANSWER:

The total amount of money that a presidential campaign can spend is determined by the amount of money that it can raise—not by the virtually unlimited opportunities for spending money available if the campaign had access to unlimited funds.

There are two major steps in campaign budgeting.

First, presidential campaigns will try to raise as much money as possible from all sources available to them. All serious presidential campaigns raise money nationally. Table 10.2 shows the contributions to the 2008 presidential campaign by state.

Second, after a presidential campaign ascertains how much money it can raise, the campaign engages in a resource-allocation process in order to decide how to spend the money in the most advantageous way. The resource-allocation process is controlled by the prevailing "rules of the game." Currently, the controlling factor in allocating resources is the state-by-state winner-take-all method of awarding electoral votes.

Under the current state winner-take-all statutes, campaigns concentrate their spending on a handful of closely divided battleground states. They do this because they have nothing to lose, and nothing to gain, by paying attention to the two-thirds of the states where they are safely ahead or hopelessly behind. Under the current system, about two-thirds of the money raised in the 2004 presidential campaign was spent in five closely divided "battleground states." About 80% was spent in just nine states, and 99% was spent in just 16 states. In 2008, candidates concentrated over two-thirds of their campaign events and ad money in just six states, and 98% in just 15 states.[153]

In short, a rational resource-allocation process for presidential campaigns, under the current system, involves ignoring about two-thirds of the United States.

The National Popular Vote plan would not increase the total number of dollars available, because candidates already raise money on a national basis. The mere existence of additional places to campaign productively does not, itself, generate any additional money. Moreover, candidates would continue to spend whatever amount of money that they can raise under a national popular vote.

However, the resource-allocation process under the National Popular Vote plan would be very different. The reason is that every vote would matter in all 50 states and the District of Columbia under a national popular vote. Therefore, no serous national campaign would concentrate 99.75% of all advertising spending in just 18 states, while ignoring 32 states. The available amount of money would be reallocated because every vote in every state would matter in every presidential election.

If exactly the same amount of money were raised under both systems, it would be impossible to operate a campaign in all 50 states at the same per-capita level of intensity as recent campaigns in battleground states such as Pennsylvania.

Although Pennsylvania would not be ignored under a national popular vote, some of the available money that was previously spent in Pennsylvania would be reallocated to other states. As an example, given that both Pennsylvania and Illinois each have 20 electoral votes (2010 census), it is likely that Pennsylvania and Illinois would receive more or less equal attention. Although one cannot predict exactly how a future political campaign will unfold, it is a certainty that Illinois would receive considerably more than the paltry $53,896 (Table 10.2) that it received under the current state-by-state winner-take-all method of awarding electoral votes (while Pennsylvania received about $25,000,000).

---

[153] http://fairvote.org/tracker/?page=27&pressmode=showspecific&showarticle=230.

10.13 Myths about Election Administration

10.13.1 MYTH: Local election officials would be burdened by the National Popular Vote compact.

QUICK ANSWER:

- The mechanics for counting and tallying votes at the local, county, and state levels would be the same as they are now in presidential elections.

MORE DETAILED ANSWER:

Local and county elections officials would conduct elections exactly as they do now.

10.13.2 MYTH: The state's chief elections official would be burdened by the National Popular Vote compact.

QUICK ANSWER:

- The state's chief election official would not be burdened by the National Popular Vote compact, because the only difference is that the chief elections official would add up the popular vote totals for each presidential slate in all 50 states and the District of Columbia to determine the national popular vote winner.

MORE DETAILED ANSWER:

The only administrative difference between the National Popular Vote plan and the current system is that the state's chief elections official (typically the Secretary of State) of each state belonging to the National Popular Vote compact would determine the number of votes for each presidential slate in all 50 states and the District of Columbia in which votes have been cast in a statewide popular election and would add such votes together to produce a "national popular vote total" for each presidential slate.

The chief election official would then designate the presidential slate with the largest national popular vote total as the "national popular vote winner."

Finally, the presidential elector certifying official of each state belonging to the National Popular Vote compact would certify the appointment in that official's own state of the elector slate nominated in that state in association with the national popular vote winner.

10.13.3 MYTH: The National Popular Vote compact would burden the state's chief election official with the need to evaluate the election returns of other states.

QUICK ANSWER:

- The National Popular Vote compact would operate in a manner identical to the current system in that no state election official has any power to examine or judge the presidential election returns of any other state.

- Each candidate's popular vote total in each state will be certified using the same "certificates of ascertainment" as are currently required by existing federal law.

MORE DETAILED ANSWER:

The mechanics for counting and tallying votes at the precinct, local, county, and state levels would be the same under the National Popular Vote compact as they are under the current system.

Neither the current system nor the National Popular Vote compact permits any state to become involved in judging the election returns of other states. Existing federal law (the "safe harbor" provision in section 5 of title 3 of the United States Code) specifies that a state's "final determination" of its presidential election returns is "conclusive" in the counting of votes by Congress (if done in a timely manner and in accordance with laws that existed prior to Election Day).

The wording of the National Popular Vote compact is patterned directly after the existing federal "safe harbor" provision. It would require each state to treat as "conclusive" each other state's "final determination" of its vote for President. Clause 5 of article III of the National Popular Vote compact provides:

> "The chief election official of each member state shall treat as conclusive an official statement containing the number of popular votes in a state for each presidential slate made by the day established by federal law for making a state's final determination conclusive as to the counting of electoral votes by Congress."

Thus, no state would have any power to examine or judge the presidential election returns of any other state under the National Popular Vote compact.

10.13.4 MYTH: The National Popular Vote compact would be costly.

QUICK ANSWER:

- The National Popular Vote compact would not impose any fiscal burden on any state, because voting in presidential elections would be conducted at the precinct, local, and county levels in the same manner as it is today.
- When the National Popular Vote bill has been considered by state legislatures, state fiscal officials have uniformly concluded that it would have no significant fiscal impact.

MORE DETAILED ANSWER:

Under the National Popular Vote compact, the mechanics for counting votes for President at the precinct, local, county, and state levels would be the same as they are today.

The only administrative difference would be that, after counting all the votes in the state, each state's chief elections officer would add up the popular vote totals from all 50 states and the District of Columbia to determine which slate of presidential electors would be called upon to cast the state's electoral votes.

When the National Popular Vote bill has been introduced in state legislatures, state fiscal officials have uniformly concluded that it has no significant fiscal impact on the state. In most states, this determination has been explicitly stated in the financial analysis that is routinely produced when a legislature considers a piece of legislation.

10.13.5 MYTH: Post-election audits cannot be conducted under a national popular vote.

QUICK ANSWER:

- There is nothing in the National Popular Vote plan that prevents audits of election results. Post-election audits can be conducted for any election.

MORE DETAILED ANSWER:

Post-election audits can be conducted for any election. The arguments in favor of conducting audits apply to all elections, regardless of the office being filled. The statistical procedures for conducting audits are applicable to all elections.

Audits are conducted in some states today, thanks to statutory audit procedures and administratively established audit procedures.

In addition, federal legislation has been proposed to require audits in all federal elections—including presidential elections. For example, the proposed Voter Confidence and Increased Accessibility Act of 2009 (H.R. 2894 of 111th Congress introduced by Representative Rush Holt of New Jersey and supported by a considerable number of congressional co-sponsors) requires audits for all federal elections, including presidential elections.

One important difference between presidential elections and elections for the U.S. House and U.S. Senate is that the U.S. Constitution establishes a strict overall national schedule for finalizing the results of a presidential election. The existing constitutional provision (and existing supporting federal statutes) apply equally to elections conducted under both the National Popular Vote plan and the current system.

Specifically, the U.S. Constitution requires that the Electoral College meet on a uniform nationwide day in every state.[154] Congress has specified the Monday after the second Wednesday in December as the date for the meeting of the Electoral College.[155]

Moreover, the U.S. Supreme Court has made it clear that the states are expected to make their "final determination" six days before the Electoral College meets (the so-called "safe harbor" day established by section 5 of title 3 of the United States Code).[156]

Thus, under both the current system and the National Popular Vote plan, all counting, recounting, and judicial proceedings must be conducted so as to reach a "final determination" by the "safe harbor" day prior to the uniform nationwide date for the meeting of the Electoral College in mid-December.

Many of the most important reasons for conducting an audit are lost if insufficient time remains available to conduct a full recount if the audit discovers a problem. Indeed, in the "Principles and Best Practices for Post-Election Audits" endorsed by numerous organizations involved in

---

[154] U.S. Constitution. Article II, section 1, clause 4.

[155] United States Code. Title 3, chapter 1, section 7.

[156] For example, in 2008, the election was Tuesday, November 4, and the "safe harbor" day was 33 days later on Monday, December 8. The Electoral College met on the following Monday, December 15 (the Monday after the second Wednesday in December). Congress met to count votes on January 6, 2009. According to the Constitution, the outgoing President's term ended on January 20, 2009.

election-administration issues (including the Brennan Center for Justice, Common Cause, Verified Voting, and numerous state-level groups), one of the best practices is

> "Post-election audits must be completed prior to finalizing official election results and must either verify the outcome or, through a 100% recount, correct the outcome."

Thus, in the case of presidential elections, a practical and realistic schedule for audits must allow time for a potential full recount (and also time for potential post-recount litigation) prior to the uniform nationwide day for meeting of the Electoral College. Thus, audits in presidential elections must be conducted in an expeditious and timely manner (soon after Election Day) so as to allow time for a potential full recount and potential post-recount litigation.

Fortunately, audits do not take a lot of time. Today, audits are routinely conducted within a couple of days by the states that have statutory audit procedures or administratively established audit procedures. There is thus no reason why audits cannot be conducted for presidential elections under either the current system or the National Popular Vote approach.

Proposed legislation such as H.R. 2894 already provides for audits of presidential elections. This excellent proposal could be improved by amending the formula for determining the intensity of auditing that is required in presidential elections so that the level of intensity of the audit is determined by the apparent margin in the nationwide count (as opposed to the apparent statewide count) in case the appointment of presidential electors is based on the national popular vote. Alternatively, the highest level of intensity already provided for in H.R. 2894 for the audit might be automatically applied to presidential counts. Note that this suggested improvement concerning the issue of intensity does not relate to whether an audit will be conducted—but merely to the audit's level of intensity.

In short, there is nothing in the National Popular Vote plan that would prevent a post-election audit.

10.14 Myths about Lack of an Official National Count for Presidential Elections and Secret Elections

10.14.1 MYTH: There is no official count of the national popular vote.

QUICK ANSWER:

- Current federal law provides for an official count of the popular vote for President from each state in the form of a public "certificate of ascertainment."

MORE DETAILED ANSWER:

It is sometimes asserted that there is no official national count of the national popular vote for President and, therefore, the National Popular Vote compact would be impossible to implement.

In his testimony on February 19, 2010, to the Alaska Senate Judiciary Committee, Professor Robert Hardaway of the University of Denver Sturm College of Law claimed that there was uncertainty in this area:

> "Under the Koza scheme, **who would be the national official who would decide what the popular vote is**?"
> [Emphasis added]

Existing federal law (section 6 of Title 3 of the United States Code) requires that an official count of the popular vote for President from each state be certified and sent to various federal officials in the form of a "certificate of ascertainment."

> "It shall be the duty of the executive of each State, as soon as practicable after the conclusion of the appointment of the electors in such State by the final ascertainment, under and in pursuance of the laws of such State providing for such ascertainment, to communicate by registered mail under the seal of the State to the Archivist of the United States **a certificate of such ascertainment** of the electors appointed, setting forth the names of such electors and **the canvass or other ascertainment under the laws of such State of the number of votes given or cast for each person for whose appointment any and all votes have been given or cast....**" [Emphasis added]

Appendices E, F, G, H, and I show examples of certificates of ascertainment from several states. The certificates of ascertainment from all 50 states and the District of Columbia are available on-line for the 2000, 2004, and 2008 presidential elections.[157]

10.14.2 MYTH: A single state could frustrate the National Popular Vote compact by making its election returns a state secret.

QUICK ANSWER:

- Current federal law provides for an official public count of the popular vote for President in each state.

MORE DETAILED ANSWER:

It has been suggested on a blog that a state might pass a law making its election returns secret at the precinct, local, county, and state levels:

"Couldn't [a state] decide to turn its popular vote totals into a state secret, thereby ruining the pact? What's to stop a state from choosing to count votes behind closed doors?"

Existing federal law (section 6 of Title 3 of the United States Code) requires each state to certify the number of popular votes cast for each presidential elector in a public document, called a "certificate of ascertainment," prior to the mid-December meeting of the Electoral College.

"It shall be the duty of the executive of each State, as soon as practicable after the conclusion of the appointment of the electors in such State by the final ascertainment, under and in pursuance of the laws of such State providing for such ascertainment, to communicate by registered mail under the seal of the State to the Archivist of the United States a certificate of such ascertainment of the electors appointed, setting forth the names of such electors and the canvass or other ascertainment under the laws of such State of the number of votes given or cast for each person for whose appointment any and all votes have been given or cast; and it shall also thereupon be the duty of the executive of each State to deliver to the electors of such State, on or before the day on which they are required by sec-

[157] For the 2004 presidential election, see http://www.archives.gov/federal-register/electoral-college/2004/certificates_of_ascertainment.html.

tion 7 of this title to meet, six duplicate-originals of the same certificate under the seal of the State; and if there shall have been any final determination in a State in the manner provided for by law of a controversy or contest concerning the appointment of all or any of the electors of such State, it shall be the duty of the executive of such State, as soon as practicable after such determination, to communicate under the seal of the State to the Archivist of the United States a certificate of such determination in form and manner as the same shall have been made; and the certificate or certificates so received by the Archivist of the United States shall be preserved by him for one year and shall be a part of the public records of his office and shall be open to public inspection; and the Archivist of the United States at the first meeting of Congress thereafter shall transmit to the two Houses of Congress copies in full of each and every such certificate so received at the National Archives and Records Administration." [Emphasis added]

Appendices E, F, G, H, and I show the certificates of ascertainment from several states. The certificates of ascertainment from all 50 states and the District of Columbia are available on-line for the 2000, 2004, and 2008 elections.[158]

Of course, making election returns secret is not within the realm of political possibility in the real world. This question assumes that there is a state in the United States whose legislature, governor, and voters would permit making election returns secret for any reason. The question also assumes that there is a state whose public has a strong affection and attachment to the current winner-take-all rule (i.e., awarding all of a state's electoral votes to the candidate who receives the most votes in the state). In fact, more than 70% of the American people have favored a nationwide election for President since the Gallup poll started asking this question in 1944.[159] The 2007 *Washington Post*, Kaiser Family Foundation, and Harvard University poll showed 72% support for direct nationwide election of the President. Numerous state-level polls confirm this high level of support.

---

[158] http://www.archives.gov/federal-register/electoral-college/2004/certificates_of_ascertainment.html.

[159] Numerous polls are available on National Popular Vote's web site at http://www.nationalpopularvote.com/pages/polls.

10.15 Myths about Recounts

10.15.1 MYTH: The current system typically produces undisputed outcomes, and problems are rare.

QUICK ANSWER:

- There have been five litigated state counts in the nation's 56 presidential elections under the current state-by-state winner-take-all system. This rate is dramatically higher than the historical 1-in-160 rate for elections in which there is a single statewide pool of votes and in which the winner is the candidate who receives the most popular votes.

- The current state-by-state winner-take-all system repeatedly creates artificial crises because every presidential election generates 51 separate opportunities for a razor-thin margin.

- Recounts would be far less likely under the National Popular Vote bill than under the current system because there would be a single pool of votes. Given that there is a recount only once in about 160 statewide elections, and given there is a presidential election once every four years, one would expect a recount about once in 640 years under the National Popular Vote approach. The actual probability of a close national election would be even less than that because recounts are less likely with larger pools of votes.

- The average change in the margin of victory as a result of a statewide recount was a mere 296 votes in a 10-year study of 2,884 elections.

- Three-quarters of all recounts do not change the outcome.

- No recount would have been warranted in any of the nation's 56 previous presidential elections if the outcome had been based on the nationwide count.

MORE DETAILED ANSWER:

Tara Ross, an opponent of the National Popular Vote plan, has stated:

> "The Electoral College **typically produces** quick and **undisputed outcomes.**"[160] [Emphasis added]

---

[160] Written testimony submitted by Tara Ross to Delaware Senate in June 2010.

Ross has also said:

"The Electoral College encourages stability and certainty in our political system. **Events such as those that occurred in 2000 are rare.**" [161] [Emphasis added]

Nothing could be further from the truth.

There have been five litigated state counts in the nation's 56 presidential elections under the current state-by-state winner-take-all system (i.e., awarding of all a state's electoral votes to the candidate who receives the most popular votes in the state). This rate is dramatically higher than the historical 1-in-160 rate for elections in which there is a single statewide pool of votes and in which the winner is the candidate who receives the most popular votes.

The current state-by-state winner-take-all system repeatedly creates artificial crises on a regular basis because every presidential election generates 51 separate opportunities for a dispute. This fact is illustrated by examining the five litigated state counts in the nation's 56 presidential elections.

The 2000 presidential election was an artificial crisis created because of George W. Bush's lead of 537 popular votes in the state of Florida. Gore's nationwide lead was 537,179 popular votes (1,000 times larger than the disputed 537-vote margin Florida). Given the miniscule number of votes that are changed by the typical recount (about 296 votes), no one would have requested a recount or disputed the results in 2000 if the national popular vote had controlled the outcome. In the absence of the state-by-state winner-take-all system, no one (except perhaps almanac writers and trivia buffs) would have cared that one particular candidate happened to have a 537-vote margin in one particular state.

There was a recount, a court case, and a reversal of the original outcome in Hawaii in 1960. Kennedy ended up with a 115-vote margin in Hawaii in an election in which his nationwide margin was 118,574.

Samuel Tilden's 3% nationwide lead in 1876 was a solid victory in terms of the national popular vote (equal to George W. Bush's nationwide percentage lead in the 2004 election). However, an artificial crisis was created because of the razor-thin margins of 889 votes in South Carolina,

---

[161]   Oral and written testimony presented by Tara Ross at Nevada Senate Committee on Legislative Operations and Elections on May 7, 2009.

922 in Florida, and 4,807 in Louisiana. No one would have cared who received more popular votes in these three closely divided states if the President had been elected by a nationwide popular vote. Again, the state-by-state winner-take-all system created an artificial crisis.

Recounts in presidential elections would be far less likely to occur under a national popular vote system than under the current state-by-state winner-take-all system.

Table 10.11 shows that there were 18 recounts in 2,884 statewide general elections in the 10-year period from 2000 through 2009—that is, one recount for every 160 elections. This table is based on research work by FairVote.[162]

TABLE 10.11 THE 18 RECOUNTS IN 2,884 STATEWIDE GENERAL ELECTIONS 2000-2009

OFFICE	NUMBER OF STATEWIDE ELECTIONS	NUMBER OF STATEWIDE RECOUNTS
President	150	1
U.S. Senator	170	3
U.S. Representative	35	0
Governor	118	1
Lieutenant Governor	44	0
Secretary of State	81	1
Attorney General	100	1
Treasurer	79	0
Auditor	58	1
Controller	18	0
Public Service Commissioner	16	0
Agriculture or Industries Commissioner	27	0
Labor Commissioner	8	0
Insurance Commissioner	23	0
Public Lands Commissioner	11	0
Tax Commissioner	3	0
Corporation Commissioner	13	0
Railroad Commissioner	6	0
Public Utilities Commissioner	6	0
Mine Commissioner	2	0
Supt. of Public Instruction or Education	34	1

[162] Richie, Rob; Talukdar, Monideepa; and Hellman, Emily. 2010. *A Survey and Analysis of Statewide Election Recounts, 2000–2009*. FairVote.

TABLE 10.11 THE 18 RECOUNTS IN 2,884 STATEWIDE GENERAL ELECTIONS 2000–2009 (CONT.)

OFFICE	NUMBER OF STATEWIDE ELECTIONS	NUMBER OF STATEWIDE RECOUNTS
Board of Education or Governors	9	1
University Regent	8	0
Trustee	6	0
Judicial positions and retention	601	3
Ballot question	1,245	5
Other	13	0
Total	**2,884**	**18**

Historically, 0.15% is well beyond the largest shift that occurred as a result of any of the 18 recounts. Using this percentage as the dividing line, FairVote then called 11 of the 18 recounts in the 10-year period from 2000 through 2009 "consequential" because the original margin of victory was less than 0.15%. Table 10.12 shows these 11 "consequential" recounts. Three of these 11 "consequential" recounts changed original outcomes (about a quarter).

TABLE 10.12 THE 11 "CONSEQUENTIAL" RECOUNTS IN STATEWIDE GENERAL ELECTIONS 2000–2009

STATE	YEAR	OFFICE OR PROPOSITION	RECOUNT RESULT	ORIGINAL MARGIN	MARGIN IN RECOUNT	CHANGE IN VOTES
Alabama	2004	Amendment 2	Upheld	1,850	1,846	4
Colorado	2000	State Education Board	Upheld	1,211	90	1,121
Florida	2000	President	Upheld	1,784	537	1,247
Georgia	2004	Court of Appeals Judge	Upheld	348	363	-15
Minnesota	2008	U.S. Senate	Overturned	215	-225	440
Montana	2000	Superintendent of Public Instruction	Upheld	64	61	3
Oregon	2008	Measure 53	Upheld	550	681	-131
Vermont	2006	Auditor of Accounts	Overturned	137	-102	239
Virginia	2005	Attorney General	Upheld	323	360	-37
Washington	2000	U.S. Senate	Upheld	1,953	2,229	-276
Washington	2004	Governor	Overturned	261	-129	390
Average						**271**

Seventeen states provide for automatic recounts of elections. Part of the reason to conduct automatic recounts is to maximize public confidence in elections. However, in many of these legislatively mandated automatic recounts, no one (including the candidate who is behind in the initial count) realistically expects any change in the outcome.

Table 10.13 shows seven of the 18 recounts in the 10-year period from 2000 to 2009 in which the original margin of victory was greater than 0.15%. FairVote calls these seven recounts "inconsequential." As can be seen, the original outcomes were not changed by any of these "inconsequential" recounts.

TABLE 10.13 THE SEVEN "INCONSEQUENTIAL" RECOUNTS IN STATEWIDE GENERAL ELECTIONS 2000–2009 (WHERE THE ORIGINAL MARGIN OF VICTORY WAS GREATER THAN 0.15%)

STATE	YEAR	OFFICE OR PROPOSITION	RECOUNT RESULT	ORIGINAL MARGIN	MARGIN AFTER RECOUNT	CHANGE IN VOTES
Alabama	2006	Consititutional Amendment	Upheld	2,642	3,150	-508
Alaska	2004	U.S. Senate	Upheld	9,568	9,349	219
North Carolina	2006	Court of Appeals Judge	Upheld	3,416	3,466	-50
Pennsylvania	2009	Superior Court Race	Upheld	83,693	83,974	-281
Washington	2000	Secretary of State	Upheld	10,489	10,222	267
Wyoming	2004	Amendment A	Upheld	25,221	25,276	-55
Wyoming	2004	Amendment C	Upheld	13,959	14,009	-50
Average						**-65**

Using the 1-in-160 statistic (based on all 18 recounts in the 2,884 statewide elections over the 10-year period) and given that presidential elections occur once every four years, one would, therefore, expect a national recount about once every 640 years under a national popular vote.[163]

---

[163] For decades, banks, credit-card processors, and state lotteries have routinely accurately handled and accounted for far more transactions than the mere 130 million votes cast in a presidential election. Unfortunately, the technology for handling ballots is several decades behind that of the financial institutions and state lotteries. No doubt, the technology for more accurately handling and accounting for large number of transactions will improve over the next decade or so (and certainly in the next 640 years) to the point where no one even worries about recounts.

In fact, the probability of a presidential recount under a national popular vote system would be even less than 1-in-160 because a close result is less likely to occur as the size of the jurisdiction increases. As previously mentioned, the 1-in-160 statistic is based on data from 2,884 statewide elections.

In any event, when there is a single pool of votes, this 1-in-160 frequency of problematic elections is dramatically lower than the five litigated state counts in 56 presidential elections that we have experienced under the current state-by-state winner-take-all system.

The reason there have been so many disputes in the mere 56 presidential elections is that there are 51 separate opportunities for recounts in every presidential election under the current state-by-state winner-take-all system. Our nation's 56 presidential elections have really been 2,135 separate state-level elections. Thus, the current system repeatedly creates artificial crises in which the vote is extremely close in particular states, while not at all close on a nationwide basis.

One good way to visualize the difference between the two systems is to think of the chance of a recount as being represented by one bullet in a 160-chamber gun. Under a national popular vote, the trigger is pulled once every four years. Based on history, we can reasonably expect the gun to fire once every 640 years. In contrast, under the current state-by-state winner-take-all system, the trigger is pulled 51 times every four years. Thus, we should not be surprised to have had so many disputed counts in a mere 56 presidential elections.

The average change in the margin of victory as a result of a statewide recount was a mere 296 votes in the 10-year study of 2,884 elections.

In the 10-year study of 2,884 elections, there were only three elections in which the result was altered by a recount namely, the

- 2004 governor's race in Washington state (where the original 261-vote lead became a 129-vote loss),
- 2006 state auditor's race in Vermont (where the original 137-vote lead became a 102-vote loss), and
- 2008 U.S. Senate election in Minnesota (where the original 215-vote lead became a 225-vote loss).

Moreover, it should also be noted that if the nationwide count were extremely close at some time in the future, the current system would very likely also produce a disputed count in one or more states because roughly a third of the 50 states would be closely divided battleground states.

Criticism of the National Popular Vote plan in connection with recounts is yet another example of a criticism that actually applies to the current state-by-state winner-take-all system more than the National Popular Vote plan. Indeed, the question of recounts comes to mind in connection with presidential elections only because the current system so frequently creates artificial crises and unnecessary disputes. If we were debating whether to elect a governor by a popular vote, the issue of recounts would never even come to mind, because everyone knows that recounts rarely occur in elections in which there is a single pool of votes and in which the winner is the candidate who receives the most popular votes.

10.15.2 MYTH: The current system acts as a firewall that helpfully isolates recounts to particular states.

QUICK ANSWER:
- The current system does not act as a firewall that helpfully isolates recounts to particular states but, instead, is the repeated cause of unnecessary fires.
- The current system repeatedly creates artificial crises because every presidential election generates 51 separate opportunities for a dispute.
- There have been five litigated state counts in the nation's 56 presidential elections under the current state-by-state winner-take-all system. This rate is dramatically higher than the historical 1-in-160 rate for elections in which there is a single pool of votes and in which the winner is the candidate who receives the most popular votes.

MORE DETAILED ANSWER:
Brendan Loy claims that the current state-by-state winner-take-all system acts as a helpful firewall that

"isolate[es] post-election disputes to individual close states."[164]

In fact, the winner-take-all system is not a helpful firewall but, instead, the repeated cause of unnecessary fires.

---

[164] Loy, Brendan Loomer, "Count Every Vote—All 538 of Them" *Social Science Research Network*. September 12, 2007. Available at http://ssrn.com/abstract=1014431.

Under the current winner-take-all system, there are 51 separate statewide vote pools in every presidential election. Thus, our nation's 56 presidential elections have really been 2,135 separate state-level elections. These 51 separate pools regularly generate 51 separate opportunities for artificial crises in elections in which the vote is not at all close on a nationwide basis (but close in particular states). This is the reason why there have been five litigated state counts in the nation's 56 presidential elections. This rate is dramatically higher than the historical 1-in-160 rate for elections in which there is a single statewide pool of votes and in which the winner is the candidate who receives the most popular votes.

If anyone is genuinely concerned about minimizing the possibility of recounts, then a single national pool of votes provides the way to drastically reduce the likelihood of recounts and eliminate the artificial crises that are regularly produced by the current state-level winner-take-all system.

Trent England, an opponent of the National Popular Vote plan, has stated:

> **"Containing elections within state lines also means containing election problems. The Electoral College turns the states into the equivalent of the watertight compartments on an ocean liner.** Fraud or process failures can be isolated in the state where they occur and need not become national crises.[165] [Emphasis added]

The current system does not contain and isolate problems but, instead, creates artificial crises.

10.15.3 MYTH: Resolution of a presidential election could be prolonged beyond the inauguration date because of recounts.

QUICK ANSWER:

- The U.S. Constitution establishes a strict overall national schedule for finalizing the results of presidential elections. These existing provisions apply equally to elections conducted under the current system as well as elections conducted under the National Popular Vote plan.

---

[165] England, Trent. Op-Ed: Bypass the Electoral College? *Christian Science Monitor.* August 12, 2010.

- Under both the current system and the National Popular Vote plan, all counting, recounting, and judicial proceedings must be conducted so as to reach a "final determination" prior to the uniform nationwide date for the meeting of the Electoral College in mid-December.

MORE DETAILED ANSWER:

Brendan Loy warns that if we had a national popular vote:

"Post-election uncertainty could stretch well into January, raising doubt about whether we would have a clear winner by inauguration day." ...

"With two centuries of legal precedent tossed aside, courts would have a very difficult time managing it all."[166]

Loy's scenario for a prolonged and unsettled election is based on the incorrect assumption that the existing U.S. Constitution, existing federal statutes, and existing state statutes would somehow be "tossed aside" after the National Popular Vote compact comes into effect. In fact, the National Popular Vote compact was drafted so as to rely on existing constitutional and statutory provisions in the same way that the current system does.

Finality of presidential elections would be ensured under the National Popular Vote compact by the same machinery that applies to the current system namely, the existing U.S. Constitution, existing federal statutes, and existing state statutes.

The U.S. Constitution establishes a strict overall national schedule for finalizing the results of a presidential election. These existing provisions would apply to elections conducted under the proposed National Popular Vote legislation in the same way that they apply to elections conducted under the current system. No prolongation of a U.S. presidential election until January is possible, thanks to these existing constitutional provisions and existing federal and state statutory provisions.

The U.S. Constitution provides:

"The Congress may determine the Time of chusing the Electors, and **the Day on which they shall give their**

[166] Loy, Brendan Loomer, "Count Every Vote—All 538 of Them" *Social Science Research Network*. September 12, 2007. Available at http://ssrn.com/abstract=1014431.

Votes; which Day shall be the same throughout the United States."[167] [Spelling as per original] [Emphasis added]

Congress has exercised this constitutional power to set the uniform nationwide date for meeting of the Electoral College.

"The electors of President and Vice President of each State shall meet and give their votes on the **first Monday after the second Wednesday in December** next following their appointment at such place in each State as the legislature of such State shall direct."[168] [Emphasis added]

Under both the current system and the National Popular Vote approach, all counting, recounting, and judicial proceedings must be conducted so as to reach a "final determination" prior to the uniform nationwide date for the meeting of the Electoral College in mid-December.

The U.S. Supreme Court has made it clear that the states are expected to make their "final determination" six days before the Electoral College meets (the so-called "safe harbor" date established by section 5 of title 3 of the United States Code).[169]

In addition, in most states, state statutes already impose independent earlier deadlines for finalizing the count for a presidential election. The U.S. Supreme Court has ruled that state election officials and the state judiciary must conduct counts and recounts in presidential elections within the confines of existing state election laws.

It should be noted that the laws governing the finalization of the count (and completion of any recount) for a presidential election are entirely different from those governing, say, a disputed race for, say, one of the 100 seats in the U.S. Senate (e.g., the 2008 Senate race in Minnesota).

It may be argued that the schedule established by the U.S. Constitution, existing federal statutes, and existing state statutes may sometimes rush the count (and possibly even create injustice). However, there can be no

---

[167] U.S. Constitution. Article II, section 1, clause 4.

[168] United States Code. Title 3, chapter 1, section 7.

[169] For example, in 2008, the election was Tuesday November 4, and the "safe harbor" date was 33 days later on Monday, December 8. The Electoral College met on the following Monday, December 15 (the Monday after the second Wednesday in December). Congress met to count votes on January 6, 2009. According to the Constitution, the outgoing President's term ended on January 20, 2009.

argument that this schedule exists in the U.S. Constitution, federal statutes, and state statutes and that this existing schedule guarantees "finality" prior to the meeting of the Electoral College in mid-December. The existing constitutional and statutory schedule would govern the National Popular Vote compact in exactly the same way that it governs elections under the current system.

Tara Ross, an opponent of the National Popular Vote plan, asks:

"How much litigation would ensue before the presidential election could be resolved?"[170]

The answer is the same under both the current system and the National Popular Vote compact—there would be as much litigation as can fit into the time period between Election Day (the Tuesday after the first Monday in November) and the "safe harbor" day coming six days prior to the meeting date for the Electoral College (the first Monday after the second Wednesday in December).

10.15.4 MYTH: Conducting a recount would be a logistical impossibility under a national popular vote.

QUICK ANSWER:

* As a matter of routine and prudent planning, state elections officials have contingency plans to conduct a recount for every election.
* The personnel and resources necessary to conduct a recount are indigenous to each state. Thus, a state's ability to conduct a recount inside its own borders is unrelated to whether a recount is being conducted in another state.

MORE DETAILED ANSWER:

A recount is not an unimaginable horror or a logistical impossibility. A recount is a recognized contingency that is sometimes required in the context of conducting elections for dozens of elective offices and ballot propositions. As a matter of routine and prudent planning, state elections officials have contingency plans to conduct a recount of every election.

No state needs the help of any other state in order to conduct its own recount. The personnel and resources necessary to conduct a recount

---

[170] Written testimony submitted by Tara Ross to Delaware Senate in June 2010.

are indigenous to each state. Thus, a state's ability to conduct a recount inside its own borders is unrelated to whether a recount is being conducted in another state.

Under both the current system and the National Popular Vote approach, all counting, recounting, and judicial proceedings must be conducted so as to reach a "final determination" prior to the uniform nationwide date for the meeting of the Electoral College in mid-December.

In fact, the U.S. Supreme Court has made it clear that the states are expected to make their "final determination" six days before the Electoral College meets (the so-called "safe harbor" date established by section 5 of title 3 of the United States Code).

Because all states must finalize their count (or finish their recount) by the "safe harbor" date in early December, and because the only remaining step required by the National Popular Vote bill is to add up the vote totals from all 50 states and the District of Columbia, the final national vote totals would be available before the Electoral College meets.

10.15.5 MYTH: States would be put in the uncomfortable position of judging election returns from other states under a national popular vote.

QUICK ANSWER:

- No state government has any obligation or power to judge the presidential election returns of any other state under either the current system or the National Popular Vote compact.

MORE DETAILED ANSWER:

No state government has any obligation or power to judge the presidential election returns of any other state under either the current system or the National Popular Vote compact.

Existing federal law specifies that each state's own "final determination" of its presidential election returns is "conclusive" (if done in a timely manner and in accordance with laws in existence prior to Election Day).

In particular, the "safe harbor" provision of federal law specifies the conditions under which a state's "final determination" is considered "conclusive."

"**If any State shall have provided**, by laws enacted prior to the day fixed for the appointment of the electors, **for its final determination** of any controversy or contest concerning the appointment of all or any of the electors of such State, by judicial or other methods or procedures, and such determination shall have been made **at least six days before the time fixed for the meeting of the electors, such determination** made pursuant to such law so existing on said day, and made at least six days prior to said time of meeting of the electors, **shall be conclusive, and shall govern in the counting of the electoral votes as provided in the Constitution**, and as hereinafter regulated, so far as the ascertainment of the electors appointed by such State is concerned."[171] [Emphasis added]

The nation's long-standing policy of deferring to the states is echoed in the National Popular Vote compact. In particular, the compact's wording compact is directly patterned after this existing federal law and requires each state to treat as "conclusive" each other state's "final determination" of its presidential vote. The fifth clause of article III of the National Popular Vote compact provides:

"The chief election official of each member state shall treat as conclusive an official statement containing the number of popular votes in a state for each presidential slate made by the day established by federal law for making a state's final determination conclusive as to the counting of electoral votes by Congress."

10.15.6 MYTH: Fraud and mischief would be magnified under a national popular vote.

QUICK ANSWER:

- Under the current state-by-state winner-take-all system, there are huge incentives and major consequences for fraud and mischief, because a small number of popular votes can swing a large number of electoral votes.

---

[171] United States Code. Section 5 of title 3, chapter 1.

- The two conditions for successfully carrying out electoral fraud are that a very small number of people can have a large effect. Only the current system offers that.

MORE DETAILED ANSWER:

The potential for political fraud and mischief is not uniquely associated with either the current system or a national popular vote. In fact, the current state-by-state winner-take-all system magnifies the incentives for fraud and mischief because all of a state's electoral votes are awarded to the candidate who receives a bare plurality of the popular votes in each state.

Under the current system, the national outcome can be affected by mischief in one of the closely divided battleground states (e.g., by placing insufficient or defective voting equipment into the other party's precincts, or by selectively and overzealously purging voter rolls).

The ill-advised use of the butterfly ballot by a Democratic election official in one county in Florida cost Gore an estimated 6,000 votes—far more than the 537 popular votes that he needed to carry Florida and win the White House in 2000. However, an incident involving 6,000 votes would have been a mere footnote if the nationwide count (where Gore led by 537,179) had governed the presidential election.

Senator Birch Bayh (D–Indiana) summed up the concerns about possible fraud in a 1979 Senate speech by saying:

> "One of the things we can do to limit fraud is to limit the benefits to be gained by fraud. Under a direct popular vote system, one fraudulent vote wins one vote in the return. In the electoral college system, one fraudulent vote could mean 45 electoral votes."[172]

In the 1950s and 1960s, accusations of voter fraud by both political parties were commonplace in Illinois and various other states. In 1960, a switch of 4,430 votes in Illinois and a switch of 4,782 votes in South Carolina would have given Nixon a majority of the electoral votes. However, 4,430 votes in Illinois were only a focus of controversy in 1960 because of the statewide winner-take-all rule. John F. Kennedy led Richard M. Nixon by 118,574 popular votes nationwide. Four or five thousand votes in two states would not have been decisive in 1960 in

---

[172] *Congressional Record.* March 14, 1979. Page 5000.

terms of changing the national popular vote. If Nixon had carried Illinois and South Carolina in 1960, he would have won a majority of the votes in the Electoral College without receiving a majority of the popular votes nationwide.

Under a national popular vote, there would be fewer incentives for fraud and mischief, and the consequences would be less drastic for whatever fraud and mischief does occur.[173]

Tara Ross, an opponent of the National Popular Vote plan, made the following comment about fraud under the current system.

> "Fraud is minimized because it is hard to predict where stolen votes will matter."[174]

Contrary to what Ross asserts, someone intent on fraud would have no difficulty deciding where to steal votes under the current system. Stolen votes matter in closely divided battleground states, such as Florida and Ohio.

10.15.7 MYTH: A recount might be warranted, but unobtainable, under the National Popular Vote compact.

QUICK ANSWER:

- The reality today, under current laws, is that a timely recount in a presidential race might be warranted, but impossible to obtain in practice in many states.
- A recount would be less likely to be needed under the National Popular Vote plan than under the current state-by-state winner-take-all system. There have been five litigated state counts in the nation's 56 presidential elections under the current state-by-state winner-take-all system. This rate is dramatically higher than the historical 1-in-160 rate for elections in which there is a single statewide pool of votes and in which the winner is the candidate who receives the most popular votes. Given that a recount has occurred only about once in 160 statewide elections and that presidential elections occur once every four years, one would expect a national recount about once every 640 years under the National Popular Vote plan.

---

[173] For more information, see section 9.2.

[174] Written testimony submitted by Tara Ross to Delaware Senate in June 2010.

- Enactment of the National Popular Vote compact would provide impetus for states to review their imperfect existing laws regarding timely recounts in presidential elections.

- Given that Congress has the authority over the count and schedule for presidential elections, federal legislation would be the most expeditious solution to the problem of guaranteeing a timely recount in a presidential election under the current system (or the National Popular Vote approach). Such legislation is needed because the current state-by-state winner-take-all system has resulted in such a high frequency of disputes in presidential elections (five litigated state counts in a mere 56 presidential elections) and because the nation has been in an era of non-landslide presidential elections since 1988. Such a federal law would also be beneficial under the national popular vote approach, even though recounts would be less likely because there would a single national pool of votes—instead of 51 separate pools.

MORE DETAILED ANSWER:

Tara Ross criticizes the National Popular Vote plan by saying:

"States have different criteria for what does (or does not) trigger recounts within their borders. These differences could cause a whole host of problems. What if the national total is close—**close enough to warrant a recount**—but **a recount can't be conducted** because the margins in individual states were not close?"[175] [Emphasis added]

Of course, the ability to obtain a recount in situations "close enough to warrant a recount" is hardly assured under the current state-by-state winner-take-all system, as demonstrated by the nation's experience with Florida in 2000.

Moreover, there is no ability under the current system to obtain a recount in situations "close enough to warrant a recount" in the two states that do not have recount laws. If, for sake of argument, the 537-popular-vote margin that determined the 2000 presidential election had occurred in Mississippi (instead of Florida), there would have been

---

[175] Written testimony submitted by Tara Ross to Delaware Senate in June 2010.

no possibility of a recount. The initial count in Mississippi would have been the first, only, and final count.

In criticizing the National Popular Vote plan, Ross creates an additional misimpression by mentioning only automatic recounts (that is, recounts triggered merely because the original difference between the candidates is less than some fixed legislatively specified threshold). However, automatic recounts are not the only way to obtain a recount (or even the most usual way). In fact, only 17 states have such automatic recount laws.[176] In most states, there are numerous avenues available for obtaining a recount (with some state statutes providing as many as six ways). For example, 42 states allow candidates to petition for a recount. One of the most common forms of state recount laws is to permit a recount if the disgruntled candidate pays for all of the recount's administrative costs in advance (with the candidate typically being reimbursed if he or she is vindicated).

Obtaining a recount under a national popular vote would not be as difficult as Ross suggests (even under Ross's questionable assumption that no changes would be made to existing laws in response to enactment of the National Popular Vote compact).

As will be seen below:

- Under the current system, a timely recount in a presidential race may be warranted, but impossible to obtain in practice.
- A recount would be less likely to be needed under a national popular vote than under the current state-by-state winner-take-all system.
- Enactment of the National Popular Vote compact would provide impetus for the states to modify their existing laws to ensure timely recounts in presidential elections.
- Federal legislation would be an expeditious solution to the problem of guaranteeing a timely recount in a presidential election under the current system (and any future system).

THE REALITY TODAY IS THAT A TIMELY RECOUNT IN A PRESIDENTIAL RACE UNDER THE CURRENT SYSTEM MAY BE WARRANTED, BUT IMPOSSIBLE TO OBTAIN IN PRACTICE, IN MANY STATES.

Presidential elections must be conducted within the constraints of the

---

[176] Richie, Rob; Talukdar, Monideepa; and Hellman, Emily. 2010. *A Survey and Analysis of Statewide Election Recounts, 2000–2009.* FairVote.

strict overall national schedule for finalizing the results of a presidential election established by the U.S. Constitution.

In particular, all counting, recounting, and judicial proceedings concerning presidential elections must be conducted so as to reach a "final determination" six days prior to the uniform nationwide date for the meeting of the Electoral College in mid-December. This principle applies equally to both the current state-by-state winner-take-all system of electing the President and the National Popular Vote compact.

The U.S. Constitution (Article II, section 1, clause 4) provides:

> "**The Congress may determine the Time** of chusing the Electors, and **the Day on which they shall give their Votes; which Day shall be the same throughout the United States**." [Spelling as per original] [Emphasis added]

Congress has exercised its constitutional power to set the uniform nationwide date for the meeting of the Electoral College. Title 3, chapter 1, section 7 of the United States Code states:

> "**The electors** of President and Vice President of each State **shall meet and give their votes on the first Monday after the second Wednesday in December** next following their appointment at such place in each State as the legislature of such State shall direct." [Emphasis added]

This statute was enacted in 1934, just after ratification of the 20th Amendment in 1933. Prior to the 20th Amendment, the President was inaugurated on March 4. The amendment advanced the inauguration to January 20.

Moreover, the U.S. Supreme Court has made it clear that the states are expected to make their "final determination" six days before the Electoral College meets (the so-called "safe harbor" date established by section 5, chapter 1 of title 3 of the United States Code).

The important point is that there is not much time between Election Day in early November and the "safe harbor" date. For example, in 2008, Election Day was Tuesday, November 4, and the "safe harbor" date was 33 days later on Monday, December 8. In 2008, the Electoral College met on the following Monday, December 15 (the Monday after the second Wednesday in December). Congress met to count votes on January 6, 2009. The outgoing President's term ended on January 20, 2009.

The schedule imposed by the "safe harbor" date was one of the major factors preventing a hand recount of presidential ballots in Florida in 2000.

In 1960, Hawaii conducted a recount under judicial supervision (which reversed Nixon's original lead). However, the recount and judicial proceedings were not completed until after the Electoral College had met. As it happened, Hawaii's three electoral votes did not affect the outcome of the presidential election in 1960. Congress met in joint session in January 1961 to count the electoral votes. The losing presidential candidate, Vice President Richard M. Nixon, presided over the joint session and graciously permitted Hawaii's electoral votes to be counted for John F. Kennedy (while ruling that this action would not constitute a precedent). The reality, however, was that the recount was not timely.

In summary, no recount has ever been completed in a timely fashion for any U.S. presidential election.

The actual work of a recount does not itself consume a lot of time.

However, one of the obstacles to obtaining a timely recount in a presidential race is that there can't be a recount until there is a count.

Unofficial numbers are, of course, generally available from virtually every precinct and various units of local government on election night (or, in any case, on the day after an election). Candidates typically know by then whether a recount is warranted. Nonetheless, under existing laws, a candidate's request for a recount is generally not legally "ripe" until after the official initial statewide count is complete.

The official initial statewide count typically takes several weeks. The reason for the delay is that official documents certifying the count from each county (or other unit of local government) must be sent to the state's chief election official or state canvassing board. Then, the vote counts contained in these documents are added together to yield the official initial statewide count. The results are often not official until some board meets.

In the context of presidential elections (where there are strict overall national deadlines), this relaxed schedule may leave no time for a recount.

In most states, there is no deadline for completing the initial official count in sufficient time to permit the conducting of a recount (and likely post-recount litigation) that is consistent with the federal "safe harbor" date and uniform nationwide date for the meeting of the Electoral College.

Moreover, many state chief election officers have the effective ability to preclude a recount merely by "slow-walking" the initial count so that it is not completed until just before the "safe harbor" date—thus preventing a candidate's request for a recount from being legally "ripe" until it is too late to conduct the recount.

With the rising volume of voting by mail in many states, thousands of ballots are often counted at the local level after Election Day, thereby delaying completion of the initial count.

Thus, at the present time, a timely recount is impossible to obtain, in practice, under the current system in many states.

A RECOUNT WOULD BE LESS LIKELY TO BE NEEDED UNDER THE NATIONAL POPULAR VOTE PLAN THAN UNDER THE CURRENT STATE-BY-STATE WINNER-TAKE-ALL SYSTEM.

There have been five litigated state counts in our nation's 56 presidential elections. All five of these disputed state counts were the result of the state-by-state winner-take-all rule in elections that had a clear nationwide popular vote winner. Far from serving as a firewall that helpfully isolates problems to particular states, the current state-by-state winner-take-all system repeatedly creates artificial crises in situations where no problem existed in the first place.

Five litigated state counts in a mere 56 elections is a dramatically higher rate than the historical 1-in-160 rate for recounts in statewide elections in which there is a single pool of votes and the winner is the candidate who receives the most popular votes.

Given that a recount has occurred only about once in 160 elections and that presidential elections occur once every four years, one could expect a recount about once in 640 years under the National Popular Vote plan.

The reason why there have been so many disputes in a mere 56 presidential elections is that each presidential election is really 51 separate state-level elections—with 51 separate opportunities for close results warranting a recount. Our 56 presidential elections have really been 2,135 separate state-level elections. The current winner-take-all system has repeatedly created artificial crises, because the vote was close in one particular state while not at all close nationwide. This can be seen by reviewing the five litigated state counts in our nation's 56 presidential elections.

The 2000 presidential election was an artificial crisis created because of George W. Bush's lead of 537 popular votes in Florida. Al Gore's nationwide lead was 537,179 popular votes (1,000 times larger). Given the miniscule number of votes that are changed by a typical recount (averaging only 296 votes), there would not have been a dispute in an election where one candidate had a margin of 537,179 votes.

A recount, court case, and reversal of the original outcome occurred in Hawaii in 1960. John F. Kennedy ended up with a 115-vote margin over Richard Nixon in Hawaii in an election in which his nationwide margin was 118,574. There would have been no recount in Hawaii in 1960 if the President had been elected by a nationwide popular vote.

In 1876, Samuel Tilden's 3% lead over Rutherford B. Hayes was a solid victory in terms of the national popular vote (equal to Bush's percentage lead in the 2004 election). However, an artificial crisis was created because of the razor-thin margins of 889 votes in South Carolina, 922 in Florida, and 4,807 in Louisiana. The candidate who received more popular votes in these three closely divided states would have been a mere footnote if the President had been elected by a nationwide popular vote.

In short, recounts would be far less likely under the National Popular Vote bill than under the current system.

ENACTMENT OF THE NATIONAL POPULAR VOTE COMPACT WOULD PROVIDE IMPETUS FOR THE STATES TO REVIEW THEIR LAWS REGARDING TIMELY RECOUNTS IN PRESIDENTIAL ELECTIONS.

Ross's observation that existing state recount laws are not based on national popular vote totals is something of a straw man in that it suggests that existing state recount laws are permanent and unchangeable.

When the U.S. House of Representatives passed a constitutional amendment in 1969 for a national popular vote, by a 338–70 margin, there were no specific provisions in the amendment for recounts. It was, of course, generally understood that implementing legislation would have been enacted if the amendment had been ratified. The ratification of the amendment would have provided the impetus to update existing laws.

Similarly, the enactment of the National Popular Vote compact would provide impetus for the states to review their laws regarding timely recounts in presidential elections.

GIVEN THAT CONGRESS HAS THE AUTHORITY OVER THE COUNT AND SCHEDULE FOR PRESIDENTIAL ELECTIONS, FEDERAL LEGISLATION IS ANOTHER WAY TO SOLVE THE PROBLEM OF GUARANTEEING A TIMELY RECOUNT IN A PRESIDENTIAL ELECTION UNDER THE CURRENT SYSTEM (OR THE NATIONAL POPULAR VOTE PLAN).
One way to remedy the existing practical difficulties of obtaining a timely recount in a presidential election would be to amend state election laws. However, there is another way.

As previously mentioned, Congress does not have authority over the manner of awarding a state's electoral votes. Fortuitously, however, Congress does have constitutional authority over both the count and schedule for presidential elections (from both article II and the 12th Amendment).

One example of the exercise of existing federal authority over the count and schedule is the current federal law requiring states to produce (prior to the meeting of the Electoral College in mid-December) a "certificate of ascertainment" including the state's "final determination" of the number of popular votes cast in the state for each individual presidential candidate (section 6, chapter 1 of title 3 of the United States Code). The number of popular votes cast in the state for each individual presidential candidate (contained in the state's "certificate of ascertainment") supports the state's "certificate of election" of presidential electors when Congress meets in joint session in January to count the results of the presidential election.

One way to solve the problem of guaranteeing a timely recount in a presidential election would be for Congress to pass a law guaranteeing presidential candidates a timely recount.

Such a law would acknowledge the historical fact that the current state-by-state winner-take-all method for awarding electoral votes has resulted in a high frequency of disputes in presidential elections (five litigated state counts in a mere 56 presidential elections). Such a law would also be beneficial under the national popular vote approach, even though the probability of recounts would be substantially reduced under a national popular vote because there would a single national pool of votes (instead of 51 separate pools).

Such federal legislation might include the following:
- Require each state's chief election official to prepare a plan for conducting a timely initial count and a full recount

involving a one-by-one examination (to the extent possible given the state's voting equipment and procedures). The plan would list all reasonable costs associated with accelerating the initial count and conducting the recount. It would also be desirable for the plan to include standards for determining voter intent for all cases that may be reasonably anticipated given the state's voting equipment and procedures.

- Give any presidential candidate on the ballot in a state the right to call for a full statewide recount in the state, provided the candidate pays for all reasonable costs of accelerating the initial count and conducting the recount. This right would have to be exercised within six days after Election Day. In practice, this choice would be made (in most states) on the basis of available unofficial returns. This right should be extended to the candidate's successor if the candidate dies or resigns. The recount would be a full statewide recount—in order to avoid the appearance of selectivity, in order to avoid the delay that would be necessary to allow other candidates to select additional parts of the state to be recounted, and in order to limit the complexity of the cost estimate to be developed by the state's chief election official to just one overall statewide number.

- Give the presidential candidate on the ballot (or his successor) the right to sue to enforce all the provisions of title 3. To avoid forum-shopping within the state, the action should be brought in the federal district court located in the state capital (or the district court located nearest to the state capital if no federal district court is located in the capital).

- Make clear that any recount made available by federal legislation is an additional option to any procedure available under state law, administrative procedures, or judicial determinations.

- Move the uniform national day for the meeting of the Electoral College (currently established as the Monday after the second Wednesday in December) to December 30 (or to the previous Friday, if December 30 falls on a weekend). If there is no controversy, the meeting date of the Electoral College is ceremonial and irrelevant to a presidential transition. If there is a controversy, as much time as possible should be allowed to arrive at an accurate presidential vote count.

• Clarify that the "safe harbor" date (defined in the existing section 5 of title 3 of the United States Code) is the deadline for each state to complete its "final determination" of the presidential count in the state.

Using calendar year 2012 as an example, possible federal legislation could establish a schedule such as shown in Table 10.14.

TABLE 10.14 POSSIBLE RECOUNT SCHEDULE

DATE	EVENT
Tuesday August 7, 2012	**90 days prior to Election Day**—Each state's chief elections official prepares and publishes a plan for conducting a timely initial count and a full recount of the presidential election—along with all reasonable costs of accelerating the initial count and conducting the recount, with such plan including standards for determining voter intent for all cases that may be reasonably anticipated given the state's voting equipment and procedures.
Tuesday November 6, 2012	**Election Day**
Monday November 12, 2012	**Last day for a presidential candidate to request a recount under this federal bill**—such request to be accompanied by payment of the costs specified in the chief elections official's plan.
Monday December 10, 2012	Last day for completing both the initial count and the recount—10 days before the "safe harbor" day.
Tuesday December 11, 2012	**Beginning of 10-day period for post-recount litigation**
Friday December 21, 2012	**"Safe harbor" day** — day for making "final determination" of count in each state
Friday December 28, 2012	**Meeting of the Electoral College**

10.16 Myth about Federalism

10.16.1 MYTH: Federalism would be undermined by a national popular vote.

QUICK ANSWER:

• Federalism concerns the distribution of power between state governments and the national government.
• The powers of state governments would not be increased

or decreased relative to the federal government based on whether presidential electors are elected along state boundary lines (as is the case under the current state-by-state winner-take-all system) or national lines (as would be the case under the National Popular Vote plan).

- The National Popular Vote approach preserves the power of the states to control elections—an important element of federalism.

MORE DETAILED ANSWER:

Federalism concerns the distribution of power between state governments and the national government.

John Samples (an economist) argues that a national popular vote would "weaken federalism."

> "Anti-federalists feared the new Constitution would centralize power and threaten liberty....
>
> "The founders sought to fashion institutional compromises that responded to the concerns of the states and yet created a more workable government than had existed under the Articles of Confederation....
>
> "The national government would [be] part of a larger design of checks and balances that would temper and restrain political power."...
>
> "The realization of **the NPV plan would continue [the] trend toward nationalization and centralized power.**"[177] [Emphasis added]

Daniel H. Lowenstein has argued:

> "Against all the pressures of nationalization, **it is important to maintain the states as strong and vital elements of our system.**"[178] [Emphasis added]

[177] Samples, John. *A Critique of the National Popular Vote Plan for Electing the President*. Cato Institute Policy Analysis No. 622. October 13, 2008.

[178] Debate entitled "Should We Dispense with the Electoral College?" sponsored by PENNumbra (University of Pennsylvania Law Review) available at http://www.pennumbra.com/debates/pdfs/electoral_college.pdf.

However, the National Popular Vote plan is not concerned with how much power state governments possess relative to the federal government. Those issues are controlled by the U.S. Constitution, state constitutions, and various federal and state laws.

The powers of state governments are neither increased nor decreased based on whether presidential electors are selected along state boundary lines (as is currently the case in 48 states), along district boundary lines (as is currently the case in Nebraska and Maine), or national lines (as would be the case under the National Popular Vote plan).

When the Founding Fathers from Virginia, Massachusetts, and North Carolina returned from the Constitutional Convention and organized the first presidential election in their respective states in 1789, they certainly did not undermine federalism or the powers of their state governments when they chose to elect their state's presidential electors by district (rather than the statewide winner-take-all method).

Similarly, the powers of the state governments of Virginia, Massachusetts, and North Carolina were not enhanced relative to the federal government when those states subsequently decided to switch (in the early 1800s) from the district system to the winner-take-all rule (i.e., awarding all of a state's electoral votes to the candidate who receives the most popular votes in each separate state).

Surely no one would argue that Nebraska and Maine diminished the powers of their respective state governments relative to the federal government when they decided (in 1992 and 1969, respectively) to award their electoral votes by congressional district.

There is no connection between the way power is—or should be—distributed between the state and federal governments and the boundary lines used to tally votes for presidential electors.

Finally, the National Popular Vote approach preserves the Electoral College and preserves the power of the states to control elections—an important element of federalism.

10.17 Myths about Interstate Compacts and Congressional Consent

10.17.1 MYTH: Interstate compacts are exotic and fishy.

QUICK ANSWER:
- Interstate compacts are authorized by the U.S. Constitution and are in widespread use by every state.

MORE DETAILED ANSWER:

The National Popular Vote plan is an interstate compact—a type of state law that is explicitly authorized by the U.S. Constitution to enable otherwise sovereign states to enter into legally enforceable contractual obligations with one another.

There are hundreds of major interstate compacts, including the

- Colorado River Compact (allocating water among seven western states),
- Multi-State Tax Compact (whose membership includes 23 states and the District of Columbia),
- Interstate Oil and Gas Compact,
- Interstate Corrections Compact,
- Mutual Aid Compact,
- Great Lakes Basin Compact (to which the province of Ontario is a party along with various states),
- Port Authority of New York and New Jersey (a two-state compact), and
- Multi-State Lottery Compact (which operates the Powerball lotto game in 21 states).

Numerous other compacts are listed in appendix M. Some compacts include all 50 states and the District of Columbia.

Interstate compacts existed under the Articles of Confederation. The U.S. Constitution explicitly continued compacts that were in existence when the Constitution came into force.

Interstate compacts are legally enforceable against the states because the Impairments Clause of the U.S. Constitution provides:

"No State shall ... pass any ... Law impairing the Obligation of Contracts."[179]

The Council of State Governments summarizes the nature of interstate compacts as follows:

"Compacts are agreements between two or more states that bind them to the compacts' provisions, just as a contract binds two or more parties in a business deal. As such, compacts are subject to the substantive principles of contract law and are protected by the constitutional prohibition against laws that

---

[179] U.S. Constitution. Article I, section 10, clause 1.

impair the obligations of contracts (U.S. Constitution, Article I, Section 10).

"That means that compacting states are bound to observe the terms of their agreements, even if those terms are inconsistent with other state laws. In short, compacts between states are somewhat like treaties between nations. Compacts have the force and effect of statutory law (whether enacted by statute or not) and they take precedence over conflicting state laws, regardless of when those laws are enacted.

"However, unlike treaties, compacts are not dependent solely upon the good will of the parties. Once enacted, compacts may not be unilaterally renounced by a member state, except as provided by the compacts themselves. Moreover, Congress and the courts can compel compliance with the terms of interstate compacts."[180]

For additional information about interstate compacts, see chapter 5.

10.17.2 MYTH: The National Popular Vote compact is defective because Congress did not consent to the compact prior to its consideration by state legislatures.

QUICK ANSWER:
* Advance congressional consent is not the norm in the field of interstate compacts. Instead, Congress typically considers a compact only after the compact has been approved by the combination of states required to bring the compact into effect.

MORE DETAILED ANSWER:
Advance congressional consent is not the norm in the field of interstate compacts. Instead, Congress typically considers a compact only after the compact has been approved by the combination of states required to bring the compact into effect.

The occasions on which Congress has given advance consent to a compact have been relatively rare.

---

[180] Council of State Governments. 2003. *Interstate Compacts and Agencies 2003.* Lexington, KY: The Council of State Governments. Page 6.

In 1934, Congress consented in advance to interstate crime control compacts in the Crime Control Consent Act of 1934.

In 1910, Congress gave its consent in advance to four states (Illinois, Indiana, Michigan, and Wisconsin) to enter into an agreement with respect to the exercise of jurisdiction "over offenses arising out of the violation of the laws" of these states on the waters of Lake Michigan.

10.17.3 MYTH: The National Popular Vote compact is defective because it fails to mention Congress in its text.

QUICK ANSWER:

* As a matter of practice, most modern-day compacts do not specifically mention congressional consent, regardless of whether the states involved intend to seek it.

MORE DETAILED ANSWER:

As a matter of practice, most modern-day compacts do not specifically mention congressional consent, regardless of whether the states involved intend to seek it.

There have been compacts (e.g., the Port Authority of New York and New Jersey) where the states involved originally did not intend to seek congressional consent at the time that they entered into the compact, but later decided to seek it (and received it).

Conversely, there have been compacts where the states involved sought congressional consent, but, when the states discovered that they could not obtain congressional consent, they then went ahead and implemented the compact without congressional consent. The Multistate Tax Compact is an example of such a compact. This compact was the subject of the leading recent case on congressional consent of interstate compacts namely, *U.S. Steel Corporation v. Multistate Tax Commission.*[181]

10.17.4 MYTH: The National Popular Vote compact requires congressional consent to become effective.

QUICK ANSWER:

* Under prevailing U.S. Supreme Court rulings, congressional consent is not required for the National Popular Vote compact to become effective.

---

[181] *U.S. Steel Corporation v. Multistate Tax Commission.* 434 U.S. 452. 1978.

- Nevertheless, National Popular Vote is seeking support in Congress for the National Popular Vote compact.

MORE DETAILED ANSWER:

Under prevailing U.S. Supreme Court rulings, congressional consent is not required for the National Popular Vote compact to become effective. The U.S. Constitution provides:

> "No state shall, without the consent of Congress,… enter into any agreement or compact with another state…."[182]

However, the U.S. Supreme Court has ruled, in 1893 and again in 1978, that the Compacts Clause can "not be read literally." In deciding the 1978 case of *U.S. Steel Corporation v. Multistate Tax Commission*,[183] the Court wrote:

> "Read literally, the Compact Clause would require the States to obtain congressional approval before entering into any agreement among themselves, irrespective of form, subject, duration, or interest to the United States.

> "The difficulties with such an interpretation were identified by Mr. Justice Field in his opinion for the Court in [the 1893 case] *Virginia v. Tennessee*.[184] His conclusion [was] that the Clause could not be read literally [and this 1893 conclusion has been] approved in subsequent dicta."[185]

Specifically, the Court's 1893 ruling in *Virginia v. Tennessee* stated:

> "Looking at the clause in which the terms 'compact' or 'agreement' appear, **it is evident that the prohibition is directed to the formation of any combination tending to the increase of political power in the states, which may encroach upon or interfere with the just supremacy of the United States.**" [186] [Emphasis added]

---

[182] U.S. Constitution. Article I, section 10, clause 3.

[183] *U.S. Steel Corporation v. Multistate Tax Commission*. 434 U.S. 452. 1978.

[184] *Virginia v. Tennessee*. 148 U.S. 503. 1893.

[185] *U.S. Steel Corporation v. Multistate Tax Commission*. 434 U.S. 452. at 459. 1978.

[186] *Virginia v. Tennessee*. 148 U.S. 503 at 519. 1893.

The state power involved in the National Popular Vote compact is specified in Article II, section 1, clause 2 of the U.S. Constitution:

> "Each State shall appoint, in such Manner as the Legislature thereof may direct, a Number of Electors...."[187]

In the 1892 case of *McPherson v. Blacker*, the Court wrote:

> "The appointment and mode of appointment of electors belong **exclusively** to the states under the constitution of the United States"[188] [Emphasis added]

The National Popular Vote compact does not "encroach upon or interfere with the just supremacy of the United States" because there is no federal power whatsoever in the area of awarding of electoral votes in the first place—much less federal supremacy.

The 1978 case of *U.S. Steel Corporation v. Multistate Tax Commission* concerned a compact that specified that it would come into force when any seven or more states enacted it. The compact, like most modern-day compacts, was silent as to the role of Congress. The compact was submitted to Congress for its consent. After encountering fierce political opposition from various business interests concerned about the more stringent tax audits anticipated under the compact, the compacting states proceeded with the implementation of the compact without congressional consent. U.S. Steel challenged the states' action. In upholding the constitutionality of the implementation of the compact by the states without congressional consent, the U.S. Supreme Court applied the interpretation of the Compact Clause from its 1893 holding in *Virginia v. Tennessee*, writing that:

> "**the test is whether the Compact enhances state power quaod [with regard to] the National Government.**"[189] [Emphasis added]

The Court also noted that the compact did not

---

[187] U.S. Constitution. Article II, section 1, clause 2.

[188] *McPherson v. Blacker.* 146 U.S. 1 at 29. 1892.

[189] *Virginia v. Tennessee.* 148 U.S. 503. 1893.

"authorize the member states to exercise any powers they could not exercise in its absence."[190]

Of course, there is always the possibility that the U.S. Supreme Court might change the legal standards concerning congressional consent contained in its 1893 and 1978 rulings.

One dissenting justice of the U.S. Supreme Court (Byron White) suggested, in his opinion in *U.S. Steel v. Multi-State Tax Commission,* that courts could consider the possible adverse effects of a compact on non-compacting states in deciding whether congressional consent is required.

Even if Justice White's minority view were to become the majority view, it is not clear what adverse effect might be attributed to the National Popular Vote compact.

The National Popular Vote compact would treat votes cast in all 50 states and the District of Columbia equally. A vote cast in a compacting state would be, in every way, equal to a vote cast in a non-compacting state. The National Popular Vote compact would not confer any advantage on states belonging to the compact as compared to non-compacting states. The National Popular Vote compact certainly would not reduce the voice of voters in non-compacting states relative to the voice of voters in member states.

It has always been the case that one state's choice of the manner of appointing its presidential electors has affected the political value of a vote cast in other states. For example, the use of the winner-take-all rule by a closely divided battleground state arguably diminishes the political value of the votes cast by citizens in the approximately 35 non-battleground states. It is inherent in the grant by the U.S. Constitution to each state of the power to choose the method of appointing its presidential electors that one state's decision can have a political impact on other states. This is a direct consequence of federalism and the fact that the Constitution gives the states control over elections.

A current battleground state could, of course, eliminate its political effect on other states by changing its method of awarding its electoral votes. For example, if a current battleground state were to change its winner-take-all statute to a proportional method for awarding elec-

---

[190] *U.S. Steel Corporation v. Multistate Tax Commission.* 434 U.S. 454 at 473. 1978. Justice Powell wrote the opinion of the Court, joined by Chief Justice Burger and Justices Brennan, Stewart, Marshall, Rehnquist, and Stevens.

toral votes, presidential candidates would pay less attention to that state because only one electoral vote would probably be at stake in the state. However, we are not aware of anyone who currently argues that a current battleground state is obligated, under the Constitution, to make such a change in order to reduce its political effect on the approximately 35 non-battleground states.

If the Constitution gives a closely divided battleground state the power to choose a method of awarding its electoral votes that gives it a political advantage, it also gives the power to another state to choose its method for awarding its electoral votes that counter-balances the first state's advantage (and arguably creates a better overall system in the process).

In any case, the electoral votes of non-compacting states would continue to be cast in the manner specified by the laws of those states. In practical terms, that means that the non-compacting states would continue to cast their votes for the winner of the statewide popular vote (or district-wide popular vote in Maine and Nebraska), even after the National Popular Vote compact is implemented. The National Popular Vote compact would not invalidate or negate the electoral votes cast by non-compacting states. Nor would it require non-compacting states to cast their electoral votes for the winner of the national popular vote. No non-compacting state would be compelled to cast its electoral votes for the winner of the national popular vote.

The political impact of the winner-take-all rule on other states has long been recognized as a political reality. It is not California's winner-take-all rule or Wyoming's winner-take-all rule that makes votes in California and Wyoming unimportant in presidential elections. Instead, it is the winner-take-all rule in a closely divided battleground state, such as Pennsylvania, that diminishes the political value of the votes cast in California and Wyoming.

Of course, political impact does not create a legal basis for overturning another state's winner-take-all rule. In 1966, the U.S. Supreme Court declined to act in response to a complaint concerning the political impact of one state's choice of the manner of appointing its presidential electors on another state. Delaware led a group of 12 predominantly low-population states (including North Dakota, South Dakota, Wyoming, Utah, Arkansas, Kansas, Oklahoma, Iowa, Kentucky, Florida, Pennsylvania) in suing New York in the U.S. Supreme Court. Delaware argued that New

York's decision to use the winner-take-all rule effectively disenfranchised voters in the 12 plaintiff states.[191] New York's (defendant) brief is especially pertinent. Despite the fact that the case was brought under the Court's original jurisdiction, the Court declined to hear the case (presumably because of the well-established constitutional provision that the manner of awarding electoral votes is exclusively a state decision).

Nevertheless, because there could be time-consuming litigation about congressional consent, National Popular Vote is working to obtain support for the compact in Congress.[192]

Because Congress typically considers a compact only after the compact has been approved by the combination of states required to bring the compact into effect, one would expect that any action in Congress would occur after the compact had been approved by the approximately 25 states needed to give the compact the support of states possessing a majority of the electoral votes (i.e., 270 of 538).

Congressional consent can be explicitly conferred by a majority vote in both the U.S. House and Senate and approval of the President (or enactment by a two-thirds majority if the President vetoes the bill).

The question of congressional consent is discussed in greater detail in chapter 5.

10.18 Myths about Encroaching on Federal Sovereignty and State Sovereignty

10.18.1 MYTH: The National Popular Vote compact encroaches on federal sovereignty.

QUICK ANSWER:

- The power to choose the method of awarding a state's electoral votes is (as the U.S. Supreme Court has stated) an "exclusive" and "plenary" state power.
- A state does not encroach on federal sovereignty when it exercises a power that belongs exclusively to the states.
- The National Popular Vote compact would not encroach on federal sovereignty, because the federal government has no power in this area in the first place.

---

[191] The pleadings are found at http://www.nationalpopularvote.com/pages/misc/de_lawsuit.php.

[192] Congressional consent is ordinarily embodied in a statute or joint resolution.

MORE DETAILED ANSWER:

Tara Ross, an opponent of the National Popular Vote plan, asserts:

> "If ever a compact encroached on federal ... sovereignty, this is it."[193]

However, the U.S. Constitution gives the federal government no role in choosing the manner by which states award their electoral votes:

> "**Each State** shall appoint, in such Manner **as the Legislature there of may direct**, a Number of Electors...."[194] [Emphasis added]

As the U.S. Supreme Court ruled in the 1892 case of *McPherson v. Blacker*:

> "The constitution does not provide that the appointment of electors shall be by popular vote, nor that the electors shall be voted for upon a general ticket [the winner-take-all rule] nor that the majority of those who exercise the elective franchise can alone choose the electors. It recognizes that **the people act through their representatives in the legislature**, **and leaves it to the legislature exclusively to define the method of effecting the object....**

> "In short, **the appointment and mode of appointment of electors belong exclusively to the states** under the constitution of the United States."[195] [Emphasis added]

In *Bush v. Gore* in 2000, the Court approvingly referred to *McPherson v. Blacker* and called section 1 of article II of the Constitution:

> "The source for the statement in *McPherson v. Blacker* ... that the State legislature's power to select the manner for appointing electors is **plenary**."[196] [Emphasis added]

The choice of method for appointing presidential electors is a state power—not a federal power.

A state does not encroach on federal sovereignty when it exercises a power that belongs exclusively to the states.

---

[193] Ross, Tara. 2010. Federalism & Separation of Powers: Legal and Logistical Ramifications of the National Popular Vote Plan. *Engage.* Volume 11. Number 2. September 2010.

[194] U.S. Constitution. Article II, section 1, clause 2.

[195] *McPherson v. Blacker.* 146 U.S. 1 at 29. 1892.

[196] *Bush v. Gore.* 531 U.S. 98. 2000.

In short, the National Popular Vote compact would not encroach on federal sovereignty, because the federal government has no power in this area in the first place.

10.18.2 MYTH: The National Popular Vote compact encroaches on state sovereignty.

QUICK ANSWER:

- The power to choose the method of awarding a state's electoral votes is (as the U.S. Supreme Court has stated) an "exclusive" and "plenary" state power.
- The National Popular Vote compact is an exercise of state sovereignty—not an encroachment.
- A state cannot encroach on state sovereignty when a state exercises one of its "exclusive" and "plenary" powers.

MORE DETAILED ANSWER:

Tara Ross, an opponent of the National Popular Vote plan, asserts:

"If ever a compact encroached on ... state sovereignty, this is it."[197]

The U.S. Supreme Court ruled in the 1892 case of *McPherson v. Blacker* that the choice of method for appointing a state's presidential electors is an "exclusive" and "plenary" state power (quoted in section 10.18.1). Moreover, the U.S. Supreme Court approvingly referred to *McPherson v. Blacker* as recently as the 2000 case of *Bush v. Gore.*

How is it possible for a state to "encroach" on state sovereignty when the state is exercising one of its "exclusive" and "plenary" powers?

States enter into interstate compacts because they choose to do so. Moreover, except for boundary-settlement contracts (which are intended to be permanent), virtually every interstate compact (including the National Popular Vote compact) permits a state to withdraw. [198]

The 10th Amendment reinforces standard rules of constitutional and

---

[197] Ross, Tara. 2010. Federalism & Separation of Powers: Legal and Logistical Ramifications of the National Popular Vote Plan. *Engage.* Volume 11. Number 2. September 2010.

[198] In particular, clause 2 of article IV of the National Popular Vote compact would permit a state to withdraw from the compact by simply repealing the statute under which it entered the compact. The effective date of the withdrawal is immediate during 3½ years of every four-year presidential election cycle. The withdrawal is subject to a delay until after inauguration day if the withdrawal occurs during a blackout period running between July 20 of a presidential election year and the following January 20 (inauguration day).

statutory interpretation by addressing the question of whether the states are prohibited from exercising a particular power when the Constitution contains no specific prohibition against it.

"**The powers** not delegated to the United States by the Constitution, **nor prohibited by it to the States, are reserved to the States** respectively, or to the people." [Emphasis added]

In short, the National Popular Vote compact would be an exercise of state sovereignty—not an encroachment on it.

10.19 Myth about Our Republican Form of Government

10.19.1 MYTH: A national popular vote violates the concept that the United States is a republic, not a democracy.

QUICK ANSWER:
- In a republic, the citizens do not rule directly but, instead, elect officeholders to represent them and conduct the business of government in the period between elections.
- Thus, the United States is a republic, not a democracy.
- The United States will remain a republic—with or without the National Popular Vote approach to appointing presidential electors.

MORE DETAILED ANSWER:
In a republic, the citizens do not rule directly but, instead, elect officeholders to represent them and conduct the business of government in the period between elections.

In the United States, legislation is crafted by officeholders who serve for a term of two years (in the U.S. House of Representatives) and six years (in the U.S. Senate). Laws are executed and administered by an officeholder (the President) who serves for a term of four years. The United States has a "Republican form of government" because of this division of power between the citizenry and these elected officials who act on behalf of the citizenry between elections. Therefore, the United States is a republic, not a democracy.

The division of power between the citizenry and elected officeholders is not affected by the boundaries of the regions used to tally popular votes in choosing presidential electors. The United States is neither less nor more a "republic" if its chief executive is elected under the state-by-state winner-take-all method (i.e., awarding all of a state's electoral votes to the candidate who receives the most popular votes in each separate state), under a district system (such as used by Maine and Nebraska), or under the proposed national popular vote system (in which the winner would be the candidate receiving the most popular votes in all 50 states and the District of Columbia).

The United States is a republic under current state winner-take-all statutes, and it would remain so under the National Popular Vote compact.

Direct popular election of the chief executive is not incompatible with a "republican form of government." The specific meaning of the word "republic" and the phrase "republican form of government" can be ascertained by examining the single place in the U.S. Constitution where these words appear namely, the Guaranty Clause:

> "The United States shall guarantee to every State in this Union a Republican Form of Government."[199]

At the time of the Constitutional Convention in 1789, state governors were selected by state legislatures (except in Connecticut and Rhode Island). Today, the governor of every state is elected by a direct popular vote. No one has ever argued that the states denied their citizens a "Republican form of government" when they switched to direct popular election of their chief executives (or adopted it at the time when they were first admitted to the Union). No one has ever argued that the federal government should have invoked the Guaranty Clause and intervened (militarily or otherwise) to prevent the states from electing their chief executives by popular vote.

10.20 Myths about Mob Rule

10.20.1 MYTH: A national popular vote would be mob rule.

QUICK ANSWER:

- The American people currently cast votes for President in 100% of the states, and they have done so in 100% of the states since the 1880 election. If anyone thinks it is appropriate to characterize the American electorate as a "mob," it is now long-settled political reality that the "mob" rules in

---

[199] U.S. Constitution. Article IV, section 4, clause 1.

American presidential elections.

MORE DETAILED ANSWER:

This myth apparently originates from the failure (by some) to realize that the American people cast votes for President in 100% of the states, and they have done so in 100% of the states since the 1880 election.

If anyone thinks it is appropriate to characterize the American electorate as a "mob," it is now long-settled political reality that the "mob" rules in American presidential elections.[200]

The choice presented by the National Popular Vote is not whether the "mob" is going to control presidential elections, but whether the mob's votes are tallied on a state-by-state basis versus a nationwide basis.

The National Popular Vote bill is concerned with the relative political importance of popular votes cast in different states for presidential electors. The currently prevailing winner-take-all method (i.e., awarding all of a state's electoral votes to the candidate who receives the most popular vote in a state) makes popular votes unequal from state to state. Under the current system, presidential candidates concentrate their attention on voters from a small handful of closely divided battleground states, while ignoring voters in two-thirds of the states.

The National Popular Vote plan would address the shortcomings of the current system by making every vote equally important in every state in every presidential election. Thus, the issue presented by the National Popular Vote bill is not whether the "mob" will vote for President, but whether the "mobs" in certain closely divided battleground states should be more important than the "mobs" in the remaining two-thirds of the states.

10.20.2 MYTH: The Electoral College acts as a buffer and damper against popular passions.

QUICK ANSWER:

- The Electoral College has never operated as a buffer and damper against popular passions.
- The Electoral College will not operate as a buffer and damper against popular passions—with or without the National Popular Vote approach to appointing presidential electors.

---

[200] State legislatures frequently chose presidential electors in the nation's early years; however, the last time presidential electors were chosen by a state legislature was the 1876 election (in Colorado).

MORE DETAILED ANSWER:

This myth apparently originates from the failure (by some) to realize that the Electoral College currently does not act as a buffer and damper against popular passions—and indeed never did.

It is true that the Founding Fathers intended that the Electoral College would provide a buffer against the will of the people. They anticipated that the Electoral College would consist of "wise men" who would deliberate on the choice of the President and "judiciously" select the best candidate for the office. However, the vision of the Founding Fathers was never realized in practice because the Founders did not anticipate the emergence of political parties.

In the nation's first two presidential elections (1789 and 1792), the Electoral College did not act as a buffer against popular passions but, instead, acceded to the nationwide consensus that George Washington should be the President.

As soon as George Washington announced that he would not run for a third term in 1796, political parties emerged. The competition for power was between two opposing groups holding two very different visions about how the country should be governed.

In 1796, both the Federalist and Anti-Federalist parties nominated their presidential and vice-presidential candidates at national meetings composed of the party's members of Congress. As soon as there were national nominees, both parties presented the public with candidates for the position of presidential elector who made it known that they intended to act as willing "rubberstamps" for the nominees of their respective political parties when the Electoral College met. In 1796, all but one of the presidential electors then dutifully voted as expected when the Electoral College met. Moreover, that election established the expectation that presidential electors should "act" and not "think."[201]

---

[201] A Federalist supporter famously complained in the December 15, 1796, issue of *United States Gazette* that Samuel Miles, a Federalist presidential elector, had voted for Thomas Jefferson, instead of John Adams, by saying, "What, do I chufe Samuel Miles to determine for me whether John Adams or Thomas Jefferfon is the fittest man to be President of the United States? No, I chufe him to act, not to think." [Spelling per original]. Of the 22,453 electoral votes cast for President in the nation's 56 presidential elections, only 11 were cast in an unexpected way. As explained in greater detail in section 2.12, the vote of Federalist elector Samuel Miles for Anti-Federalist Thomas Jefferson in 1796 remains the only instance when the elector might have intended, at the time he cast his unexpected vote, that his vote might affect the national outcome.

The U.S. Supreme Court noted this history in its opinion in the 1892 case of *McPherson v. Blacker*:

"Doubtless it was supposed that the electors would exercise a reasonable independence and fair judgment in the selection of the chief executive, but experience soon demonstrated that, **whether chosen by the legislatures or by popular suffrage on general ticket or in districts, they were so chosen simply to register the will of the appointing power** in respect of a particular candidate. In relation, then, to the independence of the electors, the original expectation may be said to have been frustrated."[202] [Emphasis added]

Thus, as early as the nation's first competitive presidential election in 1796, the principle was established that the Electoral College would act as a rubberstamp for the "the will of the appointing power." Since then, the Electoral College has reliably elected the nominees determined by extra-constitutional bodies (namely, the nominating meetings of political parties).

In reality, the Electoral College has never acted as a buffer or damper against popular passions.

Similarly, the Electoral College would not act as a buffer or damper against popular passions under the National Popular Vote plan.

10.21 Myth about an Incoming President's Mandate

10.21.1 MYTH: The current winner-take-all system gives the incoming President a "mandate" in the form of an exaggerated lead in the Electoral College.

QUICK ANSWER:

- The current system of electing the President does not reliably generate a "mandate" in the form of a larger percentage share of the electoral vote than the candidate's share of the national popular vote.
- If anyone believes that an exaggerated margin in the Electoral College is desirable in that it enhances a new president's ability to lead, the National Popular Vote plan would do an even better job of creating this illusion than the current system.

---

[202] *McPherson v. Blacker.* 146 U.S. 1 at 36. 1892.

MORE DETAILED ANSWER:

Daniel H. Lowenstein has argued:

> **"The Electoral College** turns the many winners who fail to win a majority of the popular vote into majority winners. It also **magnifies small majorities in the popular vote into large majorities.** These effects of the Electoral College enhance Americans' confidence in the outcome of the election and thereby **enhance the new president's ability to lead.**"[203] [Emphasis added]

The historical record shows that the above statement is false about as often as it is true. It is, therefore, not an accurate characterization of what actually happens in the real world.

The current state-by-state winner-take-all system does not reliably deliver an exaggerated margin to the incoming President. For example, despite winning by almost two million votes nationwide, Jimmy Carter won the Electoral College in 1976 with only 297 electoral votes (27 over the 270 needed for election). Despite winning by over three million votes in 2004, George W. Bush won the Electoral College with only 286 electoral votes (16 over the 270 needed).

Moreover, the current state-by-state winner-take-all system does not reliably confer an illusory mandate on an incoming President. There is certainly no historical evidence that the Congress, the public, the media, or anyone else has been more deferential to an incoming President after an election in which he received a larger percentage of the electoral vote than his percentage of the popular vote. As a recent example, Bill Clinton did not receive such deference when he came into office with an eye-catching 370 electoral votes but only 43% of the popular vote in 1992.

However, if anyone believes that an exaggerated margin will "enhance the new president's ability to lead," the National Popular Vote plan would do an even better job of creating this illusion than the current system.

Under the National Popular Vote compact, the nationwide winning candidate would generally receive an exaggerated margin (roughly 75%) of the votes in the Electoral College in any given presidential election.

---

[203] Debate entitled "Should We Dispense with the Electoral College?" sponsored by PENNumbra (University of Pennsylvania Law Review) available at http://www.pennumbra.com/debates/pdfs/electoral_college.pdf.

The reason is that the National Popular Vote bill guarantees that the presidential candidate receiving the most popular votes in all 50 states and the District of Columbia would receive at least 270 electoral votes (of 538) from the states belonging to the compact. Then, in addition to this guaranteed minimum bloc of at least 270 electoral votes, the nationwide winning candidate would generally receive some additional electoral votes from whichever non-compacting states he or she happened to carry. Because the non-compacting states would likely be divided approximately equally between the candidates, the nationwide winning candidate would generally receive an exaggerated margin (roughly 75%) of the votes in the Electoral College (that is, about 404 out of 538 electoral votes).

Of course, the current system often does more than just exaggerate an incoming President's percentage in the Electoral College as compared to his or her percentage in the nationwide popular vote. In four out of the nation's 56 presidential elections, the current system has actually awarded the Presidency to a candidate who did not receive the most popular votes nationwide. This is a failure rate of 1 in 14. Moreover, because about half of American presidential elections are popular-vote landslides (i.e., a margin of greater than 10%), the failure rate is actually 1 in 7 among non-landslide elections.

10.22   Myth about Presidential Power

10.22.1 MYTH: The President's powers would be changed by a national popular vote.

QUICK ANSWER:

- Because the National Popular Vote compact is state legislation that would not alter the U.S. Constitution, no power that the President possesses under the U.S. Constitution would be enhanced or diminished by it.

MORE DETAILED ANSWER:

The National Popular Vote compact is state legislation. It would not alter the U.S. Constitution. In particular, it does not augment or diminish any power possessed by the President under the U.S. Constitution.

The National Popular Vote compact would, in effect, make a change in the "district" from which presidential electors are elected. Under current state winner-take-all statutes, state boundary lines define the "districts" used to elect presidential electors. Under the National Popular Vote compact, presidential electors would be elected from a single national "district." Changing these "district" boundaries would not diminish or augment any power possessed by the President under the U.S. Constitution.

10.23 Myth about the 12th Amendment

10.23.1 MYTH: The Meeting Clause of the 12th Amendment precludes the National Popular Vote compact.

QUICK ANSWER:
- The 12th Amendment does not address, much less restrict, the states in the manner of choosing their presidential electors.
- The Meeting Clause of the 12th Amendment requires that the physical location of the meeting of presidential electors be inside each respective state.
- The National Popular Vote compact would not affect the meeting place for presidential electors.

MORE DETAILED ANSWER:
The Meeting Clause of the 12th Amendment (ratified in 1804) specifies that the meeting of the presidential electors must be physically conducted in each state.

The 12th Amendment states:

> "**The Electors shall meet in their respective states**, and vote by ballot for President and Vice-President, one of whom, at least, shall not be an inhabitant of the same state with themselves; they shall name in their ballots the person voted for as President, and in distinct ballots the person voted for as Vice-President, and they shall make distinct lists of all persons voted for as President...."[204] [Emphasis added]

Congress has implemented the Meeting Clause of the 12th Amendment by enacting section 7 of chapter 1 of title 3 of the United States Code:

> "The electors of President and Vice President of each State

---

[204] The full text of the 12th Amendment is available in appendix A.

shall meet and give their votes on the first Monday after the second Wednesday in December next following their appointment **at such place in each State as the legislature of such State shall direct.**" [Emphasis added]

Individual states, in turn, have further implemented the Meeting Clause of the 12th Amendment and section 7.

For example, current Alaska law provides that Alaska's presidential electors shall meet at the offices of the Director of the Division of Elections located in Juneau:

"The electors shall meet at the office of the director or other place designated by the director at 11:00 o'clock in the morning on the first Monday after the second Wednesday in December following their election. If Congress fixes a different day for the meeting, the electors shall meet on the day designated by the Act of Congress."[205]

The 12th Amendment does not contain any restriction on the manner of choosing presidential electors.

The National Popular Vote compact would not affect the meeting place for presidential electors.

10.24 Myths about the 14th Amendment

10.24.1 MYTH: Section 2 of the 14th Amendment precludes the National Popular Vote compact.

QUICK ANSWER:
* The U.S. Supreme Court has considered, and rejected, the argument that section 2 of the 14th Amendment made the statewide winner-take-all method of awarding electoral votes the only constitutional method of appointment of presidential electors.

MORE DETAILED ANSWER:
Section 2 of the 14th Amendment reads:

"Representatives shall be apportioned among the several States according to their respective numbers, counting the

---

[205]   Section 15.30.070.

whole number of persons in each State, excluding Indians not taxed. **But when the right to vote at any election for the choice of electors for President and Vice President of the United States**, Representatives in Congress, the Executive and Judicial officers of a State, or the members of the Legislature thereof, is denied to any of the male inhabitants of such State, being twenty-one years of age, and citizens of the United States, or in any way abridged, except for participation in rebellion, or other crime, the basis of representation therein shall be reduced in the proportion which the number of such male citizens shall bear to the whole number of male citizens twenty-one years of age in such State. [Emphasis added]

Section 2 of the 14th Amendment does not prescribe any action by the states. Instead, it provides a remedy if a state denies or abridges any person's right to vote. The remedy is in the form of reduced congressional representation.

The National Popular Vote compact would not deny or abridge any person's right to vote for any office. Under the National Popular Vote compact, voters will continue to vote for their "choice of electors for President and Vice President of the United States." Therefore, the remedy provided by section 2 (namely, reduced congressional representation) would not apply.

Section 2 of the 14th Amendment does not give the voters the right to vote for President nor does it require that the state-by-state winner-take-all rule be used to appoint presidential electors.

The losing attorney (F.A. Baker) in the 1892 case of *McPherson v. Blacker* strenuously argued before the U.S. Supreme Court that section 2 of the 14th Amendment limited the states in their choice of manner of electing presidential electors.

"The electoral system as it actually exists is recognized by the 14th and 15th amendments, and by necessary implication, **the general ticket method [i.e., the winner-take-all rule] for choosing presidential electors is made permanent, and the only constitutional method of appointment.**"[206] [Emphasis added]

---

[206] *Brief of F.A. Baker for Plaintiffs in Error in McPherson v. Blacker.* 1892. Page 64.

As pointed out in the brief[207] of the winning attorney (Otto Kirchner) in *McPherson v. Blacker*, one deficiency in Baker's interpretation of section 2 of the 14th Amendment is that "judicial officers of a state" are also mentioned in section 2 and, of course, judges were not elected by the people in a number of states—either before or immediately after ratification of the 14th Amendment.

Even more pertinently, the 14th Amendment was never intended to restrict the states in their choice of method of appointing presidential electors. Immediately before and after the 14th Amendment was ratified in 1867, some state legislatures appointed presidential electors without a vote by the people (e.g., South Carolina in 1860, Florida in 1868, and Colorado in 1876).

In addition, the congressional act providing for Colorado's statehood in 1876 included a specific reference to the fact that the Colorado legislature would be appointing the state's presidential electors for the 1876 election.

No contemporary argued that these actions were unconstitutional.

If Baker's interpretation of the 14th Amendment had any validity, the appointment of presidential electors by the Florida legislature in 1868 and by the Colorado legislature in 1876 would have been unconstitutional.

If contemporaries thought the 14th Amendment required popular election of presidential electors, that legal argument would certainly have been employed during the contentious dispute over the 1876 presidential election (where Colorado's three electoral votes would have been decisive). If the Colorado legislature's appointment of the state's three presidential electors favoring Hayes in 1876 were invalid, Tilden would have had the required "majority of the whole number of Electors *appointed*"[208] and, therefore, would have become President—even after losing the contested electoral votes of Louisiana, Florida, and South Carolina.

The history and practices used to choose presidential electors were exhaustively reviewed during the dispute over the 1876 election. In particular, the report of the Senate Committee on Privileges and Elections

---

[207] *Brief of Otto Kirchner for Defendants in Error in McPherson v. Blacker.* 1892.

[208] The Constitution does not require an absolute majority of the electoral votes to become President but only an absolute majority of the electoral votes appointed. There have been occasional cases when a state failed to appoint its presidential electors. For example, New York did not in 1789 because the legislature could not agree on how to appoint them. Notably, the southern states did not appoint presidential electors in 1864.

reviewed the history concerning the appointment of presidential electors and stated:

> **"The appointment of these electors is thus placed absolutely and wholly with the Legislatures of the several states.** They may be chosen by the Legislature, or the Legislature may provide that they shall be elected by the people of the State at large, or in districts, as are members of Congress, which was the case formerly in many States, and **it is no doubt competent for the Legislature to authorize the governor, or the Supreme Court of the State, or any other agent of its will, to appoint these electors.**"[209] [Emphasis added]

In any event, the U.S. Supreme Court was not moved by Baker's argument that section 2 of the 14th Amendment made the state-by-state winner-take-all rule permanent and binding on the states. The Court unanimously ruled in *McPherson v. Blacker* that:

> **"The constitution does not provide that the appointment of electors shall be by popular vote, nor that the electors shall be voted for upon a general ticket [i.e., the 'winner-take-all' rule],** nor that the majority of those who exercise the elective franchise can alone choose the electors."[210] [Emphasis added]

In 2000, the U.S. Supreme Court wrote:

> **"The individual citizen has no federal constitutional right to vote for electors for the President of the United States unless and until the state legislature chooses a statewide election as the means to implement its power to appoint members of the Electoral College**. U.S. Const., Art. II, §1.

> "This is the source for the statement in *McPherson v. Blacker* ... that the State legislature's power to select the manner for appointing electors is plenary"...

---

[209] Senate Report 395. Forty-Third Congress.

[210] *McPherson v. Blacker.* 146 U.S. 1 at 27. 1892.

"There is no difference between the two sides of the present controversy on these basic propositions."[211] [Emphasis added]

Far from denying or abridging "the right to vote at any election for the choice of electors for President and Vice President of the United States," the National Popular Vote compact actually would establish the people's right to vote for President in compacting states. Article II of the compact states.

"Each member state shall conduct a statewide popular election for President and Vice President of the United States."[212]

10.24.2 MYTH: The Privileges and Immunities Clause of the 14th Amendment precludes the National Popular Vote compact.

QUICK ANSWER:
- The National Popular Vote compact would not abridge any protection that citizens currently possess relative to abridgments of their rights by the federal government.

MORE DETAILED ANSWER:
The Privileges and Immunities Clause of the 14th Amendment (ratified in 1867) reads:

"No State shall make or enforce any law which shall abridge the privileges or immunities of citizens of the United States."

The Privileges and Immunities Clause gives each citizen the same protection against abridgments by state governments as each citizen already possessed, by virtue of national citizenship, relative to abridgments by the federal government.

The National Popular Vote compact would not deny or abridge any existing constitutional privilege or immunity possessed by citizens of the United States.

In particular, as discussed in section 10.24.1, there is no federal right to vote for President conferred by section 2 of the 14th Amendment.[213]

---

[211] *Bush v. Gore.* 531 U.S. 98. 2000.

[212] The term "statewide popular election" is defined in article V of the compact as "a general election at which votes are cast for presidential slates by individual voters and counted on a statewide basis."

[213] Even if there were a federal right to vote for President, the National Popular Vote bill would do nothing to abridge that right.

10.24.3 MYTH: The Due Process Clause of the 14th Amendment precludes the National Popular Vote compact.

QUICK ANSWER:

- The National Popular Vote compact would not deprive any person of life, liberty, or property.

MORE DETAILED ANSWER:

The Due Process Clause of the 14th Amendment says:

"... nor shall any State deprive any person of life, liberty, or property, without due process of law ..."

The National Popular Vote compact would not deny any person of life, liberty, or property in any way.

10.24.4 MYTH: The Equal Protection Clause of the 14th Amendment precludes the National Popular Vote compact.

QUICK ANSWER:

- The Equal Protection Clause of the 14th Amendment reads: "no state shall ... deny to any person within its jurisdiction the equal protection of the laws."
- No state would deny equal protection of the laws to any person within its jurisdiction as a result of electing its presidential electors in accordance with the National Popular Vote compact.

MORE DETAILED ANSWER:

The Equal Protection Clause of the 14th Amendment reads:

"no state shall ... deny **to any person within its jurisdiction** the equal protection of the laws" [Emphasis added]

Some have argued that it is not permissible, under the Equal Protection Clause, for some states to permit ex-felons to vote while others prohibit it (absent a pardon), and for some states (e.g., Kentucky and Indiana) to close their polls at 6:00 P.M. while others close later in the evening; and for some states to conduct their election entirely by mail while other states conduct their (non-absentee) voting at the polls.

However, the U.S. Constitution does not require that the election laws of all 50 states be identical in every respect. In fact, the Constitution gives the states control over elections. Differences in election laws are inherent in our federalist system, which gives the states control over elections.

The Equal Protection Clause of the 14th Amendment restricts a particular state in the manner in which it treats persons "within its jurisdiction." The Equal Protection Clause imposes no obligation on a given state concerning a "person" in another state who is not "within its [the first state's] jurisdiction."

State election laws are not identical now, nor is there anything in the National Popular Vote compact that would force them to become identical. Indeed, the U.S. Constitution anticipates diversity of election laws among the states because it explicitly gives the states control over the conduct of presidential elections (article II) as well as congressional elections (article I). The fact is that the Founding Fathers intended, and the U.S. Constitution permits, states to conduct elections in diverse ways.

The National Popular Vote plan would not violate the Equal Protection Clause of the 14th Amendment.

10.25 Myths about the Voting Rights Act

10.25.1 MYTH: Section 2 of the Voting Rights Act precludes the National Popular Vote compact.

QUICK ANSWER:

- The National Popular Vote compact would not deny or abridge the right to vote. It would make every person's vote for President equal—consistent with a main goal of the Voting Rights Act.

MORE DETAILED ANSWER:

The purpose of the Voting Rights Act is to guarantee voting equality throughout the United States (particularly in relation to racial minorities that historically suffered discrimination in certain states or areas). Section 2 of the Act prohibits the denial or abridgment of the right to vote. Section 5 requires certain states (that historically violated the right to vote) to obtain advance approval for proposed changes in their state election laws to ensure that they do not have a discriminatory purpose or effect. The advance approval can be in the form of a favorable declaratory judgment from the U.S. District Court for the District of Columbia or pre-clearance by the U.S. Department of Justice (the more commonly chosen path).

The National Popular Vote compact manifestly would make every person's vote for President equal throughout the United States in an election to fill a single office (the Presidency). It is, therefore, consistent with the goals of the Voting Rights Act.

There have been court cases under the Voting Rights Act concerning contemplated changes in voting methods for various representative legislative bodies (e.g., city councils, county boards). However, these cases do not bear on elections to fill a single office (i.e., the Presidency).

In *Butts v. City of New York*, the United States Court of Appeals for the Second Circuit addressed the question of whether the Voting Rights Act applies to a run-off election for the single office of mayor, council president, or city comptroller in a New York City primary election. The court opined:

> "We cannot…take the concept of a class's impaired opportunity for equal representation and uncritically transfer it from the context of elections for multi-member bodies to that of elections for single-member officers."[214]

The court also stated:

> "**There is no such thing as a 'share' of a single member office.**" [Emphasis added]

The court then added:

> "It suffices to rule in this case that a run-off election requirement in such an election does not deny any class an opportunity for equal representation and therefore cannot violate the Act."

In *Dillard v. Crenshaw County*, the Eleventh Circuit addressed the question of whether the at-large elected chairperson of the Crenshaw County Commission in Alabama is a single-member office. The office's duties are primarily administrative and executive, but also include presiding over meetings of the commissioners and voting to break a tie. The court stated that it was unsatisfied that

---

[214] *Butts v. City of New York*, 779 F.2d 141 at 148 (1985).

"The chairperson will be sufficiently uninfluential in the activities initiated and in the decisions made by the commission proper to be evaluated as a single-member office."[215]

The case was remanded to the U.S. District Court for either "a reaffirmation of the rotating chairperson system" or approval of an alternative proposal preserving "the elected integrity of the body of associate commissioners."

In 1989, in *Southern Leadership Conference v. Siegelman*,[216] the U.S. District Court for the Middle District of Alabama distinguished between election of a single judge to a one-judge court and the election of multiple judges to a single Alabama circuit court or judicial court. Pre-clearance was required when more than one judge was to be elected, but not when one judge was to be elected.

In any event, those who argue that section 2 of the Voting Rights Act precludes the National Popular Vote compact do, however, concede that congressional consent to the National Popular Vote compact would eliminate the basis for any litigation under section 2.

10.25.2 MYTH: The political influence of racial and ethnic minorities would be diminished by a national popular vote.

QUICK ANSWER:

- Given that every vote would be equal under the National Popular Vote compact, then the assertion that the compact would diminish the influence of minorities must be based on the premise that current state winner-take-all statutes give minorities more than their fair share of influence. There is no evidence that this is the case.

MORE DETAILED ANSWER:

Six Colorado professors issued a written statement at a committee hearing in Colorado in 2007, arguing that the National Popular Vote plan would

"diminish the political influence of racial and ethnic minorities in the United States in presidential elections."[217]

---

[215] *Dillard v. Crenshaw County*, 831 F.2d 246 at 253 (11th Cir. 1987).

[216] *Southern Leadership Conference v. Siegelman*, 714 F. Supp. 511 at 518 (M.d. Ala. 1989).

[217] Statement signed by Professors Robert D. Loevy, Danial Clayton, Edward Roche, Robert M. Hardaway, Jim L. Riley, and Dennis Steele.

Curtis Gans (another opponent of the National Popular Vote plan) made a similar claim in a speech at the National Civic Summit in Minneapolis on July 17, 2009.

Given that every vote would be equal under the National Popular Vote compact, then the assertion that the compact would diminish the influence of minorities must be based on the premise that the current state-by-state winner-take-all system of electing the President gives minorities *more than their fair share of influence.*

The facts do not support the notion that minorities receive more than their fair share of influence under current state winner-take-all statutes. As FairVote's *Presidential Election Inequality* report points out:

"In the 1976 presidential election, 73% of African Americans were in a classic swing voter position; they lived in highly competitive states (where the partisanship is 47.5%–52.5%) in which African Americans made up at least 5% of the population. By 2000, that percentage of potential swing voters declined to 24%. In 2004, it fell to just 17%."[218]

The National Popular Vote bill has been sponsored by 135 minority state legislators and endorsed by organizations such as the National Black Caucus of State Legislators, the National Latino Congreso, and the NAACP.

In endorsing the National Popular Vote bill, the NAACP cited the fact that it supported "the ideal of one person, one vote."

10.26 Myth about a Federal Election Bureaucracy

10.26.1 MYTH: A federal election bureaucracy would be created by the National Popular Vote compact.

QUICK ANSWER:

- The National Popular Vote compact would not create any bureaucracy—much less a federal election bureaucracy.
- Implementation of the National Popular Vote compact would merely involve adding up the popular vote totals that are already being routinely tabulated by existing state officials under existing laws and procedures.

---

[218] Fair Vote. *Presidential Elections Inequality: The Electoral College in the 21st Century.* http://www.fairvote.org/media/perp/presidentialinequality.pdf.

MORE DETAILED ANSWER:

A brochure published by the Evergreen Freedom Foundation of Olympia, Washington, suggests that the National Popular vote plan would result in

"**nationalizing election administration**, potentially putting presidential appointees in charge of presidential elections."[219] [Emphasis added]

Trent England, an opponent of the National Popular Vote compact working for the Evergreen Freedom Foundation, writes:

"Because of the Electoral College, **the United States has no national election bureaucracy**—no presidential appointee in charge of presidential elections."[220] [Emphasis added]

Professor Robert Hardaway of the University of Denver Sturm College of Law repeated this theme in his testimony on February 19, 2010, to the Alaska Senate Judiciary Committee:

"Under the Koza scheme, who would be the **national official** who would decide what the popular vote is? And what would happen if a state officer decides that the popular vote tally is one figure, and **someone from the federal government**, like the Congressional Budget Office, the *Congressional Quarterly*, decides that it's something else?"

The National Popular Vote compact provides for the adding up of the vote totals for President from all 50 states and the District of Columbia. These vote totals are election results that are created by, and certified by, state election officials under existing laws and procedures.

These state-level vote totals would be generated by each state in exactly the same manner as they are today. Each state's vote totals would be officially recorded in a "certificate of ascertainment"[221]—just as they are today. Each state's results would then be reported to Congress as required under the 12th Amendment—just as they are today.

---

[219] Evergreen Freedom Foundation. Olympia, Washington.

[220] England, Trent. Op-Ed: Bypass the Electoral College? *Christian Science Monitor*. August 12, 2010.

[221] Appendices E, F, G, H, and I show examples of certificates of ascertainment from several states. The certificates of ascertainment from all 50 states and the District of Columbia are available online for the 2000, 2004, and 2008 presidential elections. For the 2004 presidential election, see http://www.archives.gov/federal-register/electoral-college/2004/certificates_of_ascertainment.html.

The National Popular Vote compact does not create any bureaucracy—much less a federal bureaucracy.

The states would continue to control elections, as provided by the U.S. Constitution—just as they do today.

Note that the Congressional Budget Office has nothing to do with elections, and the Congressional Quarterly is a private publishing corporation.

10.27 Myths about the District of Columbia

10.27.1 MYTH: The National Popular Vote compact would permit the District of Columbia to vote for President, even though it is not a state.

QUICK ANSWER

- The District of Columbia has had the vote for President since ratification of the 23rd Amendment to the U.S. Constitution in 1961.

MORE DETAILED ANSWER:

This myth stems from a failure to realize that the District of Columbia has had the vote for President and Vice President since ratification of the 23rd Amendment in 1961.

The 23rd Amendment specifies that presidential electors representing the District of Columbia

> "**shall be considered**, for the purposes of the election of President and Vice President, to be electors appointed by a state." [Emphasis added]

The National Popular Vote compact is consistent with the existing U.S. Constitution in that it treats the District of Columbia as a state for the purposes of presidential elections.

10.27.2 MYTH: Because it is not a state, the District of Columbia may not enter into interstate compacts.

QUICK ANSWER

- The District of Columbia may be a party to interstate compacts, and already belongs to numerous compacts.

MORE DETAILED ANSWER:

The Council of State Governments (CSG) lists 17 major interstate compacts to which the District of Columbia is a party.[222] Examples include the Interstate Compact on Juveniles and the Interstate Compact on the Placement of Children (both of which are compacts to which all 50 states and the District of Columbia belong). The Interstate Compact for Education encompasses 48 states, including the District of Columbia.

10.27.3 MYTH: Only Congress may enter into interstate compacts on behalf of the District of Columbia.

QUICK ANSWER:

- The District of Columbia Council may enter into interstate compacts under Congress's delegation of authority to the Council by the District of Columbia Home Rule Act of 1973, and it has done so on numerous occasions.

MORE DETAILED ANSWER:

Prior to 1973, it was customary for Congress to enact interstate compacts on behalf of the District of Columbia.

However, in the District of Columbia Home Rule Act of 1973, Congress delegated its authority to pass laws concerning the District to the District of Columbia Council in all but 10 specifically identified areas listed in section 602(a) of the Act.[223]

None of the 10 specific restrictions in section 602(a) of the Home Rule Act prevents the District of Columbia from entering into interstate compacts. Accordingly, the District of Columbia Council has itself entered into numerous interstate compacts. For example, the Council entered into the Interstate Parole and Probation Compact[224] in 1976 (three years after enactment of the Home Rule Act). In 2000, the Council entered into the Interstate Compact on Adoption and Medical Assistance.[225] In 2002, the Council entered into the Emergency Management Assistance Compact.[226]

---

[222] Council of State Governments. 2003. *Interstate Compacts and Agencies 2003* Lexington, KY: The Council of State Governments.

[223] D.C. Code § 1-233.

[224] D.C. Code § 24-452.

[225] Title 4, Chapter 3, D.C. ST § 4-326, June 27, 2000, D.C. Law 13-136, § 406, 47 DCR 2850.

[226] Interestingly, the Council originally entered into this compact on an emergency 90-day temporary basis (by D.C. Council Act 14-0081) under the authority of section 412(a) of the Home Rule Act. The Council subsequently entered into this same compact (by D.C. Council Act A14-0317) under the authority of section 602(c)(1) of the Home Rule Act (providing for the usual 30-day congressional review period).

10.27.4 MYTH: Only Congress may change the winner-take-all rule for the District of Columbia.

QUICK ANSWER:

- The District of Columbia Council has authority to change its election laws under Congress's delegation of authority to the Council by the District of Columbia Home Rule Act of 1973.

MORE DETAILED ANSWER:

This question arises because of the appearance of the word "Congress" in the 23rd Amendment to the U.S. Constitution (ratified in 1961):

"Section 1. The District constituting the seat of government of the United States shall appoint **in such manner as the Congress may direct**:

"A number of electors of President and Vice President equal to the whole number of Senators and Representatives in Congress to which the District would be entitled if it were a state, but in no event more than the least-populous state; they shall be in addition to those appointed by the states, but they shall be considered, for the purposes of the election of President and Vice President, to be electors appointed by a state; and they shall meet in the District and perform such duties as provided by the twelfth article of amendment.

"Section 2. The Congress shall have power to enforce this article by appropriate legislation." [Emphasis added].

Of course, the word "Congress" also appears in Article I, section 8, clause 17 of the original U.S. Constitution containing the enumerated powers of Congress in connection with the District of Columbia:

"The **Congress shall have Power … to exercise exclusive Legislation in all Cases whatsoever, over such District** (not exceeding ten Miles square) as may, by Cession of particular States, and the Acceptance of Congress, become the Seat of the Government of the United States…."

After ratification of the 23rd Amendment to the Constitution in 1961, Congress enacted a law establishing the winner-take-all method of awarding the District of Columbia's electoral votes (which, at the time, was the method used by all 50 states).

The winner-take-all method for awarding the District of Columbia's electoral votes is currently contained in section 1-1001.10(a)(2) of the D.C. Code:

> "The electors of President and Vice President of the United States shall be elected on the Tuesday next after the 1st Monday in November in every 4th year succeeding every election of a President and Vice President of the United States. Each vote cast for a candidate for President or Vice President whose name appears on the general election ballot shall be counted as a vote cast for the candidates for presidential electors of the party supporting such presidential and vice presidential candidate. **Candidates receiving the highest number of votes in such election shall be declared the winners.**" [Emphasis added].

In the District of Columbia Home Rule Act of 1973, Congress delegated its authority to pass laws concerning the District to the District of Columbia Council in all but 10 specifically identified areas listed in section 602(a) of the Act.[227]

Election law is not one of the 10 specifically excluded areas in section 602(a) of the Home Rule Act.

Moreover, section 752 of the District of Columbia Self-Government and Governmental Reorganization Act passed by Congress in 1973 specifically states:

> "Notwithstanding any other provision of this Act [Home Rule Act] or of any other law, the Council shall have authority to enact **any act or resolution with respect to matters involving or relating to elections in the District.**"[228] [Emphasis added]

Therefore, the District of Columbia Council may change section 1-1001.10(a)(2) of the D.C. Code establishing the winner-take-all rule as the method for awarding the District's electoral votes.

---

[227] D.C. Code § 1-233.

[228] P.L. 93-198 , 87 Stat. 774, (1973), codified at D.C. Statutes section 1-207.52.

10.27.5 MYTH: Because it is not a state, the District of Columbia cannot bind itself by means of an interstate compact.

QUICK ANSWER:

- The District of Columbia Home Rule Act of 1973 specifically applied the Impairments Clause of the U.S. Constitution to the District, thereby permitting the District to bind itself to an interstate compact in the same manner as a state is bound.

MORE DETAILED ANSWER:

Because the District of Columbia is not a state, the question has been raised[229] concerning whether the District can bind itself by means of an interstate compact in the same way that a state can.

Section 302 of the District of Columbia Home Rule Act states:

"Except as provided in sections 601, 602, and 603, the legislative power of the District shall extend to all rightful subjects of legislation within the District consistent with the Constitution of the United States and the provisions of this Act **subject to all the restrictions and limitations imposed upon the States by the tenth section of the first article of the Constitution** of the United States." [Emphasis added].

Section 10 of article I of the U.S. Constitution contains about three dozen restrictions on states. In particular, clause 1 of section 10 contains the Impairments Clause, stating that:

"No State shall ... pass any ... Law impairing the Obligation of Contracts."[230]

The Impairments Clause prevents states from violating the terms of an interstate compact.

Section 302 of the Home Rule Act applies the Impairments Clause to the District, thereby preventing it from violating the terms of any interstate compact to which it is a party. The Impairments Clause is discussed in greater detail in section 10.11.1.

---

[229] The issue was raised on an elections blog on September 23, 2010.

[230] U.S. Constitution. Article I, section 10, clause 3.

10.27.6 MYTH: The enactment of the National Popular Vote compact by the District of Columbia Council is incomplete because Congress has not approved the Council's action.

QUICK ANSWER:

- The process by which Congress approves of the District of Columbia's action on the National Popular Vote compact is specified by the District of Columbia Home Rule Act of 1973, and all of the requirements of the process were completed on December 7, 2010.

MORE DETAILED ANSWER:

The enactment of the National Popular Vote compact in the District of Columbia in 2010 was governed by the District of Columbia Home Rule Act of 1973.[231]

Under the Home Rule Act, Congress delegated its plenary authority to pass laws concerning the District regarding certain matters (including elections) to the District of Columbia Council.

Section 102 of the Act states:

"Subject to the retention by Congress of the ultimate legislative authority over the nation's capital granted by article I, 8, of the Constitution, **the intent of Congress is to delegate certain legislative powers to the government of the District of Columbia....**" [Emphasis added]

Section 601 provides:

"Notwithstanding any other provision of this Act, the Congress of the United States reserves the right, at any time, to exercise its constitutional authority as legislature for the District, by enacting legislation for the District on any subject, whether within or without the scope of legislative power granted to the Council by this Act, including legislation to amend or repeal any law in force in the District prior to or after enactment of this Act and any act passed by the Council."

The District of Columbia Council gave its final approval to the bill (B18-0769) on September 21, 2010. Bill B18-0769 contained the following provision:

---

[231] D.C. Code § 1-233.

"This act shall take effect following **approval by the Mayor** (or in the event of veto by the Mayor, action by the Council to override the veto), **a 30-day period of Congressional review** as provided in section 602(c)(l) of the District of Columbia Home Rule Act, approved December 21 1973 (87 Stat. 813; D.C. Official Code § 1-206.02(c)(l)), and **publication in the District of Columbia Register.**" [Emphasis added]

On September 22, 2010, Tara Ross, an opponent of the National Popular Vote plan, wrote:

"And so the dominoes continue to fall. The D.C. Council yesterday approved the National Popular Vote plan that has been pending before several state legislatures. D.C.'s approval comes less than two months after Massachusetts approved the plan. **Two procedural steps remain before NPV is officially enacted in D.C.: The mayor must sign the legislation and Congress has 30 days to review it.** If these two hurdles are overcome, then D.C.'s approval will bring the total number of entities supporting the bill to seven: Hawaii, Illinois, Maryland, Massachusetts, New Jersey, and Washington."[232] [Emphasis added]

Ross then issued a call to action:

"The Council's action gives constitutionalists in both parties an excellent opportunity to highlight their allegiance to the Constitution during this election season. **Constitutionalists in the House and Senate should sponsor resolutions of disapproval** if and when NPV is signed by D.C.'s mayor."[233] [Emphasis added]

The bill was signed by Mayor Adrian Fenty on October 12, 2010.[234]

On October 18, 2010, the bill was transmitted to the Senate Committee on Homeland Security and Governmental Affairs and the

---

[232] Ross, Tara. The electoral college takes another hit. *National Review.* September 22, 2010. http://www.nationalreview.com/corner/247368/electoral-college-takes-another-hit-tara-ross.

[233] *Id.*

[234] The entire legislative history of bill B18-0769 is available at http://www.dccouncil.us/lims/legislation.aspx?LegNo=B18-0769.

House Committee on Oversight and Government Reform. In the Senate, the bill was referred to the Subcommittee on Oversight of Government Management, the Federal Workforce, and the District of Columbia. In the House committee, the bill was referred to the Federal Workforce, Postal Service and the District of Columbia Subcommittee.

On October 22, 2010, the bill was published in the District of Columbia Register.[235]

The procedure for congressional consideration of an action of the District of Columbia Council is contained in section 604 of the District of Columbia Home Rule Act of 1973.

"This section is enacted by Congress—

"(1) as an exercise of the rulemaking power of the Senate and the House of Representatives, respectively, and as such these provisions are deemed a part of the rule of each House, respectively, but applicable only with respect to the procedure to be followed in that House in the case of resolutions described by this section; and they supersede other rules only to the extent that they are inconsistent therewith; and

"(2) with full recognition of the constitutional right of either House to change the rule (so far as relating to the procedure of that House) at any time, in the same manner and to the same extent as in the case of any other rule of that House.

"(b) For the purpose of this section, 'resolution' means only a joint resolution, the matter after the resolving clause of which is as follows: 'That the ___ approves/disapproves of the action of the District of Columbia Council described as follows: ___, the blank spaces therein being appropriately filled, and either approval or disapproval being appropriately indicated; but does not include a resolution which specifies more than 1 action.

"(c) A resolution with respect to Council action shall be referred to the Committee on the District of Columbia of the House of Representatives [now the House Committee on Oversight and Government Reform], or the Committee on the District of Columbia of the Senate [now the Senate Committee on Homeland Security and Governmental Affairs], by the President of the Senate or the Speaker of the House of Representatives, as the case may be.

"(d) If the Committee to which a resolution has been referred has not reported it at the end of 20 calendar days after its introduction, it is in order to move to discharge the Committee from further consideration of any other resolution with respect to the same Council action which has been referred to the Committee.

"(e) A motion to discharge may be made only by an individual favoring the resolution, is highly privileged (except that it may not be made after the Committee has reported a resolution with respect to the same action), and debate thereon shall be limited to not more than 1 hour, to be divided equally between those favoring and those opposing the resolution. An amendment to the motion is not in order, and it is not in order to move to reconsider the vote by which the motion is agreed to or disagreed to.

"(f) If the motion to discharge is agreed to or disagreed to, the motion may not be renewed, nor may another motion to discharge the Committee be made with respect to any other resolution with respect to the same action.

"(g) When the Committee has reported, or has been discharged from further consideration of, a resolution, it is at any time thereafter in order (even though a previous motion to the same effect has been disagreed to) to move to proceed to the consideration of the resolution. The motion is highly privileged and is not debatable. An amendment to the motion is not in order, and it is not in order to move to reconsider the vote by which the motion is agreed to or disagreed to.

"(h) Debate on the resolution shall be limited to not more than 10 hours, which shall be divided equally between those favoring and those opposing the resolution. A motion further to limit debate is not debatable. An amendment to, or motion to recommit, the resolution is not in order, and it is not in order to move to reconsider the vote by which the resolution is agreed to or disagreed to.

"(i) Motions to postpone made with respect to the discharge from Committee or the consideration of a resolution, and motions to proceed to the consideration of other business, shall be decided without debate.

"(j) Appeals from the decisions of the chair relating to the application of the rules of the Senate or the House of Representatives, as the case may be, to the procedure relating to a resolution shall be decided without debate."

All of the requirements of the District of Columbia Home Rule Act of 1973 concerning congressional consideration were completed on December 7, 2010, and the National Popular Vote compact became law number 18-274 in the District of Columbia.

Representative Chellie Pingree of Maine made the following remarks on the floor of the U.S. House of Representatives:

"Madam Speaker, I rise today to recognize and congratulate the District of Columbia for its recent enactment of the National Popular Vote bill, which would guarantee the Presidency to the candidate who receives the most popular votes in all 50 states and the District.

"Just a few weeks ago, Mayor Fenty signed this important legislation, which was passed by unanimous consent by the D.C. Council. National Popular Vote is now law in 7 jurisdictions, and has been passed by 31 legislative chambers in 21 states.

"The shortcomings of the current system stem from the winner-take-all rule. Presidential candidates have no reason to pay attention to the concerns of voters in states where they are comfortably ahead or hopelessly behind. In 2008, candidates concentrated over two-thirds of their campaign visits and ad money in just six closely divided 'battleground' states. A total of 98 percent of their resources went to just 15 states. Voters in two-thirds of the states are essentially just spectators to presidential elections.

"Under the National Popular Vote, all the electoral votes from the enacting states would be awarded to the presidential candidate who receives the most popular votes in all 50 states and DC. The bill assures that every vote will matter in every state in every Presidential election.

"I look forward to more states, all across the country passing this important piece of legislation."[236]

10.28   Myths about Congressional or Proportional Allocation of Electoral Votes

10.28.1 MYTH: It would be better to allocate electoral votes by congressional district.

QUICK ANSWER:

* Allocating electoral votes by congressional district would make a bad system even worse.
* District allocation would reduce the percentage of Americans living in closely divided battleground areas.
* District allocation would not guarantee the Presidency to the candidate who receives the most popular votes nationwide.
* District allocation would not make every vote equal.

MORE DETAILED ANSWER:

Under the congressional-district approach for allocating electoral votes (as currently used in Maine and Nebraska), the voters elect two presidential electors statewide and one presidential elector for each of a state's congressional districts.

In addition, there are variations on the district approach. For example, in the nation's first presidential election in 1789, when Virginia had 12 electoral votes, Virginia choose electors from 12 special presidential elector districts. In 1892, Michigan chose one presidential elector from

---

[236] *Congressional Record.* December 15, 2010. Page E2143.

each of its 12 congressional districts and one additional elector from each of two special districts (each encompassing six congressional districts).

The congressional-district approach fails when evaluated against the criteria of whether it would make presidential elections more competitive, whether it would accurately reflect the nationwide popular vote, and whether it would make every vote equal. In short, allocating electoral votes by congressional district would make a bad system even worse.

As to competitiveness, even fewer Americans live in presidentially competitive congressional districts than live in battleground states. In the 2000 presidential election, there were only 55 congressional districts (out of 435 districts) in which the difference between George W. Bush and Al Gore was 4% or less in the district. Similarly, in 2004, there were only 42 congressional districts nationwide in which the difference between George W. Bush and John Kerry was 4% or less in the district. That is, only about a tenth of the population of the country lives in a congressional district that is closely divided in presidential elections. In contrast, about a third of the country's population currently lives in a battleground state.

One reason why the congressional-district approach is so much less competitive than the existing statewide winner-take-all approach is that congressional districts are often gerrymandered in favor of one party or the other in many states. This gerrymandering is sometimes done to give one party an unfair political advantage, and it is sometimes done as part of a bipartisan agreement to ensure safe seats to incumbents of both parties. If electoral votes were allocated by congressional district, state legislatures would have even greater incentives to gerrymander districts than they now do.

As to accurately reflecting the nationwide popular vote, a second-place candidate could easily win the Presidency under the congressional-district approach. If the congressional-district approach had been applied to the results of the closest of the nation's most recent presidential elections (2000), then Bush would have received 288 electoral votes (53.3% of the total number of electoral votes), and Gore would have received 250 electoral votes (46.5% of the total). That is, the congressional-district approach would have given Bush a 6.8% lead in electoral votes over Gore in 2000. Under the existing system, Bush received 271 electoral votes in 2000 (50.4% of the total number of electoral votes)—a 0.8% lead in electoral votes over Gore. The congressional district approach would have greatly magnified Bush's lead in electoral votes in an election in which Gore received 50,992,335 popular votes (50.2% of the two-party popular vote) nationwide compared to Bush's 50,455,156 votes. In summary, the congressional-district approach would have been even less accurate than the existing statewide winner-take-all system in terms of reflecting the nationwide will of the voters.

In the 2004 presidential election, George W. Bush carried 255 (59%) of the 435 congressional districts, whereas John Kerry carried 180. Bush also carried 31 (61%) of the 51 jurisdictions (the 50 states plus the District of Columbia) entitled to appoint presidential electors. If the congressional-district approach had been used nationwide for the 2004 presidential election, Bush would have won 317 (59%) of the 538 electoral votes in an election in which he received 51.5% of the two-party nationwide popular vote.

As to making every vote equal, there is a wide disparity in the number of votes cast in various congressional districts for a variety of reasons. Inside many states, there is a three-to-one disparity in the number of votes cast in particular districts (due to factors such as population changes since the last federal census and variations in turnout level among districts).

The congressional-district approach could be implemented in two ways.

First, an individual state could decide to allocate its electoral votes by district (as Maine and Nebraska currently do).

Second, a federal constitutional amendment could be adopted to implement the congressional-district approach on a nationwide basis.

Of course, passing a constitutional amendment requires an enormous head of steam at the beginning of the process (i.e., getting a two-thirds vote in both houses of Congress). There have been only 17 amendments ratified since the Bill of Rights. The last time Congress successfully launched a federal constitutional amendment (voting by 18-year-olds) was in 1971.

There is a prohibitive, additional political impediment associated with the adoption of the congressional-district approach on a piecemeal basis by individual states. In 1800, Thomas Jefferson argued that Virginia should switch from its then-existing district system of electing presidential electors to the statewide winner-take-all system because of the political disadvantage suffered by states that divided their electoral votes by districts in a political environment in which other states used the winner-take-all approach:

> "while 10. states chuse either by their legislatures or by a general ticket [winner-take-all], it is folly & worse than folly for the other 6. not to do it."[237] [Spelling and punctuation as per original]

Indeed, the now-prevailing statewide winner-take-all system became entrenched in the political landscape in the 1830s precisely because dividing a state's electoral votes diminishes the state's political influence relative to states employing the statewide winner-take-all approach.

The "folly" of individual states adopting the congressional-district approach on a piecemeal basis is shown by the fact that there were only 55 congressional districts in which the difference between George W. Bush and Al Gore was 4% or less in the 2000 presidential election. Suppose that as many as 48 or 49 states were to allocate electoral votes by district, but that one or two large, closely divided battleground states did not. The one or two state(s) retaining the winner-take-all system would immediately become the only state(s) that would matter in presidential politics. Thus, if states were to start adopting the congressional-district approach on a piecemeal basis, each state adopting the approach would increase the influence of the remaining winner-take-all states and thereby decrease the chance that the remaining states would adopt that approach. A state-by-state process of adopting the congressional-district approach would bring itself to a halt.

Finally, it should be noted that if a constitutional amendment were used to install the congressional-district approach, the states would no longer have the power to decide on the manner of awarding their electoral votes.

For more details on the congressional-district approach, see sections 3.3 and 4.2.

---

[237] The January 12, 1800, letter is discussed in greater detail and quoted in its entirety in section 2.2.3. Ford, Paul Leicester. 1905. *The Works of Thomas Jefferson*. New York: G.P. Putnam's Sons. 9:90.

10.28.2 MYTH: It would be better to allocate electoral votes proportionally.

QUICK ANSWER:

- Allocating electoral votes proportionally would make a bad system even worse.

- Proportional allocation would not guarantee the Presidency to the candidate who receives the most popular votes nationwide.

- Proportional allocation would not make every vote equal.

- The proportional system would result in most states being ignored in presidential elections if it were implemented on a piecemeal state-by-state basis (which inherently would permit candidates to receive only a whole number of electoral votes from each state).

MORE DETAILED ANSWER:

Proportional allocation of electoral votes could be implemented in two ways, and there are significant differences between the two approaches.

First, a federal constitutional amendment could be adopted to implement the system on a nationwide basis. If an amendment were used, it would be possible to divide a state's electoral votes into small decimal fractions (say, one-thousandth of an electoral vote).

Second, an individual state could decide to allocate its own electoral votes proportionally. For example, Colorado voters considered a ballot initiative to divide their state's nine electoral votes proportionally in 2004 (but rejected it by a two-to-one margin). If the proportional approach were implemented on a piecemeal state-by-state basis, the Electoral College and the position of presidential elector would remain in existence. A presidential elector is, after all, a person, and a person's vote cannot be divided into fractions. Absent a constitutional amendment, there is no way for legislation in an individual state to introduce fractional voting into the Electoral College. As a result, small fractions would not be possible, and each state would have to allocate its electoral votes in whole numbers.

Both forms of the proportional approach fail when evaluated against the criteria of whether it would accurately reflect the nationwide popular vote and whether it would make every vote equal.

Concerning the criterion of accurately reflecting the nationwide popular vote, the fractional proportional allocation approach does not ensure election of the winner of the nationwide popular vote.

If the whole-number proportional approach had been in use throughout the country in the nation's closest recent presidential election (2000), it would not have awarded the most electoral votes to the candidate receiving the most popular votes nationwide. Instead, the result would have been a tie of 269–269 in the Electoral College, even though Al Gore led by 537,179 popular votes across the nation. The presidential election would have been thrown into Congress. Given the composition of Congress in January 2001, the whole-number proportional approach would have resulted in the election of the second-place candidate in terms of the national popular vote.

Similarly, if the fractional proportional approach had been used in 2000, it would not have awarded the most electoral votes to the candidate receiving the most popular votes nationwide. Al Gore would have received 259.969 electoral votes; George W. Bush would have received 260.323 electoral votes; and Ralph Nader would have received 17.707 electoral votes.[238] Moreover, the election would have been thrown into Congress. Given the composition of Congress at the time, the whole-number proportional approach would have resulted in the election of the second-place candidate in terms of the national popular vote.

Concerning the criterion of making every vote equal, every vote would not be equal under the proportional approach. The proportional approach would disadvantage fast-growing states because electoral votes are only redistributed among the states every 10 years (after each federal census). The proportional approach would penalize states with a high degree of civic participation and high voter turnout (e.g., Oregon, Utah). The proportional approach would disadvantage certain states in relation to other states. For example, Montana and Wyoming each have one congressman and hence three electoral votes. However, Wyoming has a population of 495,304 in 2010, whereas Montana has a population of 905,316.

If a federal constitutional amendment were adopted along the lines of proposals that have been previously introduced in Congress, the Electoral College and presidential electors would be abolished. Under

---

[238] See table 3.1.

these proposals, the electoral votes of each state and the District of Columbia would be divided proportionally according to the percentage of votes (carried out to three decimal places) received in that state by each presidential slate.

The fractional proportional approach would, in fact, succeed in making voters relevant in all 50 states and the District of Columbia because some fraction of an electoral vote would always be at stake in every state. However, as already noted, it would not guarantee the Presidency to the candidate who receives the most popular votes nationwide, and it would not make every vote equal.

If, on the other hand, individual states were to adopt the proportional system on a piecemeal basis through state legislation, the proportional system would be constrained to operating with whole numbers (not fractions carried out to several decimal places). Each participating state's electoral vote would have to be rounded off to the nearest whole number. This rounding-off has counter-intuitive effects. In particular, there would be fewer battleground states under this system than under the current system.

This counter-intuitive result comes about because of the rounding-off to whole numbers. In the seven low-population states with three electoral votes, one electoral vote would correspond to 33% of the popular vote. Overall, the average state has 11 electoral votes (and, in fact, two-thirds of the states have fewer than 11). If one considers an average-sized state, one electoral vote would correspond to 9% of the popular vote in that state. Nine percent is a rather wide range when talking about practical politics.

Campaigning is rarely capable of shifting more than 8% of the vote during a typical presidential campaign. Thus, the only battleground states would be those where popular sentiment in the state fortuitously hovers right at the critical boundary point where one electoral vote might be shifted. The vast majority of the states would not be poised anywhere near that critical boundary point. Presidential campaigns would ignore every state where not even one electoral vote would appear to be at stake. In the states hovering right at the boundary, the only "battle" in these states would be for one electoral vote. That is, the proportional system would be, in effect, a "winner-take-one" system (that is, the candidate receiving the most popular votes in the state would win an advantage of one electoral vote). Among the 50 states and the District of Columbia, California is the only jurisdiction where as many as two electoral votes might be in play under the proportional approach. Most states would not hover right at the critical boundary point and hence would be ignored by presidential campaigns.[239]

There is a prohibitive, additional political impediment associated with the adoption of the proportional approach on a piecemeal basis by individual states. Any state that enacts the proportional approach on its own would reduce its own influence. This was the most telling argument that caused Colorado voters to agree with Republican Governor Owens and to reject the ballot measure in November 2004 by a two-to-one margin. This inherent defect cannot be remedied unless all 50 states simultaneously enact the proportional approach. This inherent defect cannot be remedied if, for example, 10, 20, 30, or even 40 states were to enact the proportional system on a piecemeal basis. If as many as 48 or 49 states were to allocate electoral votes proportionally, but one or two large, closely divided battleground winner-take-all states did not, the state(s) continuing to use the winner-take-all system would immediately become the only state(s) that would matter in presidential politics. Thus, if states were to start adopting the proportional approach on a piecemeal basis, each additional state adopting the approach would increase the influence of the remaining winner-take-all states and thereby decrease the chance that the additional states would adopt the approach. A state-by-state process of adopting the proportional approach would bring itself to a halt.

Finally, it should be noted that if a constitutional amendment were used to install the proportional approach, the states would no longer have the power to decide on the manner of awarding their electoral votes.

For more details on the proportional approach, see section 3.1.

10.29 Myth That One State Can Derail the National Popular Vote Compact

10.29.1 MYTH: There is an "Achilles' heel" that enables one discordant state to derail the National Popular Vote compact.

QUICK ANSWER:

- The National Popular Vote compact was specifically written to prevent a single discordant state from derailing the

---

[239] For more details, see section 3.1 and chapter 4.

operation of the compact by abolishing the short presidential ballot (or by abolishing popular voting for President).

MORE DETAILED ANSWER:

All 50 states and the District of Columbia currently permit the people to
vote for President.

In addition, all 50 states and the District of Columbia currently use
the so-called "short presidential ballot." That is, all of these jurisdictions
permit their voters to vote for President and Vice President with a convenient single vote.

The "short presidential ballot" permitted a California voter in 2008,
for example, to cast a convenient single vote for McCain-Palin and to
have that single vote count as if the voter had separately voted for each
of the 55 Republican candidates for the position of presidential elector
in California. Similarly, the "short presidential ballot" meant that a single
vote for Obama-Biden would be treated as a vote for each of the 55
Democratic elector candidates in California.

Professor Alexander S. Belenky suggests that:

"Opposing states can turn the plenary right of every state to
choose a manner of appointing its electors ... into the **NPV's
Achilles' heel**.

"By allowing voters to favor individual electors of their
choice from any slate of state electors..., the legislature of
each opposing state can make it impossible to tally votes cast
there as part of the national popular vote for president."[240]
[Emphasis added]

If Belenky's hypothetical change had been in effect in 2008 in
California, a voter would not have been able to cast a convenient single
vote for McCain-Palin or Obama-Biden (or any of the four minor-party
slates for President and Vice President on the ballot). Instead, each voter
would have had to cast a separate vote for the Democratic candidate,
the Republican candidate, or the candidate of one of the four minor parties for elector position no. 1. Then, the voter would have had to make a
separate choice for elector position no. 2, and so on. Because California

[240] Belenky, Alexander S. The Achilles Heel of the popular vote plan. Guest column. *Daily
New Tribune.* January 30, 2009. http://www.dailynewstribune.com/opinion/x625264242/
Belenky-The-Achilles-Heel-of-the-popular-vote-plan.

has 55 electoral votes, each voter would have had to vote on 55 separate races for presidential elector. In total, the voter would have had to choose among 330 separate candidates for the 55 positions in California.

Because some voters would inevitably get tired or confused in the process of choosing among 330 names for 55 separate races, each of the 55 winning elector candidates would have received a slightly different total number of popular votes statewide. Consequently, there would be no single number of popular votes associated with the candidacy of McCain-Palin or Obama-Biden in California.

Belenky's proposed ballot is, of course, constitutional. Indeed, the "short presidential ballot" was not used in the nation's first presidential election in 1789 in the five states that permitted voters to participate in the presidential election.

In 1960, Alabama used a ballot such as Belenky describes (and it is shown in figure 2.13). In that election, voters cast 10 separate votes for presidential electors.

Although Belenky's proposed ballot format is constitutional, it is not an "Achilles' heel" that would paralyze the operation of the National Popular Vote compact. In fact, the National Popular Vote compact was specifically written to prevent a single discordant state from derailing the operation of the compact along the lines of Belenky's scenario.

Article II of the National Popular Vote compact creates a legally binding obligation to conduct a popular election for President and Vice President in each member state.

> "Each member state shall conduct a **statewide popular election** for President and Vice President of the United States." [Emphasis added]

The term "statewide popular election" is specifically defined in article V of the compact as

> "a general election at which **votes are cast for presidential slates** by individual voters and counted on a statewide basis." [Emphasis added]

The term "presidential slate" is defined in article V of the compact in the following way:

> " 'Presidential slate' shall mean a slate of two persons, the first

of whom has been nominated as a candidate for President of the United States and the second of whom has been nominated as a candidate for Vice President of the United States, or any legal successors to such persons, regardless of whether both names appear on the ballot presented to the voter in a particular state."

That is, the National Popular Vote compact commits each member state to continue to allow its people to vote for President (something the state is not required to do by the U.S. Constitution) and also to vote for "presidential slates" as opposed to individual candidates for presidential elector (something else that the state is clearly not required to do). These two requirements guarantee that each member state will generate a single popular vote count for each presidential-vice-presidential slate as part of a "statewide popular election."

Of course, non-member states are not bound by the compact. Although all 50 states and the District of Columbia currently employ the "short presidential ballot," a non-member state is not obligated to continue to give its own voters the convenience of casting a single vote for a presidential slate consisting of a named candidate for President and a named candidate for Vice President. Moreover, a non-member state is not obligated to continue to permit its own voters to vote for President.

Thus, a non-member state may effectively opt out of participation in the national popular vote either by repealing its current law establishing the "short presidential ballot" or by repealing its current law of permitting its own voters to vote for President.[241]

The National Popular Vote compact deals with both of these unlikely possibilities by specifying that the popular votes that are to be included in the "national popular vote total" are those that are

"… cast for each presidential slate in each State of the United States and in the District of Columbia **in which votes have been cast in a statewide popular election.**" [Emphasis added]

If a state continues to let its people vote for President and continues

---

[241] The Colorado Constitution is unique in that it establishes the right of the people to vote for President (starting in 1880). Thus, legislation alone could not deprive the people of the right to vote for President in Colorado. Such a change would require a state constitutional amendment in Colorado.

to employ the convenient "short presidential ballot," it will be conducting a "statewide popular election" (as that term is specifically defined in the compact). That state will, therefore, be automatically included in the "national popular vote total" computed under the National Popular Vote compact.

In the unlikely event that a non-member state were to pass a law abolishing the "short presidential ballot" or abolishing popular voting for President, that state would be effectively opting out of the National Popular Vote compact. In that event, the President and Vice President would be elected by the voters from the remaining 49 states and the District of Columbia.

There is no "Achilles' heel" in the National Popular Vote compact; however, there would be an "Achilles' heel" awaiting any governor and legislature that implemented Belenky's hypothetical scenario. They would have to answer to their own voters for taking the extraordinary step of disenfranchising their own voters in the presidential election.

Belenky's hypothetical scenario involving abolition of the short presidential ballot (and the idea of taking the vote for President away from the people) is, of course, a parlor game devoid of any connection to political reality. Both of these hypothetical scenarios assume that there is some governor and state legislature that is so fanatically opposed to a nationwide vote for President that they would disenfranchise their own state's voters in order to protest a national popular vote.

The political reality is that the public strongly favors a nationwide vote for President. Recent polls show high levels of public support for a national popular vote for President in battleground states, low-population states, southern and border states, and elsewhere.

High support for a national popular vote exists in recent battleground states polled such as Colorado (68%), Florida (78%), Iowa (75%), Michigan (73%), Missouri (70%), New Hampshire (69%), Nevada (72%), New Mexico (76%), North Carolina (74%), Ohio (70%), Pennsylvania (78%), Virginia (74%), and Wisconsin (71%). The National Popular Vote bill passed the Michigan House of Representatives by a 65–36 vote in 2008. It also passed the New Mexico House, the Nevada Assembly, and both houses in Colorado (although in different years).

Among Southern and border states polled, support is strong in Arkansas (80%), Florida (78%), Kentucky (80%), Mississippi (77%),

Missouri (70%), North Carolina (74%), and Virginia (74%). The National Popular Vote bill passed the Arkansas House and North Carolina Senate in 2007.

In low-population states polled, support is strong in Delaware (75%), Maine (71%), Rhode Island (74%), and Vermont (75%). The National Popular Vote compact is law in Hawaii and the District of Columbia. As of 2010, it has passed nine legislative chambers in the less-populous states.

Support is also strong in California (70%), Connecticut (73%), Massachusetts (73%), Minnesota (75%), Nebraska (74%), New York (78%), Oregon (76%), and Washington (77%).

The National Popular Vote bill has passed, as of 2010, a total of 31 state legislative houses in 21 states.

Nationwide, the *Washington Post*, Kaiser Family Foundation, and Harvard University poll in 2007 showed 72% support for direct nationwide election of the President.[242]

10.30 Myth about Decline in Voter Turnout

10.30.1 MYTH: A national popular vote will decrease turnout.

QUICK ANSWER:

- Voter turnout averages about 7% higher in battleground states than spectator states. Therefore, one would reasonably expect that voter turnout would rise in the two-thirds of the country that is currently ignored by presidential campaigns.

MORE DETAILED ANSWER:

Curtis Gans, in a speech at the National Civic Summit in Minneapolis on July 17, 2009, claimed that a national popular vote would decrease turnout in presidential elections.

In *America Goes to the Polls: A Report on Voter Turnout in the 2008 Election*, the Nonprofit Voter Engagement Network found that

> "Voter turnout in the 15 battleground states averaged seven points higher than in the 35 non-battleground states."[243]

---

[242] These polls (and many others) are available on National Popular Vote's web site at http://www.nationalpopularvote.com/pages/polls.

[243] *America Goes to the Polls: A Report on Voter Turnout in the 2008 Election.* Nonprofit Voter Engagement Network. 2008.

If presidential campaigns did not ignore 200,000,000 of 300,000,000 Americans, one would reasonably expect that voter turnout would rise in the two-thirds of the country that is currently ignored by presidential campaigns.

10.31 The National Popular Vote Compact Is a Conspiracy

10.31.1 MYTH: The National Popular Vote compact is a conspiracy.

QUICK ANSWER:
- An interstate compact is not a "conspiracy" but a mechanism provided by the U.S. Constitution that enables sovereign states to enter voluntarily into binding contractual arrangements with one another.

MORE DETAILED ANSWER:
Professor Robert Hardaway of the University of Denver Sturm College of Law presented the following testimony on February 19, 2010, to the Alaska Senate Judiciary Committee:

> "And what would happen if, under the Koza scheme, some of the states decided to withdraw from the **conspiracy**? What federal organ would be empowered to enforce the original terms of that **conspiracy**?" [Emphasis added]

An interstate compact is not a "conspiracy" but a mechanism provided by the U.S. Constitution that enables sovereign states to enter voluntarily into binding contractual arrangements with one another.

The National Popular Vote compact would be an interstate compact based on the exclusive and plenary power of the states to choose the manner of awarding their electoral votes (as provided by section 1 of article II of the U.S. Constitution):

> "Each State shall appoint, in such Manner **as the Legislature thereof may direct**, a Number of Electors...."[244] [Emphasis added]

[244] U.S. Constitution. Article II, section 1, clause 2.

10.32   Myth that our Nation's Freedom, Security, and Prosperity Are Protected by the Winner-Take-All Rule

10.32.1 MYTH: Our nation's freedom, security, and prosperity are protected by the current winner-take-all method of awarding electoral votes.

QUICK ANSWER:

* The state-by-state winner-take-all method of awarding electoral votes has no connection with our nation's freedom, security, or prosperity.

MORE DETAILED ANSWER:

Tara Ross, an opponent of the National Popular Vote plan, argues:

"This important aspect of our Constitution [the Electoral College] continues to protect our freedom, just as it did when it was created in 1787."[245] [Emphasis added]

A brochure published by the Evergreen Freedom Foundation of Olympia, Washington states:

"[The Electoral College is] essential to our security and prosperity and, in the end, to keeping America free."[246] [Emphasis added]

Neither Ross nor the Evergreen Freedom Foundation offers any argument that establishes a cause-and-effect relationship between our nation's prosperity and state winner-take-all statutes (i.e., awarding all of a state's electoral votes to the candidate who receives the most votes in the state).

Similarly, there is no argument as to how the nation's security is enhanced by the winner-take-all rule.

Is there any evidence that our nation's "freedom" was endangered by the fact that only three states used the winner-take-all rule in our nation's first presidential election in 1789?

Was prosperity reduced when Nebraska in 1992, and Maine in 1969, adopted the congressional district system of awarding electoral votes? It should be noted that all the states had winner-take-all statutes during the Great Depression.

---

[245] Written testimony submitted by Tara Ross to Delaware Senate in June 2010.

[246] Evergreen Freedom Foundation. 2010. Olympia, Washington.

10.33 Myth about the Replacement of a Dead, Disabled, or Discredited Presidential Candidate

10.33.1 MYTH: The Electoral College provides a way to replace a dead, disabled, or discredited President-Elect after the people vote in November, but before the Electoral College meets in December.

QUICK ANSWER:

* The National Popular Vote compacts would not abolish the Electoral College. Therefore, a dead, disabled, or discredited President-Elect could be replaced in the same manner as would currenly be the case.

MORE DETAILED ANSWER:

Daniel H. Lowenstein points out that the Electoral College provides a way to replace a dead, disabled, or discredited President-Elect after the people vote in November, but before the Electoral College meets in December.

Lowenstein calls this

"what might some day turn out to be the Electoral College's greatest benefit."

Lowenstein continues:

"What is needed for such problems is a political solution. And the Electoral College is ideal for the purpose. The decision would be made by people in each state selected for their loyalty to the presidential winner. Therefore, abuse of the system to pull off a coup d'etat would be pretty much out of the question. But in a situation in which the death, disability or manifest unsuitability plainly existed, the group would be amenable to a party decision, which seems to me the best solution."

The National Popular Vote compact would not abolish the Electoral College. It simply would reform the method of choosing the presidential electors so that they reflect the choice of all the people of the United States, instead of the choice of the people on a state-by-state basis using the winner-take-all rule.

The same presidential electors would be available under the National Popular Vote compact to replace the dead, disabled, or discredited President-Elect as would be available under the current system. The presidential electors would presumably vote for the winning party's vice-presidential nominee.

10.34 Myth That the Winner-Take-All Rule Produces Good Presidents

10.34.1 MYTH: The winner-take-all method for awarding electoral votes produces good Presidents.

QUICK ANSWER:

* State winner-take-all statutes have nothing to do with producing good Presidents.

MORE DETAILED ANSWER:

Daniel H. Lowenstein has argued that there are "11 good reasons"[247] not to change the current system of electing the President:

> "The Electoral College produces good presidents.... The Electoral College has produced Washington, Jefferson, Jackson, Lincoln, Cleveland, Theodore Roosevelt, Wilson, Franklin Roosevelt, Truman, Eisenhower, and Reagan."[248]

Although these 11 Presidents were indeed distinguished, Lowenstein does not offer any argument connecting the ascension of these 11 individuals to the Presidency and the state-by-state winner-take-all rule (i.e., awarding all of a state's electoral votes to the candidate who receives the most votes in the state). Moreover, he does not offer any argument as to why these same talented individuals (or other equally talented individuals) could not have risen to the Presidency without the winner-take-all rule. How, for example, was the winner-take-all rule essential to the emergence of, say, Eisenhower or Reagan? He also offers no argument as to why a system in which the candidate who receives the most popular votes in all 50 states and the District of Columbia would necessarily not produce good Presidents.

---

[247] Panel discussion at the Commonwealth Club in San Francisco on October 24, 2008.

[248] Debate entitled "Should We Dispense with the Electoral College?" sponsored by PENNumbra (University of Pennsylvania Law Review) available at http://www.pennumbra.com/debates/pdfs/electoral_college.pdf.

Lowenstein includes two Presidents on his list who were defeated in the Electoral College by a candidate who received fewer popular votes nationwide namely, Andrew Jackson in 1824 and Grover Cleveland in 1888. Why does Lowenstein credit the winner-take-all rule with success when it elected "good Presidents" such as Jackson in 1828 and Cleveland in 1892, but not acknowledge the failure of the Electoral College when it rejected the very same Andrew Jackson in 1824 and the very same Grover Cleveland in 1888?[249]

Why does Lowenstein credit the Electoral College with success when it elected "good Presidents" such as Thomas Jefferson in 1804, but not acknowledge the failure of the Electoral College when it defeated Jefferson in 1796 and handed Jefferson a tie in the Electoral College in 1800?

Moreover, Lowenstein includes three Presidents on his list who were elected before the era when the state-by-state winner-take-all rule became widespread. Only three states used the state-by-state winner-take-all rule when George Washington was elected in 1789 and 1792.[250] Only one state used the state-by-state winner-take-all rule when Thomas Jefferson was elected in 1800.[251]

Lowenstein also credits the winner-take-all rule for producing Theodore Roosevelt and Harry Truman, even though they both ascended to the Presidency on the death of their predecessor.

Tellingly, Lowenstein's list of 11 Presidents fails to account for the 33 remaining Presidents, including those who were exceedingly corrupt (e.g., Harding, Grant), totally ineffectual and damaging to the country (e.g., Buchanan), and thoroughly mediocre and forgettable.

---

[249] Lowenstein includes Thomas Jefferson on his list even though the Electoral College defeated Jefferson in 1796.

[250] New Hampshire, Maryland, and Pennsylvania used the winner-take-all rule in the nation's first presidential election (1789) and in the second (1792).

[251] Only Virginia used the winner-take-all rule in the 1800 election. The legislatures of New Hampshire and Pennsylvania directly appointed presidential electors in 1800, and Maryland switched to a district system in 1796.

11 | Epilogue

The epilogue to this book will be written by the people, the state legislatures, and the Congress as they consider the proposed "Agreement Among the States to Elect the President by National Popular Vote" described in this book.

APPENDIX A
U. S. Constitutional Provisions on Presidential Elections

ARTICLE II, SECTION 1, CLAUSE 1

The executive Power shall be vested in a President of the United States of America. He shall hold his Office during the Term of four Years, and, together with the Vice President, chosen for the same Term, be elected, as follows

ARTICLE II, SECTION 1, CLAUSE 2

Each State shall appoint, in such Manner as the Legislature thereof may direct, a Number of Electors, equal to the whole Number of Senators and Representatives to which the State may be entitled in the Congress: but no Senator or Representative, or Person holding an Office of Trust or Profit under the United States, shall be appointed an Elector.

ARTICLE II, SECTION 1, CLAUSE 3

The Electors shall meet in their respective States, and vote by Ballot for two Persons, of whom one at least shall not be an Inhabitant of the same State with themselves. And they shall make a List of all the Persons voted for, and of the Number of Votes for each; which List they shall sign and certify, and transmit sealed to the Seat of the Government of the United States, directed to the President of the Senate. The President of the Senate shall, in the Presence of the Senate and House of Representatives, open all the Certificates, and the Votes shall then be counted. The Person having the greatest Number of Votes shall be the President, if such Number be a Majority of the whole Number of Electors appointed; and if there be more than one who have such Majority, and have an equal Number of Votes, then the House of Representatives shall immediately chuse by Ballot one of them for President; and if no Person have a Majority, then from the five highest on the List the said House shall in like

Manner chuse the President. But in chusing the President, the Votes shall be taken by States, the Representation from each State having one Vote; A quorum for this Purpose shall consist of a Member or Members from two thirds of the States, and a Majority of all the States shall be necessary to a Choice. In every Case, after the Choice of the President, the Person having the greatest Number of Votes of the Electors shall be the Vice President. But if there should remain two or more who have equal Votes, the Senate shall chuse from them by Ballot the Vice President.

ARTICLE II, SECTION 1, CLAUSE 4

The Congress may determine the Time of chusing the Electors, and the Day on which they shall give their Votes; which Day shall be the same throughout the United States.

12th AMENDMENT

The Electors shall meet in their respective states, and vote by ballot for President and Vice-President, one of whom, at least, shall not be an inhabitant of the same state with themselves; they shall name in their ballots the person voted for as President, and in distinct ballots the person voted for as Vice-President, and they shall make distinct lists of all persons voted for as President, and of all persons voted for as Vice-President, and of the number of votes for each, which lists they shall sign and certify, and transmit sealed to the seat of the government of the United States, directed to the President of the Senate;—The President of the Senate shall, in the presence of the Senate and House of Representatives, open all the certificates and the votes shall then be counted;—The person having the greatest number of votes for President, shall be the President, if such number be a majority of the whole number of Electors appointed; and if no person have such majority, then from the persons having the highest numbers not exceeding three on the list of those voted for as President, the House of Representatives shall choose immediately, by ballot, the President. But in choosing the President, the votes shall be taken by states, the representation from each state having one vote; a quorum for this purpose shall consist of a member or members from two-thirds of the states, and a majority of all the states shall be necessary to a choice. And if the House of Representatives shall not choose a President whenever the right of choice shall devolve upon them, before the fourth day of March next following, then the Vice-President shall act as President, as in the case of the death or other constitutional disability of the President. The person having the greatest number of votes as Vice-President, shall be the Vice-President, if such number be a majority of the whole number of Electors appointed, and if no person have a majority, then from the two highest numbers on the list, the Senate shall choose the Vice-President; a quorum for the purpose shall consist of two-thirds of the whole number of Senators, and a majority of the whole number shall be necessary to a choice. But no person constitutionally ineligible to the office of President shall be eligible to that of Vice-President of the United States.

14th AMENDMENT-SECTIONS 2 AND 3

Section 2. Representatives shall be apportioned among the several States according to their respective numbers, counting the whole number of persons in each State, excluding Indians not taxed. But when the right to vote at any election for the choice of electors for President and Vice President of the United States, Representatives in Congress, the Executive and Judicial officers of a State, or the members of the Legislature thereof, is denied to any of the male inhabitants of such State, being twenty-one years of age, and citizens of the United States, or in any way abridged, except for participation in rebellion, or other crime, the basis of representation therein shall be reduced in the proportion which the number of such male citizens shall bear to the whole number of male citizens twenty-one years of age in such State.

Section 3. No person shall be a Senator or Representative in Congress, or elector of President and Vice President, or hold any office, civil or military, under the United States, or under any State, who, having previously taken an oath, as a member of Congress, or as an officer of the United States, or as a member of any State legislature, or as an executive or judicial officer of any State, to support the Constitution of the United States, shall have engaged in insurrection or rebellion against the same, or given aid or comfort to the enemies thereof. But Congress may by a vote of two-thirds of each House, remove such disability.

15th AMENDMENT-SECTION 1

Section 1. The right of citizens of the United States to vote shall not be denied or abridged by the United States or by any State on account of race, color, or previous condition of servitude.

19th AMENDMENT

The right of citizens of the United States to vote shall not be denied or abridged by the United States or by any State on account of sex.

Congress shall have power to enforce this article by appropriate legislation.

20th AMENDMENT – SECTIONS 1-5

Section 1. The terms of the President and Vice President shall end at noon on the 20th day of January, and the terms of Senators and Representatives at noon on the 3d day of January, of the years in which such terms would have ended if this article had not been ratified; and the terms of their successors shall then begin.

Section 2. The Congress shall assemble at least once in every year, and such meeting shall begin at noon on the 3d day of January, unless they shall by law appoint a different day.

Section 3. If, at the time fixed for the beginning of the term of the President, the President elect shall have died, the Vice President elect shall become President. If a President shall not have been chosen before the time fixed for the beginning of his term, or if the President elect shall have failed to qualify, then the Vice President elect shall act as President until a President shall have qualified; and the Congress may by law provide for the case wherein neither a President elect nor a Vice President elect shall have qualified, declaring who shall then act as President, or the manner in which one who is to act shall be selected, and such person shall act accordingly until a President or Vice President shall have qualified.

Section 4. The Congress may by law provide for the case of the death of any of the persons from whom the House of Representatives may choose a President whenever the right of choice shall have devolved upon them, and for the case of the death of any of the persons from whom the Senate may choose a Vice President whenever the right of choice shall have devolved upon them.

Section. 5. Sections 1 and 2 shall take effect on the 15th day of October following the ratification of this article.

22nd AMENDMENT – SECTION 1

Section 1. No person shall be elected to the office of the President more than twice, and no person who has held the office of President, or acted as President, for more than two years of a term to which some other person was elected President shall be elected to the office of the President more than once. But this Article shall not apply to any person holding the office of President when this Article was proposed by the Congress, and shall not prevent any person who may be holding the office of President, or acting as President, during the term within which this Article becomes operative from holding the office of President or acting as President during the remainder of such term.

23rd AMENDMENT

Section 1. The District constituting the seat of government of the United States shall appoint in such manner as the Congress may direct:

A number of electors of President and Vice President equal to the whole number of Senators and Representatives in Congress to which the District would be entitled if it were a state, but in no event more than the least populous state; they shall be in addition to those appointed by the states, but they shall be considered, for the purposes of the election of President and Vice President, to be electors appointed by a state; and they shall meet in the District and perform such duties as provided by the twelfth article of amendment.

Section 2. The Congress shall have power to enforce this article by appropriate legislation.

24th AMENDMENT

Section 1. The right of citizens of the United States to vote in any primary or other election for President or Vice President, for electors for President or Vice President, or for Senator or Representative in Congress, shall not be denied or abridged by the United States or any state by reason of failure to pay any poll tax or other tax.

Section 2. The Congress shall have power to enforce this article by appropriate legislation.

25th AMENDMENT

Section 1. In case of the removal of the President from office or of his death or resignation, the Vice President shall become President.

Section 2. Whenever there is a vacancy in the office of the Vice President, the President shall nominate a Vice President who shall take office upon confirmation by a majority vote of both Houses of Congress.

Section 3. Whenever the President transmits to the President pro tempore of the Senate and the Speaker of the House of Representatives his written declaration that he is unable to discharge the powers and duties of his office, and until he transmits to them a written declaration to the contrary, such powers and duties shall be discharged by the Vice President as Acting President.

Section 4. Whenever the Vice President and a majority of either the principal officers of the executive departments or of such other body as Congress may by law provide, transmit to the President pro tempore of the Senate and the Speaker of the House of Representatives their written declaration that the President is unable to discharge the powers and duties of his office, the Vice President shall immediately assume the powers and duties of the office as Acting President.

Thereafter, when the President transmits to the President pro tempore of the Senate and the Speaker of the House of Representatives his written declaration that no inability exists, he shall resume the powers and duties of his office unless the Vice President and a majority of either the principal officers of the executive department or of such other body as Congress may by law provide, transmit within four days to the President pro tempore of the Senate and the Speaker of the House of Representatives their written declaration that the President is unable to discharge the powers and duties of his office. Thereupon Congress shall decide the issue, assembling within forty-eight hours for that purpose if not in session. If the Congress, within twenty-one days after receipt of the latter written declaration, or, if Congress is not in session, within twenty-one days after Congress is required to assemble, determines by two-thirds vote of both Houses that the President is unable to discharge the powers and duties of his office, the Vice President shall continue to discharge the same as Acting President; otherwise, the President shall resume the powers and duties of his office.

26th AMENDMENT

Section 1. The right of citizens of the United States, who are eighteen years of age or older, to vote shall not be denied or abridged by the United States or by any State on account of age.

Section 2. The Congress shall have the power to enforce this article by appropriate legislation.

APPENDIX B
Federal Law on Presidential Elections

UNITED STATES CODE
TITLE 3, CHAPTER 1. PRESIDENTIAL ELECTIONS AND VACANCIES

Time of appointing electors

§1. The electors of President and Vice President shall be appointed, in each State, on the Tuesday next after the first Monday in November, in every fourth year succeeding every election of a President and Vice President.

Failure to make choice on prescribed day

§2. Whenever any State has held an election for the purpose of choosing electors, and has failed to make a choice on the day prescribed by law, the electors may be appointed on a subsequent day in such a manner as the legislature of such State may direct.

Number of electors

§3. The number of electors shall be equal to the number of Senators and Representatives to which the several States are by law entitled at the time when the President and Vice President to be chosen come into office; except, that where no apportionment of Representatives has been made after any enumeration, at the time of choosing electors, the number of electors shall be according to the then existing apportionment of Senators and Representatives.

Vacancies in electoral college

§4. Each State may, by law, provide for the filling of any vacancies which may occur in its college of electors when such college meets to give its electoral vote.

Determination of controversy as to appointment of electors

§5. If any State shall have provided, by laws enacted prior to the day fixed for the appointment of the electors, for its final determination of any controversy or contest concerning the appointment of all or any of the electors of such State, by judicial or other methods or procedures, and such determination shall have been made at least six days before the time fixed for the meeting of the electors, such determination made pursuant to such law so existing on said day, and made at least six days prior to said time of meeting of the electors, shall be conclusive, and shall govern in the counting of the electoral votes as provided in the Constitution, and as hereinafter regulated, so far as the ascertainment of the electors appointed by such State is concerned.

Credentials of electors; transmission to archivist of the united states and to congress; public inspection

§6. It shall be the duty of the executive of each State, as soon as practicable after the conclusion of the appointment of the electors in such State by the final ascertainment, under and in pursuance of the laws of such State providing for such ascertainment, to communicate by registered mail under the seal of the State to the Archivist of the United States a certificate of such ascertainment of the electors appointed, setting forth the names of such electors and the canvass or other ascertainment under the laws of such State of the number of votes given or cast for each person for whose appointment any and all votes have been given or cast; and it shall also thereupon be the duty of the executive of each State to deliver to the electors of such State, on or before the day on which they are required by section 7 of this title to meet, six duplicate-originals of the same certificate under the seal of the State; and if there shall have been any final determination in a State in the manner provided for by law of a controversy or contest concerning the appointment of all or any of the electors of such State, it shall be the duty of the executive of such State, as soon as practicable after such determination, to communicate under the seal of the State to the Archivist of the United States a certificate of such determination in form and manner as the same shall have been made; and the certificate or certificates so received by the Archivist of the United States shall be preserved by him for one year and shall be a part of the public records of his office and shall be open to public inspection; and the Archivist of the United States at the first meeting of Congress thereafter shall transmit to the two Houses of Congress copies in full of each and every such certificate so received at the National Archives and Records Administration.

Meeting and vote of electors

§7. The electors of President and Vice President of each State shall meet and give their votes on the first Monday after the second Wednesday in December next following their appointment at such place in each State as the legislature of such State shall direct.

Manner of voting

§8. The electors shall vote for President and Vice President, respectively, in the manner directed by the Constitution.

Certificates of votes for president and vice president

§9. The electors shall make and sign six certificates of all the votes given by them, each of which certificates shall contain two distinct lists, one of the votes for President and the other of the votes for Vice President, and shall annex to each of the certificates one of the lists of the electors which shall have been furnished to them by direction of the executive of the State.

Sealing and endorsing certificates

§10. The electors shall seal up the certificates so made by them, and certify upon each that the lists of all the votes of such State given for President, and of all the votes given for Vice President, are contained therein.

Disposition of certificates

§11. The electors shall dispose of the certificates so made by them and the lists attached thereto in the following manner:

First. They shall forthwith forward by registered mail one of the same to the President of the Senate at the seat of government.

Second. Two of the same shall be delivered to the secretary of state of the State, one of which shall be held subject to the order of the President of the Senate, the other to be preserved by him for one year and shall be a part of the public records of his office and shall be open to public inspection.

Third. On the day thereafter they shall forward by registered mail two of such certificates and lists to the Archivist of the United States at the seat of government, one of which shall be held subject to the order of the President of the Senate. The other shall be preserved by the Archivist of the United States for one year and shall be a part of the public records of his office and shall be open to public inspection.

Fourth. They shall forthwith cause the other of the certificates and lists to be delivered to the judge of the district in which the electors shall have assembled.

Failure of certificates of electors to reach president of the senate or archivist of the united states; demand on state for certificate

§12. When no certificate of vote and list mentioned in sections 9 and 11 and of this title from any State shall have been received by the President of the Senate or by the Archivist of the United States by the fourth Wednesday in December, after the meeting of the electors shall have been held, the President of the Senate or, if he be absent from the seat of government, the Archivist of the United States shall request, by the most expeditious method available, the secretary of state of the State to send up the certificate and list lodged with him by the electors of such State; and it shall be his duty upon receipt of such request immediately to transmit same by registered mail to the President of the Senate at the seat of government.

Same; demand on district judge for certificate

§13. When no certificates of votes from any State shall have been received at the seat of government on the fourth Wednesday in December, after the meeting of the electors shall have been held, the President of the Senate or, if he be absent from the seat of government, the Archivist of the United States shall send a special messenger to the district judge in whose custody one certificate of votes from that State has been lodged, and such judge shall forthwith transmit that list by the hand of such messenger to the seat of government.

Forfeiture for messenger's neglect of duty

§14. Every person who, having been appointed, pursuant to section 13 of this title, to deliver the certificates of the votes of the electors to the President of the Senate, and having accepted such appointment, shall neglect to perform the services required from him, shall forfeit the sum of $1,000.

Counting electoral votes in congress

§15. Congress shall be in session on the sixth day of January succeeding every meeting of the electors. The Senate and House of Representatives shall meet in the Hall of the House of Representatives at the hour of 1 o'clock in the afternoon on that day, and the President of the Senate shall be their presiding officer. Two tellers shall be previously appointed on the part of the Senate and two on the part of the House of Representatives, to whom shall be handed, as they are opened by the President of the Senate, all the certificates and papers purporting to be certificates of the electoral votes, which certificates and papers shall be opened, presented, and acted upon in the alphabetical order of the States, beginning with the letter A; and said tellers, having then read the same in the presence and hearing of the two Houses, shall make a list of the votes as they shall appear from the said certificates; and the votes having been ascertained and counted according to the rules in this subchapter provided, the result of the same shall be delivered to the President of the Senate, who shall thereupon announce the state of the vote, which announcement shall be deemed a sufficient declaration of the persons, if any, elected President and Vice President of the United States, and, together with a list of the votes, be entered on the Journals of the two Houses. Upon such reading of any such certificate or paper, the President of the Senate shall call for objections, if any. Every objection shall be made in writing, and shall state clearly and concisely, and without argument, the ground thereof, and shall be signed by at least one Senator and one Member of the House of Representatives before the same shall be received. When all objections so made to any vote or paper from a State shall have been received and read, the Senate shall thereupon withdraw, and such objections shall be submitted to the Senate for its decision; and the Speaker of the House of Representatives shall, in like manner, submit such objections to the House of Representatives for its decision; and no electoral vote or votes from any State which shall have been regularly given by electors whose appointment has been lawfully certified to according to section 6 of this title from which but one return has been received shall be rejected, but the two Houses concurrently may reject the vote or votes when they agree that such vote or votes have not been so regularly given by electors whose appointment has been so certified. If more than one return or paper purporting to be a return from a State shall have been received by the President of the Senate, those votes, and those only, shall be counted which shall have been regularly given by the electors who are shown by the determination mentioned in section 5 of this title to have been appointed, if the determination in said section provided for shall have been made, or by such successors or substitutes, in case of a vacancy in the board of electors so ascertained, as have been appointed to fill such vacancy in the mode provided by the laws of the

State; but in case there shall arise the question which of two or more of such State authorities determining what electors have been appointed, as mentioned in section 5 of this title, is the lawful tribunal of such State, the votes regularly given of those electors, and those only, of such State shall be counted whose title as electors the two Houses, acting separately, shall concurrently decide is supported by the decision of such State so authorized by its law; and in such case of more than one return or paper purporting to be a return from a State, if there shall have been no such determination of the question in the State aforesaid, then those votes, and those only, shall be counted which the two Houses shall concurrently decide were cast by lawful electors appointed in accordance with the laws of the State, unless the two Houses, acting separately, shall concurrently decide such votes not to be the lawful votes of the legally appointed electors of such State. But if the two Houses shall disagree in respect of the counting of such votes, then, and in that case, the votes of the electors whose appointment shall have been certified by the executive of the State, under the seal thereof, shall be counted. When the two Houses have voted, they shall immediately again meet, and the presiding officer shall then announce the decision of the questions submitted. No votes or papers from any other State shall be acted upon until the objections previously made to the votes or papers from any State shall have been finally disposed of.

Same; seats for officers and members of two houses in joint meeting

§16. At such joint meeting of the two Houses seats shall be provided as follows: For the President of the Senate, the Speaker's chair; for the Speaker, immediately upon his left; the Senators, in the body of the Hall upon the right of the presiding officer; for the Representatives, in the body of the Hall not provided for the Senators; for the tellers, Secretary of the Senate, and Clerk of the House of Representatives, at the Clerk's desk; for the other officers of the two Houses, in front of the Clerk's desk and upon each side of the Speaker's platform. Such joint meeting shall not be dissolved until the count of electoral votes shall be completed and the result declared; and no recess shall be taken unless a question shall have arisen in regard to counting any such votes, or otherwise under this subchapter, in which case it shall be competent for either House, acting separately, in the manner hereinbefore provided, to direct a recess of such

House not beyond the next calendar day, Sunday excepted, at the hour of 10 o'clock in the forenoon. But if the counting of the electoral votes and the declaration of the result shall not have been completed before the fifth calendar day next after such first meeting of the two Houses, no further or other recess shall be taken by either House.

Same; limit of debate in each house

§17. When the two Houses separate to decide upon an objection that may have been made to the counting of any electoral vote or votes from any State, or other question arising in the matter, each Senator and Representative may speak to such objection or question five minutes, and not more than once; but after such debate shall have lasted two hours it shall be the duty of the presiding officer of each House to put the main question without further debate.

Same; parliamentary procedure at joint meeting

§18. While the two Houses shall be in meeting as provided in this chapter, the President of the Senate shall have power to preserve order; and no debate shall be allowed and no question shall be put by the presiding officer except to either House on a motion to withdraw.

Vacancy in offices of both president and vice president; officers eligible to act

§19. (a)

    (1) If, by reason of death, resignation, removal from office, inability, or failure to qualify, there is neither a President nor Vice President to discharge the powers and duties of the office of President, then the Speaker of the House of Representatives shall, upon his resignation as Speaker and as Representative in Congress, act as President.

    (2) The same rule shall apply in the case of the death, resignation, removal from office, or inability of an individual acting as President under this subsection.

  (b) If, at the time when under subsection (a) of this section a Speaker is to begin the discharge of the powers and duties of the office of President, there is no Speaker, or the Speaker fails to qualify as Acting President, then the President pro tempore of the Senate shall, upon his resignation as President pro tempore and as Senator, act as President.

(c) An individual acting as President under subsection (a) or subsection (b) of this section shall continue to act until the expiration of the then current Presidential term, except that

(1) if his discharge of the powers and duties of the office is founded in whole or in part on the failure of both the President-elect and the Vice-President-elect to qualify, then he shall act only until a President or Vice President qualifies; and

(2) if his discharge of the powers and duties of the office is founded in whole or in part on the inability of the President or Vice President, then he shall act only until the removal of the disability of one of such individuals.

(d)

(1) If, by reason of death, resignation, removal from office, inability, or failure to qualify, there is no President pro tempore to act as President under subsection (b) of this section, then the officer of the United States who is highest on the following list, and who is not under disability to discharge the powers and duties of the office of President shall act as President: Secretary of State, Secretary of the Treasury, Secretary of Defense, Attorney General, Secretary of the Interior, Secretary of Agriculture, Secretary of Commerce, Secretary of Labor, Secretary of Health and Human Services, Secretary of Housing and Urban Development, Secretary of Transportation, Secretary of Energy, Secretary of Education, Secretary of Veterans Affairs.

(2) An individual acting as President under this subsection shall continue so to do until the expiration of the then current Presidential term, but not after a qualified and prior-entitled individual is able to act, except that the removal of the disability of an individual higher on the list contained in paragraph (1) of this subsection or the ability to qualify on the part of an individual higher on such list shall not terminate his service.

(3) The taking of the oath of office by an individual specified in the list in paragraph (1) of this subsection shall be held to constitute his resignation from the office by virtue of

the holding of which he qualifies to act as President.

(e) Subsections (a), (b), and (d) of this section shall apply only to such officers as are eligible to the office of President under the Constitution. Subsection (d) of this section shall apply only to officers appointed, by and with the advice and consent of the Senate, prior to the time of the death, resignation, removal from office, inability, or failure to qualify, of the President pro tempore, and only to officers not under impeachment by the House of Representatives at the time the powers and duties of the office of President devolve upon them.

(f) During the period that any individual acts as President under this section, his compensation shall be at the rate then provided by law in the case of the President.

Resignation or refusal of office

§20. The only evidence of a refusal to accept, or of a resignation of the office of President or Vice President, shall be an instrument in writing, declaring the same, and subscribed by the person refusing to accept or resigning, as the case may be, and delivered into the office of the Secretary of State.

Definitions

§21. As used in this chapter the term –

(a) "State" includes the District of Columbia.

(b) "executives of each State" includes the Board of Commissioners * of the District of Columbia.

APPENDIX C
U. S. Constitution on Interstate Compacts and Contracts

ARTICLE I, SECTION 10, CLAUSE 3

No State shall, without the Consent of Congress, lay any Duty of Tonnage, keep Troops, or Ships of War in time of Peace, enter into any Agreement or Compact with another State, or with a foreign Power, or engage in War, unless actually invaded, or in such imminent Danger as will not admit of delay.

ARTICLE I, SECTION 10, CLAUSE 1

No State shall enter into any Treaty, Alliance, or Confederation; grant Letters of Marque and Reprisal; coin Money; emit Bills of Credit; make any Thing but gold and silver Coin a Tender in Payment of Debts; pass any Bill of Attainder, ex post facto Law, or Law impairing the Obligation of Contracts, or grant any Title of Nobility.

APPENDIX D
Minnesota Laws on Presidential Elections

208.02. ELECTION OF PRESIDENTIAL ELECTORS

Presidential electors shall be chosen at the state general election held in the year preceding the expiration of the term of the president of the United States.

208.03. NOMINATION OF PRESIDENTIAL ELECTORS

Presidential electors for the major political parties of this state shall be nominated by delegate conventions called and held under the supervision of the respective state central committees of the parties of this state. On or before primary election day the chair of the major political party shall certify to the secretary of state the names of the persons nominated as Presidential electors and the names of the party candidates for president and vice-president.

208.04. PREPARATION OF BALLOTS

Subdivision 1. When Presidential electors are to be voted for, a vote cast for the party candidates for president and vice-president shall be deemed a vote for that party's electors as filed with the secretary of state. The secretary of state shall certify the names of all duly nominated Presidential and vice-Presidential candidates to the county auditors of the counties of the state. Each county auditor, subject to the rules of the secretary of state, shall cause the names of the candidates of each major political party and the candidates nominated by petition to be printed in capital letters, set in type of the same size and style as for candidates on the state white ballot, before the party designation. To the left of, and on the same line with the names of the candidates for president and vice-president, near the margin, shall be placed a square or box, in which the voters may indicate their choice by marking an "X."

The form for the Presidential ballot and the relative position of the several candidates shall be determined by the rules applicable to other state officers. The state ballot, with the required heading, shall be printed on the same piece of paper and shall be below the Presidential ballot with a blank space between one inch in width.

Subdivision 2. The rules for preparation, state contribution to the cost of printing, and delivery of Presidential ballots are the same as the rules for white ballots under section 204D.11, subdivision 1.

208.05. STATE CANVASSING BOARD

The state canvassing board at its meeting on the second Tuesday after each state general election shall open and canvass the returns made to the secretary of state for Presidential electors, prepare a statement of the number of votes cast for the persons receiving votes for these offices, and declare the person or persons receiving the highest number of votes for each office duly elected. When it appears that more than the number of persons to be elected as Presidential electors have the highest and an equal number of votes, the secretary of state, in the presence of the board shall decide by lot which of the persons shall be declared elected. The governor shall transmit to each person declared elected a certificate of election, signed by the governor, sealed with the state seal, and counter-signed by the secretary of state.

208.06. ELECTORS TO MEET AT CAPITOL; FILLING OF VACANCIES

The Presidential electors, before 12:00 M. on the day before that fixed by congress for the electors to vote for president and vice-president of the United States, shall notify the governor that they are at the state capitol and ready at the proper time to fulfill their duties as electors. The governor shall deliver to the electors present a certificate of the names of all the electors. If any elector named therein fails to appear before 9:00 a.m. on the day, and at the place, fixed for voting for president and vice-president of the United States, the electors present shall, in the presence of the governor, immediately elect by ballot a person to fill the vacancy. If more than the number of persons required have the highest and an equal number of votes, the governor, in the presence of the electors attending, shall decide by lot which of those persons shall be elected.

208.07. CERTIFICATE OF ELECTORS

Immediately after the vacancies have been filled, the original electors present shall certify to the governor the names of the persons elected to complete their number, and the governor shall at once cause written notice to be given to each person elected to fill a vacancy. The persons so chosen shall be Presidential electors and shall meet and act with the other electors.

208.08. ELECTORS TO MEET AT STATE CAPITOL

The original and substituted Presidential electors, at 12:00 M., shall meet in the executive chamber at the state capitol and shall perform all the duties imposed upon them as electors by the constitution and laws of the United States and this state.

204B.07. NOMINATING PETITIONS

Subdivision 1. Form of petition. A nominating petition may consist of one or more separate pages each of which shall state:

(a) The office sought;

(b) The candidate's name and residence address, including street and number if any; and

(c) candidate's political party or political principle expressed in not more than three words. No candidate who files for a partisan office by nominating petition shall use the term "nonpartisan" as a statement of political principle or the name of the candidate's political party. No part of the name of a major political party may be used to designate the political party or principle of a candidate who files for a partisan office by nominating petition, except that the word "independent" may be used to designate the party or principle. A candidate who files by nominating petition to fill a vacancy in nomination for a nonpartisan office pursuant to section 204B.13, shall not state any political principle or the name of any political party on the petition.

Subdivision 2. Petitions for presidential electors. This subdivision does not apply to candidates for Presidential elector nominated by major political parties. Major party candidates for Presidential elector are certified under section 208.03. Other Presidential electors are nominated by petition pursuant to this section. On petitions nominating Presidential electors, the names of the candidates for president and vice-president shall be added to the political party or political principle stated on the petition. One petition may be filed to nominate a slate of Presidential electors equal in number to the number of electors to which the state is entitled.

Subdivision 3. Number of candidates nominated. No nominating petition shall contain the name of more than one candidate except a petition jointly nominating individuals for governor and lieutenant governor or nominating a slate of Presidential electors.

Subdivision 4. Oath and address of signer. Following the information required by subdivisions 1 and 2 and before the space for signing, each separate page that is part of the petition shall include an oath in the following form:

> "I solemnly swear (or affirm) that I know the contents and purpose of this petition, that I do not intend to vote at the primary election for the office for which this nominating petition is made, and that I signed this petition of my own free will."

Notarization or certification of the signatures on a nominating petition is not required. Immediately after the signature, the signer shall write on the petition the signer's residence address including street and number, if any, and mailing address if different from residence address.

Subdivision 5. Sample forms. An official with whom petitions are filed shall make sample forms for nominating petitions available upon request.

Subdivision 6. Penalty. An individual who, in signing a nominating petition, makes a false oath is guilty of perjury.

204B.09. TIME AND PLACE OF FILING AFFIDAVITS AND PETITIONS

Subdivision 1. Candidates in state and county general elections.

(a) Except as otherwise provided by this subdivision, affidavits of candidacy and nominating petitions for county, state, and federal offices filled at the state general election shall be filed not more than 70 days nor less than 56 days before the state primary. The affidavit may be prepared and signed at any time between 60 days before the filing period opens and the last day of the filing period.

(b) Notwithstanding other law to the contrary, the affidavit of candidacy must be signed in the presence of a notarial officer or an individual authorized to administer oaths under section 358.10.

(c) This provision does not apply to candidates for Presidential elector nominated by major political parties. Major party candidates for Presidential elector are certified under section 208.03. Other candidates for Presidential electors may file petitions on or before the state primary day pursuant to section 204B.07. Nominating petitions to fill vacancies in nominations shall be filed as provided in section 204B.13. No affidavit or petition shall be accepted later than 5:00 p.m. on the last day for filing.

(d) Affidavits and petitions for offices to be voted on in only one county shall be filed with the county auditor of that county. Affidavits and petitions for offices to be voted on in more than one county shall be filed with the secretary of state.

Subdivision 1a. Absent candidates. A candidate for special district, county, state, or federal office who will be absent from the state during the filing period may submit a properly executed affidavit of candidacy, the appropriate filing fee, and any necessary petitions in person to the filing officer. The candidate shall state in writing the reason for being unable to submit the affidavit during the filing period. The affidavit, filing fee, and petitions must be submitted to the filing officer during the seven days immediately preceding the candidate's absence from the state. Nominating petitions may be signed during the 14 days immediately preceding the date when the affidavit of candidacy is filed.

Subdivision 2. Other elections. Affidavits of candidacy and nominating petitions for city, town or other elective offices shall be filed during the time and with the official specified in chapter 205 or other applicable law or charter, except as provided for a special district candidate under subdivision 1a. Affidavits of candidacy and applications filed on behalf of eligible voters for school board office shall be filed during the time and with the official specified in chapter 205A or other applicable law.

Subdivision 3. Write-in candidates.

(a) A candidate for state or federal office who wants write-in votes for the candidate to be counted must file a written request with the filing office for the office sought no later than the fifth day before the general election. The filing officer shall provide copies of the form to make the request.

(b) A candidate for president of the United States who files a request under this subdivision must include the name of a candidate for vice-president of the United States. The request must also include the name of at least one candidate for Presidential elector. The total number of names of candidates for Presidential elector on the request may not exceed the total number of electoral votes to be cast by Minnesota in the presidential election.

(c) A candidate for governor who files a request under this subdivision must include the name of a candidate for lieutenant governor.

APPENDIX E
Minnesota 2004 Certificate of Ascertainment

STATE of MINNESOTA

EXECUTIVE DEPARTMENT

TIM PAWLENTY
GOVERNOR

CERTIFICATE OF ASCERTAINMENT
OF APPOINTMENT OF ELECTORS
FOR PRESIDENT AND VICE PRESIDENT
OF THE UNITED STATES
FOR THE STATE OF MINNESOTA

To: John W. Carlin
        Archivist of the United States
        National Archives and Records Administration
        c/o Office of the Federal Register (NF)
        8601 Adelphi Road
        College Park, MD 20740-6001

I, Tim Pawlenty, Governor of the State of Minnesota, do hereby certify the following:

In accordance with Article 2, Section 1 of the Constitution of the United States, the Legislature of the State of Minnesota directed that the electors for President and Vice President of the United States be elected at the General Election conducted on November 2, 2004.

At the General Election held in this State on November 2, 2004, the following persons received the greatest number of votes cast for the office of Electors for President and Vice President of the United States, and are duly elected to fill such office:

State of Minnesota
Certificate of Ascertainment, 2004, Page 2 of 8

Minnesota Democratic-Farmer-Labor Party
Electors pledged to John F. Kerry for President of the United States
and John Edwards for Vice President of the United States.
These candidates for presidential elector each received 1,445,014
votes:

> Sonja Berg, of St. Cloud
> Vi Grooms-Alban, of Cohasset
> Matthew Little, of Maplewood
> Michael Meuers, of Bemidji
> Tim O'Brien, of Edina
> Lil Ortendahl, of Osakis
> Everett Pettiford, of Minneapolis
> Jean Schiebel, of Brooklyn Center
> Frank Simon, of Chaska
> Chandler Harrison Stevens, of Austin

I further certify that the returns of the votes cast for Presidential Electors at the
General Election were canvassed and certified by the State Canvassing Board
on the 16th day of November, 2004 in accordance with the laws of the State of
Minnesota, and that the number of votes cast for each candidate for Presidential
Elector at the General Election is as follows:

Green Party of Minnesota
Electors pledged to David Cobb for President of the United States
and Pat LaMarche for Vice President of the United States.
These candidates for presidential elector each received 4,408 votes:

> Scott Bol
> Kellie Burriss
> Michael Cavlan
> Amber Garlan
> Jenny Heiser
> Molly Nutting
> Douglas Root
> Mark Wahl
> Annie Young
> Dean Zimmermann

State of Minnesota
Certificate of Ascertainment 2004, Page 3 of 8

Republican Party of Minnesota
Electors pledged to George W. Bush for President of the United States
and Dick Cheney for Vice President of the United States.
Each elector received 1,346,695 votes:

George Cable
Jeff Carnes
Ronald Eibensteiner
Angie Erhard
Eileen Fiore
Walter Klaus
Michelle Rifenberg
Julie Rosendahl
Lyall Schwarzkopf
Armin Tesch

Socialist Equality Party
Electors pledged to Bill Van Auken for President of the United States
and Jim Lawrence for Vice President of the United States.
These candidates for presidential elector each received 539 votes:

Nathan Andrew
Dan W. Blais
William J. Campbell-Bezat
Christopher M. Isett
Cory R. Johnson
Cynthia B. Moore
Thomas G. Moore
Stephen M. Paulson
Emanuele Saccarelli
James Strouf

State of Minnesota
Certificate of Ascertainment 2004, Page 4 of 8

Socialist Workers Party
Electors pledged to Roger Calero for President of the United States
and Arrin Hawkins for Vice President of the United States.
These candidates for presidential elector each received 416 votes:

> Dennis Drake
> Rebecca L. Ellis
> Catherine S. Fowlkes
> Allan J. Grady
> Bryce J. Grady
> Louise M. Halverson
> Bernadette Kuhn
> Thomas O'Brien
> Michael Pennock
> Sandra M. Sherman

Christian Freedom Party
Electors pledged to Thomas J. Harens for President of the United States
and Jennifer A. Ryan for Vice President of the United States.
These candidates for presidential elector each received 2,387 votes:

> Gail Froncek
> Brian Harens
> Kaja R. King
> Wayne Kruekeberg
> Sally Paulsen
> Janine Quaile
> Susan Smith
> Nadine Snyder
> Susan M. Style
> John Vinje

State of Minnesota
Certificate of Ascertainment 2004, Page 5 of 8

Better Life Party
Electors pledged to Ralph Nader for President of the United States
and Peter Miguel Camejo for Vice President of the United States.
These candidates for presidential elector each received 18,683 votes:

Cassandra Lynn Carlson
Enrique Pedro Gentzsch
Rhoda Jean Gilman
Kari Elizabeth Kyle
Linda Shannon Mann
Corey Scott Mattson
Lois Minna Piper
Preston George Piper
Matthew Alan Ryg
Suzanne Shelley Skorich

Constitution Party
Electors pledged to Michael Peroutka for President of the United States
and Chuck Baldwin for Vice President of the United States.
These candidates for presidential elector each received 3,074 votes:

Arthur Becker
Patricia Becker
Kent Berdahl
Bill Dodge
Rev. Dr. Tom Jestus Sr.
Lars Johnson
Don Koehler
Marilyn Nibbe
John Robillard
Wayne Zimmerscheid

State of Minnesota
Certificate of Ascertainment 2004, Page 6 of 8

Libertarian Party
Electors pledged to Michael Badnarik for President of the United States
and Richard Campagna for Vice President of the United States.
These candidates for presidential elector each received 4,639 votes:

      Stephen Baker
      Kathy Helwig
      Beatrice Kurk
      Jeremy Mackinney
      Mary O'Connor
      Corey Stern
      Shelby Thorsted
      David Wiester
      Colin Wilkinson
      Jill Wilkinson

Elector Pledged to Declared Write-In Candidates
Debra Joyce Renderos for President of the United States
and Oscar Renderos Castillo for Vice President of the United States.
This candidate for presidential elector received 2 votes:

      Henry Ford

Elector Pledged to Declared Write-In Candidates
Martin Wishnatsky for President of the United States
and Andrew Vanyo for Vice President of the United States.
This candidate for presidential elector received 2 votes:

      Chris Welle

State of Minnesota
Certificate of Ascertainment 2004, Page 7 of 8

Elector Pledged to Declared Write-In Candidates
Walt Brown for President of the United States
and Mary Alice Herbert for Vice President of the United States.
This candidate for presidential elector received 2 votes:

> Kari B. Garcia-Fisher

Electors Pledged to Declared Write-In Candidates
John Joseph Kennedy for President of the United States
and Daniel Robert Rezac for Vice President of the United States.
These candidates for presidential elector each received 4 votes:

> Donna Finnala
> Leonard Finnala
> Anita Hameister
> Jeff Hovde
> Darlene Jaskulke
> Jesse James Morris
> Joshua J. Morris
> Teresa A. Morris
> Julie Wellen

Electors Pledged to Declared Write-In Candidates
Joy Elaina Graham-Pendergast for President of the United States
and Ronald M. LeFeber for Vice President of the United States.
These candidates for presidential elector each received 1 vote:

> Daniel J. Coellinger
> Chris Haness
> B. Johnson

State of Minnesota
Certificate of Ascertainment 2004, Page 8 of 8

IN WITNESS WHEREOF,
I have set my hand and the Great Seal
of the State of Minnesota at the Capitol
in Saint Paul this 8th day of December,
2004, being the 228th year of
Independence, and the 146th year of
Statehood.

TIM PAWLENTY
Governor

ATTEST:

MARY KIFFMEYER
Secretary of State

APPENDIX F
Maine 2004 Certificate of Ascertainment

STATE OF MAINE

Certificate of Ascertainment of Electors

I, John Elias Baldacci, Governor of the State of Maine, *do hereby certify that Jill Duson of Portland; Samuel Shapiro of Waterville; Lu Bauer of Standish and David Garrity of Portland have been duly chosen and appointed*

ELECTORS OF PRESIDENT AND VICE PRESIDENT
OF THE UNITED STATES

for the State of Maine, at an election for that purpose which was held on the Tuesday following the first Monday in November, in the year two thousand and four, in accordance with the provisions of the laws of the State of Maine and in conformity with the Constitution and laws of the United States, for the purpose of giving their votes for President and Vice President of the United States for the respective terms commencing on the twentieth day of January, in the year two thousand and five; and

I further certify, that, *the votes given at said election for Electors of President and Vice President of the United States as appears by the returns from the several cities, towns and plantations in the State, which were duly received and examined by me in accordance with the laws, were as follows:*

The LIBERTARIAN PARTY Electors supporting the candidacy of Michael Badnarik for President and Richard Campagna for Vice President received the following votes:

First Congressional District
Mark Cenci, Portland   1,047

Second Congressional District
Dana Snowman, Alton   918

At-Large
Richard W. Eaton, Westbrook   1,965

At-Large
Geoffrey H. Keller, Dayton   1,965

The REPUBLICAN PARTY Electors supporting the candidacy of George W. Bush for President and Dick Cheney for Vice President received the following votes:

First Congressional District
Kenneth M. Cole, III, Falmouth   165,824

Second Congressional District
Katherine L. Watson, Pittsfield   164,377

At-Large
Peter E. Cianchette, South Portland   330,201

At-Large
James D. Tobin, Bangor   330,201

The GREEN INDEPENDENT PARTY Electors supporting the candidacy of David Cobb for President and Patricia LaMarche for Vice President received the following votes:

First Congressional District
Larry Dean Lofton-McGee, Augusta   1,468

Second Congressional District
Heather E. Garrold, Brooks   1,468

At-Large
Charlene Decker, Machias   2,936

At-Large
Ruth Z. Gabey, West Gardiner   2,936

The DEMOCRATIC PARTY Electors supporting the candidacy of John F. Kerry for President and John Edwards for Vice President received the following votes:

First Congressional District
Jill Duson, Portland   211,703

Second Congressional District
Samuel Shapiro, Waterville   185,139

At-Large
Lu Bauer, Standish   396,842

At-Large
David Garrity, Portland   396,842

The BETTER LIFE PARTY Electors supporting the candidacy of Ralph Nader for President and Peter Miguel Camejo for Vice President received the following votes:

First Congressional District
Rosemary L. Whittaker, South Portland   4,004

Second Congressional District
Christopher M. Droznick, Auburn   4,065

At-Large
Nancy Oden, Jonesboro   8,069

At-Large
J. Noble Snowdeal, Jonesboro   8,069

The CONSTITUTION PARTY Electors supporting the candidacy of Michael Anthony Peroutka for President and Chuck Baldwin for Vice President received the following votes:

First Congressional District
Stanley Jones, Hallowell   346

Second Congressional District
Harvey R. Lord, Paris   389

At-Large
Mary-Ann Greiner, St. George   735

At-Large
Patricia Truman, Hallowell   735

In Testimony Whereof, I have caused the Great Seal of the State of Maine to be hereunto affixed, given under my hand, this twenty-third day of November in the year two thousand and four.

John Elias Baldacci, Governor

Dan A. Gwadosky, Secretary of State

APPENDIX G
Nebraska 2004 Certificate
of Ascertainment

STATE OF NEBRASKA
ELECTORAL COLLEGE
CERTIFICATE OF ASCERTAINMENT

We, Mike Johanns, Governor of the State of Nebraska, and John A. Gale, Secretary of State of the State of Nebraska, do hereby certify the following is a certified list of the five Presidential Electors in and for the State of Nebraska, including the names of the Presidential and Vice Presidential candidates and the votes received by each as duly canvassed by the State Canvassing Board on November 29, 2004.

Republican Party **George W. Bush, President/Dick Cheney, Vice President**
Statewide Total Votes Received: 512,814

Electors: Ms. Kay Orr 1610 Brent Blvd. Lincoln, NE 68506 (At Large)
Mr. Ken Stinson 14349 Hamilton St. Omaha, NE 68154 (At Large)

First Congressional District Total Votes Received: 169,888
The Honorable Curt Bromm 1448 N Pine St. Wahoo, NE 68066 (1st District)

Second Congressional District Total Votes Received: 153,041
Mr. Michael John Hogan 16212 Wakely St. Omaha, NE 68118 (2nd District)

Third Congressional District Total Votes Received: 189,885
Mr. Bill Barrett P.O. Box 366 Lexington, NE 68850 (3rd District)

Democratic Party **John F. Kerry, President/John Edwards, Vice President**
Statewide Total Votes Received: 254,328

Electors: Ms. Carol Yoakum 1145 Rose St., #117 Lincoln, NE 68502-2268 (At Large)
Mr. Frank Johannsen HC 86, Box 149 Bayard, NE 69334 (At Large)

First Congressional District Total Votes Received: 96,314
The Honorable Diana Schimek 2321 Camelot Ct. Lincoln, NE 68512 (1st District)

Second Congressional District Total Votes Received: 97,858
Ms. Sandi Skorniak 6324 Blondo St. Omaha, NE 68104 (2nd District)

Third Congressional District Total Votes Received: 60,156
Deb Hardin Quirk P.O. Box 1142 Hastings, NE 68902 (3rd District)

Libertarian Party **Michael Badnarik, President/Richard V. Campagna, Vice President**
Statewide Total Votes Received: 2,041

Electors: Mr. Paul Tripp 12216 Poppleton Plz., #238 Omaha, NE 68144 (At Large)
Ms. Nydra Smart 310 Fawn Ct. Bellevue, NE 68005-2006 (At Large)

First Congressional District Total Votes Received: 656
Mr. Gerald F. Kosch 775 N 11th St. #4 David City, NE 68632 (1st District)

Second Congressional District Total Votes Received: 813
Mr. Jack Graziano 1513 N 112th Ct., #5413 Omaha, NE 68154

Third Congressional District Total Votes Received: 572
Mr. Jerry Hickman Rt. 2 Box 91 Loup City, NE 68853-9632

<u>Nebraska Party</u>   **Michael Anthony Peroutka, President/Chuck Baldwin, Vice President**
Statewide Total Votes Received: 1,314

Electors: Mr. Duane Dufek Box 555 Creighton, NE 68729 (At Large)
Mr. Gene Dobias 510 Washington Ave. Creighton, NE 68729 (At Large)

First Congressional District Total Votes Received: 405
Mr. Peter Rosberg 83626 557 Ave. Norfolk NE 68701 (1st District)

Second Congressional District Total Votes Received: 305
Mr. Tim Larson 15709 O Cir. Omaha, NE 68135 (2nd District)

Third Congressional District Total Votes Received: 604
Mr. Joseph Rosberg 54288 874 Rd. Wausa, NE 68786

<u>Green Party</u>   **David Cobb, President/Patricia LaMarche, Vice President**
Statewide Total Votes Received: 978

Electors: Mr. Tim Jensen 307 W. Charleston, #1232 Lincoln, NE 68528 (At Large)
Ms. Elaine Santore 609 N 17th St. Lincoln, NE 68508 (At Large)

First Congressional District Total Votes Received: 453
Ms. Ginny Crisco 1601 F St. Lincoln, NE 68508 (1st District)

Second Congressional District Total Votes Received: 261
Mr. Charles Ostdiek 3808 Harney St., #4 Omaha, NE 68131(2nd District)

Third Congressional District Total Votes Received: 264
Mr. Josh Skufca 3058 S. 41 Omaha, NE 68105 (3rd District)

<u>By Petition</u>   **Roger Calero, President/Arrin Hawkins, Vice President**
Statewide Total Votes Received: 82

Electors: Mr. Nelson F. Gonzalez 4731 S 24th St., Apt. 209 Omaha, NE 68107 (At Large)
Mr. David Z. Rosenfeld 4841 S 24th St. Omaha, NE 68107 (At Large)

First Congressional District Total Votes Received: 30
Ms. Lisa J. Krueger 5951 Oakridge Dr. Lincoln, NE 68516 (1st District)

Second Congressional District Total Votes Received: 23
Ms. Lisa M. Rottach 4841 S 24th St. Omaha, NE 68107 (2nd District)

Third Congressional District Total Votes Received: 29
Mr. Wayne Honsermeier 1206 Nebraska Hwy 2 Phillips, NE 68865 (3rd District)

<u>By Petition</u>   **Ralph Nader, President, Peter Miguel Camejo, Vice President**
Statewide Total Votes Received: 5,698

Electors: Ms. Diana McIntyre-Wright 5621 Dogwood Dr. Lincoln, NE 68516 (At Large)
Ms. Irma Sarata 2000 SW 47th St. Lincoln, NE 68522 (At Large)

First Congressional District Total Votes Received: 2,025
Ms. Amber McIntyre 5621 Dogwood Dr. Lincoln, NE 68516 (1st District)

Second Congressional District Total Votes Received: 1,731
Ms. Susan Robinson 9815 Pasadena Ave. Omaha, NE 68124 (2nd District)

Third Congressional District Total Votes Received: 1,942
Mr. Lee R. Heerten HC 81 PO Box 121 Springview, NE 68778

We hereby certify the names of the Republican Party Electors associated with the Bush-Cheney ticket have been duly appointed and notified by certified mail by the Governor and will appear at the State Capitol, Lincoln, Nebraska on the 13th day of December 2004, for the purpose of casting Nebraska's five Electoral College votes.

We hereunto affix our signatures this 13th day of December, 2004, at Lincoln, Nebraska.

Mike Johanns
Governor

John A. Gale
Secretary of State

APPENDIX H
New York 2004 Certificate
of Ascertainment

STATE OF NEW YORK

BY

George E. Pataki

GOVERNOR

I, **GEORGE E. PATAKI**, Governor of the State of New York, do hereby certify, that the statement containing the Canvass and Certificate of Determination by the State Board of Canvassers of the State of New York, as to **ELECTORS of PRESIDENT and VICE-PRESIDENT** hereto annexed, and certified by the Chairperson of the State Board of Elections of said State, under her seal of office, contains a true and correct list setting forth the names of Electors of President and Vice-President, elected in said State, at the General Election held in said State on the Tuesday after the First Monday in November (November second), in the year two thousand four, pursuant to the Constitution and Laws of the United States and of the State of New York, to wit:

Joseph Ashton	Bertha Lewis
Bill De Blasio	Alan Lubin
Molly Clifford	Thomas Manton
Lorraine Cortes-Vazquez	Dennis Mehiel
Inez Dickens	June O'Neill
Danny Donahue	David Paterson
Herman D. Farrell	Jose Rivera
Virginia Fields	Rich Schaffer
Emily Giske	Chung Seto
Bea Gonzalez	Sheldon Silver
Alan Hevesi	Eliot Spitzer
Frank Hoare	Antoine Thompson
Virginia Kee	Paul Tokasz
Peggy Kerry	Bill Wood
Denise King	Robert Zimmerman
Len Lenihan	

And further that the Statement of Canvass and Certificate of Determination certified by the Chairperson of the State Board of Elections of said State, as aforesaid, correctly sets forth the Canvass of Determination under the Laws of said State of New York, of the number of votes given or cast for each person for whose elections any and all votes have been given or cast at said election as aforesaid.

In Testimony Whereof, The Great Seal of the State is hereunto affixed.

Witness my hand at the City of Albany, the tenth day of December, in the year two thousand four.

....

Attested by

....
Secretary of State

654

We, the State Board of Elections, constituting the State Board of Canvassers, having canvassed the whole number of votes given for the office of ELECTOR of PRESIDENT and VICE-PRESIDENT at the general election held in said State, on the Second day of November, 2004, according to the certified statement of canvass received by the State Board of Elections, in the manner directed by law, do hereby determine, declare and certify that

Joseph Ashton	Bertha Lewis
Bill De Blasio	Alan Lubin
Molly Clifford	Thomas Manton
Lorraine Cortes-Vazquez	Dennis Mehiel
Inez Dickens	June O'Neill
Danny Donahue	David Paterson
Herman D. Farrell	Jose Rivera
Virginia Fields	Rich Schaffer
Emily Giske	Chung Seto
Bea Gonzalez	Sheldon Silver
Alan Hevesi	Eliot Spitzer
Frank Hoare	Antoine Thompson
Virginia Kee	Paul Tokasz
Peggy Kerry	Bill Wood
Denise King	Robert Zimmerman
Len Lenihan	

were, by the greatest number of votes given at said election duly elected ELECTOR of PRESIDENT and VICE-PRESIDENT of the United States.

GIVEN under our hands in Sloatsburg, New York, the 6th day of December in the year two thousand four.

Carol Berman — Commissioner
Neil W. Kelleher — Commissioner
Evelyn J. Aquila — Commissioner
Helena Moses Donohue — Commissioner

STATE OF NEW YORK :
: ss:
STATE BOARD OF ELECTIONS :

I certify that I have compared the foregoing with the original certificate filed in this office, and that the same is a correct transcript therefrom and of the whole of such original.

GIVEN under my hand and official seal of office of the State Board of Elections, in Sloatsburg, New York, this 6th day of December in the year two thousand four.

Carol Berman

Carol Berman — Chairperson

STATE OF NEW YORK, ss:

Statement of the whole number of votes cast for all the candidates for the office of ELECTOR OF PRESIDENT and VICE-PRESIDENT at a General Election held in said State on the Second day of November, 2004.

The whole number of votes given for the office of ELECTOR OF PRESIDENT and VICE-PRESIDENT was **7,448,266** of which

		REPUBLICAN	CONSERVATIVE	TOTAL
George E. Pataki	received	2,806,993	155,574	2,962,567
Alexander F. Treadwell	received	2,806,993	155,574	2,962,567
Joseph Bruno	received	2,806,993	155,574	2,962,567
Charles Nesbitt	received	2,806,993	155,574	2,962,567
Mary Donohue	received	2,806,993	155,574	2,962,567
Rudolph Giuliani	received	2,806,993	155,574	2,962,567
Charles Gargano	received	2,806,993	155,574	2,962,567
Joseph Mondello	received	2,806,993	155,574	2,962,567
J. Patrick Barrett	received	2,806,993	155,574	2,962,567
John F. Nolan	received	2,806,993	155,574	2,962,567
Robert Davis	received	2,806,993	155,574	2,962,567
Peter J. Savago	received	2,806,993	155,574	2,962,567
Maggie Brooks	received	2,806,993	155,574	2,962,567
Catherine Blaney	received	2,806,993	155,574	2,962,567
Howard Mills	received	2,806,993	155,574	2,962,567
John Cahill	received	2,806,993	155,574	2,962,567
Rita DiMartino	received	2,806,993	155,574	2,962,567
Libby Pataki	received	2,806,993	155,574	2,962,567
Stephen Minarik	received	2,806,993	155,574	2,962,567
Raymond Meier	received	2,806,993	155,574	2,962,567
Thomas M. Reynolds	received	2,806,993	155,574	2,962,567
Adam Stoll	received	2,806,993	155,574	2,962,567
Herman Badillo	received	2,806,993	155,574	2,962,567
Jane Forbes Clark	received	2,806,993	155,574	2,962,567
James Garner	received	2,806,993	155,574	2,962,567
Shawn Marie Levine	received	2,806,993	155,574	2,962,567
Viola J. Hunter	received	2,806,993	155,574	2,962,567
Laura Schreiner	received	2,806,993	155,574	2,962,567
Carmen Gomez Goldberg	received	2,806,993	155,574	2,962,567
Bernadette Castro	received	2,806,993	155,574	2,962,567
Cathy Jimino	received	2,806,993	155,574	2,962,567

		DEMOCRATIC	WORKING FAM.	TOTAL
Joseph Ashton	received	4,180,755	133,525	4,314,280
Bill De Blasio	received	4,180,755	133,525	4,314,280
Molly Clifford	received	4,180,755	133,525	4,314,280
Lorraine Cortes-Vazquez	received	4,180,755	133,525	4,314,280
Inez Dickens	received	4,180,755	133,525	4,314,280
Danny Donahue	received	4,180,755	133,525	4,314,280
Herman D. Farrell	received	4,180,755	133,525	4,314,280
Virginia Fields	received	4,180,755	133,525	4,314,280
Emily Giske	received	4,180,755	133,525	4,314,280
Bea Gonzalez	received	4,180,755	133,525	4,314,280
Alan Hevesi	received	4,180,755	133,525	4,314,280
Frank Hoare	received	4,180,755	133,525	4,314,280
Virginia Kee	received	4,180,755	133,525	4,314,280
Peggy Kerry	received	4,180,755	133,525	4,314,280
Denise King	received	4,180,755	133,525	4,314,280
Len Lenihan	received	4,180,755	133,525	4,314,280
Bertha Lewis	received	4,180,755	133,525	4,314,280
Alan Lubin	received	4,180,755	133,525	4,314,280
Thomas Manton	received	4,180,755	133,525	4,314,280
Dennis Mehiel	received	4,180,755	133,525	4,314,280
June O'Neill	received	4,180,755	133,525	4,314,280
David Paterson	received	4,180,755	133,525	4,314,280
Jose Rivera	received	4,180,755	133,525	4,314,280
Rich Schaffer	received	4,180,755	133,525	4,314,280
Chung Seto	received	4,180,755	133,525	4,314,280
Sheldon Silver	received	4,180,755	133,525	4,314,280
Eliot Spitzer	received	4,180,755	133,525	4,314,280
Antoine Thompson	received	4,180,755	133,525	4,314,280
Paul Tokasz	received	4,180,755	133,525	4,314,280
Bill Wood	received	4,180,755	133,525	4,314,280
Robert Zimmerman	received	4,180,755	133,525	4,314,280

		INDEPENDENCE	TOTAL
Fran Siems	received	84,247	84,247
Barbara Smith	received	84,247	84,247
Theresa Smith	received	84,247	84,247
Joseph Baruth	received	84,247	84,247
Howard Edelbaum	received	84,247	84,247
Bryan Puertas	received	84,247	84,247
Barbara Pershay	received	84,247	84,247
Elizabeth Allen	received	84,247	84,247
Paul Gouldin	received	84,247	84,247
Joan Fleischman	received	84,247	84,247
Ken Gallashaw	received	84,247	84,247
Robert Conroy	received	84,247	84,247
Bobby Soto	received	84,247	84,247
Lenora Fulani	received	84,247	84,247
Harry Kresky	received	84,247	84,247
Amy Jo Butler	received	84,247	84,247
Rebecca Seward	received	84,247	84,247
Lili Vega	received	84,247	84,247
Jeff Graham	received	84,247	84,247
Patricia Anken	received	84,247	84,247
Judith Resen	received	84,247	84,247
Paul Caputo	received	84,247	84,247
Jessie Field	received	84,247	84,247
Sarah Lyons	received	84,247	84,247
Judith A. Orsini	received	84,247	84,247
Lee Kolesnikoff	received	84,247	84,247
Ben Curtis	received	84,247	84,247
Lorraine Stevens	received	84,247	84,247
Frank Mackay	received	84,247	84,247
Eileen Trace	received	84,247	84,247
Richard Schulman	received	84,247	84,247

		PEACE & JUSTICE	TOTAL
Sally J. Cass	received	15,626	15,626
Mitchel Cohen	received	15,626	15,626
Millicent Y. Collins	received	15,626	15,626
Edward T. Dodge	received	15,626	15,626
Mark A. Dunlea	received	15,626	15,626
J. David Edelstein	received	15,626	15,626
James Farney	received	15,626	15,626
Leslie Farney	received	15,626	15,626
Anthony Gronowicz	received	15,626	15,626
Howie Hawkins	received	15,626	15,626
Gerald F. Kann	received	15,626	15,626
Alan B. Kendrick-Bowser	received	15,626	15,626
James C. Lane	received	15,626	15,626
Peter LaVenia	received	15,626	15,626
Daniella Liebling	received	15,626	15,626
Joseph Lombardo	received	15,626	15,626
Ronald J. MacKinnon	received	15,626	15,626
Jessica L. Maxwell	received	15,626	15,626
Robin L. Miller	received	15,626	15,626
Steven Penn	received	15,626	15,626
Stephen H. Reynolds	received	15,626	15,626
Rebecca Rotzler	received	15,626	15,626
Leigh C. Safford	received	15,626	15,626
Eric Salzman	received	15,626	15,626
Lorna Salzman	received	15,626	15,626
Rachel Treichler	received	15,626	15,626
Jason West	received	15,626	15,626
Betty K. Wood	received	15,626	15,626
Paul H. Zulkowitz	received	15,626	15,626

		SOCIALIST WORKERS	TOTAL
Michael J. Fitzsimmons	received	2,405	2,405
Olga L. Rodriguez	received	2,405	2,405

		LIBERTARIAN	TOTAL
Richard A. Cooper	received	11,607	11,607
Dawn Davis	received	11,607	11,607
Donald H. Davis	received	11,607	11,607
Robert S. Flanzer	received	11,607	11,607
Christopher B. Garvey	received	11,607	11,607
David A. Harnett	received	11,607	11,607
James E. Harris	received	11,607	11,607
Loretta K. Hetzner	received	11,607	11,607
Werner Hetzner	received	11,607	11,607
David J. Hopwood	received	11,607	11,607
Nicolas Leobold	received	11,607	11,607
Jim Lesczynski	received	11,607	11,607
Adam Martin	received	11,607	11,607
Bruce A. Martin	received	11,607	11,607
Crystal Martin	received	11,607	11,607
William P. McMillen	received	11,607	11,607
Ronald G. Moore	received	11,607	11,607
John C. Mounteer	received	11,607	11,607
Christian Padgett	received	11,607	11,607
Audrey M. Pappaeliou	received	11,607	11,607
Gary S. Popkin	received	11,607	11,607
Louise Popkin	received	11,607	11,607
Eleanor Rosenblatt	received	11,607	11,607
Catherine Ruks	received	11,607	11,607
Thomas Ruks	received	11,607	11,607
Norma Segal	received	11,607	11,607
Donald Silberger	received	11,607	11,607
Sam Sloan	received	11,607	11,607
Thomas Robert Stevens	received	11,607	11,607
Michael L. Trombetta	received	11,607	11,607
Alexander E. Ulmann, III	received	11,607	11,607

GIVEN under our hands in Sloatsburg, New York, the 6th day of December in the year two thousand four.

Carol Berman	Commissioner
Neil W. Kelleher	Commissioner
Evelyn J. Aquila	Commissioner
Helena Moses Donohue	Commissioner

STATE OF NEW YORK :
: ss:
STATE BOARD OF ELECTIONS :

I certify that I have compared the foregoing with the original certificate filed in this office, and that the same is a correct transcript therefrom and of the whole of such original.

GIVEN under my hand and official seal of office of the State Board of Elections, in the City of Albany, this 6th day of December, 2004.

Peter S. Kosinski   Deputy Executive Director

APPENDIX I
Mississippi 2004 Certificate of Ascertainment

CERTIFICATE OF ASCERTAINMENT

TO: THE HONORABLE JOHN W. CARLIN
ARCHIVIST OF THE UNITED STATES
NATIONAL ARCHIVES AND RECORDS ADMINISTRATION

I, HALEY BARBOUR, Governor of the State of Mississippi, in accordance with Chapter 1, Section 6 of Title 3, United States Code, do hereby certify as follows:

At the General Election held on Tuesday, November 2, 2004, the qualified electors of the state at large elected and appointed six (6) Presidential and Vice Presidential Electors for the State of Mississippi; and

There was no controversy or contest concerning the election of all or of any of such Electors; and

Pursuant to the applicable laws of this state, final ascertainment has now been made of the results of the November 2, 2004, General Election, and the following named persons have been elected and appointed to serve as, and to discharge the duties of, Presidential and Vice Presidential Electors for the State of Mississippi:

ELECTORS FOR GEORGE W. BUSH FOR PRESIDENT AND DICK CHENEY FOR VICE PRESIDENT (REPUBLICAN PARTY)

Mr. James H. "Jimmy" Creekmore	684,981
Mr. Victor Mavar	684,981
Mr. W.D. "Billy" Mounger	684,981
Mr. Wayne Parker	684,981
Mr. John F. Phillips	684,981
Dr. Kelly S. Segars	684,981.

I do further certify that the number of votes cast at the November 2, 2004, General Election for the other candidates for election as Presidential and Vice Presidential Electors has been finally ascertained to be:

ELECTORS FOR JOHN F. KERRY FOR PRESIDENT AND JOHN EDWARDS FOR VICE PRESIDENT (DEMOCRATIC PARTY)

Mr. Gary Bailey	458,094
Ms. Janice Carr	458,094
Mr. Robert Hooks	458,094
Ms. Tamara Longmire	458,094
Mrs. Tyna Stewart	458,094
Mr. Al Tate	458,094

ELECTORS FOR MICHAEL BADNARIK FOR PRESIDENT AND RICHARD V. CAMPAGNA FOR VICE PRESIDENT (LIBERTARIAN PARTY)

Mr. Mark G. Bushman	1,793
Mr. Victor G. Dostrow	1,793
Ms. Lana Renee Ethridge	1,793
Mr. Lewis W. Napper	1,793
Mr. Harold M. Taylor	1,793
Ms. Leighanne A. Taylor	1,793

ELECTORS FOR DAVID COBB FOR PRESIDENT AND PATRICIA LAMARCHE FOR VICE PRESIDENT (GREEN PARTY)

Mr. Sherman Lee Dillon	1,073
Mr. Ray Gebhart	1,073
Ms. Jan Hillegas	1,073
Mr. Greg Johnson	1,073
Mr. Claude Evan Peacock	1,073
Ms. Gwendolyn M. Wages	1,073

ELECTORS FOR JAMES HARRIS FOR PRESIDENT AND MARGARET TROWE FOR VICE PRESIDENT (INDEPENDENT)

Ms. Barbara Bell	1,268
Mr. Roy Bell	1,268
Ms. Joann Hogan	1,268
Ms. Penny Hogan	1,268
Mr. R.C. Howard	1,268
Ms. Linda Miles	1,268

ELECTORS FOR RALPH NADER FOR PRESIDENT AND PETER MIGUEL CAMEJO FOR VICE PRESIDENT (REFORM PARTY)

Mr. Rodney (Billy) Fulgham	3,177
Ms. Carroll Grantham	3,177
Mr. John A. Hailey	3,177
Ms. Lamonica L. Magee	3,177
Mr. Billy Minshew	3,177
Mr. Christopher Minshew	3,177

ELECTORS FOR MICHAEL A. PEROUTKA FOR PRESIDENT AND CHUCK BALDWIN FOR VICE PRESIDENT (CONSTITUTION PARTY)

Mr. John C. Bethea	1,759
Mr. Jim Bourland	1,759
Mr. Tim Delrie	1,759
Mr. Thomas R. Floyd	1,759
Mr. Leslie Riley	1,759
Mr. Steve C. Thornton	1,759.

IN WITNESS WHEREOF, I have hereunto set my hand and caused the Great Seal of the State of Mississippi to be affixed.

DONE at the Capitol, in the City of Jackson, this the 22nd day of March, in the year of our Lord, Two thousand and five, and of the Independence of the United States of America, the two hundred and twenty ninth.

GOVERNOR

BY THE GOVERNOR

SECRETARY OF STATE

APPENDIX J
Dates Appearing on Certificates of Ascertainment for 2000 and 2004 Presidential Elections

TABLE J.1 KEY DATES IN 2000 AND 2004 PRESIDENTIAL ELECTION PROCESS

	DATE FOR 2000	DATE FOR 2004
Election day	November 7, 2000	November 2, 2004
Safe harbor day	December 12, 2000	December 7, 2004
Electoral college meeting day	December 18, 2000	December 13, 2004

TABLE J.2 DATES APPEARING ON 2000 AND 2004 CERTIFICATES OF ASCERTAINMENT

JURISDICTION	DATE FOR 2000	DATE FOR 2004
Alabama	December 8, 2000	November 29, 2004
Alaska	December 5, 2000	December 7, 2004
Arizona	December 4, 2000	November 22, 2004
Arkansas	November 30, 2000	November 23, 2004
California	December 14, 2000	December 13, 2004
Colorado	December 4, 2000	December 13, 2004
Connecticut	November 29, 2000	November 24, 2004
Delaware	December 4, 2000	November 30, 2004
District of Columbia	December 6, 2000	December 7, 2004
Florida	November 26, 2000	November 18, 2004
Georgia	December 1, 2000	November 23, 2004
Hawaii	November 27, 2000	November 22, 2004
Idaho	November 22, 2000	November 17, 2004
Illinois	November, 27, 2000	December 3, 2004
Indiana	December 5, 2000	December 7, 2004
Iowa	December 14, 2000	December 13, 2004
Kansas	December 6, 2000	December 8, 2004
Kentucky	December 4, 2000	December 1, 2004
Louisiana	November 21, 2000	November 16, 2004
Maine	November 27, 2000	November 23, 2004
Maryland	December 18, 2000	December 13, 2004
Massachusetts	December 6, 2000	December 13, 2004

TABLE J.2 DATES APPEARING ON 2000 AND 2004 CERTIFICATES OF ASCERTAINMENT *(cont.)*

JURISDICTION	DATE FOR 2000	DATE FOR 2004
Michigan	November 30, 2000	November 30, 2004
Minnesota	December 5, 2000	November 30, 2004
Mississippi	December 7, 2000	December 13, 2004
Missouri	December 11, 2000	December 13, 2004
Montana	December 6, 2000	December 8, 2004
Nebraska	December 18, 2000	December 13, 2004
Nevada	December 4, 2000	December 7, 2004
New Hampshire	December 6, 2000	December 1, 2004
New Jersey	December 8, 2000	December 13, 2004
New Mexico	December 5, 2000	December 3, 2004
New York	December 12, 2000	December 6, 2004
North Carolina	December 8, 2000	December 1, 2004
North Dakota	November 27, 2000	December 3, 2004
Ohio	December 11, 2000	December 6, 2004
Oklahoma	December 8, 2000	December 13, 2004
Oregon	No date	No date
Pennsylvania	December 14, 2000	December 10, 2004
Rhode Island	November 22, 2000	November 23, 2004
South Carolina	November 28, 2000	December 3, 2004
South Dakota	November 28, 2000	December 13, 2004
Tennessee	November 28, 2000	December 7, 2004
Texas	November 27, 2000	November 18, 2004
Utah	December 1, 2000	December 13, 2004
Vermont	December 9, 2000	December 3, 2004
Virginia	November 29, 2000	December 13, 2004
Washington	December 7, 2000	December 9, 2004
West Virginia	December 11, 2000	December 13, 2004
Wisconsin	December 11, 2000	December 6, 2004
Wyoming	November 22, 2000	December 2, 2004

APPENDIX K
Ohio Adoption of the
Great Lakes Basin Compact

SECTION 6161.01 (EFFECTIVE ON OCTOBER 9, 1963)

The "great lakes basin compact" is hereby ratified, enacted into law, and entered into by this state as a party thereto with any other state or province which, pursuant to Article II of said compact, has legally joined in the compact as follows:

GREAT LAKES BASIN COMPACT

The party states solemnly agree:

ARTICLE I

The purposes of this compact are, through means of joint or co-operative action:

(A) To promote the orderly, integrated, and comprehensive development, use, and conservation of the water sources of the great lakes basin (hereinafter called the basin);

(B) To plan for the welfare and development of the water resources of the basin as a whole, as well as for those portions of the basin which may have problems of special concern;

(C) To make it possible for the states of the basin and their people to derive the maximum benefit from utilization of public works, in the form of navigational aids or otherwise, which may exist or which may be constructed from time to time;

(D) To advise in securing and maintaining a proper balance among industrial, commercial, agricultural, water supply, residential, recreational, and other legitimate uses of the water resources of the basin;

(E) To establish and maintain an intergovernmental agency to the end that the purposes of this compact may be accomplished more effectively.

ARTICLE II

(A) This compact shall enter into force and become effective and binding when it has been enacted by the legislatures of any four of the states of Illinois, Indiana, Michigan, Minnesota, New York, Ohio, Pennsylvania, and Wisconsin and thereafter shall enter into force and become effective and binding as to any other of said states when enacted by the legislature thereof.

(B) The province of Ontario and the province of Quebec, or either of them, may become states party to this compact by taking such action as their laws and the laws of the government of Canada may prescribe for adherence thereto. For the purpose of this compact the word "state" shall be construed in include a province of Canada.

ARTICLE III

The great lakes commission created by Article IV of this compact shall exercise its powers and perform its functions in respect to the basin which, for the purposes of this compact, shall consist of so much of the following as may be within the party states:

(A) Lakes Erie, Huron, Michigan, Ontario, St. Clair, Superior, and the St. Lawrence River, together with any and all natural or man-made water interconnections between or among them;

(B) All rivers, ponds, lakes, streams, and other watercourses which, in their natural state or in their prevailing condition, are tributary to Lakes Erie, Huron, Michigan, Ontario, St. Clair, and Superior, or any of them, or which comprise part of any watershed draining into any of said lakes.

ARTICLE IV

(A) There is hereby created an agency of the party states to be known as the great lakes commission (hereinafter called the commission). In that name the commission may sue and be sued, acquire, hold and convey real and personal property, and any interest therein. The commission shall have a seal with the words "the great lakes commission" and such other design as it may prescribe engraved thereon by which it shall authenticate its proceedings. Transactions involving real or personal property shall conform to the laws of the state in which the property is located, and the commission may by bylaws provide for the execution and acknowledgement of all instruments in its behalf.

(B) The commission shall be composed of not less than three commissioners nor more than five commissioners from each party state designated or appointed in accordance with the law of the state which they represent and serving and subject to removal in accordance with such law.

(C) Each state delegation shall be entitled to three votes in the commission. The presence of commissioners from a majority of the party states shall constitute a quorum for the transaction of business at any meeting of the commission. Actions of the commission shall be by a majority of the votes cast except that any recommendations made pursuant to Article VI of this compact shall require an affirmative vote of not less than a majority of the votes cast from each of a majority of the states present and voting.

(D) The commissioners of any two or more party states may meet separately to consider problems of particular interest to their states but no action taken at any such meeting shall be deemed an action of the commission unless and until the commission shall specifically approve the same.

(E) In the absence of any commissioner, his vote may be cast by another representative or commissioner of his state provided that said commissioner or other representative casting said vote shall have a written proxy in proper form as may be required by the commission.

(F) The commission shall elect annually from among its members a chairman and vice-chairman. The commission shall appoint an executive director who shall also act as secretary-treasurer, and who shall be bonded in such amount as the commission may require. The executive director shall serve at the pleasure of the commission and at such compensation and under such terms and conditions as may be fixed by it. The executive director shall be custodian of the records of the commission with authority to affix the commission's official seal and to attest and certify such records or copies thereof.

(G) The executive director, subject to the approval of the commission in such cases as its bylaws may provide, shall appoint and remove or discharge such personnel as may be necessary for the performance of the commission's functions. Subject to the aforesaid approval, the executive director may fix their compensation, define their duties, and require bonds of such of them as the commission may designate.

(H) The executive director, on behalf of, as trustee for, and with the approval of the commission, may borrow, accept, or contract for the services of personnel from any state or government or any subdivision or agency thereof, from any intergovernmental agency, or from any institution, person, firm, or corporation; and may accept for any of the commission's purposes and functions under this compact any and all donations, gifts, and grants of money, equipment, supplies, materials, and services from any state or government or any subdivision or agency thereof or intergovernmental agency or from any institution, person, firm, or corporation and may receive and utilize the same.

(I) The commission may establish and maintain one or more offices for the transacting of its business and for such purposes the executive director, on behalf of, as trustee for, and with the approval of the commission, may acquire, hold, and dispose of real and personal property necessary to the performance of its functions.

(J) No tax levied or imposed by any party state or any political subdivision thereof shall be deemed to apply to property, transactions, or income of the commission.

(K) The commission may adopt, amend, and rescind bylaws, rules, and regulations for the conduct of its business.

(L) The organization meeting of the commission shall be held within six months from the effective date of this compact.

(M) The commission and its executive director shall make available to the party states any information within its possession and shall always provide free access to its records by duly authorized representatives of such party states.

(N) The commission shall keep a written record of its meetings and proceedings and shall annually make a report thereof to be submitted to the duly designated official of each party state.

(O) The commission shall make and transmit annually to the legislature and governor of each party state a report covering the activities of the commission for the preceding year and embodying such recommendations as may have been adopted by the commission. The commission may issue such additional reports as it may deem desirable.

ARTICLE V

(A) The members of the commission shall serve without compensation, but the expenses of each commissioner shall be met by the state which he represents in accordance with the law of that state. All other expenses incurred by the commission in the course of exercising the powers conferred upon it by this compact, unless met in some other manner specifically provided by this compact, shall be paid by the commission out of its own funds.

(B) The commission shall submit to the executive head or designated officer of each party state a budget of its estimated expenditures for such period as may be required by the laws of the state for presentation to the legislature thereof.

(C) Each of the commission's budgets of estimated expenditures shall contain specific recommendations of the amount or amounts to be appropriated by each of the party states. Detailed commission budgets shall be recommended by a majority of the votes cast, and the costs shall be allocated equitably among the party states in accordance with their respective interests.

(D) The commission shall not pledge the credit of any party state. The commission may meet any of it obligations in whole or in part with funds available to it under Article IV (H) of this compact, provided that the commission takes specific action setting aside such funds prior to the incurring of any obligations to be met in whole or in part in this manner. Except where the commission makes use of funds available to it under Article IV (H) hereof, the commission shall not incur any obligations prior to the allotment of funds by the party states adequate to meet the same.

(E) The commission shall keep accurate accounts of all receipts and disbursements. The receipts and disbursements of the commission shall be subject to the audit and accounting procedures established under the bylaws. However, all receipts and disbursements of funds handled by the commission shall be audited yearly by a qualified public accountant and the report of the audit shall be included in and become a part of the annual report of the commission.

(F) The accounts of the commission shall be open at any reasonable time for inspection by such agency, representative, or representatives of the party states as may be duly constituted for that purpose and by others who may be authorized by the commission.

ARTICLE VI

The commission shall have power to:

(A) Collect, correlate, interpret, and report on data relating to the water resources and the use thereof in the basin or any portion thereof;

(B) Recommend methods for the orderly, efficient, and balanced development, use, and conservation of the water resources of the basin or any portion thereof to the party states and to any other governments or agencies having interests in or jurisdiction over the basin or any portion thereof;

(C) Consider the need for and desirability of public works and improvements relating to the water resources in the basin or any portion thereof;

(D) Consider means of improving navigation and port facilities in the basin or any portion thereof;

(E) Consider means of improving and maintaining the fisheries of the basin or any portion thereof;

(F) Recommend policies relating to water resources including the institution and alteration of flood plain and other zoning laws, ordinances, and regulations;

(G) Recommend uniform or other laws, ordinances, or regulations relating to the development, use, and conservation of the basin's water resources to the party states or any of them and to other governments, political subdivisions, agencies, or intergovernmental bodies having interests in or jurisdiction sufficient to affect conditions in the basin or any portion thereof;

(H) Consider and recommend amendments or agreements supplementary to this compact to the party states or any of them, and assist in the formulation and drafting of such amendments or supplementary agreements;

(I) Prepare and publish reports, bulletins, and publications appropriate to this work and fix reasonable sale prices therefor;

(J) With respect to the water resources of the basin or any portion thereof, recommend agreements between the governments of the United States and Canada;

(K) Recommend mutual arrangements expressed by concurrent or reciprocal legislation on the part of congress and the parliament of Canada including but not limited to such agreements and mutual arrangement as are provided for by Article XIII of the Treaty of 1909 Relating to Boundary Waters and Questions Arising Between the United States and Canada. (Treaty Series, No. 548);

(L) Co-operate with the governments of the United States and of Canada, the party states and any public or private agencies or bodies having interests in or jurisdiction sufficient to affect the basin or any portion thereof;

(M) At the request of the United States, or in the event that a province shall be a party state, at the request of the government of Canada, assist in the negotiation and formulation of any treaty or other mutual arrangement or agreement between the United States and Canada with reference to the basin or any portion thereof;

(N) Make any recommendation and do all things necessary and proper to carry out the powers conferred upon the commission by this compact, provided that no action of the commission shall have the force of law in, or be binding upon, any party state.

ARTICLE VII

Each party state agrees to consider the action the commission recommends in respect to:

(A) Stabilization of lake levels;

(B) Measures for combating pollution, beach erosion, floods, and shore inundation;

(C) Uniformity in navigation regulations within the constitutional powers of the states;

(D) Proposed navigation aids and improvements;

(E) Uniformity or effective co-ordinating action in fishing laws and regulations and co-operative action to eradicate destructive and parasitical forces endangering the fisheries, wild life, and other water resources;

(F) Suitable hydroelectric power developments;

(G) Co-operative programs for control of soil and bank erosion for the general improvement of the basin;

(H) Diversion of waters from and into the basin;

(I) Other measures the commission may recommend to the states pursuant to Article VI of this compact.

ARTICLE VIII

This compact shall continue in force and remain binding upon each party state until renounced by act of the legislature of such state, in such form and manner as it may choose and as may be valid and effective to repeal a statute of said state, provided that such renunciation shall not become effective until six months after notice of such action shall have been officially communicated in writing to the executive head of the other party states.

ARTICLE IX

It is intended that the provisions of this compact shall be reasonably and liberally construed to effectuate the purposes thereof. The provisions of this compact shall be severable and if any phrase, clause, sentence, or provision of this compact is declared to be contrary to the constitution of any party state or of the United States, or in the case of a province, to the British North America Act of 1867 as amended, or the applicability thereof to any state, agency, person, or circumstance is held invalid, the constitutionality of the remainder of this compact and the applicability thereof to any state, agency, person, or circumstance shall not be affected thereby, provided further that if this compact shall be held contrary to the constitution of the United States, or in the case of a province, to the British North America Act of 1867 as amended, or of any party state, the compact shall remain in full force and effect as to the remaining states and in full force and effect as to the state affected as to all severable matters.

APPENDIX L
Congressional Consent to the Interstate Agreement on Detainers

PUBLIC LAW 91-538 OF 1970

AN ACT
To enact the Interstate Agreement on Detainers into law

Be it enacted by the Senate and House of Representatives of the United States of America in congress assembled, That this Act may be cited as the "Interstate Agreement on Detainers Act".

Sec. 2. The Interstate Agreement on Detainers is hereby enacted into law and entered into by the United States on its own behalf and on behalf of the District of Columbia with all jurisdictions legally joining in substantially the following form:

"The contracting States solemnly agree that:

"Article I

"The party States find that charges outstanding against a prisoner, detainers based on untried indictments, informations, or complaints and difficulties in securing speedy trial of persons already incarcerated in other jurisdictions, produce uncertainties which obstruct programs of prisoner treatment and rehabilitation. Accordingly, it is the policy of the party States and the purpose of this agreement to encourage the expeditious and orderly disposition of such charges and determination of the proper status of any and all detainers based on untried indictments, informations, or complaints. The party States also find that proceedings with reference to such charges and detainers, when emanating from another jurisdiction, cannot properly be had in the absence of cooperative procedures. It is the further purpose of this agreement to provide such cooperative procedures.

"Article II

"As used in this agreement:

"(a) 'State' shall mean a State of the United States; the United States of America; a territory or possession of the United States; the District of Columbia; the Commonwealth of Puerto Rico.

"(b) 'Sending State' shall mean a State in which a prisoner is incarcerated at the time that he initiates a request for final disposition pursuant to article III hereof or at the time that a request for custody or availability is initiated pursuant to article IV hereof.

"(c) 'Receiving State' shall mean the State in which trial is to be had on an indictment, information, or complaint pursuant to article III or article IV hereof.

"Article III

"(a) Whenever a person has entered upon a term of imprisonment in a penal or correctional institution of a party State, and whenever during the continuance of the term of imprisonment there is pending in any other party State any untried indictment, information, or complaint on the basis of which a detainer has been lodged against the prisoner, he shall be brought to trial within one hundred and eighty days after he shall have caused to be delivered to the prosecuting officer and the appropriate court of the prosecuting officer's jurisdiction written notice of the place of his imprisonment and his request for a final disposition to be made of the indictment, information, or complaint: Provided, That, for good cause shown in open court, the prisoner or his counsel being present, the court having jurisdiction of the matter may grant any necessary or reasonable continuance. The request of the prisoner shall be accompanied by a certificate of the appropriate official having custody of the prisoner, stating the term of commitment under which the prisoner is being held, the time already served, the time remaining to be served on the sentence, the amount of good time earned, the time of parole eligibility of the prisoner, and any decision of the State parole agency relating to the prisoner.

"(b) The written notice and request for final disposition referred to in paragraph (a) hereof shall be given or sent by the prisoner to the warden, commissioner of corrections, or other official having custody of him, who shall promptly forward it together with the certificate to the appropriate prosecuting official and court by registered or certified mail, return receipt requested.

"(c) The warden, commissioner of corrections, or other official having custody of the prisoner shall promptly inform him of the source and contents of any detainer lodged against him and shall also inform him of his right to make a request for final disposition of the indictment, information, or complaint on which the detainer is based.

"(d) Any request for final disposition made by a prisoner pursuant to paragraph (a) hereof shall operate as a request for final disposition of all untried indictments, informations, or complaints on the basis of which detainers have been lodged against the prisoner from the State to whose prosecuting official the request for final disposition is specifically directed. The warden, commissioner of corrections, or other official having custody of the prisoner shall forthwith notify all appropriate prosecuting officers and courts in the several jurisdictions within the State to which the prisoner's request for final disposition is being sent of the proceeding being initiated by the prisoner. Any notification sent pursuant to this paragraph shall be accompanied by copies of the prisoner's written notice, request, and the certificate. If trial is not had on any indictment, information, or complaint contemplated hereby prior to the return of the prisoner to the original place of imprisonment, such indictment, information, or complaint shall not be of any further force or effect, and the court shall enter an order dismissing the same with prejudice.

"(e) Any request for final disposition made by a prisoner pursuant to paragraph (a) hereof shall also be deemed to be a waiver of extradition with respect to any charge or proceeding contemplated thereby or included therein by reason of paragraph (d) hereof, and a waiver of extradition to the receiving State to serve any sentence there imposed upon him after completion of his term of imprisonment in the sending State. The request for final disposition shall also constitute a consent by the prisoner to the production of his body in any court where his presence may be required in order to effectuate the purposes of this agreement and a further consent voluntarily to be returned to the original place of imprisonment in accordance with the provisions of this agreement. Nothing in this paragraph shall prevent the imposition of a concurrent sentence if otherwise permitted by law.

"(f) Escape from custody by the prisoner subsequent to his execution of the request for final disposition referred to in paragraph (a) hereof shall void the request.

"Article IV

"(a) The appropriate officer of the jurisdiction in which an untried indictment, information, or complaint is pending shall be entitled to have a prisoner against whom he has lodged a detainer and who is serving a term of imprisonment in any party State made available in accordance with article V(a) hereof upon presentation of a written request for temporary custody or availability to the appropriate authorities of the State in which the prisoner is incarcerated: Provided, That the court having jurisdiction of such indictment, information, or complaint shall have duly approved recorded, and transmitted the request: And provided further, That there shall be a period of thirty days after receipt by the appropriate authorities before the request be honored, within which period the Governor of the sending State may disapprove the request for temporary custody or availability, either upon his own motion or upon motion of the prisoner.

"(b) Upon request of the officer's written request as provided in paragraph (a) hereof, the appropriate authorities having the prisoner in custody shall furnish the officer with a certificate stating the term of commitment under which the prisoner is being held, the time already served, the time remaining to be served on the sentence, the amount of good time earned, the time of parole eligibility of the prisoner, and any decisions of the State parole agency relating to the prisoner. Said authorities simultaneously shall furnish all other officers and appropriate courts in the receiving State who has lodged detainers against the prisoner with similar certificates and with notices informing them of the request for custody or availability and of the reasons therefor.

"(c) In respect of any proceeding made possible by this article, trial shall be commenced within one hundred and twenty days of the arrival of the prisoner in the receiving State but for good cause shown in open court, the prisoner or his counsel being present, the court having jurisdiction of the matter may grant any necessary or reasonable continuance.

"(d) Nothing contained in this article. shall be construed to deprive any prisoner of any right which he may have to contest the legality of his delivery as provided in paragraph (a) hereof, but such delivery may not be opposed or denied on the ground that the executive authority of the sending State has not affirmatively consented to or ordered such delivery.

"(e) If trial is not had on any indictment, information, or complaint contemplated hereby prior to the prisoner's being returned to the original place of imprisonment pursuant to article V(e) hereof, such indictment, information, or complaint shall not be of any further fore or effect, and the court shall enter an order dismissing the same with prejudice.

"Article V

"(a) In response to a request made under article III or article IV hereof, the appropriate authority in it sending State shall offer to deliver temporary custody of such prisoner to the appropriate authority in the State Where such indictment, information, or complaint is pending against such person in order that speedy and efficient prosecution may be had. If the request for final disposition is made by the prisoner, the offer of temporary custody shall accompany the written notice provided for in article III of this agreement. In the case of a

Federal prisoner, the appropriate authority in the receiving State shall be entitled to temporary custody as provided by this agreement or to the prisoner's presence in Federal custody at the place of trial, whichever custodial arrangement may be approved by the custodian.

"(b) The officer or other representative of a State accepting an offer of temporary custody shall present the following upon demand:

"(1) Proper identification and evidence of his authority to act for the State into whose temporary custody this prisoner is to be given.

"(2) A duly certified copy of the indictment, information, or complaint on the basis of which the detainer has been lodged and on the basis of which the request for temporary custody of the prisoner has been made.

"(c) If the appropriate authority shall refuse or fail to accept temporary custody of said person, or in the event that an action on the indictment, information, or complaint on the basis of which the detainer has been lodged is not brought to trial within the period provided in article III or article IV hereof, the appropriate court of the jurisdiction where the indictment, information, or complaint has been pending shall enter an order dismissing the same with prejudice, and any detainer based thereon shall cease to be of any force or effect.

"(d) The temporary custody referred to in this agreement shall be only for the purpose of permitting prosecution on the charge or charges contained in one or more untried indictments, informations or complaints which form the basis of the detainer or detainers or for prosecution on any other charge or charges arising out of the same transaction. Except for his attendance at court and while being transported to or from any place at which his presence may be required, the prisoner shall be held in a suitable jail or other facility regularly used for persons awaiting prosecution.

"(e) At the earliest practicable time consonant with the purposes of this agreement, the prisoner shall be returned to the sending State.

"(f) During the continuance of temporary custody or while the prisoner is otherwise being made available for trial as required by this agreement, time being served on the sentence shall continue to rim but good time shall be earned by the prisoner only if, and to the extent that, the law and practice of the jurisdiction which imposed the sentence may allow.

"(g) For all purposes other than that for which temporary custody as provided in this agreement is exercised, the prisoner shall be deemed to remain in the custody of and subject to the jurisdiction of the sending State and any escape from temporary custody may be dealt with in the same manner as an escape from the original place of imprisonment or in any other manner permitted by law.

"(h) From the time that a party State receives custody of a prisoner pursuant to this agreement until such prisoner is returned to the territory and custody of the sending State, the State in which the one or more untried indictments informations, or complaints are pending or in which trial is being had shall be responsible for the prisoner and shall also pay all costs of transporting, caring for, keeping, and returning the prisoner. The provisions of this paragraph shall govern unless the States concerned shall have entered into a supplementary agreement providing for a different allocation of costs and responsibilities as between or among themselves. Nothing herein contained shall be construed to alter or affect any internal relationship among the departments, agencies, and officers of and in the government of a party State, or between a party State and its subdivisions, as to the payment of costs, or responsibilities therefor.

"Article VI

"(a) In determining the duration and expiration dates of the time periods provided in articles III and IV of this agreement, the running of said time periods shall be tolled whenever and for as long as the prisoner is unable to stand trial, as determined by the court having jurisdiction of the matter.

"(b) No provision of this agreement, and no remedy made

available by this agreement shall apply to any person who is adjudged to be mentally ill.

"Article VII

"Each State party to this agreement shall designate an officer who, acting jointly with like officers of other party States shall promulgate rules and regulations to carry out more effectively the terms and provisions of this agreement, and who shall provide, within and without the State, information necessary to the effective operation of this agreement.

"Article VIII

"This agreement shall enter into full force and effect as to a party State when such State has enacted the same into law. A State party to this agreement may withdraw herefrom by enacting a statute repealing the same. However, the withdrawal of any State shall not affect the status of any proceedings already initiated by inmates or by State officers at the time such withdrawal takes effect, nor shall it affect their rights in respect thereof.

"Article IX

"This agreement shall be liberally construed so as to effectuate its purposes. The provisions of this agreement shall be severable and if any phrase, clause, sentence, or provision of this agreement is declared to be contrary to the constitution of any party State or of the United States or the applicability' thereof to any government, agency, person, or circumstance is held invalid the validity of the remainder of this agreement and the applicability thereof to any government, agency, person or circumstance shall not be affected thereby. If this agreement shall be held contrary to the constitution of any State party hereto, the agreement shall remain in full force and effect as to the remaining States and in full force and effect as to the State affected as to all severable matters."

Sec. 3. The term "Governor" as used in the agreement on detainers shall mean with respect to the United States, the Attorney General, and with respect to the District of Columbia, the Commissioner of the District of Columbia.

Sec. 4. The term "appropriate court" as used in the agreement on detainers shall mean with respect to the United States, the courts of the United States, and with respect to the District of Columbia, the courts of the District of Columbia, in which indictments, informations, or complaints, for which disposition is sought, are pending.

Sec. 5. All courts, departments, agencies officers, and employees of the United States and of the District of Columbia are hereby directed to enforce the agreement on detainers and to cooperate with one another and with all party States in enforcing the agreement and effectuating its purpose.

Sec. 6. For the United States, the Attorney General, and for the District of Columbia, the Commissioner of the District of Columbia, shall establish such regulations, prescribe such forms, issue such instructions, and perform such other acts as he deems necessary for carrying out the provisions of this Act.

Sec. 7. The right to alter, amend, or repeal this Act is expressly reserved.

Sec. 8. This Act shall take effect on the ninetieth day after the date of its enactment.

APPENDIX M:
List of Interstate Compacts

The National Center for Interstate Compacts of the Council of State Governments has compiled the following list of 196 interstate compacts believed to be currently in force. The National Center for Interstate Compacts (NCIC) is designed to be an information clearinghouse, a provider of training and technical assistance, and a primary facilitator in assisting states in their review, revision, and creation of new interstate compacts to solve multi-state problems or, provide alternatives to federal preemption. As such, the NCIC combines policy research and best practices, and functions as a membership association, serving the needs of compact administrators, compact commissions, and state agencies where interstate compacts are in effect.

For additional information on the National Center for Interstate Compacts (NCIC), contact John Mountjoy, Director of the National Center for Interstate Compacts at 859-244-8256 or jmountjoy@csg.org. The web address of NCIC is http://www.csg.org/CSG/Programs/National+Center+for+I nterstate+Compacts/default.htm. The web address of the Council of state governments is http://www.csg.org.

LIST OF INTERSTATE COMPACTS
- Apalachicola-Chattahoochee-Flint River Basin Compact,
- Alabama-Coosa-Tallapossa River Basin Compact,
- Animas-La Plata Project Compact,
- Appalachian States Low-Level Radioactive Waste Compact,
- Arkansas-Mississippi Great River Bridge Construction Compact Arkansas,
- Arkansas River Basin Compact of 1970,
- Arkansas River Compact of 1949,

- Arkansas River Compact of 1965 (Arkansas River Basin Compact, Kansas, Oklahoma),
- Atlantic States Marine Fisheries Compact Delaware,
- Bay State–Ocean State Compact,
- Bear River Compact,
- Belle Fourche River Compact,
- Chesapeake Bay Commission Agreement (Bi/Tri-State Agreement on the Chesapeake Bay) – Chesapeake Bay Commission,
- Bi-State Criminal Justice Center Compact Arkansas,
- Bi-State Development Agency Compact Missouri (Bi-State Metropolitan District),
- Boating Offense Compact,
- Breaks Interstate Park Compact,
- Buffalo and Fort Erie Bridge Compact New York,
- Bus Taxation Proration and Reciprocity Agreement,
- California-Nevada Compact for Jurisdiction on Interstate Waters,
- Canadian River Compact – Canadian River Compact Commission,
- Central Interstate Low-Level Radioactive Waste Compact – Central Interstate Low-Level Radioactive Waste Commission,
- Central Midwest Low-Level Radioactive Waste Compact,
- Chesapeake Regional Olympic Games Authority,
- Chickasaw Trail Economic Development Compact,
- Colorado River Compact,
- Colorado River Crime Enforcement Compact (Interstate Compact for Jurisdiction on the Colorado River),
- Columbia River Compact (Oregon-Washington Columbia River Fish Compact),
- (Columbia River Gorge Compact) – Columbia River Gorge Commission,
- Compact for Pension Portability for Educators,
- (Connecticut–New York) Railroad Passenger Transportation Compact,
- Connecticut River Atlantic Salmon Compact – Connecticut River Atlantic Salmon Compact Commission,
- Connecticut River Valley Flood Control Compact,
- Costilla Creek Compact Colorado,
- Cumberland Gap National Park Compact Virginia,

- Cumbres and Toltec Scenic Railroad Compact,
- Delaware River and Bay Authority Compact (Delaware–New Jersey Compact),
- Delaware River Basin Compact – Delaware River Basin Commission,
- Delaware River Joint Toll Bridge Compact,
- Delaware River and Port Authority Compact – Delaware River Port Authority,
- Delaware Valley Urban Area Compact – Delaware Valley Regional Planning Commission,
- Delmarva Advisory Council Agreement Virginia,
- Desert Pacific Economic Region Compact
- Drivers' License Compact–American Association of Motor Vehicle Administrators,
- Emergency Management Assistance Compact,
- Great Lakes Basin Compact Indiana – Great Lakes Basin Commission,
- Great Lakes Forest Fire Compact – Great Lakes Forest Fire Compact Board,
- Gulf States Marine Fisheries Compact,
- Historic Chattahoochee Compact,
- International Registration Plan,
- International Fuel Tax Agreement (Motor Carriers),
- Interpleader Compact,
- Interstate Adoption Assistance Compact,
- (Interstate) Agreement on Qualification of Educational Personnel,
- (Interstate) Civil Defense (and Disaster Compact),
- (Interstate) Compact for (on) Adoption and Medical Assistance,
- Interstate Compact for Adult Offender Supervision,
- (Interstate) Compact for Education (Compact) – Education Commission of the States,
- (Interstate) Compact(s) on Parole and Probation (the Supervision of Parolees and Probationers) (for the Supervision of) (Interstate Compact for Supervision of Parolees and Probationers),
- (Interstate) Civil Defense (and Disaster) Compact,
- Interstate Compact on Energy (Midwest Energy Compact),
- Interstate Compact on Industrialized/Modular Buildings,

- Interstate Compact on Juveniles – Association of Juvenile Compact Administrators,
- Interstate Compact on Licensure of Participants in Live Racing with Parimutuel Wagering,
- Interstate (Compact on) Pest Control Compact – Interstate Pest Control Governing Board,
- (Interstate) Compact on (The) Placement of Children,
- Interstate (Compact to Conserve) Oil and Gas Compact Illinois – Interstate Oil and Gas Compact Commission,
- Interstate Corrections Compact,
- Interstate Dealer Licensing Compact,
- Interstate Earthquake Emergency Compact,
- Interstate Forest Fire Suppression Compact,
- Interstate Furlough Compact Utah,
- Interstate High Speed Intercity Rail Passenger Network Compact/Interstate High Speed Rail Compact,
- Interstate Insurance Receivership Compact,
- Interstate Jobs Protection Compact,
- Interstate Library Compact,
- Interstate Mining Compact – Interstate Mining Compact Commission,
- (Interstate) Mutual Aid (Agreements) Compact,
- Interstate Rail Passenger Network Compact,
- Interstate Solid Waste Compact,
- (Interstate) (Uniform) Agreement on Detainers (Interstate Compact on),
- Interstate Water Supply Compact (Vermont-New Hampshire),
- (Interstate) Wildlife Violator Compact,
- Jennings Randolph Lake Project Compact,
- Kansas City Area Transportation District and Authority Compact,
- Kansas-Missouri Flood Prevention and Control Compact Missouri,
- (Kansas/Nebraska) Big Blue River Compact,
- Klamath River Compact,
- La Plata River Compact,
- Low-Level Radioactive Waste Disposal,

- Live Horseracing Compact (the Interstate Compact on Licensure of Participants in Horse Racing with Pari-Mutuel Wagering),
- Maine-New Hampshire School District Compact,
- Mentally Disordered Offender Compact,
- Middle Atlantic (Interstate) Forest Fire Protection Compact,
- Midwestern Higher Education Compact – Midwestern Higher Education Commission,
- Midwest Interstate Passenger Rail Compact,
- Midwest Interstate Low-Level Radioactive Waste Compact,
- Minnesota-Wisconsin Boundary (Area) Compact,
- Mississippi River Interstate Pollution Phase Out Compact,
- Missouri And Kansas Metropolitan Culture District Compact,
- Missouri River Toll Bridge Compact,
- Motor Vehicle Safety Equipment Compact,
- Multistate Highway Transportation Agreement,
- Multistate Lottery Agreement
- Multistate Tax Compact–the Multistate Tax Commission,
- Mutual Interstate Aid Agreements and Compacts,
- Mutual/Military Aid Compact,
- National Crime Prevention and Privacy Compact,
- National Guard Mutual Assistance Compact,
- National Guard Mutual Assistance Counter-Drug Activities Compact,
- New England Compact on Radiological Health Protection,
- New England Compact on Involuntary Detention for Tuberculosis Control,
- New England (Interstate) Corrections Compact,
- New England Higher Education Compact – New England Board of Higher Education,
- New England Interstate Water Pollution Control Compact – New England Interstate Water Pollution Control Commission,
- New England States Emergency Military Aid Compact,
- New England (State) Police Compact Massachusetts,
- New England Truckers Compact,
- New England Truck Permit Agreement for Oversize, Non-Divisible, Interstate Loads,

- New Hampshire–Massachusetts Interstate Sewage and Waste Disposal Facilities Compact,
- New Hampshire-Vermont Interstate School Compact (Hanover-Norwich District),
- New Hampshire-Vermont Interstate Sewage And Waste Disposal Facilities Compact,
- New Jersey–Pennsylvania Turnpike Bridge Compact,
- New York–New Jersey Port Authority Compact – The Port Authority of New York & New Jersey,
- New York-Vermont Interstate School Compact,
- Nonresident Violator Compact – American Association of Motor Vehicle Administrators,
- Northern New England Low-Level Radioactive Waste Compact,
- Northeast Interstate Dairy Compact,
- Northeast Interstate Low-Level Radioactive Waste Management Compact,
- Northeast Mississippi – Northwest Alabama Railroad Authority Compact,
- Northeastern (Interstate) Forest Fire Protection Compact – Northeastern Forest Fire Protection Commission,
- Northeast Interstate Dairy Compact – Northeast Interstate Dairy Compact Committee,
- Northeast Interstate Low-Level Radioactive Waste Management Compact,
- Northwest (Interstate) Compact on Low-Level Radioactive Waste Management,
- Nurse Licensure Compact,
- Ogdensburg Bridge and Port Authority,
- Ohio River Valley Water Sanitation Compact – Ohio River Valley Sanitation Commission,
- Out-of-State Parollee Supervision,
- Pacific Marine Fisheries Compact – Pacific States Marine Fisheries Commission,
- Pacific Ocean Resources Compact,
- Pacific States Agreement on Radioactive Materials Transportation,
- Palisades Interstate Park Compact New Jersey – Palisades Interstate Park Commission,

- Pecos River Compact Texas – Pecos River Compact Commission,
- Portsmouth-Kittery Bridge Compact,
- Potomac Highlands Airport Authority,
- Potomac River Bridges Towing Compact,
- Potomac River Compact of 1958,
- Potomac Valley Compact (Conservancy District) (Potomac River Basin Interstate Compact of 1940),
- Pymatuning Lake Compact,
- Quad Cities Interstate Metropolitan Authority Compact,
- Red River Compact – Red River Compact Commission,
- Republican River Compact,
- Rio Grande Interstate Compact – Rio Grande Compact Commission,
- Rocky Mountain Low-Level Radioactive Waste Compact,
- Sabine River Compact,
- Snake River Compact,
- South Central (Interstate) Forest Fire Protection Compact,
- South Platte River Compact,
- Southern Dairy Compact,
- Southern Growth Policies (Agreements) (Board) (Compact) – Southern Growth Policies Board,
- Southern (Interstate) (Energy) (Nuclear) Compact (Southern States Energy Compact),
- Southeastern (Interstate) Forest Fire Protection Compact,
- Southeast Interstate Low-Level Radioactive Waste (Management) Compact – Southeast Interstate Low-Level Radioactive
- Waste Commission,
- (Southern) Rapid Rail Transit Compact (Mississippi-Louisiana-Alabama-Georgia Rapid Rail Transit Compact),
- Southern Regional Education Compact – Southern Regional Education Board,
- Southwestern Low-Level Radioactive Waste Disposal Compact,
- Susquehanna River Basin Compact – Susquehanna River Basin Commission,
- Tahoe Regional Planning Compact,
- Tangipahoa River Waterway Compact,

- Taxation of Motor Fuels Consumed by Interstate Buses,
- Tennessee-Tombigbee Waterway Development Compact Compact – Tennessee Tombigbee Waterway Development Authority,
- Tennessee Interstate Furlough Compact,
- (Texas) Low-Level Radioactive Waste Disposal Compact,
- (The) Interstate Compact on Agricultural Grain Marketing,
- (The) (Interstate) Compact on Mental Health,
- Thames River Flood Control Compact,
- Tri-State Agreement on the Chesapeake Bay,
- Tri-State Delta Economic Compact,
- Tri-State Lotto Compact,
- Tri-State Sanitation Compact (Interstate Environmental Commission, Tri-State Compact),
- Tuberculosis Control Compact,
- Unclaimed (Abandoned or Uniform) Property Compact (Act) (Uniform Disposition of Unclaimed Property Act),
- Upper Colorado River Basin Compact,
- Upper Niobrara River Compact,
- Vehicle Equipment Safety Compact – American Association of Motor Vehicle Administrators,
- Wabash Valley Compact,
- Washington Metropolitan Area Transit Authority – Washington Metropolitan Area Transit Authority,
- Washington Metropolitan Area Transit District,
- Waterfront Commission Compact,
- Western (Interstate) Corrections Compact,
- Western Interstate Nuclear (Energy) (Cooperation) Compact,
- Western Regional (Higher) Education Compact – Western Interstate Commission for Higher Education,
- Wheeling Creek Watershed Protection and Flood Prevention Compact,
- Woodrow Wilson Bridge and Tunnel Compact, and
- Yellowstone River Compact.

The above information is reprinted here with the kind permission of the National Center for Interstate Compacts.

APPENDIX N:
Congressional Consent to the Emergency Management Assistance Compact

PUBLIC LAW 104-321 OF 1996

JOINT RESOLUTION
Granting the consent of Congress to
the Emergency Management Assistance Compact

Resolved by the Senate and House of Representatives of the United States of America in Congress assembled,

SECTION 1. CONGRESSIONAL CONSENT.

The Congress consents to the Emergency Management Assistance Compact entered into by Delaware, Florida, Georgia, Louisiana, Maryland, Mississippi, Missouri, Oklahoma, South Carolina, South Dakota, Tennessee, Virginia, and West Virginia. The compact reads substantially as follows:

"Emergency Management Assistance Compact

"ARTICLE I.
"PURPOSE AND AUTHORITIES.

"This compact is made and entered into by and between the participating member states which enact this compact, hereinafter called party states. For the purposes of this compact, the term 'states' is taken to mean the several states, the Commonwealth of Puerto Rico, the District of Columbia, and all U.S. territorial possessions.

"The purpose of this compact is to provide for mutual assistance between the states entering into this compact in managing any emergency disaster that is duly declared by the Governor of the affected state, whether arising from natural disaster, technological hazard, man-made disaster, civil emergency aspects of resources shortages, community disorders, insurgency, or enemy attack.

"This compact shall also provide for mutual cooperation in emergency-related exercises, testing, or other training activities using equipment and personnel simulating performance of any aspect of the giving and receiving of aid by party states or subdivisions of party states during emergencies, such actions occurring outside actual declared emergency periods. Mutual assistance in this compact may include the use of the states' National Guard forces, either in accordance with the National Guard Mutual Assistance Compact or by mutual agreement between states.

"ARTICLE II.
"GENERAL IMPLEMENTATION.

"Each party state entering into this compact recognizes that many emergencies transcend political jurisdictional boundaries and that intergovernmental coordination is essential in managing these and other emergencies under this compact. Each state further recognizes that there will be emergencies which require immediate access and present procedures to apply outside resources to make a prompt and effective response to such an emergency. This is because few, if any, individual states have all the resources they may need in all types of emergencies or the capability of delivering resources to areas where emergencies exist.

"The prompt, full, and effective utilization of resources of the participating states, including any resources on hand or available from the federal government or any other source, that are essential to the safety, care, and welfare of the people in the event of any emergency or disaster declared by a party state, shall be the underlying principle on which all articles of this compact shall be understood.

"On behalf of the Governor of each state participating in the compact, the legally designated state official who is assigned responsibility for emergency management will be responsible for formulation of the appropriate interstate mutual aid plans and procedures necessary to implement this compact.

"ARTICLE III.

"PARTY STATE RESPONSIBILITIES.

"A. It shall be the responsibility of each party state to formulate procedural plans and programs for interstate cooperation in the performance of the responsibilities listed in this article. In formulating such plans, and in carrying them out, the party states, insofar as practical, shall:

"1. Review individual state hazards analyses and, to the extent reasonably possible, determine all those potential emergencies the party states might jointly suffer, whether due to natural disaster, technological hazard, man-made disaster, emergency aspects of resources shortages, civil disorders, insurgency, or enemy attack;

"2. Review party states' individual emergency plans and develop a plan which will determine the mechanism for the interstate management and provision of assistance concerning any potential emergency;

"3. Develop interstate procedures to fill any identified gaps and to resolve any identified inconsistencies or overlaps in existing or developed plans;

"4. Assist in warning communities adjacent to or crossing the state boundaries;

"5. Protect and assure uninterrupted delivery of services, medicines, water, food, energy and fuel, search and rescue, and critical lifeline equipment, services, and resources, both human and material;

"6. Inventory and set procedures for the interstate loan and delivery of human and material resources, together with procedures for reimbursement or forgiveness; and

"7. Provide, to the extent authorized by law, for temporary suspension of any statutes or ordinances that restrict the implementation of the above responsibilities.

"B. The authorized representative of a party state may

request assistance to another party state by contacting the authorized representative of that state. The provisions of this compact shall only apply to requests for assistance made by and to authorized representatives. Requests may be verbal or in writing. If verbal, the request shall be confirmed in writing within thirty days of the verbal request. Requests shall provide the following information:

"1. A description of the emergency service function for which assistance is needed, including, but not limited to, fire services, law enforcement, emergency medical, transportation, communications, public works and engineering, building, inspection, planning and information assistance, mass care, resource support, health and medical services, and search and rescue;

"2. The amount and type of personnel, equipment, materials and supplies needed, and a reasonable estimate of the length of time they will be needed; and

"3. The specific place and time for staging of the assisting party's response and a point of contact at that location.

"C. There shall be frequent consultation between state officials who have assigned emergency management responsibilities and other appropriate representatives of the party states with affected jurisdictions and the United States Government, with free exchange of information, plans, and resource records relating to emergency capabilities.

"ARTICLE IV.

"LIMITATIONS.

"Any party state requested to render mutual aid or conduct exercises and training for mutual aid shall take such action as is necessary to provide and make available the resources covered by this compact in accordance with the terms hereof; provided that it is understood that the state rendering aid may withhold resources to the extent necessary to provide reasonable protection for such state.

"Each party state shall afford to the emergency forces of any party state, while operating within its state limits under the terms and conditions of this compact, the same powers, except that of arrest unless specifically authorized by the receiving state, duties, rights, and privileges as are afforded forces of the state in which they are performing emergency services. Emergency forces will continue under the command and control of their regular leaders, but the organizational units will come under the operational control of the emergency services authorities of the state receiving assistance. These conditions may be activated, as needed, only subsequent to a declaration of a state emergency or disaster by the governor of the party state that is to receive assistance or upon commencement of exercises or training for mutual aid and shall continue so long as the exercises or training for mutual aid are in progress, the state of emergency or disaster remains in effect, or loaned resources remain in the receiving state, whichever is longer.

"ARTICLE V.
"LICENSES AND PERMITS.
"Whenever any person holds a license, certificate, or other permit issued by any state party to the compact evidencing the meeting of qualifications for professional, mechanical, or other skills, and when such assistance is requested by the receiving party state, such person shall be deemed licensed, certified, or permitted by the state requesting assistance to render aid involving such skill to meet a declared emergency or disaster, subject to such limitations and conditions as the Governor of the requesting state may prescribe by executive order or otherwise.

"ARTICLE VI.
"LIABILITY.
"Officers or employees of a party state rendering aid in another state pursuant to this compact shall be considered agents of the requesting state for tort liability and immunity purposes. No party state or its officers or employees rendering aid in another state pursuant to this compact shall be liable on account of any act or omission in good faith on the part of such forces while so engaged or on account of the mainte-

nance or use of any equipment or supplies in connection therewith. Good faith in this article shall not include willful misconduct, gross negligence, or recklessness.

"ARTICLE VII.

"SUPPLEMENTARY AGREEMENTS.

"Inasmuch as it is probable that the pattern and detail of the machinery for mutual aid among two or more states may differ from that among the states that are party hereto, this compact contains elements of a broad base common to all states, and nothing herein shall preclude any state entering into supplementary agreements with another state or affect any other agreements already in force between states. Supplementary agreements may comprehend, but shall not be limited to, provisions for evacuation and reception of injured and other persons and the exchange of medical, fire, police, public utility, reconnaissance, welfare, transportation and communications personnel, and equipment and supplies.

"ARTICLE VIII.

"COMPENSATION.

"Each party state shall provide for the payment of compensation and death benefits to injured members of the emergency forces of that state and representatives of deceased members of such forces in case such members sustain injuries or are killed while rendering aid pursuant to this compact, in the same manner and on the same terms as if the injury or death were sustained within their own state.

"ARTICLE IX.

"REIMBURSEMENT.

"Any party state rendering aid in another state pursuant to this compact shall be reimbursed by the party state receiving such aid for any loss or damage to or expense incurred in the operation of any equipment and the provision of any service in answering a request for aid and for the costs incurred in connection with such requests; provided, that any aiding party state may assume in whole or in part such loss, damage, expense, or other cost, or may loan such equipment or donate such services to the receiving party state without charge or cost; and provided further, that any two or more party states may enter into supplementary agreements establishing a different allocation of costs among those states. Article VIII expenses shall not be reimbursable under this article.

"ARTICLE X.

"EVACUATION.

"Plans for the orderly evacuation and interstate reception of portions of the civilian population as the result of any emergency or disaster of sufficient proportions to so warrant, shall be worked out and maintained between the party states and the emergency management/services directors of the various jurisdictions where any type of incident requiring evacuations might occur. Such plans shall be put into effect by request of the state from which evacuees come and shall include the manner of transporting such evacuees, the number of evacuees to be received in different areas, the manner in which food, clothing, housing, and medical care will be provided, the registration of the evacuees, the providing of facilities for the notification of relatives or friends, and the forwarding of such evacuees to other areas or the bringing in of additional materials, supplies, and all other relevant factors. Such plans shall provide that the party state receiving evacuees and the party state from which the evacuees come shall mutually agree as to reimbursement of out-of-pocket expenses incurred in receiving and caring for such evacuees, for expenditures for transportation, food, clothing, medicines, and medical care, and like items. Such expenditures shall be reimbursed as agreed by the party state from which the evacuees come. After the termination of the emergency or disaster, the party state from which the evacuees come shall assume the responsibility for the ultimate support of repatriation of such evacuees.

"ARTICLE XI.

"IMPLEMENTATION.

"A. This compact shall become effective immediately upon its Effective date. enactment into law by any two states. Thereafter, this compact shall become effective as to any other state upon enactment by such state.

"B. Any party state may withdraw from this compact by enacting a statute repealing the same, but no such withdrawal shall take effect until thirty days after the Governor of the withdrawing state has given notice in writing of such withdrawal to the Governors of all other party states. Such action shall not relieve the withdrawing state from obligations assumed hereunder prior to the effective date of withdrawal.

"C. Duly authenticated copies of this compact and of such supplementary agreements as may be entered into shall, at the time of their approval, be deposited with each of the party states and with the Federal Emergency Management Agency and other appropriate agencies of the United States Government.

"ARTICLE XII.

"VALIDITY.

"This compact shall be construed to effectuate the purposes stated in Article I. If any provision of this compact is declared unconstitutional, or the applicability thereof to any person or circumstances is held invalid, the constitutionality of the remainder of this compact and the applicability thereof to other persons and circumstances shall not be affected.

"ARTICLE XIII.

"ADDITIONAL PROVISIONS.

"Nothing in this compact shall authorize or permit the use of military force by the National Guard of a state at any place outside that state in any emergency for which the President is authorized by law to call into federal service the militia, or for any purpose for which the use of the Army or the Air Force would in the absence of express statutory authorization be prohibited under § 1385 of Title 18 of the United States Code.".

SEC. 2. RIGHT TO ALTER, AMEND, OR REPEAL.

The right to alter, amend, or repeal this joint resolution is hereby expressly reserved. The consent granted by this joint resolution shall-

  (1) not be construed as impairing or in any manner affecting any right or jurisdiction of the United States in and over the subject of the compact;

  (2) not be construed as consent to the National Guard Mutual Assistance Compact;

  (3) be construed as understanding that the first paragraph of Article II of the compact provides that emergencies will require procedures to provide immediate access to existing resources to make a prompt and effective response;

  (4) not be construed as providing authority in Article III A. 7. that does not otherwise exist for the suspension of statutes or ordinances;

  (5) be construed as understanding that Article III C. does not impose any affirmative obligation to exchange information, plans, and resource records on the United States or any party which has not entered into the compact; and

  (6) be construed as understanding that Article XIII does not affect the authority of the President over the National Guard provided by article I of the Constitution and title 10 of the United States Code.

SEC. 3. CONSTRUCTION AND SEVERABILITY.

It is intended that the provisions of this compact shall be reasonably and liberally construed to effectuate the purposes thereof. If any part or application of this compact, or legislation enabling the compact, is held invalid, the remainder of the compact or its application to other situations or persons shall not be affected.

SEC. 4. INCONSISTENCY OF LANGUAGE.

The validity of this compact shall not be affected by any insubstantial difference in its form or language as adopted by the States.

APPENDIX O:
U. S. Supreme Court Decision in *McPherson v. Blacker* (1892)

U.S. SUPREME COURT
146 U.S. 1
McPherson et al. v. Blacker, Secretary of State
No. 1,170
October 17, 1892

Statement by Mr. Chief Justice FULLER:

William McPherson, Jr., Jay A. Hubbell, J. Henry Carstens, Charles E. Hiscock, Otto Ihling, Philip T. Colgrove, Conrad G. Swensburg, Henry A. Haigh, James H. White, Fred. Slocum, Justus S. Stearns, John Millen, Julius T. Hannah, and J. H. Comstock filed their petition and affidavits in the supreme court of the state of Michigan on May 2, 1892, as nominees for presidential electors, against Robert R. Blacker, secretary of state of Michigan, praying that the court declare the act of the legislature, approved May 1, 1891, (Act No. 50, Pub. Acts Mich. 1891,) entitled "An act to provide for the election of electors of president and vice president of the United States, and to repeal all other acts and parts of acts in conflict herewith," void and of no effect, and that a writ of mandamus be directed to be issued to the said secretary of state, commanding him to cause to be delivered to the sheriff of each county in the state, between the 1st of July and the 1st of September, 1892, "a notice in writing that at the next general election in this state, to be held on Tuesday, the 8th day of November, 1892, there will be chosen (among other officers to be named in said notice) as many electors of president and vice president of the United States as this state may be entitled to elect senators and representatives in the congress."

The statute of Michigan (1 How. Ann. St. Mich. 147, c. 9, p. 133) provided: "The secretary of the state shall, between the 1st day of July and the 1st day of September preceding a general election, direct and cause to be delivered to the sheriff of each county in this state a notice in writing that, at the next general election, there will be chosen as many of the following officers as are to be elected at such general election, viz.: A governor, lieutenant governor, secretary of state, state treasurer, auditor general, attorney general, superintendent of public instruction, commissioner of state land office, members of the state board of education, electors of president and vice president of the United States, and a representative in congress for the district to which each of such counties shall belong."

A rule to show cause having been issued, the respondent, as secretary of state, answered the petition, and denied that he had refused to give the notice thus required, but he said "that it has always been the custom in the office of the secretary of state, in giving notices under said section 147, to state in the notice the number of electors that should be printed on the ticket in each voting precinct in each county in this state, and following such custom with reference to such notice, it is the intention of this respondent in giving notice under section 147 to state in said notice that there will be elected one presidential elector at large and one district presidential elector and two alternate presidential electors, one for the elector at large and one for the district presidential elector, in each voting precinct, so that the election may be held under and in accordance with the provisions of Act No. 50 of the Public Acts of the state of Michigan of 1891."

By an amended answer the respondent claimed the same benefit as if he had demurred.

Relators relied in their petition upon various grounds as invalidating Act No. 50 of the Public Acts of Michigan of 1891, and, among them, that the act was void because in conflict with clause 2 of section 1 of article 2 of the constitution of the United States, and with the fourteenth amendment to that instrument, and also in some of its provisions in conflict with the act of congress of February 3, 1887, entitled "An act to fix the day for the meeting of the electors of president and vice president, and to provide for and regulate the counting of the votes for president and vice president, and the decision of questions arising thereon." The supreme court of Michigan unanimously held that none of the objections urged against the validity of the act were tenable; that it did not conflict with clause 2, 1, art. 2, of the constitution, or with the fourteenth amendment thereof; and that the law was only inoperative so far as in conflict with the law of congress in a matter in reference to which congress had the right to legislate. The opinion of the court will be found reported, in advance of the official series, in 52 N. W. Rep. 469.

Judgment was given, June 17, 1892, denying the writ of mandamus, whereupon a writ of error was allowed to this court.

The October term, 1892, commenced on Monday, October 10th, and on Tuesday, October 11th, the first day upon which the application could be made, a motion to advance the case was submitted by counsel, granted at once in view of the exigency disclosed upon the face of the papers, and the cause heard that day. The attention of the court having been called to other provisions of the election laws of Michigan than those supposed to be immediately involved, (Act No. 190, Pub. Acts Mich. 1891, pp. 258, 263,) the chief justice, on Monday, October 17th, announced the conclusions of the court, and directed the entry of judgment affirming the judgment of the supreme court of Michigan, and ordering the mandate to issue at once, it being stated that this was done because immediate action under the state statutes was apparently required and might be affected by delay, but it was added that the court would thereafter file an opinion stating fully the grounds of the decision.

Act No. 50 of the Public Acts of 1891 of Michigan is as follows:

"An act to provide for the election of electors of president and vice president of the United States, and to repeal all other acts and parts of acts in conflict herewith.

"*Section 1.* The people of the state of Michigan enact that, at the general election next preceding the choice of president and vice president of the United States, there shall be elected as many electors of president and vice president as this state may be entitled to elect of senators and representatives in congress in the following manner, that is to say: There shall be elected by the electors of the districts hereinafter defined one elector of president and vice president of the United States in each district, who shall be known and designated on the ballot, respectively, as 'eastern district elector of president and vice president of the United States at large,' and 'western district elector of president and vice president of the United States at large.' There shall also be elected, in like manner, two alternate electors of president and vice president, who shall be known and designated on the ballot as 'eastern district alternate elector of president and vice president of the United States at large,' and 'western district alternate elector of president and vice president of the United States at large;' for which purpose the first, second, sixth, seventh, eighth, and tenth congressional districts shall compose one district, to be known as the 'Eastern Electoral District,' and the third, fourth, fifth, ninth, eleventh, and twelfth congressional districts shall compose the other district, to be known as the 'Western Electoral District.' There shall also be elected, by the electors in each congressional district into which the state is or shall be divided, one electors of president and vice president, and one alternate elector of president and vice president, the ballots for which shall designate the number of the congressional district and the persons to be voted for therein, as 'district elector' and 'alternate district elector' of president and vice president of the United States, respectively.

"*Sec. 2.* The counting, canvassing, and certifying of the votes cast for said electors at large and their alternates, and said district electors and their alternates, shall be done as near as may be in the same manner as is now provided by law for the election of electors or president and vice president of the United States.

"*Sec. 3.* The secretary of state shall prepare three lists of the names of the electors and the alternate electors, procure thereto the signature of the governor, affix the seal of the state to the same, and deliver such certificates thus signed and sealed to one of the electors, on or before the first Wednesday of December next following said general election. In case of death, disability, refusal to act, or neglect to attend, by the hour of twelve o'clock at noon of said day, of either of said electors at large, the duties of the office shall be performed by the alternate electors at large, that is to say: The eastern district alternate elector at large shall supply the place of the eastern district elector at large, and the western district alternate elector at large shall supply the place of the western district elector at large. In like case, the alternate congressional district elector shall supply the place of the congressional district elector. In case two or more persons have an equal and the highest number of votes for any office created by this act as canvassed by the board of state canvassers, the legislature in joint convention shall choose one of said persons to fill such office, and it shall be the duty of the governor to convene the legislature in special session for such purpose immediately upon such determination by said board of state canvassers.

"*Sec. 4.* The said electors of president and vice president shall convene in the senate chamber at the capital of the state at the hour of twelve o'clock at noon, on the first Wednesday of December immediately following their election, and shall proceed to perform the duties of such electors as required by the constitution and the laws of the United States. The alternate electors shall also be in attendance, but shall take no part in the proceedings, except as herein provided.

"*Sec. 5.* Each of said electors and alternate electors shall receive the sum of five dollars for each day's attendance at the meetings of the electors as above provided, and five cents per mile for the actual and necessary distance traveled each way in going to and returning from said place of meeting, the same to be paid by the state treasurer upon the allowance of the board of state auditors.

"*Sec. 6.* All acts and parts of acts in conflict with the provisions of this act are hereby repealed." Pub. Acts Mich. 1891, pp. 50, 51.

Section 211 of Howell's Annotated Statutes of Michigan (volume 1, c. 9, p. 145) reads:

"For the purpose of canvassing and ascertaining the votes given for electors of president and vice president of the United States, the board of state canvassers shall meet on the Wednesday next after the third Monday of November, or on such other day before that time as the secretary of state shall appoint; and the powers, duties, and proceedings of said board, and of the secretary of state, in sending for, examining, ascertaining, determining, certifying, and recording the votes and results of the election of such electors, shall be in all respects, as near as may be, as hereinbefore provided in relation to sending for, examining, ascertaining, determining, certifying, and recording the votes and results of the election of state officers."

Section 240 of Howell's Statutes, in force prior to May 1, 1891, provided: "At the general election next preceding the choice of president and vice president of the United States, there shall be elected by general ticket as many electors of president and vice president as this state may be entitled to elect of senators and representatives in congress."

The following are sections of article 8 of the constitution of Michigan:

"*Sec. 4.* The secretary of state, state treasurer, and commissioner of the state land office shall constitute a board of state auditors, to examine and adjust all claims against the state, not otherwise provided for by general law. They shall constitute a board of state canvassers, to determine the result of all elections for governor, lieutenant governor, and state officers, and of such other officers as shall by law be referred to them.

"*Sec. 5.* In case two or more persons have an equal and the highest number of votes for any office, as canvassed by the board of state canvassers, the legislature in joint convention shall choose one of said persons to fill such office. When the determination of the board of state canvassers is contested, the legislature in joint convention shall decide which person is elected." 1 How. Ann. St. Mich. p. 57.

Reference was also made in argument to the act of congress of February 3, 1887, to fix the day for the meeting of the electors of president and vice president, and to provide for and regulate and counting of the votes. 24 St. p. 373.

Henry M. Duffield, W. H. H. Miller, and Fred A. Baker, for plaintiff in error.

Otto Kirchner, A. A. Ellis, and John W. Champlin, for defendant in error.

Mr. Chief Justice FULLER, after stating the facts in the foregoing language, delivered the opinion of the court. The supreme court of Michigan held, in effect, that if the act in question were invalid, the proper remedy had been sought. In other words, if the court had been of opinion that the act was void, the writ of mandamus would have been awarded.

And having ruled all objections to the validity of the act urged as arising under the state constitution and laws adversely to the plaintiffs in error, the court was compelled to, and did, consider and dispose of the contention that the act was invalid because repugnant to the constitution and laws of the United States.

We are not authorized to revise the conclusions of the state court on these matters of local law, and, those conclusions being accepted, it follows that the decision of the federal questions is to be regarded as necessary to the determination of the cause. *De Saussure v. Gaillard*, 127 U.S. 216, 8 Sup. Ct. Rep. 1053.

Inasmuch as, under section 709 of the Revised Statutes of the United States, we have jurisdiction by writ of error to re-examine and reverse or affirm the final judgment in any suit in the highest court of a state in which a decision could be had, where the validity of a statute of the state is drawn in question on the ground that it is repugnant to the constitution and laws of the United States, and the decision is in favor of its validity, we perceive no reason for holding that this writ was improvidently brought.

It is argued that the subject-matter of the controversy is not of judicial cognizance, because it is said that all questions connected with the election of a presidential elector are political in their nature; that the court has no power finally to dispose of them; and that its decision would be subject to review by political officers and agencies, as the state board of canvassers, the legislature in joint convention, and the governor, or, finally, the congress.

But the judicial power of the United States extends to all cases in law or equity arising under the constitution and laws of the United States, and this is a case so arising, since the validity of the state law was drawn in question as repugnant to such constitution and laws, and its validity was sustained. *Boyd v. State*, 143 U.S. 135, 12 Sup. Ct. Rep. 375. And it matters not that the judgment to be reviewed may be rendered in a proceeding for mandamus. *Hartman v. Greenhow*, 102 U.S. 672.

As we concur with the state court, its judgment has been affirmed; if we had not, its judgment would have been reversed. In either event, the questions submitted are finally and definitely disposed of by the judgment which we pronounce, and that judgment is carried into effect by the transmission of our mandate to the state court.

The question of the validity of this act, as presented to us by this record, is a judicial question, and we cannot decline the exercise of our jurisdiction upon the inadmissible suggestion that action might be taken by political agencies in disregard of the judgment of the highest tribunal of the state, as revised by our own.

On behalf of plaintiffs in error it is contended that the act is void because in conflict with (1) clause 2, 1, art. 2, of the constitution of the United States; (2) the fourteenth and fifteenth amendments to the constitution; and (3) the act of congress, of February 3, 1887.

The second clause of section 1 of article 2 of the constitution is in these words: "Each state shall appoint, in such manner as the legislature thereof may direct, a number of electors, equal to the whole number of senators and representatives to which the state may be entitled in the congress; but no senator or representative, or person holding an office of trust or profit under the United States, shall be appointed an elector."

The manner of the appointment of electors directed by the act of Michigan is the election of an elector and an alternate elector in each of the twelve congressional districts into which the state of Michigan is divided, and of an elector and an alternate elector at large in each of two districts defined by the act. It is insisted that it was not competent for the legislature to direct this manner of appointment, because the state is to appoint as a body politic and corporate, and so must act as a unit, and cannot delegate the authority to subdivisions created for the purpose; and it is argued that the appointment of electors by districts is not an appointment by the state, because all its citizens otherwise qualified are not permitted to vote for all the presidential electors.

"A state, in the ordinary sense of the constitution," said Chief Justice Chase, (*Texas v. White*, 7 Wall. 700, 731,) "is a political community of free citizens, occupying a territory of defined boundaries, and organized under a government sanctioned and limited by a written constitution, and established by the consent of the governed." The state does not act by its people in their collective capacity, but through such political agencies as are duly constituted and established. The legislative power is the supreme authority, except as limited by the constitution of the state, and the sovereignty of the people is exercised through their representatives in the legislature, unless by the fundamental law power is elsewhere reposed. The constitution of the United States frequently refers to the state as a political community, and also in terms to the people of the several states and the citizens of each state. What is forbidden or required to be done by a state is forbidden or required of the legislative power under state constitutions as they exist. The clause under consideration does not read that the people or the citizens shall appoint, but that "each state shall;" and if the words, "in such manner as the legislature thereof may direct," had been omitted, it would seem that the legislative power of appointment could not have been successfully questioned in the absence of any provision in the state constitution in that regard. Hence the insertion of those words, while operating as a limitation upon the state in respect of any attempt to circumscribe the legislative power, cannot be held to operate as a limitation on that power itself.

If the legislature possesses plenary authority to direct the manner of appointment, and might itself exercise the appointing power by joint ballot or concurrence of the two houses, or according to such mode as designated, it is difficult to perceive why, if the legislature prescribes as a method of appointment choice by vote, it must necessarily be by general ticket, and not by districts. In other words, the act of appointment is none the less the act of the state in its entirety because arrived at by districts, for the act is the act of political agencies duly authorized to speak for the state, and the combined result is the expression of the voice of the state, a result reached by direction of the legislature, to whom the whole subject is committed.

By the first paragraph of section 2, art. 1, it is provided: "The house of representatives shall be composed of members chosen every second year by the people of the several states, and the electors in each state shall have the qualifications requisite for electors of the most numerous branch of the state legislature;" and by the third paragraph, "when vacancies happen in the representation from any state, the executive authority thereof shall issue writs of election to fill such vacancies." Section 4 reads: "The times, places, and manner of holding elections for senators and representatives shall be prescribed in each state by the legislature thereof; but the congress may at any time by law make or alter such regulations, except as to the places of choosing senators."

Although it is thus declared that the people of the several states shall choose the members of congress, (language which induced the state of New York to insert a salvo as to the power to divide into districts, in its resolutions of ratification,) the state legislatures, prior to 1842, in prescribing the times, places, and manner of holding elections for representatives, had usually apportioned the state into districts, and assigned to each a representative; and by act of congress of June 25, 1842 , (carried forward as section 23 of the Revised Statutes,) it was provided that, where a state was entitled to more than one representative, the election should be by districts. It has never been doubted that representatives in congress thus chosen represented the entire people of the state acting in their sovereign capacity.

By original clause 3, 1, art. 2, and by the twelfth amendment, which superseded that clause in case of a failure in the election of president by the people the house of representatives is to choose the president; and "the vote shall be taken by states, the representation from each state having one vote." The state acts as a unit, and its vote is given as a unit, but that vote is arrived at through the votes of its representatives in congress elected by districts.

The state also acts individually through its electoral college, although, by reason of the power of its legislature over the manner of appointment, the vote of its electors may be divided.

The constitution does not provide that the appointment of electors shall be by popular vote, nor that the electors shall be voted for upon a general ticket, nor that the majority of those who exercise the elective franchise can alone choose the electors. It recognizes that the people act through their representatives in the legislature, and leaves it to the legislature exclusively to define the method of effecting the object.

The framers of the constitution employed words in their natural sense; and, where they are plain and clear, resort to collateral aids to interpretation is unnecessary, and cannot be indulged in to narrow or enlarge the text; but where there is ambiguity or doubt, or where two views may well be entertained, contemporaneous and subsequent practical construction is entitled to the greatest weight. Certainly, plaintiffs in error cannot reasonably assert that the clause of the constitution under consideration so plainly sustains their position as to entitle them to object that contemporaneous history and practical construction are not to be allowed their legitimate force, and, conceding that their argument inspires a doubt sufficient to justify resort to the aids of interpretation thus afforded, we are of opinion that such doubt is thereby resolved against them, the contemporaneous practical exposition of the constitution being too strong and obstinate to be shaken or controlled. *Stuart v. Laird*, 1 Cranch, 299, 309.

It has been said that the word "appoint" is not the most appropriate word to describe the result of a popular election. Perhaps not; but it is sufficiently comprehensive to cover that mode, and was manifestly used as conveying the broadest power of determination. It was used in article 5 of the articles of confederation, which provided that "delegates shall be annually appointed in such manner as the legislature of each state shall direct;" and in the resolution of congress of February 21, 1787, which declared it expedient that "a convention of delegates who shall have been appointed by the several states" should be held. The appointment of delegates was, in fact, made by the legislatures directly, but that involved no denial of authority to direct some other mode. The constitutional convention, by resolution of September 17, 1787, expressed the opinion that the congress should fix a day "on which electors should be appointed by the states which shall have ratified the same," etc., and that, "after such publication, the electors should be appointed, and the senators and representatives elected."

The journal of the convention discloses that propositions that the president should be elected by "the citizens of the United States," or by the "people," or "by electors to be chosen by the people of the several states," instead of by the congress, were voted down, (Jour. Conv. 286, 288; 1 Elliot, Deb. 208, 262,) as was the proposition that the president should be "chosen by electors appointed for that purpose by the legislatures of the states," though at one time adopted, (Jour. Conv. 190; 1 Elliot, Deb. 208, 211, 217;) and a motion to postpone the consideration of the choice "by the national legislature," in order to take up a resolution providing for electors to be elected by the qualified voters in districts, was negatived in committee of the whole, (Jour. Conv. 92; 1 Elliot, Deb. 156.) Gerry proposed that the choice should be made by the state executives; Hamilton, that the election be by electors chosen by electors chosen by the people; James Wilson and Gouverneur Morris were strongly in favor of popular vote; Ellsworth and Luther Martin preferred the choice by electors elected by the legislatures; and Roger Sherman, appointment by congress. The final result seems to have reconciled contrariety of views by leaving it to the state legislatures to appoint directly by joint ballot or concurrent separate action, or through popular election by districts or by general ticket, or as otherwise might be directed.

Therefore, on reference to contemporaneous and subsequent action under the clause, we should expect to find, as we do, that various modes of choosing the electors were pursued, as, by the legislature itself on joint ballot; by the legislature through a concurrent vote of the two houses; by vote of the people for a general ticket; by vote of the people in districts; by choice partly by the people voting in districts and partly by the people voting in districts and partly by the candidates voted for by the people in districts; and in other ways, as, notably, by North Carolina in 1792, and Tennessee in 1796 and 1800. No question was raised as to the power of the state to appoint in any mode its legislature saw fit to adopt, and none that a single method, applicable without exception, must be pursued in the absence of an amendment to the constitution. The district system was largely considered the most equitable, and Madison wrote that it was that system which was contemplated by the framers of the constitution, although it was soon seen that its adoption by some states might place them at a disadvantage by a division of their strength, and that a uniform rule was preferable.

At the first presidential election, the appointment of electors was made by the legislatures of Connecticut, Delaware, Georgia, New Jersey, and South Carolina. Pennsylvania, by act of October 4, 1788, (Acts Pa. 1787-88, p. 513,) provided for the election of electors on a general ticket. Virginia, by act of November 17, 1788, was divided into 12 separate districts, and an elector elected in each district, while for the election of congressmen the state was divided into 10 other districts. Laws Va. Oct. Sess. 1788, pp. 1, 2. In Massachusetts, the general court, by resolve of November 17, 1788, divided the state into districts for the election of representatives in congress, and provided for their election, December 18, 1788, and that at the same time the qualified inhabitants of each district should give their votes for two persons as candidates for an elector of president and vice president of the United States, and, from the two persons in each district having the greatest number of votes, the two houses of the general court by joint ballot should elect one as elector, and in the same way should elect two electors at large. Mass. Resolves 1788, p. 53. In Maryland, under elected on general ticket, five being residents elected on general ticket, five being residents of the Western Shore, and three of the Eastern Shore. Laws Md. 1788, c. 10. In New Hampshire an act was passed November 12, 1788, (Laws N. H. 1789, p. 169,) providing for the election of five electors by majority popular vote, and in case of no choice that the legislature should appoint out of so many of the candidates as equaled double the number of electors elected. There being no choice, the appointment was made by the legislature. The senate would not agree to a joint ballot, and the house was compelled, that the vote of the state might not be lost, to concur in the electors chosen by the senate. The state of New York lost its vote through a similar contest. The assembly was willing to elect by joint ballot of the two branches or to divide the electors with the senate, but senate would assent to nothing short of a complete negative upon the action of the assembly, and the time for election passed without an appointment. North Carolina and Rhode Island had not then ratified the constitution.

Fifteen states participated in the second presidential election, in nine of which electors were chosen by the legislatures. Maryland, Laws Md. 1790, c. 16; Laws 1791, c. 62,) New Hampshire, (Laws N. H. 1792, pp. 398, 401,) and Pennsylvania, (Laws Pa. 1792, p. 240,) elected their electors on a general ticket, and Virginia by districts, (Laws Va. 1792, p. 87.) In Massachusetts the general court, by resolution of June 30, 1792, divided the state into four districts, in each of two of which five electors were elected, and in each of the other two three electors. Mass. Resolves, June, 1792, p. 25. Under the apportionment of April 13, 1792, North Carolina was entitled to ten members of the house of representatives. The legislature was not in session, and did not meet until November 15th, while under the act of congress of March 1, 1792, (1 St. p. 239,) the electors were to assemble on December 5th. The legislature passed an act dividing the state into four districts, and directing the members of the legislature residing in each district to meet on the 25th of November, and choose three electors. 2 Ired. N. C. Laws, 1715-1800, c. 15 of 1792. At the same session an act was passed dividing the state into districts for the election of electors in 1796, and every four years thereafter. Id. c. 16.

Sixteen states took part in the third presidential election, Tennessee having been admitted June 1, 1796. In nine states the electors were appointed by the legislatures, and in Pennsylvania and New Hampshire by popular vote for a general ticket. Virginia, North Carolina, and Maryland elected by districts. The Maryland law of December 24, 1795, was entitled "An act to alter the mode of electing electors," and provided for dividing the state into ten districts, each of which districts should "elect and appoint one person, being a resident of the said district, as an elector." Laws Md. 1795, c. 73. Massachusetts adhered to the district system, electing one elector in each congressional district by a majority vote. It was provided that, if no one had a majority, the legislature should make the appointment on joint ballot, and the legislature also appointed two electors at large in the same manner. Mass. Resolves, June, 1796, p. 12. In Tennessee an act was passed August 8, 1796, which provided for the election of three electors, "one in the district of Washington, one in the district of Hamilton, and one in the district of Mero," and, "that the said electors may be elected with as little trouble to the citizens as possible," certain persons of the counties of Washington, Sullivan, Green, and Hawkins were named in the act and appointed electors to elect an elector for the district of Washington; certain other persons of the counties of Knox, Jefferson, Sevier, and Blount were by name appointed to elect an elector for the district of Hamilton; and certain others of the counties of Davidson, Sumner, and Tennessee to elect an elector for the district of Mero. Laws Tenn. 1794, 1803, p. 209; Acts 2d Sess. 1st Gen. Assem. Tenn. c. 4. Electors were chosen by the persons thus designated.

In the fourth presidential election, Virginia, under the advice of Mr. Jefferson, adopted the general ticket, at least "until some uniform mode of choosing a president and vice president of the United States shall be prescribed by an amendment to the constitution." Laws Va. 1799-1800, p. 3. Massachusetts passed a resolution providing that the electors of that state should be appointed by joint ballot of the senate and house. Mass. Resolves, June, 1800, p. 13. Pennsylvania appointed by the legislature, and, upon a contest between the senate and house, the latter was forced to yield to the senate in agreeing to an arrangement which resulted in dividing the vote of the electors. 26 Niles" Reg. 17. Six states, however, chose electors by popular vote, Rhode Island supplying the place of Pennsylvania, which had theretofore followed that course. Tennessee, by act October 26, 1799, designated persons by name to choose its three electors, as under the act of 1796. Laws Tenn, 1794-1803, p. 211; Acts 2d Sess. 2d Gen. Assem, Tenn. c. 46.

Without pursuing the subject further, it is sufficient to observe that, while most of the states adopted the general ticket system, the district method obtained in Kentucky until 1824; in Tennessee and Maryland until 1832; in Indiana in 1824 and 1828; in Illinois in 1820 and 1824; and in Maine in 1820, 1824, and 1828. Massachusetts used the general ticket system in 1804, (Mass. Resolves, June, 1804, p. 19;) chose electors by joint ballot of the legislature in 1808 and in 1816, (Mass. Resolves 1808, pp. 205, 207, 209; Mass. Resolves 1816, p. 233;) used the district system again in 1812 and 1820, (Mass. Resolves 1812, p. 94; Mass. Resolves 1820, p. 245;) and returned to the general ticket system in 1824, (Mass. Resolves 1824, p. 40.) In New York the electors were elected in 1828 by districts, the district electors choosing the electors at large. Rev. St. N. Y. 1827, tit. 6, p. 24. The appointment of electors by the legislature, instead of by popular vote, was made use of by North Carolina, Vermont, and New Jersey in 1812.

In 1824 the electors were chosen by popular vote, by districts, and by general ticket, in all the states excepting Delaware, Georgia, Louisiana, New York, South Carolina, and Vermont, where they were still chosen by the legislature. After 1832 electors were chosen by general ticket in all the states excepting South Carolina, where the legislature chose them up to and including 1860. Journals 1860, Senate, pp. 12, 13; House, 11, 15, 17. And this was the mode adopted by Florida in 1868, (Laws 1868, p. 166,) and by Colorado in 1876, as prescribed by section 19 of the schedule to the constitution of the state, which was admitted into the Union, August 1, 1876, (Gen. Laws Colo. 1877, pp. 79, 990.) [1]

Mr. Justice Story, in considering the subject in his Commentaries on the Constitution, and writing nearly 50 years after the adoption of that instrument, after stating that "in some states the legislatures have direct-

---

[1] See Stanwood, Presidential Elections, (3d Ed.) and Appleton, Presidential Counts, passim; 2 Lalor, Enc. Pol. Science, 68; 4 Hild. Hist. U. S. (Rev. Ed.) 39, 382, 689; 5 Hild. Hist. U. S. 389, 531; 1 Schouler, Hist. U. S. 72, 334; 2 Schouler, Hist. U. S. 184; 3 Schouler, Hist. U. S. 313, 439; 2 Adams, Hist. U. S. 201; 4 Adams, Hist. U. S. 285; 6 Adams, Hist. U. S. 409, 413; 9 Adams, Hist. U. S. 139; 1 McMaster, Hist. Peopel U. S. 525; 2 McMaster, Hist. People U. S. 85, 509; 3 McMaster, Hist. People U. S. 188, 189, 194, 317; 2 Scharf, Hist. Md. 547; 2 Bradf. Mass. 335; Life of Plumer, 104; 3 Niles' Reg. 160; 5 Niles' Reg. 372; 9 Niles' Reg. 319, 349; 10 Niles' Reg. 45, 177, 409; 11 Niles' Reg.

ly chosen the electors by themselves; in others, they have been chosen by the people by a general ticket throughout the whole state; and in others, by the people by electoral districts, fixed by the legislature, a certain number of electors being apportioned to each district,"-adds: "No question has ever arisen as to the constitutionality of either mode, except that by a direct choice by the legislature. But this, though often doubted by able and ingenious minds, (3 Elliot, Deb. 100, 101,) has been firmly established in practice ever since the adoption of the constitution, and does not now seem to admit of controversy, even if a suitable tribunal existed to adjudicate upon it." And he remarks that "it has been thought desirable by many statesmen to have the constitution amended so as to provide for a uniform mode of choice by the people." Story, Const. (1st Ed.) 1466.

Such an amendment was urged at the time of the adoption of the twelfth amendment, the suggestion being that all electors should be chosen by popular vote, the states to be divided for that purpose into districts. It was brought up again in congress in December, 1813, but the resolution for submitting the amendment failed to be carried. The amendment was renewed in the house of representatives in December, 1816, and a provision for the division of the states into single districts for the choice of electors received a majority vote, but not two thirds. Like amendments were offered in the senate by Messrs. Sanford of New York, Dickerson of New Jersey, and Macon of North Carolina. December 11, 1823, Senator Benton introduced an amendment providing that each legislature should divide its state into electoral districts, and that the voters of each district "should vote, in their own proper persons," for president and vice president, but it was not acted upon. December 16 and December 24, 1823, amendments were introduced in the senate by Messrs. Dickerson, of New Jersey, and Van Buren, of New York, requiring the choice of electors to be by districts; but these and others failed of adoption, although there was favorable action in that direction by the senate in 1818, 1819, and 1822. December 22, 1823, an amendment was introduced in the house by Mr. McDuffie, of South Carolina, providing that electors should be chosen by districts assigned by the legislatures, but

---

[2] 1 Benton, Thirty Years' View, 37; 5 Benton, Cong. Deb. 110, 677; 7 Benton, Cong. Deb. 472-474, 600; 3 Niles' Reg. 240, 334; 11 Niles' Reg. 258, 274, 293, 349; Annals Cong. (1812-13,) 847.

action was not taken[2]. The subject was again brought forward in 1835, 1844, and subsequently, but need not be further dwelt upon, except that it may be added that, on the 28th of May, 1874, a report was made by Senator Morton, chairman of the senate committee on privileges and elections, recommending an amendment dividing the states into electoral districts, and that the majority of the popular vote of each district should give the candidate one presidential vote, but this also failed to obtain action. In this report it was said: "The appointment of these electors is thus placed absolutely and wholly with the legislatures of the several states. They may be chosen by the legislature, or the legislature may provide that they shall be elected by the people of the state at large, or in districts, as are members of congress, which was the case formerly in many states; and it is not doubt competent for the legislature to authorize the governor, or the supreme court of the state, or any other agent of its will, to appoint these electors. This power is conferred upon the legislatures of the states by the constitution of the United States, and cannot be taken from them or modified by their state constitutions any more than can their power to elect senators of the United States. Whatever provisions may be made by statute, or by the state constitution, to choose electors by the people, there is no doubt of the right of the legislature to resume the power at any time, for it can neither be taken away nor abdicated." Senate Rep. 1st Sess. 43d Cong. No. 395.

From this review, in which we have been assisted by the laborious research of counsel, and which might have been greatly expanded, it is seen that from the formation of the government until now the practical construction of the clause has conceded plenary power to the state legislatures in the matter of the appointment of electors.

Even in the heated controversy of 1876-77 the electoral vote of Colorado cast by electors chosen by the legislature passed unchallenged, and our attention has not been drawn to any previous attempt to submit to the courts the determination of the constitutionality of state action.

In short, the appointment and mode of appointment of electors belong exclusively to the states under the constitution of the United States. They are, as remarked by Mr. Justice Gray *in Re Green*, 134 U.S. 377, 379, 10 S. Sup. Ct. Rep. 586, "no more officers or agents of the United States than are the members of the state legislatures when acting as electors of federal senators, or the people of the states when acting as the electors of representatives in congress." Congress is empowered to determine the time of choosing the electors and the day on which they are to give their votes, which is required to be the same day throughout the United States; but otherwise the power and jurisdiction of the state is exclusive, with the exception of the provisions as to the number of electors and the ineligibility of certain persons, so framed that congressional and federal influence might be excluded.

The question before us is not one of policy. but of power; and, while public opinion had gradually brought all the states as matter of fact to the pursuit of a uniform system of popular election by general ticket, that fact does not tend to weaken the force of contemporaneous and long-continued previous practice when and as different views of expediency prevailed. The prescription of the written law cannot be overthrown because the states have laterally exercised, in a particular way, a power which they might have exercised in some other way. The construction to which we have referred has prevailed too long and been too uniform to justify us in interpreting the language of the constitution as conveying any other meaning than that heretofore ascribed, and it must be treated as decisive.

It is argued that the district mode of choosing electors, while not obnoxious to constitutional objection, if the operation of the electoral system had conformed to its original object and purpose, had become so in view of the practical working of that system. Doubtless it was supposed that the electors would exercise a reasonable independence and fair judgment in the selection of the chief executive, but experience soon demonstrated that, whether chosen by the legislatures or by popular suffrage on general ticket or in districts, they were so chosen simply to register the will of the appointing power in respect of a particular candidate. In relation, then, to the independence of the electors, the original expectation may be said to have been frustrated. Miller, Const. Law, 149; Rawle, Const. 55; Story, Const. 1473; Federalist, No. 68. But we can perceive no reason for holding that the power confided to the states by the constitution has ceased to exist because the operation of the system has not fully realized the hopes of those by whom it was created. Still less can we recognize the doctrine that because the constitution has been found in the march of time sufficiently comprehensive to be applicable to conditions not within the minds of its framers, and not arising in their time, it may therefore be wrenched from the subjects expressly embraced within it, and amended by judicial decision without action by the designated organs in the mode by which alone amendments can be made. Nor are we able to discover any conflict between this act and the fourteenth and fifteenth amendments to the constitution. The fourteenth amendment provides:

> *"Section 1.* All persons born or naturalized in the United States, and subject to the jurisdiction thereof, are citizens of the United States and of the state wherein they reside. No state shall make or enforce any law which shall abridge the privileges or immunities of citizens of the United States; nor shall any state deprive any person of life, liberty, or property without due process of law, nor deny to any person within its jurisdiction the equal protection of the laws.
>
> *"Sec. 2.* Representatives shall be apportioned among the several states according to their respective numbers, counting the whole number of persons in each state, excluding Indians not taxed. But when the right to vote at any election for the choice of electors for president and vice president of the United States, representatives in congress, the executive and judicial officers of a state, or the members of the legislature thereof, is denied to any of the male inhabitants of such state, being twenty-one years of age, and citizens of the United States, or in any way abridged, except for participation in rebellion or other crime, the basis of representation therein shall be reduced in the proportion which the number of such male citizens shall bear to the whole number of male citizens twenty-one years of age in such state."

The first section of the fifteenth amendment reads: "The right of citizens of the United States to vote shall not be denied or abridged by the United States or by any state on account of race, color, or previous condition of servitude."

In the Slaughterhouse Cases, 16 Wall. 36, this court held that the first clause of the fourteenth amendment was primarily intended to confer citizenship on the negro race; and, secondly, to give definitions of citizenship of the United States, and citizenship of the states; and it recognized the distinction between citizenship of a state and citizenship of the United States by those definitions; that the privileges and immunities of citizens of the states embrace generally those fundamental civil rights for the security and establishment of which organized society was instituted, and which remain, with certain exceptions mentioned in the federal constitution, under the care of the state governments; while the privileges and immunities of citizens of the United States are those which arise out of the nature and essential character of the national government, the provisions of its constitution, or its laws and treaties made in pursuance thereof; and that it is the latter which are placed under the protection of congress by the second clause of the fourteenth amendment.

We decided in *Minor v. Happersett*, 21 Wall. 162, that the right of suffrage was not necessarily one of the privileges or immunities of citizenship before the adoption of the fourteenth amendment, and that that amendment does not add to these privileges and immunities, but simply furnishes an additional guaranty for the protection of such as the citizen already has; that, at the time of the adoption of that amendment, suffrage was not coextensive with the citizenship of the state, nor was it at the time of the adoption of the constitution; and that neither the constitution nor the fourteenth amendment made all citizens voters.

The fifteenth amendment exempted citizens of the United States from discrimination in the exercise of the elective franchise on account of race, color, or previous condition of servitude. The right to vote in the states comes from the states, but the right of exemption from the prohibited discrimination comes from the United States. The first has not been granted or secured by the constitution of the United States, but the last has been. *U. S. v. Cruikshank*, 92 U.S. 542; *U. S. v. Reese*, Id. 214.

If, because it happened, at the time of the adoption of the fourteenth amendment, that those who exercised the elective franchise in the state of Michigan were entitled to vote for all the presidential electors, this right was rendered permanent by that amendment, then the second clause of article 2 has been so amended that the states can no longer appoint in such manner as the legislatures thereof may direct; and yet no such result is indicated by the language used, nor are the amendments necessarily inconsistent with that clause. The first section of the fourteenth amendment does not refer to the exercise of the elective franchise, though the second provides that if the right to vote is denied or abridged to any male inhabitant of the state having attained majority, and being a citizen of the United States, then the basis of representation to which each state is entitled in the congress shall be proportionately reduced. Whenever presidential electors are appointed by popular election, then the right to vote cannot be denied or abridged without invoking the penalty; and so of the right to vote for representatives in congress, the executive and judicial officers of a state, or the members of the legislature thereof. The right to vote intended to be protected refers to the right to vote as established by the laws and constitution of the state. There is no color for the contention that under the amendments every male inhabitant of the state, being a citizen of the United States, has from the time of his majority a right to vote for presidential electors.

The object of the fourteenth amendment in respect of citizenship was to preserve equality of rights and to prevent discrimination as between citizens, but not to radically change the whole theory of the relations of the state and federal governments to each other, and of both governments to the people. *In re Kemmler,* 136 U.S. 436, 10 Sup. Ct. Rep. 930.

The inhibition that no state shall deprive any person within its jurisdiction of the equal protection of the laws was designed to prevent any person or class of persons from being singled out as a special subject for discriminating and hostile legislation. *Milling Co. v. Pennsylvania,* 125 U.S. 181, 188, Sup. Ct. Rep. 737.

In *Hayes v. Missouri,* 120 U.S. 68, 71, 7 S. Sup. Ct. Rep. 350, Mr. Justice Field, speaking for the court, said: "The fourteenth amendment to the constitution of the United States does not prohibit legislation which is limited either in the objects to which it is directed or by the territory within which it is to operate. It merely requires that all persons subjected to such legislation shall be treated alike, under like circumstances and conditions, both in the privileges and in the liabilities imposed. As we said in *Barbier v. Connolly,* speaking of the fourteenth amendment: 'Class legislation, discriminating against some and favoring others, is prohibited; but legislation which, in carrying out a public purpose, is limited in its application, if within the sphere of its operation it affects alike all persons similarly situated, is not within the amendment' 113 U.S. 27, 32, 5 S. Sup. Ct. Rep. 357."

If presidential electors are appointed by the legislatures, no discrimination is made; if they are elected in districts where each citizen has an equal right to vote, the same as any other citizen has, no discrimination is made. Unless the authority vested in the legislatures by the second clause of section 1 of article 2 has been divested, and the state has lost its power of appointment, except in one manner, the position taken on behalf of relators is untenable, and it is apparent that neither of these amendments can be given such effect.

The third clause of section 1 of article 2 of the constitution is: "The congress may determine the time of choosing the electors, and the day on which they shall give their votes; which day shall be the same throughout the United States."

Under the act of congress of March 1, 1792, (1 St. p. 239, c. 8,) it was provided that the electors should meet and give their votes on the first Wednesday in December at such place in each state as should be directed by the legislature thereof, and by act of congress of January 23, 1845, (5 St. p. 721,) that the electors should be appointed in each state on the Tuesday next after the first Monday in the month of November in the year in which they were to be appointed: provided, that each state might by law provide for the filling of any vacancies in its college of electors when such college meets to give its electoral vote: and provided that when any state shall have held an election for the purpose of choosing electors, and has failed to make a choice on the day prescribed, then the electors may be appointed on a subsequent day, in such manner as the state may by law provide. These provisions were carried forward into sections 131, 133, 134, and 135 of the Revised Statutes, (Rev. St. tit. 3, c. 1, p. 22.)

By the act of congress of February 3, 1887, entitled "An act to fix the day for the meeting of the electors of president and vice president," etc., (24 St. p. 373.) it was provided that the electors of each state should meet and give their votes on the second Monday in January next following their appointment. The state law in question here fixes the first Wednesday of December as the day for the meeting of the electors, as originally designated by congress. In this respect it is in conflict with the act of congress, and must necessarily give way. But this part of the act is not so inseparably connected, in substance, with the other parts as to work the destruction of the whole act. Striking out the day for the meeting, which had already been otherwise determined by the act of congress, the act remains complete in itself, and capable of being carried out in accordance with the legislative intent. The state law yields only to the extent of the collision. *Cooley, Const. Lim.* *178; *Com. v. Kimball,* 24 Pick. 359; *Houston v. Moore,* 5 Wheat. 1, 49. The construction to this effect by the state court is of persuasive force, if not of controlling weight.

We do not think this result affected by the provision in Act No. 50 in relation to a tie vote. Under the constitution of the state of Michigan, in case two or more persons have an equal and the highest number of votes for any office, as canvassed by the board of state canvassers, the legislature in joint convention chooses one of these persons to fill the office. This rule is recognized in this act, which also makes it the duty of the governor in such case to convene the legislature in special session for the purpose of its application, immediately upon the determination by the board of state canvassers.

We entirely agree with the supreme court of Michigan that it cannot be held, as matter of law, that the legislature would not have provided for being convened in special session but for the provision relating to the time of the meeting of the electors contained in the act, and are of opinion that that date may be rejected, and the act be held to remain otherwise complete and valid.

And as the state is fully empowered to fill any vacancy which may occur in its electoral college, when it meets to give its electoral vote, we find nothing in the mode provided for anticipating such an exigency which operates to invalidate the law. We repeat that the main question arising for consideration is one of power, and not of policy, and we are unable to arrive at any other conclusion than that the act of the legislature of Michigan of May 1, 1891, is not void as in contravention of the constitution of the United States, for want of power in its enactment.

The judgment of the supreme court of Michigan must be affirmed.

APPENDIX P:
U. S. Supreme Court Decision in *State of Ohio Ex Rel. Davis v. Hildebrandt* (1916)

U.S. Supreme Court

241 U.S. 565

STATE OF OHIO ON RELATION OF DAVID DAVIS, Plff. in Err.,

v.

CHARLES Q. HILDEBRANT,

Secretary of State of Ohio, State Supervisor and Inspector of Elections, and State Supervisor of Elections, et al.

No. 987

Submitted May 22, 1916

Decided June 12, 1916

Messrs. Sherman T. McPherson and J. Warren Keifer for plaintiff in error.

Mr. Edward C. Turner, Attorney General of Ohio, and Messrs. Edmond H. Moore and Timothy S. Hogan for defendants in error.

Mr. Chief Justice White delivered the opinion of the court:

By an amendment to the Constitution of Ohio, adopted September 3d, 1912, the legislative power was expressly declared to be vested not only in the senate and house of representatives of the state, constituting the general assembly, but in the people, in whom a right was reserved by way of referendum to approve or disapprove by popular vote any law enacted by the general assembly. And by other constitutional provisions the machinery to carry out the referendum was created. Briefly they were this: Within a certain time after the enactment of a law by the senate and house of representatives, and its approval by the governor, upon petition of 6 per centum of the voters, the question of whether the law should

723

become operative was to be submitted to a vote of the people, and, if approved, the law should be operative; and, if not approved, it should have no effect whatever.

In May, 1915, the general assembly of Ohio passed an act redistricting the state for the purpose of congressional elections, by which act twenty-two congressional districts were created, in some respects differing from the previously established districts, and this act, after approval by the governor, was filed in the office of the secretary of state. The requisite number of electors under the referendum provision having petitioned for a submission of the law to a popular vote, such vote was taken and the law was disapproved. Thereupon, in the supreme court of the state, the suit before us was begun against state election officers for the purpose of procuring a mandamus, directing them to disregard the vote of the people on the referendum, disapproving the law, and to proceed to discharge their duties as such officers in the next congressional election, upon the assumption that the action by way of referendum was void, and that the law which was disapproved was subsisting and valid. The right to this relief was based upon the charge that the referendum vote was not and could not be a part of the legislative authority of the state, and therefore could have no influence on the subject of the law creating congressional districts for the purpose of representation in Congress. Indeed, it was in substance charged that both from the point of view of the state Constitution and laws and from that of the Constitution of the United States, especially 4 of article 1, providing that 'the times, places and manner of holding elections for Senators and Representatives, shall be prescribed in each state by the legislature thereof; but the Congress may at any time by law, make or alter such regulations, except as to the places of choosing Senators;' and also from that of the provisions of the controlling act of Congress of August 8, 1911 (chap. 5, 37 Stat. at L. 13, Comp. Stat. 1913, 15), apportioning representation among the states, the attempt to make the referendum a component part of the legislative authority empowered to deal with the election of members of Congress was absolutely void. The court below adversely disposed of these contentions, and held that the provisions as to referendum were a part of the legislative power of the state, made so by the Constitution, and that nothing in the act of Congress of 1911, or in the constitutional provision, operated to the contrary, and that therefore the disapproved law had no existence and was not entitled to be enforced by mandamus.

Without going into the many irrelevant points which are pressed in the argument, and the various inapposite authorities cited, although we have considered them all, we think it is apparent that the whole case and every real question in it will be disposed of by looking at it from three points of view,-the state power, the power of Congress, and the operation of the provision of the Constitution of the United States, referred to.

1. As to the state power, we pass from its consideration, since it is obvious that the decision below is conclusive on that subject, and makes it clear that, so far as the state had the power to do it, the referendum constituted a part of the state Constitution and laws, and was contained within the legislative power; and therefore the claim that the law which was disapproved and was no law under the Constitution and laws of the state was yet valid and operative is conclusively established to be wanting in merit.

2. So far as the subject may be influenced by the power of Congress, that is, to the extent that the will of Congress has been expressed on the subject, we think the case is equally without merit. We say this because we think it is clear that Congress, in 1911, in enacting the controlling law concerning the duties of the states, through their legislative authority, to deal with the subject of the creation of congressional districts, expressly modified the phraseology of the previous acts relating to that subject by inserting a clause plainly intended to provide that where, by the state Constitution and laws, the referendum was treated as part of the legislative power, the power as thus constituted should be held and treated to be the state legislative power for the purpose of creating congressional districts by law. This is the case since, under the act of Congress dealing with apportionment, which preceded the act of 1911, by 4 if was commanded that the existing districts in a state should continue in force 'until the legislature of such state, in the manner herein prescribed, shall redistrict such state' (act of February 7, 1891, chap. 116, 26 Stat. at L. 735); while in the act of 1911 there was substituted a provision that the redistricting should be made by a state 'in the manner provided by the laws thereof.' And the legislative history of this last act leaves no room for doubt that the prior words were stricken out and the new words inserted for the express purpose, in so far as Congress had power to do it, of excluding the possibility of making the contention as to referendum which is now urged. Cong. Rec. vol. 47, pp. 3436, 3437, 3507

3. To the extent that the contention urges that to include the referendum within state legislative power for the purpose of apportionment is repugnant to 4 of article 1 of the Constitution and hence void, even if sanctioned by Congress, because beyond the constitutional authority of that body, and hence that it is the duty of the judicial power so to declare, we again think the contention is plainly without substance, for the following reasons: It must rest upon the assumption that to include the referendum in the scope of the legislative power is to introduce a virus which destroys that power, which in effect annihilates representative government, and causes a state where such condition exists to be not republican in form, in violation of the guaranty of the Constitution. Const. 4, art. 4. But the proposition and the argument disregard the settled rule that the question of whether that guaranty of the Constitution has been disregarded presents no justiciable controversy, but involves the exercise by Congress of the authority vested in it by the Constitution. *Pacific States Teleph. & Teleg. Co. v. Oregon*, 223 U.S. 118 , 56 L. ed. 377, 32 Sup. Ct. Rep. 224. In so far as the proposition challenges the power of Congress, as manifested by the clause in the act of 1911, treating the referendum as a part of the legislative power for the purpose of apportionment, where so ordained by the state Constitutions and laws, the argument but asserts, on the one hand, that Congress had no power to do that which, from the point of view of 4 of article 1, previously considered, the Constitution expressly gave the right to do. In so far as the proposition may be considered as asserting, on the other hand, that any attempt by Congress to recognize the referendum as a part of the legislative authority of a state is obnoxious to a republican form of government as provided by 4 of article 4, the contention necessarily but reasserts the proposition on that subject previously adversely disposed of. And that this is the inevitable result of the contention is plainly manifest, since at best the proposition comes to the assertion that because Congress, upon whom the Constitution has conferred the exclusive authority to uphold the guaranty of a republican form of government, has done something which it is deemed is repugnant to that guaranty, therefore there was automatically created judicial authority to go beyond the limits of judicial power, and, in doing so, to usurp congressional power, on the ground that Congress had mistakenly dealt with a subject which was within its exclusive control, free from judicial interference.

It is apparent from these reasons that there must either be a dismissal for want of jurisdiction, because there is no power to re- examine the state questions foreclosed by the decision below, and because of the want of merit in the Federal questions relied upon, or a judgment of affirmance, it being absolutely indifferent, as to the result, which of the two be applied. In view, however, of the subject-matter of the controversy and the Federal characteristics which inhere in it, we are of opinion, applying the rule laid down in *Swafford v. Templeton*, 185 U.S. 487 , 46 L. ed. 1005, 22 Sup. Ct. Rep. 783, the decree proper to be rendered is one of affirmance, and such a decree is therefore ordered.

Affirmed.

APPENDIX Q:
Maine Supreme Court Opinion for
In re Opinion of the Justices (1919)

Maine Supreme Court

107 A. 705

In re Opinion of the Justices

August 28, 1919

Answer to question propounded to the Justices of the Supreme Judicial Court by the Governor.

To the Honorable Carl E. Milliken, Governor of Maine:

The undersigned Justices of the Supreme Judicial Court, having considered the question propounded by you under date of July 9, 1919, concerning the necessity of submitting by referendum to the qualified voters of the state a certain act of the Legislature of Maine, entitled "An act granting to women the right to vote for presidential electors," respectfully submit the following answer:

The request contains certain recitals of fact, the substance of which is that the above statute was passed by the concurrent action of both branches of the Legislature and was duly approved by the Governor; that the Legislature adjourned without day on April 4, 1919, and within 90 days thereafter petitions, apparently bearing the requisite number of signatures, were filed with the secretary of state, requesting that this act be referred to the people under Amendment 31 of article 4 of the Constitution of Maine, known as the initiative and referendum amendment.

QUESTION.

"Is the effect of the act of the Legislature of Maine of 1919, entitled 'An act granting to women the right to vote for presidential electors,' approved by the Governor on March 28, 1919, suspended by valid written petitions of not less than 10,000 electors, addressed to the Governor and filed in the office of the secretary of state within 90 days after the recess of the Legislature, requesting that it be referred to the people, and should the act be referred to the people as provided in article 4 of the Constitution of Maine, as amended by Amendment 31, adopted September 14, 1908?"

ANSWER.

This question we answer in the affirmative. In our opinion this legislative act comes within the provisions of the initiative and referendum amendment, and should be referred to the people for adoption or rejection by them.

To solve this problem it is necessary to pursue the same general course as in deciding the question concerning the prohibitory amendment to the federal Constitution, by an examination, first, of the provisions and requirements of the Constitution of the United States relating to this subject-matter, and, second, of the provisions and requirements of the Constitution of Maine.

The first question that naturally arises is this: Where, under the federal Constitution, is lodged the power of determining in what manner presidential electors shall be chosen and of prescribing the qualifications of the voters therefor?

It was competent for the people of the United States, in creating the compact known as the federal Constitution, to lodge this power wherever they saw fit. It was a matter wholly within their discretion. It is a well-known historical fact that there was a long and spirited debate in the constitutional convention over this very question; that is, the method to be adopted in electing the chief magistrate of the nation. Many plans were submitted, such as election by Congress, by the people at large, by the chief executives of the several states, and by electors appointed by the Legislatures. 1 Elliot, Deb. 208, 211, 217, 262.

Finally the following provisions, which were presented by Gouveneur Morris for the special committee, were adopted by the convention after much discussion, and were incorporated in article 11 of the perfected instrument, where they stand unchanged today, viz.:

"Each state shall appoint, in such manner as the Legislature thereof may direct, a number of electors equal to the whole

730 | Appendix Q

number of Senators and Representatives to which the state may be entitled in the Congress," etc. Article 2, § 1, subd. 2. "The Congress may determine the time of choosing the electors, and the day on which they shall give their votes, which day shall be the same throughout the United States." Article 2, § 1, subd. 4.

These two subdivisions comprise all the provisions of the federal Constitution applicable to the point in issue here. Under section 1, subd. 4, Congress is given the power to determine the date of holding presidential elections and of the meeting of the electors, but that marks the limit of its constitutional power. *In re Green*, 134 U. S. 377, 10 Sup. Ct. 586, 33 L. Ed. 951. All other powers in connection with this subject are expressly reserved to the states. *McPherson v. Blacker*, 146 U. S. 1, 13 Sup. Ct. 3, 36 L. Ed. 869; *Pope v. Williams*, 193 U. S. 621, 24 Sup. Ct. 573, 48 L. Ed. 817 .

In the case last cited the Supreme Court of the United States say:

"The privilege to vote in a state is within the jurisdiction of the state itself, to be exercised as the state may direct, and upon such terms as to it may seem proper, provided, of course, no discrimination is made between individuals in violation of the federal Constitution."

The word "appoint" as employed in subdivision 2 has been interpreted to be sufficiently comprehensive to include the result of a popular election and to convey the broadest powers of determination. *McPherson v. Blacker*, 146 U. S. 1, 27, 13 Sup. Ct. 3, 36 L. Ed. 869.

The language of section 1, subd. 2, is clear and unambiguous. It admits of no doubt as to where the constitutional power of appointment is vested, namely, in the several states. "Each state shall appoint in such manner as the Legislature thereof may direct" are the significant words of the section, and their plain meaning is that each state is thereby clothed with the absolute power to appoint electors in such manner as it may see fit, without any interference or control on the part of the federal government, except, of course, in case of attempted discrimination as to race, color, or previous condition of servitude under the fifteenth amendment. The clause, "in such manner as the Legislature thereof may direct," means, simply that the state shall give expression to its will, as it must, of necessity, through its law-making body, the Legislature. The will of the state in this respect must be voiced in legislative acts or resolves, which shall prescribe in detail the manner of choosing electors, the qualifications of voters therefor, and the proceedings on the part of the electors when chosen.

But these acts and resolves must be passed and become effective in accordance with and in subjection to the Constitution of the state, like all other acts and resolves having the force of law. The Legislature was not given in this respect any superiority over or independence from the organic law of the state in force at the time when a given law is passed. Nor was it designated by the federal Constitution as a mere agency or representative of the people to perform a certain act, as it was under article 5 in ratifying a federal amendment, a point more fully discussed in the answer to the question concerning the federal prohibitory amendment. 107 Atl. 673. It is simply the ordinary instrumentality of the state, the legislative branch of the government, the law-making power, to put into words the will of the state in connection with the choice of presidential electors. The distinction between the function and power of the Legislature in the case under consideration and its function and power as a particular body designated by the federal Constitution to ratify or reject a federal amendment is sharp and clear and must be borne in mind.

It follows, therefore, that under the provisions of the federal Constitution the state by its legislative direction may establish such a method of choosing its presidential electors as it may see fit, and may change that method from time to time as it may deem advisable; but the legislative acts both of establishment and of change must always be subject to the provisions of the Constitution of the state in force at the time such acts are passed and can be valid and effective only when enacted in compliance therewith.

In the exercise of the power thus conferred by the federal Constitution, various methods of electing presidential electors were adopted in the early days by the several states, as set forth in detail in *McPherson v. Blacker*, 146 U. S. at pages 29 to 35, 13 Sup. Ct. 3, 36 L. Ed. 869.

In our own state the same holds true to a certain extent. Prior to 1847 the legislative direction expressed itself in the form of a joint resolution, passed every fourth year, at the session immediately preceding a presidential election. These resolves had the force of law, and with the exception of those of 1820 and 1824 they were uniformly presented to and were approved by the Governor. Prior to 1840 the district prevailed in whole or in part. Res. 1820, c. 19; 1824, c. 76; 1828, c. 23; 1832, c. 65; 1836, c. 9. In 1840 (Res c. 55) 10 electors at large were provided for, and since that time the electors have been chosen at large upon a single ballot. This method was followed in 1844. Res. 1844, c. 295.

Under the resolves of 1820, 1824, and 1828, the qualifications of voters for representatives and senators to the Legislature were made the qualifications of voters for presidential electors. By the resolves of 1832 and 1836, the qualifications of voters for representatives alone were made the test, and by the resolve of 1840 this was changed to qualifications of voters for senators alone.

The Legislature of 1847 directed for the first time by a general act, instead of by a quadrennial resolve, the manner in which the voters should proceed in the election of presidential electors (Pub. L. 1847, c. 26), and, following the resolves of 1840 and 1844, prescribed the qualified voters therefor to be "the people of this state qualified to vote for senators in its Legislature." This qualification established by the act of 1847 has been preserved in all the subsequent revisions. R. S. 1857, c. 4, § 79; R. S. 1871, c. 4, § 78; R. S. 1883, c. 4, § 86; R. S. 1903, c. 6, § 123; R. S. 1916, c. 7, § 57. And such was the law of this state when the act in question (chapter 120 of the Public Laws of 1919) was passed. The qualification of voters for senators, as well as for representatives, is fixed by the Constitution of Maine as "every male citizen of the United States of the age of twenty-one years and upwards," etc. Article 2, § 1. Therefore, prior to the act of 1919, only male citizens could vote for presidential electors. It is clear that this act, extending this privilege to women, constitutes a change in the method of electing presidential electors, and is a virtual amendment of R. S. 1916, c. 7, § 57, not in express terms, but by necessary implication.

In other words, this state during the century of its existence prior to 1919, had by appropriate legislative act or resolve directed that only male citizens were qualified to vote for presidential electors. By the act of 1919 it has attempted to change that direction, by extending the privilege of suffrage, so far as presidential electors are concerned, to women. Had this act been passed prior to the adoption of the initiative and referendum amendment in 1908, it would have become effective, so far as legal enactment is concerned, without being referred to the people; but now under Amendment 31 such reference must be had, if the necessary steps therefor are taken.

The language of that amendment is as follows:

> "No act or joint resolution of the Legislature, except such orders or resolutions as pertain solely to facilitating the performance of the business of the Legislature, of either branch, or of any committee or officer thereof, or appropriate money therefor or for the payment of salaries fixed by law, shall take effect until ninety days after the recess of the Legislature passing it, unless in case of emergency," etc.

None of the exceptions applies here. Section 17 provides that upon written petition of not less than 10,000 electors, filed in the office of the Secretary of State within 90 days after the recess of the Legislature, requesting that-

> "one or more acts, bills, resolves or resolutions, or part or parts thereof passed by the Legislature, not then in effect by reason of the provisions of the preceding section be referred to the people, such acts, bills, resolves or resolutions shall not take effect until thirty days after the Governor shall have announced by public proclamation that the same have been ratified by a majority of the electors voting thereon at a general or special election."

It is evident that the act in question falls within the terms and scope of this amendment. This is an ordinary legislative act, a bill in the form prescribed by Amendment 31. It is entitled "An act granting," etc. The enacting clause is, "Be it enacted by the people of the state of Maine." It was presented to the Governor for his approval, and was signed by him, as required by section 2 of part third of article 4 of the Constitution of Maine, viz.:

> "Every bill or resolution having the force of law, to which the concurrence of both houses may be necessary, ... which shall have passed both houses, shall be presented to the Governor,

and if he approves, he shall sign it," etc.

It has been published as chapter 120 of Public Laws of 1919.

This is not a mere joint resolution, addressed to the Governor, asking for the removal of a public official, as in *Moulton v. Scully*, 111 Me. 428, 89 Atl. 944, nor is it a joint resolution ratifying an amendment to the federal Constitution, as in the other question propounded to us herewith, in neither of which cases did the referendum attach, because neither resolution had the force of law. This is the public statute of a law-making body, and is as fully within the control of the referendum amendment as is any other of the 239 public acts passed at the last session of the Legislature, excepting, of course, emergency acts. It is shielded from the jurisdiction of that referendum neither by the state nor by the federal Constitution. In short, the state, through its Legislature, has taken merely the first step toward effecting a change in the appointment of presidential electors; but, because of the petitions filed, it must await the second step which is the vote of the people. The legislative attempt in this case cannot be fully effective until "thirty days after the Governor shall have announced by public proclamation that the same has been ratified by a majority of the electors voting thereon at a general or special election."

It follows that, for the reasons already stated, this question is answered in the affirmative.

Very respectfully,

LESLIE C. CORNISH

ALBERT M. SPEAR

GEORGE M. HANSON

WARREN C. PHILBROOK

CHARLES J. DUNN

JOHN A. MORRILL

SCOTT WILSON

LUERE B. DEASY

APPENDIX R:
State Constitutional Provisions Relating to Repealing or Amending Voter Initiatives

ALASKA CONSTITUTION-ARTICLE XI

SECTION 6. ENACTMENT. If a majority of the votes cast on the proposition favor its adoption, the initiated measure is enacted. If a majority of the votes cast on the proposition favor the rejection of an act referred, it is rejected. The lieutenant governor shall certify the election returns. An initiated law becomes effective ninety days after certification, is not subject to veto, and may not be repealed by the legislature within two years of its effective date. It may be amended at any time. An act rejected by referendum is void thirty days after certification. Additional procedures for the initiative and referendum may be prescribed by law.

ARIZONA CONSTITUTION-ARTICLE 4, PART 1(6)

(A) Veto of initiative or referendum. The veto power of the governor shall not extend to an initiative measure approved by a majority of the votes cast thereon or to a referendum measure decided by a majority of the votes cast thereon.

(B) Legislature's power to repeal initiative or referendum. The legislature shall not have the power to repeal an initiative measure approved by a majority of the votes cast thereon or to repeal a referendum measure decided by a majority of the votes cast thereon.

(C) Legislature's power to amend initiative or referendum. The legislature shall not have the power to amend an initiative measure approved by a majority of the votes cast thereon, or to amend a referendum measure decided by a majority of the votes cast thereon, unless the amending legislation furthers the purposes of such measure and at least three-fourths of the members of each house of the legislature, by a roll call of ayes and nays, vote to amend such measure.

ARKANSAS CONSTITUTION-AMENDMENT

No Veto: The veto power of the Governor or Mayor shall not extend to measures initiated by or referred to the people.

Amendment and Repeal: No measure approved by a vote of the people shall be amended or repealed by the General Assembly or by any City Council, except upon a yea and nay vote on roll call of two-thirds of all the members elected to each house of the General Assembly, or of the City Council, as the case may be.

CALIFORNIA CONSTITUTION-ARTICLE 2, SECTION 10(C)

The Legislature may amend or repeal referendum statutes. It may amend or repeal an initiative statute by another statute that becomes effective only when approved by the electors unless the initiative statute permits amendment or repeal without their approval.

MASSACHUSETTS CONSTITUTION-AMENDMENT ARTICLE 4

Section 3. Amendment of Proposed Amendments. – A proposal for an amendment to the constitution introduced by initiative petition shall be voted upon in the form in which it was introduced, unless such amendment is amended by vote of three-fourths of the members voting thereon in joint session, which vote shall be taken by call of the yeas and nays if called for by any member.

MICHIGAN CONSTITUTION-ARTICLE 2, SECTION 9

Initiative; duty of legislature, referendum. Any law proposed by initiative petition shall be either enacted or rejected by the legislature without change or amendment within 40 session days from the time such petition is received by the legislature. If any law proposed by such petition shall be enacted by the legislature it shall be subject to referendum, as hereinafter provided.

Legislative rejection of initiated measure; different measure; submission to people. If the law so proposed is not enacted by the legislature within the 40 days, the state officer authorized by law shall submit such proposed law to the people for approval or rejection at the next general election. The legislature may reject any measure so proposed by initiative petition and propose a different measure upon the same subject by a yea and nay vote upon separate roll calls, and in such event both measures shall be submitted by such state officer to the electors for approval or rejection at the next general election.

Initiative or referendum law; effective date, veto, amendment and repeal. Any law submitted to the people by either initiative or referendum petition and approved by a majority of the votes cast thereon at any election shall take effect 10 days after the date of the official declaration of the vote. No law initiated or adopted by the people shall be subject to the veto power of the governor, and no law adopted by the people at the polls under the initiative provisions of this section shall be amended or repealed, except by a vote of the electors unless otherwise provided in the initiative measure or by three-fourths of the members elected to and serving in each house of the legislature. Laws approved by the people under the referendum provision of this section may be amended by the legislature at any subsequent session thereof. If two or more measures approved by the electors at the same election conflict, that receiving the highest affirmative vote shall prevail.

NEBRASKA CONSTITUTION-ARTICLE III, SECTION 2

... The Legislature shall not amend, repeal, modify, or impair a law enacted by the people by initiative, contemporaneously with the adoption of this initiative measure or at any time thereafter, except upon a vote of at least two -thirds of all the members of the Legislature.

NEVADA CONSTITUTION-ARTICLE 19, SECTION 2

3. ... An initiative measure so approved by the voters shall not be amended, annulled, repealed, set aside or suspended by the legislature within 3 years from the date it takes effect....

NORTH DAKOTA CONSTITUTION-ARTICLE 3, SECTION 8

... A measure approved by the electors may not be repealed or amended by the legislative assembly for seven years from its effective date, except by a two-thirds vote of the members elected to each house...

WASHINGTON CONSTITUTION, ARTICLE 2, SECTION 41

... No act, law or bill approved by a majority of the electors voting thereon shall be amended or repealed by the legislature within a period of two years following such enactment: Provided, That any such act, law or bill may be amended within two years after such enactment at any regular or special session of the legislature by a vote of two-thirds of all the members elected to each house with full compliance with section 12, Article III, of the Washington Constitution, and no amendatory law adopted in accordance with this provision shall be subject to referendum. But such enactment may be amended or repealed at any general regular or special election by direct vote of the people thereon. These provisions supersede the provisions of subsection (c) of section 1 of this article as amended by the seventh amendment to the Constitution of this state.

WYOMING CONSTITUTION-ARTICLE 3, SECTION 52

(f) If votes in an amount in excess of fifty percent (50%) of those voting in the general election are cast in favor of adoption of an initiated measure, the measure is enacted. If votes in an amount in excess of fifty percent (50%) of those voted in the general election are cast in favor of rejection of an act referred, it is rejected. The secretary of state shall certify the election returns. An initiated law becomes effective ninety (90) days after certification, is not subject to veto, and may not be repealed by the legislature within two (2) years of its effective date. It may be amended at any time. An act rejected by referendum is void thirty (30) days after certification. Additional procedures for the initiative and referendum may be prescribed by law.

APPENDIX S:

Supporters in Congress of Nationwide Popular Election of the President in Roll Calls and Sponsors of Constitutional Amendments

S.1 ALABAMA

SPONSOR OF A CONSTITUTIONAL AMENDMENT	VOTED FOR SJR 28 IN 1979 ROLL CALL	VOTED FOR HJR 681 IN 1969 ROLL CALL
Rep. John H. Buchanan (R) • HJR 228 - 95th Congress • HJR 288 - 96th Congress		Rep. John H. Buchanan (R)
		Rep. William Dickinson (R)
Rep. William Edwards (R) • HJR 138 - 95th Congress • HJR 189 - 96th Congress • HJR 195 - 97th Congress		Rep. William Edwards (R)
	Sen. Donald Stewart (D)	

S.2 ALASKA

SPONSOR OF A CONSTITUTIONAL AMENDMENT	VOTED FOR SJR 28 IN 1979 ROLL CALL	VOTED FOR HJR 681 IN 1969 ROLL CALL
Sen. Maurice Gravel (D) • SJR 1 - 94th Congress • SJR 1 - 95th Congress • SJR 1 - 96th Congress • SJR 28 - 96th Congress	Sen. Maurice Gravel (D)	

S.3 ARIZONA

SPONSOR OF A CONSTITUTIONAL AMENDMENT	VOTED FOR SJR 28 IN 1979 ROLL CALL	VOTED FOR HJR 681 IN 1969 ROLL CALL
		Rep. John Rhodes (R)
		Rep. Sam Steiger (R)
Rep. Morris K. Udall (D) • HJR 168 - 95th Congress		Rep. Morris K. Udall (D)
Sen. Dennis DeConcini (D) • SJR 1 - 95th Congress • SJR 1 - 96th Congress • SJR 28 - 96th Congress • SJR 3 - 97th Congress • SJR 17 - 98th Congress • SJR 297 - 102nd Congress	Sen. Dennis DeConcini (D)	

S.3 ARKANSAS

SPONSOR OF A CONSTITUTIONAL AMENDMENT	VOTED FOR SJR 28 IN 1979 ROLL CALL	VOTED FOR HJR 681 IN 1969 ROLL CALL
Rep. William Vollie Alexander Jr. (D) • HJR 137 - 93rd Congress		Rep. William Vollie Alexander Jr. (D)
		Rep. John Hammerschmidt (R)
		Rep. Wilbur Mills (D)
Sen. David H. Pryor (D) • SJR 1 - 96th Congress • SJR 28 - 96th Congress • SJR 3 - 97th Congress • SJR 17 - 98th Congress • SJR 163 - 101st Congress • SJR 297 - 102nd Congress	Sen. David H. Pryor (D)	Rep. David H. Pryor (D)

S.5 CALIFORNIA

SPONSOR OF A CONSTITUTIONAL AMENDMENT	VOTED FOR SJR 28 IN 1979 ROLL CALL	VOTED FOR HJR 681 IN 1969 ROLL CALL
		Rep. Glenn Anderson (D)
Rep. Jim Bates (D) • HJR 137 - 101st Congress		
Rep. Anthony Beilenson (D) • HJR 9 - 102nd Congress		
Rep. Alphonza Bell (R) • HJR 237 - 93rd Congress		Rep. Alphonza Bell (R)
Sen. Barbara Boxer (D) • HJR 5 - 100th Congress		
Rep. George Brown (D) • HJR 228 - 95th Congress • HJR 254 - 96th Congress		Rep. George Brown (D)
Rep. Clair Burgener (R) • HJR 228 - 95th Congress		
		Rep. Phillip Burton (D)
Rep. Tom Campbell (R) • HJR 180 - 104th Congress • HJR 43 - 105th Congress		
		Rep. Donald Clausen (R)
		Rep. Delwin Clawson (R)
Rep. Anthony Coelho (D) • HJR 254 - 96th Congress		
		Rep. Jeffery Cohelan (D)
		Rep. James Corman (D)
Sen. Alan Cranston (D) • SJR 1 - 94th Congress • SJR 1 - 95th Congress • SJR 1 - 96th Congress • SJR 28 - 96th Congress • SJR 3 - 97th Congress • SJR 297 - 102nd Congress	Sen. Alan Cranston (D)	
Rep. George Danielson (D) • HJR 207 - 93rd Congress • HJR 149 - 95th Congress • HJR 7 - 96th Congress		
Rep. Ronald Dellums (D) • HJR 117 - 104th Congress		

S.5 CALIFORNIA *(cont.)*

SPONSOR OF A CONSTITUTIONAL AMENDMENT	VOTED FOR SJR 28 IN 1979 ROLL CALL	VOTED FOR HJR 681 IN 1969 ROLL CALL
Rep. Calvin Dooley (D) • HJR 28 - 103rd Congress		
		Rep. William Edwards (D)
Rep. Vic Fazio (D) • HJR 254 - 96th Congress		
Sen. Diane Feinstein (D) • SJR 11 - 109th Congress		
Rep. Bob Filner (D) • HJR 103 - 108th Congress		
		Rep. Charles Gubser (R)
		Rep. Richard Hanna (D)
Rep. Mark W. Hannaford (D) • HJR 229 - 95th Congress		
Rep. Augustus Hawkins (D) • HJR 384 - 95th Congress		Rep. Augustus Hawkins (D)
Rep. Andrew Hinshaw (R) • HJR 207 - 93rd Congress		
Rep. Chester Holifield (D) • HJR 207 - 93rd Congress		Rep. Chester Holifield (D)
		Rep. Craig Hosmer (R)
		Rep. Harold Johnson (D)
Rep. William M. Ketchum (R) • HJR 168 - 95th Congress • HJR 230 - 95th Congress • HJR 384 - 95th Congress		
Rep. Jay Kim (R) • HJR 28 - 103rd Congress		
Rep. John H. Krebs (D) • HJR 228 - 95th Congress		
Rep. Robert L. Leggett (D) • HJR 207 - 93rd Congress • HJR 231 - 95th Congress		Rep. Robert L. Leggett (D)
Rep. James F. Lloyd (D) • HJR 168 - 95th Congress		

S.5 CALIFORNIA *(cont.)*

SPONSOR OF A CONSTITUTIONAL AMENDMENT	VOTED FOR SJR 28 IN 1979 ROLL CALL	VOTED FOR HJR 681 IN 1969 ROLL CALL
Rep. Zoe Lofgren (D) • HJR 112 - 108th Congress • HJR 50 - 109th Congres		
		Rep. William Mailliard (R)
Rep. Matthew Martinez (D) • HJR 137 - 101st Congress		
		Rep. Robert Mathias (R)
Rep. Alfred McCandless (R) • HJR 28 - 103rd Congress		
		Rep. Paul McCloskey (R)
		Rep. John McFall (D)
		Rep. George Miller (D)
Rep. John Moss (D) • HJR 70 - 95th Congress • HJR 168 - 95th Congress		Rep. John Moss (D)
Rep. Jerry M. Patterson (D) • HJR 231 - 95th Congress • HJR 397 - 95th Congress • HJR 254 - 96th Congress		
Rep. Nancy Pelosi (D) • HJR 137 - 101st Congress		
		Rep. Jerry Pettis (R)
Rep. Shirley N. Pettis (R) • HJR 228 - 95th Congress		
		Rep. Thomas Rees (D)
Rep. Edward R. Roybal (D) • HJR 228 - 95th Congress		
Rep. Bernice Sisk (D) • HJR 207 - 93rd Congress		
		Rep. Allen Smith (R)
Rep. Fortney Stark (D) • HJR 228 - 95th Congress • HJR 299 - 96th Congress • HJR 36 - 109th Congress • HJR 50 - 109th Congress		

S.5 CALIFORNIA *(cont.)*

SPONSOR OF A CONSTITUTIONAL AMENDMENT	VOTED FOR SJR 28 IN 1979 ROLL CALL	VOTED FOR HJR 681 IN 1969 ROLL CALL
		Rep. Burt Talcott (R)
Rep. Walter R. Tucker III (D) • HJR 65 - 103rd Congress		
Sen. John Tunney (D) • SJR 1 - 94th Congress		Rep. John Tunney (D)
Rep. Lionel Van Deerlin (D) • HJR 254 - 96th Congress		Rep. Lionel Van Deerlin (D)
		Rep. Jerome Waldie (D)
		Rep. Charles Wiggins (R)
Rep. Charles H. Wilson (D) • HJR 231 - 95th Congress		Rep. Charles H. Wilson (D)
		Rep. Robert Wilson (R)
Rep. Lynn Woolsey (D) • HJR 50 - 109th Congress		

S.6 COLORADO

SPONSOR OF A CONSTITUTIONAL AMENDMENT	VOTED FOR SJR 28 IN 1979 ROLL CALL	VOTED FOR HJR 681 IN 1969 ROLL CALL
	Sen. William Armstrong (R)	
		Rep. Wayne Aspinall (D)
		Rep. Donald Brotzman (R)
Sen. Ben Campbell (R) • HJR 9 - 102nd Congress		
Rep. Frank Evans (D) • HJR 137 - 93rd Congress		Rep. Frank Evans (D)
Sen. Gary W. Hart (D) • SJR 1 - 94th Congress • SJR 1 - 95th Congress	Sen. Gary W. Hart (D)	
Sen. Floyd Haskell (D) • SJR 1 - 95th Congress • SJR 1 - 99th Congress		
		Rep. Byron Rogers (D)

S.7 CONNECTICUT

SPONSOR OF A CONSTITUTIONAL AMENDMENT	VOTED FOR SJR 28 IN 1979 ROLL CALL	VOTED FOR HJR 681 IN 1969 ROLL CALL
		Rep. Emilio Daddario (D)
Rep. Robert Giaimo (D) • HJR 137 - 93rd Congress		Rep. Robert Giaimo (D)
Rep. Stewart McKinney (R) • HJR 197 - 95th Congress		
		Rep. Thomas Meskill (R)
		Rep. John Monagan (D)
Rep. Bill Ratchford (D) • HJR 254 - 96th Congress		
Sen. Abaraham A. Ribicoff (D) • SJR 1 - 94th Congress • SJR 1 - 95th Congress • SJR 1 - 96th Congress • SJR 28 - 96th Congress	Sen. Abaraham A. Ribicoff (D)	
Rep. Ronald A. Sarasin (R) • HJR 300 - 93rd Congress • HJR 230 - 95th Congress		
		Rep. William St. Onge (D)
		Rep. Lowell Palmer Weicker (R)

S.8 DELAWARE

SPONSOR OF A CONSTITUTIONAL AMENDMENT	VOTED FOR SJR 28 IN 1979 ROLL CALL	VOTED FOR HJR 681 IN 1969 ROLL CALL
		Rep. William Victor Roth (R)
Sen. Thomas Carper (D) • HJR 137 - 101st Congress		

| *Appendix S*

S.9 FLORIDA

SPONSOR OF A CONSTITUTIONAL AMENDMENT	VOTED FOR SJR 28 IN 1979 ROLL CALL	VOTED FOR HJR 681 IN 1969 ROLL CALL
Rep. Jim Bacchus (D) • HJR 506 - 102nd Congress • HJR 28 - 103rd Congress		
Rep. Charles E. Bennett (D) • HJR 13 - 93rd Congress • HJR 3 - 94th Congress • HJR 33 - 95th Congress • HJR 24 - 96th Congress • HJR 20 - 97th Congress • HJR 11 - 98th Congress • HJR 19 - 99th Congress • HJR 12 - 100th Congress • HJR 11 - 101st Congress • HJR 9 - 102nd Congress		Rep. Charles E. Bennett (D)
		Rep. Herbert Burke (R)
		Rep. William Cramer (R)
Rep. Dante Fascell (D) • HJR 207 - 93rd Congress		Rep. Dante Fascell (D)
		Rep. Louis Frey (R)
Rep. Don Fuqua (D) • HJR 31 - 93rd Congress		
Rep. Sam Gibbons (D) • HJR 228 - 95th Congress • HJR 261 - 96th Congress		Rep. Sam Gibbons (D)
Rep. Alcee Hastings (D) • HJR 28 - 103rd Congress • HJR 17 - 109th Congress		
Rep. Claude Pepper (D) • HJR 207 - 93rd Congress • HJR 228 - 95th Congress • HJR 288 - 96th Congress		Rep. Claude Pepper (D)
		Rep. Paul Rogers (D)

S.10 GEORGIA

SPONSOR OF A CONSTITUTIONAL AMENDMENT	VOTED FOR SJR 28 IN 1979 ROLL CALL	VOTED FOR HJR 681 IN 1969 ROLL CALL
		Rep. John Davis (D)
		Rep. Phillip Landrum (D)
Rep. John Lewis (D) • HJR 137 - 101st Congress • HJR 9 - 102nd Congress		
		Rep. Robert G. Stephens, Jr. (D)
		Rep. Standish Thompson (R)

S.11 HAWAII

SPONSOR OF A CONSTITUTIONAL AMENDMENT	VOTED FOR SJR 28 IN 1979 ROLL CALL	VOTED FOR HJR 681 IN 1969 ROLL CALL
Rep. Cecil Heftel (D) • HJR 168 - 95th Congress		
Sen. Daniel K. Inouye (D) • SJR 1 - 94th Congress • SJR 1 - 95th Congress • SJR 1 - 96th Congress • SJR 28 - 96th Congress • SJR 3 - 97th Congress • SJR 362 - 100th Congress	Sen. Daniel K. Inouye (D)	
Sen. Spark Matsunaga (D) • SJR 1 - 95th Congress • SJR 1 - 96th Congress • SJR 28 - 96th Congress • SJR 3 - 97th Congress • SJR 17 - 98th Congress	Sen. Spark M. Matsunaga (D)	Rep. Spark M. Matsunaga (D)
		Rep. Patsy Mink (D)

S.12 IDAHO

SPONSOR OF A CONSTITUTIONAL AMENDMENT	VOTED FOR SJR 28 IN 1979 ROLL CALL	VOTED FOR HJR 681 IN 1969 ROLL CALL
Sen. Frank F. Church (D) • SJR 1 - 94th Congress • SJR 1 - 95th Congress	Sen. Frank F. Church (D)	
		Rep. Orval Hansen (R)
Rep. George Hansen (R) • HJR 207 - 93rd Congress		

S.13 ILLINOIS

SPONSOR OF A CONSTITUTIONAL AMENDMENT	VOTED FOR SJR 28 IN 1979 ROLL CALL	VOTED FOR HJR 681 IN 1969 ROLL CALL
Rep. John Anderson (R) • HJR 228 - 95th Congress • HJR 288 - 96th Congress		Rep. John Anderson (R)
Rep. Frank Annunzio (D) • HJR 137 - 93rd Congress		Rep. Frank Annunzio (D)
		Rep. Leslie Arends (R)
Rep. Rod Blagojevich (D) • HJR 23 - 106th Congress		
Rep. Harold Collier (R) • HJR 137 - 93rd Congress • HJR 462 - 93rd Congress		Rep. Harold Collier (R)
		Rep. George Collins (D)[1]
Rep. Cardiss Collins (D) • HJR 229 - 95th Congress • HJR 137 - 101st Congress • HJR 28 - 103rd Congress • HJR 117 - 104th Congress		
Rep. Philip Crane (R) • HJR 28 - 105th Congress		
Sen. Richard Durbin (D) • HJR 60 - 103rd Congress • SJR 56 -106th Congress		
		Rep. John Erlenborn (R)

---

[1] The roll call does not make clear whether this Representative Collins or the one from Texas voted for HJR 681 in 1969.

S.13 ILLINOIS *(cont.)*

SPONSOR OF A CONSTITUTIONAL AMENDMENT	VOTED FOR SJR 28 IN 1979 ROLL CALL	VOTED FOR HJR 681 IN 1969 ROLL CALL
Rep. Lane Evans (D) • HJR 506 - 102nd Congress • HJR 28 - 103rd Congress • HJR 23 - 106th Congress • HJR 17 - 109th Congress		
		Rep. Paul Findley (R)
		Rep. Kenneth Gray (D)
Rep. Robert Hanrahan (R) • HJR 207 - 93rd Congress		
Rep. Jesse Jackson Jr. (D) • HJR 109 - 108th Congress • HJR 36 - 109th Congress		
		Rep. John Kluczynski (D)
Rep. Ray LaHood (R) • HJR 28 - 105th Congress • HJR 23 - 106th Congress		
Rep. William O. Lipinski (D) • HJR 9 - 102nd Congress • HJR 28 - 105th Congress		
Rep. Robert McClory (R) • HJR 118 - 95th Congress • HJR 197 - 95th Congress • HJR 240 - 96th Congress		Rep. Robert McClory (R)
		Rep. Robert Michel (R)
		Rep. Abner Mikva (D)
		Rep. William Murphy (D)
Rep. Charles Price (D) • HJR 228 - 95th Congress • HJR 261 - 96th Congress		Rep. Charles Price (D)
		Rep. Roman Pucinski (D)
		Rep. Thomas Railsback (R)
		Rep. Charlotte Reid (R)
		Rep. Daniel Rostenkowski (D)

S.13 ILLINOIS *(cont.)*

SPONSOR OF A CONSTITUTIONAL AMENDMENT	VOTED FOR SJR 28 IN 1979 ROLL CALL	VOTED FOR HJR 681 IN 1969 ROLL CALL
Rep. Martin A. Russo (D) • HJR 288 - 96th Congress • HJR 384 - 96th Congress		
Rep. Janice Schakowsky (D) • HJR 109 - 108th Congress		
		Rep. George Shipley (D)
		Rep. William Springer (R)
Sen. Aldai Stevenson III (D) • SJR 1 - 94th Congress • SJR 1 - 95th Congress • SJR 1 - 96th Congress • SJR 28 - 96th Congress	Sen. Aldai Stevenson III (D)	
		Rep. Sidney Yates (D)

S.14 INDIANA

SPONSOR OF A CONSTITUTIONAL AMENDMENT	VOTED FOR SJR 28 IN 1979 ROLL CALL	VOTED FOR HJR 681 IN 1969 ROLL CALL
		Rep. Edwin Adair (R)
Sen. Birch E. Bayh (D) • SJR 1 - 94th Congress • SJR 1 - 95th Congress • SJR 123 - 95th Congress • SJR 1 - 96th Congress • SJR 28 - 96th Congress	Sen. Birch E. Bayh (D)	
Rep. Adam Benjamin Jr. (D) • HJR 384 - 95th Congress		
		Rep. John Brademas (D)
Rep. William Bray (R) • HJR 137 - 93rd Congress		Rep. William Bray (R)
Rep. Floyd Fithian (D) • HJR 521 - 94th Congress • HJR 350 - 95th Congress • HJR 208 - 96th Congress • HJR 254 - 96th Congress		
Rep. Lee Hamilton (D) • HJR 137 - 93rd Congress • HJR 207 - 95th Congress • HJR 137 - 101st Congress • HJR 9 - 102nd Congress • HJR 28 - 103rd Congress • HJR 28 - 105th Congress		Rep. Lee Hamilton (D)
Rep. Andrew Jacobs Jr. (D) • HJR 28 - 103rd Congress • HJR 33 - 103rd Congress • HJR 117 - 104th Congress • HJR 180 - 104th Congress		Rep. Andrew Jacobs Jr. (D)
		Rep. Ray Madden (D)
		Rep. John Myers (R)
Rep. Tim Roemer (D) • HJR 506 - 102nd Congress		
		Rep. Richard Roudebush (R)
Rep. John Roush (D) • HJR 106 - 93rd Congress		
		Rep. Roger Zion (R)

S.15 IOWA

SPONSOR OF A CONSTITUTIONAL AMENDMENT	VOTED FOR SJR 28 IN 1979 ROLL CALL	VOTED FOR HJR 681 IN 1969 ROLL CALL
Rep. Berkley W. Bedell (D) • HJR 229 - 95th Congress • HJR 230 - 95th Congress • HJR 254 - 96th Congress		
Rep. Michael T. Blouin (D) • HJR 1100 - 94th Congress • HJR 676 - 95th Congress		
Sen. Richard Clark (D) • SJR 1 - 94th Congress • SJR 1 - 95th Congress		
	Sen. John Culver (D)	Rep. John Culver (D)
Rep. James Leach (R) • HJR 585 - 96th Congress • HJR 516 - 102nd Congress • HJR 113 - 106th Congress		
		Rep. Frederick Schwengel (R)

S.16 KANSAS

SPONSOR OF A CONSTITUTIONAL AMENDMENT	VOTED FOR SJR 28 IN 1979 ROLL CALL	VOTED FOR HJR 681 IN 1969 ROLL CALL
Sen. Robert J. Dole (R) • SJR 1 - 94th Congress • SJR 1 - 95th Congress • SJR 1 - 96th Congress • SJR 28 - 96th Congress • SJR 3 - 97th Congress • SJR 17 - 98th Congress	Sen. Robert J. Dole (R)	
Rep. Dan Glickman (D) • HJR 673 - 100th Congress • HJR 137 - 101st Congress • HJR 516 - 102nd Congress • HJR 28 - 103rd Congress		
Sen. James Pearson (R) • SJR 1 - 94th Congress		
Rep. William Roy (D) • HJR 207 - 93rd Congress		
		Rep. Garner Shriver (R)
		Rep. Joe Skubitz (R)
Rep. James Slattery (D) • HJR 137 - 101st Congress		
Rep. Edward Winn (R) • HJR 231 - 95th Congress		Rep. Edward Winn (R)

S.17 KENTUCKY

SPONSOR OF A CONSTITUTIONAL AMENDMENT	VOTED FOR SJR 28 IN 1979 ROLL CALL	VOTED FOR HJR 681 IN 1969 ROLL CALL
Rep. Scotty Baesler (D) • HJR 28 - 103rd Congress		
Rep. John Breckinridge (D) • HJR 384 - 95th Congress		
		Rep. Tim Carter (R)
		Rep. William Cowger (R)
Sen. Wendell H. Ford (D) • SJR 1 - 94th Congress • SJR 1 - 95th Congress • SJR 1 - 96th Congress • SJR 28 - 96th Congress • SJR 3 - 97th Congress • SJR - 17 - 98th Congress	Sen. Wendell H. Ford (D)	
Sen. Walter Huddleston (D) • SJR 1 - 94th Congress • SJR 1 - 95th Congress • SJR 1 - 96th Congress • SJR 28 - 96th Congress • SJR 3 - 97th Congress • SJR 17 - 98th Congress	Sen. Walter Huddleston (D)	
		Rep. William Natcher (D)
Rep. Carl D. Perkins (D) • HJR 228 - 95th Congress		Rep. Carl D. Perkins (D)
		Rep. Marion Snyder (R)
		Rep. Frank Stubblefield (D)
		Rep. John Watts (D)

S.18 LOUISIANA

SPONSOR OF A CONSTITUTIONAL AMENDMENT	VOTED FOR SJR 28 IN 1979 ROLL CALL	VOTED FOR HJR 681 IN 1969 ROLL CALL
		Rep. Thomas Hale Boggs (D)
Sen. John Breaux (D) • HJR 229 - 95th Congress		
		Rep. Edwin Edwards (D)
Rep. Thomas J. Huckaby (D) • HJR 516 - 102nd Congress • HJR 526 - 102nd Congress		
Sen. John B. Johnston Jr. (D) • SJR 1 - 96th Congress • SJR 28 - 96th Congress	Sen. John B. Johnston Jr. (D)	
Rep. Richard A. Tonry (D) • HJR 228 - 95th Congress		

S.19 MAINE

SPONSOR OF A CONSTITUTIONAL AMENDMENT	VOTED FOR SJR 28 IN 1979 ROLL CALL	VOTED FOR HJR 681 IN 1969 ROLL CALL
Rep. Thomas Andrews (D) • HJR 28 - 103rd Congress		
Rep. David Emery (R) • HJR 228 - 95th Congress		
Sen. William Hathaway (D) • SJR 1 - 94th Congress)		Rep.. William Hathaway (D
		Rep. Peter Kyros (D)

S.20 MARYLAND

SPONSOR OF A CONSTITUTIONAL AMENDMENT	VOTED FOR SJR 28 IN 1979 ROLL CALL	VOTED FOR HJR 681 IN 1969 ROLL CALL
		Rep. John Glenn Beall (R)
Rep. Elijah E. Cummings (D) • HJR 109 - 108th Congress		
		Rep. George Fallon (D)
		Rep. Samuel Friedel (D)
		Rep. Edward Garmatz (D)
		Rep. Gilbert Gude (R)
		Rep. Lawrence Hogan (R)
		Rep. Clarence Long (D)
Sen. Charles McCurdy Mathias Jr. (R) • SJR 1 - 94th Congress • SJR 1 - 95th Congress • SJR 1 - 96th Congress • SJR 28 - 96th Congress • SJR 8 - 97th Congress • SJR 17 - 98th Congress	Sen. Charles McCurdy Mathias Jr. (R)	
Rep. Kweisi Mfume (D) • HJR 117 - 104th Congress		
Rep. Parren Mitchell (D) • HJR 229 - 95th Congress • HJR 261 - 96th Congress		
		Rep. Rogers Morton (R)
Rep. Gladys Spellman (D) • HJR 384 - 95th Congress		
Rep. Albert Wynn (D) • HJR 103 - 108th Congress		

S.21 MASSACHUSETTS

SPONSOR OF A CONSTITUTIONAL AMENDMENT	VOTED FOR SJR 28 IN 1979 ROLL CALL	VOTED FOR HJR 681 IN 1969 ROLL CALL
Rep. Chester Atkins (D) • HJR 137 - 101st Congress		
Rep. Edward Boland (D) • HJR 137 - 93rd Congress		Rep. Edward Boland (D)
Sen. Edward W. Brooke (R) • SJR 1 - 94th Congress • SJR 1 - 95th Congress		
		Rep. James Burke (D)
Rep. Silvio Conte (R) • HJR 300 - 93rd Congress • HJR 38 - 94th Congress • HJR 45 - 95th Congress • HJR 230 - 95th Congress • HJR 231 - 95th Congress • HJR 373 - 95th Congress • HJR 150 - 96th Congress		Rep. Silvio Conte (R)
Rep. William D. Delahunt (D) • HJR 5 - 107th Congress • HJR 103 - 108th Congress • HJR 8 - 109th Congress		
Rep. Brian Donnelly (D) • HJR 288 - 96th Congress		
		Rep. Harold Donohue (D)
Rep. Barney Frank (D) • HJR 137 - 101st Congress • HJR 9 - 102nd Congress • HJR 28 - 103rd Congress • HJR 117 - 104th Congress • HJR 28 - 105th Congress • HJR 17 - 109th Congress • HJR 36 - 109th Congress		
		Rep. Margaret Heckler (R)
		Rep. Hastings Keith (R)
Sen. Ted Kennedy (D) • SJR 1 - 94th Congress • SJR 1 - 95th Congress • SJR 1 - 96th Congress • SJR 28 - 96th Congress	Sen. Ted Kennedy (D)	

S.21 MASSACHUSETTS *(cont.)*

SPONSOR OF A CONSTITUTIONAL AMENDMENT	VOTED FOR SJR 28 IN 1979 ROLL CALL	VOTED FOR HJR 681 IN 1969 ROLL CALL
Rep. Torbert MacDonald (D) • HJR 336 - 94th Congress		Rep. Torbert MacDonald (D)
Rep. Edward Markey (D) • HJR 373 - 95th Congress		
		Rep. Frank Morse (R)
		Rep. David Obey (D)
		Rep. Thomas O'Neill (D)
		Rep. Philip Philbin (D)
Rep. Gerry Studds (D) • HJR 208 - 93rd Congress • HJR 384 - 95th Congress • HJR 261 - 96th Congress • HJR 591 - 96th Congress • HJR 70 - 97th Congress • HJR 124 - 98th Congress • HJR 137 - 101st Congress • HJR 117 - 104th Congress		
Sen. Paul Tsongas (D) • SJR 1 - 96th Congress • SJR 28 - 96th Congress	Sen. Paul Tsongas (D)	

S.22 MICHIGAN

SPONSOR OF A CONSTITUTIONAL AMENDMENT	VOTED FOR SJR 28 IN 1979 ROLL CALL	VOTED FOR HJR 681 IN 1969 ROLL CALL
Rep. James A. Barcia (D) • HJR 117 - 104th Congress		
Rep. James J. Blanchard (D) • HJR 168 - 95th Congress		
Rep. David Bonior (D) • HJR 230 - 95th Congress • HJR 145 - 102nd Congress • HJR 28 - 103rd Congress		
Rep. William Broomfield (R) • HJR 137 - 93rd Congress • HJR 288 - 94th Congress		Rep. William Broomfield (R)
		Rep. Garry Brown (R)
Rep. Milton R. Carr (D) • HJR 397 - 95th Congress • HJR 261 - 96th Congress		
Rep. Elford Cederberg (R) • HJR 168 - 95th Congress		Rep. Elford Cederberg (R)
Rep. Charles Chamberlain (R) • HJR 202 - 93rd Congress		Rep. Charles Chamberlain (R)
Rep. John Conyers Jr. (D) • HJR 137 - 93rd Congress • HJR 109 - 108th Congress		Rep. John Conyers Jr. (D)
Rep. George Crockett (D) • HJR 137 - 101st Congress		
Rep. John David Dingell Jr. (D) • HJR 137 - 93rd Congress		Rep. John David Dingell Jr. (D)
Rep. Marvin Esch (R) • HJR 137 - 93rd Congress		Rep. Marvin Esch (R)
		Rep. Gerald Ford (R)
Rep. W. D. Ford (D) • HJR 137 - 93rd Congress • HJR 229 - 95th Congress • HJR 288 - 96th Congress		Rep. W. D. Ford (D)
Sen. Robert Griffin (R) • SJR 1 - 94th Congress		

S.22 MICHIGAN *(cont.)*

SPONSOR OF A CONSTITUTIONAL AMENDMENT	VOTED FOR SJR 28 IN 1979 ROLL CALL	VOTED FOR HJR 681 IN 1969 ROLL CALL
Sen. Philip Hart (D) • SJR 1 - 94th Congress		
Sen. Rupert Hartke (D) • SJR 1 - 94th Congress		
Rep. James Harvey (R) • HJR 207 - 93rd Congress		Rep. James Harvey (R)
Rep. Dale E. Kildee (D) • HJR 229 - 95th Congress • HJR 254 - 96th Congress • HJR 261 - 96th Congress		
Sen. Carl Levin (D) • SJR 1 - 96th Congress • SJR 28 - 96th Congress • SJR 3 - 97th Congress • SJR 17 - 98th Congress • SJR 362 - 100th Congress • SJR 163 - 101st Congress	Sen. Carl Levin (D)	
		Rep. Jack McDonald (R)
Rep. Lucien Nedzi (D) • HJR 168 - 95th Congress • HJR 231 - 95th Congress • HJR 384 - 95th Congress		Rep. Lucien Nedzi (D)
Rep. James O'Hara (D) • HJR 137 - 93rd Congress • HJR 139 - 93rd Congress • HJR 207 - 93rd Congress • HJR 208 - 93rd Congress		Rep. James O'Hara (D)
Rep. Carl D. Pursell (R) • HJR 168 - 95th Congress • HJR 230 - 95th Congress		
Sen. Donald Riegle (D) • SJR 1 - 95th Congress • SJR 1 - 96th Congress • SJR 28 - 96th Congress	Sen. Donald Riegle (D)	Rep. Donald Riegle (D)
		Rep. Philip Ruppe (R)
Rep. Harold Sawyer (R) • HJR 384 - 95th Congress		

S.22 MICHIGAN *(cont.)*

SPONSOR OF A CONSTITUTIONAL AMENDMENT	VOTED FOR SJR 28 IN 1979 ROLL CALL	VOTED FOR HJR 681 IN 1969 ROLL CALL
Rep. Bart Stupak (D) • HJR 28 - 103rd Congress		
		Rep. Guy Vander Jagt (R)
Rep. Howard Wolpe (D) • HJR 288 - 96th Congress		

S.23 MINNESOTA

SPONSOR OF A CONSTITUTIONAL AMENDMENT	VOTED FOR SJR 28 IN 1979 ROLL CALL	VOTED FOR HJR 681 IN 1969 ROLL CALL
Sen. Wendell Anderson (D) • SJR 1 - 95th Congress		
		Rep. John Blatnik (D)
Sen. Dave Durenberger (R) • SJR 1 - 96th Congress • SJR 28 - 96th Congress • SJR 3 - 97th Congress	Sen. Dave Durenberger (R)	
Rep. Donald Fraser (D) • HJR 207 - 93rd Congress • HJR 384 - 95th Congress		Rep. Donald Fraser (D)
Rep. William Frenzel (R) • HJR 300 - 93rd Congress • HJR 253 - 95th Congress		
Sen. Hubert Humphrey (D) • SJR 1 - 94th Congress • SJR 1 - 95th Congress		
Rep. Joseph Karth (D) • HJR 204 - 94th Congress		Rep. Joseph Karth (D)
		Rep. Odin Langen (R)
Rep. Bill Luther (D) • HJR 117 - 104th Congress • HJR 28 - 105th Congress		
		Rep. Clark MacGregor (R)
Rep. Betty McCollum (D) • HJR 103 - 108th Congress		
Rep. David Minge (D) • HJR 28 - 103rd Congress • HJR 23 - 106th Congress		

S.23 MINNESOTA

SPONSOR OF A CONSTITUTIONAL AMENDMENT	VOTED FOR SJR 28 IN 1979 ROLL CALL	VOTED FOR HJR 681 IN 1969 ROLL CALL
Sen. Walter Mondale (D) • SJR 1 - 94th Congress		
		Rep. Ancher Nelsen (R)
Rep. Richard M. Nolan (D) • HJR 229 - 95th Congress • HJR 308 - 96th Congress		
Rep. Collin Peterson (D) • HJR 28 - 103rd Congress		
Rep. Albert H. Quie (R) • HJR 151 - 94th Congress • HJR 434 - 95th Congress		Rep. Albert H. Quie (R)
Rep. Bruce F. Vento (D) • HJR 288 - 96th Congress • HJR 137 - 101st Congress		
		Rep. John Zwach (R)

S.24 MISSISSIPPI

SPONSOR OF A CONSTITUTIONAL AMENDMENT	VOTED FOR SJR 28 IN 1979 ROLL CALL	VOTED FOR HJR 681 IN 1969 ROLL CALL
Rep. Gene Taylor (D) • HJR 506 - 102nd Congress		

S.25 MISSOURI

SPONSOR OF A CONSTITUTIONAL AMENDMENT	VOTED FOR SJR 28 IN 1979 ROLL CALL	VOTED FOR HJR 681 IN 1969 ROLL CALL
Rep. Richard Bolling (D) • HJR 207 - 93rd Congress		
Rep. William D. Burlison (D) • HJR 137 - 93rd Congress • HJR 786 - 94th Congress • HJR 39 - 95th Congress • HJR 228 - 95th Congress • HJR 229 - 95th Congress • HJR 281 - 95th Congress • HJR 384 - 95th Congress • HJR 397 - 95th Congress • HJR 254 - 96th Congress • HJR 261 - 96th Congress • HJR 288 - 96th Congress • HJR 299 - 96th Congress • HJR 308 - 96th Congress • HJR 332 - 96th Congress		Rep. William D. Burlison (D)
Sen. John C. Danforth (R) • SJR 1 - 95th Congress • SJR 1 - 96th Congress • SJR 28 - 96th Congress	Sen. John C. Danforth (R)	
Rep. Pat Danner (D) • HJR 117 - 104th Congress • HJR 28 - 105th Congress		
Rep. Richard Gephardt (D) • HJR 228 - 95th Congress		
		Rep. William Raleigh Hull (D)
		Rep. William Hungate (D)
		Rep. Richard Ichord (D)
		Rep. William Randall (D)
Sen. William Symington (D) • SJR 1 - 94th Congress		
Rep. James Symington (D) • HJR 300 - 93rd Congress		Rep. James Symington (D)

S.25 MISSOURI *(cont.)*

SPONSOR OF A CONSTITUTIONAL AMENDMENT	VOTED FOR SJR 28 IN 1979 ROLL CALL	VOTED FOR HJR 681 IN 1969 ROLL CALL
Rep. Alan Wheat (D) • HJR 137 - 101st Congress • HJR 145 - 102nd Congress • HJR 65 - 103rd Congress		
Rep. Robert Young (D) • HJR 261 - 96th Congress		

S.26 MONTANA

SPONSOR OF A CONSTITUTIONAL AMENDMENT	VOTED FOR SJR 28 IN 1979 ROLL CALL	VOTED FOR HJR 681 IN 1969 ROLL CALL
Sen. Max Baucus (D) • HJR 197 - 95th Congress • HJR 229 - 95th Congress • HJR 230 - 95th Congress • SJR 3 - 97th Congress • SJR 17 - 98th Congress	Sen. Max Baucus (D)	
Sen. Michael Mansfield (D) • SJR 1 - 94th Congress		
		Rep. Arnold Olsen (D)

S.27 NEBRASKA

SPONSOR OF A CONSTITUTIONAL AMENDMENT	VOTED FOR SJR 28 IN 1979 ROLL CALL	VOTED FOR HJR 681 IN 1969 ROLL CALL
Rep. John J. Cavanaugh (D) • HJR 228 - 95th Congress • HJR 332 - 96th Congress		
		Rep. Glenn Cunningham (R)
		Rep. Robert Denney (R)
Sen. J. James Exon (D) • SJR 3 - 97th Congress • SJR 362 - 100th Congress • SJR 163 - 101st Congress • SJR 302 - 102nd Congress • SJR 173 - 103rd Congress	Sen. J. James Exon (D)	
		Rep. David Martin (R)
Sen. Edward Zorinsky (D) • SJR 1 - 95th Congress • SJR 1 - 96th Congress • SJR 28 - 96th Congress	Sen. Edward Zorinsky (D)	

S.28 NEVADA

SPONSOR OF A CONSTITUTIONAL AMENDMENT	VOTED FOR SJR 28 IN 1979 ROLL CALL	VOTED FOR HJR 681 IN 1969 ROLL CALL
Sen. Harry M. Reid (D) • SJR 297 - 102nd Congress		

S.29 NEW HAMPSHIRE

SPONSOR OF A CONSTITUTIONAL AMENDMENT	VOTED FOR SJR 28 IN 1979 ROLL CALL	VOTED FOR HJR 681 IN 1969 ROLL CALL
Sen. Thomas J. McIntyre (D) • SJR 1 - 94th Congress • SJR 1 - 95th Congress		
		Rep. Louis Wyman (R)

S.30 NEW JERSEY

SPONSOR OF A CONSTITUTIONAL AMENDMENT	VOTED FOR SJR 28 IN 1979 ROLL CALL	VOTED FOR HJR 681 IN 1969 ROLL CALL
		Rep. William Cahill (R)
Rep. Dominick Daniels (D) • HJR 137 - 93rd Congress		Rep. Dominick Daniels (D)
		Rep. Florence Dwyer (R)
Rep. Edwin Forsythe (R) • HJR 207 - 93rd Congress		
		Rep. Peter Frelinghuysen (R)
		Rep. Cornelius Gallagher (D)
		Rep. Henry Helstoski (D)
Rep. James J. Howard (D) • HJR 228 - 95th Congress • HJR 288 - 96th Congress • HJR 130 - 97th Congress		Rep. James J. Howard (D)
Rep. William J. Hughes (D) • HJR 114 - 95th Congress		
		Rep. John Hunt (R)
Rep. Joseph G. Minish (D) • HJR 231 - 95th Congress		Rep. Joseph G. Minish (D)
Rep. Edward Patten (D) • HJR 820 - 93rd Congress		Rep. Edward Patten (D)
Rep. Matthew Rinaldo (R) • HJR 300 - 93rd Congress		
Rep. Peter Rodino (D) • HJR 144 - 95th Congress		Rep. Peter Rodino (D)
		Rep. Charles Sandman (R)
		Rep. Frank Thompson (D)
Rep. William Widnall (R) • HJR 208 - 93rd Congress		Rep. William Widnall (R)
Sen. Harrison Williams (D) • SJR 1 - 94th Congress • SJR 1 - 95th Congress • SJR 1 - 96th Congress • SJR 28 - 96th Congress	Sen. Harrison Williams (D)	

S.31 NEW MEXICO

SPONSOR OF A CONSTITUTIONAL AMENDMENT	VOTED FOR SJR 28 IN 1979 ROLL CALL	VOTED FOR HJR 681 IN 1969 ROLL CALL
		Rep. Manuel Lujan (R)
Sen. Joseph Montoya (D) • SJR 1 - 94th Congress		

S.32 NEW YORK

SPONSOR OF A CONSTITUTIONAL AMENDMENT	VOTED FOR SJR 28 IN 1979 ROLL CALL	VOTED FOR HJR 681 IN 1969 ROLL CALL
Rep. Joseph P. Addabbo (D) • HJR 207 - 93rd Congress • HJR 168 - 95th Congress		Rep. Joseph P. Addabbo (D)
Rep. Herman Badillo (D) • HJR 207 - 93rd Congress		
		Rep. Mario Biaggi (D)
Rep. Jonathan Bingham (D) • HJR 352 - 95th Congress • HJR 384 - 95th Congress		Rep. Jonathan Bingham (D)
Rep. Frank James Brasco (D) • HJR 137 - 93rd Congress		Rep. Frank James Brasco (D)
		Rep. Daniel Button (R)
		Rep. Hugh Carey (D)
		Rep. Emanuel Celler (D)
Rep. Shirley A. Chisholm (D) • HJR 137 - 93rd Congress • HJR 300 - 93rd Congress • HJR 254 - 96th Congress		Rep. Shirley A. Chisholm (D)
		Rep. Barber Conable (R)
		Rep. James Delaney (D)
Rep. Thomas J. Downey (D) • HJR 229 - 95th Congress • HJR 288 - 96th Congress		
		Rep. Thaddeus Dulski (D)
Rep. Eliot L. Engel (D) • HJR 17 - 109th Congress		
		Rep. Leonard Farbstein (D)

S.32 NEW YORK *(cont.)*

SPONSOR OF A CONSTITUTIONAL AMENDMENT	VOTED FOR SJR 28 IN 1979 ROLL CALL	VOTED FOR HJR 681 IN 1969 ROLL CALL
Rep. Hamilton Fish Jr. (R) • HJR 137 - 93rd Congress • HJR 50 - 94th Congress		Rep. Hamilton Fish Jr. (R)
		Rep. Jacob Gilbert (D)
Rep. James Russell Grover Jr. (R) • HJR 137 - 93rd Congress		Rep. James Russell Grover Jr. (R)
		Rep. Seymour Halpern (R)
Rep. James Hanley (D) • HJR 228 - 95th Congress • HJR 261 - 96th Congress		Rep. James Hanley (D)
Rep. James Hastings (R) • HJR 207 - 93rd Congress		Rep. James Hastings (R)
		Rep. Frank Horton (R)
Sen. Jacob Javits (R) • SJR 1 - 94th Congress • SJR 1 - 95th Congress • SJR 1 - 96th Congress • SJR 28 - 96th Congress	Sen. Jacob Javits (R)	
		Rep. Carleton King (R)
		Rep. Edward Koch (D)
		Rep. Allard Lowenstein (D)
		Rep. Richard McCarthy (D)
		Rep. Robert McEwen (R)
		Rep. Martin McKneally (R)
Rep. Michael McNulty (D) • HJR 28 - 103rd Congress • HJR 60 - 103rd Congress • HJR 28 - 105th Congress • HJR 23 - 106th Congress • HJR 103 - 108th Congress • HJR 17 - 109th Congress		
Rep. Donald Mitchell (R) • HJR 750 - 94th Congress • HJR 168 - 95th Congress • HJR 228 - 95th Congress • HJR 288 - 96th Congress		

S.32 NEW YORK *(cont.)*

SPONSOR OF A CONSTITUTIONAL AMENDMENT	VOTED FOR SJR 28 IN 1979 ROLL CALL	VOTED FOR HJR 681 IN 1969 ROLL CALL
Rep. Susan Molinari (R) • HJR 28 - 103rd Congress		
		Rep. John Murphy (D)
Rep. Jerrold Nadler (D) • HJR 109 - 108th Congress		
Rep. Richard L. Ottinger (D) • HJR 231 - 95th Congress • HJR 384 - 95th Congress • HJR 288 - 96th Congress		Rep. Richard L. Ottinger (D)
Rep. Major Owens (D) • HJR 117 - 104th Congress • HJR 109 - 108th Congress		
		Rep. Otis Pike (D)
		Rep. Alexander Pirnie (R)
Rep. Bertram Podell (D) • HJR 207 - 93rd Congress		Rep. Bertram Podell (D)
Rep. Charles B. Rangel (D) • HJR 300 - 95th Congress		
		Rep. Ogden Reid (D)
Rep. Frederick Richmond (D) • HJR 229 - 95th Congress • HJR 254 - 96th Congress		
		Rep. Howard Robison (R)
		Rep. John Rooney (D)
Rep. Benjamin Rosenthal (D) • HJR 207 - 93rd Congress		Rep. Benjamin Rosenthal (D)
		Rep. William Ryan (D)
		Rep. James Scheuer (D)
Rep. Jose E. Serrano (D) • HJR 103 - 108th Congress • HJR 50 - 109th Congress		
		Rep. Henry Smith (R)
		Rep. Samuel Stratton (D)
Rep. Anthony Weiner (D) • HJR 103 - 108th Congress		

S.32 NEW YORK *(cont.)*

SPONSOR OF A CONSTITUTIONAL AMENDMENT	VOTED FOR SJR 28 IN 1979 ROLL CALL	VOTED FOR HJR 681 IN 1969 ROLL CALL
Rep. Theodore S. Weiss (D) • HJR 228 - 95th Congress		
Rep. Lester L. Wolff (D) • HJR 208 - 93rd Congress • HJR 228 - 95th Congress		Rep. Lester L. Wolff (D)
		Rep. John Wydler (R)

S.33 NORTH CAROLINA

SPONSOR OF A CONSTITUTIONAL AMENDMENT	VOTED FOR SJR 28 IN 1979 ROLL CALL	VOTED FOR HJR 681 IN 1969 ROLL CALL
		Rep. James Broyhill (R)
		Rep. Lawrence Fountain (D)
		Rep. Nick Galifianakis (D)
		Rep. David Henderson (D)
		Rep. Charles Jonas (R)
Rep. Walter Beaman Jones Sr. (D) • HJR 207 - 93rd Congress		Rep. Walter Beaman Jones Sr. (D)
		Rep. Wilmer Mizell (R)
		Rep. Lunsford Preyer (D)
		Rep. Earl Ruth (R)
		Rep. Roy Taylor (D)

S.34 NORTH DAKOTA

SPONSOR OF A CONSTITUTIONAL AMENDMENT	VOTED FOR SJR 28 IN 1979 ROLL CALL	VOTED FOR HJR 681 IN 1969 ROLL CALL
		Rep. Mark Andrews (R)
Sen. Quentin N. Burdick (D) • SJR 1 - 94th Congress • SJR 1 - 96th Congress • SJR 28 - 96th Congress • SJR 17 - 98th Congress	Sen. Quentin N. Burdick (D)	

S.35 OHIO

SPONSOR OF A CONSTITUTIONAL AMENDMENT	VOTED FOR SJR 28 IN 1979 ROLL CALL	VOTED FOR HJR 681 IN 1969 ROLL CALL
Rep. Thomas Ashley (D) • HJR 137 - 93rd Congress		Rep. Thomas Ashley (D)
		Rep. William Ayers (R)
		Rep. Jackson Betts (R)
		Rep. Frank Bow (R)
		Rep. Clarence J. Brown (R)
Rep. Charles J. Carney (D) • HJR 35 - 94th Congress • HJR 40 - 95th Congress • HJR 384 - 95th Congress		
		Rep. Donald Clancy (R)
Rep. Dennis Eckart (D) • HJR 9 - 102nd Congress		
		Rep. Michael Feighan (D)
Sen. John H. Glenn Jr. (D) • SJR 1 - 94th Congress • SJR 1 - 95th Congress • SJR 1 - 96th Congress • SJR 3 - 97th Congress • SJR 17 - 98th Congress	Sen. John H. Glenn Jr. (D)	
		Rep. William Harsha (R)
		Rep. Wayne Hays (D)
Rep. Dennis J. Kucinich (D) • HJR 109 - 108th Congress		
		Rep. Delbert Latta (R)
Rep. Thomas Luken (D) • HJR 228 - 95th Congress		
		Rep. William McCulloch (R)
Sen. Howard M. Metzenbaum (D) • SJR 1 - 95th Congress • SJR 1 - 96th Congress • SJR 3 - 97th Congress • SJR 17 - 98th Congress	Sen. Howard M. Metzenbaum (D)	
		Rep. Clarence Miller (R)
		Rep. William Minshall (R)

S.35 OHIO *(cont.)*

SPONSOR OF A CONSTITUTIONAL AMENDMENT	VOTED FOR SJR 28 IN 1979 ROLL CALL	VOTED FOR HJR 681 IN 1969 ROLL CALL
		Rep. Charles Mosher (R)
Rep. Ronald Mottl (D) • HJR 168 - 95th Congress		
Rep. Donald J. Pease (D) • HJR 168 - 95th Congress • HJR 229 - 95th Congress • HJR 288 - 96th Congress		
Rep. John F. Seiberling (D) • HJR 229 - 95th Congress		
		Rep. John Stanton (R)
Rep. Louis Stokes (D) • HJR 254 - 96th Congress		Rep. Louis Stokes (D)
Sen. Robert Taft Jr. (R) • SJR 1 - 94th Congress		Rep. Robert Taft Jr. (R)
Rep. James A. Traficant Jr. (D) • HJR 511 - 102nd Congress • HJR 117 - 104th Congress		
Rep. Charles Vanik (D) • HJR 139 - 93rd Congress		Rep. Charles Vanik (D)
Rep. Charles Whalen (R) • HJR 300 - 93rd Congress • HJR 345 - 94th Congress • HJR 238 - 95th Congress		Rep. Charles Whalen (R)
		Rep. Chalmers Wylie (R)

S.36 OKLAHOMA

SPONSOR OF A CONSTITUTIONAL AMENDMENT	VOTED FOR SJR 28 IN 1979 ROLL CALL	VOTED FOR HJR 681 IN 1969 ROLL CALL
		Rep. Carl Albert (D)
Sen. Dewey F. Bartlett (R) • SJR 1 - 95th Congress		
		Rep. Page Belcher (R)
Sen. Henry Bellmon (R) • SJR 101 - 93rd Congress • SJR 1 - 94th Congress • SJR 1 - 95th Congress • SJR 1 - 96th Congress • SJR 28 - 96th Congress	Sen. Henry Bellmon (R)	
Sen. David L. Boren (D) • SJR 3 - 97th Congress • SJR 17 - 98th Congress • SJR 297 - 102nd Congress • SJR 302 - 102nd Congress	Sen. David L. Boren (D)	
		Rep. John Camp (R)
		Rep. Edmond Edmondson (D)
		Rep. John Jarman (D)
		Rep. Thomas Steed (D)

S.37 OREGON

SPONSOR OF A CONSTITUTIONAL AMENDMENT	VOTED FOR SJR 28 IN 1979 ROLL CALL	VOTED FOR HJR 681 IN 1969 ROLL CALL
Rep. John Dellenback (R) • HJR 78 - 93rd Congress • HJR 137 - 93rd Congress		Rep. John Dellenback (R)
Rep. Robert B. Duncan (D) • HJR 229 - 95th Congress • HJR 230 - 95th Congress		
		Rep. Edith Green (D)
Sen. Mark O. Hatfield (R) • SJR 1 - 94th Congress • SJR 1 - 95th Congress • SJR 1 - 96th Congress • SJR 28 - 96th Congress • SJR 8 - 97th Congress • SJR 17 - 98th Congress	Sen. Mark O. Hatfield (R)	
Sen. Robert W. Packwood (R) • SJR 1 - 94th Congress • SJR 1 - 95th Congress • SJR 1 - 96th Congress • SJR 28 - 96th Congress	Sen. Robert W. Packwood (R)[2]	
Rep. Albert Ullman (D) • HJR 384 - 95th Congress		Rep. Albert Ullman (D)
		Rep. Wendell Wyatt (R)

[2] Senator Packwood was announced in favor of SJR 28, but did not cast a vote in the roll call.

S.38 PENNSYLVANIA

SPONSOR OF A CONSTITUTIONAL AMENDMENT	VOTED FOR SJR 28 IN 1979 ROLL CALL	VOTED FOR HJR 681 IN 1969 ROLL CALL
Rep. Joseph Ammerman (D) • HJR 384 - 95th Congress		
		Rep. William Barrett (D)
Rep. Edward George Biester Jr. (R) • HJR 207 - 93rd Congress		Rep. Edward George Biester Jr. (R)
		Rep. James Byrne (D)
Rep. Frank Clark (D) • HJR 137 - 93rd Congress		Rep. Frank Clark (D)
		Rep. Robert Corbett (R)
		Rep. Robert Coughlin (R)
		Rep. John Dent (D)
Rep. Robert Edgar (D) • HJR 230 - 95th Congress • HJR 384 - 95th Congress		
Rep. Joshua Eilberg (D) • HJR 127 - 95th Congress		Rep. Joshua Eilberg (D)
Rep. Allen E. Ertel (D) • HJR 384 - 95th Congress • HJR 288 - 96th Congress		
		Rep. Edwin Eshleman (R)
Rep. Daniel J. Flood (D) • HJR 137 - 93rd Congress • HJR 288 - 96th Congress		Rep. Daniel J. Flood (D)
		Rep. James Fulton (R)
Rep. Joseph Gaydos (D) • HR 2063 - 95th Congress		Rep. Joseph Gaydos (D)
Rep. William F. Goodling (R) • HJR 150 - 96th Congress		
		Rep. George Goodling (R)
		Rep. William Green (D)
Rep. James Greenwood (R) • HJR 28 - 103rd Congress		
		Rep. Albert Johnson (R)

S.38 PENNSYLVANIA

SPONSOR OF A CONSTITUTIONAL AMENDMENT	VOTED FOR SJR 28 IN 1979 ROLL CALL	VOTED FOR HJR 681 IN 1969 ROLL CALL
Rep. Joseph P. Kolter (D) • HJR 506 - 102nd Congress		
Rep. Peter H. Kostmayer (D) • HJR 506 - 102nd Congress		
Rep. Joseph McDade (R) • HJR 207 - 93rd Congress		Rep. Joseph McDade (R)
Rep. Paul McHale (D) • HJR 28 - 103rd Congress		
		Rep. William Moorhead (D)
		Rep. Thomas Morgan (D)
Rep. Austin Murphy (D) • HJR 228 - 95th Congress • HJR 288 - 96th Congress		
		Rep. Robert Nix (D)
		Rep. Frederick Rooney (D)
		Rep. John Saylor (R)
		Rep. Herman Schneebeli (R)
Sen. Richard Schweiker (R) • SJR 1 - 94th Congress • SJR 1 - 95th Congress		
		Rep. Joseph Vigorito (D)
		Rep. George Watkins (R)
		Rep. Lawrence Williams (R)
Rep. Gus Yatron (D) • HJR 139 - 93rd Congress • HJR 168 - 95th Congress • HJR 231 - 95th Congress • HJR 261 - 96th Congress		Rep. Gus Yatron (D)

S.39 RHODE ISLAND

SPONSOR OF A CONSTITUTIONAL AMENDMENT	VOTED FOR SJR 28 IN 1979 ROLL CALL	VOTED FOR HJR 681 IN 1969 ROLL CALL
Rep. Edward P. Beard (D) • HJR 168 - 95th Congress		
Sen. John H. Chafee (R) • SJR 1 - 95th Congress • SJR 1 - 96th Congress • SJR 28 - 96th Congress • SJR 3 - 97th Congress • SJR 17 - 98th Congress	Sen. John H. Chafee (R)	
Sen. John Pastore (D) • SJR 1 - 94th Congress		
Sen. Claiborne Pell (D) • SJR 1 - 94th Congress • SJR 1 - 95th Congress • SJR 1 - 96th Congress • SJR 28 - 96th Congress • SJR 3 - 97th Congress • SJR 17 - 98th Congress	Sen. Claiborne Pell (D)	
		Rep. Fernand St. Germain (D)
Rep. Robert Tiernan (D) • HJR 208 - 93rd Congress		Rep. Robert Tiernan (D)

S.40 SOUTH CAROLINA

SPONSOR OF A CONSTITUTIONAL AMENDMENT	VOTED FOR SJR 28 IN 1979 ROLL CALL	VOTED FOR HJR 681 IN 1969 ROLL CALL
Rep. John Wilson Jenrette Jr. (D) • HJR 384 - 95th Congress		

S.41 SOUTH DAKOTA

SPONSOR OF A CONSTITUTIONAL AMENDMENT	VOTED FOR SJR 28 IN 1979 ROLL CALL	VOTED FOR HJR 681 IN 1969 ROLL CALL
Sen. James G. Abourezk (D) • SJR 1 - 94th Congress • SJR 1 - 95th Congress		
Sen. Thomas A Daschle (D) • SJR 297 - 102nd Congress		
Sen. Tim Johnson (D) • HJR 145 - 102nd Congress • HJR 28 - 103rd Congress • SJR 56 - 106th Congress		
Sen. George McGovern (D) • SJR 1 - 94th Congress	Sen. George McGovern (D)	

S.42 TENNESSEE

SPONSOR OF A CONSTITUTIONAL AMENDMENT	VOTED FOR SJR 28 IN 1979 ROLL CALL	VOTED FOR HJR 681 IN 1969 ROLL CALL
		Rep. William Anderson (D)
Sen. Howard H. Baker Jr. (R) • SJR 1 - 94th Congress • SJR 1 - 95th Congress • SJR 1 - 96th Congress • SJR 28 - 96th Congress • SJR 3 - 97th Congress	Sen. Howard H. Baker Jr. (R)	
		Rep. Leonard Blanton (D)
Rep. William Boner (D) • HJR 252 - 96th Congress		
Rep. Bob Clement (D) • HJR 28 - 103rd Congress		
		Rep. Richard Fulton (D)
		Rep. John Kyl (R)
	Sen. James Sasser (D)	

S.43 TEXAS

SPONSOR OF A CONSTITUTIONAL AMENDMENT	VOTED FOR SJR 28 IN 1979 ROLL CALL	VOTED FOR HJR 681 IN 1969 ROLL CALL
	Sen. Lloyd Millard Bentsen Jr. (D)	
Rep. Jack Bascom Brooks (D) • HJR 137 - 93rd Congress • HJR 80 - 97th Congress • HJR 5 - 98th Congress • HJR 5 - 99th Congress • HJR 5 - 100th Congress • HJR 2 - 101st Congress		Rep. Jack Bascom Brooks (D)
		Rep. George H.W. Bush (R)
		Rep. Earle Cabell (D)
		Rep. Robert Casey (D)
		Rep. James Collins (R)[3]
Rep. Lloyd Doggett (D) • HJR 36 - 109th Congress		Rep. Henry Gonzalez (D)
Rep. Henry Gonzalez (D) • HJR 167 - 93rd Congress		Rep. Henry Gonzalez (D)
Rep. Gene Green (D) • HJR 28 - 103rd Congress • HJR 117 - 104th Congress • HJR 180 - 104th Congress • HJR 28 - 105th Congress • HJR 132 - 106th Congress • HJR 3 - 107th Congress • HJR 103 - 108th Congress • HJR 8 - 109th Congress		
Rep. Sam Blakeley Hall (D) • HJR 384 - 95th Congress		
		Rep. Abraham Kazen (D)
Rep. Dale Milford (D) • HJR 239 - 93rd Congress • HJR 230 - 95th Congress		
		Rep. Herbert Roberts (D)
Rep. Bill Sarpalius (D) • HJR 28 - 103rd Congress		

[3] The roll call does not make clear whether this Representative Collins or the one from Illinois voted for HJR 681 in 1969.

S.43 TEXAS *(cont.)*

SPONSOR OF A CONSTITUTIONAL AMENDMENT	VOTED FOR SJR 28 IN 1979 ROLL CALL	VOTED FOR HJR 681 IN 1969 ROLL CALL
		Rep. Olin Teague (D)
		Rep. Richard White (D)
		Rep. James Claude Wright (D)
		Rep. John Young (D)

S.44 UTAH

SPONSOR OF A CONSTITUTIONAL AMENDMENT	VOTED FOR SJR 28 IN 1979 ROLL CALL	VOTED FOR HJR 681 IN 1969 ROLL CALL
Sen. E. J. Garn (R) • SJR 1 - 95th Congress • SJR 1 - 96th Congress • SJR 28 - 96th Congress • SJR 3 - 97th Congress	Sen. E. J. Garn (R)	
Rep. James Hansen (R) • HJR 28 - 103rd Congress		
		Rep. Sherman Lloyd (R)
Sen. Frank Moss (D) • SJR 1 - 94th Congress		
Rep. Bill Orton (D) • HJR 506 - 102nd Congress • HJR 169 - 103rd Congress • HJR 36 - 104th Congress		
Rep. Douglas Owens (D) • HJR 347 - 93rd Congress		
Rep. Karen Shepherd (D) • HJR 28 - 103rd Congress		

S.45 VERMONT

SPONSOR OF A CONSTITUTIONAL AMENDMENT	VOTED FOR SJR 28 IN 1979 ROLL CALL	VOTED FOR HJR 681 IN 1969 ROLL CALL
Sen. Patrick J. Leahy (D) • SJR 1 - 95th Congress • SJR 1 - 96th Congress • SJR 28 - 96th Congress • SJR 3 - 97th Congress	Sen. Patrick J. Leahy (D)	
Rep. Bernard Sanders (I) • HJR 28 - 103rd Congress		
Sen. Robert T. Stafford (R) • SJR 1 - 94th Congress • SJR 1 - 95th Congress • SJR 1 - 96th Congress • SJR 28 - 96th Congress • SJR 17 - 98th Congress	Sen. Robert T. Stafford (R)	Rep. Robert T. Stafford (R)

S.46 VIRGINIA

SPONSOR OF A CONSTITUTIONAL AMENDMENT	VOTED FOR SJR 28 IN 1979 ROLL CALL	VOTED FOR HJR 681 IN 1969 ROLL CALL
Rep. Rick Boucher (D) • HJR 28 - 105th Congress • HJR 23 - 106th Congress		
		Rep. Joel Broyhill (R)
Rep. Leslie Byrne (D) • HJR 28 - 103rd Congress		
Rep. Thomas Downing (D) • HJR 207 - 93rd Congress • HJR 43 - 94th Congress		Rep. Thomas Downing (D)
		Rep. John Marsh (D)
		Rep. Richard Poff (R)
		Rep. William Scott (R)
		Rep. William Wampler (R)
		Rep. George Whitehurst (R)

S.47 WASHINGTON

SPONSOR OF A CONSTITUTIONAL AMENDMENT	VOTED FOR SJR 28 IN 1979 ROLL CALL	VOTED FOR HJR 681 IN 1969 ROLL CALL
		Rep. Brockman Adams (D)
Rep. Brian Baird (D) • HJR 103 - 108th Congress • HJR 8 - 109th Congress		
Rep. Norman Dicks (D) • HJR 384 - 95th Congress		
		Rep. Thomas Foley (D)
		Rep. Julia Hansen (D)
Rep. Floyd Hicks (D) • HJR 300 - 93rd Congress		Rep. Floyd Hicks (D)
Sen. Henry M. Jackson (D) • SJR 1 - 94th Congress • SJR 1 - 95th Congress • SJR 1 - 96th Congress • SJR 28 - 96th Congress • SJR 3 - 97th Congress • SJR 17 - 98th Congress	Sen. Henry M. Jackson (D)	
Sen. Warren G. Magnuson (D) • SJR 1 - 94th Congress • SJR 1 - 95th Congress • SJR 1 - 96th Congress • SJR 28 - 96th Congress	Sen. Warren G. Magnuson (D)	
		Rep. Catherine May (R)
Rep. Mike McCormack (D) • HJR 281 - 95th Congress		
Rep. Jim McDermott (D) • HJR 117 - 104th Congress • HJR 50 - 109th Congress		
Rep. Lloyd Meeds (D) • HJR 66 - 94th Congress • HJR 228 - 95th Congress		Rep. Lloyd Meeds (D)
		Rep. Thomas Pelly (R)
Rep. Joel Pritchard (R) • HJR 384 - 95th Congress		

S.48 WEST VIRGINIA

SPONSOR OF A CONSTITUTIONAL AMENDMENT	VOTED FOR SJR 28 IN 1979 ROLL CALL	VOTED FOR HJR 681 IN 1969 ROLL CALL
	Sen. Robert Byrd (D)	
		Rep. Kenneth Hechler (D)
		Rep. James Kee (D)
Rep. Robert H. Mollohan (D) • HJR 197 - 95th Congress • HJR 308 - 96th Congress		Rep. Robert H. Mollohan (D)
Sen. Jennings Randolph (D) • SJR 1 - 94th Congress • SJR 1 - 95th Congress • SJR 1 - 96th Congress • SJR 28 - 96th Congress • SJR 3 - 97th Congress • SJR 17 - 98th Congress	Sen. Jennings Randolph (D)	
		Rep. John Mark Slack (D)
		Rep. Harley Staggers (D)
Rep. Robert E. Wise Jr. (D) • HJR 137 - 101st Congress • HJR 28 - 103rd Congress • HJR 117 - 104th Congress • HJR 28 - 105th Congress		

S.49 WISCONSIN

SPONSOR OF A CONSTITUTIONAL AMENDMENT	VOTED FOR SJR 28 IN 1979 ROLL CALL	VOTED FOR HJR 681 IN 1969 ROLL CALL
Rep. Alvin J. Baldus (D) • HJR 231 - 95th Congress		
		Rep. John Byrnes (R)
Rep. Robert J. Cornell (D) • HJR 229 - 95th Congress		
		Rep. Glenn Davis (R)
Rep. Robert Kastenmeier (D) • HJR 62 - 94th Congress • HJR 70 - 95th Congress • HJR 57 - 96th Congress		Rep. Robert Kastenmeier (D)
Rep. Gerald D. Kleczka (D) • HJR 145 - 102nd Congress • HJR 60 - 103rd Congress		
Sen. Gaylord Nelson (D) • SJR 1 - 94th Congress	Sen. Gaylord Nelson (D)	
Sen. William Proxmire (D) • SJR 1 - 94th Congress • SJR 1 - 95th Congress • SJR 1 - 96th Congress • SJR 28 - 96th Congress • SJR 3 - 97th Congress • SJR 17 - 98th Congress	Sen. William Proxmire (D)	
		Rep. Henry Reuss (D)
		Rep. Henry Schadeberg (R)
Rep. William Steiger (R) • HJR 207 - 93rd Congress		Rep. William Steiger (R)
		Rep. Vernon Thomson (R)
		Rep. Clement Zablocki (D)

S.50 WYOMING

SPONSOR OF A CONSTITUTIONAL AMENDMENT	VOTED FOR SJR 28 IN 1979 ROLL CALL	VOTED FOR HJR 681 IN 1969 ROLL CALL
		Rep. John Wold (R)

APPENDIX T:
State Statutory Deadlines for Certification of Elections

TABLE T.1 STATE STATUTORY DEADLINES FOR CERTIFICATION OF ELECTIONS FOR THE 50 STATES AND DISTRICT OF COLUMBIA

JURISDICTION	CERTIFIER	CERTIFICATION DEADLINE
Alabama	Governor	Within 22 days after the election
Alaska	Director	No date specified
Arizona	Secretary of State	On the third Monday following a general election
Arkansas	Governor	Within 20 days after the election
California	Secretary of State	On the first Monday in the month following the election
Colorado	Secretary of State	No later than the fifteenth day after any election
Connecticut	Secretary of State/ Superior Court	Last Wednesday in the month in which votes were cast
Delaware	Board of Elections	No date specified
District of Columbia	Superior Court	No date specified
Florida	Canvassing Commission	No date specified
Georgia	Secretary of State	No later than 5:00 p.m. on the four-teenth ay following the date on which such election was conducted
Hawaii	Governor	No later than 4:30 p.m. on the last day in the month of the election or as soon as returns received from all counties
Idaho	Secretary of State	On or before the second Wednesday in December next after such election
Illinois	Governor	Within 31 days after holding the election
Indiana	Secretary of State	Not later than noon on the last Tuesday in November
Iowa	Governor	At the expiration of 10 days after the completed canvass
Kansas	Governor	Before the first Wednesday in December next after such election

TABLE T.1 STATE STATUTORY DEADLINES FOR CERTIFICATION OF ELECTIONS FOR THE 50 STATES AND DISTRICT OF COLUMBIA (cont.)

Kentucky	State Board	State Board shall meet to count when all the returns are in or no later than the third Monday after the election
Louisiana	Governor	On or before the 12th day after the general election
Maine	Governor	Within 20 days after the election.
Maryland	Board of Canvassers	Within 35 days of the election
Massachusetts	Governor	Within 10 days after they have been transmitted to the Secretary of State
Michigan	Secretary of State	On or before the 20th day after the election and no later than the 40th day
Minnesota	Governor	On the second Tuesday after each state general election the state canvassing board shall open and canvass the returns
Mississippi	Secretary of State	Within 30 days after the date of the election
Missouri	Governor	Within two days after the election, the clerks shall, within eight days after they receive the returns, certify and transmit them to the Governor
Montana	Secretary of State	No date specified
Nebraska	Secretary of State	Within 40 days
Nevada	Governor	On the fourth Tuesday of November open canvass the vote, must be completed within 20 days
New Hampshire	Governor	No date specified
New Jersey	Secretary of State	No later than the 28th day after the election
New Mexico	Secretary of State	On the third Tuesday after each election board will meet to canvass and declare the results of the election
New York	State Board of Elections	No date specified
North Carolina	Governor	Board of elections shall meet at 11:00 a.m. on the seventh day after every election or a reasonable time thereafter if the counting of the votes has not been completed
North Dakota	Secretary of State	Within ten days and before 4 p.m. on the tenth day following any general election
Ohio	Board of Elections	No date specified

TABLE T.1 STATE STATUTORY DEADLINES FOR CERTIFICATION OF ELECTIONS FOR THE 50 STATES AND DISTRICT OF COLUMBIA (cont.)

Oklahoma	Secretary of State	Election board shall convene on the day of and remaining session until all returns are delivered
Oregon	Secretary of State	No later than the 30th day after any election
Pennsylvania	Governor	No date specified
Rhode Island	State Board	State board shall commence the canvass at 9:00 p.m. on election day and shall continue and complete the tabulation with all reasonable expedition
South Carolina	State Board	State board shall meet within 10 days after any general election
South Dakota	Governor	Within seven days after the day of election
Tennessee	Secretary of State	No date specified
Texas	Secretary of State	No date specified
Utah	Lieutenant Governor	Fourth Monday of November at noon
Vermont	Canvassing Committee	Canvassing committee shall meet at 10:00 A.M. one week after the day of the election
Virginia	State Board	Fourth Monday in November, if the Board is unable to ascertain results on that day, the meeting shall stand adjourned for not more three days
Washington	Secretary of State	Not later than 30 days after the election
West Virginia	Board of Canvassers	Fifth day after every election
Wisconsin	Elections Board	The first day of December following a general election
Wyoming	Canvassing Board	No later than the second Wednesday following the election

Appendix U:
U. S. Supreme Court Decision in *Hawke v. Smith*

U.S. SUPREME COURT
253 U.S. 221
HAWKE V. SMITH, SECRETARY OF STATE OF OHIO. NO. 582.
ARGUED APRIL 23, 1920
DECIDED JUNE 1, 1920

Mr. J. Frank Hanly, of Indianapolis, Ind., for plaintiff in error.

Mr. Lawrence Maxwell, of Cincinnati, Ohio, for defendant in error.

Mr. Justice DAY delivered the opinion of the Court.

Plaintiff in error (plaintiff below) filed a petition for an injunction in the court of common pleas of Franklin county, Ohio, seeking to enjoin the secretary of state of Ohio from spending the public money in preparing and printing forms of ballot for submission of a referendum to the electors of that state on the question of the ratification which the General Assembly had made of the proposed Eighteenth Amendment to the federal Constitution. A demurrer to the petition was sustained in the court of common pleas. Its judgment was affirmed by the Court of Appeals of Franklin County, which judgment was affirmed by the Supreme Court of Ohio, and the case was brought here.

A joint resolution proposing to the states this amendment to the Constitution of the United States was adopted on the 3d day of December, 1917. 40 Stat. 1050. The amendment prohibits the manufacture, sale or transportation of intoxicating liquors within, the importation thereof into, or the exportation thereof from, the United States and all territory subject to the jurisdiction thereof for beverage purposes. The several states were given concurrent power to enforce the amendment by appropriate legislation. The resolution provided that the amendment should be inoperative unless ratified as an amendment of the

Constitution by the Legislatures of the several states, as provide in the Constitution, within seven years from the date of the submission thereof to the states. The Senate and House of Representatives of the state of Ohio adopted a resolution ratifying the proposed amendment by the General Assembly of the state of Ohio, and ordered that certified copies of the joint resolution of ratification be forwarded by the Governor to the Secretary of State at Washington and to the presiding officer of each House of Congress. This resolution was adopted on January 7, 1919; on January 27, 1919, the Governor of Ohio complied with the resolution. On January 29, 1919, the Secretary of State of the United States proclaimed the ratification of the amendment, naming 36 states as having ratified the same, among them the state of Ohio.

The question for our consideration is: Whether the provision of the Ohio Constitution, adopted at the general election, November, 1918, extending the referendum to the ratification by the General Assembly of proposed amendments to the federal Constitution is in conflict with article 5 of the Constitution of the United States. The amendment of 1918 provides:

> "The people also reserve to themselves the legislative power of the referendum on the action of the General Assembly ratifying any proposed amendment to the Constitution of the United States."

Article 5 of the federal Constitution provides:

> "The Congress, whenever two-thirds of both houses shall deem it necessary, shall propose amendments to this Constitution, or, on the application of the Legislatures of two-thirds of the several states, shall call a convention for proposing amendments, which, in either case, shall be valid to all intents and purposes, as part of this Constitution, when ratified by the Legislatures of three-fourths of the several states, or by conventions in three-fourths thereof, as the one or the other mode of ratification may be proposed by the Congress: Provided that no amendment which may be made prior to the year one thousand eight hundred and eight shall in any manner affect the first and fourth clauses in the ninth section of the first article; and that no state, without its consent, shall be

deprived of its equal suffrage in the Senate."

The Constitution of the United States was ordained by the people, and, when duly ratified, it became the Constitution of the people of the United States. *McCulloch v. Maryland*, 4 Wheat. 316, 402. The states surrendered to the general government the powers specifically conferred upon the nation, and the Constitution and the laws of the United States are the supreme law of the land.

The framers of the Constitution realized that it might in the progress of time and the development of new conditions require changes, and they intended to provide an orderly manner in which these could be accomplished; to that end they adopted the fifth article.

This article makes provision for the proposal of amendments either by two-thirds of both houses of Congress, or on application of the Legislatures of two-thirds of the states; thus securing deliberation and consideration before any change can be proposed. The proposed change can only become effective by the ratification of the Legislatures of three-fourths of the states, or by conventions in a like number of states. The method of ratification is left to the choice of Congress. Both methods of ratification, by Legislatures or conventions, call for action by deliberative assemblages representative of the people, which it was assumed would voice the will of the people.

The fifth article is a grant of authority by the people to Congress. The determination of the method of ratification is the exercise of a national power specifically granted by the Constitution; that power is conferred upon Congress, and is limited to two methods, by action of the Legislatures of three-fourths of the states, or conventions in a like number of states. *Dodge v. Woolsey*, 18 How. 331, 348. The framers of the Constitution might have adopted a different method. Ratification might have been left to a vote of the people, or to some authority of government other than that selected. The language of the article is plain, and admits of no doubt in its interpretation. It is not the function of courts or legislative bodies, national or state, to alter the method which the Constitution has fixed.

All of the amendments to the Constitution have been submitted with a requirement for legislative ratification; by this method all of them have been adopted.

The only question really for determination is: What did the framers of the Constitution mean in requiring ratification by "legislatures"? That was not a term of uncertain meaning when incorporated into the Constitution. What it meant when adopted it still means for the purpose of interpretation. A Legislature was then the representative body which made the laws of the people. The term is often used in the Constitution with this evident meaning. Article 1, section 2, prescribes the qualifications of electors of Congressmen as those "requisite for electors of the most numerous branch of the state Legislature." Article 1, section 3, provided that Senators shall be chosen in each state by the Legislature thereof, and this was the method of choosing senators until the adoption of the Seventeenth Amendment, which made provision for the election of Senators by vote of the people, the electors to have the qualifications requisite for electors of the most numerous branch of the state Legislature. That Congress and the states understood that this election by the people was entirely distinct from legislative action is shown by the provision of the amendment giving the Legislature of any state the power to authorize the executive to make temporary appointments until the people shall fill the vacancies by election. It was never suggested, so far as we are aware, that the purpose of making the office of Senator elective by the people could be accomplished by a referendum vote. The necessity of the amendment to accomplish the purpose of popular election is shown in the adoption of the amendment. In article 4 the United States is required to protect every state against domestic violence upon application of the Legislature, or of the executive when the Legislature cannot be convened. Article 6 requires the members of the several Legislatures to be bound by oath, or affirmation, to support the Constitution of the United States. By article 1, section 8, Congress is given exclusive jurisdiction over all places purchased by the consent of the Legislature of the state in which the same shall be. Article 4, section 3, provides that no new states shall be carved out of old states without the consent of the Legislatures of the states concerned.

There can be no question that the framers of the Constitution clearly understood and carefully used the terms in which that instrument referred to the action of the Legislatures of the states. When they intended that direct action by the people should be had they were no less accurate in the use of apt phraseology to carry out such purpose. The members of the House of Representatives were required to be chosen by the people of the several states. Article 1, section 2.

The Constitution of Ohio in its present form, although making provision for a referendum, vests the legislative power primarily in a General Assembly, consisting of a Senate and House of Representatives. Article 2, section 1, provides:

> "The legislative power of the state shall be vested in a General Assembly consisting of a Senate and House of Representatives, but the people reserve to themselves the power to propose to the General Assembly laws and amendments to the Constitution, and to adopt or reject the same at the polls on a referendum vote as hereinafter provided."

The argument to support the power of the state to require the approval by the people of the state of the ratification of amendments to the federal Constitution through the medium of a referendum rests upon the proposition that the federal Constitution requires ratification by the legislative action of the states through the medium provided at the time of the proposed approval of an amendment. This argument is fallacious in this—ratification by a state of a constitutional amendment is not an act of legislation within the proper sense of the word. It is but the expression of the assent of the state to a proposed amendment.

At an early day this court settled that the submission of a constitutional amendment did not require the action of the President. The question arose over the adoption of the Eleventh Amendment. *Hollingsworth et al. v. Virginia*, 3 Dall. 378. In that case is was contended that the amendment had not been proposed in the manner provided in the Constitution as an inspection of the original roll showed that it had never been submitted to the President for his approval in accordance with article 1, section 7, of the Constitution. The Attorney General answered that the case of amendments is a substantive act, unconnected with the ordinary business of legislation, and not within the policy or terms of the Constitution investing the President with a qualified negative on the acts and resolutions of Congress. In a footnote to this argument of the Attorney General, Justice Chase said:

> "There can, surely, be no necessity to answer that argument. The negative of the President applies only to the ordinary cases of legislation. He has nothing to do with the proposi-

tion, or adoption, of amendments to the Constitution."

The court by a unanimous judgment held that the amendment was constitutionally adopted.

It is true that the power to legislate in the enactment of the laws of a state is derived from the people of the state. But the power to ratify a proposed amendment to the federal Constitution has its source in the federal Constitution. The act of ratification by the state derives its authority from the federal Constitution to which the state and its people have alike assented.

This view of the amendment is confirmed in the history of its adoption found in 2 Watson on the Constitution, 1301 et seq. Any other view might lead to endless confusion in the manner of ratification of federal amendments. The choice of means of ratification was wisely withheld from conflicting action in the several states.

But it is said this view runs counter to the decision of this court in *Davis v. Hildebrant*, 241 U.S. 565, 36 S. Ct. 708. But that case is inapposite. It dealt with article 1 section 4, of the Constitution, which provides that the times, places, and manners of holding elections for Senators and Representatives in each state shall be determined by the respective Legislatures thereof, but that Congress may at any time make or alter such regulations, except as to the place for choosing Senators. As shown in the opinion in that case, Congress had itself recognized the referendum as part of the legislative authority of the state for the purpose stated. It was held, affirming the judgment of the Supreme Court of Ohio, that the referendum provision of the state Constitution, when applied to a law redistricting the state with a view to representation in Congress, was not unconstitutional. Article 1, section 4, plainly gives authority to the state to legislate within the limitations therein named. Such legislative action is entirely different from the requirement of the Constitution as to the expression of assent or dissent to a proposed amendment to the Constitution. In such expression no legislative action is authorized or required.

It follows that the court erred in holding that the state had authority to require the submission of the ratification to a referendum under the state Constitution, and its judgment is reversed and the cause remanded for further proceedings not inconsistent with this opinion.

Reversed.

Appendix V:
U. S. Supreme Court Decision in *Smiley v. Holm* (1932)

U.S. SUPREME COURT
SMILEY V. HOLM, 285 U.S. 355 (1932)
285 U.S. 355
SMILEY V. HOLM, AS SECRETARY OF STATE OF MINNESOTA
NO. 617.
ARGUED MARCH 16, 17, 1932
DECIDED APRIL 11, 1932

Messrs. George T. Simpson, Alfred W. Bowen, W. Yale Smiley, John A. Weeks, and F. J. Donahue, all of Minneapolis, Minn., for petitioner.

Messrs. Henry N. Benson, Atty. Gen., and William H. Gurnee, Asst. Atty. Gen., both of St. Paul, Minn., for respondent.

Mr. Chief Justice HUGHES delivered the opinion of the Court.

Under the reapportionment following the fifteenth decennial census, as provided by the Act of Congress of June 18, 1929 (c. 28, 22, 46 Stat. 21, 26 (2 USCA 2a)), Minnesota is entitled to nine Representatives in Congress, being one less than the number previously allotted. In April, 1931, the bill known as House File No. 1456 (Laws Minn. 1931, p. 640), dividing the state into nine congressional districts and specifying the counties of which they should be composed, was passed by the House of Representatives and the Senate of the state, and was transmitted to the Governor, who returned it without his approval. Thereupon, without further action upon the measure by the House of Representatives and the Senate, and in compliance with a resolution of the House of Representatives, House File No. 1456 was deposited with the secretary of state of Minnesota. This suit was brought by the petitioner as a "citizen, elector and taxpayer" of the state to obtain a judgment declaring invalid all fillings for nomination for the office of Representative in Congress, which should designate a subdivision of the state as a congressional district, and to enjoin the secretary of state from giving notice of the holding of elections for that office in such subdivisions. The petition alleged that House File No. 1456 was a nullity, in that, after the Governor's veto, it was not repassed by the Legislature as required by law, and also in that the proposed congressional districts were not "compact" and did not "contain an equal number of inhabitants as nearly as practicable" in accordance with the Act of Congress of August 8, 1911.[1]

The respondent, secretary of state, demurred to the petition upon the ground that it did not state facts sufficient to constitute a cause of action. He maintained the validity of House File No. 1456 by virtue of the authority conferred upon the Legislature by article 1, 4, of the Federal Constitution, and he insisted that the act of Congress of August 8, 1911, was no longer in force, and that the asserted inequalities in redistricting presented a political and not a judicial question. The trial court sustained the demurrer, and its order was affirmed by the Supreme Court of the state. 238 N. W. 494. The action was then dismissed upon the merits, and the Supreme Court affirmed the judgment upon its previous opinion. 238 N. W. 792. This Court granted a writ of certiorari. 284 U.S. 616, 52 S. Ct. 266, 76 L. Ed.

---

[1] The Act of August 8, 1911, c. 5, 37 Stat. 13 (2 USCA 2 and note, 3-5), provided for the apportionment of Representatives in Congress among the several states under the thirteenth census. After fixing the total number of Representatives and their apportionment, in sections 1 and 2, the act provided as follows:

"Sec. 3. That in each State entitled under this apportionment to more than one Representative, the Representatives to the Sixty-third and each subsequent Congress shall be elected by districts composed of a contiguous and compact territory, and containing as nearly as practicable an equal number of inhabitants. The said districts shall be equal to the number of Representatives to which such State may be entitled in Congress, no district electing more than one Representative.

"Sec. 4. That in case of an increase in the number of Representatives in any State under this apportionment such additional Representative or Representatives shall be elected by the State at large and the other Representatives by the districts now prescribed by law until such State shall be redistricted in the manner provided by the laws thereof and in accordance with the rules enumerated in section three of this Act; and if there be no charge in the number of Representatives from a State, the Representatives thereof shall be elected from the districts now prescribed by law until such State shall be redistricted as herein prescribed.

"Sec. 5. That candidates for Representative or Representatives to be elected at large in any State shall be nominated in the same manner as candidates for governor, unless otherwise provided by the laws of such State."

Article 1, 4, of the Constitution of the United States, provides:

"The times, places and manner of holding elections for senators and representatives, shall be prescribed in each state by the legislature thereof; but the Congress may at any time by law make or alter such regulations, except as to the places of choosing senators."

Under the Constitution of Minnesota, the "legislature" consists "of the senate and house of representatives." Const. Minn. art. 4, 1. Before any bill passed by the Senate and House of Representatives "becomes a law," it must "be presented to the governor of the state," and if he returns it, within the time stated, without his approval, the bill may become a law provided it is reconsidered and thereupon passed by each house by a two-thirds vote. *Id.* art. 4, 11. The state Constitution also provides that, after each Federal census, "the legislature shall have the power to prescribe the bounds of congressional ... districts." *Id.* art. 4, 23. We do not understand that the Supreme Court of the state has held that, under these provisions, a measure redistricting the state for congressional elections could be put in force by the Legislature without participation by the Governor, as required in the case of legislative bills, if such action were regarded as a performance of the function of the Legislature as a lawmaking body. No decision to that effect has been cited. It appears that "on seven occasions" prior to the measure now under consideration the Legislature of Minnesota had "made state and federal reapportionments in the form of a bill for an act which was approved by the Governor."[2] While, in the instant case, the Supreme Court regarded that procedure as insufficient to support the petitioner's contention as to practical construction, that question was dismissed from consideration because of the controlling effect which the court ascribed to the federal provision. 238 N. W. page 500. The court expressed the opinion that "the various provisions of our state Constitution cited in the briefs are of little importance in relation to the matter now in controversy"; that "the power of the state Legislature to prescribe congressional districts rests exclusively and solely in the language of article 1, 4, of the United States Constitution." *Id.* 238 N. W. page 497. Construing that provision, the court reached the conclu-

---

[2] See Laws of Minnesota 1858, c. 83; 1872, c. 21; 1881, c. 128; 1891, c. 3; 1901, c. 92; 1913, c. 513; 1929, c. 64.

sion that the Legislature in redistricting the state was not acting strictly in the exercise of the lawmaking power, but merely as an agency, discharging a particular duty in the manner which the Federal Constitution required. Upon this point the court said (*Id.* 238 N. W. page 499):

"The Legislature in districting the state is not strictly in the discharge of legislative duties as a lawmaking body, acting in its sovereign capacity, but is acting as representative of the people of the state under the power granted by said article 1, 4. It merely gives expression as to district lines in aid of the election of certain federal officials; prescribing one of the essential details serving primarily the federal government and secondly the people of the state. The Legislature is designated as a mere agency to discharge the particular duty. The Governor's veto has no relation to such matters; that power pertains, under the state Constitution, exclusively to state affairs. The word 'legislature' has reference to the well-recognized branch of the state government-created by the state as one of its three branches for a specific purpose-and when the framers of the Federal Constitution employed this term, we believe they made use of it in the ordinary sense with reference to the official body invested with the functions of making laws, the legislative body of the state; and that they did not intend to include the state's chief executive as a part thereof. We would not be justified in construing the term as being used in its enlarged sense as meaning the state or as meaning the lawmaking power of the state."

The question then is whether the provision of the Federal Constitution, thus regarded as determinative, invests the Legislature with a particular authority, and imposes upon it a corresponding duty, the definition of which imports a function different from that of lawgiver, and thus renders inapplicable the conditions which attach to the making of state laws. Much that is urged in argument with regard to the meaning of the term "Legislature" is beside the point. As this Court said in *Hawke v. Smith*, No. 1, 253 U.S. 221, 227, 40 S. Ct. 495, 497, 10 A. L. R. 1504, the term was not one "of uncertain meaning when incorporated into the Constitution. What it meant when adopted it still means for the purpose of interpretation. A Legislature was then the representative body which made the laws of the people." The question here is not with respect to the "body" as thus described but as to the function to be performed. The use in the Federal Constitution of the same term in different relations does not always imply the performance of the same function. The Legislature may act as an electoral body, as in the choice of United States Senators under article 1, 3, prior to the adoption of the Seventeenth Amendment. It may act as a ratifying body, as in the case of proposed amendments to the Constitution under article 5. *Hawke v. Smith*, No. 1, supra; *Hawke v. Smith*, No. 2, 253 U.S. 231, 40 S. Ct. 498; *Leser v. Garnett*, 258 U.S. 130, 137, 42 S. Ct. 217. It may act as a consenting body, as in relation to the acquisition of lands by the United States under article 1, 8, par. 17. Wherever the term "legislature" is used in the Constitution, it is necessary to consider the nature of the particular action in view. The primary question now before the Court is whether the function contemplated by article 1, 4, is that of making laws.

Consideration of the subject-matter and of the terms of the provision requires affirmative answer. The subject-matter is the "times, places and manner of holding elections for senators and representatives." It cannot be doubted that these comprehensive words embrace authority to provide a complete code for congressional elections, not only as to times and places, but in relation to notices, registration, supervision of voting, protection of voters, prevention of fraud and corrupt practices, counting of votes, duties of inspectors and canvassers, and making and publication of election returns; in short, to enact the numerous requirements as to procedure and safeguards which experience shows are necessary in order to enforce the fundamental right involved. And these requirements would be nugatory if they did not have appropriate sanctions in the definition of offenses and punishments. All this is comprised in the subject of "times, places and manner of holding elections," and involves lawmaking in its essential features and most important aspect.

This view is confirmed by the second clause of article 1, 4, which provides that "the Congress may at any time by law make or alter such regulations," with the single exception stated. The phrase "such regulations" plainly refers to regulations of the same general character that the legislature of the State is authorized to prescribe with respect to congressional elections. In exercising this power, the Congress may supplement these state regulations or may substitute its own. It may impose additional penalties for the violation of the state laws or provide independent sanctions. It "has a general supervisory power over the whole subject." *Ex parte Siebold*, 100 U.S. 371, 387; *Ex parte Yarbrough*, 110 U.S. 651, 661, 4 S. Ct. 152; *Ex parte Clarke*, 100 U.S. 399 ; *United States v. Mosley*, 238 U.S. 383, 386, 35 S. Ct. 904; *Newberry v. United States*, 256 U.S. 232, 255, 41 S. Ct. 469. But this broad authority is conferred by the constitutional provision now under consideration, and is exercised by the Congress in making "such regulations"; that is, regulations of the sort which, if there be no overruling action by the Congress, may be provided by the Legislature of the state upon the same subject.

The term defining the method of action, equally with the nature of the subject matter, aptly points to the making of laws. The state Legislature is authorized to "prescribe" the times, places, and manner of holding elections. Respondent urges that the fact that the words "by law" are found in the clause relating to the action of the Congress, and not in the clause giving authority to the state Legislature, supports the contention that the latter was not to act in the exercise of the lawmaking power. We think that the inference is strongly to the contrary. It is the nature of the function that makes the phrase "by law" apposite. That is the same whether it is performed by state or national Legislature, and the use of the phrase places the intent of the whole provision in a strong light. Prescribing regulations to govern the conduct of the citizen, under the first clause, and making and altering such rules by law, under the second clause, involve action of the same inherent character.

As the authority is conferred for the purpose of making laws for the state, it follows, in the absence of an indication of a contrary intent, that the exercise of the authority must be in accordance with the method which the state has prescribed for legislative enactments. We find no suggestion in the federal constitutional provision of an attempt to endow the Legislature of the state with power to enact laws in any manner other than that in which the Constitution of the state has provided that laws shall be enacted. Whether the Governor of the state, through the veto power, shall have a part in the making of state laws, is a matter of state polity. Article 1, 4, of the Federal Constitution, neither requires nor excludes such participation. And provision for it, as a check in the legislative process, cannot be regarded as repugnant to the grant of legislative authority. At the time of the adoption of the Federal Constitution, it appears that only two states had provided for a veto upon the passage of legislative bills; Massachusetts, through the Governor, and New York, through a council of revision.[3] But the restriction which existed in the case of these states was well known. That the state Legislature might be subject to such a limitation, either then or thereafter imposed as the several states might think wise, was no more incongruous with the grant of legislative authority to regulate congressional elections than the fact that the Congress in making its regulations under the same provision would be subject to the veto power of the President, as provided in article 1, 7. The latter consequence was not expressed, but there is no question that it was necessarily implied, as the Congress was to act by law; and there is no intimation, either in the debates in the Federal Convention or in contemporaneous exposition, of a purpose to exclude a similar restriction imposed by state Constitutions upon state Legislatures when exercising the lawmaking power.

The practical construction of article 1, 4, is impressive. General acquiescence cannot justify departure from the law, but long and continuous interpretation in the course of official action under the law may aid in removing doubts as to its meaning. This is especially true in the case of constitutional provisions governing the exercise of political rights, and hence subject to constant and careful scrutiny. Certainly, the terms of the constitutional provision furnish no such clear and definite support for a contrary construction as to justify disregard of the established practice in the states. *McPherson v. Blacker*, 146 U.S. 1, 36, 13 S. Ct. 3; *Missouri Pacific Railway Co. v. Kansas*, 248 U.S. 276, 284, 39 S. Ct. 93, 2 A. L. R. 1589; *Myers v. United States*, 272 U.S. 52, 119, 136 S., 47 S. Ct. 21; The *Pocket Veto Case*, 279 U.S. 655, 688-690, 49 S. Ct. 463, 64 A. L. R. 1434. That

---

[3] The Constitution of Massachusetts of 1780 provided for the Governor's veto of "bills" or "resolves." Part Second, ch. 1, 1, art. 2; 3 Thorpe, *American Charters, Constitutions and Organic Laws*, 1893, 1894. The council of revision in New York, which had the veto power under the first Constitution of 1777 (art. 3), was composed of the Governor, the chancellor, and the judges of the Supreme Court, "or any two of them, together with the Governor." The veto power was given to the Governor alone by the Constitution of 1821. Article 1, 12, 3 Thorpe, op. cit. 2628, 2641, 2642. In South Carolina, the veto power had been given by the Constitution of 1776 to the "president" (article 7), but under the Constitution of 1778 the Governor had no veto power; see article 14, 6 Thorpe, op. cit., 3244, 3252.

practice is eloquent of the conviction of the people of the states, and of their representatives in state Legislatures and executive office, that in providing for congressional elections, and for the districts in which they were to be held, these Legislatures were exercising the lawmaking power and thus subject, where the state Constitution so provided, to the veto of theGovernor as a part of the legislative process. The early action in Massachusetts under this authority was by "resolves," and these, under the Constitution of 1780, were required to be submitted to the Governor, and it appears that they were so submitted and approved by him.[4] In New York, from the outset, provision for congressional districts was made by statute,[5] and this method was followed until 1931. The argument based on the disposition, during the early period, to curtail executive authority in the states, and on the long time which elapsed in a number of states before the veto power was granted to the Governor, is of slight weight in the light of the fact that this power was given in four states shortly after the adoption of the Federal Constitution,[6] that the use of this check has gradually been extended, and that the uniform practice (prior to the questions raised in relation to the present reapportionment) has been to provide for congressional districts by the enactment of statutes with the participation of the Governor wherever the state Constitution provided for such participation as part of the process of making laws. See *Moran v. Bowley*, 347 Ill. 148, 179 N. E. 526, 527; *Koening v. Flynn*, 258 N. Y. 292, 300, 179 N. E. 705; *Carroll v. Becker* (Mo. Sup.) 45 S.W.(2d) 533; *State ex rel. Schrader v. Polley*, 26 S. D. 5, 7, 127 N. W. 848. The Attorney General of Minnesota, in his argument in the instant case, states: "It is conceded that until 1931 whenever the State of Minnesota was divided into districts for the purpose of congressional elections such action was taken by the legislature in the form of a bill and presented to and approved by the governor." That the constitutional provision contemplates the exercise of the

---

[4] Const. Mass. 1780; 3 Thorpe, op. cit. 1893, 1894, Mass. Resolves, Oct.Nov., 1788, c. XLIX, p. 52; May-June, 1792, c. LXIX, p. 23.

[5] New York, Laws of 1789, c. 11; 1797, c. 62; 1802, c. 72. See Koenig v. Flynn, 258 N. Y. 292.

[6] Georgia, Const. 1789, art. 2, 10, 2 Thorpe, op. cit. 788; Pennsylvania, Const. 1790, art. 1, 22, 5 Thorpe, op. cit., 3094; New Hampshire, Const. 1792; Part Second, 44, 4 Thorpe, op. cit., 2482; Kentucky, Const. 1792, art. 1, 28, 3 Thorpe, op. cit., 1267. In Vermont, the Constitution of 1793 (chapter 2, 16) gave the Governor and council a power of suspension similar to that for which provision had been made in the Constitution of 1786 (chapter 2, 14) before the admission of Vermont to the Union. See, also, Constitution of 1777 (chapter 2, 14), 6 Thorpe, op. cit., 3744, 3757, 3767.

lawmaking power was definitely recognized by the Congress in the Act of August 8, 1911,[7] which expressly provided in section 4 for the election of Representatives in Congress, as stated, "by the districts now prescribed by law until such State shall be redistricted in the manner provided by the laws thereof, and in accordance with the rules enumerated in section three of this Act." The significance of the clause "in the manner provided by the laws thereof" is manifest from its occasion and purpose. It was to recognize the propriety of the referendum in establishing congressional districts where the state had made it a part of the legislative process. "It is clear," said this Court in *Davis v. Hildebrant*, 241 U.S. 565, 568, 36 S. Ct. 708, 710, "that Congress, in 1911, in enacting the controlling law concerning the duties of the states, through their legislative authority, to deal with the subject of the creation of congressional districts, expressly modified the phraseology of the previous acts relating to that subject by inserting a clause plainly intended to provide that where, by the state Constitution and laws, the referendum was treated as part of the legislative power, the power as thus constituted should be held and treated to be the state legislative power for the purpose of creating congressional districts by law."

The case of *Davis v. Hildebrant*, supra, arose under the amendment of 1912 to the Constitution of Ohio reserving the right "by way of referendum to approve or disapprove by popular vote any law enacted by the general assembly." *Id.*, 241 U. S. page 566, 36 S. Ct. 708, 709. The act passed by the General Assembly of Ohio in 1915, redistricting the state for the purpose of congressional elections, was disapproved under the referendum provision, and the validity of that action was challenged under article 1, 4, of the Federal Constitution. The Supreme Court of the state, denying a mandamus to enforce the disapproved act, "held that the provisions as to referendum were a part of the legislative power of the state, made so by the Constitution, and that nothing in the act of Congress of 1911, or in the constitutional provision, operated to the contrary, and that therefore the disapproved law had no existence." *Id.* 241 U. S. page 567, 36 S. Ct. 708, 709. This Court affirmed the judgment of the state court. It is manifest that the Congress had no power to alter article 1, 4, and that the act of 1911, in its reference to state laws, could but operate as a legislative recognition of the nature of the authority deemed to have been

---

[7] See note 1.

conferred by the constitutional provision. And it was because of the authority of the state to determine what should constitute its legislative process that the validity of the requirement of the state Constitution of Ohio, in its application to congressional elections, was sustained. This was explicitly stated by this Court as the ground of the distinction which was made in *Hawke v. Smith No. 1*, supra, where, referring to the Davis Case, the Court said: "As shown in the opinion in that case, Congress had itself recognized the referendum as part of the legislative authority of the state for the purpose stated. It was held, affirming the judgment of the Supreme Court of Ohio, that the referendum provision of the state Constitution, when applied to a law redistricting the state with a view to representation in Congress, was not unconstitutional. Article 1, section 4, plainly gives authority to the state to legislate within the limitations therein named. Such legislative action is entirely different from the requirement of the Constitution as to the expression of assent or dissent to a proposed amendment to the Constitution. In such expression no legislative action is authorized or required."

It clearly follows that there is nothing in article 1, 4, which precludes a state from providing that legislative action in districting the state for congressional elections shall be subject to the veto power of the Governor as in other cases of the exercise of the lawmaking power. Accordingly, in this instance, the validity of House File No. 1456 cannot be sustained by virtue of any authority conferred by the Federal Constitution upon the Legislature of Minnesota to create congressional districts independently of the participation of the Governor as required by the state Constitution with respect to the enactment of laws.

The further question has been presented whether the Act of Congress of August 8, 1911,[8] is still in force. The state court held that it was not, that it had been wholly replaced by the Act of June 18, 1929. Sections 1 and 2 of the former act, making specific provision for the apportionment under the thirteenth census, are, of course, superseded; the present question relates to the other sections. These have not been expressly repealed. The act of 1929 repeals "all other laws and parts of laws" that are inconsistent with its provisions (section 21 (46 Stat. 26, 13 USCA 1 note)). The petitioner urges that this act contains nothing inconsistent with sections 3, 4,

---

[8] See note 1.

and 58 of the act of 1911, and the only question is whether these sections by their very terms have ceased to be effective. It is pointed out that the provisions of the act of 1911 were carried into the United States Code. U. S. C., tit. 2, 2-5 (2 USCA 2 and note 3-5). Inclusion in the Code does not operate as a re-enactment; it establishes "prima facie the laws of the United States, general and permanent in their nature, in force on the 7th day of December, 1925." Act of June 30, 1926, c. 712, 44 Stat. 777. While sections 3 and 4 of the act of 1911 expressly referred to "this apportionment" (the one made by that Act), the argument is pressed that they contain provisions setting forth a general policy which was intended to apply to the future creation of congressional districts, and the election of Representatives, until Congress should provide otherwise.

There are three classes of states with respect to the number of Representatives under the present apportionment pursuant to the act of 1929, (1) where the number remains the same, (2) where it is increased, and (3) where it is decreased. In states where the number of Representatives remains the same, and the districts are unchanged, no question is presented; there is nothing inconsistent with any of the requirements of the Congress in proceeding with the election of Representatives in such states in the same manner as heretofore. Section 4 of the act of 1911 (2 USCA 4) provided that, in case of an increase in the number of Representatives in any state, "such additional Representative or Representatives shall be elected by the State at large and the other Representatives by the districts now prescribed by law" until such state shall be redistricted. The Constitution itself provides in article 1, 2, that "The house of representatives shall be composed of members chosen every second year by the people of the several states," and we are of the opinion that under this provision, in the absence of the creation of new districts, additional Representatives allotted to a state under the present reapportionment would appropriately be elected by the state at large. Such a course, with the election of the other Representatives in the existing districts until a redistricting act was passed, would present no inconsistency with any policy declared in the act of 1911.

Where, as in the case of Minnesota, the number of Representatives has been decreased, there is a different situation, as existing districts are not at all adapted to the new apportionment. It follows that in such a case, unless and until new districts are created, all Representatives allotted to the state must be elected by the state at large. That would be required, in the absence of a redistricting act, in order to afford the representation to which the state is constitutionally entitled, and the general provisions of the act of 1911 cannot be regarded as intended to have a different import. This conclusion disposes of all the questions properly before the Court. Questions in relation to the application of the standards defined in section 3 of the act of 1911 to a redistricting statute, if such a statute should hereafter be enacted, are wholly abstract. The judgment is reversed, and the cause is remanded for further proceedings not inconsistent with this opinion.

It is so ordered.

Mr. Justice CARDOZO took no part in the consideration and decision of this case.

Bibliography

Abbott, David W. and Levine, James P. 1991. *Wrong Winner: The Coming Debacle in the Electoral College.* Westport, CT: Praeger.

Amar, Akhil Reed and Amar, Vikram David Amar. 2001. How to achieve direct national election of the president without amending the constitution: Part three of a three-part series on the 2000 election and the electoral college. *Findlaw's Writ.* December 28, 2001. http://writ.news.findlaw.com/amar/20011228.html.

Amar, Akhil Reed and Amar, Vikram David. 2001. Rethinking the electoral college debate: The Framers, federalism, and one person, one vote. 114 *Harvard Law Review* 2526.

American Bar Association Commission on Electoral College Reform. 1967. *Electing the President: A Report of the Commission on Electoral College Reform.* Chicago, IL: American Bar Association.

American Enterprise Institute for Public Policy Research. 1969. *Proposals for Revision of the Electoral College System: Legislative Analysis.* Washington, DC: AEI.

Barone, Michael; Cohen, Michael; and Ujifusa, Grant. 2003. *The 2004 Almanac of American Politics.* Washington, DC: National Journal Group.

Barton, Weldon V. 1967. *Interstate Compacts in the Political Process.* Chapel Hill, NC: University of North Carolina Press.

Bayh, Birch. 1969. Electing a president: The case for direct election. 6 *Harvard Journal on Legislation* 1.

Bennett, Robert W. 2001. Popular election of the president without a constitutional amendment. 4 *Green Bag.* Spring 2001. Posted on April 19, 2001.

Bennett, Robert W. 2002. Popular election of the president without a constitutional amendment. In Jacobson, Arthur J. and Rosenfeld, Michel (editors). *The Longest Night: Polemics and Perspectives on Election 2000.* Berkeley, CA: University of California Press. Pages 391-396.

Bennett, Robert W. 2002. Popular election of the president II: State coordination in popular election of the president without a constitutional amendment. *Green Bag.* Winter 2002.

Bennett, Robert W. 2006. *Taming the Electoral College.* Stanford, CA: Stanford University Press.

Berns, Walter (editor). 1992. *After the People Vote: A Guide to the Electoral College.* Washington, DC: The AEI Press.

Best, Judith A. 1996. *Choice of the People? Debating the Electoral College.* Lanham, MD: Rowman & Littlefield.

Best, Judith Vairo. 1975. *The Case Against Direct Election of the President: A Defense of the Electoral College.* Ithaca, NY: Cornell University Press.

Bowman, Ann O'M. 2004. Trends and issues in interstate cooperation. In *The Book of the States 2004 Edition.* Chicago, IL: The Council of State Governments.

Brams, Steven J. 1978. *The Presidential Election Game.* New Haven, CT: Yale University Press.

Brown, Everett Sumerville. 1938. *Ratification of the Twenty-First Amendment to the Constitution of the United States.* Ann Arbor, MI: The University of Michigan Press.

Busch, Andrew E. 2001. The development and democratization of the electoral college. In Gregg, Gary L. II (editor). *Securing Democracy: Why We Have an Electoral College.* Wilmington, DE: ISI Books.

Chace, James. 2004. *1912: Wilson, Roosevelt, Taft & Debs—The Election that Changed the Country.* New York, NY: Simon and Schuster.

Committee for the Study of the American Electorate (2004). "President Bush, Mobilization Drives Propel Turnout to Post-1968 High." November 4, 2004.

Congressional Quarterly. 1979. *Presidential Elections Since 1789.* Second Edition. Washington, DC: CQ Press.

Congressional Quarterly. 2002. *Presidential Elections 1789–2002.* Washington, DC: CQ Press.

Cook, Charlie. 2004. Convention dispatches—As the nation goes, so do swing states. *Charlie Cook's Political Report.* August 31, 2004.

Cook, Charlie. 2005. Off to the races: 435 ways to parse the presidential election results. *Charlie Cook's Political Report.* March 29, 2005.

Council of State Governments. 2003. *Interstate Compacts and Agencies 2003.* Lexington, KY: The Council of State Governments.

Council of State Governments. 2005. *The Book of the States.* Lexington, KY: The Council of State Governments. 2005 Edition. Volume 37.

DenBoer, Gordon; Brown, Lucy Trumbull; and Hagermann, Charles D. (editors). 1984. *The Documentary History of the First Federal Elections 1788–1790.* Madison, WI: University of Wisconsin Press. Volume II.

DenBoer, Gordon; Brown, Lucy Trumbull; and Hagermann, Charles D. (editors). 1986. *The Documentary History of the First Federal Elections 1788–1790.* Madison, WI: University of Wisconsin Press. Volume III.

DenBoer, Gordon; Brown, Lucy Trumbull; Skerpan, Alfred Lindsay; and Hagermann, Charles D. (editors). 1989. *The Documentary History of the First Federal Elections 1788-1790*. Madison, WI: University of Wisconsin Press. Volume IV.

Dover, Edwin D. 2003. *The Disputed Presidential Election of 2000: A History and Reference Guide*. Westport, CT: Greenwood Press.

Dunn, Susan. 2004. Jefferson's Second Revolution: *The Elections Crisis of 1800 and the Triumph of Republicanism*. Boston, MA: Houghton Mifflin.

Edwards, George C., III. 2004. *Why the Electoral College Is Bad for America*. New Haven, CT: Yale University Press.

FairVote. 2005. *The Shrinking Battleground: The 2008 Presidential Election and Beyond*. Takoma Park, MD: The Center for Voting and Democracy. www.fairvote.org/shrinking.

FairVote. 2005. *Who Picks the President?* Takoma Park, MD: The Center for Voting and Democracy. www.fairvote.org/whopicks.

Ferling, John. 2004. *Adams vs. Jefferson: The Tumultuous Election of 1800*. Oxford, UK: Oxford University Press.

Ford, Paul Leicester. 1905. *The Works of Thomas Jefferson*. New York, NY: G.P. Putnam's Sons. 9:90.

Fortier, John C. and Ornstein, Norman. 2004. If Terrorists Attack Our Presidential Elections. 3 *Election Law Journal* 4, 597–612.

Frankfurter, Felix and Landis, James. 1925. The compact clause of the constitution—A study in interstate adjustments. 34 *Yale Law Journal* 692–693 and 730–732. May 1925.

Gallup News Service. 2000. Americans have Historically Favored Changing Way Presidents Are Elected. November 10, 2000.

Gettleman, Marvin E. 1973. *The Dorr Rebellion: A Study in American Radicalism 1833–1849*. New York, NY: Random House.

Goldfeder, Jerry H. 2005. Could Terrorists Derail a Presidential Election. 32 *Fordham Urban Law Journal* 3, 523–566. May 2005.

Gordon, James D. and Magleby, David B. 1989. Pre-Election Judicial Review of Initiatives and Referendums. 64 *Notre Dame Law Review* 298–320.

Grace, Adam S. 2005. *Federal-State "Negotiations" over Federal Enclaves in the Early Republic: Finding Solutions to Constitutional Problems at the Birth of the Lighthouse System*. Berkeley, CA: Berkeley Electronic Press. Working Paper 509. http://law.bepress.com/expresso/eps/509.

Grant, George. 2004. *The Importance of the Electoral College*. San Antonio, TX: Vision Forum Ministries.

Gregg, Gary L. II. (editor). 2001. *Securing Democracy: Why We Have an Electoral College.* Wilmington, DE: ISI Books.

Hardy, Paul T. 1982. *Interstate Compacts: The Ties That Bind.* Athens, GA: Institute of Government, University of Georgia.

Jacobson, Arthur J. and Rosenfeld, Michel (editors). 2002. *The Longest Night: Polemics and Perspectives on Election 2000.* Berkeley, CA: University of California Press.

Jensen, Merrill and Becker, Robert A. (editors). 1976. *The Documentary History of the First Federal Elections 1788–1790.* Madison, WI: University of Wisconsin Press. Volume I.

Kirby, J. 1962. Limitations on the powers of the state legislatures over presidential elections. 27 *Law and Contemporary Problems* 495.

Kole, Edward A. 1999. *The First 13 Constitutions of the First American States.* Haverford, PA: Infinity Publishing.

Kole, Edward A. 1992. *The True Intent of the First American Constitutions of 1776–1791.* Haverford, PA: Infinity Publishing.

Kuroda, Tadahisa. 1994. *The Origins of the Twelfth Amendment: The Electoral College in the Early Republic, 1787–1804.* Westport, CT: Greenwood Press.

Leach, Richard H. and Sugg, Redding S. Jr. 1959. *The Administration of Interstate Compacts.* Louisiana State University Press.

LeVert, Suzanne. 2004. *The Electoral College.* New York, NY: Franklin Watts.

Longley, Lawrence D. and Braun, Alan G. 1972. *The Politics of Electoral College Reform.* New Haven, CT: Yale University Press.

Longley, Lawrence D. and Peirce, Neal R. 1999. *The Electoral College Primer 2000.* New Haven, CT: Yale University Press.

Morris, Roy B. 2003. *Fraud of the Century: Rutherford B. Hayes, Samuel Tilden, and the Stolen Election of 1876.* Waterville, ME: Thorndike Press.

Nelson, Suzanne. Three-Month Period Imperils Presidency. *Roll Call.* November 2, 2004.

New York Daily News. 2000. Bush Set to Fight an Electoral College Loss: They're Not Only Thinking the Unthinkable, They're Planning for It. *New York Daily News.* November 1, 2000.

Nivola, Pietro S. 2005. *Thinking About Political Polarization.* Washington, DC: The Brookings Institution. Policy Brief 139. January 2005.

Orfield, Lester Bernhardt. 1942. *The Amending of the Federal Constitution.* Ann Arbor, MI: The University of Michigan Press.

Ornstein, Norman. 2004. *Roll Call.* October 21, 2004.

Peirce, Neal R. 1968. *The People's President: The Electoral College in American History and Direct-Vote Alternative*. New York, NY: Simon and Schuster.

Peirce, Neal R. and Longley, Lawrence D. 1981. *The People's President: The Electoral College in American History and the Direct-Vote Alternative, Revised Edition*. New Haven, CT: Yale University Press.

Peterson, Svend. 1981. *A Statistical History of the American Presidential Elections: With Supplementary Tables Covering 1968–1980*. Westport, CT: Greenwood Press Reprint.

Posner, Richard A. 2001. *Breaking the Deadlock: The 2000 Election, the Constitution, and the Courts*. Princeton, NJ: Princeton University Press.

Rehnquist, William H. 2004. *Centennial Crisis: The Disputed Election of 1876*. New York, NY: Alfred A. Knopf.

Ridgeway, Marian E. 1971. *Interstate Compacts: A Question of Federalism*. Carbondale, IL: Southern Illinois University Press.

Robinson, Lloyd. 1996. *The Stolen Election: Hayes versus Tilden—1876*. New York, NY: Tom Doherty Associates Books.

Ross, Tara. 2004. *Enlightened Democracy: The Case for the Electoral College*. Los Angeles, CA: World Ahead Publishing Company.

Schumaker, Paul D. and Loomis, Burdett A. (editors). 2002. *Choosing a President*. New York, NY: Chatham House Publishers.

Schlesinger, Arthur M., Jr. and Hewson, Martha S. 2002. Philadelphia, PA: Chelsea House Publishers.

Schlesinger, Arthur M., Jr. and Israel, Fred L. (editors). 2002. *History of American Presidential Elections 1878–2001*. Philadelphia, PA: Chelsea House Publishers. (11 volumes).

Shambon, Leonard M. 2004. Electoral-College Reform Requires Change of Timing. *Roll Call*. June 15, 2004.

Smith, Hayward H. 2001. *Symposium, Law of Presidential Elections: Issues in the Wake of Florida 2000*. History of the Article II Independent State legislature Doctrine. 29 *Florida State University Law Review* 731–785. Issue 2.

Stanwood, Edward. 1912. *A History of the Presidency from 1897 to 1909*. Boston, MA: Houghton Mifflin Company.

Stanwood, Edward. 1916. *A History of the Presidency from 1897 to 1916*. Boston, MA: Houghton Mifflin Company.

Stanwood, Edward. 1924. *A History of the Presidency from 1788 to 1897*. Boston, MA: Houghton Mifflin Company.

Tribe, Laurence H. 2000. *American Constitutional Law*. Third Edition. Volume 1. New York, NY: Foundation Press.

U.S. House of Representatives Committee on the Judiciary. 1969. *Electoral College Reform: Hearings on H.J. Res. 179, H.J. Res. 181, and Similar Proposals to Amend the Constitution Relating to Electoral College Reform.* 91st Congress, 1st Session. February 5, 6, 19, 20, 26, and 27; March 5, 6, 12, and 13, 1969. Washington, DC: U.S. Government Printing Office.

U.S. House of Representatives Committee on the Judiciary. 1999. *Proposals for Electoral College Reform: Hearing on H.J. Res. 28 and H.J. Res. 43.* 105th Congress, 1st Session. September 4, 1997. Washington, DC: U.S. Government Printing Office.

U.S. Senate Committee on the Judiciary. 1967. *Election of the President: Hearings on S.J. Res. 4, 7, 11, 12, 28, 58, 62, 138; and 139, 89th Congress; and S.J. Res. 2, 3, 6, 7, 12, 15, 21, 25, 55, 84, and 86.* 89th Congress, 2nd Session and 90th Congress, 1st Session. February 28–August 23, 1967. Washington, DC: U.S. Government Printing Office.

U.S. Senate Committee on the Judiciary. 1969. *Electing the President: Hearings on S.J. Res. 1, S.J. Res. 2, S.J. Res. 4, S.J. Res. 12, S.J. Res. 18, S.J. Res. 20, S.J. Res. 25, S.J. Res. 30, S.J. Res. 31, S.J. Res. 33, S.J. Res. 71, and S.J. Res. 72 to Amend the Constitution Relating to Electoral College Reform.* 91st Congress, 1st Session. January 23 and 24; March 10, 11, 12, 13, 20 and 21; April 30; and May 1 and 2, 1969. Washington, DC: U.S. Government Printing Office.

U.S. Senate Committee on the Judiciary. 1969. *Direct Popular Election of the President: Report, with Additional Minority, Individual, and Separate Views on H.J. Res. 681, Proposing an Amendment to the Constitution of the United States Relating to the Election of the President and Vice President.* 91st Congress, 1st Session. Washington, DC: U.S. Government Printing Office.

U.S. Senate Committee on the Judiciary. 1975. *Direct Popular Election of the President: Report (to Accompany S.J. Res. 1).* 94th Congress, 1st Session. Washington, DC: U.S. Government Printing Office.

U.S. Senate Committee on the Judiciary. 1977. *The Electoral College and Direct Election: Hearings on the Electoral College and Direct Election of the President and Vice President (S.J. Res. 1, 8, and 18): Supplement.* 95th Congress, 1st Session. July 20, 22 and 28; and August 2, 1977. Washington, DC: U.S. Government Printing Office.

U.S. Senate Committee on the Judiciary. 1979. *Direct Popular Election of the President and Vice President of the United States: Hearings on S.J. Res. 28, Joint Resolution Proposing an Amendment to the Constitution to Provide for the Direct Popular Election of the President and Vice President of the United States.* 96th Congress, 1st Session. March 27 and 30; and April 3, and 9, 1979. Washington, DC: U.S. Government Printing Office.

U.S. Senate Committee on the Judiciary. 1993. *The Electoral College and Direct Election of the President: Hearing on S.J. Res. 297, S.J. Res. 302, and S.J. Res 312, Measures Proposing Amendments to the Constitution Relating to the Direct Election of the President and Vice President of the United States.* 102nd Congress, 2nd Session. July 22, 1992. Washington, DC: U.S. Government Printing Office.

White, Theodore H. 1969. *The Making of the President 1968.* New York, NY: Atheneum Publishers.

Wiecek, William M. 1972. *The Guarantee Clause of the U.S. Constitution.* Ithaca, NY: Cornell University Press.

Wilmerding, Lucius Jr. 1958. *The Electoral College.* Boston, MA: Beacon Press.

Zimmermann, Frederick L. and Wendell, Mitchell. 1976. *The Law and Use of Interstate Compacts.* Lexington, KY: Council of State Governments.

Zimmerman, Joseph F. 1992. *Contemporary American Federalism.* Westport, CT: Praeger.

Zimmerman, Joseph F. 1996. *Interstate Relations: The Neglected Dimension of Federalism.* Westport, CT: Praeger.

Zimmerman, Joseph F. 1997. *The Recall: Tribunal of the People.* Westport, CT: Praeger.

Zimmerman, Joseph F. 1997. *The Referendum: The People Decide Public Policy.* Westport, CT: Praeger.

Zimmerman, Joseph F. 1999. *The Initiative: Citizen Law-Making.* Westport, CT: Praeger.

Zimmerman, Joseph F. 2002. *Interstate Cooperation: Compacts and Administrative Agreements.* Westport, CT: Praeger.

Zimmerman, Joseph F. 2004. *Interstate Economic Relations.* Albany, NY: State University of New York Press.

Zimmerman, Joseph F. 2005. *Congressional Preemption: Regulatory Federalism* Albany, NY: State University of New York Press.

INDEX

NOTE: Notations such as 12*n* refer to a footnote on page 12.

H

I